Robert S. Taylor:
THE MAKING OF A LIBRARY

Herman M. Weisman:
INFORMATION SYSTEMS, SERVICES, AND CENTERS

Jesse H. Shera:
THE FOUNDATIONS OF EDUCATION FOR LIBRARIANSHIP

Charles T. Meadow:
THE ANALYSIS OF INFORMATION SYSTEMS, Second Edition

Stanley J. Swihart and Beryl F. Hefley:
COMPUTER SYSTEMS IN THE LIBRARY

F. W. Lancaster and E. G. Fayen:
INFORMATION RETRIEVAL ON-LINE

Richard A. Kaimann:
STRUCTURED INFORMATION FILES

Thelma Freides:
LITERATURE AND BIBLIOGRAPHY OF THE SOCIAL SCIENCES

Manfred Kochen:
PRINCIPLES OF INFORMATION RETRIEVAL

Dagobert Soergel:
INDEXING LANGUAGES AND THESAURI: CONSTRUCTION AND MAINTENANCE

Robert M. Hayes and Joseph Becker:
HANDBOOK OF DATA PROCESSING FOR LIBRARIES, Second Edition

Andrew E. Wessel:
COMPUTER-AIDED INFORMATION RETRIEVAL

Lauren Doyle
INFORMATION RETRIEVAL AND PROCESSING

Charles T. Meadow:
APPLIED DATA MANAGEMENT

Andrew E. Wessel
THE SOCIAL USE OF INFORMATION—OWNERSHIP AND ACCESS

Hans H. Wellisch:
THE CONVERSION OF SCRIPTS: ITS NATURE, HISTORY, AND UTILIZATION

The Conversion of Scripts—Its Nature, History, and Utilization

Hans H. Wellisch
University of Maryland

A WILEY-INTERSCIENCE PUBLICATION

JOHN WILEY & SONS
NEW YORK ● CHICHESTER ● BRISBANE ● TORONTO

Library of Congress Cataloging in Publication Data

Wellisch, Hanan.
 The conversion of scripts, its nature, history, and utilization.

 (Information sciences series)
 "A Wiley-Interscience publication."
 Bibliography: p.
 Includes index.
 1. Transliteration. 2. Writing. 3. Bibliography—
Theory, methods, etc. I. Title.

P226.W4 411 77–2205
ISBN 0-471-01620-9

Printed in the United States of America

10 9 8 7 6 5 4 3 2 1

Foreword

It is a rare privilege to receive a manuscript that is simultaneously scholarly, literate, readable, and important. When this one came to me, my first reaction was scepticism which rapidly turned to unalloyed enthusiasm. The scholarship of the book speaks for itself; everything in it is thoroughly documented and based on facts. The literacy and readability are shown on every page. Those aspects, though, I leave to the readers to judge themselves, and will comment no further on them except to say that I found this to be an exciting book to read.

The importance of this work is so great, however, that I do want to bring out some of the relevant issues—all of them things that Hans Wellisch has said far better and more concretely that I can. They relate to the fundamental nature of information science, at least as I see it.

On numerous occasions I have defined information science as ''the study of information-generating transformations of recorded data.'' In that definition the phrase ''information-generating transformation'' embodies the primary focus of study, the aim of information science being to identify, characterize, and measure them. But the term ''recorded data'' is taken as a primitive, to be interpreted in the form most appropriate to any particular focus of information science study, depending on the specific form for their representation.

The most obvious examples of recorded data, of course, are those that use printed symbols—numbers, letters, etc.—as the means for their representation. The colloquial use of the word ''data'' usually implies numbers as the symbols; by extension ''data processing'' encompasses alphabetic as well as numeric data.

The value of treating the term ''recorded data'' as a primitive, however, is that it allows us to consider other examples in which the symbols used for this representation may be dramatically different. Amino acids, for example, have been regarded as the means for representation of the genetic data recorded in DNA and RNA. As a result, processes quite different from what we would normally interpret as ''data processing'' can be viewed in abstract form as such, giving us greater insight into the processes themselves.

Thus the symbols or means for representation of recorded data have an interesting dual character. They *can* be treated as symbols for recording data, and that is what makes them of interest to information science—but they are also something else, something real and tangible rather than simply representational.

Characters printed in a book are both representations and actual imprints of ink. Data recorded in a computer are represented by binary symbols—the magnetized states of cores or the surfaces of recording media. The amino acids in an RNA chain are both symbols and actual chemical compounds.

It is that other aspect of the symbols, their reality in contrast to their symbolism, that leads us from information science into the world of art, psychology, anthropology, chemistry, economics, ...

And that to me is the most valuable contribution made by this book. The scripts by which mankind has recorded data are both symbols for accomplishing that aim and a reality in themselves. They embody a complex of cultural, economic, religious, and political issues far transcending their role as representations of recorded data.

To the data processing specialist, the conversion of scripts is a technical problem. It may be simple, such as conversion from ASCII to EBCDIC, or it may be complex, such as conversion from Chinese logograms into Roman alphabet. Sometimes the conversion may be one to one; other times, ambiguous or unresolvable. But in every case, the technical problems are still fundamentally solvable.

Yet the problems posed by conversion of scripts, especially in the context of bibliographic control, are not merely of a technical nature. Rather, they occur on the cultural, societal, and psychological levels, and concern the question of how best to serve users of information recorded in various scripts and languages.

In addressing and exploring these aspects, Wellisch answers many specific questions about the conversion of scripts. He illuminates and thoroughly illustrates the purely technical problems. He shows where and when conversion can be one-to-one, where and when it is ambiguous or unresolvable. And he tells us why. In doing so, though, he always places the why in the larger context of the real world—the world in which the scripts may still be symbols, but not solely of recorded data. They are symbols of life, of conflict, of the history of civilization.

R. M. HAYES

Sherman Oaks, California
March 1977

Information Sciences Series

Information is the essential ingredient in decision making. The need for improved information systems in recent years has been made critical by the steady growth in size and complexity of organizations and data.

This series is designed to include books that are concerned with various aspects of communicating, utilizing, and storing digital and graphic information. It will embrace a broad spectrum of topics, such as information system theory and design, man-machine relationships, language data processing, artificial intelligence, mechanization of library processes, non-numerical applications of digital computers, storage and retrieval, automatic publishing, command and control, information display, and so on.

Information science may someday be a profession in its own right. The aim of this series is to bring together the interdisciplinary core of knowledge that is apt to form its foundation. Through this consolidation, it is expected that the series will grow to become the focal point for professional education in this field.

Preface

Conversion of scripts—transliteration and transcription—is a phenomenon with which almost every literate person is thoroughly familiar. The daily press, television news captions, and many books and articles convey the names of persons and places that were originally written in one of the many non-Roman scripts in a form readily discernible by Western readers, namely in Roman script. The practice of converting one script into another has been in use ever since man began to create graphic records in different scripts, whenever two or more such scripts came into close contact and had to be made intelligible to those who could read only one of them.

Yet, despite the pervasiveness and long tradition of script conversion, the topic has not, to the best of my knowledge, been explored in its various ramifications. At first sight one may wonder whether any far-reaching investigation is warranted at all. There would seem to be nothing more to it than rendering the name of, say, a Russian or Chinese personality and the title of a book written in an "exotic" script so that an English-speaking reader could readily read it and even pronounce it after a fashion. But conversion of scripts is by no means merely a technical operation, nor is it a simple process of substituting letters of script *A* for corresponding letters of script *B*. Indeed, such is the complexity of this process that hundreds of books and articles have been written on *how* to perform the conversion of one script into another. The present work does not attempt to add yet another title to that long list. Rather, it has been my aim to explore *why* script conversion has been performed at different times, and what *effects* it has had on those who were exposed to the results.

Conversion of scripts has played an important role in the history of many nations, and its own history is intertwined with the development of civilizations and their literature. Since the late Renaissance, script conversion has also been the method commonly used in the Western world to make the literature of other peoples and cultures accessible in libraries and bibliographic lists. Chapters 1 through 3 trace these aspects, their evolution, and their social and political implications. They provide the background to the main part of the study, which is devoted to an investigation of the effectiveness of script conversion, and in particular Romanization, as it is performed in our own times in various fields, especially in the catalogs of libraries and in bibliographies that list documents written in non-Roman scripts.

Based on a comparison of various conversion schemes prescribed by national and international standards, and by the cataloging codes of many countries for more than three dozen scripts, as well as on a survey of the world's libraries that possess substantial collections of materials in scripts other than their dominant ones, the functional and systemic requirements of script conversion are analyzed. Most of these requirements are found to be mutually incompatible; unambiguous reversibility, which has always been stressed as the most important requirement for script conversion in bibliographic control, is shown to be impossible to achieve for most scripts. The theory and practice of script conversion in bibliographic control systems are further analyzed with the aid of cybernetic methods. This analysis shows that script conversion is not an effective control tool for either operators or users, because it is inherently incapable of functioning in such a capacity (and not, as is so often claimed, because we need ''better'' or more ''scientific'' transcription schemes).

Script conversion, and in particular Romanization, which has been an accepted bibliographic method for centuries, must thus be reevaluated in the light of the changed role of contemporary libraries and information services, which are no longer dominated by the ''keeper'' outlook of the past, when collection and preservation were the primary concerns of libraries, while only scant attention was paid to the needs of potential users of the stored treasures. In our time access to literature in all languages and scripts must be provided for readers and users whose skills and needs are fundamentally different from those of library patrons in the 19th century and in the earlier part of the present century, when Romanization was performed mainly for the benefit of philologists, historians, and other specialists. The book concludes, therefore, with a brief survey of possible alternative methods of bibliographic control for documents in dissimilar scripts, whith special emphasis on the role of computers and other automated devices which may contribute to the realization of Universal Bibliographic Control without the use of methods that are demonstrably unsuitable for that purpose.

Since I have been severely critical of certain library practices and the attitudes of certain librarians, I wish to emphasize that I have been a practicing librarian myself for more than two decades. My views on the use and misuse of script conversion for bibliographic control are based on my experience in multilanguage and multi-script libraries in Israel, where I practiced what I am preaching here, namely provision of direct access to documents in their original script. The theoretical foundations for this practice were, however, developed only many years later, after I had devoted myself to the teaching of librarianship and information science, first in Israel and subsequently in the United States.

In this book, too, I have made every effort to take my own medicine, and to cite names of persons and titles of works in the original language and script. Those written in a non-Roman script have also been transcribed, either according to the *Recommendations* of the International Organization for Standardization (ISO) or, for those scripts not covered by an ISO scheme, by the relevant scheme of the Library of Congress. In the Bibliography names and titles in non-Roman scripts are first briefly listed in transcribed form in the main alphabetical sequence, with references to full bibliographic data in separate listings by scripts.

I have dealt with about a dozen different scripts in more or less detail, and have mentioned the features of many others in passing. It would be preposterous to claim that I have mastered them all; at most, I am familiar with about four scripts, and I can find my way through a couple more, but I admit that I am not conversant with the scripts of South and East Asia as far as reading and writing are concerned. Obviously I had to rely on data from a large number of published (and sometimes unpublished) sources, and on the judgment of experts. I wish to express my gratitude to the many linguists, subject specialists, and librarians from many countries who generously contributed data on certain scripts and their applications, and who shared with me information on library practices regarding the treatment of dissimilar scripts.

It is also a pleasant duty to acknowledge the assistance rendered by academic and research libraries in the metropolitan Washington area, foremost among them the Library of Congress, whose collections (particularly those of the Rare Book Division) furnished most of the illustrations in Chapter 3.

I am particularly indebted to Dr. Tsung Chin of the University of Maryland, and to Mr. Frank J. Shulman, Mr. Kung-Yao Fan, Mrs. Connie Galmeijer, and Mr. Eizaburo Okuizumi of the McKeldin Library of the same University, who reviewed the sections on Chinese and Japanese, and who assisted me in unraveling some of the mysteries of these beautiful yet most intricate means of graphic communication. Dr. Karl Stowasser, also of the University of Maryland, reviewed and commented on the historical part of the study, and on the sections dealing with the Arabic language and script. Dr. Eva Verona, Chairman of the Committee of Cataloguing, International Federation of Library Associations, commented on a draft of Chapter 5, and supplied information on the Glagolitsa script and on the Arabic transliteration of Croatian. Dr. Frank Schick, Chief, Library Surveys Branch, Department of Health, Education, and Welfare, advised me on the collection and presentation of the statistical data in Chapter 4. The customary disclaimer that absolves all those mentioned from responsibility for any mistakes and errors is particularly needed here, because I am convinced that, despite all my efforts at utmost accuracy, the experts on certain languages and scripts will inevitably find inaccuracies and errors of omisson and commission, for which I alone am to blame.

I am especially grateful to my friend and mentor, Dr. Laurence B. Heilprin, now Professor Emeritus at the College of Library and Information Services of the University of Maryland, who was a constant source of inspiration and who guided me gently through the intricacies of cybernetics. Thanks are also due my colleague in the College of Library and Information Services, Dr. Michael M. Reynolds, to Dr. David E. Sparks of the University of Notre Dame, and to Dr. Jerrold Orne of the University of North Carolina, who gave freely of their time to discuss and improve the work in its earlier incarnation as a Ph.D. thesis.

Finally, I wish to express my gratitude to my wife Shulamith for her encouragement, patience, and understanding during the long period in which I conducted this study, and for the selfless efforts she made to support my work. That she is fluent in seven languages from four different linguistic families, written in three different scripts, naturally contributed to a considerable degree to the conception and accomplishment of this book.

HANS HANAN WELLISCH

College Park, Maryland
August 1977

Contents

Figures

Tables

One

Writing Systems, Scripts, and Conversion of Scripts

CLASSIFICATION, TYPOLOGY, AND DEFINITIONS

First of all it is necessary to rectify terms. If language is not correct, then what is said is not what is meant. . . . Hence there must be no arbitrariness in what is said. This matters above everything.

K'ung Fu-tzu. *Analects,* 13:3

Science begins when the meaning of words is strictly delimited. Words may be selected from the existing vocabulary or new words may be coined, but they all are given a new definition which prevents misunderstandings and ambiguities within the chapter of science where they are used.

Leon Brillouin. *Science and information theory.* 1962, p. ix.

From the days of the great Chinese sage until our own age, the importance of clarity of expression and of exact definition of terms has been stressed by orators, poets, writers, and scholars, many of whom set admirable examples in their own works. But their advice has often been neglected, and the proliferation of fuzzy notions and fancy neologisms has perhaps never been greater than in our own time. Excessive use of polysyllabic words is mistaken for erudition, and clarity of expression is hampered by the designation of vastly different concepts by the same terms while, conversely, different words are being coined for the same idea in different branches of science.

As we set out to explore the conversion of scripts, it is particularly important

1

to define our terms exactly and unambiguously for at least three reasons: first, to a large extent the phenomena to be investigated pertain to the fields of librarianship and information science, where confusing and ambiguous terminology is the rule rather than the exception; second, the terms used to indicate the methods of script conversion, namely, *transcription* and *transliteration,* are almost always loosely treated as quasi-synonyms; third, the resulting confusion is compounded by the fact that ''transcription'' also happens to be a homonym.

When, for example, a piano score of Peter Ilich Tchaikovsky's *Eugen Onegin* is cataloged by a music library, transcription is involved in three different denotations: *(a)* the work itself is a transcription in the musical sense (from a full score to a piano score); *(b)* the name of the composer and the title of the work have been transcribed for English users from the Cyrillic script[1]; *(c)* the title page of the document has to be transcribed correctly, that is, copied according to certain rules, for a catalog entry to be produced.

The major terms with which we deal in this study have, of course, been defined in general and specialized dictionaries as well as in the publications of organizations concerned with the problems of script conversion, such as the International Organization for Standardization (ISO), the United Nations Conferences on the Standardization of Geographical Names, and others. It is, however, not sufficient to define the meaning of these terms in a purely lexicographical manner, nor can such definitions be satisfactory when they are made for a relatively narrow field of application.

We attempt to clarify and to define succinctly and unambiguously the concepts and technical terms pertaining to script conversion, based on an integrated approach revealing the relationships between them as well as their structural and functional role in writing systems.

1.   WRITING SYSTEMS

Language is normally expressed in two distinct modes—speech and writing. Speech is the uttering of articulate sounds that are combined to form words and sentences to express human experience (concepts, thoughts, emotions). Writing, the making of marks on a medium, serves to record that human experience, and sometimes, but by no means always, its spoken expression. Both are means of communication, and they are often closely related, but to speak of *written language* is somewhat imprecise and may even be entirely inappropriate if it implies the ancient notion that ''written words are the signs of words spoken,'' as

---

[1]The transcription used here does not follow any of the standards otherwise used in this book but is purposely taken from a reference book for English-speaking readers, *The Concise Oxford Dictionary of Music.*

Aristotle puts it in the introduction to his tract *On interpretation*,[2] or that "writing is the mirror of speech." This, to be sure, may be true in a figurative sense as it pertains to some forms of literature, but writing is used for purposes and in circumstances in which speech is not adequate, and vice versa.[3] *Writing* is, in fact, a much too general term for what occurs when the elements of a language are permanently recorded by conventional graphic marks. Many different rules, distinctions, and traditions as well as overt and covert intentions on the part of a person who writes come into play in the act of writing and influence each other in subtle ways. The script, the letters or other signs, the spelling, the punctuation marks, and several other elements form parts of an integrated whole, namely the *writing system* of a language. Each language has its own writing system, many of whose elements have no equivalent in spoken language.

1.1 Functional Classification of Writing Systems

Writing systems can be grouped according to their sociolinguistic function, that is, according to the role they play, and the tasks for which they are employed in a language community. A language community is here understood to comprise all persons speaking the same language, irrespective of nationality or geographic contiguity of the countries in which they live. The following classification is largely based on one proposed by the English linguist John Mountford.[4]

1.1.1 Orthographies. The word *orthography* means literally "the correct kind of writing," and is often used synonymously for "correct spelling," but in the context of a writing system it has a much wider denotation.

---

[2] Aristoteles (1938), para. 1.

[3] Jones (1948). Carroll (1953) states: " . . . particularly to be avoided is any suggestion that a language may be equated to a system of writing" (p. 11); " . . . systems of written symbols may have a status and structure of their own, in some ways dependent of the spoken language system, in other ways independent of it" (p. 13). Lavelle (1947) says: "Cette action dans la parole est plus directe et plus apparente; dans l'écriture elle est plus lointaine et plus précaire. Dans la parole elle ne depasse le cercle le plus restraint, dans l'écriture elle ne s'assigne aucune borne. . . . Pourtant, on peut dire beaucoup des choses que l'on ne peut pas écrire, non pas seulement parce que la parole s'efface et que l'écriture reste, mais parce qu'on choisit celui à qui on parle, au lieu que le sort de l'écriture, même la plus secrète, c'est d'être livrée à tous" (p. 159). Wrolstad (1976) goes so far as to state that written or "visible" language preceded spoken or "audible" language in the evolution of human communication—a view not shared by linguists, but persuasively argued on the evidence of neurophysiological language processing, recent research on language performance, and the paintings and markings of prehistoric man, who, because of the anatomy of his vocal organs, was apparently not yet capable of articulated speech.

[4] Mountford (1973).

Definition 1: Orthography

An orthography is a set of rules intended to serve the general purposes of written communication for the literate members of a language community.

This set of rules is uniform, integrated, and standardized. It is *uniform;* that is to say, it is designed to apply to all possible words and sentences in the language, past, present, and future, including those words that have not yet been coined and sentences that have not yet been uttered and written. It is *integrated* in that its rules form a coherent whole and are interdependent: a change in one rule may affect all or most of the others, and such a change may actually transform one kind of orthography into another one. Finally, it is *standardized;* that is, it is the product of convention or the general consensus of the majority of its users; this consensus is usually based on traditional and historical usage, but there are also cases where it has been forcibly imposed by decree.

1.1.1.1.   STANDARDIZATION.   A language may and sometimes does have several orthographies, but only the one that has been conventionally accepted as a norm by the majority of the literate language community, for religious, historical, or political reasons, becomes the standard orthography.

The first element of an orthography to become standardized is the repertory of graphic signs used to record written communication, the script. Standardization and codification of spelling and punctuation often come much later and are a relatively recent sociolinguistic phenomenon compared with the history of writing which began more than 6000 years ago. For European languages, at any rate, standardization of orthographies dates back to 1635, when the Académie Française was founded. Until the beginning of the 20th century similar official learned bodies were established in many other countries, with the notable exception of the English-speaking nations, which left the standardization of their orthography in the hands of individual lexicographers and grammarians.

The rapid rise in the rate of literacy, coupled with the influence of modern mass communication media, is now leading inexorably toward ever greater standardization of not only the spoken language but, even more, its orthography. Perhaps the most important feature that distinguishes standard orthography from all other writing systems of a language (and in particular from transliteration and transcription, which are alternative writing systems) is that the standardized rules and conventions of an orthography are codified and exemplified in dictionaries that are freely available and are normally also comprehended and used by the literate language community. This means that all words (and many phrases) in the language can be verified as to their graphic representation by a standard authority with which all or most of the members of the language community are familiar, and to which they all submit in the interests of mutual intelligibility.

All languages for which written records exist have had several orthographies during their history, and several of them have had more than one standard orthography at one time.

Diachronic Orthographies. Many European languages, particularly those in countries with established language academies, officially changed their orthographies around the beginning of this century or somewhat later; among these are German, Swedish, Russian, and Romanian, to mention only a few. English, which has the most conservative spelling of any modern language, preserving phonological elements that have long since disappeared from the spoken language (as in *rough, through, brought,* where the same concatenation of five letters now has three completely different sound values), had a fairly standardized orthography by the time it was codified in Samuel Johnson's famous dictionary in 1755. Yet although no far-reaching changes occurred, present-day English orthography is somewhat different from the one prescribed by the learned doctor who admitted in his preface that "the pen must at length comply with the tongue. . . ."

Synchronic Orthographies. A language may be written simultaneously in more than one standard orthography, either in the same script or in various scripts. English has at present two standardized orthographies, British and American, which differ not only in spelling but also in punctuation. Concurrently, various "simplified" or "modernized" orthographies have been proposed, and some have even been used with more or less success.

Hebrew also has two officially recognized orthographies; one is known as *defective* because vowels are only partially represented by *matres lectionis* (consonants that may also be read as vowels) and must be indicated by (optional) diacritical marks, the so-called *points.* The Bible and most other liturgical literature, as well as poetry (both classical and modern), are written with these points, as are also children's books and primers. The other orthography is known as *full* because the vowels $[i]$, $[ɔ]$, and $[u]$ and the diphthongs $[ai]$, $[ɔi]$, and $[ui]$ are written with the aid of the consonants א *(alef),* ' *(yod),* and ו *(waw).* Most modern Hebrew literature, all newspapers, governmental publications, textbooks, and so forth, are written in full orthography, of which there is one officially approved version and several unauthorized modifications.

Serbo-Croatian is another language written in two standard orthographies, but in this case two different scripts are used, namely Roman and Cyrillic, largely following the spheres of influence of the Roman Catholic Church and the Greek Orthodox Church. The same phenomenon occurs in what formerly used to be called the Hindustani language, which is written by Hindus in the Devanagari script and known as Hindi, while Moslems write it in Arabic script and call it Urdu. In both instances, in the words of David Diringer, "writing follows religion."[5] We explore these aspects in more detail in Chapter 2.

[5]Diringer (1968), pp. 210, 374, 427, et passim.

1.1.1.2 ELEMENTS OF STANDARD ORTHOGRAPHIES.   A standard orthography consists of a set of rules for the proper use of all or some of the following elements:

1. *Spelling*. The graphic representation of morphemes, and the concatenation of morphemes into words.
2. *Punctuation*. The function and placement of graphic signs that do not represent either phonemes or morphemes but serve to demarcate certain parts of the graphic representation of language, as well as grammatical boundaries.
3. *Layout*. The direction of writing, for example, from left to right, from top to bottom, boustrophedon.
4. *Serialization devices*. The use of digits, letters, or logographs to indicate serial order.
5. *Referral devices*. Numerals or signs (such as asterisks and daggers) that refer from one part of a written communication to another, noncontiguous part.
6. *Abbreviation devices*. The construction and use of contractions, acronyms, and so forth.
7. *Differentiation devices*. The use of italics, letter-spacing, boldface type, and so on, for the purpose of emphasizing or otherwise distinguishing certain parts of a written communication. These devices are largely independent of script but may be characteristic for the writing system of a particular language. For example, an emphasized word in English text is generally *italicized,* whereas in German and some other languages it is l e t t e r - s p a c e d .
8. *Distinguishing devices*. Capitalization (at the beginning of a word that is not the first word in a sentence, or throughout, known in typography as SMALL CAPS). Capitalization can be used only in alphabetic writing systems and in scripts that have two different sets of letters (majuscules and minuscules, better known in English typographic usage as uppercase and lowercase); it is thus dependent on script. Occasionally, it may also be used in monomorphous alphabets such as Hebrew, where certain words in the Bible are traditionally written with a large initial, for example, in Ecclesiastes, 12: 13.
9. *Continuity devices*. Syllabification of words and the use of certain punctuation marks to distinguish a word-break at the end of a line from a hyphen at the end of a line; catchwords (now almost never used in English but still retained in Portuguese) are another such device.
10. *Script*. A set of graphic marks and their distinctive shapes that give visual representation to the elements of a writing system enumerated under points (1) through (9). It is thus, in Mountford's words, "the least linguistic aspect of writing." The linguistic characteristics of a writing system are not so much embedded in the script itself as in the rules that the orthography of a language prescribes for the use of a script. Thus, the Roman alphabet is used

to write a large number of languages, but each of these has its own orthography (in the sense of a standardized writing system, not only with regard to spelling and punctuation).

Orthographies are the most common writing systems in any language community, and other kinds of writing systems form only a small fraction of all written representations of language. They are, however, important for the purpose of this study, and we now briefly consider their main characteristics.

1.1.2. Stenographies.   These are writing systems devised for the purpose of fast recording of (mainly spoken) language. They are alternative orthographies of a language, and also follow standardized rules that are normally available to anybody interested in using these writing systems. Stenographies fall outside the scope of this study and are listed here only for the sake of completeness of the sociolinguistic classification of writing systems.

1.1.3. Cryptographies.   These are writing systems whose primary purpose is secrecy. Although they too follow strict rules and are, in fact, the most highly standardized orthographies a language might have, the rules and standards are not available to members of the language community in general, but only to a select group or, in extreme cases, only to one individual who wishes to record his experiences while at the same time trying to shield it from anyone but himself (Leonardo da Vinci, Samuel Pepys, and Bertrand Russell are some famous examples). To a native speaker of a language who is familiar only with its standard orthography, any other orthography that is markedly different from it constitutes a cryptography that he may or may not be able to decipher. This applies, *mutatis mutandis,* also to transliterations and transcriptions that are paedographies and technographies.

1.1.4. Paedographies.   These are writing systems mainly intended for language teaching, with the primary aim of giving the student a more or less precise idea of the pronunciation of a word written in conventional orthography. Paedographies are mostly found in bilingual dictionaries or in monolingual dictionaries of languages whose orthography does not give unambiguous clues to their pronunciation.

Paedographies may use several systems with varying degrees of sophistication. One of the simplest paedographic methods is to relate the indication of pronunciation of a phoneme first to the standard orthography of short words with unambiguous pronunciation in the native language of the learner, who is supposed to know these words, and then to use the orthography of the phonemes in phonetic transcription. Thus, the pronunciation of the English word *surely* could be roughly indicated in a paedographic system aimed at speakers of English as /shoorlee/, whereas a similar system for Francophones would give /chourli/, and one for speakers of German would have /schurli/. Scientific paedographies make use of Roman letters and a large number of specially invented characters and signs to convey the pronunciation with a high degree of accuracy, as in the International Phonetic Alphabet (IPA), in which *surely* is rendered as [ʃuːəlɪ]. Other paedographic systems fall somewhere in between, using predominantly Roman letters, a few special characters, and some diacritical marks to indicate quality and quantity of vowels, stress, and so forth, as in *Webster's Third New International Dictionary,* where the same word is phonetically transcribed as / shü(ə)rli/, while the *American Heritage Dictionary* uses the transcription /shŏŏr'lē/.

A great variety of paedographies exist, and there is almost no standardization. (Even the IPA is differently applied by various linguists, and practically every lexicographer and author of language textbooks devises his own system.) However, two features are common to all systems of paedography. One is the fact (or at least the conviction of their designers) that they make it possible for the reader to ascertain the correct pronunciation of a word or phrase which, when written in the standard orthography of the language, is either ambiguous or impossible to deduce; the other feature is that a paedographic writing system must be linked to a certain target language, its phonemes and their graphemic representation (as demonstrated in the various paedographic renderings of the pronunciation of *surely* for readers in three different languages). Every system must be made understandable to readers of various languages by different examples of words that contain a certain phoneme. Thus, an English reader is told that the IPA sign [ʃ] stands for the sound represented by the italicized part of the conventional spelling of *sh*ip, the explanation for a Frenchman uses the word *ch*at, a German is given the word *Sch*ule, while a Spaniard (in whose language the phoneme [ʃ]) does not exist) is referred to any of these examples on the assumption that he will be able to gather the pronunciation from other sources.

The same features are also present in most systems for the conversion of scripts used in the fields of geography (particularly in cartography) and bibliographic control. The Romanization of words written in Arabic, Hebrew, Chinese, or Japanese is intended to suit the literacy of readers unfamiliar with these scripts and the writing systems of languages that employ them, and to enable them to pronounce, however imperfectly, words and names in those languages. Generally, these Romanizations do not aim at the precision of paedographies used in certain dictionaries and in textbooks of foreign languages, but their paedographic character is nevertheless unmistakable.

1.1.5. Technographies. These are closely related to paedographies and often use the same techniques, but they differ in that the paedagogic aspect is not predominant or is often lacking altogether. Technographies, writing systems aimed at specialists, represent words and sentences of a language in a manner that highlights certain features by the use of special signs because the standard orthography of a language is either not capable of expressing these features or may even be nonexistent. The IPA, one of the most widely used technographies for linguists, can also be applied to languages that do not have any orthography because no writing system has yet been developed for them.

Systems for the conversion of scripts are also technographies, used primarily by librarians and bibliographers who have been trained to recognize special signs employed in certain Romanization schemes and to interpret them in relation to specific languages. An example is the Romanization system of the Library of Congress, in which the Cyrillic letter ц, pronounced $[ts]$ is transliterated as $\hat{ts}$ (with a ligature sign) when written in Russian, but as *ts* (without the ligature) when written in Ukrainian or White-Russian, while it is Romanized as *c* when written in Serbian or Macedonian.

In principle, the key to a technography is publicly available (otherwise it would be a cryptography), but in actual practice only few people have access to such a key and its existence is not always well publicized. Manuals of cataloging sometimes contain tables of transliteration and transcription (only rarely accompanied by examples); but even these professional tools do not always give clear guidance to librarians and bibliographers about the use of those tables, leading to discrepancies in application. The users of libraries or the readers of bibliographies, however, are normally not able to get access to the keys of the particular technography used in the conversion of scripts, so that for them these technographies become virtually cryptographies.

A technography, although following more or less strict rules and being standardized to a certain degree (thus exhibiting features of an orthography) is not codified in dictionaries. This is because a technography is normally not applied to whole portions of text; only very few books have ever been written entirely in a technography. Rather, single words, short phrases, and, in particular, names of persons or corporate bodies are the subject of technographic treatment. The specialists using such a writing system are expected to know enough both of the principles of that system and of the standard orthography of the source language to be able to make the necessary transformations.

1.1.6. Machinographies.   These are writing systems specially adapted for the direct and automatic use by machines, such as Morse telegraph keys or printout devices of computers. In fact, they are a special kind of technography with a limited number of characters, and they do not normally make use of special signs such as diacritical marks. Machines can, of course, be designed to print any character occurring in writing systems of any kind, but such special design features are costly and cannot, at least at the present time, be economically used when direct computer printout is employed. The case is entirely different for printing and typesetting produced by a mechanical or photomechanical device that is controlled by a computer, since such a mode of operation does not involve a different writing system but only special coding for the characters, which is done within the machine and does not affect the result, normally presented in the standard orthography of the language used. A good illustration of this phenomenon is a comparison of two French computer-produced bibliographies. The catalogs of the Université de Grenoble are produced by direct computer printout and do not display any diacritical marks (although French standard orthography uses 13 modified letters). The four letters COTE may represent the nouns *cote* (share), *côte* (rib), *côté* (side), or the adjective *coté* (marked); the letter *A* may be the name of an object (as in *Vitamin A*), it may be the third person singular of *avoir,* or it may be the preposition *à*. The reader must rely on the context to find out which meaning is intended—a feat that Frenchmen sometimes find annoying but with which English readers have to cope every day (words such as *bow, row,* and *sewer* can neither be understood as to their meaning nor can they be properly pronounced unless the context is given). The *Bulletin signalétique,* on the other hand, displays not only French standard orthography but also different typefaces, indentations, and so forth, all of which are controlled by a properly programmed computer driving a phototypesetting device.

Thus, the limitations of machines may make it necessary to employ an orthography that is slightly or even markedly different from the standard orthography of a language. This factor will have to be taken into consideration more and more when schemes are designed for the conversion of scripts that are intended for automated systems and direct printout.

* * *

The six sociolinguistic kinds of writing systems briefly outlined are, of course, not mutually exclusive, and some of them are, or may be, overlapping, depending on the use made of them by the language community. In principle, any language may be recorded in written form by any of these different writing systems.

1.2. Structural Features of Writing Systems

All writing systems have certain structural features by means of which they seek to represent certain elements of a spoken language. Before turning to a brief exposition of these features, we must define the term *graphic sign* in the sense in which it will be used throughout the following discussion.

Definition 2: Graphic Sign

A graphic sign is any conventional mark by which a human being intends to affect the state or behavior of other human beings.

This definition is modeled on a more general one given by Cherry[6]; it is simplified and more specific, since we are here concerned only with graphic

---

[6]Cherry (1966), p. 308.

communication and can therefore disregard spoken or gestured signs; we are also concerned only with communication between human beings, not between organisms in general.

To achieve communication, a graphic sign must also be conventional; that is to say, it must convey its intended meaning as based on a practice, procedure, or custom that is widely or almost universally accepted and observed in a group between whose members communication is to take place. If a graphic sign has meaning only to its originator, meaningful communication can occur only and exclusively with that selfsame individual when he is looking at the sign at any time after he has written it. This happens not infrequently when someone writes notes to himself, marks a passage in a book in a certain manner, or uses a privately invented stenography. But if even one other human being is to be affected by a graphic sign made by his fellow human being, there must necessarily exist a convention between them, an agreement as to what that graphic sign means. If such a convention does not exist, then the only meaningful conclusion that can be drawn from a configuration of graphic signs is: "This must have been written by someone who wanted to communicate something, but we do not know what that something is." This is the situation in which archaeologists or paleographers find themselves when they discover an inscription written in a script that has not yet been deciphered. Once they succeed in deciphering the script, they thereby become members of the group of people between whom a convention pertaining to that script existed.

Graphic conventions may thus be extended over time almost indefinitely; quite recently, an attempt was made to extend it also over space when the *Pioneer* spacecraft sent to explore the surface of Jupiter and then to move on to outer space beyond our solar system was fitted with a pictorial plaque designed to tell "scientifically educated inhabitants of some other star system" about the origin of the spacecraft and the nature of its designers.[7]

When there is no discernible regularity of form, shape, arrangement, or direction in a group of graphic signs that are written in physical proximity, it may sometimes be difficult to decide whether any kind of communication was intended at all.

The fact that graphic signs intended for communication, and therefore all writing systems and their scripts, must be based on convention has important implications for the historical development of scripts in their application to, and sometimes forced imposition on, various languages, and it has also practical consequences for script conversion in bibliographic control systems.

---

[7]Gombrich (1972) has, however, seriously questioned the validity of this approach, which presupposes that the "inhabitants of some other star system" possess the same kind of sense organs as human beings and that they also know how to interpret line drawings the way Western man has been educated to do. He points out that the gesture of greeting made by the man in the picture would be misinterpreted even by earthlings like the Chinese or Indians.

The manner in which graphic signs are used to record language gives rise to two different structural typologies of writing systems, namely graphemic and phonological typology.

1.2.1. Graphemic Typology. This is the traditional typology, best known to scholars and laymen alike, whose roots can be traced back at least to Socrates and Plato.[8] Graphemic typology is based on the nature of the graphemes used to represent the lexical and grammatical elements of a language, and distinguishes in its modern form between alphabetic, syllabic, and logographic writing systems.

1.2.1.1. ALPHABETIC WRITING SYSTEMS.   The basic graphic signs used are letters which are designed to represent a single phoneme of a spoken language. Today, only few alphabetic signs represent single phonemes unambiguously, not even in those languages that have their own specially devised alphabet, nor can all the complex phonemes of any language be represented by unique signs if the alphabet is to be kept to a reasonably small number of letters. But it is generally assumed that each letter in an alphabet was at least originally designed to represent a phoneme that could not be adequately represented by any other single letter, so that a special one had to be invented.[9]

Alphabetic writing systems are today the most widespread ones, used by all European languages as well as most Asian and African languages, with the exception of Chinese, Japanese, Korean, and Amharic.

1.2.1.2. SYLLABIC WRITING SYSTEMS.   The basic graphic signs used represent syllables, that is, a group of phonemes, consisting either of a vowel or continuant, alone or in combination with one or more consonants. Living languages using this type of writing system are Amharic and Japanese in *kana* script.

1.2.1.3. LOGOGRAPHIC WRITING SYSTEMS.   The basic graphic signs are logograms[10] designed to represent concepts, independent of their pronunciation in any spoken language. Logograms may display a more or less obvious identity between their form and the referent of a concept, such as when a road sign

---

[8]Plato's *Kratylos* (1926), para, 393D–394A and *Theaitetos* (1921), para. 205A and B, are considered to be the earliest scholarly discussions of the terms γράμματα ("alphabetic letters"), στοιχεῖα ("sounds"), συλλαβαί ("syllables"), and of the relations between the concepts they designate.

[9]This principle was applied in modern times when the Cyrillic alphabet was imposed in the early 1940s on most non-Slavic languages in the Soviet Union. Additional characters had to be added to the 32 Cyrillic letters of the Russian alphabet, and various diacritical marks had to be used to represent the phonemes of more than 40 languages for which the basic Cyrillic alphabet was not sufficient. See also Chapter 2, Section 3.2.

[10]The terms *logogram* and *logographic sign* are used here following Gelb (1963), p. 249–250 et passim. The term *ideographic*, often used for Chinese writing and Egyptian hieroglyphs in popular

showing the outline of a locomotive symbolizes an unguarded railroad crossing. But this is not a necessary condition. The sign # symbolizes the concept *number* or *pound* only by various conventions and only in the writing systems of certain languages. Living languages using this type of writing system are Chinese, Japanese in *kanji* script, and Korean (when written in Chinese logograms). All modern alphabetic writing systems also make use of logograms in the form of the so-called Arabic digits, and they employ various logographic signs such as &, %, #, and $, but these are not part of the alphabets themselves.

1.2.2. Phonological Typology. A more recent structural classification, based on contemporary linguistic theories, distinguishes among writing systems according to their phonological qualities. The following dichotomous typology has more important implications for the methods of script conversion than does the older graphemic typology because the use of transcription versus transliteration depends largely on the phonological properties of a writing system.

1.2.2.1. NONPHONOLOGICAL, OR MORPHEMIC, WRITING SYSTEMS. This is virtually identical with the logographic type. The graphic signs, which represent primarily morphemes, are entirely independent of phonemes. Again, Chinese and to a certain extent Japanese written in *kanji* and Korean written in Chinese logograms are the only representatives of nonphonological writing systems presently used.

1.2.2.2. PHONOLOGICAL WRITING SYSTEMS. All other writing systems fall in this category, since their graphic signs (single letters, letter combinations, or syllabic signs) represent more or less accurately phonemes of the languages for which they are used; in conjunction, they also represent morphemes, which makes it possible to demarcate individual words and to string them together to form sentences. One basic sign of the writing system represents at the maximum one syllable, and at the minimum one phoneme in the phonology of a language.

Table 1.1 shows the classification of writing systems in schematic form. The examples listed are, of course, only indicative. In the case of cryptographies, neither ciphers nor codes are phonological, but certain cipher systems are based on single letters or pairs of letters, while the code systems are based on whole words.

We can now proceed to formulate the following definition:

Definition 3: Writing System

A writing system is a system of rules governing the recording of words and sentences of a language by means of conventional graphic signs.

---

as well as in scholarly works is misleading because *all* writing systems are used to convey *ideas,* whereas Chinese characters represent one or more *words;* that is, they are *word-signs.* Catford (1965) also uses the term ''logographic'' and disparages the use of ''ideographic'' or ''pictographic'' writing (p. 68).

Table 1.1   Classification and Typology of Writing Systems

TYPE	PHONOLOGICAL	Phonological		Nonphonological
	GRAPHEMIC	Alphabetical	Syllabic	Logographic
FUNCTION — Orthographies	Orthographies	English Russian Arabic Hebrew Greek, etc.	Amharic Japanese *(kana)*	Chinese Japanese *(kanji)*
Stenographies	Stenographies	Gregg, Pitman, Gabelsberger, etc.[1]		
Cryptographies	Cryptographies	Vigenère cipher[2]	Playfair cipher[3]	Code systems
Paedographies	Paedographies	Transcription schemes		
Technographies	Technographies	Transliteration schemes		Road signs Drafting symbols
Machinographies	Machinographies	Morse code		

[1]Stenographies use alphabetical, syllabic, and logographic writing.
[2]Based on substitution of single letters, but not phonological.
[3]Based on substitution of letter pairs, but not phonological.

The term *writing system* is thus entirely abstract and generic, and it is neutral as to function or typology. A writing system of any kind may be of any type.

A writing system is always linked to a particular language, so that a writing system for language *A* cannot be used for language *B*. This is so because a writing system is intended to represent the morphemes of a language, and these are, by definition, different in different languages. There may be some or many similarities between the writing systems of language *A* and *B,* foremost among them the script used, but as systems they are essentially independent of script, which is only one of their elements. Writing systems are, however, entirely dependent on the conventions underlying their rules; these rules are not derived from any ''natural law,'' nor do they follow any logical pattern, but they are arbitrary inventions, accepted and observed by those who wish to communicate in writing in a certain language.

2.   SCRIPT

2.1.   Definitions

The term *script* has several denotations of which only one forms the subject of our investigation. The *Oxford English Dictionary (OED)* distinguishes five meanings, three of which are more or less general, while two are restricted to the professional usage of the word in law and theater (and more recently, films) which we shall disregard here. The first three meanings are:

(1) Something written; a piece of writing. (Now rare.)[11]
(2a) Handwriting; the characters used in handwriting (as distinguished from print).
(2b) A kind of type devised to imitate the appearance of handwriting.
(3) A kind of writing, a system of alphabetical or other written characters.

The German psychologist and linguist Friedrich Kainz[12] observed that *Schrift* (which in German has a wider range of denotations than its English counterpart) can be interpreted in four different ways, somewhat analogous to *Sprache*, following de Saussure's distinctions[13]:

Script ≅ [langage]: the forms of written marks used for the purpose of recording communication; studied by graphic artists, calligraphers.

Script ≅ [langue]: an element of a writing system; studied by linguists. (= *OED* (3))

Script ≅ [parole]: the operation of writing and its end results; studied by psychologists, literary critics. (= *OED* (1))

Script ≅ [parler]: handwriting; studied by graphologists. (= *OED* (2))

We are here concerned only with *script* in the sense of *OED* (3) or Kainz' *langue* equivalent, and define it for our purposes as follows:

Definition 4: Script

A script is the set of conventional graphic signs designed to give visual representation to the elements of a writing system.

A graphic sign, to qualify as a member of the set that constitutes a script, must consist of one or more distinctive geometrical shapes whose configuration is such that a literate person who is familiar with the conventions governing a script can identify it and use it in the manner prescribed by these conventions.

The set of graphic signs constituting a script may comprise some or all of several subsets of *characters*, each of which has certain designated functions: letters (to represent phonemes), syllable signs (to represent a group of

---

[11]The German equivalent of *script*, the word *Schrift*, still means a written work, such as a book or essay, and in the plural it means the works of a writer. The French *écriture* may also mean a body of written documents such as correspondence, and it is also used as the equivalent of the English *scripture* (sacred writings).

[12]Kainz (1967), Bd. 4, p. 14.

[13]Saussure (1949), pp. 36–39.

phonemes), logographic signs (to represent concepts), punctuation marks (to demarcate boundaries between letters, words, and sentences), diacritical marks (to modify letters so as to represent phonemes other than those represented by the basic letters), and prosodic marks (to indicate accent, pitch, cadence, pauses, and so forth).

Definition 5: Character

A character is an element of a script, representing a phoneme, syllable, word, or prosodic feature of a language by means of graphic signs.

Characters may be semantic (numerals, Chinese logograms, or other logograms[14] such as %, #, $, and &) or nonsemantic (letters, syllabic signs, punctuation marks, and prosodic marks).

Definition 6: Letter

A letter is a character, originally designed to represent one distinctive phoneme of a spoken language, that forms part of an alphabet.

A letter has a *name* by which it is commonly known to the literate users of a language, its alphabet, and its writing system. It also has a *pronunciation* which may be unique in the writing system of a particular language (i.e., a certain letter is always pronounced by uttering a certain phoneme) or variable (i.e., the same letter may be pronounced by uttering various phonemes, or even no phoneme at all, depending on the letter's concatenation with other letters or on other reasons). Certain concatenations and sequences of letters are characteristic for the orthography of a language, while others are not permitted. For example, a Czech word may begin with the letters *hr* or *sr*, but no English word could begin with these concatenations; the concatenation *szcz* is characteristic for Polish

---

[14]Logograms are increasingly used in modern technology, particularly in road signs, where quick perception by drivers and independence of spoken language is of prime importance, and in drafting practice, where each branch of science and technology has developed its own repertory of logograms. Gerlach (1953) gives the example of the following label on an electric measuring instrument:

$$1° = 10mA \approx \sqcap \angle \ \underline{\widehat{\Omega}} \ \approx \overset{1}{_{1.5}} \ \bigstar$$

This may look like hieroglyphs to the layman, but it is immediately understood—independently of any particular language—by a trained electrician to mean: "One degree of the scale is equal to 10 milliamperes; the instrument can be used for alternating or direct current; it should be used in a horizontal or inclined position (i.e., not upright); it has a moving-coil system with a permanent field magnet; the current flows through a rectifier; when used for direct current, it is rated 1; when used for alternating current, it is rated 1.5 (this is the maximum permissible error expressed in percent of deflection of the pointer); it has been tested for a voltage of 2000 volts." Compare the length of this verbal statement to the compact notation of the logograms!

orthography but cannot occur in that of any other language written in Roman script. The set of rules governing the permissible and nonpermissible letter concatenations of an orthography form its *graphotactics*.

Single letters or letter combinations, not modified in any way by devices such as diacritical marks or ligatures, may occasionally assume the role of logograms. The letter *d*, formerly used in the British notation for monetary value, was pronounced *penny;* the abbreviation *e.g.* is pronounced *for example;* and the two letters *lb* are pronounced *pound*. In these cases, there is no connection between the phonemes for which the letters or letter combinations stand; they have become logograms, exactly like Chinese characters.

In alphabetical writing systems, the subset of letters is the basic subset of a script to which all other subsets (except logographs) are ancillary; that is, letters can be used to write words, sentences, and even entire paragraphs without punctuation marks, diacritical marks, and so on, but not vice versa. The subset of letters in conjunction with the subset of diacritical marks is arranged in standardized sequences to form other subsets, namely *alphabets*.

Definition 7: Alphabet

An alphabet is a finite set of letters arranged in a standardized order and used to write a specific language.

Every language has its own specific alphabet, since only a particular set of letters, with its ordinal arrangement and a particular set of diacritical marks or ligatures, is recognized as forming a standardized alphabet, while other diacritical marks are considered "foreign" to the alphabet of that particular language. Thus, the English alphabet consists of 26 letters, *A* to *Z*, all of which exist in an upper- and lowercase form, and it has an empty set of diacritical marks. (When diacritical marks do occur in certain words such as *précis* or *rôle*, they are almost invariably of French origin, and are mostly used in Britain but almost always omitted in American usage.) German also has 26 uppercase letters, *A* to *Z*, but it has 27 lowercase letters, *a* to *z* and the ligature ß); it uses three umlauts *(ä, ö, and ü)* but has no accents; and so on. In the alphabets of some languages, certain modified letters have an ordinal value separate from that of the basic letter (e.g., in Swedish, the letters *å, ä, and ö* file after *Z* as the 27th to 29th letters), while other languages give separate ordinal values to ligatures or double letters (e.g., in Spanish, *ch, ll*, and *rr* are filed separately after *c, l,* and *r*, respectively).

2.2. Uses of Scripts

All scripts, particularly alphabetic ones, can be used for at least three different purposes which, though interrelated in various ways, must nevertheless be clearly distinguished and which have to be considered on their own merits and for their individual objectives if confusion is to be avoided.[15] As we shall see later, it is the failure to make such clear-cut distinctions between the purposes of using a script that has led to lengthy and largely fruitless discussions about the value and usefulness of different schemes for the conversion of scripts for various applications.

The first and most common use of script is in the *orthography* of a language. Although, in theory, the letters and letter combinations of an alphabetic script ought to express as unambiguously as possible the phonemes of the language for which the script was designed, this has probably never been the case even in the distant past when various alphabets were invented. In all contemporary orthographies, the phonetic requirements are subordinated to the demands of graphemic convenience and tradition (even to the extent that outright errors, once they have been repeated often enough, are retained as part of a mistaken ''historic'' spelling tradition).[16]

The second use of a script is in *transcription,* when the phonemes of a source language written in a dissimilar script (or not written at all) are represented more or less faithfully by the characters (letters and other graphic signs) of a dominant script. Transcription is inherently a paedography, since its main purpose is to ''teach'' persons who are unfamiliar with the sounds of a language (including dialectal variants of their own language) how to pronounce words and phrases; secondarily, when it is used by linguists and in particular by phoneticians, it may also be used as a technography, a convenient and highly effective means of graphic communication between experts to express phenomena that could otherwise be described only by lengthy and cumbersome circumscription.

The third use of script is in *transliteration,* when the graphemes of a source script are converted into graphemes of a target script without any regard to pronunciation and also, at least in the strictest sense, without either adding or deleting any graphemes that are not present in the source script. Transliteration is always a technography, used by specialists either when the faithful reproduction

---

[15]Alphabetical scripts can be used for several other purposes: the letters may also serve as numerals (e.g., Roman numerals); they may be used to indicate enumeration (e.g., in the designation of chapters or paragraphs, or when used in the notation of a classification scheme); and they may be used as logograms, such as in music (the tone C), in chemistry (C for carbon), mathematics ($x, y,$ and z used as conventional designations of unknown quantities), and so forth. These uses of alphabetic scripts are, however, not relevant to our topic.

[16]One example of many is the word *foreign,* derived from the Latin *foranus* (''the one from abroad''), which was variously spelled *foren, forren, forreyn,* and *forrayn* until the 16th century when, due to the affectation of some writers, it began to be spelled with an entirely superfluous *g* through a mistaken analogy with *reign* (derived from the Latin *regnum,* ''royal authority, realm''). This erroneous spelling was sanctioned by Samuel Johnson in his dictionary, and has survived ever since. English orthography is particularly rich in such pseudoetymological spellings, but many other languages also suffer from them, despite spelling reforms which could not always eradicate time-honored mistakes.

of the graphemes of a source script is technically unfeasable, or when certain purposes are more conveniently served by a graphemic representation in the target script.

The first of these three uses of script pertains only to a *single* graphemic system, while the second and third pertain always to *pairs* of graphemic systems and are employed in the conversion of one system into the other. We now proceed to define the generic operation of script conversion and the methods by which it is performed.

3. CONVERSION OF SCRIPTS

3.1. Definitions

A script, although originally always invented and designed for a specific language, is in principle independent of language. This means that any language may be written in any script. As we see in Chapter 2, there are languages that have indeed been written in two or more scripts, albeit not always with the same ease and clarity. The corollary of the independence of script and language is the fact that a language written in one script may at any time and for any purpose be written in another script. The processes involved can be described in generic terms only by the somewhat cumbersome expression *conversion of scripts,* since there is no English equivalent for the German *Umschrift* and similar terms in other languages that denote both transliteration and transcription or any blend of the two methods. (The term *metagraphy* which has been proposed[17] is a synonym for transliteration only but not for transcription, while *Romanization,* now used as a neutral term to denote both methods of script conversion, is applicable only to conversion into the Roman script, that is to say, to a subset of all possible script conversions.)

Definition 8: Conversion of Scripts

Conversion of scripts is the operation of replacing the script and writing system of a language by a different script and writing system.

When a language originally written in script A is to be written in script B, the necessary conversion is the equivalent, on the graphemic level, of translation from one language into another on the semantic level. We shall therefore use similar terminology for the designation of the pair of scripts involved in a conversion.

---

[17]Wright (1969).

Definition 9: Source Script

A source script is the script of a language that is converted into a different script.

In bibliographic control systems this is always, by definition, a dissimilar script (see Definition 12).

Definition 10: Target Script

A target script is that script into which a different script is being converted.

In bibliographic control systems this is the dominant script.

Definition 11: Dominant script

A dominant script is that script in which all or most of the written communications of a language community are recorded, and the script with which the majority of literate members of that community are most familiar.

Most language communities have only one dominant script, but there are some, notably Serbo-Croatian and Hindustani (Hindi/Urdu), that use two different dominant scripts.

Definition 12: Dissimilar Script

A dissimilar script is any script that is different from and incompatible with the dominant script because some or all of its characters exhibit features that make it impossible to integrate them with the characters of the dominant script.

A script becomes incompatible with the dominant one when it contains basic elements (letters or other characters) that are not members of the set governed by the conventions of the dominant script, and are therefore foreign to it. Even a script that has some basic elements in common with the dominant one is considered to be incompatible if it contains more than a very small number of "foreign" elements. The Icelandic alphabet, which contains two non-Roman letters, is considered a Roman alphabet, but Greek, which has nine non-Roman letters (considering only majuscules), is a dissimilar script wherever the Roman script is the dominant one.

Since bibliographic control depends on the arrangement of items in a known and predictable sequence, namely the conventional order of characters in a script, an effort is generally made to integrate the characters of a script irrespective of languages and language-specific characteristics of alphabets. To achieve this aim for Roman script on the largest possible scale, it has long been the custom to consider modified characters (such as letters with diacritical marks) as equivalents of their basic forms so far as their alphabetization is concerned. The rules of alphabetization in most European orthographies are based on this principle, the exceptions being those languages in which modified letters have their own separate place in the alphabet. For example, in most countries any of the characters ó, ò, ô, õ, ö, ő, ō, ŏ, and ǫ is considered to be the equivalent (for alphabetizing purposes) of the basic Roman letter *o,* provided it is written in conjunction with any of the other 25 letters of the Roman script. But if *o* is written in conjunction with non-Roman characters such as Ψ or ш, it becomes itself a "foreign" character and can no longer be integrated and alphabetized; it loses, so to speak, its citizenship in the Roman script and becomes a citizen of the Greek or Cyrillic script, as the case may be.

Such artificial "integration" of essentially different alphabets as has been customary for Roman script cannot, however, be performed for most other scripts that are used by more than one language; it is not entirely possible for Cyrillic, nor is it feasible for Arabic or Hebrew script, as is discussed in more detail in Chapter 4.

3.2. Absolute and Relative Conversion of Scripts

For the purpose of this study, it is necessary to distinguish between two completely different kinds of script conversion. The first, which we shall call *absolute conversion of scripts,* applies to a language originally written in a certain script, on which another script is imposed by *decree.* It is absolute in the sense that, after the conversion has been imposed, the language is no longer written in the former script; also, there is generally only one approved version of the imposed script (even though alternative versions may develop after the new script has been in use for a considerable time). An example is the Turkish language, which for centuries had been written in Arabic script until the Roman script was imposed by governmental decree. The application of a certain script to the writing of previously unwritten language may also be considered to fall into this category (the conversion being made from "zero" script, or an empty set of characters, to a particular script and its specific set of characters), because a body of men (such as the priests of a faith, a political assembly, or an academy of language) or even a single individual makes a decision to that effect. Examples include the application of the Roman script to most European languages in the past and to some African and Asian languages in our own time, and the application of Cyrillic script to some languages spoken in Central Asia and Siberia.

The second type of conversion of scripts, which we shall call *relative conversion of scripts,* occurs when a source language written in a certain script is converted into the different script of a target language for the purposes of the users of that target language. It is relative in two respects: *(a)* the purposes for which it is undertaken may be linguistic, bibliographic, geographic, commercial, or generally informational, and each of these purposes may and usually does require a different conversion method; *(b)* the writing systems of different target languages may and usually do require different conversion methods to suit the conventions underlying those writing systems, even if they use the same basic script. For example, the transcription of a Russian name for bibliographic purposes differs from that used in a newspaper, and the name is transcribed differently in England and in Germany, even though the same script is used in both target languages.

Relative conversion of scripts is never intended to supersede or replace the script of a source language. It merely enables people unfamiliar with the script of the source language to convert names and phrases written in that language into the characters of a script with which they are familiar (in most instances, the script in which their native language is written). Relative conversion of scripts is normally not used to write consecutive passages of text comprising more than a few sentences or a short paragraph.

The distinction between absolute and relative conversion of scripts makes it necessary to introduce some new terminology to avoid ambiguity. Ordinarily, the term *Romanization* is now used in both senses: one may speak of the Romanization of a Turkish text (i.e., an old one, written in Arabic script), and of the Romanization of the Turkish language (i.e., the introduction of the Roman script by Kemal Atatürk and its consequences). The context generally makes clear what is intended. But since this study deals with both phenomena, regarding not only the Roman script but also other scripts that are widely used, confusion would result from the indiscriminate use of one term for two different concepts.

We shall use terms ending in the suffix *-ification* to signify absolute conversion of scripts, while terms ending in *-ization* will be used for relative conversion of scripts. The latter practice follows established usage in ISO standards and in the schemes of the Library of Congress. The suffix *-ification* implies positive action, being derived from the Latin root for "to do," and is therefore suitable for the kind of script conversion effected by fiat (from the same Latin root), that is, by decree and enforced by political power, whereas *-ization* implies "treating in the way of" or "conforming to" *(OED)*, which is more appropriate for relative script conversion.

To be entirely consistent, the first term under Absolute Conversion should have been *Romanification,* but coining this term would have betrayed the kind of foolish consistency denounced by Emerson. The term *Latinization* already exists and has been used by several authors in the sense intended here,[18] although it is not entirely unambiguous; the verb *Latinize* from which the noun is derived, has

---

[18]For example, Braun (1930), Castagné (1927, 1928), Imart (1965), and Wood (1929).

ABSOLUTE CONVERSION OF SCRIPTS	RELATIVE CONVERSION OF SCRIPTS
results in	results in
Latinization	Romanization
Cyrillification	Cyrillization
Arabification	Arabization
Hebraification	Hebraization
.	.
.	.
.	.

several different meanings, but since only one of these is *to transcribe into Latin characters (OED),* while all others pertain to topics that fall entirely outside the scope of our investigation, there seems to be little danger in using *Latinization* for the absolute conversion of a language's non-Roman script to the Roman script.

We can now proceed to define the two kinds of script conversion.

Definition 13: Absolute Conversion of Scripts

Absolute conversion of scripts is the substitution of a script for another script in which a language was formerly written, or the application of a script to a previously unwritten language. It is introduced by decree or by the general consensus of the members of a language community.

Definition 14: Relative Conversion of Scripts

Relative conversion of scripts is the conversion of the script of a source language into the script of a target language. It is performed for the purpose of making words in the source language readable and/or pronounceable for members of the language community using the target language.

3.3.   Transcription and Transliteration

3.3.1.   Dictionary Definitions.   According to the *OED,* the verb *transcribe* appears in the middle of the 16th century in the sense of "copy out from an original" but was not used until 1724 in the sense of "to write out in other characters." The verb *transliterate* seems to have been coined relatively recently and is first recorded in 1861, when it was used by the philologist Max Müller to write about a Buddhistic text that had been converted into Chinese, and by G. Moore in relation to Hebrew texts. From then onward, the terms *transcription* and *transliteration* were used fairly indiscriminately to denote methods of script conversion. The *OED* defines *transliteration* as

The act or process of transliterating; the rendering of the letters or characters of one alphabet into those of another.

This is based on the definition of *transliterate* as

To replace (letters or characters of one language) by those of another used to represent the same sounds; to write (a word, etc.) in the characters of another alphabet.

Transcription is defined by the *OED* as synonymous with *transliteration,* to which the reader is referred.

Thus, in the early years of this century, when the relevant fascicle of the *OED* was compiled (it was first published in 1914), no difference in meaning was perceived between the two terms. As far as general dictionaries of the English language are concerned, the situation has not changed appreciably to this very day, as the latest edition of *Webster's Third New International Dictionary of the English Language* (copyright 1971) also defines *transliterate* as

To represent or spell (words, letters or characters) of another language or alphabet

and equates *transcribe* (in the relevant sense) with *transliterate*. The definitions of the respective nouns follow the same pattern. Thus, most people, including librarians who deal with the products of script conversion almost daily, do not distinguish between the two terms and use them interchangeably as quasi-synonyms.

3.3.2. Linguistic Definitions.   Linguists recognized the need for a distinction between the two methods of script conversion in the early 1920s, when attempts were made to arrive at exact definitions and systematization of conversion schemes. A conference of philologists and linguists was convened in Copenhagen in 1925 to deal with the problem, and their report constituted the basis for the present International Phonetic Alphabet. The conference concerned itself only with the linguistic aspects of the issue and did not deal with script conversion for bibliographic or cartographic purposes:

It had to provide a system of phonetic transcription of the sounds actually occurring in any language or dialect to be described scientifically without any regard to the way in which such languages or dialects may have been hitherto written down; and then, on the other hand, to indicate the best way in which Oriental and other alphabets should be transliterated in Roman type, without any regard to the manner in which words are actually pronounced in the language concerned. It is obvious that this really constitutes two different problems. . . . Nevertheless, though thus transcription and transliteration are necessarily two different things, they must be harmonized as far as possible.[19]

[19]*Phonetic Transcription and Transliteration* (1925), p. 7.

The basic principles were now established. Transcription was defined as a method that linked phonemes of a (written or unwritten) source language with their written representation in the characters of the script of the target language. It was understood that these target characters would practically always be those of the Roman script. Transliteration, on the other hand, was defined as the establishing of a strict equivalence between characters in the script of a source language and corresponding characters in the script of a target language. Again, the implication was that the target language would be one that used the Roman script. At that time no attention was paid to the fact that script conversion is a universal problem: Russians or Japanese, for example, encounter difficulties of their own in converting words or phrases in languages using the Roman script into the Cyrillic or *kanji* script.

The definitions formulated by the Copenhagen conference formed the stepping-stone for further developments, particularly those dealing with the implications of script conversion in the context of bibliographic control.

3.3.3. ISO Definitions.

The next step toward a more precise definition of the methods of script conversion was taken when the ISO began to devote itself to the task of issuing standards for the conversion of scripts.[20] We shall devote more detailed attention to the analysis of these definitions, because they were the first to be formulated expressly for the purposes of bibliographic and library work, and also because of the importance of statements and definitions emanating from a prestigious international organization, whose influence reaches far beyond that achieved by a purely professional body and even a national organization, which by necessity are often more restricted in their activities. In other words, rules for the conversion of scripts made for the particular purposes of specialists such as linguists, philologists, and cartographers cannot hope to command the universal acceptance that is so essential for universal bibliographic control intended to serve the needs of all those who wish to identify, find, and use documents of any kind anywhere. Such international and universal control cannot be based on the practices of even the largest national libraries, which must necessarily cater to certain linguistic and sometimes historical preferences of their users, but only on those accepted by the majority of the members of an international agency. The resulting standards will almost inevitably be the fruit of compromises made in the interest of mutual acceptability and interchangeability. The underlying theory, however, as expressed in the basic assumptions and

---

[20]Until 1972 the standards developed by the ISO were called *Recommendations,* and only individual national members of the ISO issued *Standards* which were either partly or wholly identical with ISO Recommendations. Since January 1972 the ISO has published *International Standards,* for which the approval of at least 75% of the member bodies is needed. The transliteration schemes of the ISO are still Recommendations and have not yet achieved the status of International Standards, which will occur only when they are revised in future or when new such schemes are published.

particularly in the definitions of purposes and methods, must be as succinct as possible and free of controversial or logically unsound statements; otherwise there could be no solid foundation on which to build the framework of individual rules and standards.

The ISO's work in the field of script conversion is discussed in Chapter 4; here, we are concerned only with the definitions of aims and methods as stated in two versions of the introductory statement printed in ISO standards dealing with the subject. The first, with the title "Introductory note on the general principles of transliteration," was written by Jean Meyriat, then the Secretary-General of the International Commitee for Social Sciences Documentation. The following excerpt is the relevant part of the official English version (the original being in French); it was first published in ISO/R 9, the recommendation on the transliteration of Cyrillic characters, issued in 1954.

Introductory Note on the
General Principles of Transliteration

Transliteration is the operation of representing the characters or signs of any one alphabet by those of any other, but this note refers only to transliteration of non-Latin alphabets into the Latin alphabet, also termed Roman alphabet. For documentation purposes, the main requirement is that non-Latin texts should be reproducible by typewriters or other devices having only Latin characters and a few additional signs (diacritical, etc.).

It is a question of representing characters or signs, not sounds—aand this is what distinguishes transliteration from transcription—a matter of representing characters as they are written, rather than according to their phonetic or etymological values. Transliteration generally can and should be automatic, so that it can be done by anyone able to identify the language of the original; and it should be possible for anyone with an adequate knowledge of this language to re-establish the text in its original characters.

This introduction and its definitions dealt primarily with transliteration, while transcription as an alternative method was only obliquely mentioned without being actually defined. At that time, it was thought that practically all major non-Roman scripts could somehow be converted into Roman script by transliteration, and that this method, when based on an unambiguous one-to-one correspondence between the characters of the two scripts involved, would also be automatic. It was realized, to be sure, that the Chinese and Japanese scripts would not be amenable to such treatment, but these problems were relegated to the more distant future.

The operational definition of *transliteration* did not go beyond the Copenhagen statement and was, as such, quite correct. The functional part of the definition, however, recognized explicitly that the standard dealt with transliteration in one direction only. Thus, it was not really international in the sense that its principles could be applied to script conversion between "any one alphabet" and any other one.

The second paragraph contains a mistake which, in somewhat different form, was also carried over into the later version of this introductory statement. After stating categorically that "transliteration can and should be automatic," its says that to transliterate one must be "able to identify the *language* of the original" (my emphasis), and that the same knowledge of language is necessary to carry out the reconversion of a converted text. What is meant here is, of course, the *script,* and not a *language* written in any particular script. (Lest it might be thought that faulty translation is involved, the original French version has the term *langue* in the same sentence.) If conversion is truly to be done by transliteration, then only two finite sets of characters are involved between which a strict one-to-one equivalence has been established. All that is necessary to do this automatically (i.e., by a purely clerical manipulation or by a machine) is the unmistakable establishment of which set of characters is the source alphabet, which one is the target alphabet, and the switching code (i.e., transliteration scheme) to be used. The language in which the text is written is of no consequence in this process, since it is expressly stated that "phonetic or etymological values" should be entirely disregarded. If the source script is the Cyrillic one, the text may be in Russian, Ukrainian, Bulgarian, or even in one of the non-Slavic languages of the USSR, such as Turkmen or Uzbek. The results of such automatic transliteration will sometimes look peculiar to a person familiar with those languages, to be sure, but that is exactly what transliteration does; it sometimes has to sacrifice intelligibility (and almost always pronounceability) for the reader who knows only the target script, in the interests of absolute and unambiguous reversibility. Meyriat probably felt uneasy about these prospects, and wrote *language* where *script* was the only possible word to use because any tampering with the automatic transliteration process by changing, inserting, or deleting letters by someone who "knew the language," done in the interests of intelligibility or proper pronunciation, would run counter to the very principle established.

Meyriat's definitions and statements, which were reprinted (with some important reservations regarding the "automatic" operation of transliteration) in the following two ISO transliteration standards for Arabic and Hebrew, were subjected to some critique by R. Frontard, the director of the Association française de normalisation (AFNOR). He was the first Westerner to point out that

ISO will have to broaden the scope of its transliteration work, at present systematically confined to the problem of the transliteration of non-Latin characters into Latin characters. It cannot indefinitely disregard the drawbacks of an asymmetrical conception of transliteration.[21]

After discussing the difficulties encountered by too strict an interpretation of transliteration when applied to scripts other than the Cyrillic, he came to the

[21]Frontard (1961), p. 80.

somewhat odd conclusion that "transliteration is therefore a particular kind of transcription and not the opposite of transcription."[22] In the light of several passages in his article, one may conclude that what he apparently wanted to say was that the ISO recommendations for the conversion of scripts, although called "transliteration schemes," were in fact transcription schemes with more or less pronounced features of transliteration (or perhaps vice versa), and that such compromise solutions were the only workable ones for practical application in bibliographic control.

Although Frontard was obviously no linguist[23] and no official spokesman for the ISO, his conception of transliteration as a species of the genus transcription was unfortunately given the stamp of quasirespectability because of his position and the prestige of the source in which his article was published, the *Unesco Bulletin for Libraries*.

About two years later, ISO's Working Party on Transliteration concluded that the wording of the "Introductory Note" was inadequate in the light of experience gained in the compilation of transliteration schemes for Arabic and Hebrew. J. Orne, then librarian of the University of North Carolina, was asked to draw up a new version in 1963 which, after many discussions and several changes, was accepted by the Working Group in 1964 and published in 1965.[24] The parts relevant to our discussion are as follows:

General principles for the conversion of one written language
into another [(ISO/TC46 (Sec. 426) 697 (Rev.)]

Various methods of conversion are used to represent one written language in the characters of another. An important function of conversion, particularly in bibliographic, documentation and library work, is to facilitate classifying, in alphabetical order, documents or cards in languages using differing alphabets. Another useful function is to permit various alphabets to be reproduced by usually available mechanical devices, such as the typewriter. The methods of conversion most commonly used are:

Transcription: The operation of representing the elements of a language, either sounds or signs, however they may be written originally, in any other system of letters or sound signs.

Transliteration: The operation of representing the characters or signs of one alphabet by those of another, in principle letter by letter. This method of conversion is applied specifically in representing the purely literal alphabets such as Cyrillic into another literal alphabet, such as Latin.

---

[22]*Ibid.*, p. 82.

[23]Frontard says that "the Arabic and Hebrew languages use what might be called stenographic [sic!] systems of writing" (*Ibid.*, p. 81).

[24]International Organization for Standardization (1964). Before the approved text appeared in two ISO Recommendations (ISO/R9 for Cyrillic and ISO/R843 for Greek, both published in 1968), it was reproduced in full in *Journal of Documentation* **21** (1965):15–16.

These methods are applicable to the conversion in different alphabets, which results in Romanization, Arabization, Cyrillization, etc.

Romanization, for example, is a form of conversion in which letters of the Latin alphabet are made to represent languages using other characters or signs.

Every effort should be made to avoid ambiguity and at the same time to maintain the utmost simplicity and the most direct relationship of each letter or sign to its counterpart in conversion.

Although the wording of the title is misleading, and some parts of the definitions are either ambiguous or erroneous (as shown in detail below), this was, on the whole, a considerable improvement on the former version, especially in light of the fact that it was the product of a committee, and had to satisfy sometimes widely divergent points of view by way of compromise. An effort was made to "internationalize" the introduction, that is, to make its provisions valid for the conversion of any script from and into any other script; also, the former emphasis on transliteration as the only valid method was dropped, as was the implication that this could and should be done "automatically."

We now take up those parts of the statement that seem to be in need of revision or amendment.

The title of the document speaks of "conversion of one written *language* into another," which seems to confuse transliteration with translation. A "written language" can only be converted into another written language by translation, that is, by rendering the expressions written in language *A* by means of its words, phrases, idioms, grammar, and syntax into more or less equivalent expressions in language *B,* using that language's words, phrases, idioms, grammar, and syntax. What ISO standards on this subject are concerned with is, of course, the conversion of *scripts* used in the writing systems of various languages. The first sentence of the text is more precise, and the title should in fact be modeled on it as follows: *General principles for the representation of one written language in the characters of another.*

The definition of *transcription* introduces an unfortunate ambiguity by saying that "either sounds or signs" are converted to "any other written system of letters or sound signs," thus not recognizing expressly that individual letters are not transcribed *qua* letters, but solely as graphic representations of sounds. The expression "Letters or sound signs" is tautological, since letters *are* sound signs; what was meant was possibly the distinction between letters and syllabic signs or logograms.

The definition of *transliteration* is correct as far as its first sentence is concerned, although the words *characters* and *signs* should be changed to *letters* since transliteration, by definition, can be applied only to those characters that are letters of an alphabet, while it is impossible to use this method for the conversion of other characters. The second sentence, however, is no longer strictly in the realm of definition, but is concerned with the *application* of the method.

The next paragraph implies that both methods can be used for conversion between any two scripts, which is simply not the case. In Arabization and Cyrillization (the two kinds of conversion mentioned) only transcription can be performed, for reasons that are discussed in Chapter 5.

So much for the shortcomings of the official version of the statement. When it was first published, however, as an introduction to ISO/R9, the second edition of the transliteration scheme for Cyrillic characters, and in ISO/R843, the transliteration scheme for Greek, the anonymous editor found it necessary to tamper with the official version by rearranging the first sentences of the introductory paragraph and making seemingly "minor" changes in other places, all of which made a mess of what had been so carefully worded in committee. This was particularly unfortunate since only very few people had access to the original version of 1964 (although it was later reprinted in the *Journal of Documentation),* while anybody using the ISO Recommendations is presented with a substantially distorted version. The first paragraph of the "Introduction" now reads as follows:

One important function of conversion of one written language in the characters of another, particularly in bibliographic, documentation and library work, is to facilitate classifying, in alphabetical order, documents or cards in languages using differing alphabets. Conversion permits also the reproduction of texts written in various alphabets by readily available mechanical devices, such as the typewriter.

The statement about methods disappeared from the telescoped first sentence, as did the phrase that explained the nature of conversion as being the representation of one written language in the characters of another. In the definition of *transliteration,* some changes in wording were introduced which, although not affecting the meaning, did nothing to clarify matters but rather obscured them. Some apparently minor changes made in the next paragraph were more serious. It now reads:

These methods are applicable to conversion from any alphabet to another, resulting in Romanization, Arabization, Cyrillization, etc.

This is considerably different from "conversion *in* different alphabets," and makes the statement even more vulnerable to the criticism voiced above. In the following paragraph, the phrase, "Every effort should be made to avoid. . . ." was watered down to, "In conversion, it is important to avoid . . ." Finally, in the paragraph on Romanization, the last word, *characters,* correctly printed in ISO/R9, which was published in September 1968, was inexplicably changed to *characteristics or signs* in ISO/R843, published only one month later. This may be due to sloppy editing (since "characteristics" is obviously a misprint for "characters"), but it did little to enhance the value and prestige of the ISO statement on transliteration.

ISO's Subcommittee on Conversion of Written Languages (ISO/TC46/SC2) decided in 1976 to draft a new introduction to ISO's standards on script conversion. The text of this draft, which is free from the distortions and ambiguities of earlier versions of the introduction, is reproduced in full in Appendix B.

3.3.4. Definitions for Geographic Purposes. The definitions of transliteration and transcription proposed by another international body, the Working Group on a Single Romanization System, convened under the auspices of the United Nations Conference on the Standardization of Geographical Names,[25] deserve close attention because of their exact wording:

Transcription: The process of recording the phonological and/or morphological elements of a language in terms of a specific writing system.

Transliteration: The process of recording the graphic symbols of one writing system in terms of the corresponding graphic symbols of a second writing system.

Although expressly formulated for the purposes of cartography, that is, primarily for the conversion of names and designations but not normally for continuous passages of text, these definitions are succinct and general enough to be applied in other contexts.

3.3.5. Definitions for Bibliographic Purposes. Our own definitions are now formulated in the light of the foregoing discussion.

Definition 15: Bibliographic Transcription

Bibliographic transcription is the operation of converting the phonemes and/or morphemes of a source language, recorded in the script of its writing system, as nearly as possible into the script of the writing system of a target language.

Definition 16: Bibliographic Transliteration

Bibliographic transliteration is the operation of converting the characters of a source script into the characters of a target script. In principle, this is a one-to-one transformation, in which one character of the source script is converted into one (and only one) specific character of the target script.

---

[25]United Nations Conference . . . (1972). *Transfer of Names From One Writing System into Another.* (E/CONF. 61/L.5, p. 3.)

3.4.   Function and Typology of Methods for Script Conversion

3.4.1.   Transcription Systems.   Typologically, transcription systems are phonological writing systems, since they are basically used for the conversion of phonemes. From a functional point of view, as pointed out before, they are paedographies as well as technographies, with the aim of conveying the sounds of a source language to the native readers of a target language in such a way as to enable them to pronounce the converted words or phrases by using sounds of their own language that approximate as far as possible those of the source language.[26]

Transcription is normally used to convert a source script into a different target script; the source script may exhibit phonological features of the language to varying extent. For example, the spelling of Finnish and Turkish is almost entirely phonetical, while the spelling of Czech, Spanish, Italian, German, French, and English, in descending order, displays fewer phonological elements,[27] and Chinese script does not exhibit any phonological features at all. Occasionally, transcription is used for two languages using the same script. In Turkish, for example, the names *Churchill* or *Shakespeare* are spelled as *Çörçil* and *Şeykspir,* according to the principle of Turkish orthography that every word, including foreign names, must be spelled phonetically. A similar phenomenon appears in Swedish orthography, where loanwords are often spelled phonetically (for Swedish speakers), for example, *fåtölj* for French *fauteuil* and *tejp* for English *tape.*

3.4.2.   Transliteration Systems.   Typologically, transliteration systems are graphemic but nonphonological writing systems; they may, of course, convey phonological elements, but do so only by virtue of such elements being phonetically rendered in the source script, and not by design or intent. In other words, they do not exhibit any structural features of their own but are entirely

---

[26]No transcription system, not even one designed especially to represent phonetic elements of a spoken language (such as the IPA) can ever do more than approximate the sounds uttered by native speakers of a language. Roman Jakobson (1956) has said: "Letters never, or only partially, reproduce the different distinctive features on which the phonemic pattern is based and unfailingly disregard the structural relationship of these features. There is no such thing in human society as the supplantation of the speech code by its visual replicas, but only a supplementation of this code by parasitic auxiliaries. . . ." (p. 17).

[27]Lundell (1930) attempted a ranking of orthographies (pp. 358–361) in terms of phonological exactitude. Serbian and Finnish were given the mark "excellent"; Croatian, Czech, Polish, Italian, and Spanish were "very good"; Swedish and German "quite bad"; and French, English, and Tibetan were rated "abominable." Regarding English in particular, Lundell says that "L'orthographie anglaise est la plus absurde." The British linguist Firth (1937) agrees: "English spelling is . . . so preposterously unsystematic that some sort of reform is undoubtedly necessary in the interest of the whole world." But nothing has been done about English spelling, and it is unlikely that anything will ever be done, because the forces of tradition are stronger than the most logical arguments of linguists.

dependent on the structure of the source script. They are derivative writing systems.

Regarding their functional classification, they are best considered as technographies (and, by extension, machinographies) for bibliographers, cartographers, and other specialists, since their purpose is the reconstruction of words, phrases, or even consecutive text in a source script through the use of characters in the target script. This process is a purely technical operation for control purposes that is essentially unrelated to any knowledge of languages or to the interpretation of meaning. Pure transliteration systems are never used in the teaching of languages, and can therefore not be considered as paedographies. Occasionally, they may assume the character of cryptographies, since they may be unintelligible (and for the most part also unpronounceable in the target language) to any person not familiar with the system used, although he may know the source language and its script and writing system. Such frustrating features are, however, only unwanted by-products; they are not intentionally built into the system. In Mountford's words, "Bibliographic transliterations are secondary orthographies, designed to suit the literacy of nonnative users of a language."[28]

Needless to say, there are no completely pure transliteration systems in practical use. Even the Romanization schemes devised for the transliteration of scripts that lend themselves well to one-to-one transformations, such as Cyrillic, sometimes ignore certain characters in the source script, and they make often concessions to phonological features for a variety of reasons that are discussed in Chapter 5. However, when transliteration schemes are used as machinographies, it is absolutely necessary to ensure complete and unambiguous one-to-one reversibility, even though the results may look unfamiliar or awkward when printed out and read by a human being. One of the best examples for such a scheme is a proposal for a completely computer-compatible transliteration of Hebrew script that uses uppercase Roman letters, punctuation marks, and other signs available on standard computer printout devices to express Hebrew consonants, vowel points, and diacritical marks.[29] A Hebrew text transliterated in this manner is not really "readable" for either an English or a Hebrew reader, as a glance at Figure 5.1 (p. 323) will show, but it can be analyzed for linguistic purposes by specially trained people, and it can actually be reconverted into the original script by back-transliteration without any ambiguity.

3.4.3. Back-transliteration and Retranscription. The reconstruction of a name or a word in the original script from its converted form is one of the principal features required of transliteration schemes. Exact back-transliteration can, however, be performed only under certain conditions which depend on the nature of the scripts and languages involved in the conversion process rather than

---

[28]Mountford (1973), p. 440.
[29]Goldman, Smith, and Tanenbaum (1971).

on the design or quality of a conversion scheme. Moreover, even when exact back-transliteration is possible, it does not always yield desirable or useful results and must be complemented by retranscription.

It is important to distinguish clearly between back-transliteration and retranscription, which are related but different processes.

Back-transliteration is performed when a name or word that has been transliterated from a source script into a target script is to be reconstituted exactly as it was written in the source script by applying the rules of the transliteration scheme in reverse. The accuracy of the original spelling in the source script is here of no importance at all; that is, even a spelling error, an archaic spelling, or a deliberately distorted spelling (as in the rendering of a dialect in literary works) will be exactly reconstituted. Back-transliteration is possible only between two fully alphabetic scripts, and depends for its execution solely on the rules governing the relationships between the graphemes of the source script and those of the target script. The process involves three distinct stages, and the last stage must yield a result that is identical with the first stage, forming a closed loop (see Figure 1.1).

Retranscription, on the other hand, is needed primarily for the rendering of proper names, and occasionally also for nouns and adjectives derived from proper names and applied to laws, theories, theorems, processes, objects, and so forth (e.g., Copernican system, Gaussian distribution, pasteurization, Diesel engine, Freudian slip). When such a name in Roman script has been Cyrillized, for example, and must be rendered back into the original Roman form, back-transliteration often results in a distorted form because Cyrillization converts

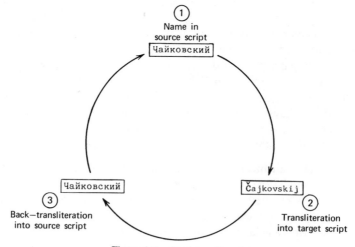

Figure 1.1.   Back-transliteration.

names and words from other scripts by phonological transcription, not by transliteration (the latter would result in a rendering unintelligible and largely unpronounceable to Russian readers). An additional step is therefore needed, namely converting the result of simple back-transliteration from a phonological transcription into the original form. Obviously this can be done only if it is known from sources outside the document that an author's name or the name of a theory or an object is spelled a certain way, and that the conversion into the target script actually referred to that particular name, and not to a similar or even a different one. Retranscription thus involves a four-stage process, and the loop can be successfully closed only if certain facts are known that are entirely independent of the graphemes of the writing systems of either language, and that are not subject to the rules of a conversion scheme (see Figure 1.2).

Stage 3 will be identical with stage 4 only occasionally, namely, when the phonological transcription of a name happens to coincide with the spelling in the source script, but this is rarely the case, particularly when the names involved have spellings that are highly unphonetic and often idiosyncratic, as in English, French, and Scandinavian. But even English, French, or German names, which readers of these languages consider to be spelled quite phonetically, will suffer in back-transliteration and must be retranscribed, as shown in Figure 1.3.

Note that the back-transliteration *Braun* may actually refer to a German author by that name (i.e., an instance of stage 3 being identical with stage 4) cited in an English text that has been translated into Russian; similarly, the alternative spellings of *Brown, Meier,* and *Mülheim* can only be transcribed correctly when

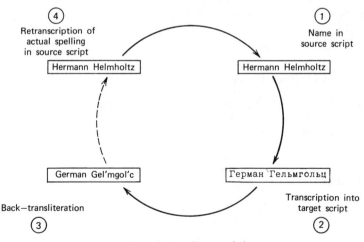

Figure 1.2. Retranscription.

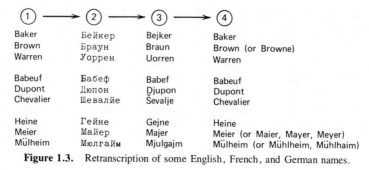

① →	② →	③ →	④
Baker	Бейкер	Bejker	Baker
Brown	Браун	Braun	Brown (or Browne)
Warren	Уоррен	Uorren	Warren
Babeuf	Бабеф	Babef	Babeuf
Dupont	Дюпон	Djupon	Dupont
Chevalier	Шевалйе	Ševalje	Chevalier
Heine	Гейне	Gejne	Heine
Meier	Майер	Majer	Meier (or Maier, Mayer, Meyer)
Mülheim	Мюлгайм	Mjulgajm	Mülheim (or Mühlheim, Mühlhaim)

Figure 1.3. Retranscription of some English, French, and German names.

it is positively known that the person referred to uses a certain spelling of his name.

For languages that lack certain phonemes common to most Western languages and that have to add or substitute other phonemes not present in the pronunciation of the original name to make the transcription pronounceable for their own speakers, the task of retranscription of a name sometimes becomes impossible without cumbersome tracing of the original name through a maze of transformations and a thorough knowledge of the conventions governing the transcription from the source language into the target language. This is the case, for example, in Japanese, where *Diesel* is rendered as *Jizeru* and *Leblanc* appears as *Reburan,* because the Japanese language lacks the phoneme $[1]$ and substitutes $[r]$ for it, while generally two consonants cannot follow each other without being separated by a vowel, most often $[u]$. Incidentally, in Japanese as well as in Chinese, retranscription is the only possible method of conversion from and to any other script, since back-transliteration is ruled out by the logographic character of the script used in these languages.

Definition 17: Back-transliteration

Back-transliteration is the operation of converting the characters of a target script into the characters of a source script. It is the exact reverse of transliteration, and is performed by applying the rules of a transliteration scheme in the opposite direction.

Definition 18: Retranscription

Retranscription is the operation of converting words that have been transcribed phonologically into a target script back into their original form (spelling, capitalization, and punctuation) in the source script.

In practice, retranscription is mainly needed for proper names and their derivatives.

4. BIBLIOGRAPHIC CONTROL

Relative conversion of scripts is today most often performed for bibliographic control purposes, and this study deals primarily with the problems posed by applications in this field, although other uses of script conversion are also considered. It is therefore necessary to define some terms that are frequently used in succeeding chapters.

Bibliographic control is a term now often encountered in publications dealing with documentation in general or with organization of recorded knowledge in libraries[30]; surprisingly, it can be found in only one of the large contemporary dictionaries and encyclopedias of library and information science,[31] but without any definition. The British librarian A. H. Chaplin defined it tersely as "an organized and accessible record of what published material exists," while his American colleague Ritvars Bregzis described it in the following terms:

Bibliographic control utilizes characteristics of bibliographic items expressed as bibliographic data which are formalized in the framework of the bibliographic record. The objectives of this control are varied, and the biblio-graphic record is required to be responsive to any of the functions relevant in attaining these objectives. The variety of the objectives of bibliographic control ranges from ability to identify the most specific aspects of a single bibliographic item to the requirement of international compatibility of bibliographic files.[32]

This description delineates both the nature and the objectives of bibliographic control quite succinctly; it forms the basis for our own definition of a bibliographic control *system.*

[30]Shera and Egan (1949) were probably the first to use the term *bibliographic control.* They saw it as an emerging American equivalent to the European term *documentation* and thought it to be "more descriptive." After explaining the role of control in machines (perhaps) inspired by Wiener's fundamental work *Cybernetics,* dealing with control in man and machine, which had appeared only one year earlier), they stressed its social function in communication and stated that "bibliographic control is thus seen to be one of the instrumental devices in our modern system of graphic communication." The term then found its way into many books and articles written since the 1950s on methods of information storage and retrieval. It was first defined authoritatively (if somewhat narrowly) in a report sponsored by Unesco, *Bibliographic Services: Their Present State and the Possibilities of Improvement* (1950), p. 1: "*Bibliographic control* is defined to mean the mastery over written and published records which is provided by and for the purposes of bibliography." The most exhaustive theoretical and philosophical treatment of the topic is Patrick Wilson's *Two Kinds of Power: an Essay on Bibliographical Control* (1968).

[31]The term *bibliographic control* is listed in *Vocabularium bibliothecarii* (1962) as a synonym for "documentation (selection, classification and dissemination of information)" but it has no equivalent in the other four languages covered by the work. The following reference works (listed here in chronological order) were searched without result: *Encyclopedia of librarianship,* 3rd ed., 1968; *Encyclopedia of library and information science,* 1968– ; L. M. Harrod, *The librarians glossary,* 3rd ed., 1971; *Elsevier's dictionary of library science, information and documentation in 6 languages,* 1973.

[32]Bregzis (1970), p. 7.

Definition 19: Bibliographic Control System

A bibliographic control system performs the operations of description and/or analysis of documents, and produces document surrogates in a standardized and uniform format.

The document surrogates may be arranged in one or more ordered sequences, the order of which must be uniquely predictable, so as to make it possible to retrieve the document surrogates by various characteristics, such as the name of the originator (author), title, subject, form of presentation, language, script, and physical properties. As a result, documents are listed in *bibliographic control tools* of various types. Best known among these are catalogs (listings of documents held by a particular library or, in the case of a union catalog, by several libraries) and bibliographies (listings of documents not restricted to the holdings of one or more more libraries but arranged according to criteria determined by the compilers, such as works written by a particular author, works emanating from a certain country or written during a certain period, works on a particular subject, or any combination of these). Abstracting and indexing services, citation indexes, and other specialized bibliographies, whether in printed form or recorded in a machine-readable format, are other types of bibliographic control tools.

All bibliographic control systems and the bibliographic control tools generated by them are subsystems or components of *documentary communication systems,* which perform a large number of operations designed to achieve the purposes of information storage and retrieval.

We now define the elements of a bibliographic control system and describe them in more detail. In conclusion, we define a documentary communication system.

Definition 20: Document

A document is a permanent record of an observed event (real or imaginary) in visible, audible, or tactile form.

This definition covers written documents, such as books, reports, articles, manuscripts, and machine-readable data bases; two-dimensional representations, such as pictures, maps, and graphs; motion pictures and videotapes; audio recordings; and three-dimensional objects that are used to convey information about themselves, such as sculptures and specimens of natural or man-made objects. Printed documents in particular, such as books and articles, are also known as *bibliographic units* and are characterized by having a title page (or its substitute) and a pagination (and/or volume numbering) that makes them bibliographically independent works.[33]

Definition 21: Document Surrogate

A document surrogate is any secondary record made of a document that is self-contained and has a unique logical structure. It must contain at least a minimal bibliographic description; it may contain an indication of the subject content and/or the form of the document.

Definition 22: Bibliographic Description

A bibliographic description is that part of a document surrogate which lists all or some of the data that identify a document uniquely and unambiguously.

The following elements, here listed in the traditional order followed by most bibliographic tools, but not necessarily named according to conventional bibliographic terminology (so as to make them applicable to all kinds of documents), may be included in the bibliographic citation:

1. Originator: author, composer, artist, performer, producer, manufacturer, and so forth;
2. Title: the name assigned to a document by its originator;
3. Title of the containing document, if the document described is part of a larger document and has its own title;
4. Edition: number or kind (revised, enlarged, etc.);
5. Place of publication or origin;
6. Publisher, distributor, or other agent of provenance (including the author as publisher);
7. Date of publication, release, and so forth;
8. Physical characteristics identifying the document as an object: number of pages or volumes, dimensions, color, rounds per minute, bits per inch, and so forth;
9. Indication of being part of a series: name of series and/or serial number;
10. Language;
11. Explanatory notes: contents, relation to other documents, and so forth.

---

[33] Although an article has a pagination which is dependent on that of another bibliographic unit (a periodical), its pagination is unique to it in that no other independent bibliographic unit can occupy the same space in the same periodical. A single issue of a periodical or a fascicle of a book published serially, on the other hand, are bibliographically dependent works and are not normally considered to be bibliographic units.

The *minimal set of data,* according to the international standard ISO 690[34] in a bibliographic description for books and other monographic publications consists of items 1, 2, 4, 5, and 7; for periodicals and other serials, items 2 and 5; for articles in periodicals, contributions in conference proceedings, or chapters in a book, items 1, 2, 3, 4, 5, 7 and 8; for nonbook materials (which are not covered by ISO 690), all items are often needed for unique identification. In bibliographic descriptions that refer to documents held in a particular collection, there must also be an indication of the document's physical location in the store (call number, serial number, etc.).

Definition 23: Documentary Communication System

A documentary communication system facilitates communication between originators of documents and their present or future users. It performs some or all of the operations of collection, evaluation, description, analysis, sotrage, retrieval, and dissemination of documents. These are known as documentary operations.

Individual libraries, library networks (national and international), or organizations that publish bibliographic reference tools such as abstracting and indexing services are documentary communication systems. Although these systems differ in nature, scope, and aims, all use essentially the same kind of subsystem to exercise bibliographic control.

[34]International Organization for Standardization (1975).

Two

The Adaptation of Scripts to Various Languages

> Convention is the ruler of all.
> Pindar, Fragment 169.

1. THE IMPOSITION OF SCRIPT CONVENTIONS

During five millennia, many hundreds of scripts have evolved, flourished, and sometimes died with the languages for which they were devised. They were adopted by or adapted to other languages, sometimes by linguistic or religious affinity, more often by conquest or colonization, and only rarely by peaceful means. We consider here primarily four alphabetical scripts which have had an influence far beyond the sphere of the language for which they were originally employed, namely the Roman, Cyrillic, Arabic, and Hebrew scripts.

When discussing the phenomenon of adaptation of a writing system and its script to a language, it is important to understand the significance of conventions (already discussed in Chapter 1 in relation to writing systems in general). The application of a writing system to a language is impossible to achieve without the imposition of conventions that are accepted as binding by practically all who read and write that language. Whether or not individuals in the language community are ready to accept the conventions of a writing system, or are ready to abandon allegiances to earlier conventions underlying a different system or even their adherence to no system at all (in the case of languages that have no written means of expression), and whether or not they do so of their own free will, is of relatively little importance, as long as the majority of the literate language community submits to the conventions of a writing system or can be forced to do so.[1]

What does matter is that, once a writing system has been successfully established for a language community, its underlying conventions become essentially indivisible, all-embracing, and intolerant of any other convention. The conventions of that writing system become so intimately amalgamated with other conventions in the realms of religion, morals, law, art, and other manifestations of a people's culture that it will be almost impossible to replace even an unsuitable system with one better geared to the character of the language. What militates against such a change is that the conventions underlying a writing system form a monolithic whole that cannot be displaced gradually by piecemeal substitution (or this can be done only to a very limited extent, such as when certain characters are removed or added to make a script more amenable to the needs of a language). Generally, a writing system can be applied to a formerly unwritten language, or can be removed in its entirety and replaced by another writing system only by force.

Such force has historically been exercised by the great religions which were usually either supported by a strong secular power or able to exercise such secular power themselves. The spread of the Roman alphabet followed the Latin cross of the Roman Catholic Church throughout Europe and later to the colonies established by European powers in Africa, Asia, and the Americas. The Cyrillic alphabet followed the Patriarchal cross of the Eastern Orthodox Church throughout the Russian empire and a large part of the Balkan. Their ancestor, the Greek alphabet, held its place where the Greek Orthodox Church wielded spiritual power; and the Arabic alphabet followed the banner of the Crescent far

---

[1] An individual may, of course, choose to adhere only partially to the conventional rules of a writing system, but he does so at the risk of not being able to use a writing system for its essential purpose, namely to communicate with other human beings. The Roman alphabet is conventionally written from left to right; anyone writing it in the other direction, or in boustrophedon manner, will be practically unable to make himself understood in writing. Most modern writing systems also have conventional rules of punctuation which say that a little dot following the last letter of a word indicates the end of a sentence, while a dot with a little tail, the comma, separates words and phrases to avoid ambiguity. One may rebel against this convention, as did Gertrude Stein when she said:

> What does a comma do. I have refused them so often and left them out so much and did without them so continually that I have come finally to be indifferent to them. I do not care whether you put them in or not but for a long time I felt very definitely about them and would have nothing to do with them. As I say commas are servile and they have no life of their own and their use is not a use it is a way of replacing one's own interest and I do decidedly like to like my own interest my own interest in what I am doing . . . the use of them was positively degrading. (Stein, 1935).

Some people may find this to be a delightful piece of prose, and freedom of poetic license has always been granted, but on the whole, we have to conform with the conventions of a writing system and its script or not use it at all.

beyond the realm of the Arabic-speaking peoples of the Mediterranean, spreading from the Atlantic to the Indian Ocean wherever Islam became the dominant religion or that of the rulers in Asia and Africa.

Christianity and Islam succeeded in imposing the writing system of their sacred scriptures where the population was totally or almost entirely illiterate, and where few or no literary works in written form existed. Subsequently, the conventions of the writing system were not only universally accepted but were in themselves held to be sacred, the more so since for many hundreds of years after the introduction of a script most or all of the written literature consisted of liturgical works or commentaries on the sacred texts, written by the clergy and also largely read only by members of an ecclesiastical hierarchy and by a few scholars.

When the power and influence of the great religions began to decline, the new forces of nationalism struggled to shake off the political fetters of a foreign colonial power or sought to gain autonomy within a monolithic empire. In most instances, these forces drew their strength from a national language.[2] The nationalistic movements of the 19th and 20th centuries were keenly aware of the importance of script as a highly visible means of demonstrating the separateness of an ethnic group, but the approaches were different. Where a script had long been established but where no large body of literature in the vernacular existed, it was often retained but given a different twist and used in a manner different from the writing system of the ruling power or that of a competing ethnic group. (The Slovaks decided to use some but not all of the Czech diacritical marks, and thus spell many words common to the two closely related languages slightly differently; the Ukrainians, White-Russians, and more recently the Macedonians introduced their own special letters into the Cyrillic script, although the existing ones could have served them very well; these and similar phenomena were not so much matters of practical utility as particularistic assertions of separate nationality.) Where both an ancient script and literáry monuments existed, as in India and to some degree in Ireland, the struggle was against the "foreign" script, no matter what advantages might be gained by the worldwide currency of the

---

[2] "The first movements against Western rule in the Middle East were Moslem movements, the first opposition to Turkish domination in the Balkans was on behalf of Orthodoxy, and looked to the distant Tsar as the champion of the Orthodox faith. But before long these movements based on religion split up, as the secular category of language became more important." (Seton-Watson, 1965, p. 9.) The author also cites many examples from Eastern Europe, the Pan-Turkic, and Pan-Arabic movements, all of which are highly relevant to our topic. See also Benjamin Akzin: "The most frequently named [characteristics of an ethnic group] are a common language and a common tradition of *mores* and culture. . . . A further characteristic, of utmost significance in the more distant past, but of rapidly diminishing importance as we approach modern times, is a common religion; still, in a number of cases it continues to be influential as basis for 'peoplehood' and its concomitant claims. Thus Catholicism in relation to Ireland, Islam in relation to Pakistan, and Judaism in relation to Israel." (Akzin, 1964, p. 30).

Roman alphabet. But where a script was felt to be the symbol of oppression, temporal or spiritual, a strong movement for script conversion became part of nationalistic programs and, in most instances, resulted in the adoption of the Roman alphabet. This was the case in Albania and in Turkey, where Latinization was instituted by decree, and to some extent also in Indonesia and Malaysia. A different manifestation of nationalism under a dictatorial regime occurred in the Soviet Union where, after an abortive attempt at Latinization, Stalinism imposed the Cyrillic alphabet on many dozens of nationalities. In these instances, too, the imposition of a new script was successful because of the high degree of illiteracy of the populations involved, and the absence or scarcity of literature in written form. But in China, where Latinization was also introduced by a dictatorial regime, and where illiteracy was as widespread as it had been in Turkey, it did not succeed; it also failed to gain acceptance in Japan. We shall explore the reasons for these phenomena in more detail later on.

Many religious, political, and cultural factors have played a role in the forcible imposition of scripts on various languages or in the more or less effective adaptation of scripts to vernaculars. The historical evolution of these processes must be briefly outlined since they are important for the understanding of the results of various script conversions, the products of which have to be handled in bibliographic systems. The records of a nation may be written in several different scripts, depending on the period in which they were created, so that literary works and their authors and titles may appear in different guises that are sometimes difficult to discern without a knowledge of the various phases through which the literature passed over the centuries and sometimes even during a few decades.[3] Conversely, the same script generally serves a number of entirely different languages, and is seldom amenable to the same methods of conversion to a target script, despite an apparent similarity of the source script.

2. LATINIZATION

2.1. Adaptation of the Roman Script to the Languages of Europe

The script that was destined to become the means of written expression for the majority of mankind developed about 2700 years ago from the Etruscan alphabet

---

[3]Examples for this phenomenon can be found among the non-Slavic nationalities of the Soviet Union. The Kalmyks adapted the Mongolian script to their language and used it from about 1650 until 1920, when they were forced to switch to Cyrillic. A few years later, they decided to adopt a Roman alphabet which they used until 1937, when the Cyrillic alphabet was again imposed on them. The Karakalpaks, a Turkic nationality of Muslim faith, used the classical Arabic script until 1924, a reformed Arabic alphabet until 1928, a Roman alphabet from 1928 to 1938, a revised form of the latter from 1938 to 1940, and finally a Cyrillic alphabet which "was far less satisfactory than either the earlier reformed Arabic or Latin alphabets had been." (Henze, 1957, p. 125.)

(which is still largely undeciphered but had probably been an adaptation of an early Greek alphabet). For 600 years, the Latin alphabet consisted of 21 letters; after the conquest of Greece in the 2nd century B.C., the letters *Y* and *Z* were added to write Greek names and loanwords such as *Zephyros,* and the digraph *CH* was used to render the Greek *X,* since Latin lacked the phoneme $[\chi]$ and did not need a special letter for it. The Latin alphabet that became standardized in the 1st century B.C., the "Golden Age" of Rome, is essentially still the one used today, as far as the basic forms of letters are concerned. No new letters were accepted after that time, and even the emperor Claudius (10 B.C.–A.D. 54) did not succeed in introducing the *digamma inversum* Ⅎ for the $[v]$ sound in an effort to distinguish it from $[u]$, the *antisigma* Ɔ for the Greek Ψ, and the letter Ⱶ (the left half of an *H*) for the sound $[ü]$.

This alphabet served the Latin language quite well, despite the redundancy in the letters *c, k,* and *q,* which may originally have stood for different phonemes but were all used to write the $[k]$ sound. It was carried by the soldiers of the Roman legions and by imperial administrators to the farthest corners of the Roman Empire, and became the dominant script of written records, especially in the western parts which had not become hellenized; in those countries that had once formed a part of Alexander's realm, Greek script also remained in use until the Arab conquest in the 7th century A.D.

After the fall of Rome, Christian missionaries spread not only the Gospel but also the Latin language and its script throughout central, western, and northern Europe. For more than a thousand years, Latin became the almost universal medium of written expression, first for theological treatises and later for literary, philosophical, and scientific discourse. It was only natural that its script became the written embodiment of the Romance languages which gradually developed from Latin, as well as of the Germanic languages, the vernaculars of the Slavic peoples who followed the Church of Rome, and later also of the Hungarian, Finnish, Estonian, Latvian, and Lithuanian languages. The alphabet had ceased to be that of Latin alone; it had become the Roman script, used to write the vernaculars of Europe in the characters employed by the nation that had once dominated the continent.

The Latinization of European languages was practically completed during the Middle Ages, but it did not result in a unification of the various writing systems, because virtually all languages had phonemes not found in classical Latin and therefore not represented by corresponding graphemes, while on the other hand some of the letters of the Latin alphabet were of no use to them because their languages lacked the equivalent phonemes. It would have been a simple matter to drop unnecessary letters and to add new ones, or even to adapt letters from other scripts so as to be able to express the phonemes of various languages more accurately than could be done by using the 23 letters of the Latin alphabet. Such methods had been successfully employed at about the same time in Eastern

Europe, when St. Cyril created the Cyrillic alphabet for Slavic peoples by adapting the Greek alphabet, adding some Hebrew letters and inventing a few entirely new characters.

But the Latin alphabet could not be altered or tampered with, because it was the script in which the Vulgate had been written. It was therefore *ipso facto* sacrosanct as the Christian embodiment of the Hebrew script which, throughout the Middle Ages and until the 18th century, was believed to have been directly inspired by the Almighty and was held to be inviolable and immutable by Jews and Christians alike.[4] The invention of entirely new characters as additions to the Latin alphabet was therefore not tolerated. Only on the islands of the Atlantic Ocean, in England and faraway Iceland, where a substantial body of written literature in runic script already existed, were some runic letters retained and added to the Latin script. Old and Middle English used the letters þ *(thorn)*, ð *(edh)*, þ *(wen)*, and ȝ *(yogh)*, but these fell gradually into disuse after the Norman conquest and disappeared in the late Middle Ages. Old Norse also used þ and ð, but in this case the Icelandic language was able to retain these useful additions until the present time, perhaps because Iceland was so remote from the continent and succeeded in preserving its cultural heritage throughout its long history. In the countries of Western and Central Europe, however, scribes had to resort to various adaptations of the basic Latin letters to write the phonemes of their vernaculars in a script invented for another language.

The most frequently used methods of adaptation (all of which are still in use today) were the following:

1. The use of letters that are redundant in Latin to differentiate between phonemes for which there is no equivalent in Latin. For example, the Polish and Czech languages use *c* for the phoneme $[\text{ts}]$ and *k* for $[\text{k}]$.

---

[4]The doctrine of Hebrew as the language spoken by the Almighty and the original tongue of mankind had been firmly enunciated in the writings of Origenes, St. Jerome, and St. Augustine. During the late Middle Ages Christian theologians added the theory that the vowel points (which had been invented by the rabbis of Tiberias sometime between the 6th and 9th centuries A.D.) were originally written by the right hand of God, the writers of the Bible having been merely *Dei calami* ("pens of God"). The Reformation by no means challenged this view, and even as late as 1678 the Calvinists of Geneva stipulated that no minister could obtain office unless he publicly proclaimed that the masoretic text of the Bible, as written by Hebrew consonants and vowel points, was of divine origin and therefore authentic. The theory found defenders down to the mid-18th century. One of the last "scholarly" attempts was made by Johann Heinrich Olpius, who attacked the blasphemers who dared to question the divine origin of the Hebrew language and script in his dissertation, שלמות הכתיב המנצחת *sive sinceritas scripturae V. T. suspicione erroris . . . abstersa . . .* (Jenae, 1717). It was found worthy of reprinting in an anthology compiled by the German theologians T. Hase and C. Iken, *Thesaurus novus theologico-philologicus* (Hase, 1732, Vol. 1, p. 53–67). For a more detailed account of the place of the Hebrew language and script in Christian theology, see White (1896), chapter 17.

2. The combination of two or more letters to represent a single phoneme. One of the worst deficiencies of the Latin alphabet is the lack of single letters to express the voiced and unvoiced palatal-alveolar fricatives and affricates which play such an important role in the phonology of most European languages. All Romance and Germanic languages use some ingenious but mutually incompatible combinations of letters to write these sounds, and some use more than one such combination (English and Swedish having the largest number). This is one of the greatest obstacles to an effective and uniform transliteration from languages that use the Cyrillic alphabet, which are fortunate to have single letters for these sounds (see Table 2.1); similar difficulties arise for languages written in other scripts, especially Arabic and Hebrew.

3. The addition of letters from other alphabets. As noted, this was only sparingly done during the Middle Ages in England and Iceland, and the practice ceased shortly after the invention of printing. The letters *j, u,* and *w* are not really additions but only adaptations of the Latin letters *i* and *v*. The letter *j* developed from the habit of medieval scribes to make the small letter *i* more conspicuous by providing it with a "tail" and a dot, especially when written together with another *i* at the end of a word, as in *filij* or in such numerals as *ij* and *vij.* The letter *u* is a cursive form of *v,* and *w,* as its English name implies, is nothing but a redoubled *v* (often so printed as late as in the 18th century). The first printer who distinguished between the letters *i* and *j,* and *u* and *v* was Louis Elzevir, who printed in Leyden between 1595 and 1616.

4. The invention of entirely new letters. This method might have been beneficial had it already been used in the early Middle Ages. It was suggested by an early German grammarian in the 16th century, Valentin Ickelsamer,[5] who pointed out that the Hebrew letters ח *(ḥet)* and שׁ *(šin)* were unambiguous and simpler than the German letter combinations *ch* and *sch,* but he did not actually propose to use these letters as additions to the Roman alphabet, probably because traditional German orthography was even in his time already too well established, and such radical innovations had no chance of being accepted by writers and scribes. The method has only been applied in modern times, under the influence of phonetic alphabets invented for philological purposes in the 19th century. Special characters are used for the Latinization of some African languages (e.g., ɖ, ɣ, ŋ, ɔ) to represent sounds that are specific to these; the Latinization scheme for Chinese tentatively proposed in 1956 (but later withdrawn) contained the specially designed letter ŋ to represent the $[ŋ]$ sound; the dependence on IPA characters is obvious here.

5. The addition of diacritical marks to the basic letters of an alphabet. This method, which was and still is the most widely used method of adaptation,

[5]Ickelsamer (1527), pp. 38 and 40.

Table 2.1 Representation of Palatal-Alveolar Fricatives and Affricates in Some European Languages

Phonemes	Romance languages					Germanic languages			Albanian	Uralic	Semitic	Slavic languages				
	Italian	French	Spanish	Portuguese	Romanian	English	German	Swedish		Hungarian	Maltese	Croatian	Czech	Polish	Russian Bulgarian	Serbian
[ʃ]	sc sci	ch		ch x	ş	sh s ch ti (+vowel)	sch s (+p,t)	sch sj skj ssj si, ssi (+ on)	sh	s	x	š	š	ś sz s (+ i)	ш	ш
[ʒ]		j g (+e,i)		z		s z			zh	zs		ž	ž	ź rz z (+ i)	ж	ж
[tʃ]	c (+e,i)		ch		c (+e,i)	ch	tsch	k (+ e,i; y, ä, ö) tj		cs ts	ċ	č	č	ć cz c (+ i)	ч	ч
[dʒ]	g (+e,i)				g (+e,i)	g, j (+e,i)			xh	gy	ġ	dž	dž	dź dz (+ i)	дж	џ
	ROMAN														CYRILLIC	

48

dates back to the Greek grammarian Aristophanes (257–180 B.C.), who was the chief librarian of the Alexandrian library and who is generally credited with having invented punctuation and accentuation (although the accents were then used to indicate tone or pitch, not stress). Diacritical marks have been employed in the writing systems of almost all languages written in Roman script, with the exception of modern English (which uses it only for foreign words).

Most diacritical marks originated in labor- and space-saving devices and abbreviations used by copyists during the Middle Ages, such as writing a small *e* over the vowels *a, o,* and *u* in German (to indicate an umlaut), or a small *n* over a regular *n* in Spanish to indicate the palatal sound (this became the modern tilde over *ñ*). Today, a large number of accents, tildes, cedillas, oblique strokes, and other modifiers of basic letters are used singly or in any combination for five different (and sometimes conflicting) purposes:

(a) To indicate vowel quantity;
(b) To indicate vowel quality;
(c) To indicate syllabic stress;
(d) To indicate diaeresis;
(e) To modify consonant letters so as to write phonemes otherwise not possible to express by an existing letter of the Latin alphabet.

Table 2.2 shows the use of various diacritical marks and special letters in the principal languages written in Roman script.

The Romance languages use diacritical marks mainly to indicate various qualities of vowels or to indicate stress; in a few cases, diacritical marks are also used to modify consonants, such as *ç* and *ñ*.

The Germanic languages make use of diacritical marks only sparingly, mainly for expressing the fronting of vowels (umlaut) and for certain other vowel modifications, but not for altering consonants or for indicating stress (except in loanwords from languages that use such stress indicators).

The Slavic languages written in Roman script (Croatian, Czech, Slovakian, Slovenian, Sorbian, and Polish) have to use a large number of diacritical marks because so many specifically Slavic sounds have no equivalent Roman letter. The first Slavic language written with the aid of diacritical marks was Czech; to begin with, the Czechs used letter combinations (following the example of their German neighbors) and added accents and dots, but in an unsystematic manner that was used differently by various writers and scribes. The great Bohemian reformer Jan Hus (1369?–1415), who was also an accomplished linguist, was the first to analyze the sounds of the Czech language in his treatise *Orthographia*

Table 2.2 Diacritical Marks and Special Letters

Afrikaans   á é è ê ë ï î ô û

Albanian   á â ç é ê ë í ó ú

Anglo-Saxon   ā æ (Æ) ǣ ē ę ī ō ǫ œ (Œ) ū ð (Ð) þ ƿ[1]

Catalan   à ç é è í ï l·l ó ò ú ü

Croatian   ć č đ (Đ) š ž

Czech   á č d' (Ď) é ě í ň ó ř š t' (Ť) ú ů ý ž

Danish   æ (Æ) å ø

Dutch   á â ä é è ê ë ï ó ô ö ú û

Esperanto   ĉ ĝ ĥ ĵ ŝ ŭ

Estonian   ä ö õ ü

Faeroese   á æ (Æ) í ó ø ú ý ð (Ð)

Finnish   ä å ö

French   à â ç é è ê ë ι ï ô œ (Œ) ù û ü

German   ä ö ü ß[2]

Hawaiian   á é í ó ú

Hungarian   á é í ó ö ő ú ü ű

Icelandic   á æ (Æ) é í ó ö ú ý ð (Ð) þ

Italian   à è ì ò ù

Latvian   ā č ē ģ (Ģ) [ȼ] ī ķ [Ķ] ļ [Ļ] ņ [Ņ]
            ō ŗ [Ŗ] ş [Ş] ū ž

Lithuanian   ą č ę ė [ë] į [ł] [m̃] [ñ] š ų ū [ů]
             ž [ż]

Maltese   ċ ġ ħ (Ħ) ż

Middle English   ȝ þ ð (Ð)

Used in Languages Written in Roman Script

Navaho   á ã a̢ æ ê ė ǧ ħ i̢ ł ṅ t'

Norwegian   ä å̊ æ (Æ) ö ø

Polish   a̢ ć e̢ ł ń ó ś ź ż

Portuguese   á à â ã ç é è ê ẽ í ì ï ĩ ó ò ô õ

            ú ù û ũ

Romanian   ă [â] [ĭ] ş ţ [ŭ]

Slovak   á ä č d' (Ď) é í í l' (Ľ) ň ó ô ŕ š

            t' (Ť) ú ý ž

Slovene   č š ž

Sorbian   High   [b́] ć č ě ł [ḿ] ń ó ò [ṕ] ř [ŕ] š [ẃ] ź ž

        Low   b́ ć č ě f' ł ḿ ń ò ṕ ŕ [ŕ] ś š ẃ ź ž

Spanish   á é í ñ ó ú ü

Swedish   ä å̊ ö

Tagalog   á à â é è ê í ì î ñg ó ò ô ú ù û

Turkish   â ç ğ i (İ) î (Î) ı (I) ö ş û ü

Vietnamese[3]   á à ă â ã a̢ å̂ å̂ ǎ a̢ đ (Đ) ơ ư

Welsh   á â ê ï ò ö ŵ ŷ

Note. All modified letters are listed in the sequence of the English alphabet, irrespective of their order in the alphabet of a specific language. Contractions are listed after their first letter; special letters are shown after *z*. Letters in parentheses are now obsolete. Uppercase letters are shown only when their form differs from or is not obvious from the form of the lowercase letter. The order of diacritical marks has been arbitrarily fixed, since there is no generally agreed-upon sequence: à á â ä ā ă ã a̢ ɜ, other marks. For special letters used in some African languages see Table 2.7.

[1] This letter, called *wen,* is now generally rendered by *w* because it can be easily mistaken for *p*.

[2] May be written *ss* (formerly also *sz*).

[3] The possible combinations of two diacritical marks are shown only for the letter *a* but may be applied also to other vowels.

bohemica.[6] He showed that plain Roman letters were unable to represent Slavic sounds adequately and proceeded to develop the system of diacritical marks that, with only minor adaptations, is still used today in the Czech writing system. The Slovak, Slovenian, and Croatian languages, (which did not become written languages until the beginning of the 19th century), used the same diacritical marks for their equivalent sounds. But the Polish language, which had been written with the aid of letter combinations and with some of the early Czech diacritical marks used before Hus, did not change its orthography. This resulted in their present use of diacritical marks, which is completely different from that of other Slavic languages written in Roman script; the same sound may be represented by three different letter combinations (see Table 2.1).

In Vietnamese, the only southeast Asian tone language written in Roman script, accents and other diacritical marks are used to express the six tones of the language, and the quality of some vowels (see Section 2.4.4, p. 93).

In many languages, modified Roman letters are counted as separate letters of the alphabet, and their position in the standardized sequence of the alphabet may be quite different from that of the basic letter. The Swedish letters *å*, *ä*, and *ö* come at the end of the alphabet, after *z*, while the equivalent letters in Danish and Norwegian are ranked *æ*, *ø*, and *å* (formerly written *aa*) after *z*, and there are other European alphabets that have variant rankings of modified letters. Other languages, such as French, which uses a large array of diacritical marks, treat all modified letters as special cases of their basic forms and lump them together in alphabetical listings.

The idiosyncratic use of diacritical marks in the writing systems of various languages is another obstacle to the compatibility of various Roman alphabets, and has also hampered the acceptance of ISO transliteration standards because

---

[6]Schröpfer (1968). In the introduction to his work, Jan Hus stated:

> Since the Latin alphabet cannot suffice for the writing of the Bohemian language . . . I have made the decision (which seems to me to be useful) to abridge the Latin alphabet somewhat for the purpose of writing Bohemian, to remedy its shortcomings and to define the differences between its letters . . . The Latin letters are not sufficient to write Bohemian, even as they are not sufficient to write the languages of the Greeks, the Jews, and the Germans, and of others, which is evident to all who wish to express the words of these languages exactly in writing. Thus, the Jews have a letter with the name *ches* and another with the name *ssyn*. And the Slavs have correspondingly their *chir* and *ssa*, which letters the Bohemians do not have. . . ." (My translation.)

This shows that Hus had a fair knowledge not only of the Slavic languages but also of German, Greek, and Hebrew (the latter in Ashkenazic pronunciation). He perceived clearly that equivalents of the Hebrew letters ⊓ and ש would have solved some of the problems of rendering Slavic sounds. His reference to the "Slavs" is to the monks of the Orthodox Slavic Church who used the Glagolitic alphabet, in which *ⱈ (her')* is the equivalent of Cyrillic x and Ⱎ *(ša)* that of Cyrillic Ш.

even in those standards the use of diacritical marks is far from uniform, quite apart from the unwillingness of English-speaking peoples to accept marks that are foreign to their own writing system.

The use of diacritical marks has always been a headache for printers, typographers, and graphic artists,[7] as well as for the ordinary reader. Modified letters are more costly to produce because of the relatively small demand and are often difficult to obtain. They are not available for all typefaces and tend to break off and wear out more quickly than regular letters; they clutter up the printed page and, if not very neatly printed, may be blurred and become illegible and outright misleading. Readers tend to overlook them (especially if they appear beneath a letter) and forget to handwrite them[8] because they slow down the even flow of the pen; when they are written, they are not always put where they belong, thus introducing another element of ambiguity (even in English, many people do not put the dots of their *i*'s and the crosses of their *t*'s where they are supposed to be). Finally, it is difficult and costly to fit typewriters with diacritical marks. No normal typewriter can accommodate all the diacritical marks used in European languages, much less those devised for some African and Asian languages; the addition of typebars with modified letters diminishes the number of other signs, while adding only the diacritical marks on so-called "dead" typebars slows down typing considerably and does not result in accurately typed modified letters.

Altogether, most writing systems could function without diacritical marks, and many languages have always had alternative ways of writing. The sound [ɲ], written in Spanish as *ñ*, is written in neighboring Portugal as *nh*, and the German umlauts may be written as the digraphs *ae, oe,* and *ue.* In mechanographies such as the Morse system, the teleprinter, and direct computer printout, diacritical marks have seldom been used because providing for them is costly and cumbersome (although technically feasible).[9] It may very well be that the increasing use of international telecommunication networks, which use teleprinters, computer consoles and video displays, may lead to a gradual abandonment

---

[7]"With the spread of religion over the world, the missionaries, usually educated men, have left, as has been said, examples of their erudition: but unfortunately they have shown little knowledge of typography, as is evidenced by the selection made by them of the miscellaneously accented characters with which they have unhappily endowed the scripts of many countries." (Legros, 1916, p. 535).

[8]The report of the *Rejaf Language Conference* (1928) stated that experience in Northern Sudan schools had shown that about half of the diacritical marks of Arabic script were omitted by the pupils.

[9]Special print chains for direct computer printout are available, but they are slower and therefore more expensive to use than print chains with upper- and lowercase letters. When a computer is used to drive a phototypesetting device, any graphic mark can be produced if suitably coded, but such devices are expensive and are generally not available in situations where day-to-day bibliographic control has to be exercised.

of diacritical marks, even in languages that have used them for many hundreds of years.[10]

The adaptation of the Roman script to the languages of Europe was practically completed by the end of the 19th century. We have already noted the Latinization of Slovak, Slovenian, and Croatian, which took place in the early 19th century. The Romanians, who had long been forced to write their language in the Cyrillic script but who were firmly conscious of its Romance origin, began to write it in Roman characters, adapted with many diacritical marks, around 1860; the Romanian orthography was, however, not fully standardized until 1954, when several diacritical marks were also eliminated.

The last Indo-European language to be Latinized was Albanian; here, political emancipation went hand in hand with script conversion. When the National Congress held at Monastir in 1909 decided to fight for autonomy (Albania was then a province of the Ottoman empire) the Roman alphabet was introduced. Previously, the Arabic script had been used, and some Albanian patriots had designed indigenous Albanian scripts based on a mixture of Greek and Roman letters which were, however, not successful. The Albanian writing system employs many diacritical marks, and uses some letters and digraphs in an unusual manner; for example, *ç* represents the $[t\int]$ sound, and *xh* stands for $[d_3]$.

The only Semitic tongue written in Roman characters (and also the only one spoken by an entirely Christian community) is Maltese, essentially a West Arabic dialect related to the Arabic spoken in Tunisia, which has absorbed many Latin, Greek, and Italian words. Since the islands of Malta and Gozo, where this language is spoken, were ruled for hundreds of years by the Knights of St. John and by the clerical hierarchy of the Catholic Church, there was never any question that the vernacular should be written in the Roman script, as were Latin and Italian, the language of the rulers. The oldest Maltese records date from the late 17th century, but the language began to be written to any extent only in the middle of the 19th century, when the Akkademja tal-Malti (Maltese Language Academy) devised a Roman alphabet that was largely based on Italian orthography and that contained three letters with diacritical marks, namely, *ġ* for $[d_3]$, *ħ* for $[\chi]$, and *ż* for $[z]$. A new phonetic alphabet proposed in 1880 by the Xirka Xemia (The Semitic Society) was used for a time in the schools but did not prevail. The next development took place in 1924, when the Ghaqda tal-kittieba tal-Malti (The Society of Maltese Writers) introduced some changes in the old orthography and added another modified letter, *ċ* for $[t\int]$, while using *x* for $[\int]$ and *w* for $[w]$; a distinction was also made between *k* and *q*, the latter being used

---

[10]Several computer-produced book catalogs in France do not contain any diacritical marks, and this does not seem to impair their function. Long before the computer age Ševčik (1947) pointed out that his Czech name *could* be spelled simply Sevcik and still be recognizable, but that it would suffer when spelled Scheftschiek, Chefftchique, or Sheftcheek.

for the glottal stop indicated in Arabic by a *hamzah*. Altogether, the Latinization of Maltese (which was codified in its final form in 1932) is somewhat clumsy but it is the only successful Latinization of a Semitic language, devised by people without much linguistic experience and in the face of opposition and disdain from the ruling class. Today, Maltese is the official language of the former British colony, and many books and newspapers are printed in that language, although both Italian and English are still widely used in speech and writing.

The letter ħ (Ħ in uppercase), which has been specially designed for Maltese, deserves attention because it avoids a diacritical mark either beneath or above the letter itself and yet conveys the impression that a fricative other than $[h]$ is represented by it; perhaps it could serve as a uniform transliteration of the Cyrillic x, the Greek χ, the Arabic $\dot{\zeta}$, and the Hebrew ח, all of which are pronounced $[\chi]$ but are rendered in ISO transliteration schemes as h, ḫ, and ḥ, respectively.

2.2. Latinization of Turkish

Mustafa Kemal Atatürk (1881–1938), who created the modern state of Turkey out of the shambles of the former Ottoman empire, became its president in 1923, when he abolished the caliphate and declared Turkey a secular republic. Since the power of the former sultan was largely based on the support of the Muslim religious scholars, the *'Ulemā'*, and the local *mullahs*, Kemal sought to eliminate their influence, which was inextricably linked to the teaching of the Qur'ān and therefore to the Arabic script. As in so many other Oriental countries, only a small elite of religious dignitaries and rich businessmen could read and write, while the masses of the people were illiterate and ignorant. Secularization and Westernization of Turkish life meant for Kemal, above all, the discarding of the Arabic script which he and many others considered to be entirely unsuited to the nature of the Turkish language[11] and the substitution of the Roman script. The question had first been discussed on the governmental level in 1923, but Latinization had then been rejected for various reasons. Meanwhile, the peoples speaking Turkic languages in the neighboring Soviet Union had decided to adopt the

---

[11]Imart (1965) cites the following witticism on the plight of a literate Turk who reads his own language in Arabic script: "All his life, like a squirrel in his cage, he turns round and round in a vicious circle in which he must restore the vowels in order to understand what he must understand in order to restore the vowels." (p. 226). While the Semitic languages can more easily dispense with written vowels because the consonants of the "root" convey the meaning of a word, the Turkish language has a very rich vocalization which is indispensable for the meaning of a word (as in English, where *pat, pet, pit, pot,* and *put* have the same consonants, with the vowel determining the meaning of the word).

Roman alphabet. This served as an example and incentive to Kemal, and in June 1928 he decided to appoint a committee to study the problem of script reform and to "examine the possibility and the manner of adopting Latin letters." The committee deliberated for several months without coming to any constructive conclusion, whereupon Kemal is said to have taken things into his own hands, designing the New Turkish Alphabet in one night and presenting it the following evening, August 9, 1928, in a dramatic manner:

> The Republican People's Party was holding a fête that night, in the park at Seraglio Point, and many of its leading figures were present. Towards eleven o'clock the President himself appeared, and after a while he rose to address them.
>
> "My friends," he said, "our rich and harmonious language will now be able to display itself with new Turkish letters. We must free ourselves from these incomprehensible signs that for centuries have held our minds in an iron vice. You must learn the new Turkish letters quickly. Teach them to your compatriots, to women and to men, to porters and to boatmen. Regard it as a patriotic and national duty . . . and when you perform this duty, bear in mind that for a nation to consist of 10 or 20 percent of literates and 80 or 90 percent of illiterates is shameful."
>
> After this call to mobilization, the Gazi set out on a tour of the country, teaching and examining the populace in village squares, schoolrooms, town halls, and cafés. The Prime Minister and other dignitaries followed his example, and soon all Turkey was a schoolroom, with the nation's intellectuals, armed with blackboard and easel, teaching people to read and write the new script.[12]

The New Turkish Alphabet consisted of the basic Roman alphabet minus the letters *q, w,* and *x,* for which there was no need; Kemal added to it the umlauts *ö* and *ü,* as used in German, and diacritical marks borrowed from French and Romanian, namely, *ç* and *ş*; his own inventions were the three letters *ğ* and *ı* (an *i* without a dot) and *k̇* (to be used in the spelling of Arabic names only as a transliteration of ق). The alphabet was completely phonetic according to the pronunciation of Turkish in Istanbul and did not contain any silent or unused letters, nor did it use any digraphs. It was promulgated by law on November 3, 1928. Thereafter, the teaching of the Arabic script was summarily prohibited, all government agencies and post offices were instructed to accept only documents written in Roman, and books, newspapers, and other publications were soon printed only in the new script. Every Turk under 40 years of age had to attend classes to learn reading and writing. Only many years later, when the Latinization of Turkish had become an irreversible fact, were the Qur'ān and other

---

[12]Lewis (1968), p. 278, where several original Turkish references are cited. The invention of the alphabet in one night may be apocryphal, although several of Kemal Atatürk's biographers mention it; se non è vero è molto ben trovato.

liturgic texts of Islam again translated and transliterated into the Turkish alphabet.

Despite Kemal's far-reaching and truly revolutionary innovations in the political and religious spheres, it was the abolishment of the Arabic script that his contemporaries considered to be the Turkish dictator's boldest venture, and many doubted whether it would be able to overcome the stubborn resistance from Muslim dignitaries and conservatives.[13] But Kemal, who in 1934 had also decreed that all Turks must take a Western-style surname, and who had adopted the name of Atatürk (Father of the Turks), succeeded and thereby achieved his political goal, the Westernization of Turkey.

The Latinization of the Turkish language, a unique example of complete script conversion for a whole nation in modern times, was achieved through a combination of four factors. Firstly, the Arabic script was badly suited to the needs of the Turkish language with its rich vocalization. Secondly, the decision to change the script of the nation overnight could be backed up by dictatorial force and had the support of the ruling class of young officers and nationalistic intellectuals. Thirdly, more than 90% of the Turkish nation was illiterate, and no new conventions of script had to be imposed on them; the new script was the only one they ever knew, and they were eager to learn it (illiteracy in Turkey is now generally not higher than in some European countries). Finally, the Turkic-speaking peoples beyond Turkey's northern border, in the Soviet republics of Azerbaijan, Turkmenistan, and Uzbekistan, had already decided to discard the Arabic script and had developed their own "New Alphabet"; this fact, as already mentioned, influenced Atatürk's decision to forge ahead with his Latinized alphabet (which, however, differed from those devised for the Turkic languages spoken in the USSR).

This brings us to a little-known and unfortunately short-lived episode in the history of script conversion, namely, the attempts to Latinize the scripts of several nationalities in the Soviet Union.

2.3. Latinization Movement in the Soviet Union

During the first two decades of the Soviet regime there existed a relatively strong and widespread movement for the adaptation of the Roman alphabet to the languages of the dozens of nationalities throughout the Soviet Union, which for the most part either did not have a written language or used an inadequate or complicated script that restricted literacy to a small elite. In its scope and ambi-

---

[13]Such resistance died only slowly. Mahmut Makal (1963) reports the case of a young schoolteacher who was beaten up in 1950 by Anatolian village elders because he had dared to teach children the Roman alphabet.

tion to adapt the Roman alphabet to the most variegated languages of entirely different origin, this movement was unlike anything that had been tried before in Latinization. During a brief period, serious consideration was given to discarding the Cyrillic script altogether and writing Russian too in Roman script; it seems that Lenin was in favor of such a revolutionary step which, had it been successful, might have changed the course of history.

Lenin and his political followers had been ardent internationalists while still in exile. When they came to power in Russia after 1917, they tried to realize their ideals on the linguistic plane also. They perceived clearly that to reach the masses illiteracy would have to be eradicated so that practically everybody could be subjected to the teachings of communism. Initially, Russian linguists tried, not very successfully, to "reform" some of the national scripts that already existed. The Cyrillic alphabet and the Russian orthography were somewhat simplified, and some rather crude "simplifications" were also decreed for the Arabic, Hebrew, and Mongol scripts used by various nationalities. But the first turbulent years of the Soviet Union were not propitious for reform movements and painstaking linguistic research into the theoretical foundations of writing systems. There was an urge to adopt radical measures, and for a number of reasons it seemed that the Roman alphabet would be the only rational solution to the problem of how to make millions of people literate. Firstly, it already existed and needed no time-consuming new inventions. Secondly, it had only a small number of basic letters which would, if necessary, need only a few diacritical marks to express specific Slavic phonemes. Thirdly, it had already proved its great versatility by being applied to many different languages, while the Cyrillic alphabet had a much larger number of letters, some of them redundant, and had in the past been applied only to Slavic languages. Finally, the Roman alphabet could easily be learned in less than two months by a five-year-old child as well as by an illiterate adult. The last argument was particularly persuasive, because in the early 1920s more than 60% of the population in the European part of the Soviet Union was still illiterate; thus, the introduction of the Roman alphabet would have involved a break with the cultural heritage of the past for only less than half of the Russian people and would not have affected the Asian nations, which were then either completely illiterate or just beginning to Latinize their indigenous scripts.

The first period of the Latinization movement encompasses the years from 1918 to 1922, when previously vague utopian dreams began to be realized. The possible introduction of the Roman alphabet had been discussed by the political leaders almost from the day they came to power, but the first actual application took place in the Yakut Soviet Socialist Republic through the endeavors of a native linguist, S. A. Novgorodov, who devised an alphabet largely based on the IPA and modified to suit the phonetic needs of the Yakut language. The new script was introduced in 1919, became officially recognized in 1921 by the local government, and was immediately applied to a wide range of literary activities, primarily in the press, the theater, and other cultural activities in the capital city of Yakutsk.

Meanwhile, there began a strong drive toward Latinization among the Turkic-speaking Muslims in the republics of the Caucasus, spearheaded mainly by teachers, journalists, and typographers who wished to eradicate illiteracy and to discard the Arabic script, which was ill-suited for expressing Turkic languages, and in which they saw the embodiment of the old regime that had been swept away by the revolution. Already in 1906, a congress of teachers and writers in Azerbaijan had decided to abandon the Arabic script and to introduce the Roman alphabet for the Turkic languages spoken there, but this could only be realized after the revolution in 1919. The new alphabet, Jeni əlefbasi, was officially adopted by decree in 1923 for all Azerbaijani publications, journals, and private communications, with a transitional period of five years provided for the gradual abandonment of the Arabic script. Indeed, four years later Arabic had practically disappeared, and the schools, the press, the administration, and even the shopkeepers used only the new Roman alphabet. The sweeping success of this Latinization of a Turkic language sent shock waves far beyond the borders of Azerbaijan. It had a decisive influence on Kemal Atatürk, and was seriously discussed in other Muslim countries such as Syria (then a French protectorate with strong sympathies for Western ideas), Iran, and the Muslim parts of India (today mainly Pakistan). Within the Soviet Union itself, the example of Azerbaijan was soon followed by other Turkic-language republics where the "Latinists," through the initiative of the Azerbaijan president Samed-aga Agamalı-Oğlu, organized themselves in a Committee for the New Turkish Alphabet and elaborated, sometimes with the aid of Russian linguists, various alphabets for their individual languages and dialects. For some time, they encountered fierce resistance from the "Arabists," who fought for the retainment of the old "sacred" script, particularly in those regions where literacy had been more widespread, such as in Daghestan and in Kazan', the capital of the Tatar Soviet Socialist Republic. But the traditionalists fought a losing battle and were soon outvoted in regional meetings and congresses called to decide on the Latinization of the Turkic languages. When Agamali-Oğlu was introduced to Leñin as chairman of the committee and reported to him on the progress made, Lenin told him, "Latinization—that is the great revolution of the Orient!"[14]

In the following years, various Roman alphabets were adopted throughout the Turkic-speaking southern and central regions of the Soviet Union. Unfortunately, they were not always mutually compatible with each other or with Kemal Atatürk's Latinization across the border, but a promising start had been made, and native linguists were already eagerly discussing theoretical and practical

---

[14] Quoted in Commission internationale de coopération intellectuelle (1934), p. 174.

questions of phonetics and vocabulary with the aim of achieving more uniformity and compatibility between the various new alphabets. For example, a typewriter keyboard was designed that could accommodate all existing Latinized Turkic alphabets. The importance of the movement was recognized by a decree of the Soviet government which, in 1930, transformed the Committee for the New Turkish Alphabet into the Central All-Union Committee on the New Latinized Alphabet for the Peoples of the USSR. This body broadened the scope of its activities from the relatively narrow circle of the Turkic languages to those of the peoples in the North, the Far East, and the Volga regions, many of which had never before had a written language. The committee had its seat in Moscow, but much of its work was performed in Leningrad, where Russian linguists, in collaboration with teachers and writers of various nationalities, adapted the Roman alphabet to no less than 36 languages. They even devised a Romanization system for Chinese, intended for use by Russian-speaking people. The various Latinization schemes were unified by the Committee in 1934 and published as the "October Alphabet,"[15] which was to be the script for most non-Slavic languages spoken in the Soviet Union, with the exception of Armenian, Greek, Georgian, and Yiddish, which were allowed (reluctantly, and only for the time being) to keep their traditional scripts.

Truly revolutionary efforts were also made to substitute the Roman script for the Cyrillic alphabet so as to Latinize Russian. To this end, another committee was appointed in 1929, and its proposals were published in 1930; they were fully endorsed by the former Commissar for Education, A. Lunačarskij.[16] The chairman of the committee, the linguist N. F. Jakovlev, explained the Latinization scheme and justified its adoption, arguing that the Cyrillic alphabet was the symbol of autocratic oppression and of Great-Russian chauvinism, and that it hindered linguistic and cultural intercourse among the peoples of the Soviet Union. He also pointed out that Latinization would have the politically important advantage of automatically making all prerevolutionary literature in Cyrillic unintelligible, so that only "valuable" material from this period would in future be reprinted in Roman script.[17]

One of the linguists from Leningrad, B. Larin, submitted a slightly different proposal, suggesting that the new alphabet should first be used for official publications, the daily press, and scientific books and journals, while the old Cyrillic script would gradually be phased out during a period of not more than 10 years, at the end of which the Roman alphabet alone would be permitted in the Soviet Union. The proposals by Jakovlev and Larin are shown in Table 2.3.

When news of these developments reached Europe and America in the early

[15]Nurmakov (1934).
[16]Lunačarskij, quoted in Weinreich (1953).
[17]Jakovlev, quoted in Weinreich (1953).

Table 2.3   Soviet Proposals for the Latinization of Cyrillic Script

Russian Cyrillic	Latinization by Jakovlev	Larin
а	a	a
б	b	b
в	v	v
г	g̦	g̦
д	d	d
е	e	e
ё	ô (jo)	ó (jo)
ж	ž	z̄
з	z	z
и	i	i
й	j	j
к	k̦	k̦
л	l	l
м	m	m
н	n	n
о	o	o
п	p	p
р	r	r
с	s	s
т	t	t
у	u	u
ф	f	f
х	x	x
ц	c	ç
ч	č	c
ш	š	ş
щ	šč	sc
з	—	—
ы	y	y
ь	′ (j)	í (j)
э	æ	—
ю	û (ju)	ú (ju)
я	â (ja)	á (ja)

1930s, experts on Slavic languages were quick to hail it as a momentous advance and hastened to offer their own advice, suggesting further "improvements" for the planned Latinization proposed by the Russian linguists.[18] These well-meant efforts may have done more harm than good, considering the suspicion with which any Western meddling in Soviet affairs was always viewed by the rulers in the Kremlin, and it may have been one of the contributing factors that led to the ultimate downfall of the whole Latinization plan.

However, the primary causes for the abrupt termination of all efforts at Latinization, and the swift and ruthless reversal leading to almost complete Cyrillification of the languages of the USSR, were the changes that took place in the political leadership after Lenin's death. Lenin, who had tried to protect the non-Russian nationalities from "Russification" and had chastised Stalin for "bullying the non-Russians,"[19] had also been favorably inclined toward the Latinization of the non-Slavic languages of the Soviet Union. But he was succeeded by that same Stalin who, himself being of non-Russian origin, tried, like all renegades, to out-Russian the Russians. Only a few years after he had seized power, a period of fierce Russian nationalism began, and the various national minorities were systematically deprived of their aspirations toward greater political autonomy and indigenous cultural achievements, the keys to which were their newly acquired Roman alphabets. Stalin temporarily abandoned the cherished idea of spreading the proletarian revolution on a worldwide scale and instead concentrated his efforts on preventing the spread of "counterrevolutionary ideas" imported into the Soviet Union from abroad. He seems to have seen a twofold danger in the Latinization movement. It would make the Soviet Union more vulnerable to "capitalistic" influences, since Western literature and ideas could much more easily be read by any literate Soviet citizen once the barrier of a different script had been removed; and the use of Roman script among the non-Slavic peoples could become a dangerous rallying point for the nationalistic and secessionist movements among minorities in Central Asia, in the Caucasus, and in the Far Eastern regions of the Soviet Union.

Thus, the Great Purges of the middle and late 1930s claimed as victims not only the political leaders of those nationalities, but also most of the poets, playwrights, novelists, and journalists who had initiated and developed the Latinization of their languages. The works of these purged writers were proscribed as treasonous, and millions of volumes were destroyed so as to make

---

[18]Braun (1930), Jopson (1934), Morison (1934).

[19]"Were we careful enough to take measures to provide the non-Russians with a real safeguard against the truly Russian bully? I do not think we took such measures although we could and should have done so. I think that Stalin's haste and his infatuation with pure administration together with his spite against the notorious 'nationalist-socialism' played a fatal role here." (Lenin, 1966, v. 36, p. 606.) See also Seton-Watson (1965), p. 21, on the policy of Russification before and after the Revolution.

anything written in a Latinized script inaccessible to coming generations which were brought up exclusively with the help of the Cyrillic script. No more was heard, of course, of any Latinization of Russian, and nothing is known about the fate of the hapless linguists who had been foolish enough to devote themselves to that subject. Beginning in 1934, all national minorities who had used a Latinized script were summarily compelled to switch to the Cyrillic script, and in 1939 the changeover was almost complete. We shall deal with the methods and results of this Cyrillification process in Section 3.2.

2.4.   Latinization of Languages Using Logographic Scripts

2.4.1.   Cybernetics of Literary Language Systems.

While it is possible to speak of the Latinization of an alphabetic script such as Cyrillic or Arabic, and such Latinization can be applied (at least in principle) to any language formerly written in either of those scripts, it is not possible to speak of the Latinization of the Chinese script. This may sound paradoxical, since it is well-known that several attempts have been made to Latinize Chinese and Japanese script (and we shall presently deal with these movements). In order to understand why logographic scripts cannot be Latinized in the same way as alphabetic ones, we must make a digression and explore the fundamental difference between the conventions governing logographic scripts and those governing languages written in alphabetic scripts. These differences can best be analyzed by structuring the model of a literary language (i.e., one that can be expressed both in spoken and in written form) as a cybernetic system.

In such a system, we can distinguish three interrelated subsystems that are necessary for the functioning of the language system as a whole (see Figure 2.1):

1. The semantic system S;
2. The phonemic system P;
3. The graphemic system G.

The semantic system S is the one that characterizes the other two as belonging to a language. The sounds emitted by speakers of the language are intended to convey meaning (they are not sneezes, coughs, etc.), and the graphic marks made by a literate member of that language community are also intended to convey meaning (they are not idle doodling). For a language to be considered literary, all three subsystems must be present, and all of them must be operative if the system as a whole is to function purposively and achieve its goal—the meaningful communication between human beings, based on concepts in their minds that are expressed by means of speech and writing.

An observer who encounters a living language, the sounds of which he does not understand and the writing system of which he cannot read, may nevertheless

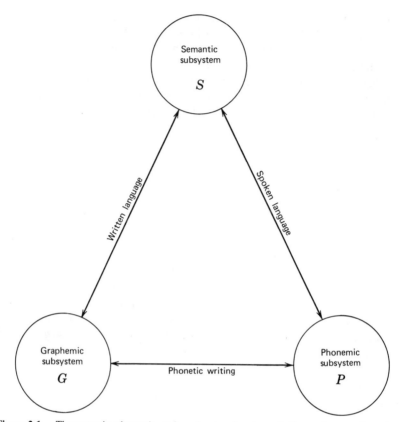

Figure 2.1.   The semantic, phonemic, and graphemic subsystems of a literary language L_A using an alphabetical writing system.

recognize subsystems P and G as existing in this language system; but neither the spoken nor the written language will communicate anything to him unless he has the key to the subsystem of meaning S, which is the focal one. Conversely, a dead language such as Old Egyptian may lack subsystem P either partially or entirely (because present-day "users" of that language know little or nothing about its phonology), but it does have a subsystem G, from which subsystem S can be inferred in one way or another, so that the purpose of communication is achieved. Pharaoh Ikhnaton still "speaks" to us in his ode to Aton, the sun god, over the span of 3400 years. But when only subsystem G is present, such as in most pre-Columbian inscriptions or in proto-Indian relics, and when neither subsystem P nor subsystem S can even be inferred, the only conclusion that can be drawn from the evidence is that these are or might have been manifestations of a language; no meaningful communication can take place.

In alphabetically written languages the conventions governing the graphemic system G are intimately connected with those governing the phonemic system P and the semantic system S. The connections between the three systems form a closed cybernetic loop; they regulate and control each other, and keep the system of meaningful communication by language in a stable state. A speaker of a language L, after having formed a concept in his mind that has (at least to him) a meaning S, must express it orally in certain conventional sounds P if he wishes to be understood; that is to say, his pronunciation may not deviate too much from the current conventions of the spoken language as accepted by the language community in a certain place and at a certain time. If he is a foreigner, a little more leeway may be granted to him by his interlocutors, who may make allowance for his foreign accent, but even then the accidental substitution of a long vowel for a short one, a hard consonant for a soft one (or vice versa), or a wrongly stressed syllable, all of which may not be crucial in the phonological system of the foreigner's mother tongue, will make him unintelligible or may change the meaning of what he wishes to say. The speaker of language L, having uttered his sounds in system P, may choose to convert these sounds into written marks in system G to express his concept in writing. He is again subject to conventions which stipulate that only certain graphic marks may be made in the writing system of language L_A (i.e., one that is written alphabetically) to express a particular sound, if others are to be able to understand what he has written. Finally, going from G to S, the conventions controlling the writing system assure that what has been written has also a meaning, and relates indeed to a certain concept. To perform this task, a small number of graphemes—26 in the Roman alphabet—suffice to express a practically infinite number of words, since the number of theoretically possible permutations is several billions of times larger than the vocabulary of any language. In the words of Wilhelm von Humboldt, a person who writes "makes infinite use of finite means."

The cybernetic loop formed by the subsystems of an alphabetically written language works in both directions, independent of where the starting point is chosen. In the preceding example we started at subsystem S and went from there to P and G. If we start at P, the sounds heard by a member of the language community, these sounds are, by convention, associated with a meaning S, and that meaning in turn may be written down following certain conventions of subsystem G. Starting at G, a reader associates a meaning S with the written marks, and he may then also utter the corresponding sounds P, conventionally expressed by G.

Natural and living languages (as opposed to artificial ones or dead languages whose phonology has been artificially reconstructed), of course, almost never have a one-to-one relationship between phonemes and graphemes, but at least in principle there is (or at least there was at the time when the writing system was first applied to the spoken language) an intimate and ideally unique bond between systems P and G. If a phonetic alphabet such as the IPA is used in system G, there exists indeed a one-to-one relationship between P and G, and the reader who knows the relevant convention is able to pronounce a word or phrase, even though he may not know the meaning of that word and may not have heard it uttered.

An important feature of the cybernetic loop in an alphabetically written language is the fact that control is also exercised by the conventions obtaining between any *two* subsystems, resulting in viable (i.e., meaningful) outcomes, without any need to go through the third subsystem. A concept that has a meaning (again, at least in the mind of the speaker of a language) is uttered by that speaker following the phonological conventions of his language, resulting in spoken language; there is obviously no need to use also subsystem G and to write down the utterance (although this may be done if desired). The same meaningful concept may also be expressed by a writer who may or may not be the same person as the speaker in the foregoing example, again following the conventions of the writing system of the language; what he has written need not necessarily be pronounced (either aloud or silently). Finally, spoken sounds can be expressed in written marks, thus resulting in a controlled outcome governed by conventions underlying a phonetic writing system. In most instances a meaning will also be attached to the phonetically written expression, but this is not necessarily a condition; a person may utter the sounds *abracadabra* or some similar string of nonsense syllables, and these can be faithfully written down in phonetic notation or in shorthand. All these relationships between any two subsystems of a language system are also bidirectional.

This analysis of the conventions governing an alphabetically written language, and the closed cybernetic control loop that they form, may seem to be trivial because in most of the world's languages we take these relationships for granted and use them every day without encountering any difficulties.

The picture that emerges from a similar analysis of logographically written languages, namely Chinese, Japanese, and Korean, is, however, entirely different. These language systems are governed not by one integrated and closed loop of conventions, but by at least *two* separate and different conventions that share only one subsystem, namely S. The first convention, which obtains between S and P, is analogous to the one examined in alphabetically written languages, except that Chinese has several dialects[20] which, although in a linguistic sense

---

[20]The standard form of modern Chinese is the Peking dialect (also known as *Mandarin)*, which is spoken by the majority of the population. In addition there are five other major dialects: Wu (in the Shanghai region), Min (in Fuchow), Cantonese (in Canton), Hakka (in Kiangsi province), and Hunanese (in Chang-sha), as well as several others. "In point of phonology, lexicon . . . and to a lesser extent in grammar, the dialects are as different from one another, as, say, English is from Dutch or French is from Spanish, and are thus often rated by linguists as different languages." (Chao, 1968, p. 96).

constituting isomorphs of an ideal "Chinese language," are mutually incomprehensible. There are, therefore, several Chinese spoken languages or control systems, $S \rightarrow P_1$, $S \rightarrow P_2$, $S \rightarrow P_3$, and so on.

The second convention governs the relations between subsystems S and G_L (the logographic graphemes or Chinese characters as they are called in popular usage), where the number of graphic signs in G_L must theoretically be equal to the number of meaningful concepts in S, because each logogram stands for a whole word or for several words expressing a concept. Since there is a practical upper limit to the number of unique logographs in subsystem G_L there must necessarily also be a limitation on the number of words in the language, as well as a large number of homophones that have to be distinguished by auxiliary phonemic and graphemic means. This is indeed the case in the Chinese language. The number of basic words is relatively small, and new concepts are expressed by the combination of existing words and by periphrasis (which leads to the erroneous impression that Chinese is a "flowery language"); moreover, words are limited in principle to single syllables, although modern Chinese has many two-syllable words. Altogether, the number of basic words in Chinese is estimated to be no more than about 2500. The problem of homophony in the spoken language is solved by a system of tones (four in the Peking dialect, up to eight in others), which allow for about 10,000–12,000 actual phonemically distinct words. In many cases, however, a large number of identically pronounced homophones still remain unresolved, and their meaning can be made clear only by the context when spoken; in written form, on the other hand, a distinct logogram exists for each of these homophones.[21] On the whole, the number of individual Chinese logograms corresponds roughly to the number of words, and is not higher than about 10,000. (The number 40,000 and more,

---

[21]"It would be possible, even easy, to write a story consisting of nothing but the syllable *hsi* in one of the four tones: ¯ (unmarked), ´, ˇ, and `, as follows:

西 溪 犀 , 喜 婧 戲.	West Creek rhinoceros enjoys romping and playing.
嬉 熙 夕 丶 丶 携 犀 戲.	Hsi Hsi every evening takes rhinoceros to play.
嬉 熙 細 丶 丶 習 洗 犀.	Hsi Hsi meticulously practices washing rhinoceros.
犀 吸 溪, 戲 襲 熙.	Rhinoceros sucks creek, playfully attacks Hsi.
嬉 熙 嘻 丶 希 息 戲.	Hsi Hsi laughing hopes to stop playing.
惜 犀 嘶 丶 喜 襲 熙.	Too bad rhinoceros neighing enjoys attacking Hsi.

It makes absolutely no sense when read aloud in modern Mandarin, but from the writing a reader of classical Chinese can make out the story [as in the translation given above]." (Chao, 1968, pp. 120–121.)

The English language and its writing a system exhibit some features that are similar to Chinese. The written form of a word does not necessarily give any clue to its pronunciation, which sometimes depends entirely on the context (e.g., *bow, row, sewer*), and it has a large number of homophones that can be distinguished only by their written form (e.g., *muscles-mussles, steal-steel, flour-flower*).

which is sometimes cited, refers to variants and different calligraphic practices.)[22]

There is, however, absolutely no direct link or governing convention between G_L and any of the phonemic subsystems P_1, P_2, P_3, and so on; that is to say, a certain logogram does not in and by itself indicate a certain pronunciation, nor does the utterance of a phoneme result in its written expression by a certain logogram, *unless* the two separate conventions are linked with each other through subsystem S, which alone can then exercise control over G_L and P, resulting in the formation of the relevant concept in the mind of the speaker-hearer-writer (see Figure 2.2).

If we now consider a potential Latinization of Chinese in the light of the foregoing observations, two facts clearly emerge. One is that an alphabetic writing system G_A can be devised for only one of the subsystems P, say, for the dominant Peking or "Mandarin" pronunciation P_1 (because the alphabetically produced visual image of a phoneme will mean different things in dialects P_2, P_3, and so on, in the same way in which the combination of letters forming the written word *most* means *greatest in number* in English, *cider* in German, and *bridge* in Czech). The same concept would have to be written in entirely different ways in the various dialects; this would, in fact, transform them into as many different written languages as there are now spoken ones, thus leading to fragmentation and disintegration of "Chinese," since a book written in Latinized Mandarin would be unintelligible to readers of Latinized Cantonese, for example, quite apart from the difficulty of using an alphabetic script to distinguish between the large number of Chinese homophones, as shown in footnote 21.

The other fact is that the logographic writing system G_L of Chinese indeed constitutes the only unifying force for the various dialects, and is also the only means by which the ambiguities of homophones can be resolved on the graphemic level. ("Chinese script is Esperanto for the eyes," as the famous Sinologist Bernhard Karlgren once put it.)

The logographic writing system of Chinese and Japanese must therefore be retained (at least in some form) side by side with a potential Latinization scheme, which can be no more than an auxiliary phonetic alphabet. As we shall see, this is exactly what happened in China and Japan when Latinization (i.e., alphabetization for native speakers of these languages, as distinct from Romanization for the benefit of foreigners) was officially proposed.

In summary, we can state that on the level of abstraction at which the intrinsic

---

[22]The classical Chinese dictionary *K'ang-hsi*, published in 1716, lists more than 40,000 characters, but according to Wieger (1927), p. 7, only about 4000 of these are "in common use," 2000 are proper names or doubles, and no less than 34,000 are considered by him to be "monstrosities of no practical use." The *Chinese–English dictionary* by Giles (1912) contains 10,926 individual logograms, while the more recent *Chinese–English dictionary* by Mathews (1943) lists 7785 distinct logograms; many of these, however, were not available at the printing press and had to be specially engraved for this work, which implies that they are only seldom used.

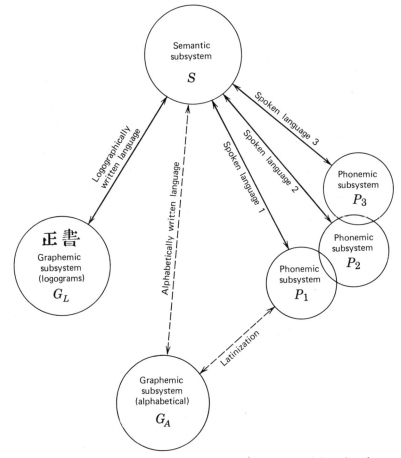

Figure 2.2. Relations between the semantic subsystem, the spoken, and the written language in Chinese. The effects of potential Latinization are indicated by broken lines.

natures of writing systems are compared, the substitution of one alphabetical script for another is ideally a one-to-one transformation, since one character of alphabet *A* is changed into one character of alphabet *B*. (Actually, all such conversions in real-life situations involve at least a few di- and trigraphs, but this does not invalidate the argument; if needed, a one-to-one transformation is always possible through use of diacritical marks and special characters, as discussed in Section 2.1.) Regarding the conversion of logographic script to an alphabetic one, however, a one-to-many transformation is needed: one Chinese logogram that is the unique visual image of one concept, is "split up," as it were, into a string of graphic signs that in themselves do not convey any meaning other than being the conventional notation for certain sounds. Since tones are not conventionally expressed by letters of an alphabet, additional graphic signs (e.g., diacritical marks or raised numerals) are needed to make the meaning of a transcribed logogram less ambiguous. (No transcription can make a Chinese logogram *entirely* unambiguous, as will be shown in Chapters 5 and 6). The somewhat different phonological renderings of a Chinese logogram in various Chinese dialects will necessarily also result in as many different alphabetical transcriptions, not to mention that many phonemes will have different alphabetical renderings in various non-Chinese languages, or even in one such language, as witness the several transcription systems from Chinese into English. These differ from each other to such a degree that it is often impossible for a person knowing Chinese to recognize a Chinese word written in certain transcription systems.[23]

Latinization of a language with the purpose of changing its writing system from a logographic to an alphabetical one therefore first requires alphabetization, or the expression of the language's phonemes by suitable graphemes that stand for individual sounds and not for the concepts expressed by those sounds or their concatenation. In other words, the Latinization of a language that uses a logographic script demands a much deeper change of convention than the one demanded from people who exchange one alphabetic script for another. Not only must a different set of graphic signs be substituted for the one in use before, but the whole conception of how to express language in written form has to be changed radically. This has always been and still is the principal obstacle to any Latinization of languages that use logographic scripts.

2.4.2.   Latinization of Chinese.   The earliest attempt at a conversion of Chinese characters into Roman script was made by Jesuit missionaries. Foremost among the them was the brilliant scholar Matteo Ricci (1552–1610), who landed in the Portuguese trading post of Macao in 1582. He began immediately to study the Chinese language, which he considered the key to a successful missionary activity. For this purpose, with the help of his colleague Michele Ruggieri (1542–1607), who had preceded him to Macao a year earlier, he compiled a Portuguese–Chinese vocabulary. The work was probably written in 1583, shortly after the two missionaries had received permission to enter Chao-ch'ing, the provincial capital of Kwang-tung. It consists of 189 handwritten pages, each of which is divided into three columns for Portuguese words, their Romanized translation into Mandarin (according to Italian orthography and pronunciation), and the corresponding Chinese characters; the first 4 pages also carry a fourth column containing an Italian translation written by Ruggieri (see Figure 2.3, which shows that for some Portuguese words no Chinese equivalents had yet been found). This vocabulary was the first systematic Romanization of

---

[23]The Chinese logogram for *to thank,* 謝 written with 17 strokes, has been variously romanized as: hsieh, shieh, xie, tse, dea, sye, sie, sieh, seay, zia, zie, jye, dere, and der.

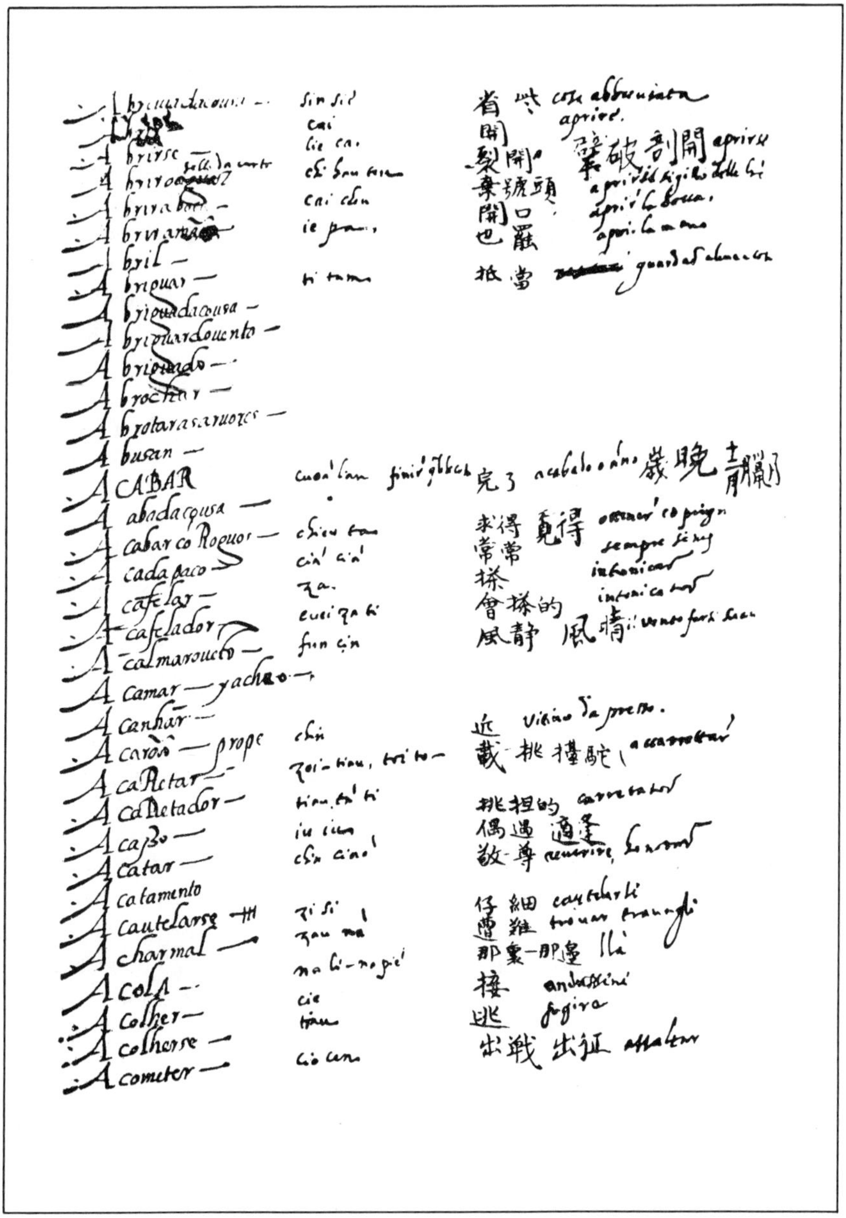

Figure 2.3. The first page of a Portuguese–Chinese vocabulary compiled by Matteo Ricci and Michele Ruggieri. (Reproduced from *Fonti Ricciane*, (1942–49), v. 2, tavola V.)

Chinese script,[24] but it lacked tone indicators. In 1598, when Ricci had become fluent in the language, he compiled a dictionary of Chinese characters with Romanized transcriptions that contained indications of aspirated syllables and diacritical marks for five tones (the latter designed by his colleague Lazzaro Cattaneo who, according to Ricci, had a better grasp of musical pitch).

Ricci spent the rest of his life in China. His name, in the Sinized form of Li Ma-t'ou (*Ricci Ma-t teo*) or in the form of the honorific appellation Hsi-t'ai ("Exalted Westerner"), became widely known among Chinese scholars and at the court of Emperor Shên-tsung, mainly through more than 20 books in Chinese on Western ideas and topics ranging from Christian theology to history, mathematics, astronomy, and cartography. Since Ricci had also made his learned Chinese friends familiar with the Western way of writing, in 1605 a scholar and maker of woodblocks for printing, Ch'eng Ta-yao, asked him to provide a text in Chinese and its Romanization. Ricci wrote three short accounts of Old and New Testament miracles in Chinese with a Romanization according to Portuguese orthography, and a dedication to Ch'eng Ta-yao. This text, together with Chinese copies of Italian woodcuts illustrating the miracles, was printed in Peking in 1606 from woodblocks under the title 西字奇蹟 ("Miracles in Western Characters")[25] (see Figure 2.4). It was the first Romanization of Chinese in printed form, though not the first Romanization of Chinese characters, which had been printed earlier by the Jesuits in Japan (see pp. 84-85).

Ricci's memoirs and reports of missionary activities in China were published posthumously by one of his colleagues, Nicolas Trigault (or Trigaut) (1577–1628), who also wrote several accounts of the Jesuit missions in China and Japan. In these works he used many examples of Chinese and Japanese names and words Romanized according to Ricci's system.[26] In 1626 Trigault published a comprehensive Chinese–Roman script dictionary under the title 西儒耳目資 ("The Western Scholar's Aid for Ear and Eye"), compiled with the aid of two Chinese converts, Wang-Cheng and Han Yün. The work consisted of a list of Romanized Chinese syllables, followed by all characters having the same pronunciation, and a corresponding list of about 20,000 Chinese characters with an indication of their pronunciation in Romanized form.[27]

These early Romanizations remained of interest mainly for Western mis-

---

[24]*Fonti Ricciane* (1942–49), v. 2, p. 32. The manuscript is preserved in the Archivum Romanum Societatis Iesu in Rome.

[25]*Fonti Ricciane* (1942–49), v. 1, p. 34, note 4. For a long time, this work was thought to be lost, and was known only by its title. It was discovered early in this century and published in 1927 in a facsimile edition by the Fu-jen University in Peking. A reprint (from which Figure 2.4 is reproduced) was published by the Chinese Written Language Reform Committee in 1957, as part of its efforts to provide source material for the Latinization of Chinese (see p. 77).

[26]Trigault (1615a, b, 1623, 1639).

[27]Trigault (1626).

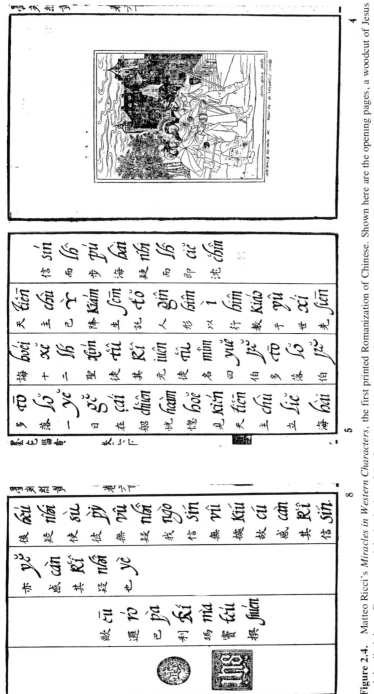

Figure 2.4. Matteo Ricci's *Miracles in Western Characters*, the first printed Romanization of Chinese. Shown here are the opening pages, a woodcut of Jesus and the disciples at Emmaus, and the beginning of the first story (right) and the last page of that story (left), with a colophon consisting of the word Europa and Ricci's name in Sinized form: *Ōu ṙó pà Rì mà toú siuén [Ou lo pa Li Ma-T'ou chuan* in modern Wade-Giles transcription]. "The European Ricci Matteo compiled [this work]" (third column from right). The two seals of the Societatis Iesu in the fourth column were used by Ricci in all his Chinese books., imitating the Chinese custom of putting seals of ownership or provenance on written works. (Reproduced from a facsimile edition published in Peking in 1957.)

73

sionaries, but Chinese scholars during the 17th and 18th centuries paid only scant attention to them. During the first half of the 19th century, Protestant missionaries working in the coastal areas of southeastern China, where a number of dialects entirely different from Mandarin are spoken, tried to Romanize these languages in religious tracts; in the province of Fukien and on the island of Amoy these Romanizations were still in use until the 1950s. However, no Romanization of Mandarin was undertaken until the 1860s, when China was forced by the Western powers to open its ports to trade. After the Second Opium War of 1860, which divided large parts of the Middle Kingdom into Western spheres of influence, the needs of businessmen and missionaries alike made it necessary to devise practical Romanization schemes for Mandarin, the predominant Chinese dialect. Sir Thomas Francis Wade (1818–1895), a British diplomat and professor of Chinese, created such a Romanization scheme in a textbook of Chinese first published in 1867. The scheme was subsequently simplified by Herbert A. Giles (1845–1935), like Wade a diplomat and philologist, in his *Chinese–English dictionary*,[28] and has become known as the Wade-Giles transcription throughout the English-speaking world.

Since any Romanization of Chinese can only be phonemical and must try to find equivalents for Chinese sounds in the phonology and writing systems of various languages, the Wade-Giles system, which was devised for speakers of English, could not serve the needs of speakers of other languages, and other Romanization schemes had to be created for them. But all these conversions of Chinese script into Roman letters were solely for the use of the "foreign devils" and did not influence the traditional mode of Chinese writing.

It was not until the war with Japan in 1894 that Latinization, or at least phonetization, was seriously considered by Chinese scholars and statesmen who began to realize that the high degree of illiteracy weakened China's potential in modern warfare. One of the earliest reform schemes was designed in 1892 by Lu Chu-chang, who proposed a Romanized "New Phonetic Alphabet." Thereafter more than two dozen reformers suggested various phonetic scripts based on simplified Chinese characters, among them Wu Chin-hen's "Beansprout Alphabet" and the "Best Alphabet for the Golden Age" by Shen Hsueh.[29] Others proposed a kind of shorthand system using parts of Chinese characters and sometimes also a few Roman letters, and even a purely numerical system of sound representation was suggested in order to overcome the difficulties of learning and using the traditional Chinese characters. Most successful among these early Chinese script reform schemes was a system of phonetic symbols similar to the Japanese *kana,* designed in 1900 by Wang Chao; this scheme was

[28]Wade (1867); Giles (1892).
[29]*Reform of the Chinese written language* (1958), pp. 63–64.

supported by government officials as well as by private individuals, and was taught for some time in special schools in 13 provinces in northern China.[30]

After the revolution of 1911, the 注 音 字 母 [Chu-yin Tzŭ-mu] ("Chinese National Phonetic Alphabet") system was introduced by the Association for Standard Pronunciation in 1913, and it was officially promulgated by the Chinese Ministry of Education in 1918 (see Table 2.4., p. 76, first column). This was not a Latinization scheme, but rather an attempt to substitute phonetic symbols consisting of the main strokes in certain Chinese logograms as pronounced in the Mandarin dialect spoken in Peking. In other words, it was a kind of phonetic alphabetization still linked to the traditional Chinese writing system. Originally there were 41 characters, a number later reduced to 37; attempts were made to use them in cursive writing like Roman letters, both vertically (i.e., in the traditional Chinese style) and horizontally, but this was not successful, mainly because many of the phonetic signs were too similar to be distinguished from each other when written together, and also because some of them represented more than one phoneme. The problem of writing foreign personal and geographic names or scientific terms remained unsolved, and the system was not applicable to the languages of non-Chinese minorities. Despite these shortcomings, the system was introduced in primary and secondary schools as a first step toward learning traditional Chinese logograms, and it is said to have contributed to the increased literacy and the widespread use of the Peking pronunciation as the standard for the spoken language.

This official phonetic transcription system, although still based on Chinese writing traditions, paved the way for alphabetization in Roman characters, and led ultimately to proposals for Latinization. The first step in this direction was the creation of the *Gwoyeu Romatzyh* ("National Romanized Writing"), devised by Chien Hsuan-tung, Li Chin-hsi, Yuen Ren Chao,* and Lin Yü-t'ang, and officially promulgated by the Ministry of Education in 1928. The scheme, which was aimed at a phonemic transcription, used a complicated system to indicate the tones (without which the many homophonous Chinese syllables remain ambiguous when written in phonemic transcription only). The scheme was well received by Chinese scholars but, because it had little governmental support, it remained largely an academic exercise.

As already noted the late 1920s was a period during which experiments in Latinization were made in the Soviet Union, and Chinese, spoken by a large number of people in the Soviet Far East, also became the subject of such attempts. The Scientific Research Institute on China at the Academy of Sciences in Moscow, after having first considered Cyrillification, decided in favor of

---

[30]Chu (1969), p. 27.

*The spelling of this name is the Romanization used by the author himself (who also wrote extensively in English); in Wade-Giles transcription his name is Yüan-jên Chao.

Table 2.4 Chinese Phonetic Alphabets

Chinese National Phonetic Alphabet[1]		Pin-yin[2]	Wade-Giles[3]
注音字母	Gwoyeu Romatzyh		
ㄅ	b	·	p
ㄆ	p	·	p'
ㄇ	m	·	·
ㄈ	f	·	·
ㄉ	d	·	t
ㄊ	t	·	t'
ㄋ	n	·	·
ㄌ	l	·	·
ㄍ	g	·	k
ㄎ	k	·	k'
ㄏ	h	·	·
ㄐ	j	·	ch
ㄑ	ch	q	ch'
ㄒ	sh	x	hs
ㄓ	j	zh	ch
ㄔ	ch	·	ch'
ㄕ	sh	·	·
ㄖ	r	·	j

Chinese National Phonetic Alphabet[1]		Pin-yin[2]	Wade-Giles[3]
注音字母	Gwoyeu Romatzyh		
ㄗ	tz	z	ts, tz
ㄘ	ts	c	ts', tz'
ㄙ	s	·	s, ss, sz
ㄚ	a	·	·
ㄛ	o	·	·
ㄜ	e, è	e	ê
ㄝ	è	·	eh
ㄞ	ai	·	·
ㄟ	ei	·	·
ㄠ	ao	·	·
ㄡ	ou	·	·
ㄢ	an	·	·
ㄣ	en	·	ên
ㄤ	ang	·	·
ㄥ	eng	·	êng
ㄦ	el	er	êrh
ㄧ	i, y	(y)i, yi	i, yi
ㄨ	u, w	(w)u, wu	u, wu
ㄩ	iu, yu	(y)u, yu	ü, yü

[1]Diphthongs written with two characters (e.g., ㄧ ㄝ) are not listed.
[2]A dot indicates that the Romanization is identical with Gwoyeu Romatzyh.
[3]Shown here for the sake of comparison.

76

Latinization as more appropriate, and devised a new transcription scheme for Chinese. This scheme influenced a group of Chinese Communist linguists, led by Chu Chiu-pai and Wu Yu-chang, who at that time studied in the Soviet Union. They, together with Soviet experts, developed it further, into a 28-letter system which was published in 1931 and became known as *Latinxua Sin Wenz* ("New Latinized Writing"). Where the *Gwoyeu Romatzyh* had been overly complicated in indicating the tones, the *Latinxua* used no tone marks at all, but despite this shortcoming it was used for several years, first in the Soviet Far Eastern Region, and later in Communist-held northwestern China, where a "Latinxua Association" was formed in 1941 to publish popular literature in this script.

In 1940 Mao Tse-tung had declared that "the written language must be reformed" through character simplification, popularization of the P'u T'ung-hua (a common or standardized Chinese, based on the pronunciation of the Peking dialect, the grammar of Northern Chinese dialects, and the vocabulary of modern colloquial Chinese), and a phonetic alphabet.[31] Less than a decade later his demands began to be put into action when, on October 10, 1949, only 10 days after the Communists had finally established their rule in China, the Association for Language Reform was founded in Peking and charged with the task of devising an improved Latinization scheme. In 1951 Mao stated, somewhat ambiguously, that "our written language must be reformed; it should take the direction of phonetization common to all the languages of the world," adding, however, that "it must be national in form".[32] The Association created in 1949 was transformed in 1952 into a Research Committee on Language Reform and was put under the direct control of the State Council in 1954. The first results of the deliberations of this committee were published in October 1955, when six different proposals were presented to a National Conference on the Reform of the Chinese Written Language, which was convened in Peking. Four of these used blocklike characters derived from traditional Chinese logograms, one proposal was based on Cyrillic letters, and one was a Romanization. The latter, named Han-yu Pin-yin, or Pin-yin ("spelled sound") for short, used all Roman letters except *v*, four modified Roman letters, namely, ç, ş,ʐ , and ŋ (all taken from the IPA), and the Cyrillic letter ч, for a total of 30 letters. This was the scheme adopted by the conference. One month later another conference in Peking devoted to the "Standardization of Modern Chinese" endorsed the P'u T'ung-hua as the standard language of the People's Republic of China. The decisions of these two conferences formed the basis for all subsequent developments in the fields of language and script reform.

The first draft of the Pin-yin scheme was submitted in 1956 to "consultative

---

[31]*Language and linguistics in the People's Republic of China* (1975), p. 43.
[32]*Ibid.*, p. 51.

conferences'' throughout China, in which more than 10,000 persons actively participated; government departments that were most affected by script reform, namely those dealing with education, post and telegraph, and the railways, held separate discussions on the scheme. Altogether 4300 suggestions for revisions or improvements were transmitted to the Committee as a result of these deliberations. At the plenary session of the State Council on November 1, 1957, a revised version of the Pin-yin system was promulgated, and this was finally adopted by the National People's Congress on February 11, 1958.

In its final form Pin-yin retained the 26 basic letters of the Roman alphabet without any modifications or additions. Three digraphs are used, namely *ch* for / tʂ /, *sh* for /ʂ/ and *zh* for / dʐ/; the umlaut *ü* represents /y/; the diacritical marks ‾, ´, ˇ, and `, are used to indicate the four tones of the P'u T'ung-hua, but their use is optional. The letter *v* is used only for the transcription of foreign names, since Chinese lacks a corresponding phoneme. A comparison of the three Chinese phonetic alphabets is shown in Table 2.4, and details of the Pin-yin scheme are given in Table 4.11 (pp. 284–287).

At that time the goal of phonetic alphabetization of Chinese was not a complete Latinization, and there was no intention of abandoning the traditional Chinese logograms altogether. Premier Chou En-lai made this quite clear when he addressed a meeting devoted to the introduction of the Pin-yin alphabet a few days before its official adoption. He elaborated on Mao's three objectives for the reform of the Chinese written language. The first was to simplify the Chinese logograms and to reduce their number; work on this task had already begun in 1956, when 515 of the most common characters had been simplified and 29 others had been eliminated entirely. Newspapers, magazines, and textbooks have been printed since then in these characters (which are partially unintelligible to readers of Chinese who know only the traditional forms). Figure 2.5 shows some of the simplified characters and their traditional forms.

The second task envisaged by Chou En-lai was the

. . . popularization of the common speech (P'u T'ung-hua). . . . People of different areas, each speaking their own dialect, can hardly understand each other. People of the same province (for example, northern and southern Fukien; northern and southern Kiangsu) find it difficult to carry on conversation. The diversity in dialects has an unfavorable effect on the political, economic and cultural life of our people. . . . It is, therefore, an important political task to popularize vigorously the common speech, with the Peking pronunciation as the standard.[33]

The third objective was to develop a phonetic alphabet, but Chou warned in no uncertain terms against any misconceptions about a complete Latinization of Chinese:

[33]*Reform of the Chinese written language* (1958), pp. 14–15.

2 笔	乡〔鄉〕	〔昇〕	邓〔鄧〕	归〔歸〕
厂〔廠〕	**4 笔**	凶〔兇〕	劝〔勸〕	叶〔葉〕②
卜〔蔔〕	**【一】**	长〔長〕	双〔雙〕	号〔號〕
儿〔兒〕	丰〔豐〕	仆〔僕〕	书〔書〕	电〔電〕
几〔幾〕	开〔開〕	币〔幣〕	**5 笔**	只〔隻〕
了〔瞭〕	无〔無〕	从〔從〕	**【一】**	〔祇〕
3 笔	韦〔韋〕	仑〔侖〕	击〔擊〕	叽〔嘰〕
干〔乾〕①	专〔專〕	仓〔倉〕	戈〔戔〕	叹〔嘆〕
〔幹〕	云〔雲〕	风〔風〕	扑〔撲〕	**【丿】**
亏〔虧〕	艺〔藝〕	仅〔僅〕	节〔節〕	们〔們〕
才〔纔〕	厅〔廳〕	凤〔鳳〕	术〔術〕	仪〔儀〕
万〔萬〕	历〔歷〕	乌〔烏〕	札〔劄〕	丛〔叢〕
与〔與〕	〔曆〕	**【、】**	〔剳〕	尔〔爾〕
千〔韆〕	区〔區〕	闩〔門〕	龙〔龍〕	乐〔樂〕
亿〔億〕	巨〔鉅〕	为〔爲〕	厉〔厲〕	处〔處〕
个〔個〕	扎〔紮〕	斗〔鬥〕	布〔佈〕	冬〔鼕〕
么〔麼〕	〔紮〕	忆〔憶〕	灭〔滅〕	鸟〔鳥〕
广〔廣〕	车〔車〕	订〔訂〕	东〔東〕	务〔務〕
门〔門〕	**【丨】**	计〔計〕	轧〔軋〕	刍〔芻〕
义〔義〕	冈〔岡〕	讣〔訃〕	**【丨】**	饥〔饑〕
卫〔衛〕	贝〔貝〕	认〔認〕	占〔佔〕	**【、】**
飞〔飛〕	见〔見〕	讥〔譏〕	卢〔盧〕	邝〔鄺〕
习〔習〕	**【丿】**	**【乛】**	业〔業〕	冯〔馮〕
	气〔氣〕	丑〔醜〕	旧〔舊〕	闪〔閃〕
	升〔陞〕	队〔隊〕	帅〔帥〕	兰〔蘭〕
		办〔辦〕		汇〔匯〕

2

Figure 2.5. Simplified and traditional Chinese characters. The simplified characters appear in the left-hand part of each column, and the corresponding traditional characters are given in brackets alongside. (From a ''List of simplified characters'' published in 1974 by the journal 人民画报 [*People's Pictorial*].)

It should be made clear at the outset that the scheme is to annotate the characters phonetically and to popularize the common speech. It is not to replace the Chinese characters.[34]

In other words, not Latinization but Romanized phonetization. Chou then outlined five functions that the new alphabet was to fulfill. The first was to indicate
unambiguously the pronunciation of a Chinese logogram. Secondly, it was to
serve as a teaching aid for the "common speech," that is, the standard Peking
pronunciation. Thirdly, it was to serve as a common basis for the reform or
creation of written languages for the more than 50 national minorities, of which
only about 20 had their own writing systems, such as Tibetan, Mongolian,
Arabic, and Korean; for all these, Chou envisaged future Latinization on the
basis of the new alphabet. The fourth function was to help foreigners learn
Chinese. The fifth was to serve as a means for the arrangement of indexes and
dictionaries, and to "transliterate" foreign personal and geographic names,
scientific terms, and technical expressions. (Inasmuch as such names are already
written in Roman script, no transliteration is actually involved, but rather a
convenient and smooth integration of such names and terms into Romanized
Chinese texts; but in the case of Russian names, for example, there would indeed
be a "Pin-yinization," if one may say so.)

Chou concluded his remarks by defending the choice of the Roman alphabet
as in no way detrimental to the "patriotism of the Chinese people" and made a
cautious assessment of possible future developments:

One remaining question with which we are all much concerned is the future of Chinese
characters. We all agree that as a written record they have made immortal contributions to
history. As to whether or not they will remain permanently unchanged, whether they will
change on the basis of their original forms, or whether they will be replaced by a phonetic
language [sic]—Latin letters or other phonetic scripts—we need not draw a hasty
conclusion.[35]

From his detailed and lengthy defense of the scheme against the accusation of
being foreign and "un-Chinese," and from some other remarks in Chou's
speech, it is obvious that the whole question of language and script reform had
provoked not only intense professional debates among writers and linguists, but
possibly even more controversies of an ideological nature among the political
leaders. The otherwise ubiquitous voice of Mao Tse-tung is conspicuously ab-
sent from the official booklet that contains Chou's speech and several other
articles by linguists as well as the tables and explanations of the Pin-yin phonetic
alphabet.

The introduction of Pin-yin in all primary and secondary schools, the printing

[34]*Reform of the Chinese written language* (1958), p. 17.
[35]*Ibid.*, p. 28.

of textbooks in this script, the creation of alphabets for the non-Chinese minorities, and the general propagation of Latinization among China's hundreds of millions of illiterates during the Second Five-Year Plan were outlined in detail and fervently advocated in that booklet. It seems, however, that these far-reaching plans were not very vigorously pursued, perhaps because so many other tasks had a higher priority during the first decade of the Communist regime, but also because the Romanized phonetic transcription of Chinese was still considered only a complement, not a substitute, for the traditional writing system which, despite its complexity, was recognized as a unifying force for the vast country and its many different tongues, and could not be easily abandoned for complete Latinization. A few years after the introduction of the Pin-yin system, street signs in major cities and place names on railroad stations and bus stops were written in Romanized form side by side with the newly simplified Chinese logograms; some (but by no means all) book titles were printed in Pin-yin, but the text was almost always in Chinese characters. This seems to be about the extent to which Romanized phonetization was employed when the Cultural Revolution put a temporary halt to further developments in the sphere of language reform.

After the Cultural Revolution had been reined in somewhat, and especially after the People's Republic of China had taken its official seat in the United Nations in 1971, language reform and particularly the propagation of Pin-yin again became official goals of the regime, even to the extent that full Romanization is now envisaged as a "final solution" to the problem of teaching and popularizing the Chinese written language, which would make the P'u T'ung-hua a true *lingua franca* throughout China. Whether all Chinese logograms and the vast number of books written in this script will be eliminated in the future or replaced by Romanized versions of Chinese literature is, however, as yet unclear. American linguists visiting China in 1974 were told by a spokesman for the Committee on Language Reform that the application of Pin-yin to various objectives was making steady progress. Textbooks are printed in Romanized versions; instructional material for foreigners (such as the language lessons in *China Reconstructs*) is now written exclusively in Pin-yin; and there is a Pin-yin based finger spelling for the deaf, a Pin-yin Braille for the blind, and a Pin-yin code for telegraphy and for naval flag signals. The scheme is also used for the alphabetizing of dictionaries and indexes, as well as for the official list of Chinese place names submitted to the United Nations for a worldwide compilation of geographical names, and it is now also being introduced in nationwide radio broadcasts. Despite all this the linguists received the impression that the government proceeded somewhat cautiously because of "unresolved differences of opinion in the leadership."[36] No doubts exist, however, about the Latiniza-

---

[36]*Language and linguistics in the People's Republic of China* (1975), p. 53.

tion of national minority languages, 54 of which have so far been officially recognized. Non-Chinese writing systems used in the past (mainly Mongolian, which had its own script; Tibetan, which was written in Devanagari; Uighur and Kazakh, in Arabic; and Korean, in Hangŭl script), are now rapidly being Romanized. This is being achieved by using the Pin-yin scheme for the expression of phonemes that are the same as or similar to Chinese ones, and Roman letters with diacritical marks for sounds that do not occur in Chinese; in certain cases, special letters are also employed. Loanwords from Chinese are, however, always written in their original Pin-yin spelling. Unlike the methods used in the Soviet Union for the Cyrillification of non-Slavic languages, the Chinese linguists who design new writing systems for hitherto unwritten languages and dialects make efforts to harmonize the alphabets of closely related languages and to introduce as few differences as possible from the Pin-yin spelling. This seems to be in accordance with the principle of making the P'u T'ung-hua a universal second language throughout China while preserving local dialects and other languages. Until the end of 1974 the following previously unwritten minority languages had been Romanized: Chuang, Miao, Yi, Tung, Puyi, Li, Hani, Lisu, Wa, and Na-hsi. The gradual introduction of Pin-yin is accompanied by continuing efforts to simplify the traditional Chinese characters. In 1964 a list was published of 2000 simplified characters and 6000 "standard" characters for printing purposes, and the number of "radicals" (the elements conveying some part of the meaning of logograms) was reduced from the classical 214 to 189. Further simplifications of characters took place in 1975.

Needless to say, the developments in the field of language and script reform that took place in the People's Republic of China after 1949 did not affect the Republic of China in Taiwan. Neither simplification of Chinese logograms nor any form of Latinization has been considered. The traditional Chinese writing system is still being taught as it has been for many centuries, while the Roman alphabet is taught to students in high school with the sole aim of enabling them to learn foreign languages, primarily English. For official transcription purposes (the rendering of personal or geographical names for use outside China) the Wade-Giles Romanization scheme is employed.

2.4.3. Latinization of Japanese.   According to tradition Japan acquired its writing system from Korea sometime after the Chinese script had been introduced there in the 3rd century A.D. With the advent of Buddhism in the 6th century A.D. many Chinese scholars and Buddhist priests came to Japan, and soon it became necessary to translate Chinese works and to adapt the Chinese writing system to Japanese. Since the Japanese language is agglutinative, not monosyllabic as is Chinese, this was an almost impossible task, but the Japanese were then not aware of any other way of graphic expression of language, and had to make the best of the Chinese writing system. They soon devised various ingenious but highly complicated ways to adapt it to the needs of their language, primarily through the addition of a syllabic alphabet. The following description of the present Japanese writing system is by no means complete and omits certain minor but important features, but it suffices as background information for our account of attempts at its Latinization and of the various systems of Romanization and Cyrillization.

The Chinese logograms, called *kanji* in Japanese, are used for the concepts they signify in Chinese, but are pronounced either as Japanese words (the *kun* "reading," which may take several forms) or as any of three "readings" derived from Chinese sounds (the *on* readings, which are further subdivided into *go-on* and *kan-on,* used for secular texts, and *to-on* for liturgical Buddhist texts). Thus, one *kanji* logogram may have as many as six (and in some cases even more) completely different phonemic realizations, as in the following example:

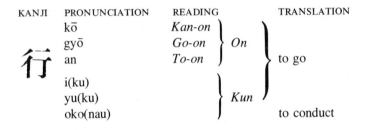

KANJI	PRONUNCIATION	READING		TRANSLATION
	kō	*Kan-on*		
	gyō	*Go-on*	*On*	
行	an	*To-on*		to go
	i(ku)			
	yu(ku)		*Kun*	
	oko(nau)			to conduct

The *kanji* logograms are supplemented by the *kana* syllabaries, graphic signs that express the traditional 47 open syllables of the Japanese language and the syllabic nasal *n* $\left[\tilde{n}\right]$, for a total of 48 signs; originally, there were 50 signs, but three open syllables, /(w)i/, /(w)u/, and /(y)e/, are now no longer used. The syllabic alphabet is called *Iroha* (after the first three syllables in a Buddhist poem), or *Goju-on* ("fifty sounds"). They are used to indicate either the proper pronunciation of a word or certain grammatical features, and are written in two different forms: *katakana,* a somewhat square style of writing, mainly used in official documents and for the phonemic transcription of foreign names and words; and *hiragana,* a cursive style, used for handwritten texts, letters, and textbooks used in elementary schools. *Katakana* may also be employed for these purposes; in poems, where the calligraphy is as much a part of the art form as the content, *hiragana* is almost always used. In modern Japan the most commonly used mode of writing is a mixture of *kanji* and *hiragana,* called *kana-majiri.*

All this relates to words and sentences, that is, to consecutive text. Regarding personal or geographical names, the situation is more complicated still. One *kanji,* when used to write a name, may have more than 20 completely different readings. For example, the simplest logograph, consisting of only one stroke ——, means "one" when it is pronounced $\left[\bar{\imath}\right]$ (with the high level tone) in

Chinese; when it means a Japanese name, however, it may be read in no less than 23 different ways: Hajime, Hajimu, Hitoshi, Makoto, Masashi, Osamu, and Susumu (as a complete name); ichi, itsu, kazu, hito, moto, katsu, ka, hi, chi, tada, kumi, nobu, hide, hiji, kata, and ma (when it is a component of a name). The name of a person who signs himself as 平平平平 (i.e., with four identical *kanji*) is pronounced *Hiradaira Heibei,* but the same signature may be pronounced in several other ways. Conversely, a name pronounced in a certain way may have numerous different written forms. The common female name *Akiko,* for example, can be written in 18 different ways, and the name *Akira* has no less than 228 different forms in the onomastic dictionary *Japanese names* by O'Neill! To alleviate the difficulties of pronouncing a personal name, it has become customary in modern Japanese books to print the name of an author in *kanji* and in *kana,* a style called *furigana;* the method is also used when the proper identification of a name is important.

It can safely be said that no other language has ever been burdened with a writing system so patently inappropriate for its structure and phonology, and at the same time so complex and ambiguous in its applications. Yet such is the power of script conventions that even the most unwieldy system, once firmly ensconced and anchored in religious tradition, a large body of literature, and national pride, is almost impossible to replace by another system save by a foreign dictatorial force bent on such a purpose. This, for better or worse, the Japanese have not yet encountered, although they came close to it after their defeat in World War II.

The earliest known Romanization of Japanese was Marco Polo's rendering of *Jih-Pen-kuo* (the Chinese name for Japan, meaning "The Land of the Rising Sun") as *Chipangu* or *Zipangu,* which was later written by Portuguese explorers as *Japão* and by Dutch merchants as *Japan,* following the Malayan pronunciation of the Chinese name. The Japanese themselves call their country *Nippon,* based on the Middle Chinese pronunciation [ńiɛt puən kuok], or *Nihon.*

The first comprehensive attempts at Romanization were those of Jesuit missionaries. The cofounder of the order, St. Francis Xavier (1506–1552) arrived in Kagoshima, on the island of Kyushyu, in 1549, and had considerable success in converting the Japanese in the province of Hizen (the present Saga prefecture) to Christianity. The Italian Jesuit Alessandro Valignani, who visited Japan in 1579 and installed the first printing press in the seminary of Katsusa near Nagasaki in 1591, was anxious to provide the Japanese converts with only those books that did not contain any trace of heresy, and he also wanted them "to learn Latin in such a way as to imbibe simultaneously Christian precepts and virtue and to abhor vice."[37] To these ends Valignani brought with him from Italy a font of Roman type and probably also metal matrices for the *katakana* signs, as well

[37]Quoted in Boxer (1951), p. 190.

as a few specimens of the most often-used *kanji*. These types, however, seem not to have been used in the beginning, because the very first book to come off the press in 1591 was *Sanctos no gosagveo* ("Life of the Saints"), which had been adapted from the *Flos sanctorum*, translated into Japanese by one of the converts, and written in a Romanization devised for that purpose by the Jesuit fathers at Katsusa. After persecutions by the local Japanese rulers, the press had to be moved to another seminary on the island of Amakusa, and in 1593 the first secular work in Romanized Japanese, the popular 13th century romance *Heike monogatari* ("The Tales of the Heike Clan") was published. The story was retold in simple colloquial language, and the preface stated that its purpose was to serve as a primer of Japanese for those Jesuits who wished to become proficient in that language; that is to say, this was a Romanization for Westerners and was not intended for use by Japanese readers. This work was printed and bound together with *Esopu no fabulas* ("Aesop's Fables") in a version written in Romanized Japanese and thoroughly edited to avoid any heathen "heresies." The Japanese converts at the seminary soon learned to cut type for *kanji* and *kana*, and the press printed a number of books in these characters, among them some linguistic works such as grammars and bilingual dictionaries "in order that the Japanese may learn Latin and we of Europe, Japanese," as the Jesuit father Francisco Pasio put it in a letter written in 1594.[38] A *Dictionarium Latino-Lusitanicum ac Iaponicum* was printed in 1595, followed by the *Racuyoxu* ("Falling Leaves," [*Rakuyōshū* in modern transcription]), a dictionary of Chinese logograms with Japanese readings, in which for the first time *kanji* and *kana* were printed together.

The press stayed at Amakusa until 1597 and was eventually moved to Nagasaki, where it remained until 1614, when the Jesuits were forcibly expelled from the city. Altogether 27 books printed by the press have survived,[39] and these *Kirishitan-ban* ("Christian books") are today as rare and highly valued as first folios of Shakespeare. The actual production of books must have been much larger; some titles, such as a number of other Romanized *monogatari* ("tales") are known to have been printed, but no copies have been found because of the wholesale destruction of all things Christian after a massacre of Christian Japanese and the final expulsion of all missionaries in 1618 by the Shogun (military ruler) Tokugawa Ieyasu, who saw the rising power of an autonomous community with ties to foreign countries as a threat to his own regime. (The ban on Christianity was not *de facto* removed until 1873.) This was also the end of any further practical attempts at Romanization of Japanese for almost 250 years.

Japan became almost entirely closed to Europeans, and only a small Dutch trading post was allowed to remain on the artificial island of Deshima in the

---

[38]Boxer (1951), p. 194.
[39]Laures (1940).

harbor of Nagasaki. Although the Japanese authorities kept a watchful eye on the foreigners, knowledge of Western things gradually spread through occasional contacts between the Dutch and the Japanese. Toward the end of the 17th century, a small *rangaku* ("Dutch studies") movement was founded by Japanese scholars interested in Western ideas, and a few decades later it was not only tolerated but actively supported by the Shogun Tokugawa Yoshimune, who decreed in 1740 that two Japanese scholars should learn Dutch in order to translate Dutch scientific works.

The influence of the *rangaku* movement also led to several proposals for a reform of the Japanese script. As early as 1715 Arai Hakuseki (1657–1726), in his book *Seiyō kibun* ("Report on Western Things"), suggested that the *kanji* be eliminated because of their extreme complexity and that Japanese be written with the Roman alphabet. The same idea was also discussed by Kamo no Mabuchi (1697–1769) in his book *Kokui Kō* ("Thoughts on Japan's Intentions"), although neither of these scholars made a practical proposal. One of the most prominent *rangaku* scholars, Honda Toshiaki (1744–1821), also urged that Japan be opened up to Western ideas, including the adoption of the Roman script. A further step toward script reform was taken in 1866, when Maejima Tsubara (later Baron Maejima) addressed an open letter to Keiki, the last Tokugawa Shogun, in which he said:

Education must encompass the whole nation. The script of a nation must be such that it is simple and easy to learn. . . . Therefore, I advise you for the sake of the education of the people, and also with regard to the European countries, to introduce the phonetic *kana* script, and to eliminate the *kanji* entirely.[40]

But only in the following Meiji period (1868–1912), during which the rapid Westernization of Japan began, did various movements for the reform and simplification of the Japanese writing system, including its possible Latinization, begin to develop. In 1869 Maejima elaborated his earlier proposals for script reform and advocated the introduction of the Roman alphabet; he was supported by Tanakadate Aikichi who, in 1870, published his *Nipponshiki Rōmazi* ("Roman Script in Japanese Style"), in which he proposed the Latinization of the *Iroha* syllabary, based on phonemic transcription. A similar plea for Latinization (but not the complete elimination of Japanese and adoption of a European language, as had been suggested by some fanatics of Westernization) was made by the linguist Kurokawa Mayori (1829–1906) in 1875. He said that "one may

---

[40]Hatsukade (1932), p. 28. The quotations taken from this source have been translated from the German original. The names of the Japanese scholars Kurokawa Mayori and Shimizu Usaburō are mentioned by Hatsukade in incomplete form, and were identified by Mr. Frank J. Shulman of the East Asia Collection, McKeldin Library of the University of Maryland; it is almost certain that these are the persons to whom the author refers.

change one's clothes but the body must remain," by which he meant that, although the body of the Japanese language must be preserved, it may be clothed in Latin garb rather than in Chinese. Others, like the scientist Shimizu Usaburō (1838–1910), preferred a purely Japanese script, and Shimizu demonstrated his method by writing a textbook on chemistry in *katakana* only. His ideas were taken up by the *Kana no tomo* ("Friends of the *Kana* Script"), founded in 1881, which later changed its name to *Kakikate kairyobu* ("Society for the Improvement of Script") and advocated an indigenous phonetic syllabic script.

In 1884 the *Rōmaji-Kai* ("Society for Roman Script") was founded, and one year later a committee published the *Rōmaji Kai-shiki* ("Script of the Romanization Society"), a phonetic scheme mainly based on the system first published in 1867 by the American missionary James Curtis Hepburn in his Japanese-English dictionary.[41] This system took into account some of Tanakadate's principles (see Figure 2.6), and Hepburn himself used this revised Romanization scheme in the third edition of his dictionary, published in 1886. The system has remained the most widely used one in the English-speaking world. The *Rōmaji-Kai* also published a periodical, the *Romāji Zasshi* ("Romanization Journal"), printed in Romanized Japanese.

Tanakadate, however, was not satisfied with this scheme and soon left the *Rōmaji-Kai* to found his own society, the *Nipponshiki Rōmazi Kai* ("Society for Romanization in Japanese Style"), which published the journal *Rōmazi Sinsi* ("New Romanization Journal"). The two rival Romanization societies henceforth engaged more in feuding with each other (mainly on the pages of their respective mouthpieces) than in promoting their avowed goal of Latinization.

The government, which by that time genuinely wished to do something about script reform and had called on scholars and experts, was caught in the middle between the proponents of two rival Latinization schemes, and several other societies that proposed the introduction of a national Japanese script based on the *kana* syllabary. It was decided to appoint a Committee of Investigation into a National Script. In 1902 this body declared, "We must adopt a phonetic script, and we have to investigate the pros and cons of a Japanese syllabic script as against the Roman script," but they procrastinated for so long that virtually nothing came of their inquiry.

In 1910 the followers of Tanakadate founded yet another society, the *Nippon Rōmazi Kai* ("Society for Japanese Romanization") and published two periodicals in Romanized Japanese, *Rōmazi no Nippon* ("Roman Script in Japan") and *Rōmazi Sekai* ("Roman Script in the World"). They also began to print scientific books in their Romanized script and published some two dozen titles until the early 1930s.

Meanwhile other developments aimed at a simplification of the *kanji* and,

---

[41]Hepburn (1867).

Tomokaku Rômaji o mochiite miyo !

Maekata Saionji-naikaku no koro ni, "Mikuni no daijin tomo aru hito ga Rômaji-Hirome-Kwai no kwaitô ya fuku-kwaitô ni natte iru to wa futsugô ja. Kamiyo konokata no kokutai o dô suru ? " to ikidôtta mono ga atta. Sokode "Anshin nasai ! warera wa Kamiyo konokata no Mikuni no kotoba o, totsukuni no hitobito nimo yoku wakaru yôni, kakeru monji o hiromeru mono de aru." to aisatsu shita to no koto de aru. Taishô no miyo no imagoro ni, mohaya monji to kokutai o hakichigaeru mono mo arumai.

Kodomo no kyôiku wa kokka no yukusue ni kakawaru mono de, shitagatte kore ni mochiiru dôgu no monji o narubeku benri na mono ni seneba naranai, to iu koto wa, ikiru tameni wa kuimono ga hitsuyô de aru kara, sono kuimono no shurui o erabaneba naranai to iu yô ni, amari wakari-sugita rikutsu de aru.

Onore no kangae o hoka no hito ni tsutaeru no ga kotoba de aru kara, kotoba wa narubeku hirataku'te, wakari-yasui ga yoi. Mata kono kotoba no kawari o suru no ga monji de aru kara, monji wa narubeku magirai no nai yôni, katsu narubeku wakari-yasui yôni, kotoba o kakeru mono ga yoi hazu de aru. Kayôna rikutsu mo, imasara noberu no ga mushiro kinodoku na kurai de aru.

Kayôni kangaeru to, yononaka no hito ga Rômaji-mondai o imani naozari ni shite iru no wa, mushiro fushigi no itari de aru. Jissai sukoshi rikutsu no wakaru hito ni, monji-kairyô no hitsuyô to

—(31)—

Figure 2.6. Specimen of *Rômaji-Kai shiki* Romanization of Japanese. (Reproduced from Hatsukade, 1932, p. 36.)

above all, at a reduction of their large number, which was the main obstacle to general education and the achievement of complete literacy throughout the nation. This movement had also arisen early in the Meiji period, when the Japanese educator, writer, and language reformer Fukuzawa Yukichi (1835–1901) argued in his book *Monji no oshie* ("Theory of script"), published in 1873, that:

It is a great inconvenience that Japan incorporated in her national script not only the indigenous syllabary but also the cumbersome Chinese logograms. Through the daily use of these logograms during hundreds of years together with our syllabary both have become amalgamated in such a way that a sudden separation from the Chinese logograms is impossible. We hope that the idea of such a separation will at some future time become a reality, but it is not possible to achieve this all at once. We must try to gradually devise methods to prepare a smooth partial separation from the complex logograms. . . . In our everyday writing we should eliminate all the particularly complex logograms and not use them at all, retaining only the easy Chinese logograms in our script.[42]

Fukuzawa's ideas were taken up in 1923 by the Ministry of Education which, in collaboration with publishers of textbooks and newspapers, published a list of 1962 logograms (chosen from the almost 50,000 that at one time or another had been in use but that, of course, were not all mastered even by the most literate Japanese). Only these *kanji* were henceforth to be used in schools and by newspapers, augmented by 154 abbreviations and by *kana* when necessary. This system became known as *tōyō-kanji* ("Everyday Characters") but was, in fact, not used as much as had been hoped. Nevertheless Japan rapidly reached the goal of almost complete nationwide literacy during the 1930s, despite the formidable obstacles posed by even the simplified writing system.

Realizing that an official Romanization scheme was needed to render Japanese personal and geographic names in publications aimed at Western readers, the government approved in 1937 the *Kokutei Rōmazi* ("Official Romanization"),[43] which was based on the principle of phonemic transcription as proposed by the linguist Takuro Tamura in 1905. This official scheme, which differed from the Hepburn scheme in several instances, was, however, not made mandatory, and the outbreak of World War II two years after its promulgation made illusory any large-scale application for internal Japanese consumption. The fiercely nationalistic atmosphere that prevailed until the surrender of Japan in 1945 made any movement for script reform suspect, and Latinization in particular was ruled out as being alien to the true Japanese spirit.

To many people in the West the allied occupation of Japan from 1945 to 1951 seemed to be the long-awaited opportunity to Latinize the Japanese language. Only eight months after the occupation had begun, a team of American

[42]Hatsukade (1932), p. 29.
[43]Carr (1939).

educators, headed by Dr. George D. Stoddard, submitted to General MacArthur recommendations for a complete restructuring of the Japanese education system, stressing the necessity for Latinization. They rejected categorically a proposal by the Japanese Ministry of Education to further reduce the number of *kanji* and to substitute the *kana* syllabary, and proposed instead

prompt establishment of a Japanese committee of scholars, educators and statesmen to formulate means of adapting the Roman alphabet to Japanese sounds, and its introduction into the schools, newspapers, magazines and books.[44]

They concluded that the present writing system wasted much useful time of Japanese students and constituted a formidable obstacle to learning.

The Japanese, on the other hand, were anxious to point out that complete Latinization would imply either that they would have to scrap all existing books and reprint them in Latinized form at a staggering cost, or that these books would be preserved in libraries, thus making it necessary for future generations to learn both traditional Japanese writing and the Roman alphabet to make use of the literary heritage of the nation.

MacArthur, who desired nothing more than to remake Japan in the image of America, realized nevertheless that enforced Latinization might become an emotional issue almost akin to the dethronement of the Emperor; he desisted from carrying out the commission's recommendations so as not to endanger almost all his other reforms. He told the committee members that he appreciated their idealism, but that such sweeping script reform could not be carried out immediately and would in any case take many years to complete. Thus the Japanese point of view prevailed. In 1946 the Japanese government published a reduced list of 1850 *kanji,* called *tōyō-kanji* ("characters for general use" or "standard characters"), and an additional 92 characters were later approved for use in personal names. Most of the characters in this list were also simplified in form so that they became easier to memorize and write, and they are now used in most official documents, textbooks, and newspapers. The most important 881 *kanji* were designated *kyōiku-kanji* ("characters for educational use"); these are taught to all pupils in elementary schools, and mastering them is considered as the absolute minimum of literacy. Words that cannot be expressed by *tōyō-kanji* are written in *kana* characters.

Romanization of Japanese, when necessary, is now performed according to three different systems. The official one, taught since 1947 in all elementary schools and last revised and codified in 1954, is the *Kunrei-shiki* ("Official Style"), a revised version of the former *Kokutei-shiki.* Most foreigners use the Hepburn system, called *Hebon-shiki* or *Hyōjun-shiki* ("Standard Style"), which

[44]*The New York Times,* April 7, 1946.

is recognized in Japan but does not enjoy official status. The third system is the *Nihon-shiki* ("Japanese Style"), a Romanization according to the principles of Tanakadate (see Chapter 4, Table 4.8, pp. 266–269).

Needless to say, some authors and editors use a mixture of the three systems, which adds to the confusion besetting all Japanese transcription, not to mention the difficulties posed by the numerous different readings of personal names.

To a Westerner it might seem that a great opportunity was missed in 1946, and that it would have been beneficial for the Japanese as well as for the rest of the world (with the possible exception of the Chinese) if they themselves had found the strength to get rid of a writing system that is difficult and awkward to use, is full of ambiguities, and has hidden pitfalls even for the native speaker of Japanese, or if such a radical solution had been imposed by the Americans, as were so many other far-reaching measures that have now become part of Japanese political, economic, and cultural life.

But such reasoning misses the point entirely. Over the centuries the Japanese language has to a considerable degree become the slave rather than the master of its writing system. It contains thousands of homophones that are distinguished by *kanji* but cannot be disambiguated phonemically by the device that serves the Chinese people so well, namely different tones, because Japanese lacks these entirely. Homophones are made intelligible in speech, if at all, by context, stress, intonation, and sometimes by additional explanation through other words. Simply writing Japanese words in phonemic or phonetic transcription (or even with pure *kana* syllabaries) does not solve this problem—quite to the contrary, it makes it knottier, as can be seen from Table 2.5, which shows the Japanese word *kaki* in unambiguous *kanji*. Neither *katakana* writing nor Romanization can express the differences between the six possible meanings.

An additional difficulty is that there exist no definite rules for punctuation or word division, which means that a sentence written in *kana* or in Romanization is generally open to several interpretations, depending on where the reader decides to separate or join syllables. The Japanese are therefore forced to cling to the

Table 2.5   Transcription of Homophonous Japanese Words

Kanji	Katakana	Transcription	Translation
柿	カキ	Kaki	Persimmon
垣	カキ	Kaki	Fence
牡蠣	カキ	Kaki	Oyster
夏季	カキ	Kaki	Summertime
火気	カキ	Kaki	Heat
火器	カキ	Kaki	Firearm

ancient Chinese logograms for their written language if they do not wish to get bogged down in almost undecipherable conundrums every time they read a street sign, open a newspaper, or receive a letter.

Latinization of Japanese in the sense of complete conversion to the Roman alphabet is thus almost impossible, not only because of the large mass of literature written in *kanji* which has accumulated over more than a thousand years, and the high degree of literacy which makes the whole nation as conscious of this rich spiritual heritage as highly literate nations of the West (although these two factors did play an important role in the rejection of complete Latinization), but rather because of the peculiar relationship between spoken and written language which has no equivalent anywhere else in the world. If it is at all permissible to speak of Latinization of the Japanese language in the strict sense, it is because the government of the country has officially recognized a Romanization scheme, and permits it to be used as an alternative writing system, albeit mainly for the benefit of foreigners. Romanization, on the other hand, takes as many forms as there are different languages, because only essentially phonemic transcription is possible for the conversion of logograms to alphabetic writing, and most languages attempt to convey the phonemes of Japanese in their own writing systems.

* * *

The two large nations that use logographic scripts and together comprise more than a fourth of the world's population failed to achieve Latinization, not because of a lack of good conversion systems or a lack of governmental support (which, as we have seen, was forthcoming at least during certain periods in China as well as in Japan), but primarily because of the sociolinguistic obstacles that apparently resist any attempts at being removed or circumvented. The loss, of course, is not so much on the side of the Chinese and Japanese, who now manage to achieve almost complete literacy in their nations through the simplification of the Chinese logograms and their reduction to a memorizable number, as rather on the part of the Western nations, and particularly their bibliographic control tools. Whatever conversion systems are used (and their number is legion) will never be compatible on a technical level, nor will they be able to convey to a reader the essence and flavor of the Chinese or Japanese language on the intellectual and emotional level. The logographs, even in their simplified forms, will still be an almost insurmountable barrier to the use of these literatures and their documents, and in particular to the recording of names in Roman script. While a large number of Chinese and Japanese scholars and scientists (other than professional linguists) have managed to learn European languages so well that they write them without any difficulty in an idiomatic and beautiful style, only a handful of Western specialists can write passable Chinese or Japanese, not to speak of idiomatic writing, which only a few people have been able to master after they had lived long enough in those countries.[45]

It is highly unlikely that any far-reaching change in this situation will occur in the foreseeable future, especially since modern technology has now found methods to reproduce Chinese logograms electronically and to store them in digital form for machine-readable records.[46] In a recent survey of library automation in Japan, it was flatly stated:

From now on, developing procedures for computerization of Chinese characters or machine-readable Chinese characters will become inevitable, since Japan and China will not abolish Chinese characters.[47]

Electronically generated and stored images of logograms may offer substantial technical advantages to Chinese and Japanese printers and to those who have to handle large numbers of graphic records in the libraries of those countries. The inherent complexity of the logograms and the ambiguities of their decoding are, however, still present. The electronic generation of characters does not solve the decoding problem any better than their production by pen and ink; the solution depends solely on the recognition of their meaning in context, a skill that cannot be reduced to an algorithm and which therefore remains a prerogative of the human mind.

2.4.4. Latinization of Vietnamese. Vietnam formed a part of the Chinese empire for more than a thousand years until A.D. 939. During this long period the Chinese language and writing system gained a status not unlike that of Latin in contemporary Europe. It was the only vehicle for official documents and literature, while the Vietnamese language was not considered worthy of any written expression and remained for a long time a spoken vernacular only. This state of affairs lasted for several hundred years after the Vietnamese had gained their political independence, and the Chinese logograms were only gradually applied to the writing of Vietnamese. The earliest evidence is a stone inscription from A.D. 1343, written in Chū nôm ("Characters of the vernacular"), a writing system in which the Chinese logograms sometimes stand for their meaning but are pronounced in Vietnamese (i.e., similar to the Japanese *kun* reading), and in which two logograms are usually written together, one to give the meaning, the other to indicate the pronunciation. Although the result looks no different from

---

[45]"It may be doubted whether an adult Westerner has ever succeeded in mastering either Chinese or Japanese well enough to compose unaided, in either of those languages, a single work of any great extent." (Boxer, 1951, p. 197.)

[46]Stallings (1975) describes a number of computerized systems for input, storage, and retrieval of Chinese logographs; some of these are still experimental, while others are in actual use.

[47]Tanabe (1972), p. 169.

any Chinese text, it is entirely incomprehensible to a Chinese reader, and can be read only by someone who knows Vietnamese. Because the system demanded many years of study, only a small number of priests and rich scholars could use it, and the masses remained illiterate.[48]

The Jesuits, who had already had such remarkable success at the Romanization of Chinese and Japanese, also Romanized Vietnamese in the missions and seminaries they established in the early 17th century in Cochinchina. Alexandre de Rhodes (1591–1660), a French Jesuit, came to Vietnam in 1624, began to learn the local language, and is said to have mastered it after only half a year. Building on earlier attempts by his Portuguese colleagues, he devised a Romanization scheme which he first used in a catechism[49] and later in a large Vietnamese–Portuguese–Latin dictionary.[50] Rhodes solved the problem of indication of the six tones of the Vietnamese language by using accents exemplified by the names of the musical scale: dò, rẻ, mi, phả, sōl, lá. He also invented four modified Roman letters, þ, đ, ơ and ư, but retained some features of the Portuguese writing system, notably the indication of $[ɲ]$ by *nh,* although he must have been familiar with the Spanish *ñ,* which would have fitted better into a scheme that used diacritical marks so heavily. However, we must remember that Portuguese was then the most widely used European language in southeast Asia because of its extensive use in trade; that was also the reason for the inclusion of Portuguese in Rhodes' trilingual dictionary. Very often two different diacritical marks are used one on top of the other over a vowel, as in the name of the Romanization scheme itself: Quốc-ngữ ("National language"). This makes the Vietnamese alphabet a printer's nightmare and is not particularly inducive to legibility.

Although they suffered severe persecution from time to time, the Jesuits and other missionaries had more success in converting the Vietnamese to Christianity than they had in any other Southeast Asian or Far Eastern country, and consequently Romanized writing of Vietnamese became fairly common. Gradually the Quốc-ngữ displaced the Chữ nôm, which today is read and studied only by a few specialized scholars. When the French established their protectorate over Indochina in 1883 they naturally used a writing system based on the Roman script for all their official documents and communications in the local language. Finally the use of Quốc-ngữ was made official and compulsory in 1910 by the French Résident supérieur of Tonkin, and it was taught exclusively in schools, which raised the literacy rate in Vietnam to a considerably higher level than in other countries of the region.

Almost no major changes were made in Rhodes' original scheme, although

---

[48]Thompson (1965), pp. 52–55.
[49]Rhodes (1651a).
[50]Rhodes (1651b).

the Vietnamese people would have benefited from a simplification. As in so many other countries the force of script convention prevented any far-reaching reform. Too much literature already existed in the Quốc-ngữ writing system, and too many people had been brought up with it and used it widely. Moreover the French were not overly interested in any reform of the Vietnamese writing system; quite to the contrary, they used it as a tool to sow discord between the various ethnic groups in the country in order to combat the growing nationalism that demanded independence. When the French colonial regime finally came to an end in 1954, the ensuing civil war deferred any possible revision of the Vietnamese writing system *ad Kalendas Graecas*.

2.5. Latinization in Indonesia and Malaysia

In the archipelago that forms today the state of Indonesia various indigenous scripts of Indian origin had evolved, foremost among them the Javanese *Kavi* script, when in the 14th and 15th century A.D. a large part of the population was converted to Islam by Muslim Indians who introduced the Arabic script. When this script was later applied to write Malayan, it became known as *Jawi*. The Dutch began to establish their colonial rule over Indonesia in the early 17th century, and their administrators, merchants, and missionaries used the Roman script, applying the spelling conventions of their language to the rendering of local names and words. The two systems of writing existed practically side by side and without much interference, since the number of literate Indonesians was at any rate very small, and the Dutch did not wish to encourage the growing Indonesian nationalism by providing the people with a common script, much less a common language.

With the proclamation of an independent state of Indonesia in 1945 and the final departure of the Dutch in 1949, one of the first steps taken by the Indonesian government was the proclamation of *Bahasa Indonesia* as the language of national unity, to be written exclusively in the Roman script. Bahasa Indonesia, which is derived from the Malay language as spoken in the northern part of Sumatra and in the Malay peninsula (with a heavy admixture of Dutch, English, Arabic, and Hindi words), was chosen because it already served as a *lingua franca* throughout the archipelago and was almost universally understood by all inhabitants. Because it was not the language of the largest ethnic group (the Javanese), it was also politically neutral and a symbol for "unity in diversity."[51] For those who were already familiar with the Roman script because they had attended Dutch schools, only two minor changes were involved: the Dutch spelling *oe* for [u] was changed to *u* (e.g., Surabaja instead of Soerabaja), and *sj*

---

[51]Nida and Wonderly (1971), p. 62.

for $[\int]$, which occurs only in foreign words and in Muslim names, was changed to *sh*. The reduplication of a word or its main part to indicate the plural was written by the raised digit 2 after the word (as had been the custom in *Jawi* writing). Muslim Indonesians, however, who had hitherto used the Arabic script, had to learn the Roman one, although Arabic script is still used for liturgic purposes and in theological seminars.

When Malaysia also became an independent state in 1963, a similar development took place there. *Bahasa Malaysia,* the Malaysian equivalent of *Bahasa Indonesia,* was declared the official language, to be written in *Rumi* (i.e., Roman) script for all official and legal purposes, while the *Jawi* script continued to be used by Muslims in worship and education, as well as in books and newspapers. Since Malaysia had formerly been under British rule, English spelling conventions were followed at first, but recently a new orthography called *Malindo,* deviating substantially from the conventional English spelling of Malay, has been promulgated simultaneously by Indonesia and Malaysia.[52] Table 2.6 shows the main differences between pre-1972 spelling and Malindo.

The use of the digit 2 to indicate reduplication was abandoned, since it proved to be ambiguous when only part of a word is repeated. Now all words are spelled out in full with a hyphen between the reduplicated parts; for example, *kata*[2] ("words") is now written *kata-kata,* and *bermain*[2] is written in full *bermain-main* ("to play [several games]").

The Latinization of the Malay language in Indonesia and Malaysia is the most recent example of conversion from Arabic to Roman script in predominantly Muslim countries by political means and as an expression of national independence. It lacked the dramatic overtones of similar developments in Turkey and the Turkic-speaking regions of the Soviet Union because it was based on already

Table 2.6   Former and Present Latinization of Malay

Phoneme	Pre-1972 spelling Bahasa Indonesia	Bahasa Malaysia	Malindo spelling
$[\,t\int\,]$	t j	ch	c
$[\,\int\,]$	sh	sh	s y
$[\,ɖ\,]$	d	dh	d
$[\,dʒ\,]$	d j	dz	z

[52]Bin Hadji Mohammad (1972).

existing script conventions that had evolved under the previous colonial regimes, and was generally welcomed by a population of highly heterogeneous ethnic elements as a unifying force and as a symbol of their nationhood. Unlike the Turkish Latinization, which was comprehensive and encompassed also Arabic given names for which a certain standardized transliteration was prescribed, neither Indonesia nor Malaysia laid down rules for the transliteration of Arabic personal names, with the result that a large variety of such transliterations or transcriptions is now used by authors. Some are not even consistent in their usage from one publication to another, or have their names printed in substantially different forms on the cover and on the title page of a book.[53] Since bibliographic control is to a large extent concerned with personal names, it might be said that in this respect at least the Latinization of Malay languages has created more problems than it has solved, until such time when some standardization in this field will be imposed by the authorities in Indonesia and Malaysia. The steadily increasing number of publications in Malay, now amounting to several hundred titles per year (whereas only 10 years ago a mere handful were published) together with the rapidly rising rate of literacy will make such standardization even more necessary and desirable not only for the national bibliographies of these countries but even more so for international bibliographic control.

2.6. Latinization of African Languages

As long as most of Africa was carved up by European countries into "protectorates" and colonies, scant attention was paid to possible Latinization of the indigenous languages by those in power, who had every reason to fear and disencourage such an inevitable incentive for the rise of nationalistic movements. Romanization of African languages was mainly the concern of missionaries and linguists who had certain limited purposes only and did not envisage the development of indigenous literature in the hundreds of vernaculars and dialects spoken in the vast area generally known as Africa south of the Sahara. Some missionaries were even severely criticized by government officials for their efforts to Romanize local vernaculars because this tended to "discourage the teaching of English by the teaching of the native languages and dialects and to seek to perpetuate them as written languages," which latter phenomenon was clearly counterproductive to the goals of the British administration in Nigeria, which issued this remarkable statement.[54]

The language most widely used throughout East Africa is Swahili, which was

---

[53]The most recent and comprehensive treatment of this problem is a paper by J. N. B. Tairas (1972), particularly the section "The spelling problem," pp. 70–71.
[54]Coleman (1958), p. 443.

initially written in Arabic but was Romanized by European missionaries during the second half of the 19th century. In this form it eventually became the official language of Tanzania, and serves as the medium of communication for many tribes also outside this country,[55] making it the seventh most important international language in the world.[56]

The Romanization of other African languages attracted the attention of ethnographers and linguists during the 1920s, and they discerned the need for a common writing system, publishing in 1930 a well-designed scheme, suitable for practically all African vernaculars, under the title *Practical Orthography of African Languages*. In the Introduction the authors state their aim as

. . . the unification and simplification of the orthography of the African languages. . . . In Africa today conditions of life are such that many thousands of natives leave their home districts and . . . settle temporarily or permanently in districts where their mother tongue is not understood. Thus . . . they are obliged to learn another language. It would obviously be a great advantage if in the orthography of the new language, the value of the letters were the same, or as nearly as possible the same, as those they have already learnt for their mother tongue.[57]

They refrained as far as possible from introducing diacritical marks, and preferred to add specially devised letters for which they also prescribed a filing order (see Table 2.7). According to the authors, some two dozen African languages had at the time of publication already adopted the scheme (see Figure 2.7), and others were expected to follow suit. The reprinting of the scheme in English, German, and French in a second edition, its reissue in 1962, and the presence of a note that mentions the availability of typewriters for the new alphabet seem to indicate that the scheme has met with considerable success.

The creation of a number of independent African states during the 1960s has, however, not been inducive to more unification of African writing systems, since many of these countries embarked on an individual policy of Latinization of their national language or languages. A statement made by the French linguist Maurice Calvet in 1971 summarizes the present situation and points out one of the main difficulties:

The transformation of traditional African societies into modern nations requires recognition of the linguistic problem which can be solved only within a multi-lingualism that will

---

[55]"Swahili . . . is not just a vehicular *lingua franca*. It is an important factor for establishing cultural, social, and political values among its interlocutors. Today in Tanzania, and indeed in the rest of East Africa, there is no serious alternative to Swahili as a basis of intertribal integration. No other tribal language in East Africa is likely to be accepted with less resistance over the whole area." (Abdulaziz, 1971, p. 173.)

[56]Mazrui (1971), pp. 186–187.

[57]International African Institute (1930), p. 3.

Table 2.7 Alphabet for African Languages Proposed by the International African Institute

Roman.	Italic.	Written Forms.	Roman.	Italic.	Written Forms.
a A	a A	a a	l L	l L	l l
b B	b B	b B	m M	m M	m m
ɓ Ɓ	ɓ Ɓ	ɓ ɦ	n N	n N	n n
c C	c C	c C	ŋ Ŋ	ŋ Ŋ	ŋ ŋ
d D	d D	d d	o O	o O	o o
ɖ Ɖ	ɖ Ɖ	ɖ or ɖ Ɖ	ɔ Ɔ	ɔ Ɔ	ɔ ɔ
e E	e E	e e	p P	p P	p p
ɛ Ɛ	ɛ Ɛ	ɛ ɛ	r R	r R	r or r R
ə Ə	ə ə	ə ə	s S	s S	s or s S
f F	f F	f f	ʃ Σ	ʃ Σ	ʃ ʃ
ƒ Ƒ	f Ƒ	ƒ ƒ	t T	t T	t t
g G	g G	g g	u U	u U	u u
ɣ Ɣ	ɣ Ɣ	ɣ ɣ	v V	v V	v V or v V
h H	h H	h H	ʋ Ʋ	ʋ Ʋ	ʋ ʋ or ʋ ʋ
x X	x X	x x	w W	w W	w w
i I	i I	i i	y Y	y Y	y y
j J	j J	j j	z Z	z Z	z Z
k K	k K	k K	ʒ Ʒ	ʒ Ʒ	ʒ ʒ

ALPHABETICAL ORDER OF THE LETTERS

The following is recommended as the alphabetical order of the principal letters:

a b ɓ c d ɖ e ɛ ə f ƒ g ɣ h x i j k l m n ŋ o ɔ p r s ʃ t u v ʋ w y z ʒ '

Nasal vowels should follow ordinary vowels, and central vowels should follow nasal vowels, thus: o õ ö. Other new letters should follow those from which they are derived: thus ɖ should follow d, and ş should follow s. If special letters are introduced to represent clicks, it is suggested that they be placed at the end of the alphabet.

It is recommended that in vocabularies and dictionaries words beginning with digraphs (dy, dz, dʒ, kp, ts, tʃ, &c.) be placed in separate groups following all the words beginning with simple d, k, t, &c.

Names of the Consonant Letters.

b	ɓ	c	d	ɖ	f	ƒ	g	ɣ	h	x	j	k	l	m	n
be	ɓa	ce	de	ɖa	ef	if	ga	ɣe	ha	ex	je	ke	el	em	en
		(tʃe)						(dʒe)							

ŋ	p	r	s	ʃ	t	v	ʋ	w	y	z	ʒ	'
iŋ	pe	ra	es	iʃ	te	ve	ʋi	wa	ya	ze	ʒi	a'a

Source. International African Institute (1930), pp. 18–19.

*Akan.**

Ɔdɔ dwo ne ani, ne yam ye, ɔdɔ nyɛ ahõɔyaw, ɔdɔ nyɛ ahoahoa, ɛŋhoraŋ, ɛnyɛ nehõ sɛnea ɛmfata, ɛŋhwehwɛ nea ɛyɛ ne aŋkasa de, ne bo ŋhaw no, ɛmfa bone ŋhyɛ ne yam, ne ani nye nea ɛntɛ̃ɛ hõ, na ɛne nokware ani gye, etie a ade nnyina, egye ade nnyina di, enya ade nnyina mu anidaso. Ɔdɔ to ntwa da. Na afei gyidi, ɔdɔ, anidaso na etrã hɔ, na ɔdɔ na ɛne mu kɛse. (From 'Ɛha amanne kwaŋ so aware Ɛso Dhyira', p. 7).

Bambara.

Kŋo sogo bee yi i nyogõ la dye k u be dlo dõ u ko sogo o sogo bee ka na ni nyo more morɛ ye. Sogo bee nana n ata ye. Suruku ba e o me mi ŋke a y ala muru ba ta, a bina a da la dia la.

Duala.

Ngɔkɔlɔ na dibobɛ ba ta dikɔm, ba yenga bɛbɔ babanɛ ponda yɛsɛ. Nde ba ta ba ja o ekwali bunya bɔɔ, nde na ngɔkɔlɔ e kwalanɛ dibobɛ na : A dikɔm lam la ndolo, na malangwea nde oa na mbalɛ, bato ba si masenga, be ndɔki. (From a text in *Africa*, vol. ii, p. 72, Jan. 1929.)

Efik.

Tiŋ enyin tim se uŋwana oro, neŋere tiene enye; ke ntre ke afo edikut inua-otop oro; tuak, ndien mɔ eyeteme fi se afo edinamde. Ndien ŋkokut ke ndap mi nte owo oro otibide itɔk efege. Ekem enye ika-ikaha kaŋa anyan usuŋ ikpɔŋ ufɔk esie; ndien kadaŋemi ŋwan esie ye nditɔ esie ekutde, mɔ etɔŋɔ ndifiori ŋkot enye, ete afiak edi; edi enye esin nuenubɔk ke utɔŋ, efege itɔk, ete, 'Uwem! uwem! nsi-nsi uwem!'

*Ewe.**

Asime. Asi ɖina le tefe geɖewo le ŋkeke ene sia ŋkeke ene megbe. Ame geɖewo va ƒoa ƒu ɖe afima. Wotsɔa bli, te, mɔli, agbeli, fofoŋ, fetri, agbitsa, atadi kple kutsetse bubu geɖewo, ɖetifu, de, nɛfi, amidzɛ̃, nɛmi, yɔkumi kple nu bubu geɖewo va dzrana. Ga si woxɔna la, wotsɔne ƒlea avɔ, ɖeti, atama, sukli, kple ŋudɔwɔnu siwo wohiã. Ɖeviwo lɔ̃a asimedede. (From 'Evegbegbalẽxɛxlẽ na Gɔmedzelawo', p. 64.)

*Ga.**

Dʒata ko hi ʃi ye dʒeŋ a·hu. Agbɛnɛ egbo hewo lɛ enyẽẽ emomo hewalɛ na· doŋŋ. Enɛ hewo lɛ eyakã ʃi ye ebu lɛ mli akɛ ehe mi· ye. Koloi lɛ ba· eŋo ekome-kome ni amɛbasra· lɛ ye ebu lɛ mli. Oso le enɛ fẽ hewo lɛ ete koni eyasra dʒata helatʃɛ nɛ. Beni ete lɛ ebotee bu lɛ mli. Edamɔ sɛ ʃoŋŋ ni ebi dʒata lɛ akɛ, 'Helatʃɛ! te oyɔ teŋŋ?' (From the *New Ga Primer*, by C. P. Moir, Part 2, p. 24.)

Figure 2.7. Specimens of actual and proposed Latinization of African languages. Items marked with an asterisk are from published documents. (Reprinted, by permission, from International African Institute, (1930), pp. 19–20.)

100

ensure the promotion of national-popular African languages. There can be no nation without a relative linguistic unity; there can be no modernity and no development without massive resort to writing in the national language. . . . The main drawback [to national consciousness through a common language] is the arbitrary outline of frontiers drawn by colonizers, and the ethnic division which results in linguistic balkanization.[58]

There are two examples of recently authorized Latinizations with a "national" twist. One is the modified Roman alphabet adopted by the Somali government in 1973, which contains two special characters, / and ∧. It superseded the Osmaniya script, a mixture of Arabic, Amharic, and Roman characters which had been invented early in the 20th century by the brother of the Somalian sultan, the poet Osman Yusuf Kanadid. The new alphabet is, however, not yet widely used in Somalia where 90% of the population are still illiterate. The same is true for Senegal, where the government decreed a Latinization of Wolof and four other languages spoken in the country; the alphabet contains the additional letters ŋ and ƌ, the former taken from the "African alphabet," the latter an adaptation of an IPA symbol.

All this, of course, is not much different from what happened in the Latinization of European languages, which also use the same letters in widely divergent ways and with many modifications; rather the important and perhaps crucial difference lies in the addition of specially designed letters to the standard Roman alphabet and in the differing uses made of them in various African languages, which pose severe problems not only for literate Africans in a multilingual environment, but even more so in bibliographic control in other countries where those special letters cannot be simply treated as mere adaptations of basic Roman letters. Although the International African Institute recognized the necessity for a prescribed filing order, the use of computers and other automated machinery for sorting and filing alphabetical entries could not possibly have been foreseen. Though it is technically feasible to provide for input and output of any nonstandard character, to program any deviant sorting routine, and also to provide for suitable printout facilities, the present small number of publications in these alphabets would not justify the costs involved. Admittedly the Latinization of most African languages could not be achieved without the use of special letters, unless a large number of diacritical marks were added to basic letters. But the inclusion of up to a dozen special letters makes this particular kind of Latinization the graphemic equivalent of the Greek alphabet, which also has 11 letters that are different from the Roman ones (if we consider only uppercase letters) and is therefore treated as a dissimilar script. It may well be that, with increasing literary production in African languages written with augmented Roman alphabets, separate filing sequences will have to be set up despite the superficial similarity of these scripts with the various manifestations of the Roman script as used in European languages.

[58] Calvet (1971), p. 274.

2.7. Illusions and Reality

In the year 1929, when the League of Nations was still thought to be a viable instrument for promoting and keeping the peace in the world, one of its agencies, the International Committee on Intellectual Cooperation (a kind of distant forebear of the present UNESCO) decided to inquire into the possibilities of encouraging the use of the Roman script throughout the world in order to achieve a better understanding between Western countries and the Orient. When the Committee started its work, the auspices for such an undertaking seemed indeed to be propitious. Turkey was just undergoing the revolution of complete Latinization; in the Soviet Union, Latinization had made considerable progress and was even contemplated for the Russian language; China had published its first official Romanization scheme; and Japan had not one but two Romanization schemes and was about to simplify the Chinese logograms. Everything seemed to point toward an almost universal adoption of the Roman script, and that was indeed the title given to the report[59] issued by the Committee five years later, which took the form of a survey of the countries in which Latinization had either been successfully introduced or had at least been considered. In the introduction to the report the famous Danish linguist Otto Jespersen made a sweeping and highly idealistic statement:

Nul doute que la coopération intellectuelle à travers tout le monde civilisé ne dût être extrêmement facilitée si l'on employait partout un même système d'écriture; la grande diversité des alphabets en usage constitue en effet l'une des plus grandes entraves au rapprochement entre les nations et les races.[60]

(Scarcely five years later, Germany and Italy, both using the Roman script, would ally themselves with the Japanese, while Britain, France, and the United States, also countries with Roman script traditions, found themselves on the same side with the Cyrillic-writing Russians. So much for the power of a worldwide unified script in bringing about "rapprochement" among nations and races!)

The report submitted by the Society for Cultural Relations between the USSR and Foreign Countries gave a detailed account of the Latinization movement and pointed out that the old "bourgeois and feudal" writing systems had now been replaced by "socialistic" Roman alphabets; they also cited proudly the rise in literacy among those nationalities that had switched from Arabic to Roman script. Little did they know that in the very year in which the report was finally published, their efforts would be nullified and repudiated as treacherous and antirevolutionary.

[59]Commission internationale de coopération intellectuelle (1934).
[60]*Ibid.*, p. 13.

A report from Greece indicated that Latinization had been widely discussed there in the late 1920s (32 references were cited), and the difficulties of transliteration of foreign names into modern Greek were pointed out. The long-standing tradition and worldwide prestige of the Greek script as well as the immense amount of literature written in this script over a period of more than 2500 years militated against any attempts at Latinization.

The Bulgarian committee reported that Latinization had been considered and was "earnestly desired," but they added the logical remark that nothing could be done about it as long as there were such wide divergences among the existing Roman alphabets, which should first be unified themselves before any Latinization was recommended to others. As shown in Table 2.1, the Bulgarians had a valid point.

The committee concluded its report with some lofty but characteristically vague resolutions concerning not only Latinization but also transcription which, for some undisclosed reason, was thought to be an instrument furthering mutual understanding between peoples:

Considérant la grande extension de l'emploi des caractères latins dans les pays civilisés, la Commission

recommande à tous les pays d'étudier la possibilité d'adopter les caractères latins dans leur language écrit, et, lorsqu'il y a des systèmes d'orthographes différents en vigueur, d'unifier l'orthographe le plus tôt possible, conformément à la nature de chaque langue;

constate la valeur que l'adoption d'une méthode de transcription uniforme des langues, à côté de l'écriture nationale, pourrait avoir pour la compréhension mutuelle des peuples.[61]

These ideas were, however, somewhat modified by a more matter-of-fact statement in the preface to the report, which was obviously not written by one of the authors of the above resolution:

On doit noter que dans les pays qui possèdent déja une méthode d'écriture très developpée, comme la Grèce, la Perse, le Chine et le Japon, par exemple, l'adoption des caractères latins ne pourra, semble-t-il, être atteinte dans un proche avenir.[62]

The report did not suggest any practical steps to promote or achieve Latinization in countries that used other scripts, and the matter was pursued no further by the Committee on Intellectual Cooperation. Only its recommendations regarding internationally accepted transcription and transliteration schemes were taken up again after World War II by the ISO.

If we for a moment make a "Gedankenexperiment" and imagine that the movements for Latinization and Romanization which flourished in the late 1920s

[61]*Ibid.*, p. 191.
[62]*Ibid.*, p. 10.

had all been as successful as in Turkey, the great majority of the world's population would today indeed be using the Roman alphabet, and the momentum of such a development would probably have brought about similar movements in countries such as India, Iran, the southeast Asian countries, and possibly even some Arab states. Would it also have meant the creation of a unifying force, breaking down the barriers to effective communication, as envisaged by the League of Nations committee? Not necessarily, since the uniformity of the Roman script as actually used today in various parts of the world and by many different languages is more apparent than real.

The Roman script was part of a uniform writing system, and therefore a truly unifying force, only when it was applied to the language for which it was designed—Latin—and only so long as this language was spoken and written throughout the Roman Empire and in early medieval Europe. But when it began to be adapted to the various European languages, the uniformity became only a superficial feature, as it was restricted to the visual image of individual basic letters, some of which were actually used in various writing systems to represent the most divergent sounds. The use of diacritical marks, as we have seen, far from making the modified letters uniform in their representation of sounds, only added to this diversity of usage. English can manage entirely without diacritical marks probably because its writing system went farthest in divorcing the letters of the Roman alphabet from the sounds they originally represented, to the degree that English spelling is now very close to logographic writing, where the visual image of a word has to be remembered together with its sound to pronounce it correctly and to understand its meaning, since the spelling of English words in most instances does not give any clue to pronunciation and often constitutes no more than a historic relic generated and venerated by grammarians.

The result is that there exist now as many Latinized writing systems as there are languages using the Roman script. It is therefore an illusion to believe that the use of this script also implies that all languages employing it are thereby "reduced" to one uniform writing system, including a uniform filing order for the 26 letters, irrespective of their modification by diacritical marks or their special place in various national alphabets. Yet most bibliographic control methods, and especially the conversion of scripts by Romanization, are based on this basically false assumption which provides for superficially facile solutions of technical problems related to alphabetization and filing of entries in library catalogs and in bibliographies. But this assumption also generates many difficulties and ambiguities for those who have to apply Romanization in cataloging as well as for the hapless users of their product, many of whom are unable to find out what had been written in the original script and, in the case of logographic scripts, are completely deprived of understanding the meaning of the transcription. We shall return to these aspects of Romanization in more detail in Chapter 6.

It is also a widespread illusion to think that the 26 letters of the present-day Roman alphabet constitute an ''ideal alphabet,'' since practically any language can be written with this small number of graphic signs and a roughly equal number of diacritical marks. We are inclined to think so because various European nations that use the Roman script have held a dominant position in world affairs during the past 500 years, and in this century English in particular has emerged as a kind of world language. Consequently, Universal Bibliographic Control is also always considered only from the point of view of the Roman script, to which all other scripts ought to be ''reduced.'' However the Roman alphabet as such is far from perfect; as already pointed out, it needs at least a few more letters for sibilants and gutturals. It is neither better nor worse suited to writing any language than other alphabetic scripts such as Cyrillic (which in some respects is actually superior to it) or, to a lesser degree, Greek, Arabic, or Hebrew,[63] all of which can be or have been adapted to write languages other than those for which they were originally designed.

However, of all the many hundreds of scripts invented during more than 5000 years, the Roman script emerged as the one that is most widely used throughout the world. More languages are now written in the Roman script than at any other time in history, and the number of people who can read and write it is now much larger than the total number of literates in all other scripts (see Chapter 4, p. 241). Its use is still rapidly rising in the developing nations of Asia and Africa, some of which adopted Roman script only recently but are already reaping the fruits of this decision in the form of higher and steadily growing literacy rates.

3. CYRILLIFICATION

3.1. Cyrillic Script and Its Application to Slavic Languages

According to tradition the Cyrillic alphabet was invented in A.D. 863 by St. Cyril (826?–869) of Salonika, who together with his brother St. Methodius (815?–885) set out to convert the pagan Slavs of Moravia. The alphabet is clearly an adaptation of the Greek one, with the addition of two Hebrew letters, **צ** *(zade)* and **ש** *(šin)*, which were modified into Ц [ts], Ч [tʃ], Ш [ʃ], and Щ [ʃtʃ] to express sounds for which there are no equivalents in the Greek alphabet, and a few other specially devised letters. The alphabet consisted originally of 43 letters and was used to write Old Church Slavic, a language based mainly on the dialect of Slavic tribes north of Salonika. In the 9th century this language was the common vernacular for the various Slavic peoples whose languages began to

---

[63] For a detailed discussion of this subject, see Gelb (1963), pp. 239–244.

diverge from each other in several respects only at a later time. The Cyrillic alphabet was first used in Bulgaria, where Cyril and Methodius carried on their missionary work after they had come into conflict with the missionaries of the Western Church in Moravia.[64]

During the Middle Ages the Cyrillic alphabet was adopted by those Slavic peoples who were converted to Greek Orthodox Christianity, while those Slavs in the sphere of influence of Western Christianity used the Roman script. The dichotomous use of two different scripts for closely related languages has persisted until our own time, and in one case, namely Serbo-Croatian, the very same language is written in two scripts. The Serbs in the southern and eastern region inhabited by this language community write it in Cyrillic, while the Croats in the northwestern region write it in Roman. By the 17th century Cyrillic in its original form (as used to write Old Church Slavic) had been firmly established throughout Russia and in the eastern part of the Balkan peninsula.

Tsar Peter the Great, as part of his program to westernize Russia, decreed in 1710 the adoption of a thoroughly modified Cyrillic alphabet in which the form of the letters resembled more closely those of Roman script, while some letters were eliminated altogether as superfluous for modern Russian. The new alphabet was called гражданский шрифт [graždanskij šrift] (civilian typeface) to distinguish it from the former "ecclesiastical" one, which henceforth was used only for liturgical purposes. In the early 19th century the гражданский шрифт was also adopted for the writing system of Bulgarian (with some minor changes) and of Serbian, for which six letters not found in Russian Cyrillic were added in order to write certain Serbian sounds, while eight Russian letters not needed for Serbian were dropped. Finally, in the 20th century, the White-Russians and Ukrainians also made some additions to and deletions from the Cyrillic alphabet, and changed the order of its letters, to suit the phonology of their languages, which for a long

---

[64]Some Slavic paleographers are of the opinion that Cyril actually invented the Glagolitsa, an alphabet possibly based on a cursive Greek hand written in the 9th century. This script, whose name was derived from Old Slavic *glagol* (to speak), was used in the oldest liturgy of the Slavs in Bohemia, Moravia, Bulgaria, the Balkans, and apparently also in Russia, where Glagolitic inscriptions have been found. The Glagolitsa script was displaced by the Roman script in Bohemia and Moravia, and by the Cyrillic script in Bulgaria and Russia, but it continued to be used for several hundred years in the liturgy of Catholic communities in Dalmatia and Istria (who became the only Roman Catholics to celebrate Mass in the vernacular before Vatican II). In the 16th and 17th centuries, secular literature and chronicles were printed in Glagolitic script, and there were even some transcriptions from Latin and Italian. From the 18th century onward the script was only seldom used to print secular literature, but liturgies continued to be printed and reprinted until the beginning of the 20th century. Some small Catholic parishes used missals written in Glagolitsa until 1965, when the Vatican Council II permitted the use of vernaculars in the Mass. The Roman script was then substituted, and the Glagolitic script thus ceased to be used entirely. It now remains of interest only to Slavic paleographers. Yugoslav libraries have sizable holdings of books written in Glagolitic script, and a Romanization scheme was therefore developed for it, so that entries for these works could be integrated with those in the Croatian language. (I am indebted for most of this information to Dr. Eva Verona, a Yugoslav librarian and an authority on the cataloging of Slavic literature.)

time had been considered by the tsarist regime as being merely "bad" Russian dialects.

After the October Revolution, the Soviet government decreed in 1918 a further reform of the Russian Cyrillic alphabet, eliminating four more redundant letters, and introduced certain simplifications of the Russian spelling.

The latest adaptation of the Cyrillic script to a Slavic language occurred in August 1944, when Macedonian became officially recognized as a literary language in Yugoslavia. Its alphabet consists of all Serbian letters except ђ and ћ, for which ѓ and ќ respectively were substituted; it also uses the letter ѕ (revived from Old Church Slavic) to represent the phoneme [dz].

Altogether 46 Slavic Cyrillic letters are currently in use, six of which are modifications of basic letters by diacritical marks; in addition there are three Russian letters and one Ukrainian letter which have not been used since 1918, and one Bulgarian letter made obsolete in 1945, which brings the total of Slavic Cyrillic letters to 51. The present Russian and Ukrainian alphabets consist of 33 letters each (but not the same set), the White-Russian alphabet has 32, the Serbian has 30, the Macedonian has 31, and the Bulgarian alphabet has 29 letters.

3.2. The Cyrillification of non-Slavic Languages

During the long reign of the tsars the Cyrillic script was adapted to only a few non-Slavic languages spoken in the Russian Empire. Romanian (essentially a Romance language containing many Slavic and Turkish loanwords and other elements from languages spoken in the Balkan peninsula) was written in Cyrillic with special diacritical marks from the late 16th century until the 1860s, when Romanian writers and educators decided to convert their writing system to the Roman script. Another Cyrillification occurred in the Caucasus region, where Ossetic, an Iranian language, began to be written in Cyrillic script in the early 19th century, augmented by some Roman letters to express certain Ossetic phonemes. Cyrillic alphabets were also devised by Russian philologists for the Chuvash, Kreshen Tatar, and Yakut languages during the latter half of the 19th century, but these were exceptions rather than the rule, since the tsarist regime followed the principle "One emperor—one religion—one language," and sought to exclude the languages and scripts of national minorities systematically from education and literary production.[65] On the other hand no efforts were

---

[65]Despite all efforts at enforced Russification, the vernaculars of Poland, the Baltic countries, and Finland continued to be spoken and were written (though not printed) in Roman script; Yiddish and Hebrew literature could be printed in Hebrew letters (although subject to the imprimatur of a Russian censor); and the Armenians and Georgians were also able to preserve their languages and scripts.

made to spread the Russian language and its script beyond the borders of the empire.

During the early years of the Soviet regime, from 1917 until about 1930, it also looked as if the Cyrillic script would be used only in the Slavic language areas of the Soviet Union, while other nationalities (most of which were entirely illiterate) would be made literate with the help of the Roman alphabet. But an abrupt change took place after the ruthless destruction of the Latinization movement by Stalin in the early 1930s. A period of fierce Russian nationalism and Russification began, resulting in enforced Cyrillification of Roman and other scripts, motivated only by political considerations and devoid of any linguistic merits. Party officials, not linguists, hastily contrived all manner of alphabets based on the Cyrillic script and fitted with peculiar diacritical marks, specially devised letters, and occasional Roman letters. The result was that no two of these new alphabets were similar or compatible even for linguistically related languages. For example, to distinguish the uvular plosive $\left[\mathrm{q}\right]$ from the velar plosive $\left[\mathrm{k}\right]$ in various Turkic languages, no less than six varieties of the Cyrillic letter к were devised: Қ, Ќ, Қ, Ҡ, Ҟ, Қ; for the same sound in Kurdish, however, the Roman letter q was used. Such a bewildering variety of letters was not accidental:

After the purges, the Communists were no longer willing to allow the Turkic peoples of the USSR even the semblance of alphabetic unity. The Cyrillic alphabets devised for the Central Asian languages were deliberately made as different from each other as possible. Likewise, dialects were chosen as norms for the Cyrillic written languages that differed as much as possible from related neighbouring languages.[66]

By 1941 the Central Asian Turkic languages as well as the Iranian languages Ossetic and Tajik had been Cyrillified, and only Mongolia held out until after the war, when the Cyrillic script was substituted there too for the ancient Mongolian alphabet. By the early 1950s more than 50 nationalities and languages had been forced to adopt Cyrillified alphabets, almost all of which contained more letters than the Russian Cyrillic alphabet.[67]

The Cyrillification drive was initiated and pursued personally by Stalin, who fancied himself an expert on linguistics, and in 1950 he pontificated at length on various philological and linguistic issues. He believed firmly in the unity of thought and language[68] and viewed script as one of the "characteristic features"

[66] Henze (1956), p. 37.

[67] A list of Cyrillified alphabets for non-Slavic nationalities in the Soviet Union appears in Diringer (1968), pp. 378–381. See also Nurmakov (1934) and Allworth (1971).

[68] "The reality of thought manifests itself in language. Only idealists can speak of thinking as not connected with the 'natural matter' of language, of thinking without language." (Stalin, 1951, p. 36.)

of a language.[69] Outwardly he seemed to favor the existence of various national vernaculars:

Is it not a fact that the Russian, Ukrainian and Uzbek languages are now serving the socialist culture of these nations just as well as they served their bourgeois cultures before the October Revolution?[70]

But he was careful not to mention that these and other languages could continue to "serve the socialist culture" only if they were subjected to complete Cyrillification, which alone, in his opinion, could foster a collective nationalism while at the same time making it more difficult for spies from the West to penetrate the Soviet system. The political purges, the atrocities of the slave labor camps, and the persecution and virtual extinction of whole national minorities (such as the Kalmycks) were mainly motivated by Stalin's paranoid fear of "spies" and "subversive elements," and the forced Russification of all nationalities in the Soviet Union and the Cyrillification of their scripts were but another manifestation of Stalinist terrorism, although Soviet officials and scholars tried to justify it on educational grounds and as a means of combating illiteracy.[71]

Only long after Stalin's death could Soviet linguists and Orientalists publish their opinion that the Roman alphabets that had been applied to the Turkic and other minority languages were more appropriate than the Cyrillic ones, which

---

[69]*Ibid.,* p. 26.

[70]*Ibid.,* p. 21. The Uzbek language is just a case in point for á multiple imposition of scripts. The Arabic script was used until 1922, when the Uzbeks decided to adopt the Roman alphabet; in 1936, they were forced to abandon it forthwith and to use only the Cyrillic script.

[71]"New alphabets for Soviet nationalities at first were compiled on the basis of the Latin alphabet. At the end of the 30's the interest in the study of Russian had grown in all the Soviet Republics. At their native language lessons the students studied the Latin alphabet, while at the Russian language lessons they studied the Russian alphabet. It was often the case that they had to spell the same words differently at their native language lessons. This hindered their progress in learning both languages. That is why at the end of the 30's almost all the nationalities of the Soviet Union changed their alphabets on the basis of the Russian alphabet which immediately made it easier for the students to learn their native and Russian languages. However, Georgians and Armenians, who had their own ancient alphabets, have preserved them until now. The alphabets of the Baltic area nationalities, Letts, Lithuanians and Estonians, as well as Karelians, are at present based on the Latin alphabet." (Serdjucenko (1965); quoted in Bowers (1968), pp. 392–393.) The author does not explain why the students of the nations mentioned in the last two sentences are not "hindered in their progress in learning both languages." The use of the phrase "at present" may hint at possible plans for future Cyrillification of these scripts too. Significantly, no mention at all is made of Yiddish which was first subjected to a "simplification" intended to sever all links with Hebrew, and was subsequently almost entirely suppressed.

suffer from mutual incompatibility and other faults caused by the ignorance of those who hurriedly devised them under orders from political commissars.[72]

Despite such criticism and some proposals for reform, nothing seems to have been done about unification of Cyrillic alphabets for the non-Slavic nationalities on whom those ill-conceived alphabets had been foisted, and these people seem not to have benefited overly much from the blessings of their new-found literacy:

> The Soviet claim that Communism has brought political emancipation to the peoples of Central Asia and has resulted in an unprecedented flowering of native cultures seems questionable in face of the fact that not even in the most basic aspects of the cultural life of these peoples—the languages which they use and the alphabets with which they write them—has stability been achieved. No wonder Central Asian literature is so barren. . . . In the Western world . . . it is the creative writers and the foremost journalists who, more than any others, set current literary standards for their languages. With Communists it is otherwise. Committees of "experts" and conferences and congresses of "cultural workers", dominated by party bureaucrats, decide these questions. They are constantly undoing and redoing what they have done a few years before. The result is linguistic and alphabetic chaos.[73]

Cyrillification of the alphabets of various minority nationalities was also considered, oddly enough, by the Chinese Communists. This happened in the early 1950s, during the same period that saw the birth of the Latin phonetic alphabet for the Chinese language, and at a time when the political relations between China and the Soviet Union were still very cordial. The Peking government decided in 1956 that the Cyrillic alphabet should be introduced in Inner Mon-

---

[72]Even shortly before Stalin's death, the Soviet Turkologist N. A. Baskakov suggested a coordination of the alphabets of the various Turkic languages in order to "bring them as close as possible to Russian and thus to remove present inconsistencies" (Baskakov, cited in Henze (1957), p. 124). He concluded with the statement, "Execution of all these tasks has been made possible by the programs and methodological instructions set forth in J. V. Stalin's work of genius," by which he meant Stalin's booklet on language cited in footnote 68. A few years later such sycophantism was no longer necessary, and the same scholar openly proposed a unified Cyrillic alphabet for all Turkic languages, containing only 42 letters (Baskakov, 1967).

Another critic was K. M. Musaev, who in the English summary of his book on the alphabets of more than 60 nationalities in the Soviet Union, declared that "as it was brought out by local national authorities without proper coordination, the existing alphabets based on Russian graphics suffer from shortcomings: lack of unification, use of several letters to designate one phoneme, designation of several phonemes by one letter, use of complicated signs, and so on." (Musaev, 1965, p. 76).

E. I. Ubriatova (1961) declared openly that the earlier Roman alphabets of the Turkic peoples and other nationalities were better and more uniform than the Cyrillified alphabets forced on them, and that unification was needed to make the literature of these peoples accessible also to those outside the areas in which it was written. A decade later both Baskakov (1972) and Musaev (1973) could indeed report some progress toward unification and simplification of the Cyrillic alphabets used by Turkic nationalities.

[73]Henze (1957), p. 129.

golia during the next four years so that Mongols on both sides of the border would read and write in the same script. Thousands of teachers were trained, and a million textbooks were prepared. Similar steps were taken in the Sinkiang region, bordering on the Soviet Union, where the Uigurs, Kazakhs, Kirgiz, Sibos, Uzbeks, and Tatars were to adopt the Cyrillic alphabets used by their respective kinsmen across the border.[74] Needless to say, these plans were not carried out after Soviet Communism had become anathema to the Chinese regime, particularly after the Cultural Revolution of 1966.

4. ARABIFICATION

4.1. Arabic Script

The Arabic script probably evolved in the 4th century A.D. from the alphabet used by the Nabataeans, an Arab (or possibly Aramaean) people whose kingdom flourished between the 2nd century B.C. and the 2nd century A.D., and who had developed their own script from the Aramaic writing system. The earliest known evidence of Arabic script is a trilingual inscription in Greek, Syriac, and Arabic dating from A.D. 512 and found in 1879 near Aleppo in Syria,[75] but the script was apparently little used since almost no written texts in Arabic remain from the period before the coming of Islām.

The Qur'ān is the first consecutive text written in the Arabic script, and it is still the most important and venerated one wherever the Arabic language is spoken or where Islām is the religion of a people. The need to codify the holy text with absolute accuracy changed the art of writing Arabic from an almost unknown occupation to one of the most highly esteemed ones, and soon also to one that produced works of art of a calligraphic beauty unrivaled by any other script. Various styles of Arabic script developed, the two most important ones being the *Kufic* and the *Nashī*. The *Kufic* (named after the town of Kūfa in Mesopotamia), was a monumental script mainly used for inscriptions, and from it the later *Maghribi* script, mainly used in North Africa, was derived. The other early style of script, the *Nashī*, was a round and cursive style of writing from which the Persian and Turkish styles of writing evolved, and which is also the source of the presently used Arabic script.

The classical Arabic alphabet consists of 28 letters, 22 of which are derived from the ancient North Semitic script that was also the common ancestor of the Phoenician and Hebrew alphabets[76]; six letters, namely ث *(ṯā')*, خ *(ḫā)*, ذ *(ḏāl)*,

[74]Henze (1957), p. 132.
[75]Diringer (1968), p. 211.
[76]Diringer (1968), pp. 158–159, 210ff.

ض‎(*ḍād*), ظ‎ (*ẓā*), and غ‎ (*ḡayn*), were added to express specific South Semitic sounds for which no equivalent existed in North Semitic scripts. A number of diacritical marks, first introduced in the early 8th century, are used to distinguish between different consonant letters of basically identical shape and also to indicate vowels. Like other Semitic alphabets, the Arabic one has no vowel letters, but three consonants, namely ا‎ (*alif*), و‎ (*waw*), and ی‎ (*ya*), may also be used in such a capacity. The letters have different forms depending on their position in a written word (beginning, middle, or end), and are always joined together, sometimes in ligatures of two and three letters which are not easily distinguishable, particularly when written in certain calligraphic styles of writing in which the aesthetics of the script are more important than the legibility. The cursive character of the Arabic script has been preserved from its beginning to the present time, and no style of writing individual letters has ever developed, although the requirements of the printing press, the typewriter, and teleprinter, not to mention computers, would make this desirable today.[77]

4.2. The Arabification of Non-Semitic Languages

Less than a decade after the death of the Prophet in A.D. 632, the whole Near East was under Arab rule, at the end of the 7th century all of North Africa had been conquered, in A.D. 711 the southern part of the Iberian peninsula had come under Muslim rule, and a few years later the regions east of Persia to the Indus river fell to the Arab invaders. Together with the new faith, the Arabic language was swiftly imposed on the conquered peoples—a phenomenon never before or since achieved in so short a time and with such far-reaching effects. What had taken the Christian Church in Europe many centuries—the imposition of one liturgical language and one script on many different peoples speaking a multitude of languages—had been accomplished in a few decades by Islām in vast areas of Asia and Africa. Less than 200 years later, Islām had spread further throughout the subcontinent of India, and from there to East Africa, the Malayan archipelago, the Philippines, and even to China. By the end of the 9th century, Arabic had become the *lingua franca* from the Atlantic to the Indian Ocean, and it was also the universal tongue of literary, philosophic, and scientific discourse

---

[77] "The classical Arabic orthography and the orthographies derived from it were most economical and efficient for the days when writing meant only calligraphy. In calligraphy it saved time and space if the orthography was cursive, if it discretely indicated all the consonantal contrasts with single graphemes but neglected some of the vowels which could be predicted, and if the letters were written in a nonlinear fashion, and were given smaller, special variants for that purpose. But these very qualities of an orthography become its worst shortcomings in these days of typewriter and printing. It is in these areas that attempts to reform the scripts should be made." This is the opinion of a Muslim scholar and linguist, C. Mohammed Naim (1971), pp. 140–141.

in spoken and written form, a role comparable only to that played in our own time by English.

To be sure, not all peoples that had embraced Islām abandoned their indigenous languages together with their former religious beliefs. The Persian and Turkic languages flourished, especially after the emergence of Persian and Turkish rulers who ascended to the thrones held earlier by the caliphs of Arab descent. These peoples have preserved their identity to this very day; the local languages of Muslims in India remained relatively little affected, and there are also other non-Arabic vernaculars that continued to be spoken by Muslims, notably the Coptic language in Egypt (the last stage of ancient Egyptian) which, although officially banned by the Arabs in A.D. 997, continued to be spoken for many centuries and ceased to be a vernacular only in the 13th century.

Although a certain degree of tolerance existed toward native languages, Arabic became the only official language throughout the realm of the caliphate, and it remained the language of administration and culture until the invasion of the Mongols in the 13th century.[78] Since the unifying force of the Islamic world was its religion, all Muslims, regardless of nation or language, had to learn at least some rudiments of Arabic so as to be able to recite their daily prayers in the language of the Qur'ān, and gradually the various languages of Muslim peoples also borrowed Arabic words for which there were no equivalent expressions in their own vocabulary.

Tolerance, however, did not pertain to script. All Muslims without exception were forced to record their languages in the Arabic script because it was unthinkable to write the Qur'ān and other liturgic and theologic literature in any script other than the one in which the Prophet had written down what Allah had revealed to him. In some instances this meant the more or less abrupt discarding of earlier writing systems, such as Latin and Greek script in Egypt and North Africa, Syriac in Syria, the Pahlavi script in Persia, various Indian and Indonesian scripts, the Kök-Turki runes and the Uighur script used by the Turkic peoples in Central Asia, as well as some others. It also became necessary, of course, to adapt the Arabic alphabet to a number of languages having widely different phonologies. Yet, unlike the adaptation of the Roman or Cyrillic script to other languages, no letters in the original Arabic alphabet could be dropped, even when they were entirely redundant in non-Semitic languages and when they made their writing systems highly ambiguous. The primary reason for this was that the elimination of even a single Arabic letter would have made it impossible to read the Qur'ān, the very source of Arabification, or to write the Arabic names adopted by converts to Islām and their descendants, even those whose language was not Arabic. The redundant letters were therefore retained, but in most non-Semitic languages they were pronounced quite differently, and in some

[78]Lewis (1966), pp. 14, 131–135.

languages they were not pronounced at all. On the other hand all non-Semitic languages to which the Arabic script was applied had to express phonemes for which there were no Arabic letter equivalents, and this they did in various ways—either by modifying Arabic letters for similar or related sounds through the device of diacritical marks, or by inventing new letters that resembled Arabic ones closely. The alphabetic sequence of letters remained exactly the same as in Arabic for all languages, and the additional or modified letters were put either before or after their prototypes in the alphabet. The Persian and Azerbaijani languages had to add 4 new letters, Ottoman Turkish and Malay 5 each (but not the ones), Urdu and Kurdish 7, Pushto 9, and Sindhi had to add the largest number of additional letters, 24—a whole new alphabet. The total number of letters in the Arabic script, including new and modified letters for non-Semitic languages, comes to 65, not counting special uses of diacritical marks to indicate vowels, especially in the writing system of the Kurdish language (see Table 2.8).

The ability to read and write either the Qur'ān and other liturgic literature, or secular works written in Arabic or in any other language written in Arabic script remained, however, the privilege of the few. Except for the "Golden Age" of Islam, from the 10th to the 12th century, when literacy was probably more widespread among Muslims than at any other period, and when, consequently, Arab arts and sciences flourished, the teaching of reading and writing was the jealously guarded monopoly of the 'Ulamā', the class of learned men and religious dignitaries. Only their own offspring and those of the rich and powerful were generally allowed to become literate, while fewer still could go on to higher studies at one of the Islamic universities which restricted themselves to the teaching of religious law. Moreover schools were, until the end of the 18th century, almost entirely confined to cities and towns, while the villages and hamlets, not to mention the tents of the nomads, were left without any means of instruction; inhabitants of the countryside remained totally illiterate. In the long twilight of Islam that lasted from the late Middle Ages until a few decades ago, literacy in Muslim countries dwindled sometimes to almost nil, and even today, despite many efforts to introduce general education and compulsory schools, most of these countries have still a very long way to go before they will reach a rate of literacy approaching that of most other developing nations. The percentage of literates among adults who speak a language written in Arabic is the lowest among users of any of the world's major scripts (see Table 4.2, p. 000).

4.2.1. Indo-Iranian Languages.   The Indo-Iranian languages on which the Arabic script was imposed are Persian, Pushto, Kurdish, Sindhi, and Urdu. Urdu is virtually the same as Hindi, this being the Indian counterpart of the phenomenon exhibited in Europe by Serbo-Croatian: one language written in two different scripts by two religious communities. The language derives from Sanskrit and is written in Devanagari script by Hindus as Hindi, whereas Mus-

Table 2.8 Classical Arabic Alphabet and Modified Letters Used in Non-Semitic Languages

CLASSICAL ARABIC Name	Letter	Sound	Added letter	PERSIAN	PUSHTO	KURDISH	URDU	SINDHI	CROATIAN	TURKISH	MALAY
ʾalif	١ ،	ʔ									
bāʾ	ب	b	پ	p	p	p	p	bh	p	p	p
tāʾ	ت	t			t			th			
ṯāʾ	ث	θ		s	s	s	s	s ṭ ṭ ḍ ṭh	s	s	s
gīm	ج	dʒ	چ چ	ʒ	dz						
ḥāʾ	ح	ħ		h	h		h	ɽ	x	h	h
ḫāʾ	خ	x			t						k
dāl	د	d	ڈ		ts	tʃ	tʃ	tʃ/h	tʃ	tʃ	tʃ
ḏāl	ذ	ð	ژ ژ	z	z	z	z	dh ɳ ɖ ɖ ɖh	z	z	
rāʾ	ر	r	ڑ		ɖ	ɽ	ɽ	ɽ			
zāy	ز	z			ʒ ʒ̃	ʒ	ʒ	ʈ	ʒ	ʒ	tʃ

CLASSICAL ARABIC Name	Letter	Sound	Added letter	PERSIAN	PUSHTO	KURDISH	URDU	SINDHI	CROATIAN	TURKISH	MALAY
sīn	س	s		s	s		s	s	s	s	s
šīn	ش	ʃ									ʃ
ṣād	ص	sˤ									
ḍād	ض	dˤ									
ṭāʾ	ط	tˤ									
ẓāʾ	ظ	ðˤ									
ʿayn	ع	ʕ									
ġayn	غ	ɣ					ph				
fāʾ	ف	f				v					
qāf	ق	q						k	k		k
kāf	ك	k	گ	g	g	g	g	g kh		g	g
lām	ل	l				ɬ					
mīm	م	m									
nūn	ن	n			ɳ ɳ	ə		ɳ	ɲ		
hāʾ	ه	h					h				
wāw	و	w		v			v	gh	v	v	
yāʾ	ي	y		y	y		y	tʃʰ dʒʰ v	y	y	

Note. The pronunciation of classical Arabic letters in non-Semitic languages is indicated by IPA symbols only when it differs from the Arabic pronunciation.

115

lims (now mainly the inhabitants of Pakistan) write it in Arabic as Urdu. Hindi and Urdu (in older literature both are sometimes subsumed under the name Hindustani) have a common structure, syntax, and grammar, and they differ only slightly in their vocabulary, in that Hindi has more words derived from Sanskrit, while Urdu borrows more from Arabic and Persian. The name *Urdu* itself, used only since 1752, is Turkish and means "army camp," which reflects its first use by the invading Muslim army in Lahore.

With the exception of Persian, which had a long-established literary tradition when the Arabs conquered its users, literature in the other Iranian languages began to be written only at a relatively late period and is not very voluminous. Most of it is heavily influenced by Persian literature, which served as a model both for writers in Pushto and Urdu in the 16th and 17th centuries, and for Sindhi, whose literature developed still later. All Arabified Indo-Iranian languages have one main problem in common, namely the expression of a large number of vowels for which there are no letters in classical Arabic. Most of these languages also contain some consonants not found in Arabic, for which suitable letters had to be devised.

4.2.2. Spanish. Over a period of more than 300 years, the Spaniards gradually regained most of the Iberian peninsula that had been conquered and ruled by the *Moros* since the beginning of the 8th century. But the Arabs who had lived in Spain for generations did not always flee when their Muslim rulers were defeated. Many thousands remained in Muslim enclaves in the Christian provinces; for a time these *Moriscos,* as they were called, were even protected by the king and were allowed to worship according to their faith. Since they were, however, isolated from the mainstream of Arab culture, they began to speak the Castilian language of their Christian neighbors, which they called العجمية [*al-aǧamīya*] ("the foreign one").

Probably from the 11th century onward, Morisco writers and poets created many works in Castilian but wrote it in Arabic script, the one they were most familiar with. This blend of Castilian language and Arabic script became known in Spanish as *Aljamía* or *Escritura aljamiada*. The oldest preserved works date from the 13th century, and the form continued to be used until the expulsion of all Muslims from Spain in 1614. Many of these works were religious poems, the most famous one being the *Poema de Yusuf* (on a theme in the 12th *sura* of the Qur'ān); there were also a number of epic legends that had been translated or adapted from Spanish and French sources. Aljamía was also used for interlinear translations of the Qur'ān into Spanish, and served as a means for secret correspondence between Muslim writers and professionals, especially after they could no longer openly follow their faith when they were forced to convert to Christianity in the 15th century. The Biblioteca Nacional in Madrid has a large collection of books written in Aljamía.

4.2.3.   Croatian.   Another European language once written in Arabic script by a Muslim minority is Croatian. From the 14th to the late 19th century, Bosnia, Macedonia, and southern Serbia formed part of the Ottoman empire. Most of the local nobility and landowners became Muslims, and they wrote their Croatian vernacular in Arabic script (adapted by diacritical marks to express Slavic sounds). This script, variously known as Arabica, Matufovica, or Al-jamiado (as in Spain), was used for private correspondence as well as for literary purposes, but only some 40 books (mostly religious tracts, poems, and legends) were printed in Arabica. Today Yugoslav Muslims use Roman script in Bosnia, and Cyrillic script in Serbia and Macedonia, for all purposes except for the Qur'ān, which is traditionally printed in Arabic script.

4.2.4.   Ottoman Turkish and Other Turkic Languages.   The Seljuks, a Turkish tribe from Turkmenistan in Central Asia, embraced Islam in the 9th century, together with most of the other Turkic-speaking peoples of the region. When they conquered Asia Minor and destroyed the last remnants of the ancient Byzantine empire in Asia, Islām supplanted the Greek Orthodox faith, and Arabic script superseded the Greek alphabet, which was henceforth only used in Greece itself and in some neighboring areas. Under the rule of the Ottomans, who came to power in the 14th century, the language spoken by the Seljuks gradually developed into Ottoman or Osmanli Turkish, a hybrid language that contained a large number of Arabic and Persian loanwords. This was used mainly by officials and in Turkish formal literature. Although it was quite different from spoken Turkish and was not even understood by the majority of the people, it remained in use until the early part of the 20th century, when modern Turkish began to be used by Turkish writers and journalists. The rich vocalization of Turkish was particularly badly served in writing by the lack of vowel signs in the Arabic script, and could only partially be indicated by the use of diacritical marks.

In the area that forms today a part of northern Persia and Afghanistan, the Caucasus, and the Central Asian regions of the Soviet Union, other Turkic peoples also adopted the Arabic script together with the Muslim faith in the 9th and 10th centuries. The Azerbaijanis, Kazakhs, Uzbeks, Uighurs, and other Turkic tribes used Arabic for almost a thousand years, until the early 20th century, but almost exclusively for liturgical purposes. The Latinization movements in the USSR and later in Turkey itself put a somewhat abrupt end to the use of a script that had hampered literary activities in the Turkic languages for so long. Outside Turkey and the Soviet Union, however, some Turkic languages are still written in Arabic script; the Azeris in northern Iran, and the Uzbeks and Turkmens in Afghanistan write their languages in the script of their countries. The Uighurs, who had been one of the few Asian peoples to have a well-developed script of their own when they adopted Islām in the 10th century, and who continued to use it until the 15th century, wrote Arabic in the Chinese province of Sinkiang until the late 1950s, although their kinsmen in the Soviet Union had been writing their language in Cyrillic since 1941.[79]

4.2.5. Malayan Languages. Muslim Indian traders brought Islam to the coasts of Malaya and the Indonesian archipelago sometime during the 13th century, and they succeeded in converting a large part of the population to the Muslim faith. The island of Mindanao and the Sulu archipelago in the Philippines also became Muslim strongholds. In the Malay languages spoken in these countries, many letters of the classical Arabic alphabet were pronounced quite differently (some of them in various ways, depending on the Arabic loanword in which they appear), while a number of new letters for Malayan phonemes had to be developed, as was the case in all other Arabified languages. The enlarged Arabic alphabet of Malayan languages is known as *Jawi* (probably because it originated on the island of Java). The introduction of Roman script for Bahasa Malaysia and Bahasa Indonesia relegated the use of Jawi in these countries to Muslim religious schools and to the liturgy of Islām.

Another Malayo-Polynesian language that used a modified Arabic script for a long period is Malagasy. The script was introduced on Madagascar probably as early as the 10th century by Arab traders, and the sacred Malagasy scriptures called *Sorabe* ("Great writings") were written in a modified Arabic script named *Katibu*. In the early 19th century British and French missionaries devised a Latinization scheme for the Malagasy language which was made official by King Radama I in 1820, and this replaced the Katibu script entirely. Today Arabic script is used only by a small number of Muslims in the northeastern part of the island for liturgical purposes.

4.2.6. African Languages.   When Arab slave traders established their rule along the East African coast, Islam gained a foothold also in that part of the continent and the local languages were strongly influenced by Arabic words and idioms.[80] Swahili, the language that became most widely used throughout the area, derived even its name from the Arabic word سواحلي [sawāḥilī] ("the coastal dweller") but was not written in Arabic script until the early 18th century. From that time until the end of the 19th century, some 60 Swahili works written in Arabic script have survived, consisting mainly of religious and epic poetry modeled on Arabic literary paradigms. As already discussed, Swahili (which had absorbed not only Arabic words but also many expressions from

---

[79]A Russian textbook of the Uighur language and a Russian–Uighur dictionary in which the Uighur part was printed in Arabic script were published in the Soviet Union in 1954 and 1955. Since the Uighurs in the USSR had at that time used the Cyrillic script for more than a decade, these reference works were probably intended for use by Uighurs in the Chinese province of Sinkiang.

[80]"Some of the vernaculars have been enriched by expressions from the Arabic for the embodiment of the higher processes of thought." (Blyden, 1887, pp. 186–187.)

Persian, Gujarati, Hindi, Portuguese, and English) began to be written in Roman script in the middle of the 19th century, and this writing system has been made official in Tanzania and other eastern African countries. However, some modern writers of Swahili prefer to use the Arabic script for contemporary works of prose and poetry, and the spread of Islam throughout Africa during the last few decades has led to a renewed interest in Arabic-written Swahili.

Other African languages sometimes written in Arabic are Hausa and Somali.

* * *

The changes in pronunciation of classical Arabic letters and the many adaptations that had to be made by various Arabified languages are the cause of many difficulties in the transliteration or transcription of names and words from these languages into other writing systems. In particular, the transliteration systems most widely adopted by libraries for Arabic are not suitable for the two languages that have produced the largest body of non-Arabic literature written in Arabic script, namely Persian and Ottoman Turkish. No satisfactory solution of this problem has yet been found; or rather, none of the proposed solutions has been officially accepted on a national or international scale. This matter is discussed in more detail in Chapter 4.

5. HEBRAIFICATION

5.1. Hebrew in the Land of Israel and in the Diaspora

The Hebrew script developed from the North Semitic alphabet, which probably originated in the second quarter of the second millennium B.C., and which is now generally considered to be the source of all alphabetic scripts. In the first half of the first millennium B.C., the script known as Early Hebrew was already widely used in the Land of Israel. After the Babylonian exile, during which the Aramaic alphabet (another branch of the ancient North Semitic script) came into use among Jews, the classical "square" Hebrew script developed from it, and this has remained essentially unchanged until present times (although many different styles of handwriting evolved later in various parts of the Diaspora).

Biblical Hebrew was the language of the Jewish people in the Kingdoms of Judah and Israel until the 6th century B.C., when Aramaic (then the *lingua franca* of the whole Near East) began to supersede it as the vernacular, but it continued to be used as a spoken language in worship and in official communications until the destruction of the Second Temple in A.D. 70 by the Romans, which marked the beginning of the Diaspora. Mishnaic Hebrew, spoken in Palestine since the

3rd century B.C., survived until about the 2nd century A.D. as a vernacular. Thereafter the use of Hebrew was limited to liturgy and literature, and it became the "Sacred Language," not considered proper for other purposes.

The Hebrew alphabet consists of 22 consonants, 4 of which, namely א *(alef)*, ה *(he)*, ו *(waw)*, and י *(yod)*, also serve to indicate the vowels; these consonants have the Hebrew name אמות קריאה ("mothers of reading") but are better known to linguists by the Latin translation *matres lectionis*. Most vowels are, however, not written but must be mentally supplied by the reader, who either knows the pronunciation of the words or can infer it from the context. When Hebrew ceased to be a spoken language, there arose the need for a graphic system to indicate vowels because words in the Bible were in danger of being mispronounced and therefore also misinterpreted, which was held to be a desecration of the holy text and a grave sin. Three different systems of vocalization developed. The "Palestinian" and "Babylonian" systems, which used supralinear marks in the form of small letters and dots respectively, were employed for a relatively short period only, and they are known only from a few surviving fragments of manuscripts. They were superseded by the "Tiberian punctuation," developed by the Masoretes in the city of Tiberias probably between the 6th and 9th centuries. This system, which uses mostly sublinear dots and dashes, was accepted as the only authorized vocalization of the Bible by all Jewish communities throughout the world, although the pronunciation of these vocalization marks came to vary considerably over more than a thousand years and in different linguistic environments.[81] The Tiberian vocalization is now also used in poetry, children's literature, and whenever the sound of a word has to be indicated unambiguously in written texts.

The destruction of the Second Temple and the expulsion of more than a million Jews from their land did not spell the doom of the Jewish people, as the Romans thought when they struck commemorative coins with the inscriptions "Iudaea capta" and "Iudaea devicta." The Jewish people survived almost 2000 years of dispersion and persecution because they had a "portable homeland": the Bible, recited and studied daily, and the interpretation of the Law in the Talmud, both written in Hebrew.

Thus the Hebrew script, the means of graphic expression for one of the smallest ethnic groups in the Roman Empire, survived not only the scripts of other more numerous and powerful nations but also the empire itself, and it attained a status on a par with the two alphabets that had also developed from the North Semitic one, and which in due time became the dominant scripts of Europe: Greek and Roman.

This was due as much to the tenacity with which the Jewish people throughout the world clung to the script of the holy language, as to the reverence with which

---

[81]*Encyclopedia Judaica* (1972), s. v. *Pronunciation of Hebrew.*

Christians of all denominations viewed the source of their versions of the Bible and of much of their liturgy and theological literature. The number of manuscripts and books written in Hebrew and preserved in libraries everywhere is therefore very large, and Hebrew is read and studied not only by Jews but also by many non-Jewish scholars in various fields. For this reason the Hebrew script and its adaptations to languages other than Hebrew are considered here, although it is today one of the ''minor'' scripts when compared in absolute figures with other scripts.

Hebrew is probably the only script that has been used to write languages other than the one for which it was originally invented without any coercive system of a religiopolitical nature. The Jewish religion does not have an established church or an ecclesiastical hierarchy that could decree the use of the Hebrew script, nor did the Jewish people in the Diaspora possess any political power to impose the script of its sacred language on either Jew or Gentile. There was not even anything to be gained by using Hebrew script for the vernacular instead of using the writing systems of the societies in which Jewish communities lived, when either the same or a very similar vernacular was written in Roman or Arabic script. Quite to the contrary, the use of a ''foreign'' script made Jews the object of suspicion and hatred. Why then did they insist on the use of the Hebrew script rather than adopting the Roman or Arabic scripts of their Gentile neighbors? First of all, the Jewish people in the Diaspora considered any foreign language (i.e., any language other than Hebrew) to be one of the temporary afflictions brought upon them by the destruction of the Temple and their dispersion among the Gentiles, whereas Hebrew alone, the ancient and sacred language of their forefathers, constituted the unifying medium of communication among Jews anywhere. Since the script first learned at an early age normally also remains the one best mastered throughout life, there was an additional strong incentive to use the Hebrew script, initially to record foreign names (for which there already existed a long-standing tradition in the Talmud for rendering Greek, Latin, Egyptian, and other names in Hebrew transcription). This practice was later extended to words and short phrases in other languages interspersed in Hebrew written communication, until finally it was quite natural to write the vernacular entirely in Hebrew characters when the daily language was used for secular purposes such as business transactions, questions concerning daily life, travel accounts, and other topics for which the Sacred Tongue came to be considered inappropriate.

Another important reason for the use of Hebrew script in the orthography of non-Hebrew languages was that the Jews identified the Roman script with Latin, the official language of the Catholic Church that oppressed and persecuted them. The Roman script became thus a symbol for persecution, not to be used under any circumstances by the persecuted themselves. To use a script other than Hebrew became almost tantamount to apostasy. Although this phenomenon may be viewed as a strong religious motive for Hebraification, it is by no means equivalent to the imposition of a script on a converted or conquered people by religious authorities, and is therefore *sui generis*.

The vernaculars spoken by the majority of the Jewish people from the late Middle Ages until the late 19th century were primarily two: Yiddish, used by Jews in Europe north of the Pyrenees and the Alps, and throughout eastern Europe to the Ukraine; and Ladino (Judezmo), the language of the Jews in Spain and, after their expulsion from the Iberian peninsula, of Jewish communities in the whole Mediterranean region from North Africa to Turkey. Some Jewish communities of relatively small size used Hebrew script for other vernaculars also.

5.2. Yiddish

Yiddish, which evolved from the Middle High German dialects spoken in the Rhineland, with a strong admixture of Hebrew and Aramaic words and phrases, became the vernacular of Jews in Germany probably during the 10th century. The oldest extant written documents in Yiddish consist of glosses in the margin of Hebrew manuscripts from the 12th century, and the first dated specimen of Yiddish writing is a pair of rhymes written in a prayerbook from Worms in the year 1272 or 1273. By then Yiddish had become firmly established as the everyday language of Jews throughout Germany and eastern Europe.

The writing of words of German origin in Hebrew script involved in every case, of course, a phonetic or phonemic transcription based on the German pronunciation at the time the word was first recorded in written form. At the end of the 14th century there was already a certain traditional Yiddish orthography for German words which was different from the one used at that time by Germans themselves in Roman script, and which preserved the pronunciation more faithfully.[82] Yiddish documents, particularly from this early period, are therefore valuable sources for students of the phonology of Middle High German.

After the expulsion of the Jews from many western European countries in the 12th and 13th centuries, and their migration to eastern Europe, the Yiddish language assimilated many Slavic words, and its grammar also changed under the influence of the surrounding Slavic languages. Its pronunciation, originally based on the sound values of Hebrew letters in the Ashkenazic pronunciation, now became differentiated, particularly regarding the pronunciation of vowels and diphthongs. The written language, however, preserved fairly uniform stan-

---

[82]Guggenheim-Grünberg (1956), who compared German legal documents found in Frankfurt and Breslau with their Yiddish transliterations, emphasizes the value of the phonetic rendering for the study of German dialects in the 13th and 14th centuries.

dards of orthography, at least until the middle of the 19th century. This is the more remarkable because Yiddish had neither a central regulating authority nor much assistance or encouragement in Jewish schools, which traditionally taught the reading and writing of Hebrew and the study of Hebrew and Aramaic sources, but left readers and writers of Yiddish pretty much to their own devices. Until the Emancipation, Yiddish was generally considered fit only for popular works written for the less well-educated and for women (who, although they were seldom given instruction in the study of the Bible or the Talmud, were practically always taught the Hebrew script so as to be able to read the prayer-book).

German books were translated and transcribed in Hebrew script as early as the 14th century, as witnessed by one of the oldest dated manuscripts in Yiddish,[83] so as to make secular works accessible to Jews who knew only the Hebrew letters, and who were both unfamiliar with and reluctant to use the Roman script. There were also translations and transcriptions into Yiddish from other languages, notably Italian.[84] The art of transcription of European languages into Hebrew script thus became quite prominent and customary in Yiddish literature before the Emancipation, in the wake of which translations from all modern languages and forms of literature were made in large numbers.

Since the 22 letters of the Hebrew alphabet were not sufficient to transcribe the phonemes of Indo-European languages, in particular their vowels and diphthongs, Yiddish orthography used three of the four Hebrew vowel-consonants or *matres lectionis*, namely א *(alef)*, ו *(waw)*, and י *(yod)*, which are used to indicate the long vowels $[a]$, $[o]$ or $[u]$, and $[i]$, to serve the same purposes in Yiddish, with the addition of the letter ע *('ayin)*, the glottal stop, for which there was no use in German or Slavic words and which was used to indicate the vowel $[e]$. Hebrew pointed vowel signs were also used, mainly to distinguish between א $[a]$ and א $[o]$, both of which written by the letter *alef*. Finally, diacritical marks in the form of a bar over a letter were used to distinguish between ב $[b]$ and ב $[v]$, and between פ $[p]$ and פ $[f]$. Modern Yiddish orthography was standardized in 1937 by the YIVO Institute for Jewish Research in Vilna,[85] and most Yiddish writers and publishers adopted this standard orthography which applies, however, only to words belonging to languages other than Hebrew or Aramaic. Hebrew names and words, which at all times formed a considerable part of the Yiddish vocabulary, were never transcribed phonemically according to their pronunciation in Yiddish but were always written in the

---

[83]See Birnbaum (1931), who published a critical edition of the Yiddish translation of a German work, *Schrift von den Kräften des Aderlassens und der Adern, nach den Schriften der Ärzte* in which he had to retransliterate the Yiddish text in order to obtain the original German text.

[84]Eliya Baḥur Levita (1468?–1549), a Hebrew grammarian who was born in Germany but lived in Italy, translated several Italian works into Yiddish.

[85]YIVO Institute for Jewish Research (1937).

original "defective" spelling (i.e., without an indication of most vowels) as written in the Bible or in the Talmud. All speakers and readers of Yiddish recognized these Hebrew words in their traditional spelling, although they pronounced them in various ways according to local usage. In effect, therefore, Yiddish orthography employs simultaneously two different spelling systems: a "traditional" consonantal spelling based on that of a Semitic language, for its Hebrew and Aramaic words; and a largely phonemic spelling, for all words derived from German, the Slavic languages, and lately also from English. For the native user of Yiddish who has been trained in the use of this mixed orthography, it does not constitute a hindrance any more than the "mixed" spelling of English does to a native user of that language who pronounces the words *bit* or *dog* according to their phonetic spelling, but "knows" that the word *gaol,* spelled according to a tradition going back to Old French, is not so pronounced.

This long-standing orthographic tradition was abruptly changed for the millions of Yiddish-speaking Jews living in the Soviet Union, another instance of a change of script and the enforced use of certain transliteration practices enacted for political, and not for linguistic, reasons. The Yiddish language was initially considered by the Soviet cultural authorities as one of the many national languages in the big mosaic of the Soviet nationalities, and as such the language and its script were not only tolerated but even encouraged to a certain degree. Soon after the October Revolution, however, it was decreed that Hebrew words must no longer be written in the orthography of the Bible, but had to be transcribed phonemically as if they were regular Yiddish words, following the pronunciation most widely used among Russian Jews. Also, some letters and letter forms were eliminated from the alphabet as "superfluous" for a purely phonemic transliteration. All this was done to sever any links with the Hebrew language and thus with the Jewish religion and its liturgical literature which, according to Communist doctrine, were nothing but "opium for the people." Another underlying motive was probably to make it more difficult for Jews to read Yiddish literature printed outside the Soviet Union which, despite heavy censorship and strict control, found its way to centers of Jewish population.[86]

After some ruthless purges of almost all prominent Yiddish writers and journalists during the 1930s, the Yiddish press and literature were barely allowed to exist during World War II but were finally eradicated in 1948, and the last

---

[86] Erlich (1973). An example of the "new" Yiddish orthography is the title of the Soviet–Yiddish newspaper דער עמעס /der emes/ ("The Truth"); the word for *truth* is the Hebrew אמת (pronounced /emes/ in Yiddish), but its spelling was changed to עמעס so as to emulate the pronunciation phonetically. The same procedure was applied to Hebrew names, for example, to the name of the famous humoristic writer who used the Hebrew phrase שלום עליכם (in Yiddish pronunciation /šolǝm aleχǝm/) as a pen name. (His real name was Šelomo Rabinovich, and his pen name is generally transcribed as Sholem Aleikhem for English readers.) In the new orthography, his name is spelled phonetically: שאלעם אלייכעם, thus hardly leaving any trace of the original spelling as used by the author himself.

surviving group of Yiddish writers was executed in 1952. Only in the late 1960s was a small monthly magazine in Yiddish allowed to appear again, still written in the Soviet version of Yiddish orthography. Thus Yiddish continues to lead a precarious existence in the Soviet Union, enduring only as an insignificant remnant, and its days in that country are probably numbered. In the United States, South America, and some other countries Yiddish is still alive, although the number of its speakers and writers is steadily declining.

5.3. Ladino

Ladino is based on Old Spanish or Castilian, the language spoken as a vernacular by the Jews in Spain since at least the 13th century. It became a written language only after the expulsion of the Jews from Spain in 1492 and from Portugal in 1497, when it began to be recorded in Hebrew characters, preserving the vocabulary, phonology, morphology, and syntax of the Castilian tongue as spoken in the 14th and 15th centuries, with the addition of Hebrew and Aramaic words for concepts not found in Castilian and for those intimately connected with the study of the Bible and the Talmud. The reasons for writing the Castilian language *(idioma castellana)* in Hebrew characters are the same as those for Yiddish, but the aversion to the use of Roman script as the literary symbol of the Roman Catholic Church and the Inquisition was, if possible, still more pronounced in Spain after the trauma of the burning of thousands of Jews at auto-da-fés and their forcible expulsion from the country.

Whereas Yiddish had almost always been written (and later printed) in square Hebrew letters, Ladino writers preferred the *Mešit* or *Raši* script, a cursive hand developed in the Middle Ages in France and widely used in Provence and in northern Spain, although Ladino documents were sometimes also written in square Hebrew letters. Hebrew and Aramaic words in Ladino were written in their original spelling (occasionally with vowel points to avoid ambiguity), while words of Castilian origin were written in phonemic or phonetic transcription. For this purpose the 22 letters of the Hebrew alphabet were not sufficient and had to be augmented by diacritical marks: the letters בֿ *(bet),* גֿ *(gimel),* דֿ *(dalet),* זֿ *(zayin),* and פֿ *(pe)* were written with a haček to render the sounds $[\beta]$, $[d_3]$ or $[t\int]$, $[\eth]$ or $[3]$, and $[f]$; the $[\lambda]$ sound was rendered by writing יי (double *yod*), ני by ייני (*nun* and double *yod*). Despite some ambiguities in vocalization (the short vowels were not written and had to be inferred from the context), the study of early Ladino is still very valuable for students of Old Spanish phonology.

The rich literature of Ladino preserved the written language almost unchanged in the form in which it was spoken in the 15th century, whereas the spoken language gradually assimilated Arabic, Greek, and Turkish words, many of which superseded the old Castilian words, so that the literature became largely incomprehensible to the less well-educated. This was certainly a contributing factor to the relatively large number of illiterates in the Ladino-speaking Jewish communities, many of which were enclaves in largely or even entirely illiterate societies throughout the Ottoman Empire and the Maghreb.

After the Latinization of the Turkish language, Ladino also began to be written in Roman script,[87] an interesting instance of retranscription at second remove, but this trend apparently did not become popular. During World War II many of the Sephardic Jewish communities in Greece and other Balkan countries were virtually annihilated. The remnants of these communities, as well as those of Bulgaria, Turkey, and the North African countries, immigrated in the 1950s to Israel, where there are now about 200,000 speakers of the language; most of these, however, are no longer able to read or write classical Ladino.

5.4. Hebraification of Other Languages

5.4.1. Judeo-Arabic. The Jews who lived in countries where the Arabic language had become the vernacular following the Arab conquests in the 7th and 8th centuries, from Babylon in the east through Egypt and to the Iberian peninsula in the west, gradually abandoned Aramaic, which had been their vernacular for more than a thousand years, and adopted Arabic as their daily language, but only scholars and wealthy businessmen could also read and write Arabic. The Hebrew script remained the only one used by the common man in Jewish communities under Arab rule. Some of the most important and influential Jewish theological and philosophical works were written in Arabic, such as Sa'adya's كتاب الأمانات والاعتقادات [*Kitāb al-Amānāt wa-al I'tiqādāt*] ("The Book of Beliefs and Opinions"), but writers who wished to reach a wider audience resorted to writing Arabic in Hebrew characters; the most famous example is דלאלת אלחאירין [*Dalālat al-Ḥa'irin*] ("Guide to the Perplexed"), by Mośe ben Maimon (Maimonides), written in 1190. (The Hebrew is the transliteration of دلالة الحايرين .)

Since both Arabic and Hebrew are Semitic languages which share a common origin and whose alphabets are structurally related, this did not pose any great difficulties. For each Arabic letter the corresponding Hebrew letter was substituted, and for those Arabic letters that have no Hebrew equivalent, Hebrew letters with superscript dots were used (see Table 2.9). In vocalized texts the Arabic vowel signs were rendered by א *(alef)*, ו *(šuruq)*, and י *(yod)*, as the case may be; the Arabic diacritical marks ٴ *(hamza)*, ٱ *(hamzat al-waṣl)*, and *(tašdīd)* were always rendered by writing the same marks over the Hebrew letters, and ة [*tā'marbūṭa*] was written ה .

---

[87] Millás-Vallicrosa (1950) cites the case of a *Haggada* printed in Istanbul in 1932 in Hebrew and Romanized Ladino; the foreword to this edition states that the text is presented "en Ebreo i en Ladino kon karakteres Latinos."

Table 2.9   Hebraization of Arabic Letters

Arabic letter	Hebraization Modern	Judeo-Arabic		Arabic letter	Hebraization Modern	Judeo-Arabic
ا	א			ض	'צ	צ֗
ب	ב			ط	ט	
ت	ת			ظ	'ט	ט֗
ث	'ת	ת֗		ع	ע	
ج	ג			غ	'ע	נ֗
ح	ח			ف	פ	
خ	'ח	נ֗		ق	ק	
د	ד			ك	כ	
ذ	'ד	ד֗		ل	ל	
ر	ר			م	מ	
ز	ז			ن	נ	
س	ס			ه	ה	
ش	שׁ			و	ו	
ص	צ			ي	י	

5.4.2.   Judeo-Persian.   Jewish communities in Persia employed Hebrew script to write various Iranian dialects as far back as the 8th century A.D., using a largely phonemic transliteration that today affords important clues to the history and dialectology of the Persian language. After the Arab conquest Persian was written in Arabic script, but the necessary addition of letters for Persian phonemes and the differences in pronunciation of some Arabic letters made transliteration of Persian into Hebrew more difficult than the transliteration of classical Arabic. Various diacritical marks were used, but the transliterated letters were ambiguous and only the context made clear which Arabic letter was written in the original Persian; for example ג *(gimel)* was written for گ *(gāf)*, while נ stood for any of the letters ج, ج, ز, and غ.

The first translation of the Pentateuch into Persian, written in Hebrew script, dates from 1319. Thereafter many Judeo-Persian commentaries on the Bible and other religious literature were written, as well as Persian-inspired Jewish poetry in Hebrew script. Judeo-Persian continued to be used for religious works until the beginning of the 20th century.

5.4.3. Judeo-French. The Jewish communities in France and in some parts of the Rhineland spoke the Old French vernacular probably from the 9th century until the beginning of the 14th century, when the Jews were expelled from France (1306) but they wrote it in Hebrew script. One of the earliest known works of this kind is a Hebrew—French glossary to the Old Testament, compiled in 1240 by Yosef ben Šimšon, in which the French words (לְעַ״זִים [la'azim], "the foreign words") were phonemically transcribed. The vocalization was so precise that it has been possible to establish the French dialect as the one spoken in Burgundy.[88] In other Judeo-French works the orthography was not phonemic but tried to preserve the Latin spelling of words that had become part of the vocabulary of Old French. In some instances diacritical marks were used, for example, when the Old French phoneme [tʃ] which had developed from Latin [k] was written ק̌ , or when Old French [y] was written יֻ (i.e., by a combination of the Hebrew consonant expressing [i] with the vowel mark for [u]).

5.4.4. Judeo-Provençal. A body of popular religious literature in the Provençal language written in Hebrew script, mainly intended for the use of Jewish women (who, in Provence as well as in central Europe, could read Hebrew script but were not taught the Hebrew language), existed from the 12th until the 15th century. The language consists almost entirely of Provençal words with only a few Hebrew expressions, and the transcription is purely phonemic. In some isolated Jewish communities in the lower Rhône valley a form of this language was still used at the end of the 18th century.

5.4.5. Judeo-Italian. A blend of several southern Italian dialects, interspersed with Hebrew expressions and "Italianized" Hebrew words such as *dabberare* (from the Hebrew root דבר [*daber*], "speak"), was used as the vernacular of Jewish communities in southern Italy, primarily in Rome, from about the 13th until the end of the 18th century; the language was written in Hebrew script. Some remnants of the spoken language are said to survive today among Jewish laborers and artisans in Rome.

5.4.6. Judeo-Greek. Most Jewish communities in Greece spoke and wrote Ladino, but there is also a body of literature in a vernacular based on Greek with many Hebrew and Aramaic expressions, and later also containing many Turkish words, all written in Hebrew script. It can be traced back to the 12th century and flourished until the end of the 17th century. The transcription is mostly phonemic.

---

[88]Sarton (1927), v. 3, p. 699.

5.4.7.   Judeo-Tat.   Tat is an Iranian language, spoken in the eastern Caucasus region. Its main dialect is Judeo-Tat, the vernacular of a Jewish community which formerly inhabited some remote mountain villages but is now concentrated in the cities of Daghestan. Religious works and poetry in the language of the *Dagh Chufuti* (Mountain Jews) were written in Hebrew script until 1929, when Soviet authorities imposed the Roman script in a secularization move. Ten years later, Judeo-Tat, like almost all other non-Slavic languages of the USSR, had to be written in Cyrillic script. It is still one of the official languages of Daghestan, though the number of its speakers is now, according to the official Soviet census taken in 1970, no more than about 12,000.[89]

5.4.8.   Karaite Turkic.   The small community of Karaite Jews who lived in the Crimea peninsula for many hundreds of years, until their extermination by the Germans in World War II, wrote the local Turkic dialect in Hebrew script.[90]

6.   ENVOI

This survey of the adaptation of the world's most important scripts to various languages is neither complete[91] nor sufficiently detailed as far as individual languages are concerned; there are now several standard works on the subject from which further details can be gleaned.[92] Rather we have been concerned with pointing out the religious and political forces that governed the imposition or change of script conventions at various times, and the changes wrought in the

[89]Western sources estimate the number of Tat-speaking Jews in Daghestan as between 40,000 and 100,000.

[90]Kowalski (1929). See also Diringer (1968), p. 440.

[91]The Greek alphabet and the Devanagari script, among others, have not been covered, for the following reasons. The Greek alphabet, although the ancestor of Roman, Cyrillic, and Coptic script, has almost never been applied to write another language (a minor exception being the use of Greek script to write Turkish by Greeks in Asia Minor, a practice that ceased after 1922 when the Greek population of Turkey was resettled in Greece). Only some Greek letters have occasionally been "borrowed" by people who devised alphabets for certain languages, for example, Albanian before 1909, but these do not qualify as adaptations of a script to another language.

Devanagari, the most widely used offshoot of the ancient Indian Brahmi script, has a large number of close and distant relatives in the scripts used for Indo-Iranian, Dravidian, Sino-Tibetan, and other South and Southeast Asian languages. In each of these, however, the original form of the characters was changed to such a degree that the relationship of these scripts to their origin is often discernible only to paleographers specializing in Indic scripts. Some of the Indic scripts are derived from different sources but have borrowed certain elements from Devanagari (see Diringer, 1968, pp. 257–313, and Chakraborti, 1971, pp. 95–102). Consequently Devanagari cannot be considered a script that has been adapted to the writing systems of various languages in the sense in which this has been the case for other scripts, namely without undergoing major changes.

[92]Cohen (1958), Diringer (1968), Jensen (1958).

graphic records of nations and language communities, which have important implications for the bibliographic control of those records.

It would be trivial to point out that, wherever a multiplicity of writing systems existed at the same time, it led inevitably to attempts at conversion from one script to another so as to make the records written in a certain script accessible to those following a different convention of graphic recording. But it is perhaps not so obvious that the absolute conversion of scripts through the power wielded by priests, kings, and dictators, who brought about large-scale changes in writing systems, has its mirror image on a smaller scale in the relative conversion of scripts. Transcription and transliteration are nothing but an artificial imposition of a dominant script convention on a language written in a dissimilar script for the convenience of those who cannot read that script, performed by those who have the power to do so, at least within the limited domain over which they hold sway—a library or other bibliographic tool. Documents written in a dissimilar script are artifically subjected to the conventions of the dominant script, and while the native speakers and writers of the language concerned would not agree to such treatment if it were performed in their own country and cultural environment, the users of a bibliographic tool that employs certain methods of script conversion have no choice but to submit to such a routine, which in most instances is designed to serve the convenience and aims of those in power but not necessarily those of the users of documentary communication systems. We discuss these aspects of script conversion in greater detail in Chapter 6.

We now take a look at the many ways in which scripts have been converted ever since men began to write down what they wished to convey, and also at the various motivations and goals of these activities, of which bibliographic control—our primary concern in this study—is only one of the more recent ones.

Three

The Historical Development of Script Conversion

עַל־כֵּן קָרָא שְׁמָהּ בָּבֶל כִּי־שָׁם בָּלַל יְהֹוָה שְׂפַת כָּל־הָאָרֶץ

Διὰ τοῦτο ἐκλήθη τὸ ὄνομα αὐτῆς, Σύγχυσις, ὅτι ἐκεῖ συνέχεε Κύριος τὰ χείλη πάσης τῆς γῆς

Therefore was the name of it called Babel, because the Lord did there confound the language of all the earth.

Genesis, 11:9.

1 SCRIPT CONVERSION IN ANTIQUITY

1.1. Early Multilingual Inscriptions

The earliest writing systems evolved independently in at least seven areas in the Orient.[1] Disregarding Proto-Elamite and Proto-Indic (which have not yet been deciphered), there are records of five ancient writing systems, of which four lasted for periods ranging from several hundred to more than 3000 years; one, the Chinese writing system, is still in use today in much the same form in which it was originally devised. In approximate chronological order of the respective earliest written documents, these are:

Sumerian cuneiform writing in Mesopotamia (3100–100 B.C.);
Egyptian hieroglyphs in the Nile valley (3000 B.C.–A.D. 400);

[1]Gelb (1963), p. 60.

Cretan hieroglyphic-linear writing in Crete and Greece (2000–1200 B.C.);
Hittite hieroglyphs in Anatolia and Syria (1500–700 B.C.);
Chinese logograms in China (1300 B.C. until the present time).

With the exception of Chinese the other four writing systems existed side by side, at least during the millenium from 2000 to 1000 B.C., in a relatively limited geographical area encompassing the Near East. Inevitably the peoples of the area and their writing systems came into frequent contact with each other, both along the trails of trade caravans and on the path of far-flung expeditions of military conquest. The natural consequence of such proximity and constant interchange between different cultures and their writing systems was a need for conversion of names for persons, places, and things from the records of one people to those of another. Thus written names were recorded as well as they could be fitted into the writing system and the speech habits of those who wished to preserve their exploits for posterity in archives and on monuments, or in the records of those who were engaged in business and administration. As to the peoples and tribes who had not yet developed a writing system when they encountered the merchants or warriors of other peoples, their names were recorded in the scripts of the traders or conquerors as they were perceived by the ears of those who could write.

That relatively few bi-or multilingual documents survived from antiquity is probably more a consequence of the perishable nature of the material on which records were generally written than to their intrinsic paucity. The Bible tells us (Esther 8: 9) that in the days of the Persian Empire

an edict was written . . . to the satraps and the governors and the princes of the provinces . . . to every province in its own script and to every people in its own language, and also to the Jews in their script and their language.

This was during the reign of Xerxes I, in the 5th century B.C., but both before and after that time very probably not only royal edicts but all kinds of documents, from legal codes to everyday business records, had to be written occasionally in more than one script, and the names of gods, persons, and places had to be transcribed. Thus there may have been thousands of bi- and polylingual documents, but since most of these were written on perishable materials such as bark, papyrus, and leather, they have not been preserved, and only the relatively few multilingual inscriptions on monuments of stone or metal, and those written on clay tablets and on earthenware utensils have come down to us. Since the beginning of the 19th century, bi- or multilingual inscriptions have played an important role in the deciphering of formerly unknown or forgotten scripts, and in the reconstruction of the morphology and sometimes even the phonology of ancient tongues (although some important decipherments have been successful even without such bilingual aids, as exemplified by the brilliant deciphering of the Cretan Linear B script by Ventris and Chadwick).[2]

The most famous of these multilingual monuments is the Rosetta stone, discovered in 1799 by French troops near Rashid (Rosetta) in the Nile delta. It is written in hieroglyphic, demotic, and Greek script, which made it possible to decipher first the demotic and later the hieroglyphic writing since one language, Greek, was known and the names of kings were rendered in both the demotic and hieroglyphic scripts by a kind of phonemic transcription, through the use of hieroglyphic logograms and phonograms. The deciphering was mainly the work of the ingenious French scholar Jean François Champollion, based on earlier partially successful attempts by the French Orientalist A. I. Silvestre de Sacy, the Swedish diplomat Jan David Åkerblad, and the British physicist Thomas Young. Another trilingual monument (also hieroglyphic–demotic–Greek), a stele containing the Decree of Canopus, was found in 1866 by the German Egyptologist Richard Lepsius, who was able to decipher it and to remove some doubts and uncertainties that still remained after the deciphering of the Rosetta stone. Lepsius too succeeded in deciphering the Canopus stele mostly because of the phonetic transcription of names, which then gave the clues to the writing and even partially to the pronunciation of other Egyptian words.

These monuments date from a late period in the history of ancient Egypt, but research into hieroglyphic writing has revealed that as early as the Middle Kingdom (ca. 2000–1800 B.C.) the Egyptians used a fairly elaborate orthography specially developed for the phonetic and phonemic writing of foreign names.[3] Several dozen such bi-and multilingual monuments have subsequently been found in the Near East, all of which bear witness to the widespread practice of phonemic-phonetic transcription of names.

1.2. The Bible

The Bible is the most ancient narrative and coherent literary work written in an alphabetic script and probably also the first one to go beyond brief inscriptions, commercial, or administrative inventories or legal codes.[4] It is also the first

---

[2]Chadwick (1958).

[3]Edgerton (1940).

[4]Diringer (1968), pp. 159–164, dismisses the opinion of Gelb (1963), pp. 147–153 et passim, that the Semitic alphabets were essentially syllabaries, and that the Greek alphabet was the first "real" alphabetic script because it was the first to represent not only consonants but also vowels and diphthongs. This controversy has not yet been resolved among the historians of script, but most scholars seem to agree on the essentially alphabetic character of the early Semitic writing system which developed into Aramaic and later into Hebrew and Arabic script.

large-scale repository of names transcribed by a writing system expressly designed to record individual sounds.

Since the majority of non-Hebrew names recorded in the Bible are of Semitic origin, the vocalization of these names as later codified by the Tiberian punctuation system probably approximates quite closely the way in which they were pronounced in their respective languages, for example, in Babylonian or Assyrian. Even the sounds of non-Semitic names, such as Egyptian or Persian ones, are reasonably well reproduced in Hebrew transcription, and are much closer to the original than are most later Greek and Latin transcriptions, even though the latter scripts had the advantage of being able to write vowels in full (see Table 3.1.).

1.3. Greek and Roman Transcriptions

The Greeks adopted the North Semitic alphabet from the Phoenicians probably around 1000 B.C., but they adapted the consonants א *(alef)*, ה *(he)*, ו *(waw)*, י *(yod)*, and ע *('ayin)* (for which they had no use in their language) to represent the vowels $[a]$, $[e]$, $[u]$, $[i]$, and $[o]$. This was a further decisive step toward a more accurate and faithful rendering of sounds by transcription, especially for names in all other languages. Most other consonants (and their names) were also incorporated in the Greek alphabet, but since the Greek language had no palatal-alveolar fricatives, the letter שׁ *(šin)*, which in the Semitic languages stood for the phoneme $[ʃ]$ as well as for an apparently closely related phoneme $[s]$, was used to express the similar phoneme $[s]$ in Greek. In form it was turned 90 degrees to become the letter Σ *(sigma)*, while the letter ס *(samek)*, pronounced $[s]$ in the Semitic languages, became the Greek Ξ *(xi)* to express the phoneme $[ks]$.

The Greek alphabet became standardized when Athens officially decreed the adoption of the Ionic alphabet in 403 B.C., and thereafter the spelling of Greek words became fairly uniform for more than 500 years. But the transcription of foreign names and words in works of fiction and history was not subject to any firm rule other than that a name should have an euphonious sound so as to blend well with Greek words and names.[5]

Because the Greek alphabet lacked letters for the gutturals and sibilants and for some dentals that occurred frequently in Oriental names, other letters had to be used to express these. Thus the foreign graphemes standing for the phoneme

---

[5]Josephus, who had to render Hebrew names in Greek script, followed a well-established custom when he gave them a Hellenized form instead of more or less faithfully transcribing them. Since Hebrew had been his mother tongue, he felt compelled to explain to his readers: "With a view to euphony and my readers' pleasure, these names have been Hellenized. The form in which they appear here is not that used in our country." *(Jewish Antiquities,* 1,129.)

Table 3.1 Transcription of Non-Hebrew Names from Biblical Times into Hebrew, Greek, and Latin

	Original form (transcribed)	Source in Bible	Hebrew	Hebrew transcribed	Greek Septuagint	Greek Other sources	Latin Vulgate	Revised Standard Version
Babylonian	Nabu-kudurri-usur	Jer. 39: 1	נְבוּכַדְרֶאצַּר	Nevukadrezar	Ναβουχοδονόσορ		Nabuchodonosor	Nebuchadrezzar
	Nergal-šar-usur	Jer. 39: 3	נֵרְגַּל שַׂרְאֶצֶר	Nergal Śarezer	Νηργαλασαρασο		Neregel, Sereser	Nergal-sharezer
Persian	Daryawuš	Ezra 4: 4	דָּרְיָוֶשׁ	Daryaweš	Δαρεῖος	Δαρειάτης[1]	Darius	Darius
	Xšayaršā	Ezra 4: 6	אֲחַשְׁוֵרוֹשׁ	Ahašweroš	Ξέρξης	Ἀσσούηρος	Assuerus	Ahasuerus
Egyptian	Š(e)š(o)nk	1 Kings 11:40	שִׁישַׁק	Šišaq	Σουσακιμ	σούσακος[2] Σεσῶγχις[3]	Sesac	Shishak
	N(i)ku-u	2 Kings 23:29	נְכֹה	Neko	Νεχαώ	Νεκώς[4]	Nechao	Neco
Hittite	Ḥatti	Josh. 1: 4	חִתִּים	Ḥittim	Χετταιοι	Κετείοι[5]	Hethaei	Hittites

NOTE. The rendering of the Revised Standard Version has been added to facilitate identification of names.

[1] Strabo.
[2] Josephus.
[3] Manetho.
[4] Herodot.
[5] Homer (?).

135

[ʃ] were usually written σ or σσ, and the phoneme [v] was rendered by β or ου, which led to further distortions and a wide range of possible phonemic renderings of foreign names.[6] Some Greek writers even went so far as to give foreign names a twist that would suggest an etymology readily discernible to Greeks, and which would reinforce the often fanciful descriptions of foreign countries. Thus the Gogra river in northern India was made into an ᾿αγοράνις ποταμός ("river of the assembly"), and Renas, a rocky stronghold in India attacked by Alexander the Great, became an ᾿άορνος πέτρα ("rock no birds [can reach]").

Even the Septuagint, which is one of the richest sources of Greek transliterations and transcriptions, and in which the translators made a genuine effort to render Hebrew names and words as accurately as possible in Greek script (because of the sanctity of the original), is often neither uniform nor accurate. The name אליהו [Eliyahu] is rendered as ᾿Ηλειού in Kings 1 and 2, while it appears as ᾿Ηλίας in Malachi; the place name רמתים [Ramatayim] became ᾿Αρμαθάιμ. Sometimes, the same name is given in transcribed form in one place but in its Greek form in another, as in the case of אחשורוש [Ahašweroš], which appears as ᾿Ασσούηρος in Ezra 4: 6, but as ᾿Αρταξέρξης in Esther 1: 1.[7]

The conquests of Alexander had spread Greek language, traditions, art, ideas, and customs to the countries bordering the eastern Mediterranean and to the Near East as far as India. The written records of the *Oikoumenē*, the "inhabited world" (i.e., the countries inhabited by peoples embracing the Hellenic culture), were collected and preserved in the great libraries of Alexandria, the Mouseion and the Serapeion, and they were, of course, written in Greek. But some evidence suggests that these libraries also contained original works of the "barbarians," namely Egyptian, Babylonian, Phoenician, Persian, and Hebrew scriptures and codices of law, such as the Pentateuch, all or most of which were also translated into Greek so as to make their contents available to the scholars of Alexandria. Certain parts of works written in scripts other than the Greek may even have been transcribed or transliterated so that they could be listed in the libraries' catalogs in an orderly manner.

---

[6]The German Orientalist Preisigke (1922) says in the preface to his *Namenbuch:* "Diese Namen sind entsprechend der verschiedenartigen Aussprache und Schreibweise ihrer Zeit in verschiedenen Schreibungen überliefert (Nebenformen)." And in the introductory note to the "Anhang" of the same work, in which the Ethiopian, Arabic, Aramaic, Canaanite (Hebrew and Phoenician), and Persian names are listed as they were rendered into Greek, he states: "Die Wiedergabe der semitischen Laute durch griechische Buchstaben ist sehr unvollkommen und in Ägypten, wie es scheint, besonders inkonsequent; da wechselt *t* mit θ und δ, κ mit χ, φ mit π und β, usw.; der Buchstabe χ kommt für semitisch *k* and *ch* und wahrscheinlich auch für h vor; häufig aber sind ch und h, ebenso wie natürlich auch ᾿ und ῾, im Griechischen gar nicht wiedergegeben; auch die Umschrift der Vokale ist nicht immer gleichmässig."

[7]Swete (1902), chapter V.

This hypothesis is based on a possible interpretation of certain passages in the pseudepigraphic book known as the *Letter of Aristeas,* which purports to tell the story of the translation of the Pentateuch by 70 (or 72) Jewish elders from the Holy Land. In that book the chief librarian of the royal library, Demetrios of Phaleron, is said to have submitted a memorandum to King Ptolemy II Philadelphos that begins with the following sentences:

. . . with respect to the completion of the collection of books in the library, that those which are wanting should be added to the collection and that those in disrepair should receive the proper attention, my efforts in the charge have not been cursory. . . . The books of the Law of the Jews together with some few others are wanting. It happens that they are written in Hebrew characters and in the Hebrew tongue, and they have been committed to writing somewhat carelessly and not adequately, according to the testimony of experts, for they have never benefited by a king's forethought.[8]

Although the story told by Aristeas has long been known to be legendary and fanciful, some facts and names mentioned in the book have been verified from other documents as authentic. It is now thought that the so-called "letter" was actually written in the style of a *diēgēsis,* a Greek literary form not unlike a romance which narrates "things which happened or which might have happened."[9] Thus Demetrios of Phaleron (345?–283 B.C.), a central character in the book, was a Peripatetic philosopher and statesman who had been forced to leave his native Athens, later to become one of the courtiers of Ptolemy I Soter (Ptolemy II's father) in Alexandria. It seems that it was indeed he who first promoted the idea of founding a large scholarly library there, but he was neither the chief librarian nor the holder of any other position under Ptolemy II, for the simple reason that the king had banished him into exile for political reasons when he succeeded to the throne. Furthermore Demetrios was already dead when the events related by Aristeas purportedly happened.

However, the words that Aristeas puts into his mouth ring true as those of a librarian concerned not only with the enrichment of his collection and its proper preservation but also with its proper cataloging. The phrase "committed to writing somewhat carelessly and not adequately" has been variously interpreted to refer either to an earlier, carelessly made translation, to a copy of the Hebrew text carelessly made by scribes, or to the Hebrew writing system itself, which does not indicate vowels and was therefore considered to be a kind of "careless writing" compared with the "perfect" Greek writing system, in which both consonants and vowels could be written. This ambiguity and Aristeas' use of two different verbs to indicate *transcription* and *copying* as distinct from *translating*

---

[8]*Aristeas to Philocrates,* ed. Hadas (1951), pp. 29–30. This and all following quotations are from this edition unless stated otherwise.

[9]*Ibid.,* pp. 55–59.

have been taken to indicate that both a transcription of the Hebrew text into Greek script and a translation into Greek had been made.[10] About the translation there can be no doubt; it exists (even though it was not created in the manner or for the reason reported by Aristeas but was made primarily for the benefit of the Alexandrian Jews, many of whom did not know Hebrew at that time). It has been suggested that the transcription was a phonemic Grecization of the entire Hebrew text of the Pentateuch, made for deposition in the royal library.[11] This is, however, highly unlikely, because the scholars and grammarians of Alexandria are not known to have studied the phonology of "barbarian" languages, and reading Hebrew in Greek transcription was of no conceivable use to them. Rather, the evidence seems to indicate that the Law of the Jews was deposited in the library both in the original Hebrew (i.e., in a "copy") and in Greek translation. For the existence of the Hebrew text we have also the testimony of Tertullian who, with reference to the source of the Septuagint, says that

To this day in the temple of Serapis, Ptolemy's library is displayed together with the Hebrew originals.[12]

But, as Aristeas is anxious to point out, the mere deposition of a good copy of the original text was not enough, as King Ptolemy seemed to assume initially, and Aristeas has Demetrios tell him: "Translation is [also] required" (Aristeas 11). Why then is transcription into Greek letters mentioned several times by Aristeas? If there was no need to transform the whole text in this manner, it seems probable that certain *parts* of this and perhaps other works in foreign languages, such as the first few sentences or verses, were phonemically transcribed so that these works could be cataloged and integrated with other entries in the *Pinakes,* the catalog and biobibliography of the library, compiled at about the same time or shortly afterward by Kallimachos (fl. ca. 265 B.C.). The phrase προνοίας γὰρ βασιλικῆς οὐ τέτευχε "for they have never benefited by a king's forethought," which has also been translated as "for they have never had a king's care to protect them,"[13] may very well imply the cataloging of the work Demetrios is anxious to add to the library, since only large libraries, collected by and for a king, were arranged in an orderly manner and were duly cataloged, while private libraries, then as now, were often mere collections of books without a written

---

[10]For a discussion of the questions raised by "transcription" and "translation" in Aristeas, see Zuntz (1959).

[11]Graberg (1974), p. 279.

[12]Tertullian, *Apologeticus,* 18.8. Although Tertullian wrote some 300 years after the events narrated by Aristeas, there is no reason to believe that the Hebrew texts in the Alexandrian library were deposited there at a later date; his account his based on a source other than Aristeas.

[13]*The Letter of Aristeas,* translated by H. T. Andrews. In *The Apocrypha and Pseudepigrapha of the O. T. in English* . . . (1913). v. 2, p. 95.

inventory. This assumption is further reinforced by another passage in Demetrios' statement, in which he speaks of the planned translation which, after its completion, "we may lay up in a distinguished manner worthy of the subject matter" (Aristeas 32). The relevant phrase, θῶμεν εὐσήμος, has also been rendered as "that we may place it on record in seemly fashion,"[14] an even stronger hint at cataloging when uttered by a librarian.

Passages in the Persian *Dēnkart* (the principal source of the Zoroastrian sacred scriptures, the Avesta) also seem to indicate that a copy of the holy books was taken by the "Rhomai" (i.e., the Macedonians) and that it was translated and possibly also transcribed into Greek.[15]

Thus transcription for bibliothecal purposes seems to go back to the days of the world's first large research library, and it was done for much the same reason advocated for the practice more than 2000 years later in Western libraries: to integrate entries for works in dissimilar languages and scripts into a catalog written in the dominant script of a library.

The sources referring to the Alexandrian libraries in the 3rd century B.C., the days of their greatest fame and splendor, have nothing to say about books in Latin. The language of Rome had not yet produced works of literature, and the Greeks still considered it a barbarian tongue. Only after the conquest of Greece in the 2nd century B.C. did Roman poets, orators, historians, and politicians begin to write in their own language, and in due course they divided the peoples of the world into three classes: Romans, Greeks, and barbarians—in that order. The general attitude of the Romans toward the Greeks, however, always remained ambivalent; they had contempt for the political inferiority of the Hellenes, from whom they had wrested the government of the *Oikoumenē,* yet admitted their cultural superiority. In the words of Cicero, "We Romans have gone to school in Greece; we read their poets and learn them by heart, and then we call ourselves scholars," and Horace wrote an often-cited verse "Graecia capta ferum victorem cepit et artes intulit agresti Latio."[16] Greek cultural influence was reflected in the infiltration of Greek words into the Latin language for almost every concept of higher culture and sophisticated thinking, such as *poeta, philosophia, rhetorica, architectura,* and many others, as well as in the emulation of Greek literary forms and verse meters. Greek language and culture became the hallmark of educated men throughout the Roman Empire and remained so for several hundred years. A man might proudly say with Cicero, "Civis Romanus sum," and feel himself a part of the mighty political and military complex of the Empire, but he could not claim to be literate unless he could read and write Greek first, Latin second.

[14]Meecham (1935), p. 203.
[15]Graberg (1974), pp. 279–284.
[16]"Greece, taken captive, captured her savage conqueror, and carried the arts into boorish Latium."
Horace, *Epistolae,* ii, 1, line 156.

Consequently the Romans used transcription only for the rendering of Greek names and loanwords when these had to be inserted into a Latin text, but never for the conversion of whole passages of Greek text into Latin characters. Names of persons and places in other languages were, of course, also transcribed phonemically in the manner in which the Greeks had been doing this, and many examples can be found in Caesar's *De Bello Gallico,* Tacitus' *Germania,* and other historical and geographical works from Rome's Golden Age.

The *bibliothecae* (another of the Greek loanwords in Latin for a cultural institution) that existed in Rome, first in the homes of wealthy and learned men, and later in temples and official buildings for use by the public, contained large collections of Latin and Greek literature written in the two nearly related yet quite different alphabets. There is evidence that the physical arrangement of collections was made by script; that is, the libraries were arranged in separate Greek and Latin sections, and each section probably also had its own librarian. A Latin inscription mentions " . . . [p]rocurator bibliothecar[um] Graec[arum] et Latin[arum] ab epistulis Graec[is],"[17] another speaks of the librarian Laryx, " . . . a bibliotheca Graeca Porticus Octaviae,"[18] while a third concerns his colleague Antiochus, " . . . a bibliotheca Latina Apollinis."[19] These seem to indicate that the Romans classified their book collections by language. More concrete testimony comes from Suetonius, who says that Caesar founded public libraries "in Greek and Latin" and that he intended to give the post of chief librarian to the famous writer Marcus Terentius Varro.[20] Suetonius also mentions another librarian, Caius Melissus, who was assigned by the Emperor Augustus to arrange the libraries in the Porticus Octaviae, which consisted of separate Greek and Latin sections.[21] The Bibliotheca Ulpia, built by Trajan on the Forum, is also known to have been divided into a Greek and Latin section on either side of the still extant column erected by that Emperor.[22]

The arrangement of Roman libraries thus obviated any need for transcription

---

[17]*Corpus inscriptionum latinarum* (1862–), III, 431.

[18]*Ibid.,* VI, 4433.

[19]*Ibid.,* VI, 5884.

[20]Suetonius, *Caesar,* 44: ". . . bibliothecas Graecas Latinasque, quas maximas posset publicare data M. Varroni cura comparandum et digerendarum. . . ."

[21]Suetonius, *De grammaticis,* 21: "[Caius Melissus] Augusto etiam insinuatus est: quo delegante, curam ordinandarum bibliothecarum in Octaviae Porticu suscepit." The libraries in the Porticus Octaviae (a temple complex between the Capitolinum and the Tiber, of which some remnants are still visible) were housed in two separate sections between which there was the *curia,* a place used occasionally for meetings of the senate (see Middleton, 1892, v. 1, p. 203). The inscription cited in footnote 18 refers to the same library and mentions the Greek part of the collection. Suetonius, *Augustus,* 29, also says of the Emperor that he built the temple of Apollo and "addidit porticus cum bibliotheca Latina Graecaque . . .," that is, two separate libraries according to the language of the works housed in each of them.

[22]Pictures of a conjectural reconstruction of the Ulpian library are shown in Pinner (1958) and are also reproduced in the *Encyclopedia of Library and Information Science* (1968), v. 1, pp. 406–407.

in their catalogs (which are known to have existed, though no trace of them has survived). Readers and librarians alike were fluent in both languages and scripts, and could switch from one to the other without any difficulty.

1.4.   Hebrew Transcription of Greek and Latin: the Talmud

Greek and Latin words and names had to be transcribed in the written languages of those peoples in the far-flung Roman Empire who, despite the dominance of the Greek and Roman alphabets, continued to use their own writing systems. We have already mentioned the Rosetta stone; several dozen other bi- and trilingual inscriptions involving different scripts have been found in various parts of the Near East, but none of these contain more than a few lines of text, and only a small number of proper names and other words had to be transcribed rather than translated. There was, of course, no uniform method of transcription; in each language a more or less successful attempt was made to render foreign names in a form that could be readily pronounced by the speakers of that language.

A much more extensive repository of transcribed Greek and Latin names and words, mainly those in use during the first five centuries of the Christian era, is the Talmud. The transcriptions in this vast collection of legal commentaries, tales, and legends are relatively uniform and consistent, considering that they were made by a large number of writers during a period of many hundreds of years, and that some of them may have been distorted by the errors of scribes. The main difficulty in transcription was the discrepancy between the Greek and Latin alphabets, which had 24 and 23 letters respectively, and the Hebrew alphabet, which had only 22 and no distinct vowel signs. It proved especially difficult to render the rich vocalization that characterizes the Greek language, with its large array of vowels and diphthongs, by means of the *matres lectionis* (see Table 3.2), although some of the variant renderings were caused by the application of the two different Hebrew spelling conventions. It is sometimes not easy to discover which Greek word was transcribed into Hebrew unless the context gives some clues, since vowels were sometimes interchanged and syllables were elided by apocope, aphaeresis, and most often by syncope. The Greek consonants θ, σ, and χ, for which Hebrew had more than one equivalent letter, were rendered differently according to the preference of the writer and the custom of the time, but such inconsistencies did not affect the pronunciation of foreign names and loanwords. The nasal sounds written in Greek as $\gamma\gamma$, $\gamma\kappa$, and $\gamma\chi$ were rendered as in Latin, that is, by writing the letter ‫ב‬ *(nun)* before the nasalized consonant, as in the following examples:

GREEK	ARAMAIC
ἄγγελος	אנגלא
’ανάγκη	אננקי
κόγχη	קונכי

Table 3.2   Hebrew Transliteration of Greek Letters in the Talmud

Greek letters	Hebrew transliteration Mostly	Sometimes	Greek letters	Hebrew transliteration Mostly	Sometimes
A	א	ע	M	מ	
AI	י , אי		N	נ	
AT	או , אב		Ξ	סp ,כס	
B	ב , ו		O	ו , או	
Γ	ג		OI	אוי	
ΓΓ	נג		OT	ו , או	
ΓΚ	נק		Π	פ , ב	
ΓΧ	נכ		P	ר	
Δ	ד		Ῥ	הר , רה	
E	א	ע , י	Σ	ס , צ , שׁ	
EI	י		T	ט	
ET	אוי, אי, או		Υ	ו	
Z	ז		TI	אוי	
H	י , אי		Φ	פ	ב
Θ	ט , ת		X	כ , ח	
I	א , אי		Ψ	פס	
K	ק , ג	כ	Ω	ו , או	
Λ	ל		᾿	א	
			῾	ה	

The transcription of Latin words posed fewer problems, because the vocalization of Latin was easier to render in Hebrew (see Table 3.3), but also because Latin loanwords constitute only a small fraction of loanwords in the Talmud, the ratio of Greek to Latin words being about 100 to 1. The variant transcriptions are again largely due to the two spelling modes, and the transcription of *F* by the voiced and unvoiced fricatives ב and פ , and that of *P* by the voiced and unvoiced bilabials ב and פ , is probably caused by variations in pronunciation as perceived by Hebrew listeners at different times.

On the whole, Talmudic transcription was phonemic and endeavored to preserve the pronunciation of foreign names and words.

As we have seen, the same cannot always be said of transcription from Hebrew into Greek, as exemplified in the Septuagint, in which the names of

Table 3.3   Hebrew Transliteration of Roman Letters in the Talmud

Roman letter	Hebrew transliteration	
	Mostly	Sometimes
A	א	ה ,ע
B	ב	ו
C	ק	ז
D	ד	
E	א	י ,ע
F	פ ,ב	
G	ג	
H	ה	
I	א ,אי ,י	
K	ק	
L	ל	
M	מ	
N	נ	
O	או ,ו	
P	פ ,ב	
Q	ק	
R	ר	
S	ס	
T	ט	ת
V	או ,ו	
X	כס ,קס	
Y	אי ,י	
Z	ז	

persons, peoples, and places were sometimes rendered in a form completely different from the original one. We now consider one of the most remarkable works of script conversion to owe its existence to that Greek translation of the Old Testament.

1.5.   Greek Transliteration of Hebrew: the Hexapla

Origenes Adamantios (A.D. 185?–254?) personified the cultural and religious turmoil of his age, when Hellenism was already on the decline while Christianity was beginning to spread despite cruel persecutions. Origenes tried to reconcile Greek philosophy with the spirit of the Bible and the Gospels. He was one of the most prolific writers of all ages (St. Jerome said of him, "Who of us can read all that he was written?"), an eloquent apologist, and deeply concerned about the Greek text of the Old Testament, which in his time existed only in more or less corrupted versions of the Septuagint, as transmitted by copyists and scribes for more than 300 years. In an effort to arrive at the "original" version of the Septuagint and at the same time to achieve a faithful rendering of the Hebrew original, he devoted 28 years of his life to the compilation of the *Hexapla* ("The Sixfold"). In this huge work, originally consisting of more than 50 volumes, of which only fragments remain today, he set out the following, arranged in six columns from right to left: the Hebrew text of the Old Testament; a phonemic transcription of the Hebrew in Greek characters; the Greek translations of the Old Testament by Aquila and by Symmachos; the Septuagint, as amended and corrected by Origenes himself; and finally, another Greek version of the Old Testament by Theodotion.

We know the reason for including the Hebrew text in this first critical edition of the Bible, because Origenes says in his letter to Julius Africanus:

As I have tried to take account of all the Hebrew editions, we ought not to find ourselves quoting for controversial purposes texts which are not in their copies, and conversely, we should be able to use texts in their copies if they are not in ours.[23]

This indicates that he considered it necessary to have the original version as much for the restoration of the Septuagint text and possible improvement on it as for theological disputations with Jews. The Hellenized Jews in the Greek cities of the Near East, particularly the large congregation in Alexandria (where Origenes was born and where he spent the earlier years of his life), had at first accepted the Septuagint and used it in their synagogues, since many Jews no longer understood the reading of the Pentateuch in the Hebrew original. But

---

[23]*Epistola ad Africanum,* 5.

when Christian apologists began to use certain passages in corrupted versions of the Septuagint to show that Christianity was superior to Judaism, most Jews repudiated it as a mutilated rendering of the Hebrew original and preferred other Greek translations, particularly the one made by Aquila (fl. A.D. 117–138), a Greek from Sinope in Asia Minor who had become a Christian but later converted to Judaism. Origenes wanted to base his apologetic writings on the original sources so that Jews could not a easily refute them. For this purpose he learned Hebrew (probably from a converted Jew), which was quite an unusual thing for a Greek to do at this time,[24] but his knowledge of the language, respectable and even remarkable as it may have been under the circumstances, was nevertheless not very profound, as is evident from certain passages in his letter to Africanus[25] and in particular from his transcription of Hebrew.

The transcription of the complete text of the Hebrew Old Testament in Greek characters by Origenes is a work not surpassed to this day in its sheer magnitude. Never before had a consecutive text of that extent been transcribed phonemically, and not until the days of modern linguistic research has anything even remotely comparable been attempted. It is, however, not quite clear why Origenes undertook this immense labor, since

a transliterated text would have been useless to those who knew no Hebrew, whereas those who understood Hebrew are unlikely to have been ignorant of the Hebrew script.[26]

Various theories have been proposed by Biblical scholars since the beginning of the 19th century. Some believe that the transcription was made for the purpose of teaching Hebrew to Greeks; others think that it was made for the benefit of Hellenized Jews who no longer knew Hebrew (or was perhaps based on such transcriptions made earlier by Jewish transcribers). According to a more recent opinion, it was made as an aid to those who knew both the Hebrew language and its alphabet but were unsure of the vocalization of the Biblical text.[27] Yet another theory suggests that some churches might have preserved the old synagogue practice of reading the Old Testament in Hebrew even though the congregation no longer understood the language, and that Origenes wished to codify this practice.[28]

Whatever his motives (and in the absence of any indication by Origenes himself we must leave this topic to the conjectures of biblical scholars), he

---

[24]Hieronymus, *De viribus illustribus*, 54, says of Origenes: "Quis autem ignoret tantum in scripturis divinis habuerit studii ut etiam Hebraeam linguam contra aetatis gentisque suae naturam edisceret?"

[25]"It is evident from the *Ep. ad Afric.* that Origen could not walk alone in Hebrew." (Bigg, 1886, p. 126.)

[26]Emerton (1956), p. 79. The same author also summarizes earlier theories on the purpose of the transcription and critically discusses them.

[27]*Ibid*.

[28]Chadwick (1966).

obviously tried to do two things: codify the original text of the Bible in Greek letters, and convey to his readers the sound of Hebrew words. To achieve this he used a transliteration scheme in which one Greek letter was substituted for each Hebrew consonant except for the gutturals and the *matres lectionis,* which were either omitted entirely or treated inconsistently (see Table 3.4). The omission of gutturals was not entirely caused by the difficulties of transliterating Hebrew letters with Greek ones but can also be ascribed to careless or outright faulty pronunciation as perceived by the transliterator. This has been pointed out by the biblical scholar Paul E. Kahle:

Whoever compares this transcribed text with the text written in Hebrew characters will come to the conclusion that the men who were responsible for this kind of transcription did not pronounce the gutturals as consonants. Now it may be said: how was it possible to render Hebrew gutturals with Greek letters? That it was really possible may be seen from the much older methods of transcription which we find in certain strata of the Septuagint.[29]

The vocalization of Hebrew words in particular was quite arbitrary, and there occurred many instances of apocope, aphaeresis, and syncope (the latter mainly caused by the omission of gutturals). Two separate Hebrew words were sometimes rendered by one continuous string of Greek letters as if they were one word, which may partly be the fault of the copying scribes but was in some instances clearly due to a lack of knowledge of the Hebrew language. Some of these shortcomings and errors can be seen in the two specimens shown in Figure 3.1, where a few verses of the Bible are shown with their transcriptions in the *Hexapla* and in a fragment of a later version of the work known as *Octapla* (which contained, as its name implies, eight columns of Hebrew and Greek renderings of the Old Testament).

Although the pronunciation of the Bible text was not codified by a vocalization system until about the 6th century A.D., there is evidence that in Origenes' time it was substantially the same as in the later Masoretic text, and that any deviation or mispronunciation "in the Greek manner" by Hellenized Jews in Caesarea was actually condemned by the rabbis as a desecration of the Scriptures.[30] Origenes happened to write most of the *Hexapla* in Caesarea, and seems to have been guided by just such a "Hellenized" pronunciation of Hebrew. Even a

---

[29]Kahle (1947).

[30]In the Jerusalem Talmud, Sota vii, 1, we are told that Rabbi Levi bar Hita heard the שׁמע *(Šemaʻ)* recited "in a Hellenistic manner" and wanted to stop such practice. J. L. Teicher, whose opinion is cited by Emerton (1970), on p. 22, interprets this to mean "that it refers to pronouncing the Hebrew language in a way that gave the vowels a Greek quality, virtually to reciting Hebrew with a Greek accent. . . . Rabbi Yosi agreed with Rabbi Levi that the recitation of the שׁמע in Hebrew with a Greek accent is wrong and then went on to give a ruling: if people cannot pronounce Hebrew correctly, they ought [rather] to use a language that they can understand." What was considered proper for the שׁמע (Deut. 6:4) was, of course, *mutatis mutandis,* binding for the recitation of any other part of the Pentateuch.

Table 3.4   Transliteration of Hebrew into Greek in the Hexapla

Hebrew letter	Greek name	Greek transliteration initial	medial	final	Hebrew letter	Greek name	Greek transliteration initial	medial	final
א	Αλεφ	1			ע	Αιν	6	7	α, ε
ב	Βηϑ	β²			פ	Φη	φ⁸		
ג	Γιμελ	γ			צ	Τσαδη	σ		
ד	Δαλεϑ	δ			ק	Κωφ	κ		
ה	Η	3			ר	Ρηχς	ρ		
ו	Ουαυ	ου	β	υ	שׁ	Χσεν	σ		
ז	Ζαιν	ζ			שׂ	–	υ		
ח	Ηϑ	χ	4	ε, η	ת	Θαυ	ϑ		
ט	Τηϑ	τ			⊤' =',=;		α		
י	Ιοδ	ι			⊤:		ε⁹		
כ	Χαφ	χ⁵			⊤..		η		
ל	Λαμεδ	λ			⊤		ει, ι¹⁰		
מ	Μημ	μ			–,ʼ		ο, ω		
נ	Νουν	ν			·׀		ου	11	
ס	Σαμεχ	σ			⊤.		ο		
					⊤		12		

¹Not realized or transcribed by relevant vowel.
²Also when written without *dageš*, i.e. [v].
³Not realized or transcribed by spiritus lenis.
⁴Not realized or transcribed by relevant vowel.
⁵Also when written with *dageš*, i.e., [k].
⁶Spiritus or relevant vowel or γ.
⁷Not realized.
⁸Also when written with *dageš*, i.e., [p].
⁹Sometimes α or ο.
¹⁰Sometimes α pr ε.
¹¹Sometimes ω.
¹²Not realized; sometimes ε or α (when next vowel is ⊤̯ or ⊤̱).

cursory look at his transcription shows that he produced no more than a travesty of what was actually the received pronunciation of Hebrew in reciting the Bible:

The reading of [the] transliterated text by a Jew who knew only Greek would ... have led to the production of sounds which bore little relation to Hebrew, and which would have been incomprehensible even to hearers who understood that language.[31]

³¹Emerton (1956), p. 81.

וֹזאת שֵׁנִית תַּעֲשׂוּ	ουζωθ σηνιθ θεσου
כַּסּוֹת דִּמְעָה אֶת־מִזְבַּח יְהוָה	χεσσουθ διμα εθμασβην ΠΙΙΙ
בְּכִי וַאֲנָקָה	βεχι ουανακα
מֵאֵין עוֹד פְּנוֹת אֶל־הַמִּנְחָה	μηην ως φεννωθ ελ αμμανα
וְלָקַחַת רָצוֹן מִיֶּדְכֶם	ουλακεθ ρασων μειδηχεμ

(a)

מֵרֶחֶם מִשְׁחָר לְךָ טַל יַלְדֻתֶךָ	μηρημ μεσσααρ λαχταλ ιελεδεθεχ

(b)

Figure 3.1. Specimens of Hebrew Old Testament texts transcribed by Greek letters in the *Hexapla* and *Octapla*. *(a)* Malachi 2:13 in the *Hexapla*. *(b)* Psalm 110:3 in the *Octapla*.

This does not mean that Origenes performed his task carelessly. To the contrary, with his lofty aim and notorious zeal, he probably strove to achieve the best and most accurate results. He failed, firstly because of an inadequate knowledge of the source language; secondly because of the lack of suitable letters in the Greek alphabet, which made transcription from Hebrew difficult and ambiguous; and thirdly because of the complete lack of any rules or systems for the transcription into Greek of languages written in different scripts, which in turn was due to a lack of incentive to invent and apply such systems. The Greeks, whose keen minds had probed the realms of logic and mathematics with such marvellous results, had also begun to explore the mysteries of language. They tried to reduce their own language, its grammar, and syntax to a system of fixed rules, and they were very much concerned with "correct" spelling. But they were also firmly convinced that anything written in a language other than Greek was hardly worth paying any attention to, and left the task of transcription from these "barbaric tongues" to anyone who felt it necessary to render the sound of foreign names and phrases in a manner suitable for Greek listeners.

The phonemic transcription of the Bible by Origenes deserves attention because of its very inadequacies. Here is perhaps the only document dating from antiquity in which the accuracy of a transcription can be checked against more or less well-known standards of pronunciation of *both* languages, and not only one out of two or three languages, as in the few other transcribed documents on which our knowledge of long-forgotten languages such as Egyptian, Accadian, or Sumerian is based. Moreover we have in the *Hexapla* thousands of words in context, while in other transcriptions we must be content largely with a few phrases and the known pronunciation of a few names. Now if Origenes, despite his aim of giving as accurate a rendering of Hebrew as possible, could produce such woefully mispronounced and misspelled transcriptions, what degree of accuracy can be expected from the relatively amateurish efforts of historiographers or royal scribes? Add to this the mistakes that the stonecutters often made when transferring the work of the scribes onto a stele or other stone monument; such errors could not easily be corrected and were often left standing rather than being corrected, which would have necessitated defacing the inscription. We know that this happened many times in Greek and Latin inscriptions, so it must have occurred many more times when stonecutters had to deal with scripts and words with which they were not familiar.

Considering these difficulties and possible pitfalls of ancient phonemic and phonetic transcriptions, we should probably be very careful when drawing conclusions regarding the possible pronunciation of languages about which little more is known than what an occasional bi- or trilingual inscription from antiquity can tell us.

2 SCRIPT CONVERSION IN THE MIDDLE AGES

2.1. Latin Transliteration of Hebrew: the Vulgate

When the Emperor Constantine transferred the capital of the Roman Empire from Rome to Byzantium in A.D. 326, the dominance of the Greek language as the tongue of culture and refinement had already begun to decline, even as the power of the Roman Empire was soon to be diminished and eroded under the onslaught of the Goths and other Teutonic tribes from the north. The almost incessant warfare, destruction, and plunder, together with the social oppression and the economic misery that were the fate of the peoples throughout the western Mediterranean, left little opportunity, time, and inclination for the pursuit of lofty philosophy in Greek, a tongue that had never become the vernacular of the man in the street but had been spoken and written only by the educated upper classes. Latin, on the other hand, the language in which the indigenous population of many lands had been governed and in which they had conversed for generations with the soldiers and officials of Rome, had a pervasive influence throughout the western part of the Empire, and was later to develop into the several Romance vernaculars.

Soon the teachings of Christianity, which had originated in the Hellenized eastern part of the Mediterranean and had used Greek as the language of its first sacred writings, had also to be translated into Latin for the benefit of the growing congregations in Italy, North Africa, Spain, and elsewhere in the western part of the Empire. The first Latin translations of parts of the Bible were probably made in North Africa in the second century A.D. All these so-called Old Latin translations were based on the Septuagint before Origenes' attempts to restore a more accurate text, and they therefore contained many errors and distortions. Because of the influence of the *Hexapla* and also because of the growing need for an authoritative text of the Scriptures in Latin, Pope Damasus entrusted the task of translating the entire Bible to his secretary, Eusebius Hieronymus Sophronius (A.D. 340?–420), better known to the English-speaking world as St. Jerome. He had already made a name for himself as a prolific writer on theological issues, and also knew Hebrew and Greek. Hieronymus began his work in Rome but soon went to the Holy Land, where he settled in Bethlehem in A.D. 385, founded its first Western monastery, and began to perfect his Hebrew with the aid of a converted local Jew to whom he refers in his works as "Hebraeus meus." He tried his hand first at a revision of the Old Latin translation of the Psalter (a version that later became known as the *Roman Psalter),* and three years later (A.D. 387) he made a second revision in which he also used the several Greek versions of the Hexapla to amend and clarify the text (this version is known as the *Gallican Psalter).* While working on these translations he realized that to achieve a good Latin translation of the Old Testament he would have to go back to the source, the Hebrew text, which at that time already existed in almost exactly the same form as the later Masoretic text. By this time his knowledge of Hebrew had also advanced to such a stage that he could confidently undertake the huge task. He began his translation, written in the plain idiom of early medieval Latin, in the year 390 and completed the work in A.D. 404. This is the Latin Bible known as the *Vulgata,* which exercised a profound influence, first on the Latin-speaking world and later on all Western Christendom, and which, except for some revisions made under Pope Clemens VIII in 1592, became the only official version for the Roman Catholic Church. All vernacular translations of the Bible until the Reformation were made from the Vulgate.

Hieronymus did not transliterate whole passages of text, as Origenes had done, but had to resort to script conversion when names of persons or places had to be rendered into Latin (and occasionally when Hebrew words such as *Halleluja* or *Amen* had to be written, which, following the practice of the Septuagint and other translations, he did not translate into Latin). He seems to have followed a rather strict transliteration scheme (see Table 3.5) in which each Hebrew letter except א *(alef),* ה *(he),* ח *(het),* and ע *('ayin)* had only one Latin equivalent, irrespective of the pronunciation as affected by the presence or absence of a *dageš* in the letters ב *(bet),* כ *(kaf),* and פ *(pe);* that is, ב was always transliterated *b,* as pronounced with *dageš,* while כ and פ were always transliterated *ch* and *ph,* as pronounced without *dageš.* In one of his commentaries Hieronymus says that Jews could not distinguish between the sounds ⌈f⌉

Table 3.5 Transliteration of Hebrew into Latin in the Vulgate

Hebrew letter	Latin name	Latin transliteration initial	medial	final	Hebrew letter	Latin name	Latin transliteration initial	medial	final
א	Aleph	1			ע	Ain	7		a,e
ב	Beth	b 2			פ	Phe	ph 8		
ג	Ghimel	g			צ	Sade	s		
ד	Daleth	d			ק	Coph	c		
ה	He	3	h	3	ר	Res	r		
ו	Vav	v			שׁ	Sin	s		
ז	Zain	z			שׂ	Sin	s		
ח	Heth	4	ch, h	4	ת	Tav	th		
ט	Teth	t			⌐ꞌ ꞊ꞌ ꞊		a		
י	Iod	i			⌐ꞌ ꞊		e		
כ	Caph	ch 5	x 6		⌐		i		
ל	Lamed	l			⌐꞉ Ꞑ		o		
מ	Mem	m			⌐ꞌ Ꞑ		u		
נ	Nun	n			⌐		9		
ס	Samech	s							

[1] Not realized or transcribed by relevant vowel.
[2] Also when written without *dageš*, i.e., [v].
[3] Not realized.
[4] Not realized; sometimes *ch*.
[5] Also when written with *dageš*, i.e., [k].
[6] When followed by שׂ .
[7] Not realized or relevant vowel.
[8] Also when written with *dageš*, i.e., [p].
[9] Not realized or *e*.

and [p], so that he therefore always transliterated פ by *ph*. Whether the Jews living in Palestine in his day actually did not make a distinction between the two sounds or Hieronymus was unable to grasp a perhaps subtle phonemic difference is impossible to decide. His opinion was challenged only some 800 years later, when Roger Bacon stated in his Hebrew grammar that the Jews not only wrote *f* and *p* differently but also pronounced the *p*.

The rendering of Hebrew vowels reveals that Hieronymus had a much better grasp of Hebrew phonology than Origenes. His vocalization usually coincides with that of the later Masoretic text, except in cases where he preferred an already existing Hellenized form of a name found in the Septuagint, such as *Darius*, or when he accepted metathesis in a Greek rendering of a name and used it for the Latin, such as in *Ezechiel* (instead of *Iechezcel*, which would have been the correct transliteration according to his own rules).

Because of the lack of two sounds in Latin, namely $[ts]$ and $[\int]$, Hieronymus had to use the letter *s* as transcription for three different Hebrew letters, ם *(samek)*, צ *(zade)*, and ש *(šin)*, although he sometimes used *ss* for the latter. This more than anything else influenced the rendering of biblical names not only in Latin but also, subsequently, in all European languages, most of which did indeed possess the equivalents of those phonemes and wrote them with various letters and letter combinations (see Table 2.1, p. 48). But by the time the Bible was translated into these languages, the Vulgate had been pronounced the sole authority for the word of God, and the translators, who for the most part knew neither Hebrew nor Greek, did not dare to tamper with the Latin spelling but transferred it unchanged into the orthography of their vernaculars. The result was that most Biblical names as written in European languages show hardly any resemblance to the Hebrew source, and the manner in which they are pronounced tends to obscure their origin even more.

2.2   From the Dark Ages to the Crusades

By the sixth century the eastern and western parts of what had once been the Roman Empire had become separated both politically and by their language. Greek became the language of the Byzantine Empire,[32] while Latin remained not only the language of Rome, gradually evolving into Italian, but also the official language of the Church, which had assumed the spiritual and secular power formerly wielded by the emperors throughout the Western Empire, now dissolving under the onslaught of the barbarians. This separation by language, which was soon followed by a schism and bitter enmity between the two parts of the Christian Church, led to the dominance of Latin and an almost complete neglect of the Greek language in western and northern Europe for almost 700 years. As early as the fourth century we find that St. Augustine could neither speak nor write Greek (although he was probably still able to read some of the Greek classics). When in 824 the Byzantine emperor Michael II (the Stammerer)

---

[32]Nevertheless the Byzantines considered themselves to the end as the true heirs of the Roman Empire and gave themselves the name ʿΡομαῖοι. The Greeks adopted that name during a later period, while the name ʿΕλληνες indicated the pagan Greeks of antiquity. The Turks and Arabs knew the Greeks under the name "Rūmī" only, and even today this is the Arabic term for the followers of the Greek-Orthodox faith. Only in the early 19th century were the names ʿΕλλάς for Greece and ʿΕλληνες for Greeks revived by the movement for national independence.

sent a Greek manuscript of *The Celestial Hierarchy* (a work that later influenced Western Christian theology and mysticism) to King Louis the Pious in France, no one in the monastery of St. Denis in Paris was able to decipher it, and the task of translating it was entrusted to the Irish scholar Johannes Scotus Erigena, one of the few truly learned men of his age.[33] Even Latin, however, fell into neglect during the 6th and 7th centuries. It took the initiative of Charlemagne (who himself remained illiterate) in the 8th century, to revive the interest in the Latin language and preserve the heritage of Rome through organized copying in his palace school and in the monasteries. Western Europe reaped at least one benefit from its almost complete isolation from other tongues and cultures: Latin became a truly universal language, the *lingua franca* of learned men from Spain in the west to Poland in the east, and from the shores of North Africa in the south to Ultima Thule in the north, and it retained this position until almost the end of the 18th century.

In the Eastern or Byzantine empire, the situation with regard to knowledge of languages was initially somewhat less parochial. Students at the school of Constantinople, founded by Theodosius II in A.D. 425, pursued studies in Greek and Latin. One of the most famous works to come from this university was a large Greek and Latin grammar by Priscian, written about A.D. 526, which became the standard textbook for those languages until the end of the Middle Ages. But gradually the Latin heritage (except for law) was forgotten in Byzantium as much as the Greek heritage was forgotten in the West.

Throughout the Dark Ages not a single book is known to have dealt with other foreign tongues, and no one cared to preserve or study these languages and the scripts in which they were written. Europe had turned from the pursuit of knowledge and science to faith, hope, and charity. Any original literature written by Christians from the 4th to the 11th century dealt with biblical and theological subjects, and names of persons or places in the Bible that had to be cited were already codified as transcribed into Greek by the Septuagint and into Latin by the Vulgate. The rich store of literature, philosophy, and theology that had developed for almost a thousand years in India, China, and Japan remained practically unknown in Europe until the 13th century.

The knights who returned from the Crusades had come into close contact with Arabs, but most were unlettered men who neither understood nor cared about the writings of the Infidels, whose scholars had inherited the wisdom of the Greeks, translated their works into Arabic, and made great advances in the sciences, particularly in medicine. It was not until the early 12th century that Jews from Moslem countries, who in ever-larger numbers migrated to Christian Europe, especially to northern Spain and to the south of France, began to translate Arabic works into Hebrew. These were in turn translated into Latin at the end of the

---

[33]Durant (1950), p. 477.

12th and the beginning of the 13th century. Some works even went through a whole chain of translations, such as the *Fables of Bidpai,* originally written in Sanskrit, then translated into Pahlavi, into Arabic, into Hebrew, into Latin, into Spanish, and into English. . . . It would be interesting to pursue the fate of names and words in this chain of transcriptions—probably no trace of the original remains in the final version.

Tangible evidence for drastic changes resulting from rough-and-ready phonemic transcriptions are the names of famous Arabic and Jewish authors which were made amenable to Latin phonology and usage: Avempace (Abū Bakr ibn Bāǧǧa), Averroës (Abū l-Walīd ibn Rušd), Avicenna (Abū ʿAlī ibn Sīnā), Avenzoar (Abū Marwān ibn Zuhr), and Avicebron (Šelomo ibn Gabirol), to name only a few. Occasionally the transcription of an Arabic name was more intelligible, as in the case of Muhammad Abū Naṣr al-Fārābī, which became the Latinized Alfarabius, but this was the exception rather than the rule. The rendering of Arabic and Hebrew phonemes into Latin had not advanced since the days of St. Jerome; rather it had seriously deteroriated, and no one had thought of devising rules for transcription.

2.3. Roger Bacon

The Latin translations of Arabic works and Arabic versions of Greek writings on philosophy, astronomy, physics, mathematics, and medicine began to influence the thinking of Latin-speaking scholars in Europe in the late 12th century. Gradually interest in these "wordly" subjects was aroused, the newly founded universities began to teach them, and theologians were soon embroiled in disputations caused by the critical thoughts of Maimonides, Ibn Sīnā, and other Jewish and Muslim philosophers. Although still hampered by gross superstitions and by the geocentric conception of the universe, experimental science was taking its first unsure steps after almost 2000 years of neglect in the Western world. One of the most eloquent and profound scholars who dared to go beyond the teachings of the Fathers was the Franciscan friar Roger Bacon (1214?–1292). While still a student, he visited Paris and was astonished at the lack of knowledge of languages other than Latin among the professors at the university. One of the few learned men of his age to perceive the importance of a thorough knowledge of languages and scripts, he began to study Greek and Hebrew. He was thus able to read the Bible in the original Hebrew and Greek, the importance of which he stressed over and over again in his works. Far from being appreciated, this made him rather suspect in the eyes of his fellow monks:

Such deep ignorance shrouded convents and hostelries that the monks and friars could not believe that any one could gain acquaintance with the learned languages except by the aid of secret intercourse with the Devil. . . . [Bacon's] books were scarcely permitted a place in the libraries of his order.[34]

Bacon planned to write a one-man encyclopedia on all that was known to mankind. He became known as the *Doctor admirabilis* and was perhaps the first modern scientist, preferring firsthand knowledge and experiment to mere bookish wisdom and scholastic disputations on the writings of Aristotle (whom he nevertheless considered an authority on almost anything). When Pope Clement IV asked him to compile "a fair copy" of his work, he wrote, in less than a year, the *Opus maius* as a kind of abstract to present the Pope with an integrated picture of science, philosophy, and religion in his age.

Bacon began his work by listing four causes of human error, and "after the four causes of error have been banished to the lower regions, I wish to show that there is one wisdom which is perfect, and that it is contained in the Scriptures." This was what all Christendom believed, but whereas "the Scriptures" meant to Bacon's contemporaries only the Latin text of the Vulgate, Bacon was convinced that Hebrew was the language in which God had revealed Himself to His chosen people, and he was therefore particularly concerned about the faithful and accurate rendering of the text of the Bible from Hebrew into Latin. In the third part of his work, in which he devoted a whole chapter to "Linguarum cognitio," he said:

There are infinite occasions for errors, because a word is reckoned according to the Latin standard which has many forms for Hebrew. And there is the greater error, because to such a word various interpretations are given, as though they belonged to the same Hebrew word, whereas each belongs to a different one, because a Hebrew word is written by us without due construction in a single way of writing, according to which it receives different meanings.[35]

In an earlier work he had stated his opinion that to avoid mistakes in translations scholars should make a systematic and comparative study of Hebrew, Aramaic, and Arabic (which he considered to be "dialects" of one and the same language, a remarkably advanced view) and also of the Greek language:

I do not mean that everyone should learn these languages as he learns his mother tongue, so as to speak them as we speak English, French, and Latin; nor again, that we should content ourselves with being able to translate into our own language the Latin versions. . . . We should be able to understand how these languages should be rendered in Latin. The point is that a man should be able to read these languages and understand their grammatical structure.[36]

[34]"Life of Roger Bacon" (from Wood's *Antiquitates Univ. Oxon.*) in Bacon (1859), pp. xcii–xciii.
[35]Bacon (1962), v. 2, p. 85. Latin text in Bacon (1897), v. 3, p. 95.
[36]*Compendium philosophiae,* in Bacon (1859), p. 433.

Thus Bacon's ultimate motive was not the study of languages, and Hebrew in particular, *per se* (despite his keen interest in the origin and affinity of languages), but one that was quite similar to that of his predecessor Origenes a millennium earlier: to render the translation of the Bible as free from errors as possible through a better understanding of the original Hebrew and Greek texts. But unlike the Alexandrian ascetic, the learned Oxonian devised a scientific method, based on his thorough knowledge of Hebrew:

> . . . the Hebrew alphabet must be given in order that the subject under discussion may be more easily understood. The letters of the Hebrew alphabet are written first, then in the line above are given their names, and last our letters corresponding to the Hebrew ones, in order that we may know the values of the letters and the sounds indicated, some being vowels and some being consonants. [Here follows the display of the Hebrew alphabet as shown in Figure 3.2.] There are six vowels, *aleph, ain, he, heth, iot, vav;* the rest are consonants; *he* and *heth* are aspirated, *he* at the beginning, *heth* not only at the beginning, but at the end, and *heth* is produced in the throat, *he* in the mouth. *Aleph* likewise in the mouth and *ain* in the throat. But we must bear in mind that *iot* has only one sound, namely *j*, like our *j*, and becomes a consonant and vowel like *j* with us. *V,* as Jerome says in his Hebrew Questions, has a double sound, namely our *v* and *o*. The remaining four have the sound of our five vowels, namely, *a, e, i, o, u,* . . .[37]

In less than 20 lines of his manuscript (as shown in the reproduction of MS Vatican 4086 in Figure 3.3) Bacon managed to give the essentials of the Hebrew

z	v	e	d	g	b	a
zain	vaf	he	dalet	gimel	bet	aleph
ז	ו	ה	ד	ג	ב	א
m	l	ch	ch	i	t	h
mem uverte	lamet	chaf	chaf	iot	teis	heis
מ	ל	ך	כ	י	ט	ח
s	s	a	s	n	n	m
sazake dreite	sazake torte	ain	samech	nun dreite	nun torte	mem close
ץ	צ	ע	ס	ן	נ	ם
	t	s	r	k	p	p
	taf	sin	ris	kof	pe	pe
	ת	ש	ר	ק	ף	פ

Figure 3.2.   Transliteration of the Hebrew alphabet in the *Opus maius.*

---

[37]Bacon (1962), pp. 82–83. Latin text in Bacon (1897), v. 3, pp. 89–90. The Hebrew alphabet and Bible quotation in Bridges' Latin edition are correct, but in the English translation by Burke it is unfortunately marred by gross typographical errors which show that the learned translator, unlike Bacon himself, did not have any knowledge of Hebrew.

alphabet and its phonology—a remarkable feat of clarity and conciseness even by modern standards. He then went on to demonstrate his method of transliteration as well as the differences between Hebrew and Aramaic, citing as an example Jer. 10: 11 (the only verse written in Aramaic in this book of the Bible), which he translated and transliterated from both languages into Latin (see Figure 3.4).[38] The naming and transliteration of the vowels and certain consonants show clearly that he had learned Hebrew in the Sephardic pronunciation. His Jewish teacher almost certainly used the standard Hebrew grammars by the brothers Moše and David Qimḥi, מהלך *(Mahalak)* and מכלול *(Miklol)*. Bacon himself may have used these works in his studies of the Hebrew language, particularly when he later compiled a Hebrew grammar (of which unfortunately only a few fragments remain).[39]

The exposition of the Hebrew alphabet is immediately followed by one of the Greek alphabet, set out in the same systematic manner, that is, phonetic transliteration, name of the letter, and the Greek character in three lines (see Figure 3.5). This is followed by a concise explanation of the vowels and diphthongs and their transliteration, from which it is evident that Bacon assigned to the Greek letters the sound values of the modern Greek pronunciation. Additional proof for this is found in his Greek grammar, from which the following passage is taken:

Now, π after μ or ν, whether pronounced together or separately, provided they are uttered without interval, has the sound of our *b,* which they do not have otherwise, such as in λαμπάς, ’άμπελον. Similarly, τ after μ or ν sound as our *d,* which they do not have otherwise, as in ’αντίχριστος.[40]

---

[38] Hirsch (1899) observed that "the vocalization in the Hebrew quotations is altogether faulty. It appears that the writer inserted the points, not from a written copy, but in accordance with the sounds the transliteration attributed to them." But this judgment seems to be too harsh, considering that Bacon was the only scholar of his age to know any Hebrew at all; moreover, as Hirsch himself points out, the scribes who were loath to copy Hebrew and Greek characters because they considered them to be the work of the devil, may well have been to blame for any errors, since the presence or absence of even a tiny dot makes all the difference between right or wrong vocalization, for example, when .. *(ẓere)* is written instead of .. *(segol).*

[39] Almost all the names of Hebrew letters are correctly rendered, or nearly so, except for the letter צ *(ẓade),* which is labeled *sazake torte* (or *saziketor)* for the regular form and *sazake dreite* (or *sazikedrait)* for the final form. The spelling *sazike* or *sazake* is almost certainly a result of copying errors (the copyists knew only Latin and made numerous mistakes even in that language!). In Bacon's Hebrew grammar the letter is correctly named *sadich.* The Norman-French adjectives *torte* ("twisted") and *draite* ("straight") are exact translations of the traditional Hebrew names sometimes given to the regular and final forms of letters respectively. Bacon uses these adjectives in the *Opus maius* also for the letter נ *(nun)* while the two forms of מ *(mem)* are called *mem uverte* for the regular form and *mem close* (or in other MSS. *mem cose* and *mem clase,* again misspellings) for the final form; that is, in this case Bacon used Norman-French equivalents for the Hebrew "open" and "closed." In the Hebrew grammar Bacon prefers Latin adjectives throughout: *sadich primum* and *secundum* (or *clausum), mem apertum* and *clausum,* and so forth. The text of the fragments of Bacon's Hebrew grammar has been edited by Nolan and Hirsch (1902).

[40] My translation of the Latin text as quoted by Bridges in Bacon (1897), v. 1, p. L, footnote 1.

Figure 3.3. Two pages of the manuscript of the *Opus maius* containing the transliteration of the Hebrew and Greek alphabets. (MS Vatican 4086, f. 15v and 16r. Courtesy Vatican Library.)

The diphthongs αυ and ευ were rendered as *af* and *ef,* respectively, which is also very similar to the modern Greek pronunciation of these diphthongs. We may assume that Bacon had learned Greek from one of the Greek scholars who had been invited to Oxford by his teacher Grosseteste.

Bacon's work must be considered the beginning of systematic transliteration schemes for non-Roman alphabets. He assigned definite phonetic values to each

Figure 3.3.   *(continued)*

letter, based on the actual pronunciation by native speakers of the languages and on a thorough knowledge of their grammar and syntax.

Since Bacon often quotes Arabic authorities and urges the study of the Arabic language, we may wonder why he restricted his efforts at transliteration schemes to Hebrew and Greek. The answer is given by Bacon himself in Chapter 25 of his *Opus tertium* (in which he generally elaborated on many points that, because of time pressure, he had treated only briefly in the *Opus maius*):

dii eis dicetis sic   } Litera Hebraica
elaa lehom temerun chidena   Sermo Chal-
אֱלָהַיָּא לְהֹם תֵּאמְרוּן כִּדְנָה   daeus.

non terram et coelum qui
la areka ve semaa di
לָא? וְאַרְקָא שְׁמַיָּא דִּי

terra de pereant fecerunt
area me iebedu ebadu
מֵאַרְעָא יֵאבַדוּ עֲבַדוּ

coelo sub de et
semaa thehot mi u
שְׁמַיָּא : וּמִן־תְּחוֹת

dii eis dicetis sic   } Literae Hebrai-
elohim lahem tomeru co   cae Sermo
אֱלֹהִים לְהֶם תֹּאמְרוּ כֹּה   Hebraicus.

fecerunt non terram et coelum qui
asu lo ares ve samaim eser
עֲשׂוּ לֹא וְאָרֶץ שָׁמַיִם אֲשֶׁר

sub de et terra de pereant
thahat mi u eres me iobedu
וּמִתַּחַת מֵאֶרֶץ יֹאבֵדוּ

isto coelo
ele samaim
אֵלֶּה : שָׁמַיִם

Figure 3.4. Translation and transliteration of Jer. 10:11 in the *Opus maius*. (Reproduced from Bridges' edition. p. 91–92.)

a	b	g	d	e	z
alpha	vita	gamma	delta	e. penti, i.e. quintum	zita
α	β	γ	δ	ε	ζ

i	th	i	k	l	m
ita	thita	iota	kappa	labda	mi
η	ϑ	ι	κ	λ	μ

n	x	o	p	r	s
ni	xi	o. micron	pi	ro	sima
ν	ξ	ο	π	ρ	σ

	y. Graecum apud Latinos				
t	y. psilo	ph	ch	ps	o
taf		phi	chi	psi	o. mega, i.e. magnum
τ	υ	φ	χ	ψ	ω

Figure 3.5. Transliteration of the Greek alphabet in the *Opus maius*.

On Arabic, I have spoken elsewhere; I do not write anything in Arabic, as I do in Hebrew, Greek and Latin, because my subject is more obviously and easily set forth in these languages. Because, for the study of theology it is worth but little, though it is very useful for philosophy and for the conversion of the infidels.[41]

Thus only the languages immediately related to the restoration of correct texts of the Bible (and to some extent of Aristotle's works), that is, Hebrew and Greek, were in Bacon's opinion worthy of scholarly attention.

But his fervent plea for a thorough study of these two languages in order to better understand the Scriptures fell on deaf ears. Pope Clement IV died shortly after Bacon had sent him his *Opus maius* without even acknowledging it, and Bacon's own order condemned him as an heretic whose "teachings contain some suspected novelties," according to a 14th century chronicle of the Franciscan order. We do not know which part of Bacon's work was considered heretical, but he spent 15 years in prison and was released only 2 years before his death. He had been far ahead of his time, both in the study of the natural sciences and in his explorations of languages beyond the all-pervasive Latin. The study of Hebrew and Greek was taken up seriously only about a hundred years later, while other languages and scripts had to wait more than two centuries for scholarly treatment.

3   FROM THE RENAISSANCE TO THE AGE OF REASON

3.1.   Revival of Philology and the First Printed Transliterations

The beginning of the Renaissance brought a study of the ancient languages in a desire to become acquainted with the sources, hitherto known only in inadequate or faulty translations into Latin, or even entirely unknown and yet to be discovered. Following the example of Petrarch and Boccaccio, who had first begun to learn classical Greek, scholars in Italy and soon also those in Western Europe began to devote themselves to the study of the heritage of Hellas; many of them also studied Hebrew in a new spirit of inquisitiveness about the sources of the Bible. Hebrew had always been considered as the first and common language of mankind, since the Book of Genesis said so, but few Christian scholars had bothered to learn the language from which the Vulgate had been translated. Now the desire to explore the sources of ancient literature, and the beginning of missionary activities in Asian countries revived the interest in Hebrew. Dante discussed the old question about which language the first man on earth had spoken in his work *De vulgari eloquentia*[42] and confirmed, of course, as had the

[41]My translation of the Latin text in Bacon (1859), p. 88.
[42]Dante Alighieri (1890), book 1, section 6; pp. 5–7.

Fathers before him, that it had been Hebrew, but he also concluded that Christ had spoken the same language.

The Spanish poet, theologian, and missionary Ramon Lull (1232?–1315) had studied not only Hebrew and Aramaic but also Arabic, which he mastered in spoken and written form so as to be able to convert the Muslim infidels by addressing them in their own language. It is unlikely that he was familiar with the works of his English contemporary Roger Bacon, but in many of his voluminous writings he also advocated the study of Oriental languages in order to train missionaries for the conversion of Jews and Saracens. In 1311 he petitioned the Council of Vienna on this matter, and the Council decreed the establishment of schools at Rome, Bologna, Paris, Oxford, and Salamanca with chairs in Hebrew, Chaldaic (i.e., Aramaic), and Arabic so that missionaries could study these languages. Meanwhile Franciscan missionaries had already begun to work in India, Pope Innocent IV and King Louis IX of France had sent emissaries to the court of the Mongols at Karakorum at about the time Bacon was preparing his great work, and shortly afterward Marco Polo returned from his famous voyage to China (1298). Thus the scholars of western and central Europe, who for hundreds of years had enjoyed the benefit of a common literary language, gradually became aware of the existence of Babel. To be sure, many different languages were spoken in late medieval Europe, but they were mainly used to conduct the affairs of everyday life, and only a few of them had been committed to writing. What little vernacular literature existed was at any rate written in Roman script, which every literate man could make out without difficulty. But in the world beyond the frontiers of the Holy Roman Empire, in the fabulous countries of the Orient, a multitude of languages were spoken, and these were written in a bewildering variety of scripts that were as strange to the eye as were their sounds to the ear.

Together with silk and spices, the expanding trade with the Near and Far East brought manuscripts from Persia, India, and China to European courts and castles, where they were kept in the libraries that now began to be collected by kings and noblemen. With the growing interest in Oriental languages and their scripts, there soon arose also a need for some kind of transcription of the foreign names that appeared in translations from Oriental literature and in the accounts of foreign countries given by European travelers and missionaries. This was still done in the same way in which the matter had been handled since writing began, namely by a rough approximation of what the ears of these men had perceived when the names of persons and places had been uttered by native speakers. They somehow noted the strange sounds in Latin script, but many of these "transcriptions" were further distorted by scribes and copyists who, of course, were entirely ignorant of the original languages.

The invention of printing from movable type in the middle of the 15th century gave a new and strong impetus to the study of various scripts. While the first printed books sought to imitate closely the finest manuscripts and were set in Gothic type (or "black letter"), printers soon began to design Roman typefaces. Within a few decades types were cut for other scripts also, and the printing presses produced books in many languages and scripts, many of which had not been known to most European scholars a generation before.[43]

One incunabulum in particular deserves to be mentioned here, not so much because it is remarkable from a typographic point of view (it is set in black letter throughout) but because it is possibly the only one that contains whole passages of Hebrew and one passage of Turkish text transcribed into Latin: *Victoria contra Iudaeos,*[44] written by a Venetian cleric, Petrus de Brutis (Piero Bruto), who lived in the second half of the 15th century. In this rabidly anti-Semitic treatise he wished to show the wickedness of the Jews, citing as testimony for his contention verses from the Old Testament and passages from the Talmud which he very often transcribed phonemically, possibly to enable others to use them in oral disputations with Jewish scholars. His transcription was apparently not based on firsthand knowledge of Hebrew, but seems to have been done by listening to the sounds of Hebrew, probably as pronounced by a converted Jew who helped him in the compilation of the book. This would explain the many mistakes and errors found in the transcribed passages, the original text of which

---

[43]The first Greek letters appeared in print in 1465, only 15 years after Gutenberg's first experiments with movable type, in a Cicero edition printed by Fust and Schöffer in Mainz. In 1474 the first full text in Greek, the pseudo-Homerian Βατραχομνομαχία, was printed in Brescia; one year later the first Hebrew book, Raši's commentary on the Pentateuch, was printed in Reggio di Calabria. In 1491 Cyrillic type was used for the first time in Krakow by Sweipolt Fiol for prayerbooks of the Orthodox church. The first book set in Arabic type, a translation of a Book of Hours, was printed in 1514 by Gregorius de Gregoriis, a Venetian, in the town of Fano in Italy; four years later the first printed *Qur'ān* was produced by Paganini of Brescia, who used a different typeface.

Less than 80 years after Gutenberg's Bible had come off the press, Geofroy Tory (1529) published his *Champ fleury,* a learned and beautifully printed treatise on typography and the art of lettering which contained specimens of one Roman and four Gothic (black letter) styles, Hebrew, Greek, Arabic (in the book designated as "Persian, Arabic, African, Turkish and Tatar," thus showing a good understanding of the various languages written in Arabic script), Chaldaic (Syriac), and Utopian (i.e., the fanciful characters printed on the last page of Sir Thomas More's *Utopia,* published only a few years earlier, in 1516). The specimens of these various alphabets were, however, engraved and not printed from movable type. It seems that at that time Hebrew, Arabic, and Syriac types were available only to a few printers in Italy but not elsewhere. Peter Giles, the printer of the *Utopia,* states in his note to the reader, appended to the first edition of the book: " . . . I have not as yet the true characters or forms of the Utopian letters. And no marvel, seeing it is a tongue much stranger to us than the Indian, the Persian, the Syrian, the Arabic, the Egyptian, the Macedonian, the Slavonian, the Cyprian, the Scythian, etc. Which tongues, though they are nothing so strange among us as the Utopian is, yet their characters we have not. . . ." This mock excuse shows that printers at the beginning of the 16th century were well aware of a great variety of languages and scripts, for many of which (despite the protestations of Peter Giles) type was readily available and used. The Utopian alphabet was printed in later editions.

[44]Brutis (1489).

can be checked against the Hebrew source since Brutis always cites chapter and verse.[45] The pronunciation is typical for a speaker from northern Italy: initial vowels are aspirated, while initial [h] is mostly rendered by *a* or *e*. It is interesting to note that ח *(ḥet)* is often transliterated by *ch,* and שׁ *(šin)* by *sch,* although there is no uniformity and the transliterations *h* and *s* are also found. The book also contains a few sentences in Turkish, likewise transcribed phonemically; since it comprises only a few lines, it is difficult to tell much about the accuracy of this transcription.[46]

The art of the printer soon advanced from printing books in one script only to the production of polyglot and polyscript works. The first and one of the most beautiful books of this kind evěr printed was the great *Biblia polyglotta Complutensis,* commissioned by the Spanish archbishop Ximenes and edited by nine scholars from 1502 until 1517, but published only in 1522 in six large volumes. It was printed by Arnold Guillen de Brocar in the city of Alcalá de Henares (the ancient Roman Complutum, hence the epithet of the work), and contained in six parallel columns the Hebrew Masoretic text, the Septuagint, the Vulgate, and a Syriac version of the Pentateuch. Only a few years later a number of secular polyscript works were printed in Italy, France, and Germany, two of which were written expressly with the purpose of making European scholars better acquainted with the languages of the East and their scripts.

Guillaume Postel (1510?–1581), a Frenchman who in his youth had studied Hebrew under the famous Jewish grammarian Eliya Baḥur Levita in Italy and had then traveled widely through the Near East, was probably the first modern Orientalist who could base his works on personal knowledge of the countries, peoples, and languages about which he wrote. In 1538 he published a book entitled *Linguarum duodecim characteribus differentium alphabetum*[47] in which he displayed the scripts and explained the grammar of Hebrew, Samaritan, Arabic, Amharic (curiously enough called *alphabetum Indicum*), Greek, Coptic (called *alphabetum Georgianorum et Iacobitorum),* Serbian (i.e., Cyrillic), Glagolitsa *(alphabetum Dalmatianum aut Illiriorum),* and Armenian, and compared them with Latin and the Roman alphabet. In the Hebrew section each character is shown in a systematic table, listing from top to bottom its numerical value, the Hebrew letter itself, its name in Latin, and its transliteration by a Roman letter (see Figure 3.6). This is followed by a table and an explanation of

---

[45]The following is a specimen, culled at random: "'Hoc idem legitur psalmo LXXXI [i.e., LXXII, 7 in the Hebrew Bible and in the Authorized Version. H. W.]: Sifrach beiamaf soddiq ve rob schalom. Had beli iareach . . . Habet hoc etiam psalmo XXI: Charu iadei ve raglav. . . .'" (Brutis, 1489, leaf 56r.)

[46]Weil (1953) has analyzed the Turkish text that deals with the Immaculate Conception, the Virgin Mary, and the archangel Gabriel. Brutis included this passage to show that even the infidel Saracens were better than the Jews.

[47]Postel (1538).

the vowels and their signs, and by a display of several verses from Proverbs and the Psalms, with a Latin translation and a transliteration that employs an unusual method: the transliteration and translation are printed upside down so that each transliterated Roman letter can be read in exact alignment with the corresponding Hebrew letter. The transliteration follows the Sephardic pronunciation. When citing the biblical verses, Postel made a mistake in the first word, but this shows that he actually knew the language and was not a mere copyist. He wrote ראשית instead of תחילת , probably confusing Prov. 9: 10 with Prov. 4: 7, since both words mean "beginning, the first thing," so that the meaning is not affected (see Figure 3.7).

The Syriac and Arabic sections are similarly treated; for Arabic, all characters are shown in a synoptic table in their various forms and with their transliteration, and there is a separate table of all diacritical marks, their names in transliteration, and an explanation of their use. Specimens of Arabic text and a Latin translation (but no transliteration) are printed on several pages in two columns, Arabic on the left and Latin on the right. The Arabic text seems to have been set from type, which makes the book one of the earliest specimens of Arabic printing. At about the same time Postel published his *Grammatica arabica,* one of the earliest works on the Arabic language written by a Christian scholar; this book too was printed in Arabic type and contained some transliterations. Postel used to refer to himself as a *Gaulois cosmopolite;* he wrote many other works on the countries and customs of the Near East and pleaded for a union of all peoples and religions—a remarkable and daring proposition at that time, and a harbinger of what was a century later to become an idea applied to the writing of "all the world's languages." His book on alphabets is an important milestone in the history of script conversion, since it is the first printed compilation of alphabets made with the clear intention of transliterating them into Roman script, set out in a systematic manner and showing an amazing familiarity with the grammar of languages that not many people in Europe had even heard of at that time.

Postel's work was soon followed by a book written by his older friend Teseo Ambrogio (1469–1540), an Italian nobleman who taught Hebrew and Aramaic at the University of Bologna. In 1539 he published *Introductio in chaldaicam linguam . . .,*[48] which dealt mainly with the Syriac and Armenian scripts, and to a lesser extent with the Hebrew and Arabic scripts. The book also contained an "Appendix multarum diversarumque literarum," which was evidently based on Postel's earlier work, displaying specimens of some 30 other alphabets, including Coptic (*alphabetum Iacobitorum*), various versions of the Greek alphabet, the Amharic syllabary (*alphabetum Indorum*), and some rather fanciful concoctions said to be the scripts of the Egyptians, Etruscans, Chinese, and others. Most of these alphabets are cut in wood, but the Syriac and Armenian

---

[48] Ambrogio (1539).

❡De lingua Hebraica cæterarum omniũ
orientalium parente.
Canon generalis .

❡In omnibus omnium gentiũ linguis a quacũ ꝗ litera no﹣
men literę incipit ipſa eſt litera, vel literæ quæ nominãtur,
vt daleth incipit a,d,ergo d.pſi a ps,ergo ps.Fallit in ſemi﹘
uocalibus latinis & aleph & ain oriẽtaliũ, alioquin ſemper
verum eſt.

❡Literæ apud Hebræos ſunt. xxij. quarum
figuræ & nomina ita habent quæ per﹣
uerſe leguntur hoc modo.

9	8	7	6	5	4	3	2	1	Numeri
ט	ח	ז	ו	ה	ד	ג	ב	א	Figura

teth,heth,zain,vau,he,daleth,gimel,beth,aleph. Nomen

z   v   h   d   g   b.v. a,e,i,o,u. Ptãs.

200	100	90	80	70	60	50	04	30	20	10
ר	ק	ץצ	ףפ	ע	ס	[ן]נ	מ	ל	]כ	י

res,coph,zadic,phe,ain,ſamec,nun,men,lamed,caph,iod.

Vbi duæ figuræ ſunt;altera in fi﹣
ne tantum ſeruit.

400 300
ת   ש
tau,Sſin.

Carent illi vocalibus quarum loco puncta habent ſupra
vel infra literas collocanda,quorum figurę & nomina ſe﹣
quuntur.

Figure 3.6. Transliteration table for Hebrew, from Guillaume Postel's *Linguarum duodecim . . . alphabetum,* pp. [8–9].

ones seem to have been printed from cast types, and they are set out in a systematic manner, showing for each letter, from top to bottom, first the letter itself, then its transliteration into Roman, followed by the name of the letter in Syriac and its transliteration into Roman (see Figure 3.8). The book also contains a letter from Postel to Ambrogio and the latter's reply on matters of Oriental alphabets and languages.

The renewed interest in Semitic languages in Italy was chiefly due to the endeavors of Pope Leo X (Giovanni de' Medici), a brilliant Renaissance scholar

Quantitas, figura, nomen, poteſtas.

	Iongum ⟨⟩	Cametz a obſcurum.
a	breue ⟨⟩	Pathah a clarum.
	breuiſſimũ ⟨⟩	Hateph pathah a declinãs ad e.
	longum ⟨⟩	tzere e clarum.
e	breue ⟨⟩	Segol e declinãs ad a, vt in vltĩa vatés.
	breuiſs. ⟨⟩	Hateph ſegol e.
i	longum ⟨⟩	hiric. Lppter puũ pũctũ ⟨⟩ aſcribitur hic
	bre. ⟨⟩	hiric vt in holem.
o	longum ⟨⟩	holem vel vau holem.o.
	breuiſs. ⟨⟩	hateph cametz, o.
u	longum ⟨⟩	furec vel vau furec.u.
	breue ⟨⟩	Kibutz vel kibutz ſephataim vel me ꞊ lopum.v.

❡Seua pũctum eſt breuiſs, valens e, dicitur alio nomine hateph, id eſt, corripiens.   e

❡Lectio ſeu ſyllabarium ex longis ſyllabis.

נוּ כׇ גְ גָ מוּ מוֹ בִּי בֵּ בָּ אָן אוֹ vel אִ אֶ אֵ אָ

gu,go, gi, ge, ga,   bu, bo, bi, be, ba, u, o,   e i e a

❡Ex breuibus & breuiſs.

תُ שׁוּ רוֹ קׇ צַ פֶּ עַ סֶ נָ מֶ לֹ כַּ יְ טֶ הִ ו! זָ ה

thu, ſa, ro, ca, tzi, fe, a, ſa, nu, mo, li, che, ia, tu, ho, zi, ue, ha,

Figure 3.6. *(continued)*

himself, who encouraged the study of Hebrew, Aramaic, and Greek, and collected ancient manuscripts in these and other languages in the Vatican library, where many scholars were employed to edit and publish them. Before long, doubts began to be voiced about the accuracy of the Vulgate. Cardinal Cajetan wrote in the preface to his commentary on the Psalms, published in 1530, that St. Jerome's Latin rendering was essentially an interpretation of the original Hebrew and Greek texts and therefore did not truly transmit the word of God.[49]

[49]*The Cambridge history of the Bible* (1963), p. 64.

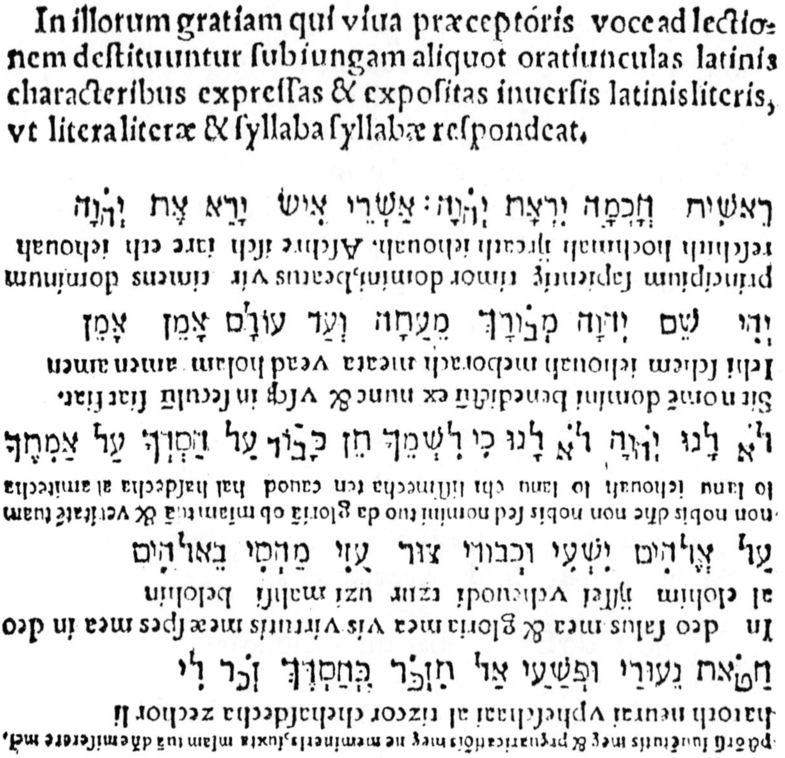

In illorum gratiam qui viua præceptóris voce ad lectio=
nem deſtituuntur ſubiungam aliquot oratiunculas latinis
characteribus expreſſas & expoſitas inuerſis latinisliteris,
vt literaliteræ & ſyllaba ſyllabæ reſpondeat.

רֵאשִׁית חָכְמָה יִרְאַת יְהֹוָה וְהָיָה יָרֵא אִישׁ אַשְׁרֵי׃

יְהִי שֵׁם יְהֹוָה מְבֹרָךְ מֵעַתָּה וְעַד עוֹלָם אָמֵן אָמֵן

לֹא לָנוּ יְהֹוָה לֹא לָנוּ כִּי לְשִׁמְךָ חֵן כָּבוֹד עַל חַסְדְּךָ עַל אֲמִתֶּךָ

עֹל אֱלֹהִים יִשְׁעִי וּכְבוֹדִי צוּר עֻזִּי מַחְסִי בֵּאלֹהִים

מֹאתֹ נְעוּרַי וּפְשָׁעַי אַל תִּזְכֹּר חַסְדְּךָ בְּחַסְדְּךָ זְכָר לִי

Figure 3.7.   Hebrew text transliterated and translated into Latin from Guillaume Postel's *Linguarum duodecim . . . alphabetum*, p. [11].

At about the same time the Reformation north of the Alps began to ask those same awkward questions: were the Pope and the Latin Vulgate to be the sole authority for God's word, or was it rather the Hebrew and Aramaic text of the Old Testament and the Greek text of the New Testament? Luther decided in favor of the original sources and translated his German Bible directly from the Hebrew and Greek (although he retained in most instances the spelling of proper names as given in the Vulgate). Following Luther's lead, many prominent Protestant theologians and scholars eagerly devoted themselves not only to the study of Hebrew and Greek, but also to the vernaculars that had been spoken in daily life for centuries, and which were now beginning to be used increasingly as literary languages, displacing Latin as the sole means of scholarly discourse.

One of the most influential of these scholars was Conrad Gessner (1516–1565), a Swiss physician and naturalist who was fluent in Latin, Greek, and Hebrew as well as in German and French, besides being able to read and

Syriam incolunt, quæ etiam Syriacæ dicuntur, & qui=
bus Antiochęna Patriarchalis Ecclesia in sacris vti=
tur, duę & viginti sunt, quę his figuris atꝗ nomi=
nibus exprimuntur. Caput. Primum.

V.	H.	D.	G.	B.	A.
Vau.	He.	Dolad.	Gomal.	Beth.	Olaph.

L.	C.	I.	T.	HH.	Z.
Lomad.	Coph.	Iud.	Teth.	Hheth.	Zain.

P.	Ga.A.	S.	N.	M.	
Phe.Pe.	Gain.Ain.	Somchath.	Nun.	Mim.	

Th.	Sc.	R.	Q.	ZZ.	
Thau.	Scin.	Ris.	Quoph.	Zzode.	

❡ Legūtur autem Hebræorum more, à dextro, in siniſtrū
latus. Habét pterea Chaldæi & Syri, alias quoꝗ minores
literas, quarum figuræ sunt infraſcrpitæ.

c

Figure 3.8. Transliteration table for the Syriac alphabet, from Teseo Ambrogio's *Introductio in chaldaicam linguam* . . . , p. 9.

write in several other languages. He is mostly known today as "the father of bibliography" because as a young man he single-handedly compiled a truly monumental work, the *Bibliotheca universalis,* the first general author bibliography in printed form. Some attempts had been made before his time to list books by various authors (mainly those who dealt with theological questions), but Gessner was the first to attempt to list the works of more than 10,000 authors who had ever written on any subject in one of the three classical languages, Latin, Greek, or Hebrew. The work was arranged in strict alphabetical order of the authors' first names (still following medieval practice), but an index of surnames and epithets was also provided. Since the text of the book was in Latin, the Latin alphabet was chosen to arrange the names of authors, and it was necessary to transcribe the names of Greek and Hebrew authors into Roman script when their names did not already have a Latinized form. Such transcriptions had, of course, been used throughout the Middle Ages, but Gessner not only founded modern bibliography as a scholarly profession, but made transcription (or Romanization, as we would say today) one of the three systematic principles on which all Western bibliographic practice has been based ever since. Firstly, he established the author entry as the main entry for a work. Secondly, he insisted on strict alphabetical order, using the word-by-word system of arrangement. Thirdly—and most important from the point of view of our present study—he listed all authors and their works in one unbroken sequence, using transcribed forms for any names not originally written in Roman script.

Gessner, who was truly a polyhistor, later devoted himself mainly to the fields of zoology, botany, and pharmacology but also made important contributions to philology and theology. He compiled extensive indexes to practically all of his works. The most elaborate was the index to his five-volume zoological encyclopedia *Historia animalium,* which was arranged in 11 languages and printed in three scripts: Roman (with German words in black letter), Greek, and Hebrew. Thus in his indexes he did not use transcription, wisely distinguishing the purposes and functions of a bibliography from an index to specific topics in a book.

Gessner's lifelong interest in languages induced him to write the first comparative philological study, *Mithridates,*[50] in which he compared the classical languages with the vernaculars of his own time; we deal with this aspect of his work in Section 4.1. Here it is of interest to mention that he appended to the book a large foldout table containing the Lord's Prayer in 22 languages, so as to demonstrate by a practical example what had been discussed in the text. The Hebrew version (to which Gessner paid particular attention since he was convinced that all languages had developed from Hebrew through successive "corruption") was transcribed phonemically both in the text and in the table according to the Sephardic pronunciation, probably following the usage in Qimḥi's Hebrew grammar, which Gessner had studied in his youth (see Figure 3.9). Gessner was

[50]Gessner (1555).

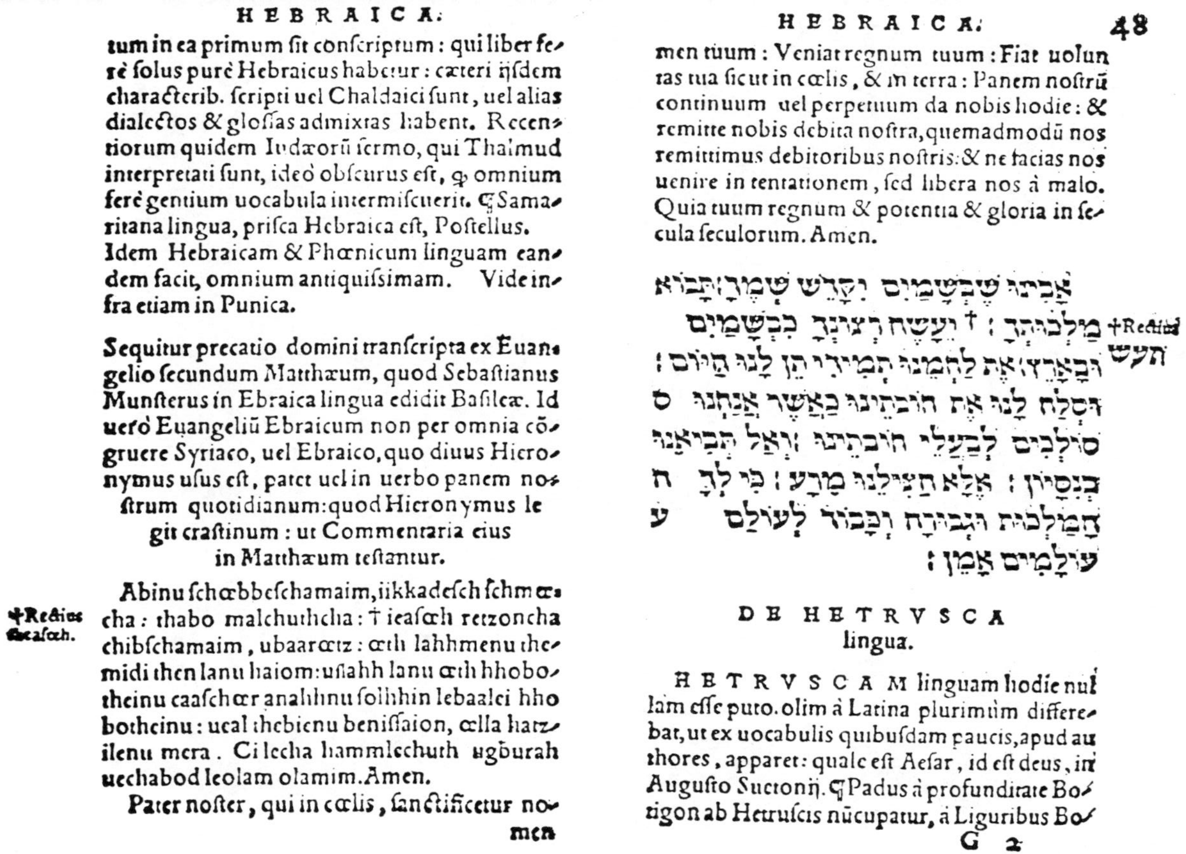

HEBRAICA.

lumina primum fit confcriptum: quiliber fe
rè folus purè Hebraicus habetur: cæteri ijfdem
characterib. fcripti uel Chaldaici funt, uel alias
dialectos & gloffas admixtas habent. Recen-
tiorum quidem Iudæorū fcrmo, qui Thalmud
interpretati funt, ideò obfcurus eft, quòd omnium
ferè gentium uocabula intermifcuerit. Sama-
riana lingua, prifca Hebraica eft, Poftellus.
Idem Hebraicam & Phœnicum linguam ean-
dem facit, omnium antiquifsimam. Videin-
fra etiam in Punica.

Sequitur precatio domini tranfcripta ex Euan-
gelio fecundum Matthæum, quod Sebaftianus
Munfterus in Ebraica lingua edidit Bafileæ. Id
ueró Euangeliū Ebraicum non per omnia cō-
gruere Syriaco, uel Ebraico, quo diuus Hieronymus ufus eft, patet uel in uerbo panem no-
ftrum quotidianum: quod Hieronymus le
git craftinum : ut Commentaria eius
in Matthæum teftantur.

†Redditⁱ Elⁱloⁱh.

Abinufchobbefchamaim, iikkadefchfchmeca-
cha : thabo malchuthcha : † icafcth retzoncha
chibefchamaim, ubaarœtz : œtl lahhmenu themidi then lanu haiom: ufahh lanu œth hhobotheinu caafchœr analihnu folihin lebaalci hho
botheinu: ueal thebienu benifaion, cella harz-
ilenu mera . Cilecha hammlechuh ugburah
ucchabod leolam olamim. Amen.

Pater nofter, qui in cœlis, fanctificetur nomen

HEBRAICA.

men tuum: Veniat regnum tuum: Fiat uolun
tas tua ficut in cœlis, & in terra: Panem noftrū
continuum uel perpetuum da nobis hodie: &
remitte nobis debita noftra, quemadmodū nos
remittimus debitoribus noftris:& ne tacias nos
uenire in tentationem, fed libera nos à malo.
Quia tuum regnum & potentia & gloria in fe-
cula feculorum. Amen.

[Hebrew text lines]

DE HETRVSCA lingua.

HETRVSCAM linguam hodie nul
lam effe puto. olim à Latina plurimùm differe-
bat, ut ex uocabulis quibufdam paucis, apud au
thores, apparet: quale eft Aefar, id eft deus, int
Augufto Suetonij. Padus à profunditate Bo-
rigon ab Hetrufcis nùcupatur, à Liguribus Bo-

G 2

Figure 3.9. The Lord's Prayer in Latin and Hebrew with Romanized transcription, from Conrad Gessner's *Mithridates* (f. 47v and 48r).

thus the first to use the Lord's Prayer as a paradigm for the exposition of various languages and scripts, and he was also the first to consider it necessary and useful to transcribe the Hebrew version in such a collection into Roman script. The trend set by Gessner continues to this day, and was particularly popular in the 18th and 19th centuries, when several collections of the Lord's Prayer were published that contained first several dozen, then 100, soon 200, 500, and nowadays 1000 or more versions,[51] all printed in their respective languages and scripts.

One of the earliest authors to follow Gessner's example was Hieronymus Megiser (1553–1618), a German philologist and geographer who sought to acquaint the reading public with the different languages spoken in Europe and elsewhere. To this end he published in 1593 a collection of the Lord's Prayer in 40 versions.[52] The Hebrew and Greek translations were printed in their original script, followed by a phonemic transcription (see Figures 3.10 and 3.11); Aramaic, Arabic, Ethiopic, Slavonic, Illyric (i.e., Serbian), Turkish, Armenian, Tataric, American Indian (no indication of which tribe) and even Chinese were rendered in transcription only. The more than 20 other languages were printed in Roman characters as used in each vernacular, but without any diacritical marks. The transcriptions were obviously intended for the use of German readers, both in orthography and in the manner in which the sounds were approximated. A second edition, enlarged to 50 languages, was published in 1603, which shows that there must have been considerable interest in such a collection of language and script specimens. The same author later also wrote a polyglot dictionary for 40 languages[53] and a Turkish grammar, the first part of which was devoted to the orthography of the language and to the Arabic script.[54] Megiser's works are necessarily quite superficial, but they are characteristic of the growing concern with foreign languages and scripts at the dawn of the Age of Reason.

The Reformation had been vitally concerned with the translation of the Bible, first into German, then into other Western vernaculars, and thereafter also into the languages and dialects of other peoples in central and eastern Europe in order to spread "the true religion" and to liberate them from "the ignorance of popery." Therefore it was only natural that the first scholars to devote themselves to the problems of diverse languages and their scripts were Protestants such as Gessner and Megiser, or "free spirits" like Postel. But the subsequent Counter-Reformation soon also made its important contribution to the growing concern with languages, primarily through the efforts of Jesuit missionaries who

---

[51]Some examples are Wilkins (1668) (see Figure 3.14), Chamberlayne (1715), Fritz (1748), Adelung (1817), *The Lord's Prayer* (1905), and North (1938). The collections by Chamberlayne and Fritz are especially interesting, because they also provide a phonemic transcription of the Lord's Prayer in most non-Roman scripts.

[52]Megiser (1593).
[53]Megiser (1603).
[54]Megiser (1612).

continued the work of their early predecessors in Asian countries, where they set out to spread the Gospel. Beginning in India, they proceeded to Nepal, Tibet, and finally even to China and Japan, countries that until the beginning of the 16th century had been practically closed to all foreigners. The Jesuits combined fervent religious zeal with sound scholarship, and above all they were eager to learn and study the languages of Southeast Asia and the Far East. They brought back with them to Europe quite accurate accounts of the geography of the countries and the customs of the peoples among whom they had lived and worked, as well as grammars of their languages, specimens of their scripts, and elaborate schemes for their transliteration into the Roman script.

To aid these missionary activities Cardinal Fernando de' Medici established a printing press in Rome to publish liturgical literature in foreign languages. The *Typographia Medicea linguarum externarum* was installed in 1585 under the supervision of the Orientalist J. B. Raimondi, and published its first book, a translation of the Gospels into Arabic, in 1591. The Arabic and Syriac type fonts of the press were cut by the famous French typographer Robert Granjon, under the guidance of Raimondi. When the Roman Catholic Church established the Congregatio de Propaganda Fide in 1622 as the central organization for missionary work in Asia and Africa, the Typographia Medicea was incorporated with it. It was at that time the only printing press to have a large number of type fonts for various non-Roman scripts.

One of its most ambitious works was a memorial volume for the French humanist, astronomer, and linguist Nicholas Claude Fabri de Peiresc (1580–1637), who had corresponded with scholars throughout Europe in several languages, had collected books and manuscripts in "exotic" scripts, and had devoted himself especially to the study of the Coptic language, thus laying the foundation for the study and ultimate deciphering of Egyptian hieroglyphic writing by his compatriots de Sacy and Champollion some 200 years later. In one part of the memorial volume in his honor, entitled *Panglossia,*[55] there were epitaphs in 40 languages, including Syriac, Georgian, Armenian, Ethiopic, Coptic, and Persian and many others, all printed in their respective original scripts. Those written in "Brachmanicum" (i.e., Sanskrit) and Japanese, however, were transcribed into Roman characters, and they are among the earliest specimens of consecutive text in these languages to be rendered in the Roman script.

3.2. Early Phonetic Alphabets

The preoccupation of Renaissance humanists with philology also led to the earliest attempts to create phonetic alphabets or at least to reform the archaic spellings of French and English, so as to make it easier to pronounce written

[55]Bouchard (1638).

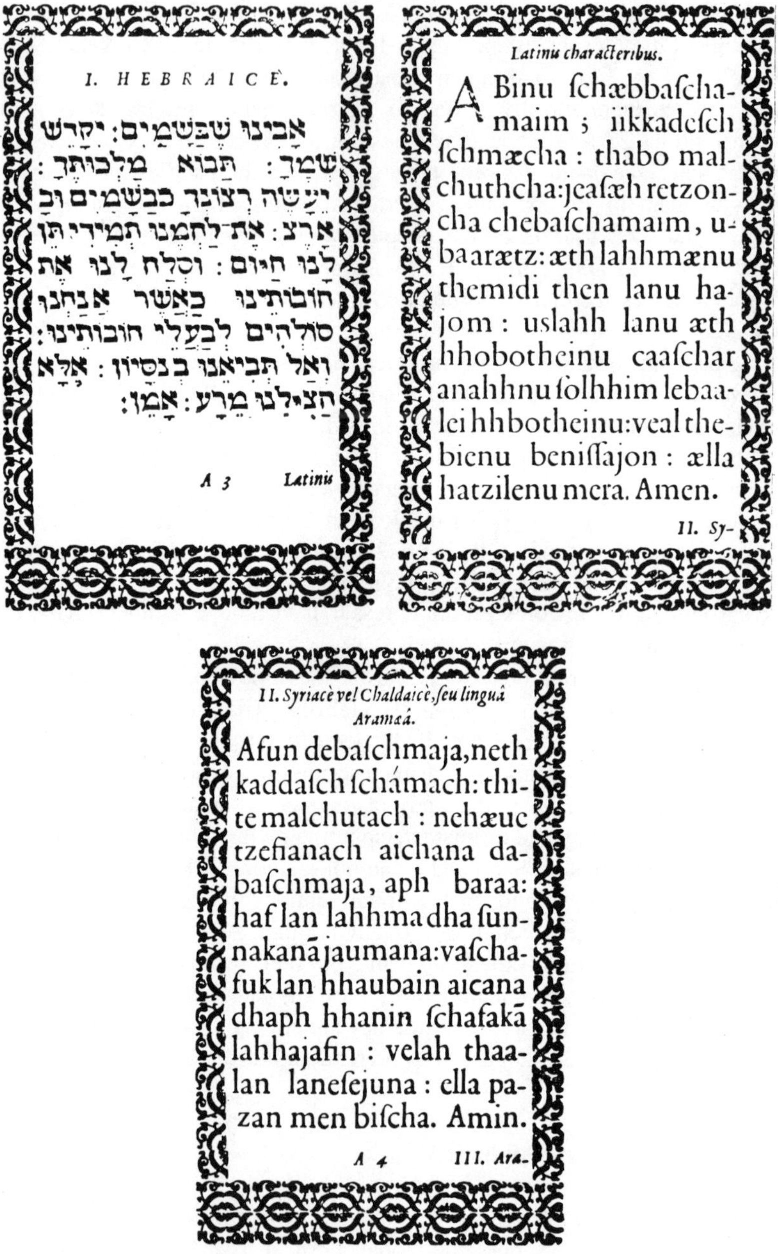

אָבִינוּ שֶׁבְּשָׁמַיִם: יְקָרֵשׁ
שֵׁמָךְ: תָּבוֹא מַלְכוּתֶךָ:
יֵעָשֶׂה רְצוֹנֶךָ כְּבְשָׁמַיִם וּבָ־
אָרֶץ: אֶת־לַחְמֵנוּ תְּמִידֵי תֵּן
לָנוּ חַיוֹם: וּסְלַח לָנוּ אֶת
חוֹבוֹתֵינוּ כַּאֲשֶׁר אֲנַחְנוּ
סוֹלְחִים לְבַעֲלֵי חוֹבוֹתֵינוּ:
וְאַל תְּבִיאֵנוּ בְּנִסָּיוֹן: אֶלָּא
חַצִּילֵנוּ מֵרַע: אָמֵן:

A 3   *Latinis*

A Binu fchæbbafcha-
maim ; iikkadefch
fchmæcha : thabo mal-
chuthcha:jcafæh retzon-
cha chebafchamaim, u-
baarætz: æth lahhmænu
themidi then lanu ha-
jom : uslahh lanu æth
hhobotheinu caafchar
anahhnu folhhim lebaa-
lei hhbotheinu:veal the-
bienu beniffajon : ælla
hatzilenu mera. Amen.

II. Sy-

Afun debafchmaja,neth
kaddafch fchámach: thi-
te malchutach : nchæue
tzefianach aichana da-
bafchmaja, aph baraa:
haf lan lahhma dha fun-
nakanā jaumana:vafcha-
fuk lan hhaubain aicana
dhaph hhanin fchafakā
lahhajafin : velah thaa-
lan lanefejuna : ella pa-
zan men bifcha. Amin.

A 4   III. Ara-

Figure 3.10. Transcription of the Hebrew and Aramaic versions of the Lord's Prayer, from Hieronymus Megister's *Specimen quadraginta linguarum.*

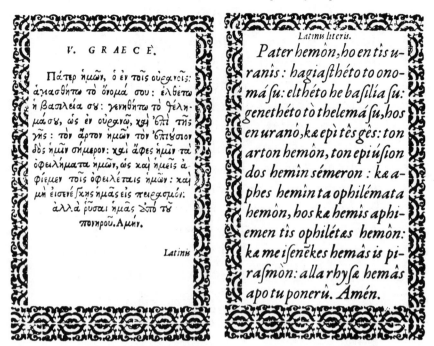

Figure 3.11. Transcription of the Greek version of the Lord's Prayer, from Hieronymus Megiser's *Specimen quadraginta linguarum.*

words "at sight." The first proposal of this kind was published by Louis Meigret (fl. 16th century) of Lyon, a member of the circle of seven poets and writers who, under the leadership of Pierre de Ronsard, had formed the *Pléiade* group. They had set themselves the aim of ridding the French language of coarse expressions and native literary forms, and casting it in the mold of classical Latin and Greek. Meigret felt that the unwieldy spelling of the language should also be reduced to something more akin to the actual pronunciation. He published his phonetic spelling scheme, on which he had worked for 12 years, under the title *Le tretté de la grammęre françoęze*[56] (see Figure 3.12). He used several modified letters and tried to eliminate some of the worst inconsistencies of French spelling, but neither his fellow poets of the *Pléiade* nor other French writers seem to have taken notice of his proposal. Perhaps it did not improve greatly on the spelling then used, but Meigret's work deserves attention as the earliest instance of a deliberately invented phonetic spelling system, devised for a language which is still badly served by its archaic spelling more than 400 years later.

---

[56]Meigret (1550).

thieu q'ęn matin:ę fubfeqęmmęnt font f,z, ę çh
qe j'eftime vne f molle . Qant a çęlles qe lę'
Gręcs tienet pour orphelines, ęlles ne lęs font
pas toutes: car l, ęn la lange Françoęze , vne
voęz plus molle qe fa primitiue: aofi a n, qi font
l, ꞧ:lęs feules m, ę i confonantes demeuret orphelines. Ao regard de x, ç'ęt vne voęs compo-
zée de cf, ou gf,ę pourtât ęlle n'aogmęte point
le nombre dę' voęs Françoęzes.Męs affin qe la
conoęffançe d'ęlles foęt plus ęzée, j'ey auizé de
lę' peindr' ę leur baller leur' noms felõ leur puif-
fançe,ę de lęs ordoner felon leur affinité.

a	*g ga ou gamma*
ę ouuert.	*ch cha afpiré*
e clós	*d de*
i Latin.	*t te*
o ouuęrt	*th the afpiré*
ou clós	*ſ, ç, s , es*
u	*ʒ ʒęd.*
y Gręc de męme puif-	*çh çhe*
fançe qe l'i	*l ęl*
b be	*l̨ ęl molle*
p pe	*m ęm*
f ef	*n ęn*
ph phi	*ꞧ ęn molle*
u confo.	*r ęr*
c ca Latin	*i ji confonante*
k ca Gręc,ou kappa	*x, cs, ks, gs, ix*
q qu	

Des

Figure 3.12. Louis Meigret's French phonetic alphabet, from his *Grammęre françoęze*, f. 15v. The text shows the application of the system.

At the same time problems of pronunciation and phonetic spelling also began to occupy the minds of scholars and statesmen across the Channel, despite the political and religious turmoil that plagued England during the reign of Edward VI and Mary Tudor. The first to propose a reformed English spelling was Sir John Cheke (1514–1557), Privy Councillor and Secretary of State to the King, and one of the most learned men of his age. He was instrumental in reviving the study of Greek in England, and devoted much effort to determining the original pronunciation of that language, an issue that involved him in a bitter controversy with other scholars and clergymen. His Greek studies also led him to consider the chaotic state of English spelling and its discrepancies from actual pronunciation, as well as what he considered the corruption of the English language by Latin and Greek words which crowded out Anglo-Saxon roots. He intended to make a new translation of the Bible, and began with the Gospel according to St. Matthew.[57] In this work he used as many Anglo-Saxon words as possible instead of those of foreign origin *(mooned* for *lunatic, gainrising* for *resurrection,* etc.), and also introduced a new phonetic spelling method. He wrote *taak* for *take, maad* for *made, giv* for *give, belev* for *believe, dai* for *day,* and so forth. Because of Cheke's early death following his imprisonment for heresy and subsequent recantation, this translation and the proposal for a reformed spelling remained in manuscript form and did not exert any influence on his contemporaries (it was edited and printed only 300 years later).

A few years later Cheke's friend and successor as Secretary of State, Sir Thomas Smith (1513–1577) also dealt with the issue of Greek pronunciation and in 1568 published a book on the topic[58] to which he appended a treatise on the reform of English spelling, *De recta et emendata linguae anglicae scriptione dialogus,* the first such proposal to be issued in printed form. In the following year, 1569, there appeared a book by John Hart (d. 1574), *An orthographie*[59] which also proposed a simplified phonetic spelling, including 6 new letters representing sounds that could not be written unambiguously with the existing 24 letters of the Roman alphabet. Hart had visited France, where he had made the acquaintance of Meigret, whose ideas on phonetic spelling influenced him. The book was based on an earlier unpublished manuscript written in 1551, in which numerous examples of French and Italian pronunciation are given and compared with English words.[60] Hart's work thus preceded those of Cheke and Smith, and it gained some posthumous fame when Sir Isaac Pitman reprinted part of it in one of his own books on "Phonography" and transcribed it into his shorthand system.

---

[57] Cheke (1843). On Cheke's attempts to reform English spelling, see Strype (1705), pp. 211–214. A specimen of the translation of Matthew, *ibid.,* pp. 214–215.
[58] Smith (1568). A table of Smith's proposed alphabet is printed in Strype (1698), appendix, p. 5.
[59] Hart (1569).
[60] Ellis (1869), v. 4, pp. 794–797.

Another effort to introduce a phonetic alphabet was made by William Bullokar (1520?–1590?) in his *Book at large for the amendment of orthographie for English speech*,[61] published in 1580. He says that "fower and twenty letters are not sufficient to picture Inglish speech" (p. 1) which "wants 40 letters altogether" (p. 21)—a remarkably accurate statement in the light of modern linguistic research, which has established that this is indeed the number of English phonemes.[62] Although Bullokar's system was rather complicated, he went one step further than his predecessors and transcribed existing works of literature into his phonetic alphabet to show how it worked. He published the fables of Aesop, some works by Cicero, and other books which thus became the first books in English to be printed in phonetic transcription.

Possibly inspired by Bullokar was the work of a clergyman, Alexander Gill (1564–1635), who in his *Logonomia anglica*,[63] published in 1619, also proposed the use of a phonetic alphabet of exactly 40 letters. He had as little success as any of his predecessors who proposed their spelling systems at a time when English orthography was still far from uniform and standardized; indeed, this lack of uniformity was one of the principal reasons for their attempts at spelling reform. But the forces of convention governing the written language were already too strongly ensconced. Faced by the stubborn conservatism of scribes (who had a vested interest in keeping English orthography as complicated as possible) and by resistance from grammarians and lexicographers who became the self-styled guardians of the English language and its spelling, these early reforms were doomed to failure, as were those of many other keen minds in the centuries to come.

All these attempts to create phonetic alphabets were aimed at the spelling reform of *one* language (French or English) and were based on the Roman script, thus not involving any transcription in the strict sense. Some of them were more fanciful than useful, but they are nevertheless important as contributing factors in the evolution that led in the following century to the idea of an "universal alphabet," which we consider in Section 3.3. They were also the forerunners of the various phonetic writing systems developed during the 19th century which ultimately led to the International Phonetic Alphabet.

3.3. Universal Languages and "Real Characters"

The Latin language, which for more than a millenium had been the *lingua franca* of the learned world, began to lose its supremacy during the latter half of the 16th century, and the use of vernaculars in spoken and written scholarly communica-

---

[61]Bullokar (1580).
[62]Cherry (1966), p. 97.
[63]Gill (1619).

tion spread rapidly in the first half of the 17th century. The Accademia dei Lincei, founded in Rome in 1603, conducted most of its business in Italian, and Galilei, its most illustrious member, was the first to use his native tongue in a scientific treatise. The Académie Française, founded in 1635, began to devote itself to the compilation of a dictionary of the French language, and when Descartes published his *Discours de la méthode* two years later, he made a particular point in stating

And if I write in French, which is the language of my country, in preference to Latin, which is that of my preceptors, it is because I expect those who make use of their unprejudiced natural reason will be better judges of my opinions than those who give heed to the writings of the ancients only.[64]

The Royal Society adopted English as its language from its foundation in 1662, "preferring the Language of Artizans, Countrymen, and Merchants, before that of Wits, or Scholars,"[65] according to its first historian, Thomas Sprat. However the Society's Fellows were not moved, as one may think, by a spirit of democratic egalitarianism so much as by abstract and lofty philosophical principles inspired by Francis Bacon and Thomas Hobbes, which led some of them ultimately to a rejection of all natural languages and to subsequent endeavors to construct an artificial universal language with its own universal script.

The idea of a universal language and script seems to have had its roots in the reports on China and Japan and their unique writing systems that were published by Jesuit missionaries. It occurred to many philosophers and theologians that a universal language, written in a commonly understood script that would in itself express "things and notions" independent of sounds and guided only by the application of inductive reasoning, would offer an ideal means by which mankind, so long divided by various tongues, could again be united, if not in speech, then at least in writing. Many of them also foresaw unlimited possibilities of spreading the Gospel to the heathens, especially the Indians in the Puritan colonies of America.

Francis Bacon was the first to extol the virtues of the Chinese writing system in his *Advancement of Learning:*

Moreover, it is now well known that in China and the provinces of the furthest East there are in use at this day certain *real characters,* not nominal; . . . which represent neither letters nor words, but things and notions; insomuch, that a number of nations, whose languages are altogether different but who agree in the use of such characters . . . communicate with each other in writing; to such an extent indeed that any book written in characters of this kind can be read off by each nation in their own language.[66]

---

[64]Descartes (1912), p. 61.
[65]Sprat (1667), p. 113.
[66]Bacon (1605), Book VI, chapter 1, p. 439.

The term "real character," coined by Bacon, was adopted by most subsequent inventors of artificial languages and universal scripts. One of the earliest was the Dutch Jesuit Herman Hugo who, inspired by the reports of Ricci and Trigault on China and Japan, proposed in 1617 in his book *De origine scribendi* a universal language and script for all Europe to be based on the model of Chinese writing.[67]

But Bacon and his followers had also other reasons for pursuing the idea of universal language. The "old" science had been based on a thorough knowledge of Latin and Greek, and being a scientist had essentially been the equivalent of being a philologist; the "new" science, based on observation and experiment, sought to become independent of natural language, with its ambiguities and imperfections. During the 1630s the idea of a universal language as a more perfect vehicle for scientific thought and discourse began to germinate in the minds of some of Europe's most eminent scholars.

Descartes seems to have been the first to explore the idea of an artificially constructed language for philosophical purposes. In a letter to Mersenne, written in 1629, he suggested the use of universal symbols for concepts that would become the building blocks of a language more logical and precise than any of the existing natural languages.[68] His aim was apparently one that was achieved only more than 200 years later with the invention of symbolic logic; since his idea was not published at the time, it had but little immediate influence, though it was discussed in the circle of his friends and was later also pursued by Leibniz.[69]

Much more influential were the works of Jan Amos Comenius (Komenský) (1592–1670), the Moravian theologian, scientist, and educational reformer who had become famous all over Europe through his ingenious multilingual textbook of Latin grammar *Janua linguarum,* which he had first used to teach Czech children the rudiments of Latin and which was subsequently translated and augmented to comprise no fewer than 16 languages.[70] In the late 1630s he

---

[67]Hugo (1617).

[68]Letter to Mersenne, 20th November 1629. In *Oeuvres,* Paris, 1897, v. 1, p. 76.

[69]The idea of a universal system for the recording of human thought was the theme of Leibniz' inaugural thesis in Leipzig, *Dissertatio de arte combinatoria,* published in 1666, two years before Bishop Wilkins' *Essay towards a Real Character* (which, when he became acquainted with it, he rejected as being not "philosophical"). Leibniz was not at all concerned with language as a means of written or spoken communication. What he proposed was a system in which each and every idea in philosophy or science would have its own symbol or character, so that scholars could manipulate and analyze these basic building blocks to generate new ideas in a manner similar to algebraic notation. Like Beck and Wilkins, Leibniz also considered Chinese writing as a prototype of what he had in mind, and he corresponded on the subject with Jesuit missionaries who had worked in China and knew the language and script. He was also influenced by the ideas of Comenius, especially those concerning the foundation of scientific colleges, the compilation of a universal encyclopedia, and missionary work among native races.

[70]Comenius (1631). The original edition was followed only three months later by an English and French one (first published under the name of the translator, Jean Anchoranus, under the title *Porta linguarum),* and soon German, Swedish, Dutch, and other editions and versions were published, all of which were reprinted for almost 200 years and used in grammar schools all over Europe.

worked on a grandiose philosophical and theological scheme, the "Pansophia," which would harmonize all human knowledge in an encyclopedic manner through general education and a new universal language. His ideas became known to Samuel Hartlib (1599?–1662), a merchant of Anglo-Polish descent living in London, whose circle of learned friends constituted the "Invisible College" in which philosophical and scientific matters were discussed. Hartlib published Comenius' *Prodromus Pansophicus* in 1639 and wrote an introduction to it.[71] The members of the Invisible College were much impressed by Comenius' ideas, and Hartlib invited him to England to establish a pansophic college there. Comenius arrived in 1641 and immediately set forth his ideas for the college, the pursuit of its studies, and its activities in a pamphlet *Via lucis,* which was circulated secretly among Hartlib's friends because of the tense political situation in England.[72] The outbreak of civil war in 1642 forced Comenius to leave England, but his ideas led in due course to the foundation of the Royal Society, with the men of the Invisible College as its nucleus.

In the *Via lucis* Comenius concentrated on three issues: the foundation of a great scientific college, the compilation of an encyclopedia of all human knowledge, and a scheme for the conversion and education of the heathens, particularly the Indians of North America. All this was to be achieved by a universal language that would be based exclusively on "things" (as he had done in his *Janua linguarum,* in which each word was exemplified by a concrete object). The new language must be beautiful, comprehensive, and easy to learn, and above all it must become a safeguard against confused thought; it must be harmonious, with no discrepancies between things and concepts, so as to make all definitions superfluous and ensure that all men using the language would immediately understand each other.[73]

Comenius' ideas on a universal language and its use in the conversion of the heathens had an immediate and profound influence on the English Baconians, who soon went to great lengths in their efforts to disparage not only the use of Latin but also the study of any natural language, all of which were held to be impediments rather than aids to the expression of clear and rational thoughts. The most outspoken critic of languages and their study was the Puritan John Webster (1610–1682) who, in his critique of the universities, *Academiarum examen,* said:

[71]Comenius (1639). Hartlib also published an English translation of this work, *A Reformation of Schooles . . .*, London 1642.

[72]Comenius (1668). The work was published by Comenius himself only 26 years after it had been written, when it was safe to do so. In the preface he dedicated it to the Royal Society, which he praised for its scientific achievements and which he admonished to devote itself also to the study of spiritual and political issues, without a knowledge of which the education of a man would not be complete.

[73]Comenius (1938), p. 186. Comenius later elaborated on the properties of a universal language and its use in an unfinished treatise published posthumously: *De rerum humanarum emendatione consultatio . . .*, Halle, 1702. "Consultatio V: Panglottia."

The knowledge of Tongues beareth a great noise in the world and . . . there is not much profit or emolument by them . . . so for schollars to spend divers years for some small scantling and smattering in the tongues . . . is but toylsome, and almost lost labour.[74]

During the following two decades several scholars proceeded to propose or construct actual "universal languages," with the professed aim of removing the curse brought on mankind by the builders of the Tower of Babel, and thus opening a pathway to universal brotherhood among peoples and to the conversion of the heathens. One of the earliest proponents and also the one who ultimately produced the most elaborate scheme was John Wilkins (1614–1672), a remarkable man who was one of the founders of the Royal Society and for a time its secretary, a scientist, inventor, mathematician, linguist, and theologian who later became Bishop of Chester. In his *Mercury* (published in 1641, the year of Comenius' visit to England) he dealt mainly with the uses of cryptography, but also considered the creation of a universal language as a substitute for the imperfect natural languages. At that time he still thought to model such a language on Hebrew, mankind's "first" language—not only because of this ancient theological reason, but rather because he already perceived one of the main problems in the construction of an entirely unambiguous artificial language:

In the contrivance of [a universal language] there must be as many severall Characters as there are primitive Words. To which purpose the Hebrew is the best patterne, because that Language consists of fewest Radicalls.[75]

A few years later, in 1647, Robert Boyle envisaged not only a universal language but also Bacon's "real character" as being both feasible and desirable. As a scientist, he stressed the use of mathematical symbols:

If the design of the *Real Character* take effect, it will in some part make amends to mankind for what their pride lost them at the tower of *Babel*. And truly since our arithmetical characters are understood by all nations of *Europe*, though every several people express that comprehension with its own particular language, I conceive no impossibility, that opposes the doing that in words, that we see already done in Numbers.[76]

In the same year Francis Lodwick (or Lodowyck), a Dutch merchant living in London, published *A common writing,*[77] in which he advocated the use of a limited vocabulary expressed by "radicall characters in hieroglyphical representation"; the vocabulary was to be based on "primitive" words in existing languages.

[74]Webster (1654), p. 21.
[75]Wilkins (1641), p. 109.
[76]Boyle (1772), v. 1, p. 22.
[77]Lodwick (1647).

These early proposals for the construction of a universal language were aimed primarily at a more perfect substitute for the deficient and irregular natural languages. But around the middle of the century two additional requirements were made. The universal language ought to be based on a logical classification scheme, and it should be written by graphic symbols that *in themselves* would express the "nature of things," so that the new language and its script would serve as a means for the exact scientific description of "things" and learned discourse about them. The idea of a classification scheme as the basis for a universal language seems to have been introduced by Cyprian Kinner, a Silesian physician and collaborator of Comenius, in a letter to Samuel Hartlib written in 1647.[78] The desire to make the new universal language a precise scientific tool probably arose from the publication of Hobbes' *Leviathan* in 1651, a large part of which was devoted to the pitfalls and errors caused by imprecise and ambiguous language, and which contained the advice to "counselors" (throughout italicized in the original edition, to emphasize the importance of the matter) not to use "obscure, confused and ambiguous Expressions, also all metaphorical Speeches, tending to the stirring-up of Passion."[79]

In 1652 Lodwick published another work, the *New Perfect Language*,[80] in which he held that a universal language ought to be "the work of a sound philosopher, who from the knowledge of things and their order in nature" would decide on their names. There he gave an outline of his proposed characters, which were essentially logograms for basic roots and "distinctional marks" for derivatives.

In the same year another approach to the problem was taken by Sir Thomas Urquhart (1611–1660), the Scottish author and translator of Rabelais. He had also invented a universal character, apparently based on phonograms, the design of which he lost in the battle of Worcester in 1651. He first described his system in a treatise entitled *Eskybalauron*, reprinted in 1653 in his *Logopandecteison*,[81] claiming that he had "couched an alphabet materiative of all the words the mouth of man . . . is able to produce" and that he had brought "all these words within the system of a language, which, by reason of its logopandocie, may deservedly be intituled *The Universal Tongue*." He went on to expound 66 advantages of his scheme, by means of which "sooner shall one reach the understanding of things to be signified by the words of this language, than by those of any other," and used the opportunity to poke fun at the excessive use of stilted technical words.

We have already mentioned Webster's *Academiarum examen,* which was published soon afterward in 1654. Within the same year there appeared a reply

---

[78]Schulte-Albert (1974).
[79]Hobbes (1909), part 2, chapter 25, p. 199.
[80]Lodwick (1652).
[81]Urquhart (1653), as quoted in J. Cohen (1954), p. 55.

written by Seth Ward (1617–1689), a professor of astronomy at Oxford and later Bishop of Salisbury, entitled *Vindiciae academiarum,* that also contained a commentary on Hobbes' *Leviathan* and to which John Wilkins wrote a preface. In this work the idea of a universal character based entirely on mathematical symbols was clearly outlined, its inherent problems were recognized, and its purpose was set forth:

My first proposal was to find whether other things might not as well be designed by Symbols (as in Mathematics), and herein I was presently resolved that Symbols might be found for every *thing* and *notion*. . . . So that an Universal Character might easily be made wherein all Nations might communicate together, just as they do in numbers and in species. . . . And the thing proposed is feasible, but the number of several Characters will be almost infinite . . . and the learning of them either impossible or very difficult. . . . But it did presently occur to me, that by the help of Logic and Mathematics this might soon receive a mighty advantage, for all Discourses being resolved into sentences, those into words, words signifying either simple notions or being resolvable into simple notions, it is manifest, that if all the sorts of simple notions be found out, and have Symbols assigned to them, those will be extremely few in respect of the other, . . . the reason of their composition easily known, and the most compounded ones at once will be comprehended, and yet will represent to the very eye all the elements of their composition, and so deliver the natures of things.[82]

In other words, it remains only to find out what are the "simple notions" and to give them a unique notation; thus all problems of human communication are solved once and for all, the signs revealing automatically the "natures of things"! It is well to remember that the mechanical *perpetuum mobile* was at that time very much in the focus of scientific endeavor and was likewise expected to be the solution to the physical problems of energy and motion; its final invention was thought to be just around the corner. The creation of a universal language written in a universal character is the exact equivalent of the *perpetuum mobile* on the linguistic plane, and so it is not surprising that John Wilkins also occupied himself with eternal motion machines, some of which he described in his *Mathematicall magick.*[83]

So far there had been only proposals and philosophical speculations about a universal language and real characters. But now, within the span of little more than a decade, three works appeared that contained actual schemes. The first one, published in 1657 by Cave Beck (1623–1706), a clergyman, under the title *Universal character,*[84] introduced a logographic script with pronounceable digits for each English word, qualified by upper- and lowercase letters to indicate

[82]Ward (1654), pp. 20–21.
[83]Wilkins (1648) described several methods of constructing a *perpetuum mobile,* particularly one of the Archimedean screw type, of which he said, however, that "upon trial and experience I found it altogether insufficient for any such purpose."
[84]Beck (1657).

grammatical features. For example, *P* stood for "noun," *a* for the genitive case, and *s* for plural. The digit *3* in Beck's dictionary was assigned to the verb *abate;* thus *P3* meant *abater, Pa3 of abater,* and *p3s abaters.* Beck demonstrated his system by writing verses from the Bible in his universal language and script; he even envisaged a multilanguage dictionary based on his cyphers in which the same concept, however expressed in a natural language, would be denoted by a short combination of digits and letters. This was in fact one of the earliest applications of a classification system and its notation to multilingual dictionaries, an idea that was realized successfully only in our own time. Beck published his book in both an English and French edition to assure it the widest possible attention, and dedicated it to Francis Bacon.

Since John Wilkins was apparently the acknowledged authority on matters of universal languages, Beck had sent him the manuscript before its publication. Wilkins in turn showed it to George Dalgarno, a Scotsman who had taught at a grammar school in Oxford for many years, had become a member of Hartlib's circle of friends, and was also known to be engaged in a project for a universal language. As is so often the case among men working independently on the same or similar projects, Dalgarno did not think much of Beck's scheme. He held it to be "nothing else, but an Engimaticall waye of writing ye English language" (which was true enough for all of the schemes!) and stated that "I have another Treatise by me, wch was put forth ye yeare of God 1647 to that same purpose, wch doth farre exceed ye other."[85] The reference may be to Kinner's letter, to Lodwick's *Common writing,* or possibly to the beginnings of his own work, which he now hastened to get into print.

Dalgarno's *Ars signorum*[86] appeared in 1661. Like Beck's work, it was a lexicon of a universal language, but it was based on a detailed classification of "notions" and used the letters of the Roman script, augmented by the Greek letters η and υ Dalgarno's scheme is perhaps one of the distant ancestors of the International Phonetic Alphabet in its attempt to reduce the world's many languages to one universally acceptable and applicable script based on the Roman and augmented by letters borrowed from other writing systems.

Dalgarno, too, demonstrated the application of his scheme with biblical texts; his book contained a translation of the first chapter of Genesis and five Psalms, and also two fables of Aesop. The work impressed some Cambridge and Oxford dons, who recommended it to King Charles II for support; in due course the Royal Chancery issued a letter to Dalgarno that epitomized in one paragraph the ideas and aims of the bold language inventors of the age:

. . . judging it [Dalgarno's scheme] to be of singular use for facilitating the matter of communication and intercourse between people of different languages, and consequently

---

[85]Letter from Dalgarno to Hartlib, dated 20 April 1657. Quoted in Schulte-Albert (1974), p. 331.
[86]Dalgarno (1661).

a proper and effectual means for advancing all the parts of real and useful knowledge, civilizing barbarous nations, propagating the Gospel, and increasing traffic and commerce . . . for the general good of mankind.[87]

The most ambitious scheme, however (and the one to become best known to posterity), was the brainchild of John Wilkins, then Bishop of Chester. Wilkins distilled and refined the thoughts of his friends and colleagues in the Royal Society into a monumental work. Entirely abandoning his earlier plan for a universal language based on Hebrew, he presented his *Essay Towards a Real Character and a Philosophical Language*[88] in 1668 as a purely mathematico-logical construct, based on a classification scheme that was more elaborate than that of any of his predecessors. He started with the observation that many symbols such as +, −, ×, ♂, ♀, and ⊙ in mathematics and astronomy, though pronounced differently in various languages, are universally understood to sig-nify the same thing to educated men. From this he concluded that one could assign to every "thing and notion . . . a Real Character, namely, the expression of our Conceptions by Marks which should signify things, not words," similar to the Chinese writing system (of which he reproduced a specimen page in his book). Such a "real character" had necessarily to be based on a classification of all knowledge, assigning to every concept a fixed place and sign. Wilkins pro-vided for 40 main classes, which were further subdivided, resulting in a rigid system of pigeonholes for all "notions" he could think of. To each position in this system a real character was then assigned. Elaborate explanations and com-mentaries were given on the nature and composition of each logogram, for which the following, for the word *Father* in real character, may serve as an example:

⤙⤚   This next character being of bigger proportion, must therefore represent some Integral Notion. The Genus of it, viz.   ⤙   is appointed to signifie Oeconomical *Relation*. And whereas the transverse Line at the end toward the *left* hand hath an affix making the *acute* angle with the *upper* side of the Line, therefore doth it refer to the *first* difference of that Genus, which according to the Tables, is relation of Consanguinity: And there being an affix making a *Right Angle* at the other end of the same Line, therefore doth it signifie the second species under this Difference, by which the notion of *Parent* is defined. . . .[89]

Wilkins then proceeded to make each real character also pronounceable, so that the philosophical language could be spoken; for this purpose he invented a phonetic alphabet of 37 characters. The application of this script and the corres-ponding real characters are exemplified in a transcription of the Lord's Prayer (see Figure 3.13), and in a comparative table of that perennial paradigm, show-ing it in 49 languages and in real character. However only the real character

---

[87]Reprinted in Dalgarno (1834), pp. xi–xii.
[88]Wilkins (1668).
[89]*Ibid.*, p. 396.

version (no. 51) and the English one (no. 52) are transcribed phonetically (see Figure 3.14). The marginal notes indicate that 17 versions are based on Megiser, and 2 are taken from Gessner.

The Royal Society published Wilkins' work, thereby giving it the stamp of scientific respectability, but soon the Society lost all interest in languages, universal or otherwise, and the whole scheme remained an oddity, not least of all because the rapid advances in the natural sciences at the end of the 17th and the beginning of the 18th century made Wilkins' system of classification, on which in turn his real character was based, quite obsolete.[90] Still, the ingenious bishop's work, for all its whimsicality, prejudice, and preoccupation with theological dogma as displayed in his classification scheme, was not only the most ambitious of its kind, but was also the forerunner of our modern logographic writing systems in all branches of science and technology, from the letter designations for chemical elements to engineering drawing symbols and road signs, all of which, to repeat Wilkins' definition, are "marks which should signify things, and not words," and are internationally recognized and understood.[91]

The work of the inventors of universal languages may be considered early attempts at an application of the cybernetic Law of Requisite Variety. These men were primarily concerned with the bewildering variety of languages and scripts, and tried as best they could to substitute another set of variety to cope with the problem, namely one that could be controlled at will by the application of reasoning and logic. Their failure to achieve this laudable aim was caused by the fact that their "regulator" was entirely inflexible, tied as it was to a preconceived system of classification in which every "notion" had its fixed place, while the real "notions" expressed by human beings in natural language defy any such attempt (as the makers and still more the users of monohierarchical classification systems for books have come to learn the hard way). Thus the result of their systems, if ever put into use, would have been "confusion worse

---

[90]Several other attempts, both in England and on the Continent, were made to create universal alphabets, notably those by the German scholars J. J. Becher (1661) and Athanasius Kircher (1663), the famous Jesuit polymath, both of which used numerical schemes based on a Latin vocabulary. For more detailed accounts of this movement, see Funke (1929), R. F. Jones (1932), Goodhart (1952), Cohen (1954), and Cornelius (1965).

The role played by Comenius in the events that led to the foundation of the Royal Society has been explored by Young (1932), Turnbull (1947), and DeMott (1957). After the gradual demise of the idea of a universal writing system toward the end of the 18th century, it was still pursued by cranks and inveterate *Weltverbesserer*-types. Some of the more remarkable and scurrilous schemes were published by Matušík (1837), Bachmaier (1868), Rost (1891), and Parsell (1946).

[91]It is interesting to note that modern anthropologists use the logographs △ ○ for *marriage*, △ = ○ for *brother* and *sister*, and ⌐//⌐ for their *disjunction*. The similarity to Bishop Wilkins' logographs for family relationships is striking, even though it is probably entirely fortuitous.

CHAP. IV.

An Inſtance of the Philoſophical Language, both in the Lords Prayer and the Creed. A Compariſon of the Language here propoſed, with fifty others, as to the Facility and Euphonicalneſs of it.

AS I have before given Inſtances of the Real Character, ſo I ſhall here in the like method, ſet down the ſame Inſtances for the Philoſophical Language. I ſhall be more brief in the particular explication of each Word; becauſe that was ſufficiently done before, in treating concerning the Character.

The Lords Prayer.

Haɪ coba ୪୪ ɪa ril dad, ha bɑbɪ ɪo ſ୪ymtɑ, ha ſalba ɪo velcɑ, ha tɑlbɪ ɪo vemg୪, m୪ ril dady me rɪl dad ɪo velpɪ rɑl ɑi ril ɪ poto haɪ ſaba vaty, na ɪo ſ୪eldy୪s lɑl ɑɪ haɪ bɑlgas me ɑɪ ɪa ſ୪eldy୪s lɑl eɪ ୪୪ ɪɑ vɑlgas r୪ ɑɪ ɩa mɪ ɪo velco ɑɪ, rɑl bedodl୪ nil ɪo c୪albo ɑɪlal vɑgasɪe, nor ɑl ſalba, na ɑl tado, na ɑl tadalɑ ɪa ha pi୪by୪ ꝗ꜖ m୪ ɪo.

1	2	3	4	5	6	7	8	9	10	11
Haɪ	coba ୪୪	ɪa	ril	dad,	ha	bɑbɪ	ɪo ſ୪ymtɑ			ha
Our	Father	who	art	in	Heaven,	Thy	Name be Hallowed,			Thy

12	13	14	15	16	17	18	19	20	21	22	23	24	25	26
ſalba	ɪo velcɑ,	ha	tɑlbi	ɪo	vemg୪,	m୪ ril dady	me	ril	dad,	ɪo	velpɪ			
Kingdome	come,	Thy	Will	be	done,	ſo in Earth	as	in	Heaven,	Give				

27	28	29	30	31	32	33	34	35	36	37	38	39	40	41
rɑl ɑɪ ril ɪ poto haɪ ſaba vaty, na ɪo ſ୪eldi୪s lal aɪ haɪ bɑlgaɪ

to us on this day our bread expedient and forgive to us our treſpaſſes

42	43	44	45	46	47	48	49	50	51	52	53	54	55	56	57	58
me ɑɪ ɪa ſ୪eldy୪s lal eɪ ୪୪ ɪɑ vɑlgas r୪ ɑɪ, na mɪ ɪo velco aɪ rɑl

as we forgive them who treſpaſs againſt us, and lead us not into

Figure 3.13. The Lord's Prayer in "real character" and in "philosophical language," from Bishop John Wilkins' *Real character*, p. 421.

English	1. Our father who are in heaven	Hallowed be thy Name	
Hebrew	2. Abinu Shebbaſchamaim	Iikkadeſch ſchemecha	
Arabic	3. Yâ Abânalladi phiſſaꝛnawati.	Yatakaddaſu ſmoca	
Syriac	4. Abun dbaſhmajo	Nethkadeſh ſhmoch	
Æthiop	5. Abúna xabaſhamájath	Yithkadaſh-ſhimicha	
Greek	6. *Pater hemūn ho en tois ouranois*	*Hagiaſthéto tò onoma ſou*	
Copti	7. *Peniot etchenniphcoui*	*Mareſtoubonje pecran*	
Latin	8. Pater noſter qui es in cœlis	Sanctificetur nomen tuum	
Spaniſh	9. Padre nueſtro que eſtas en loscielos	Sanctificado ſea el tu nombre	
Porteguese	10. Padre noſſo que ſtas nos ceos	Sanctificado ſeja o teu nome	
French	11. Noſtre pere qui es es cieulx	Ton nom ſoit ſanctifie	
Italian	12. Padre noſtro che ſei ne' cieli	Sia ſanctificato il nome tuo	
Friulian	13. Pari neſtri ch' ees in cijl	See ſantificat la to nom	
Sardinian of the City	14. Pate noſtre che ſes in loſcels	Sia ſanctificat lo nom teu	
Sardinian of the Countrey	15. Babu noſtru ſughale ſes in ſoſchelus	Santuſiada ſu nomine tuo.	
Gryſons	16. Bab nos quel tii iſt in eſchil	Santifichio ſaia ilgtes num.	
Germ. ancient	17. Pater unſer du iu himel biſt	Din namo werde geneyliget	
Germ. modern	18. Unſer Uatter der du biſt im Him= mel	Geheyliget werde dein nahm	
Old Saxon	19. Uren fader thic arth in heofnas	Sie gehalgud thin noma	
Dutch	20. Onſe bader die in den hemelin (zijt	Uwen naem werde geheyligt	
Daniſh	21. Pader bor du ſom eſt i himmelen	Hellige boꝛde dit naffn	Megiſerus
Iſland	22. Uader to: ſun ert ai himmum	helgiſt bitt nam ti	M.
Lappian	23. Jſa incidljen joho oleoly taju abiſſa	Pulettu olbohon ſun nimeſſ	M.
Suediſh	24. Fadher war ſom eſt i himlom	helghat warde titt nampn	M.
Gothic	25. Itta unſar thu in himinina	Wihnai namo thein	M.
Carniſh	26. Ozha naſh kir ſi v' nebeſih	Poſvezhenu bodi iime tvoie	M.
Dalmatian	27. Otſce nas koyi-yeſſina nebiſſih	Szvetiſſe gyme tvoye	
Hungarian	28. *Miattyanckli vagy azmennyegbe*	*Meghſtentel teſſek az te neued.*	
Croatian	29. Ozhe naſh iſhe eſina nebeſih	Svetiſe jme tuoe	M.
Servian	30. Otze naſh iſhe jeſi v' nebeſih	Poſvetiſe jme twoje	M.
Walachian	31. *Tatal noſtru cinereſſi in ceriu*	*Sfincinſchaſe numelie teu*	M.
Bohemian	32. Otozie naſs genz ſyna nebeſich	Oſzwiet ſe meno twe	Geſberus
Luſatian	33. Woſch naſch Kenſch ſy nanebebu	Wſs weſchone buſhy me tworе	M.
Polonian	34. Ocziecz naſch ktory jeſtoſz wniebye	Swyecz ſie gymye twa	G.
Lituanian	35. Tewe muſu kurſey eſi danguy	Szweskis wardas tawo	
Livonian	36. Abes mus kas tu es eck ſckan debbeſſis	Schweitzz tows waarcz	M.
Ruſſian	37. Oche naſh Izgha ycaſe nanzbzſzgh	Da ſueateſa Ima tuoæ	
Tartarian	38. Atcha wyzom hhy hokta ſen ęguſch	Ludor ſenug adongkel ſuom	M.
Turkiſh	39. Babamoz hanghe gugteſſon	Chuduſs olſum ſsenungh adun	M.
Armenian	40. Hair mer or iercins des	Surb eglizzi anun cho	M.
Perſian	41. Ai pader makeh dar oſinàn	Pàk baſhoud nàm tou	
Chiniſh	42. *Ngò tèm fu' chè tſay thien*	*Ngo tem yuen ùl niùn chim xim*	
Welſh	43. Ein Tad yꝛ hwn wyt yn y neſo= edd	Sancteiddier dy entw	
Iriſh	44. Ir nathir atnigh air nin	Rabz far hanimti	Megiſerus
Biſcan	45. Gure aita cerue tan aicena	Sanctiſica bedi hiretcena	
Friſian	46. Us haita berſu biſſe yne hymil	Dyn name with heiligt	M.
Madagaſcar	47. Impzoy antſica tzau hanautangh and anghitſl	Ingharanan hoſiſahors	
Poconchi	48. Catat tazah bilcat	Ibi nim ta incaharcihi	
NewEngland	49. Hooſhun heſubquot	Quittiana tamunach wowſuonk	
Philoſ. Language	51. Has coba ꝟ ꝺ ril dad	Ha babꝛ io ſeynta	

52. Yur fádher hᵂitſh art in Hdlloed bꝛ dhyꝛ nm
héven: K k k 2

Figure 3.14. The Lord's Prayer in 51 languages, from Bishop John Wilkins' *Real character*, p. 435. No. 51 is the translation into "philosophical language," and no. 52 is a phonetic transcription of the English version. (Reduced size.)

189

confounded''; or in cybernetic terms, the variety threatening the well-being of such a system could not have been controlled, but would have been increased, thus leading to a more rapid destruction of the entire system (in this case, of meaningful communication).[92]

Yet the idea of imposing man-made controls on an unruly system was a true manifestation of the intellectual climate of the 17th century, when scientists occupied themselves with automata as much as those in our own time.[93] It would thus be entirely unjustified to dismiss the pathetic efforts of the universal language men to substitute an artificial *lingua franca*, intended for the use of scholars in place of the rapidly waning Latin, as merely another instance of the oddities invented by "natural philosophers" toward the end of the 17th century, something on a par with the idea of "phlogiston," which then dominated the emerging science of chemistry. Just as the phlogiston theory had its usefulness as a first approximation of a scientific explanation of the phenomenon of combustion, to be finally discarded only when advances in chemical experimentation had shown that it was untenable in the light of demonstrable facts, so also the preoccupation with universal languages, which had tried to reunite the diverse tongues of mankind by casting them all into an artificial mold, gave way to more fruitful attempts to discover unity in diversity by *comparing* languages.

What survived most definitely from the work of these men was their twofold motivation, which in due course became the reason behind the efforts to design systems of transliteration and transcription until the end of the 19th century. One was the dissemination of knowledge and through it the civilization of "wild and barbarous" peoples in Asia, Africa, and the Americas; the other motive, intimately connected with the first one, was the propagation of the Gospel, inspired by the firm belief in the superiority of the white man and the Christian faith.

3.4. The London Polyglot Bible

While the inventors of universal languages were busy with their schemes, philology had made real progress through the study of the languages actually used by various peoples, including their different writing systems. Much of this had been achieved by philologically trained missionaries who translated and transcribed the Bible, and it was thus only natural that the first truly systematic display of various scripts and their transliterations into Roman characters was produced in

---

[92] For a detailed discussion of the cybernetic aspects of script conversion see Chapter 6, Section 2 (pp. 399–413). In addition to their systemic shortcomings, the universal language systems of the 17th century were also inadequate from a linguistic point of view, as pointed out by Bodmer (1944), pp. 450–458.

[93] On the similarities in scientific and particularly linguistic conceptions in the 17th and 20th centuries, see Chomsky (1968), p. 5 et passim.

the *Biblia polyglotta* edited by Bishop Brian Walton[94] in 1657. This great work was the fruit of scholarly research by philologists and Bible scholars rather than of the somewhat fanciful attempts by earlier zealous amateurs. A whole chapter in Walton's introduction was devoted to the subject of the scripts used in the 8 languages of the work, and 13 alphabets were displayed, giving for each the name of the letters, their form and transliteration, and where applicable, their numerical value. The 13 alphabets were Hebrew (square and rabbinical script), Samaritan, Syriac, Arabic (page 11); Persian, Ethiopic, Armenian (page 12); Coptic, Cyrillic, Glagolitic, Georgian, Gothic (page 13). Chinese (in the form of a colophon) and Greek were shown only in specimens of text but were not transliterated (page 14) (see Figure 3.15). Five tone values of Chinese were explained in the accompanying text and indicated by diacritical marks: yâ, ya, yà, yá, and yǎ.

All scripts except the Chinese specimen were set from new type especially cut and cast for this typographical masterwork, which was printed by Thomas Roycroft in London. For more than a century it remained the standard source for transliteration of Oriental scripts, and some of its tables are still used today in virtually the same form by philologists and Bible scholars.

The only major script missing from this work is the Devanagari script, which was to become the focus of philological and paleographic studies about a hundred years later, ushering in the age of modern comparative philology.

4. THE AGE OF COMPARATIVE PHILOLOGY

4.1. Some Early Works

The beginnings of the comparative study of languages can be traced to Jewish grammarians in Spain and North Africa during the 10th to 12th centuries, for whom Hebrew was the liturgical (and to some degree the vernacular) language, while Arabic was the accepted medium of learned discourse and writing as well as the daily language of the societies in which they lived. They were thus in an excellent position to observe that Hebrew, Aramaic, and Arabic formed one family of languages with many similarities in vocabulary, grammatical structure, and sounds. The earliest writer to compare Hebrew and Arabic seems to have been Dunaš ibn Tamim (890?–956?), of whose works, however, no trace remains other than partial translations in Ibn Ezra's writings. Yehuda ben David Ḥayyuǧ (945?–1000?) wrote three books on Hebrew grammar, only fragments of which have survived; he also made many comparisons between Hebrew and Arabic,

---

[94]*Biblia polyglotta* (1657).

Alphabeta Linguarum Præcipuarum hodiernarum sequuntur; scil. Hebraicæ et Chaldaicæ, cum literis Rabbinicis; Samaritanæ, Syriacæ, cum literis Nestorianis & antiq. Estrangelis; Arabicæ, Persicæ, Æthiopicæ, Armeniacæ, Coptæ sive Ægyptiacæ, Illyricæ, Dalmaticæ, Georgianæ, Gothicæ; cum specimine characterum Chinensium, & Græc. in MS. Alexandrino.

1 Alphabetum Hebraicum & Chaldaicum.

Literæ Rabbinicæ.

Nomen.	Figura.	Potestas.	Ital. Germ.
1	Aleph	א	Aspiratio lenis.	ה א
2	Beth	ב	V Conf. vel B.	ב ב
3	Gimel	ג	Gh. vel G.	ב ג
4	Daleth	ד	Dh. vel D.	ד ד
5	He	ה	H.	ה ה
6	Vau	ו	V. alis W.	ו ו
7	Zain	ז	Z. vel ds.	ו ז
8	Cheth	ח	Ch. alis Hh.	ה ח
9	Teth	ט	T. alis Tt.	ט ט
10	Jod	י	J. Consonans.	' '
20	Caph	כ	Ch. vel alis K.	כ כ
30	Lamed	ל	L	ל ל
40	Mem	מ	M	ה מ
50	Nun	נ	N	ה נ
60	Samech	ס	S. acutum.	ס ס
70	Ajin	ע	Aa. alis Gn.	ע ע
80	Pe	פ	Ph. vel P.	פ פ
90	Tsade	צ	Ts. vel Sf.	ב צ
100	Koph	ק	Kalis Q.	ק ק
200	Resch	ר	R.	ו ר

300	Schin vel	ש	Sh.	ש ש
	Sin		S.	
400	Tau	ת	Th. vel T.	ת ת

Literæ Rabbinicæ finales.

Literæ communes finales. Ital. מ ם ן ף ץ
Germ. מ ם ן ף ץ
ן ו ן ן ז

3 Alphabetum Syriacum.

Literæ Syriacæ.

Nomen.	Figura. In fine. In medio. In Initio.	Potestas.	Duplices.	Nestorianæ.	Estrangelæ.
1 Olaph		Aspir.tenuiss.			
2 Beth		B			
3 Gomal		G.Gh			
4 Dolath		D.Dh			
5 He		H			
6 Wau		V vel W			
7 Zain		Z			
8 Cheth		Ch.Hh.			
9 Teth		T			
10 Jud		J conf.			
20 Coph		C			
30 Lomad		L.			
40 Mim		M			
50 Nun		N			
60 Semchath		S			
70 Ae		Aa			
80 Pe		P			
90 Tsode		Tf			
100 Koph		K			
200 Risch		R			
300 Schin		Sh			
400 Tau		T			

2 Alphabetum Samaritanum.

	Nomen.	Figura.	Potestas.
1	Aleph		א
2	Beth		ב
3	Gimel		ג
4	Daleth		ד
5	He		ה
6	Vau		ו
7	Zain		ז
8	Hheth		ח
9	Teth		ט
10	Jod		י
20	Caph		כ
30	Lamed		ל
40	Mem		מ
50	Nun		נ
60	Sameth		ס
70	Ain		ע
80	Pe		פ
90	Tsade		צ
100	Koph		ק
200	Resh		ר
300	Sha		ש
400	Tau		ת

4 Alphabetum Arabicum

	Nomen.	Figura. Final. Med. Init.	Potestas.
1	Elif		Spirit. lenis.
2	Be		B
3	Te		T

Alphabetum Arabicum.

	Nomen.	Figura. Final. Med. Init.	Potestas.
4	Thse		T tlesm.
5	Gjim		G Giemb.
6	Hha		Hh
7	Cha		Ch
8	Dal		D
9	Dshal		D tlesm.
10	Re		R
11	Ze		Z
12	Sin		S
13	Schin		Sh
14	Sad		S
15	Dad		D
16	Ta		T
17	Da		D

Alphabetum Arabicum.

	Nomen.	Figura. Final. Med. Init.	Potestas.
18	Aain		y
19	Gain		G
20	Fe		F
21	Kaf		K
22	Kef		C
23	Lam		L
24	Mim		M
25	Nun		N
26	Wau		W
27	He		H
28	Je		J conf.
	Lam elif		La

5 Alpha-

Figure 3.15. Transliteration tables from Bishop Brian Walton's introduction to the *Biblia polyglotta*, v. 1, Prolegomena ii, pp. 11–14. (Reduced size.)

5 Alphabetum Persicum.

Nomen.	Figura.				Poteſtas.
		Final.	Med.	Init.	
1 Elif	ا	ا	ا	ا	Spirit. lenis.
2 Be	ب	ب	ب	ب	B
3 Pe	پ	پ	پ	پ	P
4 Te	ت	ت	ت	ت	T
5 Se	ث	ث	ث	ث	S
6 Gjim	ج	ج	ج	ج	G Guid.
7 Che	چ	چ	چ	چ	Ch Arb.
8 Hha	ح	ح	ح	ح	Hh
9 Cha	خ	خ	خ	خ	Ch.χ.
10 Dal	د	د	د	د	D
11 Zal	ذ	ذ	ذ	ذ	Z
12 Re	ر	ر	ر	ر	R
13 Ze	ز	ز	ز	ز	Z
14 Zhe	ژ	ژ	ژ	ژ	Zh Arb.
15 Sin	س	س	س	س	S
16 Schin	ش	ش	ش	ش	Sh
17 Sad	ص	ص	ص	ص	SS Arb.
18 Zad	ض	ض	ض	ض	Z
19 Ta	ط	ط	ط	ط	T
20 Za	ظ	ظ	ظ	ظ	Z
21 Aain	ع	ع	ع	ع	A seu V
22 Gain	غ	غ	غ	غ	G Arb.
23 Fe	ف	ف	ف	ف	F
24 Kaf	ق	ق	ق	ق	K
25 Kef	ك	ك	ك	ك	C vel K.
26 Ghaf	گ	گ	گ	گ	Kh seu Gh.
27 Lam	ل	ل	ل	ل	L
28 Mim	م	م	م	م	M
29 Nun	ن	ن	ن	ن	N
30 Vau	و	و	و	و	V
31 He	ه	ه	ه	ه	H
32 Ye	ی	ی	ی	ی	Y Arb.

6 Alphabetum Æthiopicum.

Tabula ſyllabarum.

Nomen.	Figura.							Numeri.
	A	U	I	A	E	E	O	
	Brev.	long.	lon.	lon.	lon.	brev.	long.	
Hoi	ha ሀ	hu ሁ	hi ሂ	ha ሃ	he ሄ	he ህ	ho ሆ	1
Lau	la ለ	lu ሉ	li ሊ	la ላ	le ሌ	le ል	lo ሎ	2
Haut	ha ሐ	hu ሑ	hi ሒ	ha ሓ	he ሔ	he ሕ	ho ሖ	3
Mai	ma መ	mu ሙ	mi ሚ	ma ማ	me ሜ	me ም	mo ሞ	4
Saut	ſa ሠ	ſu ሡ	ſi ሢ	ſa ሣ	ſe ሤ	ſe ሥ	ſo ሦ	5
Res	ra ረ	ru ሩ	ri ሪ	ra ራ	re ሬ	re ር	ro ሮ	6
Saat	ſa ሰ	ſu ሱ	ſi ሲ	ſa ሳ	ſe ሴ	ſe ስ	ſo ሶ	7
Kaf	ka ቀ	ku ቁ	ki ቂ	ka ቃ	ke ቄ	ke ቅ	ko ቆ	8
Bet	ba በ	bu ቡ	bi ቢ	ba ባ	be ቤ	be ብ	bo ቦ	10
Tau	ta ተ	tu ቱ	ti ቲ	ta ታ	te ቴ	te ት	to ቶ	10
Hharm	ha ኀ	hu ኁ	hi ኂ	ha ኃ	he ኄ	he ኅ	ho ኆ	20
Naas	na ነ	nu ኑ	ni ኒ	na ና	ne ኔ	ne ን	no ኖ	30
Alph	a አ	u ኡ	i ኢ	a ኣ	e ኤ	e እ	o ኦ	40
Caf	ka ከ	ku ኩ	ki ኪ	ka ካ	ke ኬ	ke ክ	ko ኮ	50
Vaw	va ወ	vu ዉ	vi ዊ	va ዋ	ve ዌ	ve ው	vo ዎ	60
Ain	a ዐ	u ዑ	i ዒ	a ዓ	e ዔ	o ዕ	o ዖ	70
Zai	za ዘ	zu ዙ	zi ዚ	za ዛ	ze ዜ	ze ዝ	zo ዞ	80
Jaman	ja የ	ju ዩ	ji ዪ	ja ያ	je ዬ	je ይ	jo ዮ	90
Dent	da ደ	du ዱ	di ዲ	da ዳ	de ዴ	de ድ	do ዶ	100
Geml	ga ገ	gu ጉ	gi ጊ	ga ጋ	ge ጌ	ge ግ	gu ጎ	200
Tait	ta ጠ	tu ጡ	ti ጢ	ta ጣ	te ጤ	te ጥ	to ጦ	300
Pait	pa ጰ	pu ጱ	pi ጲ	pa ጳ	pe ጴ	pe ጵ	po ጶ	400
Zadii	za ጸ	zu ጹ	zi ጺ	za ጻ	ze ጼ	ze ጽ	zo ጾ	500
Zzap	za ፀ	zu ፁ	zi ፂ	za ፃ	ze ፄ	ze ፅ	zo ፆ	600
Af	fa ፈ	fu ፉ	fi ፊ	fa ፋ	fe ፌ	fe ፍ	fo ፎ	700
Pſa	pa ፐ	pu ፑ	pi ፒ	pa ፓ	pe ፔ	pe ፕ	po ፖ	800

Aliæ ſyllabæ extra Alphabetum.

						Numeri.
chuo	chuu	chi	chua	che		900
kuo	kuu	kui	kua	kue		1000
guo	guu	gui	gua	gue		2000
huo	huu	hui	hua	hue		

7 Alphabetum Armenium.

	Nomen.	Figura.	Poteſtas.
1	Aip	ա	A
2	Pien	բ	P
3	Chiem	գ	Ch
4	Ta	դ	T
5	Jeg	ե	Je
6	Sſa	զ	Sſ
7	E	է	E
8	Jet	ը	Je
9	Tho	թ	Th
10	Sgie	ժ	Sg
20	Ini	ի	I
30	Liun	լ	L
40	Hhe	խ	Hh
50	Za	ծ	Z
60	Ghien	կ	Gh
70	Ho	հ	H
80	Zza	ձ	Zz
90	Kat	ղ	K
100	Ge	ճ	G
200	Mien	մ	M
300	I	յ	I
400	Nu	ն	N
500	Scia	շ	Sc
600	Vua	ո	V
700	Ce	չ	Ce
800	Be	պ	B
900	Gge	ջ	Gg
1000	Rra	ռ	Rr
2000	Se	ս	S
3000	Vieu	վ	V
4000	Diun	տ	D
5000	Fre	ր	R
6000	Zzo	ց	Zz
7000	Hiun	ւ	V
8000	Ppiur	փ	Pp
9000	Che	ք	Ch
	Ieu	օ	Eu
10000	Fe	ֆ	F

Literæ quæ figura habent affinitatem.

ա, a		ա, d	
գ, ch		է, t	
է, e		է, e	
գ, ſſ		կ, k	
է, ie		է, e	
ձ, ſg		ձ, z	
ը, i		ւ, hh	
լ, l		լ, l	
ձ, zz	կ, cc		
ռ, rr		ս, ſ	ո, u

8 *Alphabetum*

Collatio literarum Arabicarum & Perſicarum cum Hebræis, quoad poteſtatem earum in numerando.

ي	ط	ح	ز	و	ه	ד	ג	ב	א
70	60	50	40	30	20	10	9	8	7	6	5	4	3	2	1

ت	ط	ض	ذ	خ	ث	ت	ش	ص	ف
1000	900	800	700	600	500	400	300	200	100	90	80

Figure 3.15. *(continued)*

193

8 *Alphabetum Coptum, seu Ægyptiacum.*		
Nomen.	Figura.	Potestas.
Alpha	Ⲁ ⲁ	A
Vida	Ⲃ ⲃ	V
Gamma	Ⲅ ⲅ	G
Dalda	Ⲇ ⲇ	D
Ei·	Ⲉ ⲉ	E
So	Ⲋ ⲋ	S
Zida	Ⲍ ⲍ	Z
Hida	Ⲏ ⲏ	I
Thita	Ⲑ ⲑ	Th
Iauda	Ⲓ ⲓ	I
Kabba	Ⲕ ⲕ	K
Lauda	Ⲗ ⲗ	L
Mi	Ⲙ ⲙ	M
Ni	Ⲛ ⲛ	N
Exi	Ⲝ ⲝ	X
O	Ⲟ ⲟ	O
Bi	Ⲡ ⲡ	P
Ro	Ⲣ ⲣ	R
Sima	Ⲥ ⲥ	S
Dau	Ⲧ ⲧ	T
H	Ⲩ ⲩ	E
Phi	Ⲫ ⲫ	F
Chi	Ⲭ ⲭ	Ch
O	Ⲱ ⲱ	O
Scei	Ϣ ϣ	Sc
Fei	Ϥ ϥ	F
Chei	Ϧ ϧ	Ch
Hori	Ϩ ϩ	H
Giangia	Ϫ ϫ	Gi
Scima	Ϭ ϭ	Sc
Dei	Ϯ ϯ	Di
Ebsi	Ⲯ ⲯ	Ps

9 *Alphabetum Illyricum, sive Serovianum.*			
Cyrillian.	Hieron.	Potestas.	N.
Ꙗ ꙗ		A a	1
Б б		B b	
В в		V v	2
Г г		G gh	3
Д д		D d	4
Е е		E e	5
		X sh	
З з		Z z	6,7
Н н		I i	8
		Th	9
І і		Y j	10
К к		K k	20
Л л		L l	30
М м		M m	40
Н н		N n	50
		X x	60
О о		O o	70
П п		P p	80
			90
Р р		R r	100
С с		S sz	200
Т т		T t	300
У у		Y y	400
		V u	500
Ф ф		F f	500
Х х		H h	600
		Ps	700
		O	800
Ш ш		Sch ch	
Ц ц		Cz ç	900
		C	1000
Ш ш		Sc	
Ь ь		I i	
		Ie ja	
		Ya	
		Ye	
Ю ю		Yo	
		Yu	

10 *Alphabetum Ibericum, sive Georgianum.*			
Figura.	Nomen.	Potestas.	
ა	An	a	
ბ	Ban	b	
გ	Ghan	gh	*al* ß, *Hebr. & Ital. ths, ghi.*
დ	Don	d	
ე	En	e	
ვ	Vin	eu	*consonans, ut ß Græc. & Ital. servo, ut Ital. vestro,*
ზ	Zen	z	
ჱ	Hai	h	
თ	Hhai	hh	*ut Ϛ Arab.*
	Than	th	*ut θ, Græc.*
ი	In	i	
კ	Kan	k	
ლ	Las	l	
მ	Man	m	
ნ	Nar	n	
ო	On	o	
პ	Par	p	
ჟ	Rai	r	
ჟ	jan	j	*Hispanicum, ut hijo.*
	San	s	
ტ	Tar	t	
უ	Vn	u	*Vocalis, ut auditor.*
ფ	Far	f, ph	
ქ	Cha	ch	
	Car	c	
ღ	Gan	g	*Italicum, ut ge, ge, gu.*
	Scin	Ici	*ut Ital. scia, scio, sciu.*
ყ	Ciûen	ci	
შ	Zan	z ç	*ut Ital. zoppe.*
	Zil, &		
ჩ	Zil	z	*sibilantem, ut Ital. zio.*
ც	Chahar	ch	*Gall. ut Charles, Hisp. ut hecho.*
	Chan	ch	*ut Ϝ Hebr.*
ჯ	Char	ch	*ut Ϛ Arab.*
ჰ	Gian	g	*Ital. ut gia, gio, giu.*
	Hhoi	hh	

11 *Alphabetum Gothicum ex Dureto.*

A.	B.	C.	D.	E.
F.	G.	H.	I.	K.
L.	M.	N.	O.	P.
Q.	R.	S.	T.	V.
X.	Y.	Z.	C.	Au.
Eu.	Ei.	oi.	œ.	Æ.

D   12 *Specimen*

Figure 3.15 *(continued)*

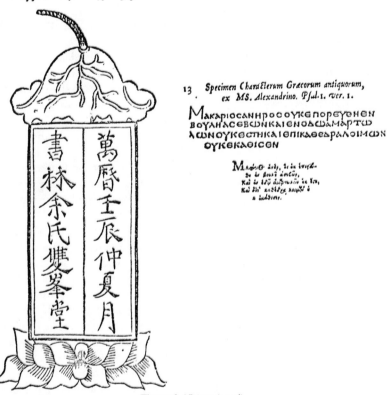

12   *Specimen Characterum Chinensium, ex initio cujusdam libri, earum typis impressi.*

13   *Specimen Characterum Græcorum antiquorum, ex MS. Alexandrino. Psal. 1. ver. 1.*

ΜΑΚΑΡΙΟCΑΝΗΡΟCΟΥΚΕΠΟΡΕΥΘΗΕΝ
ΒΟΥΛΗΑCΕΒWΝΚΑΙΕΝΟΔWΑΜΑΡΤW
ΛWΝΟΥΚΕCΤΗΚΑΙΕΠΙΚΑΘΕΔΡΑΛΟΙΜWΝ
ΟΥΚΕΚΑΘΙCΕΝ

Figure 3.15 *(continued)*

but the first scholar to devote an entire book to such comparisons was Isḥāq Abū Ibrāhīm ibn Barūn (fl. ca. 1100), whose work *The book of comparisons between the Hebrew and the Arabic language* unfortunately also has survived only in scattered fragments. These Jewish scholars and other authors of the period wrote about the Hebrew language in Arabic, but in 1101 there appeared a work written in Hebrew that has been hailed as "one of the greatest mediaeval monuments of learning,"[95] the ספר הערוך *(Sefer heʻaruk)* ("The well-prepared [or "edited"] book"), by Rabbi Natan ben Yeḥiel of Rome (1035–1106). This was a dictionary of words occurring in the Talmud and in the gaonic literature, with explana-

[95]Sarton (1927), v. 1, p. 782.

tions of their etymology by way of comparison of the Hebrew and Aramaic words with corresponding ones in Arabic, Persian, Latin, and Italian.

Soon afterward the poet, scientist, and grammarian Avraham ibn Ezra (1089–1164) summarized and partly translated the works of the earlier Jewish philologists who had written in Arabic in a Hebrew book, מאזני לשון הקודש *(Mozney lašon haqodeš)* or, for short, מאזנים *(Moznayim)* ("The balance of the Holy Language," the word *balance* being used in the sense of a weighing device). In this book he set forth the principles of Hebrew grammar and pointed out the structural affinities between the Semitic languages. Whereas the earlier Arabic treatises were soon forgotten, Ibn Ezra's work became widely known and was used as one of the textbooks for the teaching of Hebrew. No doubt Guillaume Postel was familiar with it from his intensive Hebrew studies, since he alludes several times to the similarities between Hebrew and Arabic.

But the medieval world took little notice of the comparative approach developed by Jewish scholars, being more concerned with scholastic disputations about the language of the angels and about how God had spoken to Adam in the Garden of Eden.

The first Western work of a scholarly nature that dealt with languages from a comparative point of view was Gessner's *Mithridates,* mentioned earlier. Gessner was already well acquainted with Postel's works (he devoted two and a half pages to them in his *Bibliotheca universalis* [f. 261–263]) and used them as sources for his treatment of Oriental languages. Although he still considered Hebrew the original tongue of mankind from which altogether 72 others were descended by gradual *corruptio* (by which Gessner meant change rather than deterioration), he displayed some remarkable insights into the affinities between the Romance languages, and in particular between the Germanic languages and dialects, his grouping of which into various branches coincides almost exactly with modern linguistic practice. Basing his observations mainly on personal and geographical names, Gessner rejected superficial phonetic similarities as "merae coniecturae," while pointing out some characteristic consonant shifts between various Germanic languages. The book was so successful that a second enlarged and annotated edition was published in 1610, long after the author's death.

Gessner's pioneering work was followed by a treatise from the pen of another famous polymath, Joseph Justus Scaliger (1540–1609), who divided the European languages into four major and seven minor classes, according to their words for *god.* From then until the end of the 18th century, the increasing number of languages that became known to European scholars through the accounts of explorers and travelers in Asia, Africa, and America led to the compilation of many books that treated languages from a comparative point of view, although most of these were mere vocabularies, translated into a number of tongues. Only a few followed the approach of Gessner and Scaliger, and speculated about the affinities between certain languages and their possible origin.

Two minor works based on a comparative approach to languages were published at the beginning and toward the end of the period during which some of England's best minds tried in vain to undo what the builders of the Tower of Babel had wrought. In 1617 John Minsheu published a *Guide into tongues,*[96] in which he compared the etymologies of English, Low and High Dutch (i.e., German), French, Spanish, Italian, Latin, and Hebrew. And in 1658 Henry Edmundson brought out his *Lingua linguarum,*[97] a work probably inspired by Comenius' Latin primer, in which he proposed to teach languages by emphasizing the analogies and correspondences between them. In 1675 the naturalist and philologist John Ray observed, in his treatise *A philosophical essay for the reunion of languages,* that

there is a certain accord between several languages and therefore they are attainable by comparison. . . . Latin is the daughter of the languages of the East, mother of those in the West, and sister of the more Northern.[98]

This opinion was as yet only little more than an inspired intuition and lacked a scientific basis. Soon afterward Leibniz rejected the old theory of Hebrew as the mother of all languages and postulated, on the evidence of linguistic data then available, the affinity of most European languages with those of the Near East. He assumed that they were all descended from one original language that had disappeared long since (although he could not furnish any proof for the latter assumption). Leibniz also urged the systematic collection of more linguistic data in order to better understand the mutual relationships between languages, and he succeeded in arousing the interest of Catherine II of Russia in such a project.

She entrusted the task to the German physician, naturalist, and renowned traveler Peter Simon Pallas, who published *Linguarum totum orbis vocabularium comparativa*[99] in 1787. The work consisted of a comparative vocabulary of 274 basic words in classified order. The first were *god* and *heaven,* followed by nouns selected from the fields of family relationships, anatomy, psychology, astronomy, geography, botany, zoology, and warfare, and some common adjectives, verbs, pronouns, adverbs, and interjections (in this order). There was, however, no formal grouping under any headings, and the order just named can only be inferred by scanning the list of terms, which are enumerated from 1 to 274. Each term was first listed in Russian and was then transcribed into no less than 200 languages, of which 51 were European and 149 Asiatic (including Chinese and Japanese, as well as many unwritten dialects of Central and Southern Asia). The lack of systematic arrangement and the arbitrary choice of

[96]Minsheu (1617).
[97]Edmundson (1658).
[98]Ray (1675).
[99]Pallas (1787).

terms probably did little to further the study of comparative philology, while the choice of Russian as the basic language rendered the book unintelligible to most Western scholars. What makes this "grammaticoclassified" polyglot vocabulary so remarkable is that all words, including those originally written in Roman script, were phonemically transcribed into Cyrillic. It was probably the first work in which non-Slavic languages were subjected to Cyrillization on a large scale, and it set a precedent for the future treatment of foreign scripts in Cyrillic characters.

4.2. Sir William Jones

The first Jesuit missionaries began their work in India and the Far East at about the time Gessner published his philological treatise, in which the languages of this part of the world were barely mentioned. To conduct their activities the missionaries had to learn the various vernaculars, and in many instances they also tried to devise Romanization schemes for the exotic scripts they encountered. It soon occurred to the missionaries who worked in India that certain affinities existed between the Indian languages and those spoken in Europe. One of the first to observe this phenomenon was the English Jesuit Thomas Stephens (1549–1619), who lived for 40 years in the Portuguese colony of Goa. He invented a Romanization scheme for the Konkani language (a Marathi dialect), and wrote in one of his letters:

Many are the languages of these places . . . their pronunciation is not disagreeable and their structure is allied to Greek and Latin.[100]

With the foundation of the British East India Company in 1600, which proudly declared that its aim was "to establish a large, well-grounded, sure English dominion in India for all time to come," merchants and soldiers seeking their fortunes in the ancient country were joined by missionaries who intensified their activities following the appeal of a Dutch missionary, Abraham Roger, who published his plea for the conversion of the heathens in India, *Open door to the hidden heathendom,* in 1651. From then on and throughout the 18th century, missionaries, philologists, and also some British administrators who became amateur Orientalists, devoted themselves to the study of Indian languages, particularly Sanskrit, and they began to explore the similarities between that ancient language and Greek and Latin, as well as other European languages.

   The first scholar to assert firmly the existence of an Indo-European family of

---

[100]Stephens' letter of October 1583, quoted in Firth (1937), p. 57. The Konkani language is still being written in the adapted Roman alphabet devised by Stephens and other Portuguese Jesuits in Goa, although it may also be written with Devanagari or Kannada characters.

languages by comparison of Sanskrit, Persian, Latin, Greek, and the Germanic languages was the Orientalist Sir William Jones (1746–1794). He had studied Arabic and Persian, had written a *Persian grammar* (1772), and had published translations of Arabic poems (1780) when he was appointed a judge on the Supreme Court of Bengal in 1783. There he devoted himself to the study of Sanskrit, and published his epoch-making theory in Calcutta in 1786. He became the president of the Asiatic Society in Calcutta, and wrote the introductory paper for the first issue of their *Transactions,* then entitled *Asiatick Researches.* Jones was well aware of the problems of transcription encountered by other writers on Indian languages; in the absence of any agreed-upon system each one had devised his own method, which was clearly not conducive to fruitful comparative studies of languages. Thus he devoted his paper to the problems of transliteration of Asian vernaculars:

> Every man who has occasion to compose tracts on *Asiatic* literature or to translate from the *Asiatic* languages, must always find it convenient, and sometimes necessary, to express *Arabian, Indian* and *Persian* words and sentences, in the characters generally used among *Europeans,* and almost every writer in those circumstances has a method of notation peculiar to himself: but none has yet appeared in the form of a complete system, so that each original sound may be rendered invariably by one appropriated symbol, conformably to the natural order of articulation, and with a due regard to the primitive power of the *Roman* alphabet.[101]

Jones set forth his opinion that the transliteration of a language should never use the same letter for different sounds, nor different letters for the same sound, and then proceeded to exemplify his own system, mainly for Sanskrit, with occasional reference to Arabic and Persian. The table of transliteration preceding his paper (see Figure 3.16) showed, despite the heading "The system of Indian, Arabian and Persian letters," only the Romanization of the Devanagari characters, while the latter are printed in the text of the paper (not in tabular form). Various diacritical marks were used to make the rendering of a certain sound in Roman characters unique and unambiguous. The paper marks the beginning of phonetic transcription based on scientific principles, and is expressly designed for the needs of philologists, particularly those whose mother tongue is English. The systems of transliteration presently used by the Royal Geographic Society are directly traceable to the proposals of Jones, who influenced almost all subsequent schemes for the conversion of Asian scripts (with the exception of Chinese and Japanese) until the end of the 19th century.

Sir William Jones had shown that what for centuries had been thought to be a great diversity of tongues was only apparent, and that hundreds of languages and dialects in a vast area stretching from India through almost all of Europe (and by

---

[101]Jones (1788), pp. 1–2.

The System of

INDIAN ARABIAN and PERSIAN

LETTERS

Soft and hard Breathings

	a	e	ha	hha	
Vowels	*Diphthongs*		*and*	*Semivowels*	
ă ā	aà	e	è	ya	
i	ì	o	ò	wa	
u	ù	ai	au	ra	
ṛi	ṝi	lṛi	lṝi	la	
â â	ê ê	î î	û ù	â â	

Consonants

c a	c'ha ⎫		ġha ⎫		
k a	kha ⎭	ga	gha ⎭	ṅa	
s a	sha	za	zha	śa	
t a	t́ha ⎫	'da	{ 'dha }	ṇa	
	⎭		{ 'dha }		
ta	{ t̤ha }	da	{ dha }	na	
	{ tha }		{ dha }		
pa	{ p̤ha }	ba	{ p ha }	ma	
	{ fa }		{ va }		

Compounds

cha	chha	ja	jha	ṅya
ża	z̈a	z̈a	csha	jŭya

Figure 3.16. Sir William Jones' transliteration scheme for Devanagari script. (From *Asiatick Researches*, v. 1, 1788, plate inserted before p. 1.)

200

extension to the American continent) were really all children of one large family. It now occurred to many serious and devout men that the time had come to eliminate also the bewildering and frustrating variety of scripts, about which Bishop Wilkins had already said that "the variety of letters is appendix to the curse of Babel." But unlike the good bishop, they no longer pursued the chimera of an artifically contrived universal alphabet. Since the Roman script had already unified most of the European languages on the graphemic level, it seemed only logical to substitute it also for the various scripts used for the Asian and especially the Indian branches of the great Indo-European language family. As a consequence of the unification in script and the attendant spread of literacy, it would become much easier to spread the Gospel to the millions of heathen Indians, and thus to unite them also in the Christian faith.

Among the men who believed in these goals and worked diligently toward their achievement were two British civil servants in India who devoted much of their time and energy to the problem of script conversion. William Marsden (1754–1836) served with the East India Company in Sumatra and later became First Secretary of the Admiralty and a Fellow of the Royal Society. He wrote a history of Sumatra and compiled a grammar of Malayalam, but became best known for his large library of works on Asian languages and his collection of Oriental coins, which he used as sources for the comparative study of languages and their scripts. As a result of his studies he published an essay on the application of the Roman alphabet to Oriental languages[102] with special emphasis on the Indian vernaculars written in Devanagari or scripts derived from it. Sir Charles Edward Trevelyan (1807–1886), who began his career in the Bengal civil service and became governor of Madras and finance minister of India, devoted himself to social reform, public works, and education. He too came to the conclusion that social progress could only be achieved if the Indian masses could be made literate, and in a number of publications proposed yet another transliteration scheme for Indian languages, using for the first time the term "Romanization" for the conversion of a script into Roman characters.[103]

---

[102]Marsden (1834).
[103]Trevelyan (1854).

4.3.   C. F. Volney and A. A. E. Schleiermacher

What Sir William Jones had done for English-speaking scholars, the French Orientalist Constantin François Volney[104] (1757–1820) undertook to do for French philologists. He had studied history and Oriental languages, traveled widely in Egypt and Syria, and became a member of the Constituent Assembly in 1789. In 1794 he published a phonetic transcription scheme, *Simplification des langues orientales* for Arabic, Persian, and Turkish, the principal languages of the Near East written in Arabic characters.[105] Like Jones, he pointed out that various scholars had used quite different schemes of transliteration from Arabic script, which led to confusion and inaccuracies in the rendering of Arabic proper names and place names. His scheme was adopted by the French government to transcribe place names on the map of Egypt compiled in 1803 as part of the *Description de l'Egypte,* the scientific account of Napoleon's expedition. In 1819 Volney published a much enlarged version of his work, *L'Alfabet européen appliquée aux langues asiatiques,*[106] in which he endeavored to render even the most minute nuances in the pronunciation of Arabic, Persian, Turkish, and Hebrew by means of Roman and Greek letters, diacritical marks, and small, raised letters. The application of his scheme was shown (as so many schemes before) in transcriptions of the Lord's Prayer (see Figure 3.17). To judge from the footnotes to the Hebrew version, Volney's knowledge of this language fell short of his proficiency in Arabic: si tacuisset, philosophus mansisset. Nevertheless his work exercised considerable influence on subsequent French schemes of transcription until the end of the 19th century.

In his will Volney had set out the sum of 24,000 francs as a prize to be awarded by the Institut de France to a scholar who would devise a "harmonic alphabet" in which the scripts of all languages could be expressed by Roman letters. A young German philologist, Andreas August Ernst Schleiermacher (1787–1858), submitted a proposal *De l'influence de l'écriture sur le langage* in which he outlined his scheme of a universal transliteration scheme. He was awarded the prize, which enabled him to devote himself to the intensive study of Slavic and Oriental languages. In 1835 he published a revised version of his

---

[104]Volney has often been called one of the last encyclopedists, and the scope of his activities and writings was indeed quite far-reaching. In addition to his linguistic works, he wrote a large historical treatise, *Les ruines, ou méditations sur les révolutions des empires* (1791). From 1795 to 1798 he visited the United States, where he collected material for his work *Tableau du climat et du sol des Etats Unies d'Amérique* (1803), which for a long time remained one of the standard sources of data on the climate and soil of the area covered by the original 13 states. Upon his return to France he became a member of the Académie française.

[105]Volney (1794).

[106]Volney (1819).

ARABE LITTÉRAL.

Lecture selon Volney.

Aba-na (a) ellazi fi el samaoati

l'iûtaqaddasi usm-û-ka

(b) l'tati malkot-û-ka

l'takon mafiitû-ka kama fi

el sama-i oa aʼla el arḍ-i

χobza-na kifət-na äûti-na fi el iûmi

o aqfer l'na χetaïaona kama

naqfer nahn l'man aχtaa alaina

oa la todχel-na el tatʃfareba

laken naʃʃi na men el ʃariri (c).

(a) L'arabe littéral donne la pleine valeur d'a à l'alef, que le vulgaire prononce e: il dit al, et non el.

(b) La lettre l, comme signe d'impératif n'a point besoin du kesri; l'apostrophe avertit et saute les équivoques.

(c) Délivrez-nous du malin (esprit), aucun texte oriental ne dit, délivrez-nous du mal.

PATER NOSTER HÉBREU.

Lecture de Volney.

abino fˤbˤ fˤmim (a) ˤqˤdˤʃ fˤm-kˤ (b)
Pater noster qui in cœlis   sanctificetur nomen tuum

tˤboa mˤlkot-kˤ
adveniat regnum tuum

ʒˤhˤ rˤʂon-kˤ-kˤafr   bˤ-ʃˤmim oa kˤn bˤarʂ
vivat voluntas tua ut qui   in cœlis et   sic   in terra

fˤhm-no dˤbrˤîom bˤîomo tˤn l'no lûom (c)
panem nostrum post diem   in diem   da   nobis hoc die

oa sˤlˤh bˤzo al̄ˤhobotino kˤfr
et dimitte nobis debita nostra ut qui

sˤˤhʒo fˤbălĕ (d) hobotino
dimittimus super (eos qui) debent nobis

oa al rˤbîa-no brˤʃîon
et ne inducas nos in tentationem

ki am hˤʃilno mˤrā
sed quidem solve nos ab maligno

ki kˤ kˤ lˤmˤlkot oa gˤboˤrˤh
quia tibi imperium et potentia

oa kˤbod l'iolˤm îʃolˤmin.
et gloria in sæculum sæculorum.

                            amin.

(a) On voit par les mots latins qu'il y a trois mots dans si be samin t j'écris be, parce que ba laisserait l'équivoque d'a-lef: e n'existant pas dans l'alfabet hébreu, on sent qu'il y est hors de texte.

(b) Sem-ka: les Hébreux ont pu prononcer comme l'arabe vulgaire Sem-ak: il semble que les rabbins ont emprunté leur lecture du chaldaïque qui me paraît tenir beaucoup du nahou.

(c) Chamberlayne a écrit par erreur ha dur pour he doux.

(d) Il est probable que l'Hébreu a prononcé ala comme l'Arabe, quoiqu'écrit ali, etc., etc.

Figure 3.17. C. F. Volney's transcription of the Arabic and Hebrew versions of the Lord's Prayer, from his *Alfabet européen.*

proposal[107] and a grammar of the Burmese and Malay languages.[108] By then he had been appointed chief librarian of the ducal library at Darmstadt, where he collected Orientalia and also compiled a classification system for books, *Bibliographisches System der gesammten Wissenschaftskunde,*[109] which consisted of 25 main classes and almost 13,000 subclasses. It was both the most elaborate and the most practical of all classification systems for libraries devised up to that time, and it was used for a long time not only in the library at Darmstadt but also in several German university libraries and partially in the Königliche Bibliothek in Berlin (the present Deutsche Staatsbibliothek).

But Schleiermacher's main efforts were devoted to the elaboration of his monumental treatise *Das harmonische oder allgemeine Alphabet zur Transcription fremder Schriftsysteme in lateinische Schrift,*[110] which was intended to solve once and for all the problems of transliteration from any non-Roman Script.

When Schleiermacher died in 1858, the manuscript was almost complete, but the work was not published until 1864, mainly because of the difficulties encountered in the typesetting. The print shop of Wilhelm Keller in Giessen already had Cyrillic, Hebrew, Syriac, Arabic, and Sanskrit type, but this work also required Church Slavic, Glagolitsa, Coptic, Samaritan, and Amharic characters. In addition, there were the types for the "Harmonic Alphabet" itself, which contained more than 100 different characters with diacritical marks and special forms (see Figure 3.18); further modifications of these characters (not shown in the table) were used to represent unambiguously the special characters of various scripts. There were also three series of vowels (not tabulated anywhere in the work but listed in the introduction in a discursive passage):

Short:	ă	æ̆	ĕ	ĩ	ŏ	Œ̆	ŭ	y̆
Medium:	a	æ	e	i	o	Œ	u	y
Long:	â	æ̂	ê	î	ô	Œ̂	û	ŷ

Each of these vowels could be further distinguished by accents, but since the scheme was intended for strict transliteration, no provision was made for nasalization, palatalization, and so forth. Altogether almost 300 characters had to be produced specially for this immensely thorough philological compendium, and that was probably the reason the proposed alphabet itself was never accepted for general use.

Nevertheless Schleiermacher's work constitutes the first systematic and

---

[107]Schleiermacher (1835a).
[108]Schleiermacher (1835b).
[109]Schleiermacher (1852).
[110]Schleiermacher (1864).

Uebersicht
der Consonanten des harmonischen Alphabets

Buchstaben:	einfache,	veränderte,	verstärkte, (härtere)	mouillirte,	aspirirte.
Gutturale	k, q, g, h, ʻ,	ǧ, h, h,	k, ĝ, h, b,	k̇, ġ,	k, g.
Palatale	č, ǧ, j, š,	ć, š,		č, j, š, š,	č, g.
Sibilanten	s, z,	s, s, z, z,	š, ź, ž,	ṡ, ż, ž,	ž, ž.
Linguale	t, d,	t, t, t, d, d,	t, d, d,	t, d,	t, t, d, d.
Labiale	p, b, f,	b, f,		b, p,	p, b.
Nasale	n, m,	n, g, ñ, n, m,		n, m,	
Liquide	j, r, l, v,	r, ř, r, l, w	r, ł,	r, l, v,	f.
Gemischte	x.				

Figure 3.18. A. A. E. Schleiermacher's "harmonic alphabet," from his *Das harmonische oder all gemeine Alphabet* . . . , p. 32. In the footnote to this table, the editor states that the manuscript did not contain such a systematic display but that the table is adapted from one that appears on p. 31 of Schleiermacher's earlier prize essay.

scientifically sound system for exact transliteration, irrespective of pronunciation. The editor, L. Ewald, says in his introduction:

Er gründete sein harmonisches Alphabet nicht auf die oft schwankende und in vielen Fällen kaum fest zu bestimmende Aussprache der fremden Charactere, sondern auf die *Orthographie,* um den wichtigen Vorteil zu erreichen, dass die Transcription den der fremden Sprache einigermassen kundigen Leser in den Stand setze, jeden mit dem harmonischen Alphabet geschriebenen Text unmittelbar wieder in die Originalschrift zu übertragen.[111]

This statement of Schleiermacher's intentions defines for the first time the functional aims of a transliteration scheme in operational terms. The fact that this scheme had been devised by a trained philologist who was also a librarian influenced, for better or worse, all subsequent thinking on the purposes and qualities of schemes for the conversion of scripts in the framework of bibliographic control. A scheme used by librarians had to be one that also fulfilled the needs of philologists. The operational definition "to enable a reader who has some basic knowledge of the foreign language to retransliterate immediately any text written in the Harmonic Alphabet into the original script" is almost exactly the one formulated 100 years later in the "Introductory note" to the first ISO transliteration scheme (see p. 26).

4.4. A. J. Ellis

While Schleiermacher sought to reduce Oriental and other non-Roman scripts to a uniform alphabet by strict transliteration of graphic signs, the idea of transcribing the phonemes of any and all languages now also began to find its scientific and systematic expression. One of the most remarkable men to undertake this task was Alexander John Ellis (1814–1890), who devoted almost his whole life to phonetics and phonetic transcription schemes. He studied philology and mathematics, and made brilliant contributions to both fields as well as to the theory of music. He is best known for his great work *On early English pronunciation*[112] in which he used a phonetic transcription scheme of his own invention called "Palaeotype," since to print it one had to use the

old type, παλαιοὶ τύποι (palaii·tii·pi), and no accented letters, few turned and still fewer mutilated. [It was] adapted solely to scientific, not popular use . . . and to indicate

---

[111]Schleiermacher (1864), pp. iii–iv.
[112]Ellis (1869).

the pronunciation of any language with great minuteness and much typographical convenience.[113]

The scheme consisted of 266 "letters," most of which were di- and trigraphs, and mixtures of upper- and lowercase letters, roman and italic type, and 46 "signs" to indicate stress, articulation, tone (for the tonal languages), and other phonological features. Ellis had elaborated the scheme gradually since he first published it in 1845 in his *A plea for phonotypy and phonography,*[114] but realized that it was too complicated for everyday use, even by philologists. He therefore devised a simplified version, Glossic, which was to be printed in "Glossotype" (see Figure 3.19), in which he allowed the use of some diacritical marks. This, in his words, would be

useful to all who may occasionally wish to indicate pronunciation with some degree of exactness, but do not care to enter upon general phonetic investigation.[115]

Ellis was no mere theoretician. Not only were most of his own works printed in Palaeotype whenever pronunciation had to be indicated, but he himself transcribed the New Testament and several works of literature into this scheme and also published for some time a journal, the *Fonetic Frend*. His transcription scheme had originally been devised for the English language and its dialects, and he collaborated for many years with Sir Isaac Pitman of shorthand fame to promote the use of a new English phonetic alphabet. Soon, however, he expanded his scheme to accommodate "all languages" and published a new edition of his earlier work in which he made a plea for the introduction of his "universal alphabet."[116] Needless to say, although Ellis' achievements in the field of research into early English pronunciation are still valued today, his elephantine phonetic transcription scheme did not find any followers and died with its ingenious inventor.

[113]Ellis (1869), p. 1.
[114]Ellis (1845).
[115]Ellis (1869), p. 13.
[116]Ellis (1848).

KEY TO GLOSSOTYPE.

See p. 13. Isolated letters and words in glossotype should be inclosed in ( ). (E) is never mute; all vowels and combinations having (˘) or (¯) over them, except (ŭ), are the short or long sounds of the vowels and combinations without these marks, which should not be used for any other letters, thus : (ä) is the long sound of (a) ; (ĕe) the short sound of (ee) ; (ŭ) is to be used whenever it is thought that the proper form (ou) might create confusion.

C. Cockney, *D.* Dutch, *E.* English, *F.* French, *G.* German, *I.* Italian, *P.* Provincial, *S.* Scotch, *Sw.* Swedish, *W.* Welsh.

VOWELS.		DIPHTHONGS.		CONSONANTS.	
a *gnat*	i *knit*	aiy *may*	aiw *C.*	b *bee*	n-g *ingrain*
ā *P.*	ī *S.*	ay *S.C.*	aw *C.*	ch *chest*	nk *think*
aa *ask*	ih,ĭh *P.G.ŭ*	aay *high*	aaw *how*	d *doe*	n-k *in-come*
ăa *ask*	o *not*	ucy *S.*	aew *C.*	dh *the*	p *pea*
ae *ware*	ō *P.*	ăhy *G. ai*	ăhw *G. au*	f *fee*	r *ray*
ăe *S. e*	oa, ŏa *I. d*	ahy *aye*	ahw *P.*	g *go*	'r *air*
ah *father*	oe, ŏe *G.ö*	auy *P.*	auw *P.*	gh *D.G.*	r *I.S. r*
ăh *F.G.S. a*	oh *rose*	cy *S. tide*	ew *I. eu*	н *he*	rh *P.F. r*
ai *wait*	ŏh *S.*	......	eew *I. iu*	(written *ḥ*)	s *see*
ăi *S. ai*	oɴ *F. on*	......	iw *mew*	j *jay*	sh *she*
aɴ *F. an*	oo *pool*	oy *boy*	ow *P.*	k *coo*	t *tin*
ao *S.*	ŏo *S. book*	ōy *P.*	ōw *P.*	kh *G.C. ch*	th *thin*
ăo *S. maɴ*	ou, ŭ *could*	ohy *P.*	ohw *know*	l *lo*	v *vale*
au *all*	ōu *P.*	ooy *I.F.P.*	......	'l *little*	w *wail*, or
ău *want*	u *nut*	uy *high*	uw *how*	lh *W. ll*	-w (after
e *net*	ū *P.*	uiy *F. ui*	......	m *me*	vowels)
ē *S.*	ue, ŭe *Sw.u*	cuy *F. eui*	cuw *D.*	'm *rhythm*	wh *why*
ce *meet*	uh *worth*			n *no*	y *yet*, or
če *S.I.F.*	ūh *P.*	In all these diphthongs the first element has the sound assigned in the preceding column, which is run on quickly, with a glide, to a following (ee) or (oo) written (y) or (w).		'u *open*	-y (after
cɴ *F. in*	ui, ŭi *F. u*			ɴ *F. n* (written *ŋ*)	vowels)
eu *F. eu*	uɴ *F. un*			ng *thing*	z *zeal*
ĕu *F. eu*	(') *murmur*				zh *vision*

When more than two vowels come together and the first two form one of the preceding combinations, read them as such, as (reeent·er (=ree-ent·er) =*re-enter*.

Diphthongs are also formed *P.* by affixing (') as (roh'd) almost (rohud) = *road*, and by affixing (ui), which should then be written (üi), as *D.*(ʜeuäis) = *huis*, theoretical *G.* (froüind) = *freund.*

Foreign and Oriental sounds represented by Italics and small capitals, by special convention. Accent the first syllable, unless ( ) or (·) is written after some other syllable, as : august, august·, august'.

Figure 3.19. Alexander J. Ellis' "Glossotype," from his *Early English pronunciation*, p. 16.

4.5. Richard Lepsius

The decisive step toward the design of a scientifically sound and internationally acceptable system of phonetic transcription was taken by the famous German Egyptologist Richard Lepsius (1810–1884), who had discovered and deciphered the Decree of Canopus. Since his youth he had studied Oriental languages and their alphabets; at the age of 25 he wrote his thesis *Die Anordnung und Verwandtschaft der semitischen, indischen, alt-ägyptischen und äthiopischen Alphabete,* and acquired an amazing knowledge of these and several other languages. He edited the 12-volume *Denkmäler aus Aegypten und Nubien* (1849–1860), which contained the results of his archaeological expeditions to Egypt, and wrote numerous treatises on the dead and living languages of the Near East and India, as well as on Chinese. It was only natural that he should become concerned about a uniform way of transcribing and transliterating these languages and their scripts, and in 1855 he published his first proposal for a phonetic alphabet, applicable to all languages, written or as yet unwritten, *Übertragung fremder Schriftsysteme . . . in europäische Buchstaben.*[117] The slim pamphlet of 64 pages was published simultaneously in Berlin and London in a German and English version. It displayed a large variety of typefaces, including hieroglyphics (of which only some specimens were shown), Coptic, Hebrew, Arabic, Devanagari, Avestan, Armenian, and Greek, and was printed in two colors (red being used to print non-Roman characters, earlier Romanized transcriptions, and their bibliographical references). In this first edition Lepsius applied his transcription system to 52 languages, including several African and American Indian tongues. It was the first to be based strictly on the recording of individual sounds by means of unique symbols (letters, diacritical marks, and specially devised characters) so as to make phonetic transcription independent of any national European orthography.

The work was immediately recognized as a major contribution to philology, and philologists applied it to the description of several dozen African and Asian languages. It was also used for the rendering of place names on the official map of the Austrian Empire (where the various languages and scripts posed particularly difficult problems of a cartographic as well as of a political nature).

Lepsius had conceived his scheme primarily as a scientific tool for comparative philology, but he was also a deeply religious man who sought to combine his scientific aims with practical applications for missionary activity. The Church Missionary Society in England (to whom he had dedicated and recommended the English edition) was so impressed by the potential of the scheme for its activities in Asia and Africa that it commissioned Lepsius to prepare an enlarged English edition, *Standard Alphabet for Reducing Unwritten Languages and Foreign*

----

[117]Lepsius (1855).

Graphic Systems to a Uniform Orthography in European Letters,[118] which appeared in 1863. This contained phonetic transcriptions for 83 "literary languages" and 37 "illiterate languages," as well as a learned treatise on their phonologies. The revised transcription scheme makes heavy use of diacritical marks and of some Greek letters (a summary table is shown in Figure 3.20). Lepsius wrote of his aims:

The endeavour to establish a uniform orthography for writing foreign languages in European characters has both a *scientific* and a *practical* aim. The *scientific* aim is to bring these languages with their literature more complete within our reach. . . . The *practical* aim is to facilitate the propagation of the Christian faith and the introduction of the Christian civilization among heathen nations, especially such as have no written language, by furnishing them with a suitable alphabet. The latter object is most intimately connected with the efficiency of all Christian missions. It is in this quarter that attention has lately been directed afresh to a want long felt in science, often suggested, but never yet satisfied, namely the want of a *standard* alphabet, universally current and applicable to all languages. In the Mission field, without doubt, the first decisive steps will be taken for the actual introduction of such a graphic system.[119]

He then explored in detail the need of comparative philology for a uniform system of transcription (although he did not use this term very much in the work and spoke rather of the "representation of sounds in the European alphabet"); he came to the same conclusion as Sir William Jones:

. . . the diversity of signs for one and the same sound in different languages, or even in the same language, is continually increasing; and has at length become so great, that the translator of Oriental works, the Tourist, the Geographer and Chartographer, the Naturalist, the Ethnographer, the Historian, in short everyone who has to do with the names and words of foreign languages, and above all others the *Linguist,* who studies and compares languages, find themselves entangled in an intolerable confusion of orthographic systems and signs, from which each individual finds it impossible to extricate himself. . . . We must start with . . . the construction of a complete and definite system founded on the nature of phonetic organism.[120]

Devoting himself thereafter to his "practical" aim, he revealed that despite his erudition and wide experience in linguistics and ethnography, he fully shared the prejudices of his age and society which were intertwined with deep religious convictions:

The aboriginal tribes of Africa, America, Australia and Polynesia are almost entirely destitute of written language. This fact alone characterizes them as barbarous and uncivilized. And if there be no nobler calling for the civilized and Christian world than to

[118]Lepsius (1863).
[119]*Ibid.,* p. 23. All emphases in this and the following quotations are in the original.
[120]*Ibid.,* pp. 25–26.

impart to all mankind the treasures of religious knowledge and human culture so freely entrusted to their hands by Divine Providence . . . then it is their especial duty to furnish destitute nations . . . with . . . *a written language.*[121]

Lepsius then asked the rhetorical question whether it would be

advisable to force upon those nations to which the Bible was to be presented as their first reading-book, the English orthography, which is complicated, irregular and singular even in Europe? . . . And according to what principles should those sounds be expressed which are neither found in the English alphabet nor in any other European system?[122]

and concluded that this would be neither possible nor useful, but that his proposal of a standard phonetic alphabet should be adopted forthwith by all Bible and Missionary Societies in Asia, even where native scripts and rich national bodies of literature exist, because

many important advantages would arise from the substitution of a European for all the native alphabets.[123]

During the last 12 years of his life, Lepsius served as director of the Königliche Bibliothek in Berlin. Thus both he and Schleiermacher, the two founding fathers of scientific systems for phonetic transcription and transliteration, were also actively engaged in bibliographic control and applied their systems to the collections of Orientalia in their care. They were, of course, philologists first and librarians only secondarily, or rather in consequence of their achievements in the philological field, particularly since in their time librarianship was not yet considered a profession in its own right, but only one of the so-called "Hilfswissenschaften." Yet it is significant that the first systematizations of methods for the conversion of scripts, which are so intimately connected with other aspects of bibliographic control, were formulated at about the time that the methods of cataloging and subject indexing were also beginning to be systemized in England by Anthony Panizzi,[124] in the United States by Charles

[121]*Ibid.*, p. 26. The notion that anything not yet touched by European civilization must necessarily be "savage" persisted well into the beginning of the 20th century. The author of a biographical essay on Lepsius in the *Allgemeine deutsche Biographie* (Leipzig, 1906), a certain Eduard Neville, wrote: "Sein System hat sich auch als praktisch bewährt für allerlei wilde Sprachen der jetzigen Zeit."

[122]*Ibid.*, p. 28.

[123]*Ibid.*, p. 29.

[124]British Museum (1841). The "Rules for the Compilation of the Catalogue" (v. I, pp. v–ix), which constituted the first modern cataloging code and influenced all subsequent codes in Europe and in the United States, were the work of Anthony Panizzi, an Italian lawyer who had fled to England in 1823 as a political refugee. Panizzi, also an outstanding bibliographer, was appointed Keeper of Printed Books in the British Museum in 1837, became Principal Librarian in 1855, and held this post until his retirement in 1866. He is generally considered to have been "the second founder" of the British Museum.

The Consonants of the General Alphabet.

	explosivæ or dividuæ.			fricativæ or continuæ.			ancipites.	
	fortes.	lenes.	nasales.	fortes.	lenes.	semivoc.		
I. Faucales.	ꝫ	'		k̉	h			
II. Gutturales.	k	q g	ṅ	χ	γ		ṙ	
III. Palatales.	k̉	ǵ	ń	ᶥ, ŝ, š	ǵ, ᶉ, ž y		ľ	
IV. Cerebrales. (Indicae)	ṭ	ḍ	ṇ	š̌	ᶎ		ṛ	ḷ
V. Linguales. (Arabicae)		ḏ(ṭ)		ş	ᶎ, ꝺ			
VI. Dentales.	t	d	n	s, ϑ	ᶎ, ð		r	l
VII. Labiales.	p	b	m	f	v	w		

Examples of Pronunciation.

We follow here the vertical and not the horizontal order, because we thereby keep together all the letters, which in the different classes have the same bases.

VOWELS.

ā engl. *father*, fr. *âme*.

ä ger. *Mann*, ital. *ballo*.

ę̄ fr. *mère*, ger. *Bär*.

ę́ engl. *head*, ger. *fett*.

ę̄ engl. *cane*, *vein*, fr. *donné*.

ī engl. *see*, fr. *lit*.

ĭ engl. *sin*, fr. *fil*.

ǭ engl. *all*, ital. *però*.

ǫ̆ engl. *hot*, *not*.

ō engl. *no*, fr. *faux*.

ū engl. *rule*, fr. *nous*.

ŭ engl. *foot*, fr. *ours*.

ǧ fr. *beurre*, *coeur*.

ǫ̆ engl. *cunning*, *but*.

ǭ ger. *König*, fr. *feu*.

ṇ̈ fr. *fumes*, ger. *Güte*.

ŭ fr. *but*, ger. *Glück*.

ai engl. *mine*, ger. *Kaiser*.

au engl. *house*, ger. *Haus*.

aṵ ger. *Häuser*, *heute*.

ei span. *reina*.

oi engl. *join*.

ā̃ fr. *an*, *en*.

ę̃ fr. *examen*, *Inde*.

ō̃ fr. *on*.

ǫ̃ fr. *un*.

ę engl. *nation*, ger. *Verstand*.

ṛ sanskr. ऋ.

Figure 3.20. Richard Lepsius' phonetic alphabet, from his *Standard alphabet*, pp. 76–77.

ļ sanskr. ॡ.

ẓ chin. mandar. *tsẓ.*

CONSONANTS.

A. EXPLOSIVE. *a.* Fortes.

ʾ arab. ع *(ʿaïn).*

k engl. *cool,* fr. *cause.*

k̇ old sanskr. च. [see above p. 72.]

č modern sanskr. च, engl. *ch.*

ṭ sanskr. ट.

t engl. *town,* fr. *ton.*

p engl. *pine,* fr. *peu.*

b. Lenes.

ʾ arab. ا, hebr. א, gr. spir. len. '.

q arab. ق *(qaf).*

g engl. *gold,* fr. *gauche.*

ġ old sanskr. ग.

j modern sanskr. ज, engl. *j.*

ḍ sanskr. ड.

ḏ(ṭ) arab. ظ (see below).

d engl. *dear.*

ḅ engl. *by.*

c. Nasales.

ṅ engl. *singing,* ger. *enge.*

ń sanskr. ञ, ital. *gnudo,* fr. *regner.*

ṇ sanskr. ण.

n engl. *no.*

m engl. *me.*

B. FRICATIVAE. *a.* Fortes.

ḥ arab. ح *(ḥa).*

h engl. *hand.*

χ ger. *Buch, ach;* pol. *chata.*

š engl. *show,* fr. *chat,* ger. *schon.*

χ́ ger. *ich, recht.*

ṣ́ old sanskr. ष.

ś mod. ind. श, pol. *świt.*

ṣ arab. ص *(ṣād).*

s engl. *sense,* fr. *savoir.*

θ engl. *thin,* mod. gr. ϑεός.

f engl. *fine.*

b. Lenes.

γ arab. غ *(γaïn).*

ž fr. *jeune,* pol. *bażant.*

γ́ mod. gr. γέφυρα.

ź pol. *poźno.*

z fr. *zèle,* engl. *zeal.*

ð engl. *thy,* mod. gr. δίψα.

ọ arab. ض *(ọa).*

ẓ arab. ظ *(ẓa)* (see below).

c. Semivocales.

y engl. *year,* fr. *Bayonne,* ger. *ja.*

w engl. *we.*

C. LIQUIDAE.

ŕ germ. and fr. dialects.

ṛ sanskr. र.

r engl. *very,* ital. *rabbia.*

ľ ital. *gli,* fr. *mouillé.*

ḷ sanskr. ळ.

l engl. *low.*

Figure 3.20 *(continued)*

Ammi Cutter[125] of the Boston Athenaeum, and in Germany by Karl Dziatzko[126] of the Royal Prussian library in Breslau.

5. THE TWOFOLD AIM: SUCCESS AND FAILURE

Lepsius had stipulated a twofold aim for his phonetic transcription system: a "scientific," that is, philological aim, and a "practical," or missionary aim. This was still in the tradition of those 17th century scholars who had tried to invent universal alphabets in order to "advance useful knowledge, civilize barbarous nations and propagate the Gospel," and Lepsius, who lived in an age that believed in continuous progress and the betterment of mankind, probably had no doubts that his scheme would ultimately achieve the two goals he envisaged.

From the point of view of his scientific aim, he was indeed successful. His system laid the foundations for all subsequent phonetic transcription schemes, and some of the characters and diacritical marks proposed by him were ultimately incorporated in the International Phonetic Alphabet, now universally recognized and used in linguistics and lexicography all over the world. The philological or scientific aspects of script conversion were further pursued during the last decades of the 19th century and until the outbreak of World War I, particularly in India, by professional philologists and civil servants with linguistic interests.

Among these was the German-British professor of Sanskrit at Oxford, Friedrich Max Müller (1823–1900), who devised a "Missionary Alphabet" and to whom we owe the first published use of the word *transliteration* in the context of conversion of scripts.[127] His colleague at Oxford, also a Sanskrit scholar, Sir Monier Monier-Williams (1819–1899), published several treatises on the transcription of modern Indian languages[128] and was instrumental in designing the standardized transliteration schemes for Arabic, Hebrew, and Devanagari still used by the Royal Asiatic Society.[129]

Transliteration for the purposes of geographic reference and cartography, which already had made use of the methods devised by Volney and Schleiermacher, was applied to Indian place names by Sir William W. Hunter (1840–1900) in his *Imperial Gazetteer of India*[130]; his system, as well as the more general one first adopted by the Royal Geographical Society in 1885, was

---

[125]Cutter (1876).

[126]Dziatzko (1886).

[127]In an article in *Saturday Review,* 9 March 1861, p. 247.

[128]Monier-Williams (1881, 1890).

[129]"Transliteration." *Journal of the Royal Asiatic Society* (1896), pp. 1–12 at end of volume after p. 835. This is the report of a committee appointed by the Society, following a motion by Sir Monier Monier-Williams.

[130]Hunter (1885–87).

based on the principles stated by Sir William Jones. In France a universally applicable transliteration scheme for geographic names, *Méthode de transcription rationelle générale des noms géographiques,*[131] was devised by the geographer and linguist Christian Garnier (1872–1898), who died shortly before his work was printed, and who received the Volney prize posthumously.

While the scientific aim was thus actually achieved to a considerable extent, the pious hopes of Lepsius for the practical aim were not fulfilled. The endeavors of the missionary and Bible societies during the following decades to introduce the Universal Alphabet among the heathen peoples of Asia and Africa were not crowned by success, despite their efforts to translate and transcribe the Bible in whole or in part, and to devise transliteration schemes for Indian languages. Typical of these attempts was the work of the Reverend J. Knowles, who wrote the tract *Our duty to India and Indian illiterates: Romanic letters for Indian languages*[132] and designed *A common alphabet for Indian languages: or, 53 alphabetic letters for 20,000 syllabic symbols.*[133] He also invented a Braille system for the blind speaking ''all'' Oriental languages and wrote a large number of pamphlets to promote these inventions and their use in missionary work.

Although men like Monier-Williams and Knowles started from different premises (the former concerned primarily with the needs of the philologist, the latter with the literacy of the Indian people and their subsequent conversion to Christianity), both, like Lepsius before them, considered it the sacred duty of a Christian and European to work actively toward the goal of complete conversion of Indian vernaculars to Roman script, in a spirit akin to the feelings of their compatriot Rudyard Kipling, who wrote of the ''White Man's Burden.'' Imbued by such noble sentiments, and in keeping with the general idea of ''progress'' that permeated European thought in the latter half of the 19th century, they saw themselves justified in their assumption that the general introduction of the Roman alphabet would alleviate if not altogether eliminate illiteracy in India and elsewhere. (They blandly chose to ignore the fact that a large part of Europe's rural population, though Christian throughout, was also illiterate at that time.) But such justifications proved to be feeble arguments for a cause that was doomed to failure for various reasons of a technical and sociopolitical nature.

On the technical plane the alphabet proposed by Lepsius was scarcely less complicated than the Arabic or Devanagari script (and its various derivatives). The mixture of Roman and Greek letters, inverted letters, and above all, the bewildering variety of diacritical marks, so dear to the heart of the philologist and even so useful to him, were difficult to learn and confusing to an illiterate person. Lepsius himself recognized this difficulty:

---

[131]Garnier (1899).
[132]Knowles (1910).
[133]Knowles (1913).

For the uncritical Native . . . many of the diacritical marks may be dispensed with, or will gradually drop off themselves.[134]

He did not, however, indicate which diacritical marks could be "dispensed with" (if they were expendable, why were they used at all?); at any rate no "native" could be expected to know what to retain and what to drop. Furthermore the characters of the new phonetic alphabet were not readily available from suppliers of printing equipment; even the English edition of Lepsius' book had to be printed in Berlin because apparently no printer in London had those special types available. Thus it would not have been possible to print primers, textbooks, and newspapers quickly and cheaply in countries that were (and still are) technologically far less developed than the European countries. This formidable technical obstacle to the introduction of a new alphabet containing special characters was often underestimated also by later enthusiasts of script modification, however beneficial their proposals might have been, because they were always caught in a vicious circle. The typefoundries were not ready to invest a large amount of capital in a venture whose outcome was doubtful, and even when an experiment was made, the price of the new typeface was exorbitantly high because of the small volume of sales. But without such typefaces available to printers in large quantities and at a price not higher than that of regular typefaces, no mass dissemination of a "new" or "modified" script was possible.

On the societal plane the difficulties were no less formidable. If a new script is to become the technical vehicle of communication for a whole nation that already possesses a rich literary heritage written in another script, then this literature must be transcribed into the new script. To do this the voluntary cooperation of the nation's literate elite is indispensable, because only those thoroughly familiar with the sacred scriptures and other literary works can be expected to perform the immense and demanding task of transcription. But opposition to the introduction of a new script is always strongest just from those quarters, because they are afraid of losing the cultural identity so intimately connected with the knowledge of the old script. Not only would they lose the privileged and honored status derived from their ability to read and write, worse still, they might become second-grade citizens in their own country or language community, because as adults they would probably not become as proficient in the new script as those who were formerly illiterate and learned the new script as their first and therefore best-known means of written expression. In a wholly literate nation literacy is no longer a status symbol. Examples for this phenomenon can be found in the rejection of the Ŏn-mŭn script in Korea by the literate upper classes for more

---

[134]Lepsius (1863), p. xii.

than four centuries, even though the new script had the full endorsement of the government and was infinitely better suited to writing the Korean language than were the Chinese logograms. The stubborn fight of the Turkish religious dignitaries and scholars against Kemal Atatürk's script reform is another instance.

In India, at whose scripts the European philologists-cum-theologians had aimed their efforts in particular, the religious leaders and intellectuals, whether Hindus, Buddhists, or Muslims, no matter how fiercely they hated and fought each other, were of one mind in feeling that their respective religious and literary monuments were as old and highly developed as any that the European colonists wished to foist on them.[135] They did not feel any need to be "redeemed" by foreign clergymen any more than they wished to be "civilized" by those who considered them mainly as objects of exploitation and subjugation. And the abjectly poor and illiterate Indian masses, following their quietist and introspective religions of Hinduism and Buddhism, remained apathetic and largely indifferent to the well-meant efforts to convert them to Christianity and to teach them the Roman alphabet, particularly since this was offered to them as a kind of package deal.[136]

On the political plane, finally, the emergent nationalism of Asian peoples was nurtured by strong feelings for their religions, which toward the end of the 19th century were superseded to a certain degree by a growing awareness of the importance of their language and script. One of the earliest nationalistic uprisings against a colonial power, the so-called Indian Mutiny of 1857, was motivated not only by economical and military causes but also by the suspicion that

[135] As already discussed in Chapter 2, the Arabic script is considered holy and inviolable by every Muslim, and any tampering with it by non-Muslims arouses violent feelings. As to the Devanagari script, Hindus not only consider each character to represent a certain phoneme but believe also that it has mystical powers: "To an orthodox Hindu . . . the letters of the Indian alphabet are not mere letters—they have a mystical value, particularly in Yoga and Tantric philosophy and ritual. . . . The adoption of the Roman alphabet will cut off one aspect of our religious ritual from a living contact with our daily life, which is now actually present through the Indian system of writing, and many Hindus will not contemplate this with equanimity." (Chatterji, 1935, p. 15). Note that these words were written in the 1930s—how much more must such feelings have been prevalent about a century earlier!

[136] "The labour of the Protestant missionaries resulted in the gathering of meagre fruits through much of the 19th century." *Encyclopedia Britannica,* 14th ed., 1973, s.v. "Missions," by R. P. Beaver. According to him, the Protestant mission churches in India reported a total community of 3.6 million people in 1900, which amounts to less than 1.3% of the population, then estimated to be somewhat more than 280 million. The Catholic missions, despite the fact that they had already begun their work in South and Southeast Asia in the 16th century, had even fewer converts (partly because of the temporary dissolution of the Jesuit order). The census of 1961 reported that 2.4% of the population of India belonged to Christian denominations. Conversion to Christianity, accompanied by the introduction of the Roman alphabet, was slightly more successful in Vietnam, where about 2 million people out of a population of 22 million were Christians (mostly Catholics) in 1954. (Because of the war no statistics are available for a more recent period.)

the missionaries were trying to deprive the Indian people of their cultural heritage under the guise of conversion of their script.[137]

Neither the gentle scholarly arguments of philologists nor the ardent spiritual zeal of missionaries succeeded in Latinizing Asian scripts, as Lepsius and other pious souls had hoped. The imposition of a script on entire nations or the conversion of a people's long-established writing system to a new and different one—feats that in the past had been performed by all-powerful god-kings or by the priests of great religions—could in modern times be achieved only by equally powerful secular dictators such as Atatürk and Stalin.

6. THE DEVELOPMENT OF ROMANIZATION FOR BIBLIOGRAPHIC CONTROL

6.1. Romanization in the Cataloging Codes of the 19th Century

The largely abortive attempts of Lepsius and his successors to Latinize the languages of Asia and Africa occurred during a period that saw the emergence of national and research libraries, and consequently the development of systematic bibliographic control tools in the form of author and title catalogs in which script conversion by Romanization began to become an established practice. As we have seen, the method of listing names of authors and titles of works in transcribed form may go back to the days of the Mouseion in Alexandria, and it can certainly be traced to the practice of Roman authors, who rendered Greek and other foreign names in a form suitable for the Latin language. They thus established a tradition of writing names from classical antiquity that persisted throughout the Middle Ages and during the Renaissance, when it became firmly embedded in Western bibliographic practice by Gessner's *Bibliotheca universalis,* in which the names of thousands of Greek and Hebrew authors were listed in Romanized form. Gessner's work was used by other bibliographers in aug-

---

[137]"There was an undertone of Hindu disapproval of such measures. . . . Where would the British stop? There was unease and suspicion of innovations like Western learning, with its disparagement of Oriental studies. Above all, Christian missions . . . were believed to be supported and approved by the government. There was a widespread feeling of irritation and alarm, and suspicion that the government was concerned in a deep-laid plot to subvert the established religious and social order." *Encyclopedia Britannica,* 14th ed., 1973, s.v. "Indian mutiny," by T. G. P. Spear. The situation had not changed appreciably some 80 years later: "Indian Christians were constantly accused by their fellow countrymen of being 'running dogs of imperialism' . . . [The missionaries were told by Indians] that their motive in coming to India was not really the preaching of the Gospel but the propaganda of western culture and European power." Thus Bishop Stephen Neill (1966) (who certainly cannot be accused of any antimissionary bias), in his *Colonialism and Christian missions,* p. 113, where he discusses the role and status of Indian missions in the 1930s.

mented and revised form until the middle of the 18th century, as were the bibliographical methods introduced by him. The names of Oriental authors and titles of works from Asia were also Romanized for bibliographic purposes in the manner in which this had been done during the Middle Ages for Arabic and Persian names, or the names were rendered in Roman script according to some phonological transcription, depending on the language of the first scholar to make such a transcription or on the rendering of a name and title by a translator. There were no rules of any kind, as indeed there were almost no library catalogs other than mere inventory lists, and few scholarly bibliographies before the end of the 18th century.

The problem of dealing with documents in dissimilar scripts in the catalog of a modern library was first subjected to definite rules by Anthony Panizzi, whose famous "Rules for the compilation of the catalogue" of the British Museum, published in 1841, formed the bedrock on which all subsequent catalog codes rested. He stated in Rule XXII:

All works in Oriental characters or languages, except Hebrew, to be separately catalogued in a supplementary volume, according to special rules to be framed.[138]

He was clearly of the opinion that the interests of readers would best be served by cataloging works in non-Roman scripts separately (and, except for the heading, in the original scripts), but he provided for the Romanization of names and titles, which were used as headings for filing purposes. Panizzi did not specify which kind of special treatment he envisaged for Hebrew, nor did he mention books written in Cyrillic script, of which the British Museum possessed a sizeable number, but they were actually treated according to the same principle. Russian names were Romanized, and the body of the entry was printed in Cyrillic script. The question was subsequently discussed in public hearings on Panizzi's rules, held in 1849 before a Parliamentary Commission, where a Mr. Craik proposed that the catalog be divided by alphabets (i.e., by scripts). The interrogating Commissioners seem to have been somewhat doubtful about the value of such a course of action, but Craik defended his proposal with logical arguments. His testimony is here given inasmuch as it refers to the subject of division of a catalog by script:

—I think it is very questionable whether you might not divide and simplify the catalogue by the separation, for instance, of the works in foreign languages and in ancient languages, and more especially in Oriental languages.

Q. What plan would you adopt for that purpose, taking first Oriental languages?

—I do not see upon what principle you can include works in the Oriental languages under our western alphabet.

[138]British Museum (1841), p. vi.

Q. Would you consider that Russian works ought to be excluded from the general catalogue?

—I believe they ought. Their alphabet is different from ours.

Q. Supposing an author has written partly in Latin and partly in Greek, would you admit his Latin works and exclude his Greek?

—Yes, I would, if the catalogue were compiled upon that principle.

Q. So, as to Aristotle, you would admit in your catalogue the English translations of Aristotle and the Latin translations of Aristotle, but Aristotle in the original would be entirely excluded?

—Of course it would be so if the catalogue were to be compiled upon that principle.

Q. Do not you think scholars would complain of that principle again?

—Scholars would have what they want, a complete catalogue of our Greek works.

Q. Your division would be each language that was not written in the Roman characters; would you, with regard to Oriental works, make a separate catalogue of each separate language?

—That might be a matter for consideration; probably that would be the better plan. I should think there is not much connexion between the study of Hebrew and the study of Chinese. The catalogue that would be a work of importance to the student of one language would be indifferent to the student of the other.[139]

While Craik advocated separation of catalogs by *scripts,* the Commissioners seem to have understood that he meant *languages,* including those written in Roman script, as is evident from later questions and testimony. Panizzi also defended the idea that all translations of a work should be listed together with the original, irrespective of language (but he did not say anything about non-Roman scripts). In the end the British Museum followed the practice outlined by Panizzi in rule XXII, and all Oriental languages (including Hebrew) were cataloged separately but names of authors or titles were Romanized. These individual catalogs for Oriental scripts were, however, compiled only several decades after the printing of the main catalog had begun, and supplements to them are published from time to time. Most of the catalogs contain a Romanization table for the respective script in the introductory part.

The use of Romanization by the British Museum is thus unique. It is used as a means of bibliographic control over documents in non-Roman scripts, but not in order to create one unified catalog in which Western and Oriental names are interfiled.

In the United States the question of how to deal with works written in non-

---

[139]Great Britain. Commissioners . . . (1850). Questions 5913–5923.

Roman scripts was first considered by librarians in 1883, when Melvil Dewey moved at the 6th general meeting of the American Library Association (ALA) in Buffalo, New York, that the Committee on Cataloging Rules should consider the matter and prepare a code of rules. He was supported by C. A. Nelson, the librarian of the Astor Library in New York (which later became the New York Public Library), who explained that

In his own experience, he had found a great need of definite rules for transliteration; that a perplexing want of uniformity obtained in all cases that had come under his observation and that . . . a committee . . . might perhaps, with the cooperation of eminent authorities in this country and abroad, fix upon a series of rules for transliteration, which would be recognized and adopted as the highest authority.[140]

A committee of 26 librarians was duly appointed, and a nonlibrarian, Michael Heilprin, was co-opted because he had already published various articles in the *Nation* about the need for standardized transcription systems for Russian, Greek, Hebrew, and other languages. The committee also consulted with two Harvard professors of philology, C. H. Toy, who devised the transliteration schemes for Arabic, Hebrew, Syriac, and Ethiopic, and C. R. Lanman, who contributed a scheme for Sanskrit. Heilprin elaborated the table for Cyrillic script. The report of the Committee began with the following statement:

In determining the principles of transliteration, it must be remembered that a catalog is not a learned treatise intended for special scholars, and bound to an erudite consistency, at whatever cost of convenience. It is simply a key to open the doors of knowledge to a partly ignorant and partly learned public, and it is very important that such a key should turn easily.[141]

It is clear from this and other statements made by the committee (or rather by Charles A. Cutter, who formulated the report) that they were convinced that only Romanization could solve the problem of cataloging works in non-Roman scripts. They also held the somewhat naive belief that this would somehow "open the doors of knowledge," presumably for that part of their readership they deemed "ignorant" (of languages? of scripts? of knowledge?). The subsequent discussion of the report and its recommendations at the Lake George Conference of the ALA in 1885 soon showed that ignorance was more widespread than the committee had presumed. Melvil Dewey confessed that he did not know anything about the merits and demerits of "phonetic versus literal" systems of script conversion, and W. F. Poole, another of the luminaries of librarianship at that time, urged neither the adoption nor the rejection of the report because

[140]*Library Journal*, **8** (1883), pp. 292–293.
[141]*Library Journal*, **10** (1885), p. 302.

I do not know enough about the principles of transliteration to vote upon it intelligently, and do not believe there are half-a-dozen persons who are better qualified than I am. . . . No one seems to know much about it.[142]

Charles A. Cutter also pleaded for delay because of general ignorance on the subject, and the minutes of the meeting show that the whole issue was considered to be rather amusing, and not anything to be considered very seriously:

Mr. Cutter: I do not myself feel that I know anything about it. (Laughter.) I do not think either that the Association knows anything about it. (Laughter.) And I do not think that a definitive vote at this time is desirable.[143]

Although these early efforts of the ALA did not yet result in rules "recognized and adopted as the highest authority," and American libraries continued to transcribe names and titles in non-Roman scripts as best they could and in different ways, three guiding principles for future developments clearly emerged. The first, and most important, was the unquestioned assumption that anything written in a non-Roman script must be Romanized in library catalogs, and that this was both desirable and feasible. The second was the recognition that two diametrically opposed principles were involved in Romanization, resulting in either transliteration or transcription. The third was the cooperation between librarians and philologists in the elaboration of conversion systems, which seemed to be natural (since librarians could not be expected to know all non-Roman scripts), but which led later to endless debates, delays, and changes in an attempt to create schemes that satisfied the demands of philologists more than the control functions of bibliographic tools, or the interests of library users other than philologists.

The tables of Romanization and the report that had been submitted in 1885 were first made a part of American cataloging practice when Cutter reprinted them in the second edition of his *Rules for a dictionary catalog* in 1889, and they were also included in the fourth (and last) edition of this work, published in 1904. Heilprin's original scheme for Cyrillic was there replaced by a "Table for transliteration of Slavic alphabets" compiled by a committee, one of whose members was A. V. Babine, a specialist on Russian literature at the Library of Congress. One year later the Library of Congress published its own "Supplementary Cataloging Rules 10 and 11" for Russian and modern Greek, respectively. These, as well as Romanization tables for Semitic languages and Sanskrit, were subsequently published as official ALA policy in 1908 and incorporated as Appendix 2 in what came to be known as the "Joint Anglo-American cataloging code."[144] True to the general spirit of this code, which contained

[142]*Library Journal,* **10** (1885), pp. 309–310.
[143]*Ibid.,* p. 311.
[144] American Library Association (1908), pp. 69–73.

many mutually inconsistent rules, the Romanization tables for the most important non-Roman script, namely Cyrillic, were given in three variants from which libraries could choose. The foundation was thus laid for what would soon prove to be the bane of all Romanization, namely the variant and inconsistent use of many different schemes by librarians, bibliographers, and publishers.

Curiously enough, the *principle* of Romanizing all non-Roman scripts was not expressly stated anywhere in the rules. For authors' names, it could only be inferred from the examples cited in rule 27, "Form of forenames"; rule 42, "Variations due to language, transliteration, etc." (where it was simply stated that there are "transliterated names"); and in rules 52–56, "Oriental writers and names." Regarding titles, rule 141, "Transliteration and translation of title," was permissive: titles in non-Roman scripts "may be transliterated." Nevertheless Romanization as the only officially sanctioned method for the rendering of names and titles written in non-Roman scripts, with the primary purpose of alphabetical interfiling of all entries in a unified author-title listing was established in American and British library practice by the Anglo-American code.

Meanwhile a similar development had taken place in Germany. In 1897 *Die Transscription fremder Alphabete,*[145] a comprehensive and integrated system of Romanization tables, was designed specifically "mit Berücksichtigung von Bibliothekszwecken" by the philologist E. W. A. Kuhn and the librarian H. Schnorr von Carolsfeld. In somewhat simplified form this work formed the basis for the Romanization tables of the German cataloging code known as the "Preussische Instruktionen." The tables covered a larger number of scripts than did their American counterpart (altogether 18) and also had the advantage of being more precise, not allowing for any variants, which made their application in library catalogs quite uniform. The Prussian code, like Cutter's rules and the subsequent Anglo-American code, prescribed Romanization of all non-Roman scripts. The principle was clearly stated:

§4.2 Jede andere Schriftart [i.e. other than Roman] wird nach dem anliegenden Schema (Anl. II) transkribiert, und die Bezeichnung der Schriftart vor die Transkription gesetzt.[146]

The provision for indication of the original script proved to be a very useful feature, but for some reason was never adopted in Anglo-American cataloging practice.

The Prussian code soon became the guide for all cataloging, not only throughout Germany but also in Switzerland and Austria (and later in the successor states to the Austro-Hungarian Empire), and it became the basis for national cataloging codes in the Netherlands and in the Scandinavian countries. Its

[145]Kuhn (1897).
[146]*Instruktionen für die alphabetischen Kataloge* . . . (1908), p. 5.

Romanization schemes were even adopted by several libraries in Asia and Africa.

In France, Italy, and in the libraries of the Iberian peninsula, Romanization was also performed, usually by locally devised systems based on national orthographic and phonological conventions.

The principle that all non-Roman scripts had to be rendered in library catalogs and bibliographies in Romanized form, which had guided Western librarianship since the Renaissance, had thus become the law in the national catalog codes of what was known before World War I as "the civilized world." Its value as a bibliographic control tool was accepted by all without question, and its usefulness for readers was generally taken for granted.

6.2. Romanization in Present Bibliographic Practice

Romanization as a bibliographic control method seemed to work reasonably well in European and American libraries until the 1930s and did not constitute a major problem. The amount of literature in non-Roman scripts was small or even negligible, and the number of readers interested in this literature was smaller still, most of them being specialists who had already become more or less familiar with the transcription systems through their philological or historical studies. But with the rapid growth of libraries caused by the steadily increasing number of books and other publications in a large variety of languages and scripts, it became evident that the application of Romanization as the control method for documents in non-Roman scripts caused many difficulties, mainly because of the proliferation of conversion systems and their inconsistent and often haphazard application in libraries. The focus of attention began to shift toward a never-ending search for more effective methods so that librarians could run their libraries smoothly and build up ever-larger monolithic catalogs. The "benefit of the public," which had been one of the concerns of the first ALA committee, was felt to be of less importance. Francis E. Sommer, an American librarian and linguist, tried to formulate "scientific" principles of Romanization (with which we deal in more detail in Chapter V). He also investigated the application and usefulness of the method, and in so doing stated the case of the librarian clearly:

For whose benefit is the transliteration made? Is it primarily for the readers or for the staff? On consideration, there can be but one answer: it is for the staff, or, more generally, for those who are unable to read the original script. . . .

As to the foreign readers, they naturally prefer the original script and derive practically no benefit from the transliteration.[147]

[147]Sommer (1934), p. 893.

He suggested, however, that two things be done to accommodate the needs of "foreign readers." Firstly, the rules of transliteration "should be available and the [library] assistant should be able to use it intelligently in cooperation with the readers."[148] Secondly, a file should be kept "in their native script" to enable readers of a dissimilar script to find works to which they had a citation in the original form. Unfortunately neither of Sommer's suggestions were ever taken up by any library that employed Romanization in its catalogs, although at least the first idea could easily have been performed without any additional costs or technical difficulties. Even the Library of Congress, whose Romanization schemes are widely used in the United States and elsewhere, did not publish a comprehensive edition of these schemes until 1976.[149] But among the various printed guides displayed alongside its catalog trays to aid the users, one looks in vain for even a hint about how certain foreign names written in Cyrillic, Arabic, Chinese, and so forth, are rendered and filed. The same situation prevails in all other American libraries that use Library of Congress cards or that produce their own catalog entries following the Romanization schemes used by the Library of Congress, without ever explaining to their users how a certain name is transcribed or why it is transcribed in a particular form.

As to Sommer's suggestion that a file be established in the original script (he seems to have thought primarily of title catalogs in this form, considering that Arabic, Persian, Hebrew, and other Oriental works are often better known by title than by author, and are often anonymous), this would, of course, have met with considerable difficulties of a technical nature, that is, printing in various dissimilar scripts, the very same difficulty that Romanization is designed to avoid in the first place.

Two decades later, when American research libraries had begun to compete with each other in building collections of "exotic" languages and scripts (often without having the necessary expertise), the problems of Romanization, far from being an amusing topic any more, became the subject of much professional concern among catalogers. Although it had for such a long time been taken for

---

[148]Sommer (1934), p. 893.

[149]The schemes used by the Library of Congress have been published during the past 25 years in *Cataloging Service,* a bulletin distributed to its own catalogers and interested persons in other libraries, but virtually unknown and inaccessible to the public at large. The schemes for Arabic, Cyrillic, Greek, Hebrew, and Yiddish appeared in the *ALA Cataloging rules for author and title entries* (American Library Association, 1949), and those for Chinese, Japanese, and Korean in a supplement, issued in 1959 by the Library of Congress. Both publications were normally held in the cataloging departments of libraries, that is, out of reach of the library users, and they have long been out of print. For this reason, and also because almost all schemes had been superseded by later amendments and revisions, they were reissued in a photographically reduced (and therefore often nearly illegible) format in *Cataloging Service,* Bulletin 118 (Summer 1976) and subsequent issues. For all practical purposes, the Romanization schemes of the Library of Congress are inaccessible to users of the bibliographic control tools produced by it (its own card catalog, the cards distributed to other libraries, the *National Union Catalog,* and various other bibliographies and lists).

granted, Romanization had lately been subjected to criticism. Several writers deplored the continuing proliferation of various schemes (especially for Cyrillic), which made a mockery of bibliographic consistency and compatibility. Others began to see the flaws in transcription methods for logographic scripts; and many librarians also repeated what Sommer had already recognized, namely that the users of foreign-language materials derived no benefit from Romanized entries in the catalog.[150]

These and other problems of Romanization were discussed in a paper by C. S. Spalding, an authority on cataloging and chairman of the Orientalia Processing Committee of the Library of Congress (the body responsible for the design of its Romanization schemes). It was read at the Conference on American Library Resources on Southern Asia, held in Washington, D.C., in 1957, and deserves close attention because of the official status of the author. Spalding began by stating that transliteration indeed created "a morass of problems" and admitted readily that it was not of much use to readers:

I will not attempt to support transliteration on the grounds that the actual readers of these library materials are better served by transliterated entries; I will even concede that transliteration will often impede their use of library catalogs.[151]

A large part of his paper was devoted to a detailed exposition of the flaws, difficulties, and even absurdities inherent in the Romanization of Arabic and of the various scripts used in Southern Asia. Yet despite all this, he said that he had to defend the practice of Romanization, and sought to justify it on ideological grounds. While Sommer had still considered Romanization as merely a practical tool needed primarily by a library's ordering, acquisition, and cataloging departments, Spalding now asserted that the practice was based on

great philosophical concepts: that knowledge, truth and the brotherhood of man are unitary and indivisible; . . . that a vital key to the betterment of mankind as a whole is improved communications; that languages are barriers; that language barriers are the higher and more forbidding as their written forms employ different alphabets. . . . The impetus to transliteration is part and parcel of the search for greater international understanding, of the objectives of organizations such as Unesco, of the movement to break down the compartmentalization of the world and its peoples.

How is this? It is because of the role of transliteration in the concept of the universal catalog or bibliography. . . . Through the means of transliteration, then, the universal catalog provides a key to the sum of man's knowledge and literature. . . .[152]

[150]Some of these were Palmer (1945), Shaw (1949), Bushell (1953), and Mish (1955).
[151]Spalding (1957), p. 3.
[152]*Ibid.,* pp. 3–4. After his retirement from the Library of Congress Mr. Spalding reversed his opinion radically, and recommended to abandon Romanization in favor of separate catalogs by script and language (Spalding, 1977).

The utopian belief in transliteration as a means for the betterment of mankind may be a distant echo of the pious hopes of 19th century philologists in the tradition of Lepsius, but it rests on rather shaky foundations. Neither a common script nor even a common language have ever prevented the nations of Europe from waging civil war or slaughtering each other, while on the other hand Germans and Japanese, though speaking entirely unrelated languages and using completely different scripts, made common cause in World War II. It also comes as a surprise that UNESCO is supposed to be in the business of "breaking down the compartmentalization of the world" by way of converting various peoples' writing systems to the Roman script; in fact, the opposite is true. Regarding international understanding (if that phrase is not used in a hyperbolic sense), it can be achieved only if people speaking and writing different languages can communicate with each other and can readily grasp the meaning of what others say. To this end one must learn languages, and not merely the script in which they are written. Turkish and Indonesian are now written in Roman script, but they are still incomprehensible to any European not familiar with these tongues; Romanized Arabic remains likewise a mystery unless one masters its vocabulary, grammar, and syntax. To be sure, it is easier to learn a foreign language if it is written in the same script as one's mother tongue, because a difficult initial hurdle does not have to be taken, but it is patently absurd to conclude from this that a common script constitutes in itself a means for the comprehension of a foreign language. The same applies to an even greater extent to the fallacious argument that transliteration provides a "key to the sum of man's knowledge and literature." The mere mechanical conversion of the graphemes of a dissimilar source script into the graphemes of a target script does not in itself provide such a key any more than the proverbial horde of apes pounding on typewriters for hundreds of years will produce the works of Shakespeare, or any sensible sentence at that. All they will ever produce is a jumble of letters without any meaning—and that is precisely what entries in Roman script may be to anyone not familiar with a language (even if it is originally written in Roman) and what Romanized entries are to those who know the original script that has been transmogrified in such a manner.[153] In the case of logographic scripts, Romanization, far from providing a key or aiding in the comprehension of Chinese, Japanese, or Korean, actually destroys any possibility of discovering the meaning of a written communication, as we have demonstrated in Chapter 2.

---

[153]The effect of transcription on the native reader was commented on already in 1885, when Mr. T. L. Whitney, delegate to the Lake George Conference of the American Library Association, observed: "Whichever form [of transliteration] may be chosen, the Russian student, especially if Russian born, will hold up his hands in horror and despair as he comes to the card catalogue." (*Library Journal*, **10** (1885), p. 309.)

Only thorough knowledge of a language can provide a key to the understanding of its literature, and if that language happens to be written in a dissimilar script, then that script has to be mastered in order to understand what has been written in the foreign tongue.

The naive belief in Romanization as the great equalizer seems to be based on a (psychologically understandable but nevertheless indefensible) gut reaction: "Why do those bloody foreigners write in such exotic squiggles? Let them all learn the Roman alphabet! And if they won't accept our advice—by golly, we are going to show them that it can be done!" The rationale behind such an opinion was actually stated by one of Mr. Spalding's colleagues only a few years later, when H. I. Poleman, the Chief of the Orientalia Division, in a speech before the American Oriental Society in 1963, stated:

Although we cannot reduce languages to a common denominator, we can at least Romanize all alphabets in catalogs.[154]

Poleman's paper, even more than the one by Spalding, exposed in minute detail the enormous difficulties and the sometimes hair-raising expedients that had to be resorted to in order to Romanize the scripts of India and Southeast Asia. An unbiased reader (i.e., one not brought up in the dogmatic belief that all non-Roman scripts have to be Romanized at all costs) would have expected the speaker to come to the conclusion that the system did not work, and that some better methods would have to be found for the bibliographic control of documents in non-Roman scripts. But Poleman (in a passage copied verbatim from Spalding's earlier paper) also defended Romanization as a means for "better international understanding" and saw the solution in the construction of more and "better" Romanization schemes.

One cannot help but smile wryly at the well-intentioned but wholly irrational desire for a "philosophical" justification of Romanization, propounded by men who actually knew the difficulties posed by this method very well, yet as representatives of a large national bibliographic control system traditionally committed to it, had to defend it despite its shortcomings and even inanities. Theirs was a quest for a "philosophers' stone" that would turn the base metal of "exotic" scripts into the shining gold of Roman letters from which a completely unified catalog of all the world's literature could ultimately be compiled, thus realizing the elusive dream of bibliographers since Gessner's days.

But the librarians and catalogers throughout the country who had to cope daily with the rising flood of books in non-Roman scripts, and who relied on the

---

[154] A copy of Poleman's speech, entitled "Ten Years," is preserved in the Orientalia Division of the Library of Congress; the quotation is on p. 11 of the typescript. Incidentally the exact opposite of what Poleman said is true, if one accepts the linguistic theories of Noam Chomsky; all languages do indeed have a "common denominator," while not all alphabets can be successfully Romanized.

experts of the Library of Congress to provide them with ready-made catalog entries that they themselves were unable to produce, were not concerned with philosophical or ideological issues. All they wanted was a facile means for dealing with outlandish documents that nobody in the library could read and process, but which somehow had to be brought under control so that the library could claim not only to possess such documents but also to "provide access" to them. They clamored for more Romanization, both by better bibliographic coverage of the book production in Asian countries, and by new Romanization schemes for scripts not yet covered by this method. In a sense they were more realistic, and their immediate goals were better defined than those expounded by the official spokesmen of the Library of Congress, even though few of them realized that the scripts of India, Southeast Asia, and the Far East do not lend themselves easily to the kind of Romanization that could usefully be employed in bibliographic control.

Romanization was now increasingly seen as a tool for librarians, designed to provide access to documents in dissimilar scripts for their own purposes, while little thought was given any longer to the question of whether the method actually made access possible for those able to read the original script. In a study of transliteration made in 1969 by H. C. Wright (characteristically subtitled "A discursus for catalogers"), the author dismissed the users' point of view:

It never seems to occur to the scholars, natives and others who criticize metagraphy that transliterated records are not created primarily for their enjoyment.[155]

He further declared magisterially:

As far as American librarianship is concerned, the distinction between transliteration and orthography means, among other things, that all who consult the public catalog, including natives and students of native languages, must do their bibliographical searching in terms of the Roman alphabet, *or they cannot do it at all* [my emphasis]. The problem here is not whether readers of exotic scripts prefer the native orthographies over transliterations; it is rather a matter of utilizing the catalog's ordinal machinery in order to determine whether or not a specific collection can provide access to a given document.[156]

The first part of Wright's statement seems to imply that libraries—and transliterated records, as part of their technical procedures intended to make recorded information accessible—exist for the benefit (or "enjoyment," as he would have it) of librarians rather than for users, an attitude hardly compatible with modern ideas about the functions and goals of libraries as service-oriented agencies of a community in need of information in the broadest sense. As to the second

---

[155]Wright (1969), p. 123.
[156]*Ibid.*, p. 128.

part, in Chapter 5 we deal with the fallacy of "providing access to a given document" through Romanization of dissimilar scripts which, in some cases, may actually *prevent* rather than provide access to source documents, since their authors or titles, when written in certain scripts, can never be unambiguously reconstructed or identified from a transcription. What is of concern to us here is the clear statement that transliteration and transcription are done for the sole benefit of *librarians* in order to enable them to exercise bibliographic control as they need it, while library users (especially the lowly natives!) have to comply with their terms or be damned.

Perhaps not many librarians would agree to the harsh language used by Wright, and as we shall see later, some of them continued to speak out in defense of those who are capable of reading dissimilar scripts. But it is an indisputable fact that total Romanization of all dissimilar scripts is now performed in practically all American, in many European, and even in some Asian and African libraries by librarians for librarians. This is done primarily to exercise control over documents in dissimilar scripts *as physical objects,* since lack of knowledge of those scripts on the part of most catalogers and reference librarians, and certainly of all filers of catalog cards, prevents them from making use of the documents or their surrogates as communication devices and as sources of information.

This is comparable to illiterate people trying to run a library by marking the books with signs that they can recognize, such as crosses, circles, colored dots, and the like, with literate library patrons searching for books they need, not by author or title but by those signs. The librarians' goal is to smoothly "integrate" the document surrogates in their catalogs, while adequate service to those who are most likely to make good use of documents in dissimilar scripts, namely people who can read them, is largely disregarded.

The conflict between the interests and legitimate aims of librarians and bibliographers, and those of the users of their services and products, which was recognized by almost all writers on Romanization in the past, is now either overlooked by the advocates of total Romanization and the designers of Romanization schemes, or is being dismissed as unimportant and even as preposterous.[157] The underlying causes for this conflict are explored in more

---

[157]This is essentially only one facet of the general attitude displayed by those who are in charge of the so-called "technical services" in libraries: "The most serious . . . conflict in libraries is usually between the technical services and public services. For processing units the goal becomes one of efficiency—the greatest output in least time. Of equal, if not greater, importance to them is the maintenance of their system and procedures. These goals can and do conflict with public services' goals to serve the user." (Bundy, 1966, p. 254.)

Subject specialists who were in close contact with library users had long since recognized this conflict. The former Chief of the Map Division in the Library of Congress, Dr. A. C. Gerlach, regarding the map cataloging practices of libraries, said: "Whenever there is a conflict between the

detail in Chapters 5 and 6, but before we can embark on the task of analyzing the claims of the advocates of Romanization as to the scientific basis of the method, it is necessary to examine the various conversion schemes that have been devised for the major scripts since the beginning of this century, and the attempts to unify and standardize the methods of script conversion.

---

requirement for presentation of data in an entry 'that will best meet the needs of users' and the requirement for an entry which 'can be integrated in a catalog with entries for others items', the latter principle is given priority. The *catalog* is the *thing!* Entries . . . must conform to the standards that will expedite their integration into the catalog.'' (Gerlach, 1961, p. 249). (Emphases in the original.) The last two sentences are intended to be ironical.

Four

The Major Scripts and Their Conversion Schemes

There are some "scientific systems" of transliteration, helpful to people who know enough Arabic not to need helping, but a wash-out for the world. I spell my names anyhow, to show what rot the systems are.

T. E. Lawrence. *Seven pillars of wisdom; a triumph*. London: Cape, 1935, p. 25.

1   THE WORLD'S MAJOR SCRIPTS

1.1.   Indicators of Relative Importance

In this chapter we survey the various schemes for conversion of scripts that are presently in use. For such a *tour d'horizon* it is necessary to establish a ranking of scripts by relative importance. At first glance this seems to be a fairly easy task. Most people, if asked what they consider to be the world's "major" or "most important" scripts, would give some ready answer, naming Roman, Cyrillic, Chinese, Arabic, and so on. But what makes a script "major," and how can a ranking by relative importance be ascertained? Is the criterion to be the number of people who speak the languages written in a certain script, is it the size of the geographical area in which a script is read and written, is it the number of literates, or is it perhaps the number of books published in a certain alphabet or character set? It seems that the most unlikely of these parameters, namely the geographic area, has often been taken as an indicator of relative importance of scripts, to judge from the maps of the world's major scripts found in many encyclopedias or in some works on languages and scripts, which show solid chunks of color spread over large areas of the earth and even over whole conti-

232

nents, where each color or shading represents a certain script. Most textual references to the proportional importance of various scripts simply identify them with certain languages or language families.[1] Both approaches are quite misleading, and give a distorted picture of the real proportion and relative importance of various scripts. The schematic maps show vast areas that are either entirely uninhabited or have only a very sparse (and illiterate) population, as if they were densely and uniformly populated by entirely literate people, whereas the equations between languages and scripts disregard the obvious fact that a script can, by definition, only be used by literate people, who in some countries form only a small part of the total population or language community.

In order to arrive at a more realistic picture of the relative importance of various scripts, objectively measurable parameters must be employed. Two such parameters that can be based on available statistical data are *(a)* the number of literate people who use a certain script, regardless of their language; and *(b)* the number of books published in that script.

1.2. Sources of Data

The following sources were used:
Political handbook of the world: 1976. New York: McGraw-Hill, 1976.
The statesman's yearbook, 1976–1977, New York: St. Martin's Press, 1976.
UNESCO. *Statistical yearbook, 1974.* Paris: UNESCO, 1975.
U.S. Agency for International Development. Office of Population.
Population program assistance: U.S. aid to developing countries.
Washington, D.C.: AID, 1974.

1.3. Literacy of the World's Adult Population

"Literacy" is a parameter subject to rather widely divergent interpretations in various countries, and the available figures are no more than crude indicators at best. When even highly developed countries such as England and the United States, which have an official literacy percentage of almost 100%, have to cope

---

[1]Mario Pei's *Language for everybody* contains a map "Predominant written forms of language" (Pei, 1956, pp. 184–185) which gives a distorted view of the relative importance of scripts, indicating only the geographic areas in which they are used. The same is true of a map "Systems of writing in the Old World," in M. Aurousseau's *The rendering of geographical names* (Aurousseau, 1957). These are books written for the educated layman, but even in a scholarly work such as David Diringer's *The Alphabet* the statement is made that "The Arabic alphabet is, after the Latin, the most generally used in the world today" (Diringer, 1968, p. 210); the data presented here show that this is not so.

with problems of functional illiteracy on a fairly large scale,[2] the literacy figures published by less developed countries with a much shorter history of general education must certainly be considered with some reservations, as witness the statements made by Indian experts (pp. 241–242) in the context of Devanagari. However, for the purpose of this study, all published data on literacy were necessarily taken at their face value; that is to say, the figures in Table 4.1 reflect "census literacy" and not functional literacy.

Since all figures for literacy in the UNESCO source are for the adult population 15 years of age and over, the literacy rate for each country was also calculated for that part of the population only, although the age group 10–14 at least must be considered literate in practically all countries in which compulsory elementary school systems exist, and in many instances even the age group 5–9 could be included, considering that most children are 6 years old and in some countries even younger, when they enter school. However to include one or both of these age groups in the literacy calculations would have made it impossible to compare the figures arrived at with those of the UNESCO source, in which Table 1.4, "Estimated adult population and literacy by continents" gives estimates for adults 15 years of age and over only.

The part of the total population of a country or region comprised of age groups 0–14 varies widely, and is generally much higher in the developing countries

---

[2]For an analysis of the phenomenon of functional illiteracy in the United States, see Harman (1970) and Hayes (1973), who defines functional literacy as "[an individual's] ability to recognize or call the words (word attack), know the meaning of the words (vocabulary) and understand those words in combination (comprehension) in any reading materials connected with what he is attempting to do (function or task) in a comfortable amount of time (rate). Let us include computational skills as a part of literacy, too." (Pp. 23–24). In England a conference on illiteracy "Breaking the reading barrier" was held in 1974, and the Library Association's Public Library Research Group has established a permanent Working Party on Adult Illiterates.

Key to Abbreviations and Symbols in Table 4.1

A	Arabic	K	Korean
B	Burmese	O	Other scripts
C	Cyrillic	R	Roman
D	Devanagari and scripts derived from it	T	Thai
		. . .	Data not available
E	Amharic	0.0	Magnitude less than 0.05
G	Greek	*	Estimated data
H	Hebrew	[1]	Data for 1971
J	Japanese	[2]	Data for 1972

Table 4.1 Scripts, Population, Literacy, and Book Production of the World's Countries

Country	Script	Population 1976 (Millions) Total N	Over 15 %	Over 15 N	Litera-cy rate	Literate population	Book production 1973
AFRICA							
Algeria	A	17.5	57	9.9	20	1.9	...
Angola	R	6.1	56	3.4	15	0.5	...
Benin	R	3.2	56	1.8	10	0.2	...
Botswana	R	0.8	61	0.5	25	0.1	52
Burundi	R	3.6	56	2.0	10	0.2	...
Cameroon	R	6.5	56	3.6	15	0.5	...
Central Afr. Republic	R	1.6	57	0.9	10	0.1	...
Chad	A	4.0	57	2.2	10	0.2	...
Congo Rep.	R	1.0	56	0.6	20	0.1	...
Egypt	A	38.5	57	21.9	26	5.7	2,055
Ethiopia	E	27.9	56	15.6	8	1.4	...
Gabon	R	0.6	56	0.3	12	0.0	...
Gambia	R	0.5	56	0.3	10	0.0	...
Ghana	R	10.2	56	5.7	25	1.4	136[1]
Guinea	R	4.5	56	2.5	10	0.3	. o .
Ivory Coast	R	5.0	56	2.8	20	0.6	260
Kenya	R	13.8	56	7.7	25	1.9	224
Lesotho	R	1.0	61	0.6	35	0.2	33[2]
Liberia	R	1.8	56	1.0	10	0.1	...
Libya	A	2.4	57	1.4	27	0.4	218[2]
Madagascar	R	7.3	56	4.1	40	1.6	154
Malawi	R	5.2	56	2.9	12	0.3	32
Mali	R	5.7	57	3.2	5	0.2	...
Mauritania	R	1.3	56	0.7	5	0.0	...
Mauritius	R	0.8	56	0.4	60	0.2	86
Morocco	A	17.8	57	10.1	14	1.4	122[1]
Mozambique	R	9.4	56	5.3	7	0.4	...
Niger	R	4.7	57	2.7	5	0.1	23
Nigeria	R	79.0	56	44.2	25	11.0	1,316
Rhodesia	R	6.5	57	3.7	30	1.1	...
Rwanda	R	4.4	57	2.5	10	0.3	13[2]
Senegal	R	4.5	56	2.5	10	0.3	...
Sierra Leone	R	2.8	56	1.6	10	0.2	...
Somalia	R	3.2	56	1.8	5	0.1	...
South Africa	R	25.6	61	15.6	35	5.5	2,673
Sudan	A	18.3	56	10.2	15	1.5	104
Swaziland	R	0.5	61	0.3	25	0.1	...
Tanzania	R	15.5	56	8.7	20	1.7	123[2]
Togo	R	2.3	56	1.1	10	0.1	...
Tunisia	A	6.0	56	3.4	30	1.0	82[1]
Uganda	R	11.7	57	6.7	20	1.3	205[1]
Upper Volta	R	6.1	56	3.4	10	0.3	...
Zaire	R	26.6	56	14.9	20	2.9	...
Zambia	R	4.9	56	2.7	20	0.5	...
Total		416.6		238.8		48.3	7,911

Table 4.1 *(continued)*

Country		Total N	Over 15 %	15 N	Litera-cy rate	Literate population	Book production 1973
						Population 1976 (Millions)	
NORTH & CENTRAL AMERICA							
Canada	R	23.3	71	16.5	95	15.7	4,083
Costa Rica	R	2.1	54	1.1	89	1.0	327 [1]
Cuba	R	9.5	61	5.8	78	4.5	942 [2]
Dominican R.	R	4.8	61	2.9	64	1.9	32
El Salvador	R	4.3	54	2.3	60	1.3	...
Guatemala	R	6.0	56	3.4	38	1.3	166
Haiti	R	5.5	61	3.4	10	0.3	...
Honduras	R	3.0	54	1.6	45	0.7	173
Jamaica	R	2.0	61	1.2	82	1.0	120 [2]
Mexico	R	60.4	54	32.6	76	24.8	5,455
Nicaragua	R	2.0	54	1.1	58	0.6	...
Panama	R	1.7	54	0.9	79	0.7	97 [1]
Puerto Rico	R	2.8	54	1.5	85	1.3	...
United States	R	218.0	71	155.0	98	152.0	83,724
Other	R	2.2	61	1.3	85	1.1	...
Subtotal		347.6		230.6		208.2	95,119
SOUTH AMERICA							
Argentina	R	25.4	68	17.3	91	15.7	4,578 [2]
Bolivia	R	5.7	54	3.1	40	1.2	586
Brazil	R	111.0	57	63.2	67	42.3	8,960 [2]
Chile	R	10.5	68	7.1	87	6.2	652
Colombia	R	25.5	57	14.5	63	9.2	848 [2]
Ecuador	R	6.9	57	3.9	67	2.6	32 [2]
Guyana	R	0.8	57	0.5	80	0.4	24 [2]
Paraguay	R	3.6	68	2.4	74	1.8	...
Peru	R	16.3	68	11.1	61	6.8	943
Surinam	R	0.5	57	0.3	84	0.2	...
Uruguay	R	3.1	68	2.1	90	1.9	...
Venezuela	R	12.5	57	7.1	77	5.5	...
Subtotal		221.8		132.6		93.8	16,623
Total		569.4		363.2		302.0	111,742

Table 4.1 *(continued)*

Country	Script	Population 1976 (Millions)					Book production 1973
		Total N	Over 15 %	Over 15 N	Litera- cy rate	Literate population	
ASIA							
Afghanistan	A	19.6	58	11.4	8	0.9	33
Bahrain	A	0.3	58	0.2	15	0.0	...
Bangladesh	D	79.4	56	44.5	22	9.8	...
Bhutan	D	1.0	58	0.6	5	0.0	25[2]
Burma	B	31.7	56	17.8	60	10.6	1,506
Cambodia	O	8.2	56	4.6	41	1.9	29[2]
China, P.R.	S	857.0	64	548.0	25	137.0	10,000*
China, Rep.	S	16.4	64	10.5	85	8.9	...
Cyprus	G	0.5	58	0.3	78	0.2	484
	R	0.2		0.1		0.1	
Hong Kong	S	4.4	58	2.6	80	2.0	806
India	D	615.0	58	357.0	34	121.0	14,064
Indonesia	R	134.0	56	75.0	43	32.3	1,180
Iran	A	34.4	58	19.9	23	4.6	3,353
Iraq	A	11.5	58	6.7	24	1.6	623[2]
Israel	A	0.5	58	0.2	80	0.2	2,147
	H	3.0		1.8	89	1.6	
Japan	J	111.7	76	84.9	98	83.2	35,857
Jordan	A	2.8	58	1.6	31	0.5	89
Korea, D.P.R.	K	16.4	64	10.5	73	7.7	...
Korea, Rep.	K	35.0	64	22.4	71	15.9	7,396
Kuwait	A	0.9	58	0.5	55	0.3	138
Laos	O	3.4	56	1.9	25	0.5	179[2]
Lebanon	A	3.3	58	1.9	86	1.6	...
Malaysia	R	12.0	56	6.7	43	2.9	1,082
Mongolia	C	1.5	58	0.9	96	0.8	587
Nepal	D	12.3	58	7.1	9	0.6	...
Oman	A	0.8	58	0.5	15	0.1	...
Pakistan	A	72.3	58	41.9	16	6.7	905
Papua-New G.	R	2.7	56	1.5	32	0.5	...
Philippines	R	43.9	56	24.6	72	17.7	706[1]
Qatar	A	0.2	58	0.1	15	0.0	88
Saudi Arabia	A	9.2	58	5.3	15	0.8	82
Singapore	S	2.3	58	1.3	45	0.6	201
Sri Lanka	D	14.3	58	8.3	76	6.3	1,502
Syria	A	7.6	58	4.4	31	1.4	459[2]
Thailand	T	41.0	56	23.0	68	15.6	2,255
Turkey	R	40.9	58	23.7	51	12.1	7,479
United Arab E.	A	0.3	58	0.2	15	0.0	...
Vietnam	R	45.3	56	25.4	67	17.0	729[2]
Yemen Arab R.	A	6.4	58	3.7	10	0.4	...
Yemen P.D.R.	A	1.7	58	0.9	10	0.1	...
Total		2,305.3		1,404.4		526.0	93,984

Table 4.1 *(continued)*

Country	Script	Total N	Over 15 %	Population 1976 (Millions) N	Litera- cy rate	Literate population	Book production 1973
EUROPE & USSR							
Albania	R	2.6	74	1.9	80	1.5	...
Austria	R	7.6	76	5.8	99	5.7	5,342
Belgium	R	9.9	76	7.5	97	7.3	8,953
Bulgaria	C	8.8	76	6.7	99	6.6	3,963
Czechoslovakia	R	15.2	76	11.6	99	11.5	8,567
Denmark	R	5.1	76	38.8	99	38.4	6,500
Finland	R	4.7	76	35.7	99	35.3	3,594
France	R	53.6	76	40.7	99	40.3	27,186
Germany D.R.	R	16.8	76	12.8	99	12.7	5,224
Germany F.R.	R	63.7	76	48.4	99	47.9	46,000*
Greece	G	9.1	74	6.7	82	5.5	2,007
Hungary	R	10.5	76	8.0	97	7.7	7,581
Iceland	R	0.2	76	0.2	99	0.2	617 [2]
Ireland	R	3.1	76	2.4	99	2.4	491
Italy	R	55.9	74	41.4	97	40.1	8,122
Luxembourg	R	0.4	76	0.3	99	0.3	180 [1]
Malta	R	0.3	74	0.2	70	0.2	123
Netherlands	R	14.6	76	11.1	99	11.0	11,640
Norway	R	4.0	76	3.0	99	3.0	5,694
Poland	R	34.3	76	26.1	97	25.3	10,744
Portugal	R	10.2	74	7.4	65	4.9	6,173
Romania	R	21.7	76	16.5	98	16.2	10,100
Spain	R	36.0	74	26.6	86	22.9	23,608
Sweden	R	8.4	76	6.4	99	6.3	8,242
Switzerland	R	6.7	76	5.1	99	5.0	7,942
U.K.	R	56.7	76	43.1	99	42.7	35,177
U.S.S.R.	C	258.0	72	185.8	99	183.9	80,200
Yugoslavia	C	14.4	74	10.7	80	8.5	10,110
	R	7.2		5.3		4.3	
Total		741.2		616.3		597.6	344,080
OCEANIA							
Australia	R	14.0	71	9.9	98	9.7	3,579 [2]
New Zealand	R	3.0	71	2.1	98	2.1	1,339
Total		17.0		12.0		11.8	4,918

NOTE. For each country only the script of its official or first language is listed, except for Cyprus, Israel, and Yugoslavia, where two scripts are officially used. Regarding the use of the Roman script in India see explanation in the text, p. 241.

than in the industrialized countries. Figures for each country were not always readily available; therefore the following method was adopted. The percentage of population aged 0–14 was calculated from the figures in Table 1.2 of the UNESCO source published in 1970, where a more detailed breakdown by geographical areas is provided than the one given in Table 1.4 of the 1974 edition.[3]

The most recent figures for the literacy rate of each country were derived from the AID source, generally referring to the year 1973. These were applied to the population figures of 1976. When an estimate of the literacy rate of a country had to be made, the tendency was to err on the positive side. Nevertheless the figures arrived at are sometimes lower than the UNESCO estimates, and tend to confirm the findings of other studies which show that, although the percentage of illiterates in the world is decreasing, their absolute number is increasing, due to the rapid rise in population, especially in the developing countries.[4]

1.4. Ranking of Scripts by Literacy

Table 4.2 shows the ranking of scripts by the number of adult literates in the world using them, with further breakdown by continents.

It is important to bear in mind that the figures in this table were computed by counting the literate population for each script only once for each particular country, the criterion being the language designated as the official or first language of that country. This was done to make the figures compatible with the published data or estimates, since the literacy of a population is established without regard to the number of languages and/or scripts that the inhabitants of a country are able to use. This method necessarily results in some distortion of the actual state of affairs, particularly regarding the number of people who are literate in the Roman script, because of the importance of the major European languages, which are read and written in large parts of the world, primarily English and, in descending order, French, Spanish, Portuguese, and German. There are, however, no demographically valid figures available for the number of bilingual people in many African and Asian countries where more than one language and script are widely used; much less are there such figures for the ability to read and write in more than one script, so that only approximate estimates can be made.

[3]In the explanation to that table it is stated that these "major areas . . . do not conform entirely to the conventional definition of the continents, but are so drawn as to obtain greater homogeneity for demographic analysis." (UNESCO *Statistical yearbook,* 1970, p. 24.)
[4]*Literacy and world population* (1975), p. 3.

Table 4.2 The World's Major Scripts Ranked by Number of Adult Literates

Rank	Script	AFRICA			AMERICA			ASIA			EUROPE & USSR			OCEANIA			WORLD			L % of A
		T	A	L	T	A	L	T	A	L	T	A	L	T	A	L	T	A	L	
1	Roman	284.2	164.1	34.8	569.4	363.2	302.0	279.0	157.0	82.6	453.0	409.1	393.2	17.0	12.0	11.8	1602.6	1105.4	824.3	75
2	Cyrillic							1.5	0.9	0.8	279.1	200.5	199.0				280.6	201.4	199.8	99
3	Chinese							880.1	562.4	148.5							880.1	562.4	148.5	26
4	Devanagari[1]							722.0	417.5	137.7							722.0	417.5	137.7	33
5	Japanese							111.7	84.9	83.2							111.7	84.9	83.2	98
6	Arabic	104.5	59.1	12.1				171.8	99.4	19.2							276.3	158.5	31.3	20
7	Korean							51.4	32.9	23.6							51.4	32.9	23.6	71
8	Thai							41.0	23.0	15.6							41.0	23.0	15.6	68
9	Burmese							31.7	17.8	10.6							31.7	17.8	10.6	60
10	Greek							0.5	0.3	0.2	9.1	6.7	5.5				9.6	7.0	5.7	81
11	Hebrew							3.0	1.8	1.6							3.0	1.8	1.6	89
12	Amharic	27.9	15.6	1.4													27.9	15.6	1.4	8
13	Other							11.6	6.5	2.4							11.6	6.5	2.4	37
	Total	416.6	238.8	48.3	569.4	363.2	302.0	2305.3	1404.4	526.0	741.2	616.3	597.6	17.0	12.0	11.8	4049.5	2634.7	1485.7	60

[1]Including derived and related scripts in India.

T = Total population of all countries where a script is the official or first one (millions).

A = Adults over 15 (millions).

L = Literate adults over 15 (millions).

Regarding English, it is still one of the officially recognized languages of India, and the only one that forms a common vehicle of communication between the 15 official Indian languages. It may safely be assumed that practically all functionally literate Indians are therefore also literate in the Roman script, which alone would add some 100 million literates to the figure for Roman (in Tables 4.1 and 4.2 Indian literates are counted only under Devanagari). English or French is taught at the high school level in most countries that use non-Roman scripts (those that were formerly British or French colonies, but also in the Soviet Union, in Japan, and in many other countries), probably adding as many as 200–300 million to the number of those who can at least read Roman script. This means that the actual number of adult literates who know and use Roman script is probably somewhere around 1 billion people, and may even be higher.

For Cyrillic script, some of what has been said about Roman script also applies. Because of the importance of the Soviet Union in the affairs of those eastern European countries in its political sphere of influence that use the Roman script, Russian is taught there as a second language. By now a large percentage (perhaps as many as two-thirds) of the more than 80 million adult literates in these countries are able at least to read Cyrillic, and many can also write it. A not inconsiderable number of people in Western countries are also able to read and write Cyrillic, so that an estimated 50 million should be added to the figures for Cyrillic given in Table 4.2.

Regarding Chinese, literacy figures are available only for the Republic of China (Taiwan), Hong Kong, and some other Southeast Asian countries with a sizable Chinese population. All these together are, however, numerically almost insignificant when compared to the huge number of people in the People's Republic of China, for which no data could be obtained.[5] In the absence of any official figures the AID estimate of 25% literacy was applied, although this might well be too low a percentage, since practically all children of school age are now said to be literate, so that the age group 15–19 at least must also be assumed to be highly literate.

The figures for literates in the Devanagari script (which also includes, for the purposes of this study, the scripts derived from it, that is, Assamese, Gujarati, Gurmukhi, Kannada, Oriya, Sarada, Sinhala, Telugu, Tamil, Tibetan, and others), though impressive when compared with those of only a quarter of a century ago, must nevertheless be taken with a grain of salt. As recently as 1973, S. Maitra of the Bengal Social Service League in Calcutta said: "70% of the people of India have not acquired even census literacy which is a far cry from functional literacy."[6] His colleague, P. N. Venkatachari of the *Indian National Bibliography,* elaborated further:

---

[5]Neither the official representatives of the People's Republic of China in the United States nor UNESCO could furnish any official data on literacy.

[6]Maitra (1974), p. 55.

As against the illiterates, the reading public is a microscopic minority. Whatever the percentage of literacy in India may be, it is rapidly growing [but] the actual number of people who can read a book is very much less. . . . Our literacy figure as of 1971 is 29.75% even though some Indian states like Kerala and Delhi have very high figures (60.16% and 59.65%). In other words, only three persons out of every ten are literate. If we analyze further, probably only one of these three can read a book either in his language or in English.[7]

These statements, so candidly made by representatives of a developing country that can point to truly impressive achievements in the promotion of literacy, probably apply to an even larger degree to most other Asian and African countries in which the literacy rate is still much lower than in India.

This is particularly relevant for the Arabic script, which ranks sixth according to the number of literates using it, but has the lowest literacy percentage as related to the number of potential adult literates in the countries in which this script is the official one (the Arab countries, Iran, Afghanistan, and Pakistan), even when allowance is made for several million literate and semiliterate Muslims in Africa and southeast Asia who can read at least some Arabic but have been counted as Roman script literates according to the official languages and script used in their countries (e.g., Tanzania, Malaysia, Indonesia).

The figures for Hebrew script in the table relate to Israel only (where Hebrew is the official language), but among Jews outside Israel there are probably no less than 4–5 million who can at least read Hebrew script, including an estimated 2 million Jews who read and write Yiddish, so that the actual number of literates for Hebrew is probably at least 5 million and may very well be higher. Again this does not change the relative ranking of scripts according to literacy.

Amharic, although one of the ''minor'' scripts, has been listed separately in Table 4.2 because it is the only syllabic script presently in use (except for the Japanese *kana*). According to one of the most recent sources,[8] Amharic is spoken by about half of Ethiopia's population; literacy rates range from 56% in Addis Ababa to a low 3% or less in the countryside. Official Ethiopian government figures for literacy in 1970 are 9–10%, almost double the figure for 1963, but still one of the lowest in Africa; this refers, however, to literacy in general and includes Muslims literate in Arabic, as well as people literate in the Roman script.

Table 4.3 summarizes the results of the figures given in Table 4.2, compared with the revised estimates as discussed in the preceding paragraphs. The percentage figures for literates in each script show that, even if only the first or official language and script is taken into consideration, Roman script is used by more than half of the world's literates, and probably by more than two thirds if ability

[7]Venkatachari (1974), pp. 62–63.
[8]Hess (1970), p. 157.

Table 4.3   Distribution of Literates by Major Scripts

			Literates			
Rank	Script	Number (official or first script only) (Millions)	Percentage N = 1486	Cumulative percentage	Number (revised estimate) (Millions)	Percentage
1	Roman	824	55	55	1,000[1]	67
2	Cyrillic	200	13	68	250[1]	17
3	Chinese	149	10	78	149	10
4	Devanagari	137	9	87	137	9
5	Japanese	83	6	93	83	6
6	Arabic	31	2	95	46[1]	3
7	Other	61	4	99	61	4
	Total	1,486	100			

[1]Including persons who are literate in more than one script.

to at least read it as a second script is considered. Three scripts—Roman, Cyrillic, and Chinese—account for 78% of the world's literates, and the Indic scripts, Japanese, and Arabic make up almost all the rest. Only 4% of the world's literates use a script other than one of the "big six" as their first or only means of graphic communication.

Table 4.4 shows the numerical distribution of literates by graphemic type of script; more than 80% of the world's literates use alphabetic scripts (although some of these have characteristics of syllabic scripts, and others do not normally write vowels, etc.), while the rest use logographic or logographic-syllabic scripts.

1.5.   Ranking of Scripts by Book Production

The UNESCO source lists the annual book production of many countries and also provides a breakdown by language, from which the script used can be deduced in most instances. Most countries for which no data on book production in 1973 were available play only an insignificant role in this respect, and almost all of them publish books in the Roman script, which in any case outranks all other scripts by a large margin, so that the lack of data for some smaller countries does not make any appreciable difference. The People's Republic of China announced in 1975 that about 11,000 titles had been published in 1974 (although it is not known what exactly is being counted as a "title" for the purpose of these statistics); an estimated figure of 10,000 titles was therefore assumed for 1973.

The data for book production in 1973 (or, when not available for that year, in 1972 or 1971) have been tabulated by script in Table 4.5. All figures are rounded off to the next higher hundred, which probably compensates for the lack of data from some countries. The figures show not only that the Roman script is the

Table 4.4 Distribution of Literates by Graphemic Type of Script

Graphemic type	Script	Literates Number (Millions)	Literates Percentage
Alphabetic	Roman Cyrillic Devanagari Arabic Greek Hebrew etc.	1,237	83
Logographic	Chinese Korean[1]	165	11
Logographic-syllabic	Japanese	83	6
Syllabic	Amharic	1	0
Total		1,486	100

[1]When written in Chinese script.

Table 4.5 Book Production by Script 1973

Rank	Script	Titles Roman	Titles Non-Roman	All titles Percentage N = 562,500	All titles Cumulative percentage	Non-Roman titles Percentage N = 158,500	Non-Roman titles Cumulative percentage
1	Roman	404,000		71.6	71.6		
2	Cyrillic		81,000	14.4	86.0	50.6	50.6
3	Japanese		35,500	6.3	92.3	22.2	72.8
4	Chinese		11,200	2.0	94.3	7.0	79.8
5	Devanagari		8,800	1.6	95.9	5.5	85.3
6	Arabic		7,500	1.3	97.2	4.7	90.0
7	Korean		7,400	1.3	98.5	4.6	94.6
8	Greek		2,300	0.4	98.9	1.4	96.0
9	Thai		2,200	0.4	99.3	1.4	97.4
10	Hebrew		2,000	0.4	99.7	1.3	98.7
11	Burmese		1,500	0.2	99.9	0.9	99.6
12	Other		600	0.1	100.0	0.4	100.0
	Subtotal	404,000	160,000				
	Total	564,000		100.0		100.0	

dominant and most important one in present book production—a fact that is well known to everybody—but also that the total number of books written in the Roman script is more than two and a half times that of all non-Roman scripts combined. The next five scripts together account for 90% of the world's non-Roman book production, with Cyrillic and Japanese supplying almost three-quarters of the total. These are therefore to be considered the "major" non-Roman scripts as measured by book production, all others being "minor" both in number of books published and in number of literates served.

To consider the relative importance of scripts only as manifested by their present book production would, however, result in a somewhat distorted picture. To gain a proper perspective, it must also be considered from the point of view of graphic records created in the past. Chinese and Arabic, for example, are among the major scripts whose combined output of books in 1973 was only 3.3% of the world total, but there was a time when manuscripts and books written in these scripts were more numerous than those written in Roman. A vast number of these have been preserved, and are now among the treasures of many scholarly libraries throughout the world. The same is true for two of the minor scripts, namely Greek and Hebrew, which also play an important role because of the large number of books written in these scripts during more than two millennia; these too have been collected and preserved in libraries, and are still being studied by scholars.

Any attempt to rank scripts by "intellectual impact" would therefore be presumptuous because we are dealing here with imponderables. Even the "importance of library holdings" is almost impossible to assess because data on the number of extant titles or the size of library collections by script and language are generally unavailable.

2. CONVERSION SCHEMES

2.1. Romanization

The predominance of the Roman script as the vehicle of graphic communication used by the politically most powerful Western nations and their cultural institutions is the reason that almost all efforts at script conversion for philological, cartographic, and bibliographic purposes have been made in one direction only—from non-Roman scripts into one or more of the European Roman alphabets.

As we have seen in the preceding chapter, the catalogers of the British Museum and those of the large American and German libraries developed their transcription schemes toward the end of the 19th century and published them in their catalogs or cataloging codes. When librarians in other European countries subsequently designed their own national cataloging codes during the first half of the present century, they often included Romanization tables also. Most of these deal with only one or at best a few of the most common non-Roman scripts, and all are based on one of the three models provided by the code of the British Museum, the rules followed by the Library of Congress, or the tables of the "Prussian Instructions." Many national codes expressly refer the cataloger to one of these sources. Local deviations from the chosen model were, however, almost always introduced, partly to accommodate the conventions of the national orthography, sometimes also to provide a better approximation to the pronunciation of a non-Roman character. Inevitably, these changes were labeled "minor" by the editors of codes, but they led to almost complete incompatibility between many of the codes and the catalog entries produced according to their rules.

The proliferation of mutually incompatible Romanization codes, particularly those for the most important non-Roman script, Cyrillic, led ultimately to concerted efforts on behalf of the ISO toward the design of international transliteration codes and standardization of rules. Although the resulting international standards are far from being faultless, and have by no means found as wide an application as had been hoped for, they form a useful framework for future development, and have become particularly important for Universal Bibliographic Control,[9] which is now the focus of activity in international librarianship and documentation.

Thus Romanization is at present performed at three levels. The first level is still the domain of individuals, mostly philologists who devise new schemes for scripts not yet Romanized or who attempt to improve existing schemes for their particular purposes. At the next higher level are national cataloging codes, designed by national libraries or national library associations, and often supported by officially promulgated national standards that have a wider field of application than library codes. Finally, at the top level, are international codes, primarily those designed under the auspices of the ISO, but also those developed by a few other international agencies; in most instances the latter are either virutally identical with ISO standards or at least compatible with them.

2.2. Conversion into Non-Roman Scripts

Although there is little or no coordination of efforts, resulting in much confusion and duplication in the field of Romanization, there is at least no lack of activity. Old schemes are being revised, and new schemes are frequently published. The same cannot be said about endeavors to perform conversion of scripts (both

---

[9] The International Federation of Library Associations (IFLA) devoted its entire 39th General Council Meeting in 1973 to the problems of Universal Bibliographic Control (UBC). In 1974 an International Office for UBC, working in close cooperation with the British Library, was established by the IFLA in London.

Roman and non-Roman) into any of the non-Roman scripts, for example, the rendering of English or French names into Arabic or Hindi, and the transcription of Russian into Japanese and vice versa.

The idea that conversion of scripts is a two-way street too long dominated by the one-way traffic of Romanization began to take shape only in the 1950s, concomitant with the rise in literacy in those parts of the world in which it was found necessary to render names and words from other languages and scripts into indigenous languages and scripts. The efforts at script conversion from Roman into non-Roman scripts, and between pairs of non-Roman scripts are still in their initial stages. Such conversion schemes as exist are often unsystematic, the principles of transcription are poorly understood, and there is practically no compatibility. Nevertheless this area of script conversion has increasingly important implications for Western countries and for Romanization of names in retranscribed form, particularly when these have undergone two stages of conversion, for example, when a Japanese name has been transcribed into Russian and is taken from there by a translation into English.

The conversion of non-Cyrillic scripts into Cyrillic for the benefit of users of that script dates back at least to the end of the 18th century, as we have seen. In our own time Russian, Bulgarian, and Serbian bibliographers and librarians have been concerned with the elaboration of transcription schemes since the 1950s. The schemes that have been devised deserve close attention on the part of those who use the Roman script for bibliographic work because of the problems of retranscription just mentioned.

The rendering of non-Japanese names and words for the purpose of Japanese bibliographic control is a major problem for Japanese librarians and bibliographers, who have to overcome almost insurmountable difficulties because of the phonology of the Japanese language and the complexities of its writing system. But this is not a purely local problem either. Japanese names are almost impossible to Romanize because of variant "readings" and other factors not inherent in the graphemes; these difficulties are aggravated by the Japanization of foreign names which, when retranscribed, become distorted to such an extent that they are often unrecognizable.

Similar problems confront libraries and bibliographic services in countries where the official or dominant script is Devanagari (or one of its derivatives) or Arabic script. No generally recognized conversion schemes from Roman or Cyrillic into these scripts exist as yet. The situation is not unlike the one in Europe before the mid-19th century, when every scholar who had to transcribe a name from a foreign script followed his own method, and libraries either ignored the problem or followed whatever system happened to be used by the chief librarian (who often was a philologist himself). The so-called "minor" scripts, that is, those in which relatively few books are published and which have only local or regional importance, also lack suitable transcription systems into their writing system.

2.3   Survey of Conversion Schemes

It would obviously be impractical to deal here with every single one of the many hundreds of scripts that have been transcribed at one time or another by philologists, cartographers, or other scholars by means of various conversion methods and into different scripts. To keep our survey within manageable bounds, we shall limit ourselves mainly to scripts and conversion schemes that are presently in use, and that have been published in the form of national and international standards, national cataloging codes, in general manuals of scripts and languages, and in other sources.

2.3.1.   Sources.   All data pertaining to Romanization schemes are based on the following published sources.

1.   International and national standards, identified by their official abbreviations. Scripts covered are listed in parentheses.

AFNOR   Association Française de Normalization
       (Arabic, Cyrillic, Hebrew)
ANSI   American National Standards Institute
       (Arabic, Cyrillic, Hebrew, Japanese)
BSI   British Standards Institution
       (Arabic, Cyrillic, Greek, Hebrew, Japanese)
INIS   International Atomic Energy Agency
       (Cyrillic, Greek)
ISO   International Organization for Standardization
       (Arabic, Cyrillic, Greek, Hebrew)

The national standards of other countries are listed where applicable (most of these deal only with Cyrillic script).

2.   The Romanization systems that are used in three of the four "great" national catalogs. These have also found wide application outside their respective countries of origin, thereby achieving a status commensurate with that of international codes. They are identified by the following abbreviations:

BM   British Museum
LC   Library of Congress
PI   *Preussische Instruktionen*

The BM code[10] contains Romanization tables for Gaelic (which is not really a non-Roman script, but is included here because it has been "Romanized" by

---

[10]British Museum (1936).

several cataloging codes, following the model of the code), Romanian in Cyrillic script, Bulgarian, Russian, Ukrainian, Serbian, and modern Greek (in this order). The tables for Cyrillic script have been somewhat changed and augmented for White Russian and Macedonian by means of a leaflet (undated) available in the British Museum reading room but not published anywhere else. The British Museum's *General Catalogue of Printed Books,* which contains thousands of entries transliterated according to the schemes in the BM code, does not display the tables. The Romanization schemes used for the cataloging of books and manuscripts in all other scripts appear in tabular form in some of the respective separate catalogs for each script, but in many cases they can only be inferred from the Romanized headings. Catalogs for a few scripts (Mongolian, Tibetan, Thai, and Zend) exist only in manuscript form, and have not yet been published. Altogether the published BM catalogs[11] cover 27 different scripts.

The Romanization schemes used by the Library of Congress for Arabic, Hebrew, Syriac, Amharic, Sanskrit, Cyrillic, and modern Greek were originally contained in the cataloging codes published by the American Library Association in 1908 and in 1949[12] (henceforth abbreviated as ALA 1908 and ALA 1949). Since then, most of these schemes have been slightly or substantially changed, and a large number of Romanizations for other scripts have been published at various times in *Cataloging Service* (see Chapter 3, footnote 149). The schemes now cover more than 100 languages and scripts. The printed catalogs of the Library of Congress, however, and their successor, the *National Union Catalog (NUC),* [13] do not contain any Romanization tables, nor is reference made to the source in which they have been published.

The PI code[14] contains Romanization tables that are presently used by most libraries in Germany, Austria, the German-speaking parts of Switzerland, and Luxembourg, as well as in many other countries. They cover Russian, Bulgarian, Ukrainian, Glagolitic, Serbian, Romanian, Sanskrit, Arabic, Persian, Turkish, Hindustani, Malayalam, Hebrew, Syriac, Amharic, Coptic, Armenian, and Georgian; the schemes for Arabic, Persian, and Ottoman Turkish have been updated and augmented by E. Wagner.[15] The PI code is now gradually

---

[11]A complete list of BM catalogs for non-Roman scripts is contained in Francis (1951). Since then, most of the catalogs listed there as "in the press" and supplements to several earlier catalogs have been published. There are also four new catalogs for languages and scripts not formerly covered, namely, *Catalogue of Saurashtran printed books* (1960), *Catalogue of Syrian printed books* (1962), *Catalogue of Georgian and other Caucasian printed books* (1962), and *Catalogue of Malayalam printed books* (1971).

[12]American Library Association (1908, 1949).

[13]Library of Congress (1942).

[14]*Instruktionen für die alphabetischen Kataloge* . . . (1908).

[15]Wagner (1961).

being replaced by a new German cataloging code, *Regeln für die alphabetische Katalogisierung (RAK),*[16] but its Romanization tables remain in force. The union catalog of books held in the major libraries of German-speaking countries, the *Deutsche Gesamtkatalog* (published between 1931 and 1939 but never completed), mentions in its introduction that transliteration is performed according to the PI code, but does not contain the tables themselves.

The fourth large national catalog, the *Catalogue général des livres imprimés* of the Bibliothèque Nationale in Paris (started in 1897 and still in progress), which lists the holdings of the library until 1959, also lacks any indication as to which Romanization schemes are used. The names of classical authors with Arabic, Greek, or Hebrew names are given in the form in which they have been traditionally rendered in French literature, while Slavic names are rendered in a phonemic spelling that seeks to approximate the pronunciation for Francophones. The second series of this catalog, listing books added to the collection from 1960 to 1964, is arranged according to a completely different principle. There are separate volumes for Cyrillic and Hebrew entries, in which the headings have been transliterated according to the AFNOR transliteration standards, while entries in modern Greek are printed entirely in the original script. The third series of this catalog, listing books acquired from 1960 to 1969, follows the same pattern and displays transliteration tables for Cyrillic, Hebrew, and Yiddish.

Thus, the world's largest catalogs in book form, which contain many thousands of entries with names in Romanized forms, employ entirely different conversion schemes. The Russian name Юшкевич appears therefore in the BM catalog as *Yushkevich,* in the *NUC* as *ÎUshkevich,* in the German national bibliography as *Juškevič,* and in the old French catalog as *Iouchkevitch,* that is, not only in four different Romanized forms but also in four different alphabetical positions! Yet the keys to the various conversion schemes are not displayed anywhere in easily accessible form (with the sole exception of the two last editions of the French catalog, as pointed out), perhaps because the editors of these catalogs thought that users would be as familiar with the Romanization schemes as they themselves were.

3.   The cataloging codes of 14 countries. These are identified according to the "Country of Publication Codes" used in the MARC system of the Library of Congress. The scripts covered by each code are listed in parentheses.

---

[16]The new code is a cooperative venture, produced by librarians from the Federal Republic of Germany, the German Democratic Republic, and Austria. It was published in the form of preprints between 1965 and 1975, and will probably appear in book form in 1977. Tables of Romanization will form "Anhang 5," to be published later. Until 1975 only the table for Cyrillic (almost identical with ISO 9) had been approved; other tables will cover Greek, Hebrew, Yiddish, Indic scripts, Chinese, and Japanese.

AU   Austria   Hofbibliothek. Wien. *Vorschrift für die Verfassung des alphabetischen Nominalzettelkatalogs der Druckwerke der k.k. Hofbibliothek . . .,* Wien, 1901. Beilage I. "Vorschrift für die Transscription fremder Schriftarten."*

[Amharic, Arabic, Afghan, Hindustani, Malayalam, Persian, Turkish, Armenian, Georgian, Hebrew, Zend, Huzvares (Pehlevi), Coptic, Sanskrit, Glagolitic, Bulgarian, Russian, Serbian, Syriac (Estrangelo)]

BE   Belgium   Bibliothèque royale de Belgique. *Règles cartographiques en usage à la Bibliothèque royale de Belgique.* Bruxelles, 1961.

(Amharic, Arabic, Armenian, Coptic, Cyrillic, Gaelic, modern Greek, Hebrew)

BU   Bulgaria   Народна библиотека "Васил Коларов". Правила за описване на книгите в научните и в големите библиотеки и за нареждане на фишите в азбучния каталог. Второ разширено и преработено издание. Изработиха Б. Божинова Троянова и Л. Албанска. София 1962.

(Church Slavic, Cyrillic, Greek)

CS   Czechoslovakia   Státní knihovna Československé Socialistické Republiky. Ústřední vědecko-metodický kabinet knihovnictví. *Pravidla jmenného katalogu.* 2., opravené a doplněné vydání. Praha, 1969.

(Armenian, Cyrillic, Georgian, Greek)

DK   Denmark   Bibliotekscentralen. København. *Katalogiseringsregler.* 2:a udg. København, 1970.

(Cyrillic)

FI   Finland   Yliopisto. Kirjasto. *Suomen tietellisten kirjastojen lisälvettelon luetteloimissäännöt.* Helsinki, 1949.

(Cyrillic; all other scripts by PI)

GE   Germany   Bayerische Staatsbibliothek. Kommission für alphabetische Katalogisierung. *Katalogisierungsordnung der Bayerischen Staatsbibliothek, München.* München, 1970.†

(Cyrillic, Greek)

IT   Italy   Direzione generale delle accademie e biblioteche. *Regole per la compilazione del catalogo alfabetico per autori nelle biblioteche italiane.* Roma, Palombi, 1956.

(Amharic, Arabic, Armenian, Coptic, Cyrillic, Gaelic, Greek, Hebrew, Syriac)

NO   Norway   Norsk biblioteksforening. Katalogkomité. *Katalogiseringsregler for norske biblioteker.* 4:e omarb. utg. Oslo, 1970.

(Cyrillic, Greek)

---

*This code has been superseded in Austrian libraries by the *Preussische Instruktionen* in the 1930s but is listed here because of its extensive coverage of scripts.

†This code was essentially a preliminary version of *RAK,* which superseded it in 1975.

PL   Poland   Grycz, J. *Skrócone przepisy katalogowania alfabetycznego.* Wyd. 3. Warszawa, 1961.*

(Cyrillic, Greek, Hebrew, Yiddish)

SP   Spain   Dirección general de archivos y bibliotecas. *Instrucciones para la redacción de catálogo alfabético de autores y obras anónimas en las bibliotecas públicas del estado.* 3a ed. reformada. Madrid, 1964.

(Arabic, Greek, Hebrew)

SW   Sweden   Sveriges allmänna biblioteksförening. *Katalogregler för svenska bibliotek.* 3:e uppl. Lund, Bibliotekstjänst, 1970.

(Cyrillic; all other scripts by LC)

VC   Vatican   Biblioteca Apostolica Vaticana. *Norme per il catalogo degli stampati.* Roma, 1939.

(Amharic, Arabic, Armenian, Coptic, Cyrillic, Gaelic, Greek, Hebrew, Syriac)

YU   Yugoslavia   Društvo bibliotekara Hrvatske. *Pravilnik i priručnik za izradbu abecednih kataloga.* Zagreb, 1970.

(Cyrillic, Glagolitsa, Greek, Arabic)

The cataloging codes of countries not listed under (3) do not contain transliteration tables. Some codes mention transliteration in connection with rules for the form of names, usually in general phrases such as "Oriental names are to be written in Roman characters according to the usual transcription schemes," without specifying any particular scheme.

4.   Comprehensive manuals of languages and scripts, containing Romanization tables.

Alphabete   Germany. Bundesdruckerei. *Alphabete und Schriftzeichen des Morgen- und des Abendlandes.* Berlin, 1969.

(Lists the scripts of 86 languages, 57 of which are non-Roman.)

Ostermann   Von Ostermann, G. F. *Manual of Foreign Languages.* New York, 1952.

(Lists the scripts of 132 languages, 40 of which are non-Roman.)

BGN   U.S. Board on Geographic Names. *Romanization Guide.* Washington, D.C., 1972.

(Amharic, Arabic, Bulgarian, Burmese, Chinese, Faeroese, Greek, Hebrew, Icelandic, Japanese, Khmer, Korean, Laotian, Lappish, Maldivian, Mongolian, Nepali, Pashtu, Persian, Russian, Serbian and Macedonian, Thai, Ukrainian.)

Alphabete[17] is the most comprehensive collection of non-Roman scripts and

---

*The fourth edition of this code, published in 1970, was not available to me for inspection.

[17]Germany (Federal Republic), Bundesdruckerei (1969).

their Romanization published so far. It is intended mainly for printers and typographers, but is also useful for bibliographic purposes, especially for German sources, since it is in many instances identical with the *Preussische Instruktionen*. The manual was first published in 1924 and was updated and enlarged in 1969; it covers 86 alphabets, 57 of which are in non-Roman scripts (in our tabulation only 39 of these have been listed since the other 18 are either those of dead languages or merely variants of a certain script).

Ostermann[18] has Romanization tables for 27 different scripts, and lists the pronunciation (but not transliteration) for 5 others. This work is now somewhat out of date.

BGN[19] is the official source for the Romanization of American cartographic and geographic nomenclature; most of the schemes have been devised jointly by the U.S. Board on Geographic Names and by the British Permanent Committee on Geographic Names (PCGN), and they are often designated in the literature by the acronym BGN/PCGN.

5.   Other sources.
Romanization schemes used by the *Encyclopedia Britannica,* 15th ed., 1974 *(EB),* and other encyclopedias specifically concerned with a certain script; schemes used by organizations or periodicals. These sources are listed separately under the relevant script.

Table 4.6 gives a synoptic overview of 50 scripts and languages for which tables of Romanization have been published. The first ten scripts are arranged according to the ranking established in Table 4.5; where the same script is used for various languages, these have been listed more or less by affinity; for Cyrillic, the order follows the one in the ISO standard; all other scripts are listed alphabetically.

In Tables 4.7 to 4.14, which display the various Romanization schemes used for different scripts and languages, the Romanization schemes of ISO are used as the standard of comparison, except in Tables 4.8 (Japanese), 4.9 (Devanagari), and 4.12 (Korean), in which the scheme used by the Library of Congress is the standard of comparison. The following symbols are used in all tables:

. = identical with the standard of comparison;
* = character not realized in the Romanization scheme;
a blank space indicates that the character is not included in the Romanization scheme.

[18] Von Ostermann (1952).
[19] United States, Board on Geographic Names (1972).

Table 4.6   Romanization Schemes for Non-Roman Scripts

Script	ISO	AFNOR	ANSI	BSI	Other	BM	LC	PI	Austria	Belgium	Bulgaria	Czechoslov.	Denmark	Finland	Germany	Italy	Norway	Poland	Spain	Sweden	Vatican	Yugoslavia	Alphabete	Ostermann	BGN	Other
	Standards					Cataloging codes																	Other schemes			
CYRILLIC																										
Russian	x	x	x	x	x[1]	x	x	x	x	x	x	x	x	x	x	x	x	x	x	x	x	x	x	x	x	x
Ukrainian	x	x	x	x		x	x	x	x	x		x			x	x	x		x	x	x	x	x	x	x	x
White-Russian	x	x	x	x		x	x					x			x		x		x			x	x		x	
Bulgarian	x	x	x	x	x[2]	x	x	x	x	x	x	x			x	x			x	x	x	x	x	x	x	x
Serbian	x	x	x	x		x	x	x	x		x	x			x	x			x	x	x	x	x	x	x	x
Macedonian	x	x	x	x		x						x			x				x		x		x		x	x
Church Slavonic				x			x		x						x	x					x	x	x	x		
Glagolitsa				x						x											x		x			
Romanian		x				x		x													x					
Non-Slavic	o											x											x		x	
JAPANESE	x		x	x		+	+																x	x	x	x
DEVANAGARI																										
Assamese						+	x																			
Bengali						x	x																			
Gujarati						x	x																x			
Gurmukhi						x	x																x			
Hindi						x	x																		x	x
Kannada						x	x																x	x		
Malayalam						x	x																			
Marathi						x	x																			
Oriya						+	x																x			
Sanskrit						x	x	x	x														x	x		x
Saurashtra						x																				
Sinhalese						x	x																x	x		
Tamil						x	x																x	x		
Telugu						x	x																x	x		
Tibetan						o	x																x	x		

× = Romanization scheme in tabular form.
+ = Catalog contains Romanized entries but no table.
o = Unpublished or in draft form.
* = Pronunciation indicated but no Romanization table.
[1] Brazil, Denmark, Hungary, Germany, Poland, Portugal, Romania, Sweden, USSR, INIS.
[2] Bulgaria.
[3] Hungary.
[4] Poland.
[5] INIS.

Table 4.6 *(continued)*

Script	Standards					Cataloging codes																	Other schemes			
	ISO	AFNOR	ANSI	BSI	Other	BM	LC	PI	Austria	Belgium	Bulgaria	Czechoslov.	Denmark	Finland	Germany	Italy	Norway	Poland	Spain	Sweden	Vatican	Yugoslavia	Alphabete	Ostermann	BGN	Other
ARABIC																										
Arabic	x	x	x	x		x	x	x	x	x						x		x			x	x	x	x	x	x
Persian						x	x	x	x							x					x		x	x	x	x
Pushto						+	x			x													x		x	
Urdu						x	x		x														x	x		x
Sindhi						+	x																			
Croatian																						x				
Turkish						+			x														x	x		x
Malayan						+		x	x														x			
CHINESE					x³	+	x																	x	x	+
KOREAN						+																	x	x	x	x
THAI						o	x																x	x	x	x
GREEK																										
Classical	x	x		x	x⁴	x				x	x				x	x	x	x	x	x	x	x	x	*		
Modern					x⁵	x	x			x	x				x	x	x				x		x	*	x	
HEBREW																										
Hebrew	x	x	x			x	x	x	x	x						x		x	x		x		x	*	x	x
Yiddish	o		o			x												x						+		x
OTHER																										
Amharic						+	x	x	x	x						x					x		x	*	x	
Armenian						+	x	x	x	x	x					x					x		x	x		
Burmese						x	x																x	x	x	
Coptic						+			x	x	x					x					x		x	*		
Gaelic						x		x								x					x		x			
Georgian						x	x	x			x												x		x	
Khmer						o																	x		x	
Laotian																										x
Maldivian																										x
Mongolian						o																	x	x	x	
Samaritan						+																	x	x		
Syriac						+			x							x					x		x			

255

2.3.2 Cyrillic.   All designers of Romanization schemes for Cyrillic script are confronted with two basic problems. One is that this script has a larger number of basic letters than the Roman script, which makes it necessary to transliterate certain Cyrillic letters either with the help of diacritical marks or by letter combinations (or by both methods). The other is that certain phonemes characteristic of Slavic languages cannot be expressed unambiguously by single Roman letters that stand for various other phonemes in different languages. (The English language is in this respect a particularly difficult medium into which to transform names and words written in Cyrillic; its orthography does not use any diacritical marks, and its repertory of phonemes does not contain even an approximation of certain Slavic phonemes.) These factors, together with the requirement of reversibility, are the primary reasons for the enormous proliferation of various and mutually inconsistent Romanization schemes for Cyrillic script, both within the same language community and, with even more variations, between the usage of different language communities.

The first organized attempt to design a uniform bibliographic transliteration scheme for Cyrillic script was made in 1885 by the American Library Association. The proposed scheme refrained from using diacritical marks, resorting instead to the use of the following letter combinations: *zh* for ж, *kh* for х, *tch* for ч, *sh* for ш, *shtch* for щ, *ye* for ѣ, *yu* for ю, and *ya* for я; reversibility for back-transliteration was not yet being considered. A few years later a joint committee of experts from Russia, England, and the United States elaborated another scheme, mainly for use in scientific publications, which was published in *Nature* in 1890. This scheme too used letter combinations (the main difference from the ALA scheme being the use of *ch* instead of *tch,* and *shch* instead of *shtch),* and claimed to ensure unambiguous back-transliteration. Despite various efforts to promote the uniform use of this scheme in the libraries and scientific institutions of all English-speaking countries, other transliteration schemes began to proliferate, especially since the American Library Association and the British Library Association, in their jointly issued cataloging code of 1908, permitted the use of two different schemes. One was a slight adaptation of the scheme first published in 1885, while the other one followed the Croatian method of transliteration with the help of diacritical marks. Meanwhile the Library of Congress had promulgated its own scheme in 1905, which used the by now familiar letter combinations but also employed diacritical marks (ligatures) in the interest of unambiguous back-transliteration. Despite these awkward typographical features, the LC scheme gained wide acceptance in the United States because catalog entries were available in the form of printed cards. In 1917 the British Academy produced yet another scheme[20] which did not allow for back-transliteration but differed enough from the previous schemes to generate still more confusion.

[20]British Academy (1917–18).

As already mentioned, libraries and scientific bodies in Central Europe and in the Scandinavian countries had adopted the scheme of the *Prussian Instructions,* which were almost entirely based on the Croatian model, with the exception that German-speaking countries transliterated Cyrillic x not with *h* but with *ch,* the letter combination used in their own orthography for the equivalent phoneme $[\chi]$. In France the purely phonemic rendering used in the catalog of the Bibliothèque Nationale was generally followed by all libraries.

Thus by the middle of the present century almost every European language and nation had one or more Romanization schemes for Cyrillic, most of which were not true transliterations but took into consideration the pronunciation of Russian sounds as best approximated by the national orthography.

By far the greatest diversity of schemes was (and to a large extent still is) found in the English-speaking countries, where more than a dozen schemes were in more or less extensive use. This situation caused the Royal Society to sponsor in 1953 the elaboration of yet another scheme, intended to be used "by all organizations" because

the existing schemes are so numerous that no one of them has the support of even 3.5 per cent of organizations concerned with bibliographical work.[21]

The scheme covered Russian, Serbian, and Bulgarian (but for some unexplained reason not Ukrainian, White-Russian, or Macedonian, all recognized literary languages by that time) and used practically only two diacritical marks, namely ĭ for й, and ȳ for ы, while the traditional English letter combinations were retained. Needless to say, this scheme was not any more successful in becoming a general standard than its many predecessors.

The confusion generated in catalogs, bibliographies, indexes, abstracting services, encyclopedias, and other reference works by the proliferation of so many different Romanization schemes was the main reason behind the efforts of the ISO to design an international standard for the transliteration of Cyrillic script. Its *Recommendation ISO/R9,* the first international transliteration standard ratified by a majority of ISO member nations, was published in 1954. It was based on the orthographic rules of the Croatian language, using essentially only one diacritical mark, the háček, over the letters ž, č, š, and šč to render ж, ч, ш, and щ, respectively. The system also contained the digraphs *ju* and *ja* for ю and я; for Cyrillic x, the transliteration *h* was preferred, but *ch* or *kh* were allowed as an alternative, a compromise made to accommodate long-standing German and English orthographic practice, respectively.

Quite naturally the countries that had traditionally employed the PI transliteration found the new ISO standard easy to apply, as it was almost identical. But the

[21]Bushell (1953), p. 3.

use of diacritical marks, a feature foreign to English orthography, was rejected by the British Standards Institution, which issued in 1958 its own standard (B.S. 2979:1958), retaining letter combinations. This standard was de facto endorsed also by the American Standards Association (later renamed American National Standards Institute) which, however, did not publish its own version until 1976.[21a] Thus in 1968 a second edition of ISO/R9 was published that expressly recognized the Anglo-American method as a permitted alternative; the result was a double standard that had no more pretension to being truly international than any of the other schemes that had preceded it in various countries. This basic flaw in the scheme became particularly cumbersome when transliterated texts had to be put into machine-readable form, where it is of utmost importance to provide unambiguously reversible one-to-one transformations. A third edition was therefore designed in 1975 and approved in draft form as ISO/DIS9; it will be published as International Standard ISO 9 after ratification, probably in 1977. The third edition basically reverts to the scheme of the first edition but eliminates any alternatives (including *ch* or *kh* for Cyrillic x).

Table 4.7 shows how Cyrillic script is treated by the various standards and cataloging codes. Russian Cyrillic, the most important of all non-Roman scripts, is covered by nearly all cataloging codes, and the alphabets of other Slavic languages are also fairly well represented, although some codes do not give a transliteration for certain letters. The first edition of ISO/R9 has been chosen as the standard of comparison, because all other standards or cataloging codes are either virtually identical with the first edition, or, if they follow the second edition, adopted the basic scheme (without the Anglo-American letter combinations) as their prototype.

As can be seen at a glance, the differences between the various schemes are considerable, primarily of course regarding those Cyrillic letters for which no simple or generally accepted Roman equivalent exists: ё, ж, х, ц, ч, ш, щ, ю, and я.

Several other schemes, such as those used by the New York Public Library, the *Slavonic Review,* and *Mathematical Reviews,* have been listed in a comparative table published as part of a research report by the Battelle Memorial Institute and reprinted in a paper by Neiswender.[22] Since the latter source is easily available, these schemes have not been included in Table 4.7. Although all are used in the United States, none of them is compatible with any of the others or with the ISO, BSI, LC, and BGN systems (which are also listed in the Battelle table). A reference book widely used in the United States is the *Government Printing Office Style Manual,* which lists in its section "Slavic languages" the BGN, LC, and "linguistics" (not further specified) transcription systems without indicating a preference. Dozens of individuals have at various times pro-

[21a] American National Standards Institute (1976).
[22] Neiswender (1962).

posed their own transliteration schemes for Cyrillic, each claiming that all previous schemes were deficient in some respect, and that his brainchild would solve all problems of Cyrillic transliteration. Many of these Romanizers were serious Slavic scholars, some were amateurs, and others were cranks. All have one thing in common: their schemes were not used by anyone but the inventors. Most of these proposals are listed in Hans H. Wellisch's bibliography *Transcription and Transliteration*[23] *(T & T)*, where the interested reader may find them.

Among the more recent Romanization schemes for Cyrillic typical for "private" inventors, we may mention that of J. T. Shaw,[24] who proposed no less than four different methods to be used *simultaneously* in libraries for various kinds of documents; he thus tried to exorcise the devil with Beelzebub. Another contribution comes from B. Dekleva, whose *Uniform Slavic Transliteration Alphabet (USTA)*,[25] is cleverly designed but does not stand much chance of being adopted because it consists of no less than 97 graphemes, some of which are basic Roman letters used in conjunction with a plethora of diacritical marks, some others being digraphs, thus combining the two features most obnoxious to English-speaking readers on the one hand, and Slavic readers on the other. Dekleva claims that this scheme will be amenable to machine-readable data files in which Cyrillic transliteration must be used.

The scene of Cyrillic transliteration is thus one of utter confusion and lack of compatibility, even among schemes that are extensively used in the same country, where users of libraries, maps, and encyclopedias often have to cope with names transliterated according to a bewildering array of mutually incompatible schemes. The reasons for this phenomenon are explored in Chapter 5; here we shall only state that most Romanization schemes (and in particular those for Cyrillic script) try to perform both transliteration and transcription at the same time, an inherently impossible task that is bound to lead to sometimes absurd results.

The situation is even more complex regarding the various Cyrillic alphabets designed in the Soviet Union for the languages of non-Slavic nationalities. There are at present more than 60 such alphabets, almost all of which contain special letters or Cyrillic letters with diacritical marks. The earliest scheme was published in 1960 by the Soviet bibliographers R. S. Giljarevskij and N. V. Krylova[26]; it contains a table of 52 modified letters, an indication of the languages in which each letter is used, and their Romanization. The scheme is used by the Soviet All-Union Book Chamber, mainly for the purpose of transliterating names and titles of works for the statistical publications of UNESCO. The Library of Congress designed its own Romanization tables sometime during the

[23]Wellisch (1975).
[24]J. T. Shaw (1967).
[25]Dekleva (1973).
[26]Giljarevskij (1960).

Table 4.7 Romanization Schemes for Cyrillic Script

Language[1]	Letter	ISO[2] 1 2 3	INIS	BSI	BM	LC	PI	BE	CS	DK	FI	NO	SW	VC	BGN	EB	RS[3]
	А а	a . .	•	•	°	•	•	•	•	•	•	•	•	•	•	•	•
	Б б	b . .	•	•	•	•	•	•	•	°	•	•	•	•	•	•	•
	В в	v . °	°	•	°	•	•	•	•	•	•	•	•	°	•	•	•
BMRS	Г г	g ° .	•	•	•	•	•	•	•	•	•	•	°	•	•	•	•
UW	Г г	g ° .	•	h	h	h	•	•	•	•	•	h	•	h			
UW†	Ѓ ѓ	ġ . .		g	ǵ	g	°		•			ǵ		g			
	Д д	d . .	•	•	•	•	•	°	•	•	•	•	•	•	•	•	•
S	Ђ ђ	đ . .	dj	•	•	•	d′		•			°	•	•			j′
M	Ѓ ѓ	ǵ .		•					•		g						
	Е е	e . .	°	•	•	•	°	•	•	•	•	•	e,je	•	•	e,ye	e,ye	•
R	Ё ё	ё . .	e	•	•	•	•	•	•	•	•	•	•	•	ё,yё	o,yo	•
W	Ё ё	ё ° °	e	•	îo	°	•	•			jo	•	•			
U	Є є	je . è	•	ye	îe	•	•	•			•	ye			
BRUW	Ж ж	ž . .	zh	zh	zh	zh	•	•	•	zj	•	sj	•	•	zh	zh	zh
MS	Ж ж	ž . .	zh	•	•	•	•	•	•			•	•		zh
	З з	z ° °	•	•	•	•	•	•	•	•	s	•	•	•	•	•
M	Ѕ ѕ	dz .		•					•		•	•
BMRS	И и	i . .	•	•	•	•	•	•	•	•	i,ji	°	•	•	•	•
U	И и	i . .	•	ȳ	°	y	•	•	•	•	•	1	y
RUW	І і	ї . í	yi	i	i	i	•	•	•	i	i
U	Ї ї	ï' . .	yi	yi	i	°	•	•	•	yi
MS	J j	j . .	•	•	•	•	°	•	•	•	y
BRUW	Й й	j . ј̆	•	ĭ	i[4]	ĭ	•	•	•	•	•	•	ĭ	y	y	ĭ
	К к	k . .	•	•	•	•	•	•	•	•	•	•	•	•	•	•
	Л л	l . .	•	•	•	•	•	•	•	•	•	•	•	•	•	•
MS	Љ љ	lj . .	•	°	•	•	1′	•			•	•	1′

Table 4.7 (*continued*))

Language	Letter	ISO[2] (1 2 3)	INIS	BSI	BM	LC	PI	BE	CS	DK[3]	FI	NO	SW	VC	BGN	EB	RS[3]
MS	М м	m . .	•	•	•	•	•	•	•	•	•	•	•	○	•	•	•
	Н н	n . .	•	•	•	•	•	•	•	•	•	•	•	•	•	•	•
	Њ њ	nj . .	•	•	•	•	•	ń		•			•	•	•	•	n'
	О о	o . .	•	•	•	•	•	•	•	•	•	•	•	•	•	•	•
	П п	p . .	•	•	•	•	•	•	•	○	•	•	•	•	○	•	•
	Р р	r . .	•	•	•	•	•	•	•	•	•	•	○	•	○	•	•
	С с	s . .	•	•	•	•	•	•	•	•	•	○	•	○	•	○	•
	Т т	t . .	•	•	•	•	•	•	•	•	•	•	•	•	•	•	•
S M	Ћ ћ	ć . ○	cj	•	•	•		•			•		•	○	•	t'
M	Ќ ќ	ќ .		•	•	•		•			•		○	○			
W	У у	u . .	•	•	•	•	○	•	•	•	•	•	•	•	•	○	•
	Ў ў	ŭ . .	w	w	•	•		•						•			
	Ф ф	f . .	•	•	•	•	•	•	○	•	•	•	•	•	•	•	•
BRUW	Х х	h[5] . h	kh	kh	kh	kh	kh	ch	•		•	ch	ch	kh	ch	kh	kh
MS	Х х	h . .		kh	•	•	•		•						•	•	•	kh
BRUW	Ц ц	c . .	ts	ts	ts	ts				ts		ts		ts	ts	ts	ts
MS	Ц ц	c . .		ts	•	•	•	•		•					○	•	•	ts
BRUW	Ч ч	č . .	ch	ch	ch	ch				tj		tsj			ch	ch	ch
MS	Ч ч	č . .		ch	•	•	•	•		•				○	•	•	○	ch
MS	Џ џ	dž . .	dzh	•	•	•	ǵ		•					•	•	○	dz	j
BRUW	Ш ш	š . .	sh	sh	sh	sh				sj		sj			sh	sh	sh
MS	Ш ш	š . .		sh	•	•	•	•		•					•	•	•	sh
RU	Щ щ	šč . .	shch	shch	shch	shch	○			stj					•	shch	shch	shch
B	Щ щ	št šč.	shch	○		sht	sht	•	•	•					•	sht	sht	sht
RUW†	Ъ ъ	ʺ[6] . .		•	○		•	7							•		•	ϲ

Table 4.7 *(continued)*

Language[1]	Letter	ISO[2] 1	2	3	INIS	BSI	BM	LC	PI	BE	CS	DK[5]	FI	NO	SW	VC	BGN	EB	RS[3]
B	Ъ ъ	ă	"	ă	y	ŭ	.	ŭ	ŭ	∘	∘				.	"	ŭ	ŭ	ŭ
RW	Ы ы	y	.	.		ȳ	ui	.	.	.	.	.	.	.	.	.	.	.	ȳ
BRUW	Ь ь	'	.	.			.	.	.	.	.	.	.	*	.	.	.	*	'
BRUW†	Ѣ ѣ	ě	.	.		ê	e	ı̂e	.		.			.	.			ê
RW	Э э	ė	.	.	eh	é	e	è	è	.	∘	e	.	e	.	è	e	e	é
BRUW	Ю ю	ju	∘	.		yu	yu	ı̂u	.	ı̂u	.	.	.	.	.	ı̂u	yu	yu	yu
BRUW	Я я	ja	.	.		ya	ya	ı̂a	.	ı̂a	.	.	.	.	.	ı̂a	ya	ya	ya
B†	Ѫ ѫ	ȧ	!!	ȧ		ū	ą	ŭ	ă		ă				ă	u̇			ū
R†	Ѳ ѳ	ḟ	.	.			.	.	.	.	.				.	.			th
R†	Ѵ ѵ	ẏ	.	.		y̌	i	.	.	.					.	.			ẏ
MR†UW	' '	"	\			.				.					.	.	.		

[1]B = Bulgarian, M = Macedonian, R = Russian, S = Serbian, U = Ukrainian, W = White-Russian; † after a language designation indicates that the Cyrillic letter is obsolete in the orthography of that language. Letters not marked are used in all six languages.

[2]The numbers 1, 2, and 3 refer to the editions of ISO 9; for the second edition, only the basic scheme is listed, while the alternative scheme appears in the column for ANSI and BSI; the 3rd edition is still in draft form but will probably become a standard in 1977. The national standards or cataloging codes of the following countries are identical with the first edition (ISO/R9-1954): Belgium, Bulgaria, Denmark, Germany (Federal Republic) Hungary, Italy, Norway, Portugal, and Yugoslavia. The national standards of France, Germany (Democratic Republic), Poland, Romania, and the USSR are identical with the 2nd edition (ISO/R9-1968).

[3]Royal Society.

[4]ый = *uy*.

[5]Optionally: *ch* or *kh*.

[6]Disregarded if final.

[7]Disregarded if final, indicated by - (hyphen) if medial.

1960s; these cover more than 70 languages, but were not published until 1977. The American linguist E. Allworth designed a different set of Romanization schemes for 26 Turkic, Caucasian, and Iranian languages of the USSR.[27] The ISO developed a Draft International Standard for the transliteration of 58 non-Slavic Cyrillic alphabets[28] in 1972, but this has not yet been officially ratified as

[27]Allworth (1971).
[28]International Organization for Standardization (1972).

an ISO Standard. A revision and extension of the ISO's draft to 61 languages was proposed by F. Görner in connection with the new German cataloging code *RAK*.[29] It would be desirable if agreement on a definitive ISO Standard could soon be reached, before too many different schemes are devised by eager individuals and organizations, and while the literary output in these languages remains small so that even necessary changes in already adopted library transliterations could easily be made.

The schemes considered thus far were devised by foreigners for their own use. The question of an official Romanization of Cyrillic script has, however, for a long time been considered also by the Russians themselves. As early as 1901, the Imperial Academy of Sciences in St. Petersburg elaborated a scheme for the transliteration of Russian personal and place names into Western languages written in Roman script.[30] The scheme is still in use, except for minor modifications made between 1925 and 1956 (mainly regarding the rendering of palatalized vowels). Although it has never been officially recognized as a national standard, it is employed in the publications of the Soviet Academy of Sciences, in cartographic works intended for use outside the USSR, and sometimes in bibliographic references. The scheme also served as the basis for the transliteration of Russian Cyrillic in the ISO/R9 scheme of 1954, which was subsequently adopted as an official Soviet standard for bibliographic purposes in 1957 and revised in 1971.[31]

Another transliteration standard (without diacritical marks, so as to be compatible with commercially available computer printout devices) was also promulgated in 1971, with the intention of making it mandatory for all foreign-language publications in the Soviet Union except bibliographic works, but it ran into strong opposition from various scientific bodies, and its introduction was first delayed until 1973, and has apparently since been dropped altogether. Despite these attempts at compulsory standardization, all manner of *ad hoc* transliterations and transcriptions of Russian names and words are used in foreign-language publications as well as in bilingual dictionaries and other reference works printed in the USSR. Finally, for postal services and telecommunications a completely different transliteration scheme, devised in the 19th century on French models, is still in force. Thus, even in a totalitarian state it seems to be practically impossible to make the use of a single transliteration scheme mandatory.

Cyrillization of names and words from other languages poses difficult problems for translators, bibliographers, and librarians in Slavic languages written in Cyrillic, because it can be done only by phonemic transcription, not by transliteration, as we demonstrate in Chapter 5, Section 3.4.2. We already mentioned

[29]Görner (1974).
[30]Gregory (1908), Foord (1917).
[31]USSR [All-Union Standards Committee] (1971).

the earliest attempt to Cyrillize foreign words, the multilingual dictionary by Pallas, published in 1789. Modern bibliographic practice in the USSR follows a manual by Giljarevskij and Starostin[32] which covers 18 European languages, gives rules for the transcription of the phonemes of each language as written by various graphemes, and contains lists of the most common forenames of each language and their recommended Russian Cyrillization. It is interesting to note that the manual also deals with two languages that are themselves written in Cyrillic, namely Bulgarian and Serbian, Cyrillizing their names in a form that conveys their pronunciation to Russian readers. (This is somewhat akin to the Turkish "Romanization" of Shakespeare as Şeykspir.) The same problems occur in the rendering of names from non-Slavic languages of the USSR, because the special characters and modified Cyrillic letters invented for these languages are largely unintelligible for Russian readers. Generally, the types for these special letters are available only to printers in the areas in which these languages are used. A transliteration scheme for the conversion of special non-Slavic Cyrillic letters into standard Russian Cyrillic letters has been published in a manual on the transcription of names by Starostin.[32a]

The Soviet literature on specific problems of Cyrillization, especially those in cartography, is quite voluminous, and the reader is referred to the relevant entries in the bibliography *T & T*. A series of articles in the Bulgarian linguistic periodical Български език, [Bălgarski Ezik], written by various experts, deals with the Cyrillization of names in various European and Oriental languages, adapted to the orthography of the Bulgarian language.

2.3.3. Japanese.   All standards and codes that deal with Japanese *kana* script Romanize it by means of the modified Hepburn scheme as employed in *Kenkyusha's new Japanese–English dictionary*.[33] Neither the British Museum nor the Library of Congress have a table, but ANSI, BSI, *Alphabete,* Ostermann, and BGN display tables of *kana* and their Romanization, with varying degrees of detail. The Library of Congress gives in addition many examples of word division, an aspect not dealt with in the Hepburn scheme, yet one of the thorniest problems in Japanese Romanization, since Japanese orthography does not employ any punctuation marks, and even Japanese scholars are sometimes not too sure where and how to divide words, and which meaning to assign to a sentence.[34]

---

[32] Giljarevskij (1969).

[32a] Starostin (1965).

[33] Kenkyusha (1974).

[34] Charles E. Hamilton, an American scholar of Japanese who, though in principle opposed to the Romanization of Japanese for cataloging purposes, wrote the section on word division in the LC scheme, had earlier stated: "Only a trained linguist is properly competent to discriminate in matters of word division, and since book titles often do not represent speech patterns, even the linguist's training is not proof against embarrassment." (Hamilton, 1953, p. ii).

The Hepburn scheme is essentially one designed for the needs of foreigners, more specifically those who speak English. Despite that, it has been adopted by almost all countries, but the Japanese themselves prefer their own Kunrei-shiki scheme, which is now the official one; the older Nippon-shiki Romanization is occasionally also encountered. Table 4.8 displays the three Romanization schemes and indicates the differences between them.

The various problems of Romanization for bibliographic purposes have been treated from the Japanese point of view by Shigenori Baba.[35]

Cyrillization of Japanese is performed in the Soviet Union according to the Большой Японско-русский словарь,[36] which seeks to approximate the Japanese phonemes as written in *kana* by a phonetic rendering in the equivalent Cyrillic letters, much as the Hepburn system tries to do for English readers. The Cyrillization of Japanese names for Bulgarian readers has been treated by Văglenov.[37]

Special problems arise when Japanese names referred to in Soviet sources in Cyrillized form have to be transliterated into a language written in Roman script, as is often the case when Russian scientific or technical texts are translated into English. Japanese names are notoriously difficult to Romanize even without the added complexities of being transformed by Cyrillization and subsequent Romanization. If this is done by simply applying a Romanization scheme for Russian Cyrillic, the results are often quite unlike anything produced by the Hepburn Romanization of a Japanese name; for example, the name 古島志 Cyrillized as Кодзима, содзи would be Romanized as *Kodzima, Sodzi,* but the correct Hepburn Romanization is *Kojima, Sōji.* The problem can only be solved by a system of equivalency tables for Japanese syllables in Cyrillization and in Romanization, as demonstrated by Löhr.[38]

The Japanization of non-Japanese names and words can obviously only be performed by phonemic transcription by means of a substitution of the nearest equivalent Japanese syllables. This, however, is made difficult by at least two characteristics of the Japanese language: it lacks the phoneme $[1]$, for which $[r]$ is generally substituted; and it cannot accommodate consonant clusters —between each consonant a vowel must be inserted to make the word pronounceable for a Japanese speaker. The resulting phonemic transcriptions are often quite unintelligible when seen in retranscription: Ongusutoromu (Ångstrom), Jizeru (Diesel), and Uddo (Wood) are some examples of names; purasuchikkusu (plastics), haidoro sutachikku puresu (hydrostatic pressure), and chitanyumu (titanium) are some Japanizations of technical terms adopted from English. Although the Westernization of Japan has greatly contributed to the

---

[35]Baba (1968).
[36][Great Japanese–Russian dictionary] (1970).
[37]Văglenov (1968).
[38]Löhr (1971).

Table 4.8 Romanization Systems for Japanese *Kana*

Katakana	Hiragana	Hebon-shiki	Kunrei-shiki	Nihon-shiki
ア	あ	a		
イ	い	i		
ウ	う	u		
エ	え	e		
オ	お	o		
カ	か	ka		
キ	き	ki		
ク	く	ku		
ケ	け	ke		
コ	こ	ko		
サ	さ	sa		
シ	し	shi	si	si
ス	す	su		
セ	せ	se		
ソ	そ	so		
タ	た	ta		
チ	ち	chi	ti	ti
ツ	つ	tsu	tu	tu
テ	て	te		
ト	と	to		
ナ	な	na		
ニ	に	ni		
ヌ	ぬ	nu		
ネ	ね	ne		
ノ	の	no		
ハ	は	ha		
ヒ	ひ	hi		
フ	ふ	fu	hu	hu

Table 4.8 (*continued*)

Katakana	Hiragana	Hebon-shiki	Kunrei-shiki	Nihon-shiki
ヘ	へ	he		
ホ	ほ	ho		
マ	ま	ma		
ミ	み	mi		
ム	む	mu		
メ	め	me		
モ	も	mo		
ヤ	や	ya		
ヰ	ゐ	i		
ユ	ゆ	yu		
エ	え	e		
ヨ	よ	yo		
ラ	ら	ra		
リ	り	ri		
ル	る	ru		
レ	れ	re		
ロ	ろ	ro		
ワ	わ	wa		
ヰ	ゐ	i		
ウ	う	u		
ヱ	ゑ	e		
ヲ	を	o		
ガ	が	ga		
ギ	ぎ	gi		
グ	ぐ	gu		
ゲ	げ	ge		
ゴ	ご	go		
ザ	ざ	za		
ジ	じ	ji	zi	zi
ズ	ず	zu		
ゼ	ぜ	ze		
ゾ	ぞ	zo		
ダ	だ	da		
ヂ	ぢ	ji	zi	di

Table 4.8 (*continued*)

Katakana	Hiragana	Hebon-shiki	Kunrei-shiki	Nihon-shiki
ヅ	づ	zu		
デ	で	de		
ド	ど	do		
バ	ば	ba		
ビ	び	bi		
ブ	ぶ	bu		
ベ	べ	be		
ボ	ぼ	bo		
パ	ぱ	pa		
ピ	ぴ	pi		
プ	ぷ	pu		
ペ	ぺ	pe		
ポ	ぽ	po		
ン	ん	n, m^2	n	n
ヴ	ゔ	v^3		
キヤ	きゃ	kya		
キユ	きゅ	kyu		
キヨ	きょ	kyo		
ギヤ	ぎゃ	gya		
ギユ	ぎゅ	gyu		
ギヨ	ぎょ	gyo		
シヤ	しゃ	sha	sya	sya
シユ	しゅ	shu	syu	syu
シヨ	しょ	sho	syo	syo
ジヤ	じゃ	ja	zya	zya
ジユ	じゅ	ju	zyu	zyu
ジヨ	じょ	jo	zyo	zyo
チヤ	ちゃ	cha	tya	tya
チユ	ちゅ	chu	tyu	tyu
チヨ	ちょ	cho	tyo	tyo
ニヤ	にゃ	nya		
ニユ	にゅ	nyu		
ニヨ	にょ	nyo		

Table 4.8 *(continued)*

Katakana	Hiragana	Hebon-shiki	Kunrei-shiki	Nihon-shiki
ヒ ャ	ひゃ	hya		
ヒ ュ	ひゅ	hyu		
ヒ ョ	ひょ	hyo		
ビ ャ	びゃ	bya		
ビ ュ	びゅ	byu		
ビ ョ	びょ	byo		
ピ ャ	ぴゃ	pya		
ピ ュ	ぴゅ	pyu		
ピ ョ	ぴょ	pyo		
ミ ャ	みゃ	mya		
ミ ュ	みゅ	myu		
ミ ョ	みょ	myo		
リ ャ	りゃ	rya		
リ ュ	りゅ	ryu		
リ ョ	りょ	ryo		

[1]"Hebon" is the Japanization of "Hepburn." The Hepburn scheme is virtually identical with the one used by the Library of Congress.

Only the most common combined forms are shown in this table. There are many others, some of them consisting of three characters. For example, the last syllable in this table, *ryo*, may also be written

リ ョ ウ	りょう	ryo
レ ウ	れう	ryo
レ フ	れふ	ryo

but this does not affect the pronunciation or Romanization.

[2]The letter *m* is used before *b, m,* and *p.*

[3]Used only for transcription of foreign names and words.

dimensions of the problem, Japanization of foreign names is as old as Japanese writing. The name of the legendary Buddhist saint Bodhidharma (6th century A.D.) became Ta-mo in Chinese and subsequently Daruma in Japanese; the sect founded by him under the name of Dhyāna became the Chinese Ch'an and later the Japanese Zen, under which name this form of Buddhism is now widely known in the Western world.

Kenkyusha's new Japanese–English dictionary has an appendix that contains the standard Japanization of several hundred names of well-known foreign personalities, place names, and titles of famous works of fiction, art, and architecture, all rendered in *katakana*.

2.3.4. Devanagari.   The Devanagari script probably developed during the 6th and 7th century A.D. from the ancestors of all Indic scripts, Kharosthi and Brahmi. A highly phonetic script, consisting of 14 vowels and diphthongs, and 34 basic consonants, the *aksharas,* it was first used by Brahmins to write Sanskrit, the sacred literary language, and Prakrit, the spoken language. Today it is the script in which Hindi, the most widely spoken of all Indic languages, is written.

Devanagari was first systematically transliterated by Sir William Jones, on whose scheme (see p. 200) practically all later Romanizations were based. In its classical form (as used to write Sanskrit and the Prakrits) Devanagari is covered by the BM, LC, PI, and AU schemes (see Table 4.9); in its modern form, as used to write Hindi, it has been Romanized by the BM and LC schemes. The latter also provides separate Romanizations for nine "dotted" letters used to write words of Urdu origin in Hindi (i.e., those written in Urdu with Arabic letters that have no equivalent in Devanagari). (The modern forms are not shown in Table 4.9.) In 1958 the Indian Ministry of Education promulgated an official transliteration scheme[39] that differs from the LC and BM schemes mainly in the use of various diacritical marks and the provision of transliterations for modified Devanagari letters used in languages other than Hindi. Despite the differences in the use of diacritical marks among the various schemes, there is a considerable degree of uniformity in Romanization for bibliographic control purposes, because all major schemes use the same basic Roman letters to transliterate a certain Devanagari character, while diacritical marks are commonly disregarded in the alphabetical filing of entries in catalogs and bibliographies. But Romanization as practiced outside of libraries or linguistic publications often results in widely divergent forms, especially for personal names. The very common Hindi surname चौधरी , for example, may be encountered in Romanized form as Chaudhary, Chaudharia, Chaudhery, Chaudhori, Chaudri, Chaudhuri, Chaudhury, Choudri, Choudry, Chowdhari, Chowdhary, Chowdury, and Chowdhury, depending on the predilection of the bearer of this name.[40] All these can be found on the title pages of books published in India and elsewhere, and it is not uncommon for an author to use two or three different forms of his name in his publications.

A dozen of the various scripts derived from Devanagari which are used to write the languages spoken on the Indian subcontinent and in Burma, namely Assamese, Bengali, Burmese, Gujarati, Kannada, Malayalam, Marathi, Oriya, Panjabi, Sinhalese, Tamil, and Telugu, have BM and LC Romanization

[39]India. Ministry of Education (1958).
[40]Dogra (1976), p. 346.

Table 4.9 Romanization Schemes for Devanagari Script

Letter	LC	BM	PI	IN[1]	EB
अ	a	•	•	•	•
आ	ā	•	•	•	•
इ	i	•	•	•	•
ई	ī	•	•	•	•
उ	u	•	•	•	•
ऊ	ū	•	•	•	•
ऋ	ṛ	ṛ	ṛ	r:	ṛ
ॠ	r̄		r̄	r̄:	r̄
ऌ	l		ḷ	l:	ḷ
ए	e	•	•	•	•
ऐ	ai	•	•	•	•
ओ	o	•	•	•	•
औ	au	•	•	•	•
क	k	•	•	•	•
ख	kh	•	•	•	•
ग	g	•	•	•	•
घ	gh	•	•	•	•
ङ	ṅ	•	n	n'	•
च	c	•	•	•	•
छ	ch	•	•	•	•
ज	j	•	•	•	•
झ	jh	•	•	•	•
ञ	ñ	•	n	n"	•
ट	ṭ	∘	•	t̲	•
ठ	ṭh	•	•	t̲h	•
ड	ḍ	•	•	d̲	•
ढ	ḍh	•	•	d̲h	•
ण	ṇ	•	n	n̲	•
त	t	•	•	•	•
थ	th	•	•	•	•
द	d	•	•	•	•
ध	dh	•	∘	•	∘
न	n	•	•	•	•
प	p	•	∘	•	•
फ	ph	•	•	•	•
ब	b	•	•	•	•
भ	bh	•	•	•	•
म	m	•	•	•	•
य	y	•	•	•	•
र	r	•	•	•	•
ल	l	•	•	•	•
ळ	ḷ	ḷ	l	lh	ḷ
व	v	•	•	v,w	•
श	ś	ṣ	•	s"	•
ष	ṣ	sh	•	s̲	•
स	s	•	•	•	•
ह	h	•	•	•	•
Anusvāra ं	ṃ[2]	ṃ,n̲	ṃ,n	(m:/(m,n̊)	ṃ,n̲
Anunāsika ँ	m̐	•	m	n:	ṃ,m̐
Visarga :	ḥ	•	•	h:	•

[1] Indian Ministry of Education.
[2] Exceptions: *Anusvāra* is transliterated by ṅ before gutturals, ñ before palatals, ṇ before cerebrals, n before dentals, m before labials.

schemes which are either identical or differ only in minor details. The British Museum has in addition schemes for Badaga, Kurg, Nepali, and Saurashtra. The script of Tibetan, a language whose complex and irregular orthography is rivaled only by that of English, is covered by the Library of Congress for bibliographic purposes, but there are about as many other Romanization schemes as there are Tibetan scholars in the Western world.

Some of the scripts derived from Devanagari are also transliterated in *Alphabete* and in Ostermann, but for some unexplained reason they do not appear in the BGN scheme (except for Nepali), even though there are many place names originally written in those scripts.

2.3.5. Arabic. In the words of the Orientalist G. F. Wheeler, "The Arabic character, though admirably suited to Arabic, is inelastic and does not lend itself at all readily to the transcription of other languages."[41] Nor, for that matter, is it easily rendered in Roman script. The Turkish philologist N. Danişman, who in the wake of the successful Latinization of Turkish advocated the Latinization of other languages written in Arabic, claimed that more than 2000 different Romanization schemes had been devised or proposed at various times.[42] Although this is probably an exaggeration, the fact remains that almost every Western Arabist since the Renaissance found it necessary to devise his own scheme, or tried at least to add, delete, or change a few diacritical marks of another man's transliteration, so as to make it "more scientific." This trend continues unabated, as a glance at Table 4.10 will show.

Several factors contribute to the tremendous proliferation of conversion schemes for Arabic script:

1. Several Arabic letters represent phonemes not found in other languages, and not even approximately expressed by any Roman letter or letter combination;
2. The writing system of Arabic (like those of all other Semitic languages) is "defective"; that is, vowels and diacritical marks necessary for the unambiguous identification of words (and consequently for their transliterated spelling) are not normally written but must be mentally substituted by a person who knows the language and can construe the meaning of words from their context;
3. The non-Semitic languages written in Arabic script (Persian, Pushto,* Kurdish, Urdu, Sindhi, Ottoman Turkish, Malayan, Swahili, and Croatian) use the letters of classical Arabic partly for different phonemes, but they also have to

---

[41] Wheeler (1937), p. 591.

[42] Danişman (1935).

*This is the spelling used by the Library of Congress; the British Museum uses Pushtu, the Board on Geographic Names has Pashtu, the International Congress of Orientalists uses Pakshtu, and the *OED* lists in addition Pushtoo, Pukhto, Pakhtu, and Pukshto. The differences in the rendering of the second consonant ($[\int]$ or $[\chi]$) are due to variant pronunciations in Western and Eastern Afghanistan.

use additional letters and modifications of basic Arabic letters to express phonemes not found in Arabic;
4. This in turn has led to two basically different conceptions in the design of Romanization schemes for Arabic script. One school of thought attempts to perform strict phonetic transliteration, considering only the classical Arabic letters, while the other one recognizes the variants in non-Semitic languages and allows either for additional letters and their transcription or devises entirely separate transcription schemes for each language and its writing system;
5. The latter trend is now being reinforced by the emergence of indigenous transcription schemes for Persian and Urdu (developed by native scholars from Iran and Pakistan, respectively) and by the Latinization of Turkish which, because it is *not* a transliteration of the former Arabic orthography, has important implications for the Romanization of Ottoman Turkish.

When one considers that some or all of these factors are constantly making themselves felt in the Romanization of Arabic script, it is perhaps easier to understand why no consensus has been reached on a standard scheme, either among Orientalists or among librarians and bibliographers concerned with works written in Arabic script. No Romanization system yet devised covers all applications of the Arabic script. The most extensive one is the system used by the Library of Congress, which has schemes for Arabic, Persian, Pushto, Urdu, and Sindhi, but not for Ottoman Turkish or Malay (Jawi script). The British Museum has catalogs for almost all languages, but tables have been published only for Arabic, Persian, and Urdu ("Hindustani"). The Board on Geographic Names covers Arabic, Persian, and Pushto but not Urdu and Sindhi. Croatian in Arabic script, which produced only a small body of literature, is understandably covered only by the Yugoslavian cataloging code. Kurdish has not yet been the subject of any transliteration scheme except for a tentative proposal by C. J. Edmonds,[43] probably because of the paucity of written documents in this language held in Western libraries.

Table 4.10 shows that the major schemes now in use often differ only in the application of diacritical marks, although considerable discrepancies still exist regarding the Romanization of gutturals and sibilants, resulting in a bewildering variety in the rendering of Arabic names, which is not exactly alleviated by the copious use of diacritical marks, hyphens, and other typographical devices.[44]

---

[43] Edmonds (1931).

[44] "The casual observer of Islamic names becomes confused by the amount of hyphens, apostrophes, and diacritical marks as well as by the compounded elements of the average Muslim name." (Behn and Greig, 1974, p. 13.) A German Orientalist and bibliographer who himself delights in the lavish use of diacritical marks admits that for the users of catalogs "das lateinische Schriftbild mit den vielen Bindestrichen und diakritischen Zeichen . . . hat etwas Unheimliches an sich." (Braun, 1964, p. 9.)

Table 4.10 Romanization Schemes for Arabic Script (Classical Arabic only)
(a) Consonants

Language[1]	Letter	Name	ISO, AFNOR, BSI (Std.)	BM	LC, ANSI	PI	BE, IT, VC	SP	YU[2]	ICO[3]	EI[4]	BGN	Sharify[5]	INB[6]	Birnbaum[7]	IJMES[8]	Dogra[9]	EB
	ا	alif	∅,ʾ	-	•	•	•	•	a,e,i	•	•	•	•	a	•	•	a	∘
	ب	bā	b	•	•	•	•	•	•	•	•	•	•	•	•	•	•	•
M	پ	pē				p												
PTU	پ	pē	p	∘	•	•	•			•	•	•	•	•	∘	•	•	
	ت	tā	t	•	•	•	∘	•		•	•	•		∘		•		
PTU	ث	ṯā	ṯ	th	th	•	•	ṭ		∘	th	th		th		th		th
PTU	ث	sē	ṣ	s̱	s̱		ṯ	s	s	s̱	th	s̄	s̄		s	s	s	
U	ٹ	ṭē		ṭ	ṭ	ṫ				ṣ	t′			t			ṭ	
	ج	ǧīm	ǧ	j	j	ǵ	•	ŷ		∘	dj	j	j	j		j	j	j
T M	ج	ǧīm	c		ǵ	ǧ	ǧ	ğ	dž	ǧ	dj				c	c		
P T U	چ	čē	č	ch	ch	•	•		č,ć	∘	•	ch	ch		c	ch		
				ç	c	č̣	č			č̣	č̣				ch	c	ch	
				ch		č̣				č̣	č̣							
	ح	ḥā	ḥ	ḣ	•	•	∘	•	h	•	•	ḥ	•	•	•	•	•	h
	خ	ḫā	ḫ	kh	kh	h̬	ḫ	j	-	ḫ	kh	kh	kh	kh	-	kh	kh	kh
T	ح	ḥā	ḥ			h̬	h̬		h	ḥ	kh				ḥ	ḥ		
	د	dāl	d	•	•	•	∘	•	•	•	•	•	•	•	∘	•	•	•
	ذ	ḏāl	ḏ	•	dh	•	•	•	•	dh	dh		dh		dh	ẕ	dh
PT	ذ	zāl		ẕ	ẕ	ḏ	ḏ		d	ẕ		z̄	z̄		ẕ	ẕ		
Pu	ڈ	ḍāl			ḏ̥					ḍ								
U	ڊ	ḍāl	ḍ	ḍ	ḍ	d·				ḍ	d′			d			ḍ	
	ر	rā	r	•	•	•	•	•	•	•	•	•	•	•	•	•	•	•
U	ڑ	ṛē	ṛ	ṛ	ṛ	ṙ				ṛ	ŕ			ṛ			ṛ	
	ز	zāy	z	•	•	•	•	•	•	∘	•	•	•	∘	•	•	•	•
PU	ژ	žē	ž	zh	zh	z	•			•	zh	zh	zh	zh		zh	zh	
T	ژ	žē	ž	j		z	•		•	•	zh				z	j		
Pu	ژ	žē			zh̥					g		zh						
	س	sīn	s	∘	•	•	•	∘	∘	•	∘	•	•	•	•	∘	•	•
	ش	šīn	š	sh	sh	•	•	•		∘	sh	sh	sh	sh	•	sh	sh	sh
T	ش	šīn	ṣ			sh			š	ṣ	sh				ṣ	ṣ		
Pu	ش	šē			sh̥					ksh		sh						

Table 4.10 *(continued)*

Language[1]	Letter	Name	Std. ISO, AFNOR, BSI	Cataloging codes BM	LC, ANSI	PI	BE, IT, VC	SP	YU[2]	Other schemes ICO[3]	EI[4]	BGN	Sharify[5]	INB[6]	Birnbaum[7]	IJMES[8]	Dogra[9]	EB
	ص	ṣād	ṣ	ṡ	•	•	•	•	s	•	•	ṣ	•	•	•	•	•	
	ض	ḍād	ḍ	•	•	•	•	•		•	°	ḍ	•	•	°			•
P	ض	ẕād	ḍ	ż	z	⁚	•	•		•	°	z̲	z̲			ż	z	⁚
T	ض	żād	ż	ż		ḍ	ḍ		d	ḍ	ḍ				ż	ż		
	ط	ṭā	ṭ	•	•	•	•	°	•	•	•	ṭ	•	•	•	•	•	•
Pu	ط	twē		t̤						t	ṭ							
	ظ	ẓā	ẓ	z̤	•	•	•	•	z	•	•	ẓ	•	•	•	•	•	•
	ع	ʿayn	ʿ	•	•	•	•	•	a	°	•	•	•	•	•	•	•	•
	غ	ġayn	ḡ	gh	gh	ġ	ġ	g		ġ	gh	gh	gh	gh		gh	gh	gh
M	ڠ	nga				ṅ												
T	غ	ġayn		ġ		ġ	ġ	g		ġ						ġ	ġ, ğ	
	ف	fā	f	•	•	•	•	•	•	•	°	•	•	•	•	•	•	•
	ق	qāf	q	k̤	•	•	•	•	k	•	ḳ	•	•	•	ḳ	•	•	•
	ك	kāf	k	•	°	•	•	•	•	•	•	•	•	•	•	°	•	•
PT	گ	gāf	g	•	°	•	°		▼	•	•	•	°		•	•		
T	ڭ	gāf	g[10]	ñ		ṅ	ñ,y		nj	ñ	ñ				ñ	ñ,y		
U	گ	gāf		g	g	g				g	g		g				g	
	ل	lām	l	°	•	°	•	•	°	•	•	•	•	°	•	•	•	°
	م	mīm	m	•	•	•	•	°	•	•	°	•	•	•	•	•	•	°
	ن	nūn	n	•	•	•	•	°	•	•	•	•	•	°	•	°	•	•
M	ڃ	ña				ñ												
U	ن	nūn		n̲		~			n	n			n̤			ṅ	
Pu	ڼ,ڼ	nūn		ṇ		ṇ̤				ṇ	n	n̲			ṇ		ṅ	
	ه	hā	h	°	•	•	•	•	e,h	•	•	°	•	•	•	•	•	•
	و	wāw	w	°	°	•	°	•		•	•		•	•	•	•	•	•
PTU	و	vāv	v	°	•	w	w		°		w		•		w	°	w	•
	ى	yā	y	•	•	j	•	•	j	°	•	•	•	•	•	°	•	•

[1]M = Malayam, P = Persian, Pu = Pushto, T = Turkish, U = Urdu. Language is indicated only when the transliteration of a letter differs from that of the classical Arabic letter.

[2]For Croatian only; listed under *T* because the orthography of Croatian written in Arabic was modeled on Turkish orthography.

[3]International Congress of Orientalists (= Brockelmann, 1937).

Table 4.10 *(continued)* (b) Vowels, Diphthongs, and Other Diacritical Marks

Vowel sign[11]	Name	Std. ISO, AFNOR, BSI	BM	LC, ANSI	PI	BE, IT, VC	SP	ICO[3]	EI[4]	BGN	IJMES[8]	EB
	hamzah	*, '[12]		•				•	•	•	'	•
	fatḥah	a	•	•	•	•	•	•	•	•	^a	•
	kasrah	i	•	•	•	•	•	•	•	•	^i	•
	ḍammah	u	•	•	•	•	•	•	•	•	^u	•
	fatḥah alif	ā	•	•	•	•	•	•	•	•	â	•
	kasrah yā'	ī	•	•	•	•	•	•	•	•	î	•
	ḍammah wāw	ū	•	•	•	•	•	•	•	•	û	•
	alif maqṣūrah	à		•	a			á	â		â	ā
	sukūn (jazmah)	*	•	•	•	•	•	•	•	•	•	•
	fatḥah yā' sukūn	ay	ai	•	ai	•		•	•	•	•	•
	fatḥah wāw sukūn	aw	au	•	au			•	•	•	•	•
	tanwīn fatḥah	an		•	*					aⁿ		
	tanwīn kasrah	in		•	*					iⁿ		
	tanwīn ḍammah	un		•	*					uⁿ		
	tashdīd	13	•	•		•	•	•		•	•	•
	hamzat al waṣl	'		*						•		a
	alif maddah	ā, 'ā[14]	•			ā'					•	ā

[4]*Encyclopedia of Islam,* 2nd ed.
[5]N. Sharify (1959); for Persian only.
[6]*Indian National Bibliography;* for Urdu only.
[7]E. Birnbaum (1967); for Ottoman Turkish only.
[8]*International Journal of Middle Eastern Studies.*
[9]R. C. Dogra (1973); for Urdu only.
[10]BSI has ñ.
[11]The horizontal line represents the vocalized consonant.
[12]Not realized when initial, otherwise '.
[13]Transliterated by doubling the consonant.
[14]ā when initial, otherwise 'ā.

The first Arabic Romanization scheme for library purposes was commissioned by the American Library Association in 1885, and was published as part of Cutter's *Rules for a dictionary catalog* in 1889. In the same year the British Museum published its catalog of Hindustani printed books, and this contained a transliteration table for "Persian, Arabic and Hindustani", (it actually covered only Persian and Urdu, not classical Arabic, for which a separate table was not published until 1959). Needless to say, the two schemes were quite different from each other as well as from the PI Arabic transliteration scheme and from those then used by various Orientalists.

An attempt to bring some semblance of order into the chaos of Arabic transliteration by means of concerted action on an international scale was made in 1894, when the 10th International Congress of Orientalists (ICO) adopted a scheme that covered most of the languages written in Arabic (including the variant letters used by non-Semitic languages), but it was not uniform, and left too much leeway to "permissible alternatives." New schemes continued to be hatched, and a synoptic table of Romanization schemes published in 1930 by the Orientalist A. A. Brux showed no fewer than 24 different schemes for classical Arabic alone, devised by philologists, catalogers, and editors of encyclopedias—no two of which were compatible with each other. Brux was particularly concerned with Romanization for bibliographic purposes, and proposed his own scheme, based on the principle of strictly phonetic transliteration:

The Orientalist must be able to infer at a glance the Arabic characters of each transliterated word, so that confusion with similar-sounding names and words is excluded.[45]

(This postulate is actually impossible to fulfill for "defectively" written Semitic languages.)

Following an initiative of the Deutsche Morgenländische Gesellschaft, a committee headed by the Orientalist Carl Brockelmann devised a new transliteration scheme which was adopted by the 19th International Congress of Orientalists in 1935 and was subsequently used by Brockelmann in his reference work *Geschichte der arabischen Literatur*.[46] Most Orientalists and many libraries use this scheme, and the ISO scheme is almost exactly like it, except for two diacritical marks which have been changed.

The *Encyclopedia of Islam (EI)* employed in its first edition (1911–1938) its own scheme without, however, publishing a table or dealing with the subject of transliteration in an article—a quite remarkable omission. The second edition of this work (1954–) also began without a published transliteration scheme; only in the second volume was such a table included. The scheme is unlike any other, being a mixture of some ICO and LC elements as well as some apparently

[45]Brux (1930), p. 4.
[46]Brockelmann (1937), 1. Supplementband, p. [xix].

invented by the *EI* editors. This means that names found in the *EI,* one of the main works of reference on Arabic culture, history, and literature, cannot be found in the same form in the principal library catalogs, nor do they conform with the practice of other Orientalists.

In America the transliteration tables in ALA 1908 had been reprinted, in slightly modified form, in ALA 1949 but catalogers of Arabic works found them insufficient. The Library of Congress, after lengthy consultations with other libraries and specialists, decided to adopt the BGN/PCGN scheme as revised in 1956, and published it, with some minor changes in diacritical marks, in 1958. During the 1960s the Library of Congress decided to develop separate transcription schemes for each of the non-Semitic languages written in Arabic, that is, schemes that indicate the various pronunciations. The first, for Persian, was published in 1963, followed by Urdu in 1964 and by Pushto in 1965. All Arabic Romanization schemes were reissued in slightly amended form in 1970, and the latest addition is a scheme for Sindhi, issued in 1972.[47] The ANSI standard for Arabic transliteration[48] follows the present LC scheme (for classical Arabic only).

Arabic was the second non-Roman script for which a transliteration scheme was devised by the ISO.[49] Recommendation ISO/R233 is a strict transliteration, modeled largely on the ICO scheme and on the pronunciation of the letters in classical Arabic. It contains some but not all "letters used in Arabic to represent non-Arabic sounds" (a peculiar way to indicate the additional letters used in Persian, Urdu, etc.) and gives transliterations for these, apparently based on Persian usage. The scheme is obviously intended for the specialized purposes of philologists and not for librarians; it contains features that make it impractical for normal bibliographic applications. Certain grammatical features, notably those expressed by the character ة (tā' marbūṭah) are to be "rendered by superior *h* or *t* (above the line)," thus: al-madīna[h], madīna[t] an-nabī. Such typographical niceties, difficult and costly to achieve even in the printing of philological treatises, are entirely superfluous for bibliographical purposes and are impossible to reproduce in direct teleprinter and computer printouts, or on CRT displays. Future revisions of this ISO recommendation should eliminate this feature, which is not found in any other Romanization scheme for Arabic script, including one for geographical purposes devised by Arab specialists at the Conférence

---

[47]The following Romanization schemes for languages written in Arabic script have been published in the *Cataloging Service* bulletin of the Library of Congress: Arabic (no. 91, September 1970); Persian (no. 92, September 1970); Pushto (no. 93, September 1970); Urdu (no. 94, September 1970); Sindhi (no. 104, April 1972).

[48]American National Standards Institute (1972).

[49]International Organization for Standardization (1961).

régionale des pays arabes pour la normalisation des noms géographiques, held in Beirut in 1971.[50]

It also seems advisable to develop separate Romanization tables for the non-Semitic languages written in Arabic script, as has been done by the Library of Congress and by the most recent addition to Arabic Romanization systems, the one used by the *International Journal of Middle East Studies (IJMES)*, which provides separate schemes for Arabic, Persian, Ottoman Turkish, and Modern Turkish (i.e., the official Turkish Latinization related to Arabic letters formerly used). Separate Romanizations would, of course, violate the principle of strict transliteration, according to which one and only one Roman character is used for each Arabic character. However two good reasons exist for separate Romanization tables. Firstly, every rendering of an Arabic name or word already contains elements of phonemic transcription because of the substitution of vowels not written in the original. Secondly, there are now officially endorsed Romanization schemes for Persian and Urdu, based on the phonology of these languages and not on that of classical Arabic. It would be unfortunate if the standards to be used internationally for the Romanization of these (and possibly other) languages differed from those by which Iran and Pakistan wish to render their languages into Roman script.

The scheme for Persian was designed by the Iranian librarian Nasser Sharify,[51] and is now widely used in Iranian libraries and by official bodies. It was also adopted by the LC, whose scheme differs only in the use of diacritical marks for three letters (though one wonders why it was considered necessary or useful to substitute $s̲$, for $s̲̄$, $z̄$ for $z̲$, and $z̤$ for $z̲$ as transcriptions of ث , ذ , and ض).

The Orientalist G. F. Wheeler, whose opinion on Arabic as a script for non-Semitic languages we have cited, stated that Arabic is "grievously inadequate for the exacting demands of Hindi phonetics," and so are most existing Romanization schemes for Urdu, according to Pakistani scholars. A. Moid[52] compared six schemes with the official Pakistani scheme, and a comparative study of six other schemes was made by R. C. Dogra, who found all of them to be deficient:

Transliteration schemes meant for Arabic, Persian and other languages using the same alphabet do not meet the requirements of Urdu. . . . Urdu . . . requires its own transliteration system with its own alphabet, vowels and symbols.[53]

---

[50]United Nations Conference . . . (1972). Transliteration of the Arabic alphabet. Vol. 2, p. 170.
[51]Sharify (1959).
[52]Moid (1964), pp. 73–74.
[53]Dogra (1973), pp. 365–366.

Dogra devised his own scheme (not included in the paper for technical reasons but shown here in Table 4.10), which is almost identical with the LC scheme, except for the transliteration of ‎چ‎ (*ch* instead of *c*).

A scheme for Ottoman Turkish, designed by E. Birnbaum,[54] was adopted by the British Museum and later by *IJMES*. It is interesting that the Turks themselves have not produced a bibliographic transliteration scheme for Turkish written in Arabic script, and their cataloging code contains the instruction that titles and names should be rendered "in accordance with today's pronunciation, without regard to the transcription system," although the code does provide such schemes for Arabic and Persian. Birnbaum presumes that this was done for ideological reasons, so as not to create Turkish transliterations from Arabic script that differ from the official Latinized form.

Cyrillization of Arabic, like other scripts and languages, is performed by phonemic transcription. Transcription tables for languages written in Arabic have been published by Zavadovskij,[55] and the rendering of Arabic names into Bulgarian has been treated by Nedkov.[56]

No official Arabization scheme has yet been published by any of the Arab states or other countries that use Arabic script. Names and words written in non-Arabic scripts are transcribed into Arabic in many different forms, and this is a constant source of confusion for Western Arabists as well as for Arab librarians and bibliographers, as pointed out by M. Aman.[57] It results, of course, in awkward problems of retranscription, similar to those already discussed under Cyrillic and Japanese.

2.3.6. Chinese. When the famous Sinologist B. Karlgren gave a talk in 1928 on the Romanization of Chinese, he observed wryly:

> There are as many Romanization schemes as days in the year, and in spite of energetic efforts of international congresses it has never been possible to get any one of them generally accepted.[58]

The bibliography *T & T* lists many dozens of actual and proposed schemes for the Romanization of Chinese, most of which appeared since the 1930s. Their number would seem to bear out Karlgren's somewhat fanciful "guesstimate." In a comparative study made in 1962, I. L. Legeza found 50 schemes, 29 of them no longer in active use, which still leaves the large number of 21 different transcription schemes used in various languages and writing systems, and by a number of Sinologists. Legeza says that

[54] E. Birnbaum (1967).
[55] Zavadovskij (1963).
[56] Nedkov (1963).
[57] Aman (1968), p. 263.
[58] Karlgren (1928).

although a few romanized systems can claim limited international recognition in the sense that they are used in more than one language nowadays, the use of the majority of romanized and non-romanized, currently used and outdated transliteration systems is confined to a particular language. Accordingly, one can speak about the French, German, Japanese, Arabic, Russian, etc., transliteration systems adopted for the transcription of Chinese words in the modern Peking dialect.[59]

One of the causes for this proliferation of schemes is, according to Legeza, the rejection of a proposed international scheme[60] by the 13th International Congress of Orientalists in 1902, which recommended instead that national schemes should be devised. It must be realized, however, that Chinese can only be transcribed phonemically, which means that an "international" Romanization scheme would have to be geared to the phonology of an "international" language, or, since this does not exist, to one that is internationally agreed upon as a "key" language. Actually it seems to matter relatively little that the transcriptions in different languages vary from each other, because their only function is to give an approximation of Chinese sounds to speakers of the respective languages, and they are virtually meaningless unless accompanied by the relevant Chinese logograms. The English transcription *chih,* the equivalent French *tche,* the German *dschï,* and the Russian чжи convey to readers a semblance of a Chinese syllable, phonetically expressed in the orthography of their languages, but all are equally ambiguous. It is impossible to know whether the transcriptions refer to 夂 ("step"), 支 ("branch"), 止 ("to stop"), 至 ("to reach"), or 爾 ("embroidery") without seeing the logograms.

Thus in the case of Chinese a number of transcription schemes that differ according to the orthographic conventions of various languages are virtually a necessity, and little compatibility among the schemes can be expected, even though some syllables, such as *fu, li,* and *ma,* will probably be transcribed identically in practically all languages using the Roman script.

Several concordances to a number of the most widely used schemes of transcription have been published. One of the earliest tables of this kind was issued in 1952 as an appendix to the Hungarian transcription scheme *A kínai nevek és szavak magyar átírása* (Hungarian transcription of Chinese names and words), compiled by the Hungarian Academy of Sciences.[61] This compared the Wade-Giles scheme with the French, German, and Russian schemes. A much more comprehensive work of this kind is the "Romanization Index," which forms Volume 2 of the five-volume *Chinese Character Indexes* compiled by Ching-yi Dougherty and others.[62] This is a synoptic listing of the Gwoyeu Romatzyh

[59]Legeza (1968), p. 2.
[60]Hirth (1904).
[61]Magyar Tudómanyos Akadémia (1952).
[62]Dougherty (1963).

(the official Romanization of the Chinese National Phonetic Alphabet), the Pin-yin scheme, the Wade-Giles scheme, the Yale scheme (invented in 1943 by G. A. Kennedy for instructional purposes),[63] and the Russian scheme devised by I. M. Ošanin. The transcriptions of many syllables are identical or almost so, but in many cases they are entirely different. When the Russian scheme is back-transliterated, the differences become even more obvious, as the following examples show (the back-transliterations have been added here and are not part of the tables in the work by Dougherty).

National	Pin-yin	Wade-Giles	Yale	Ošanin	Back-transliteration from Ošanin by	
					LC	ISO/R9
chai	chai	ch'ai	chai	чай	chaĭ	čaj
chiun	qun	ch'ün	chywun	цюнь	t͡sion'	cjon'

A more recent work is *A concordance to the five systems of transcription for standard Chinese* by O. B. Anderson.[64] A simplified but quite useful concordance between the Pin-yin and Wade-Giles systems appears in the booklet *Elementary Chinese for American librarians* by John T. Ma.[65] I. L. Legeza's work *Guide to transliterated Chinese in the modern Peking dialect,* already mentioned, is the most exhaustive concordance; the 407 basic Chinese syllables are shown synoptically as transcribed by 50 different schemes, including three Chinese ones (Chu-yin tzŭ-mu, Sin Wenz, and Pin-yin).

The proliferation of Romanization schemes for Chinese has had only a minor impact on bibliographic practices. The Wade-Giles scheme, although devised for English-speaking readers only, has been accepted by the majority of libraries that employ transcription for the cataloging of Chinese works, including those in non-English-speaking countries. The only cataloging code that deals with Chinese transcription is LC,[66] which has no complete tables of Romanized syllables but gives many examples illustrating the application of the Wade-Giles system as modified by the omission of the diacritical marks ˇ and ^ and the omission of the raised numbers that indicate four tones. This lack of tone markings makes the scheme highly ambiguous. The three general manuals also contain lists of words with Wade-Giles transcription (but none covers all of the more than 400 Chinese syllables). Some libraries and bibliographic works now prefer

[63]Kennedy (1944).
[64]Anderson (1975).
[65]Ma (1968).
[66]American Library Association (1959), p. 47. Partially superseded and augmented by "Chinese: Romanization, Capitalization and Punctuation," *Cataloging Service,* Bull. No. 62, September 1963, and "Chinese Romanization," *Cataloging Service,* Bull. no. 114, Summer 1975, pp. 12–30.

the official Pin-yin scheme, shown in Table 4.11; the scheme is reproduced here as originally published because the source is not easily accessible.

Cyrillization of Chinese has long been the concern of Russian Sinologists, as would be expected, since the two countries share a common border and have always had a close, if not always peaceful, relationship with each other. The multilingual dictionary by Pallas contained some Chinese words in Russian transcription, but these are now no more than an historical oddity. Present Cyrillization practices follow the standard Chinese–Russian dictionary by I. M. Ošanin,[67] which also contains a complete table of Chinese syllables and their Cyrillized forms. A more specialized manual for the use of Russian Sinologists has been compiled by Macaev and Orlov[68]; it contains tables for all Chinese syllables in their Cyrillized form and compares them with the Wade-Giles transcription and other English-oriented schemes, the French and German transcriptions, and the three Chinese schemes Latinxua, Gwoyeu Romatzyh, and Pin-yin. Back-transliteration of Cyrillized Chinese names and words into Roman script may cause considerable difficulties (as shown in the preceding comparative examples), and often results in widely disparate forms of familiar names. This problem has been treated in a paper by C. G. Allen[69] which contains many examples and a table of concordance for Chinese syllables as transcribed by Ošanin and Wade-Giles.

The rendering of non-Chinese names in Chinese script leads to difficulties similar to those already discussed under Japanization, because at best only a remotely similar transcription by logograms approximating the sounds of foreign languages is possible, and different Chinese writers produce transcriptions of such wide variation that the confusion generated by Western transcriptions appears to be a model of consistency in comparison. The name Goethe is rendered as Ch'ü-t'i but also as Ko-te, and Victor Hugo may appear as Hsiao Oo, Yü-kuo, or Yü Oo; the Indian leader Nehru becomes a Sinized Ni-ho-lu, while Marx is rendered as Ma-ke-si. Among place names, London, Paris and Rome suffer relatively little by their Sinization to Lun-tun, Pa-li, and Lo-ma, and even Washington is recognizable in Hua-sheng-tun; but New York is Niu-yüeh, and San Francisco is probably not easily identifiable in its Chinese form Chiu-chin-shan. A handbook of common and well-known English personal and place names in Sinized form has been compiled by Hua Hsin.[70]

2.3.7. Korean. The Korean language is polysyllabic and agglutinative. It may be related to the Altaic languages, but through Chinese cultural influence

---

[67] Ošanin (1959).
[68] Macaev (1966).
[69] Allen (1960).
[70] Hsin (1965).

Table 4.11 The Official Chinese Romanization Scheme Pin-yin
1. THE ALPHABET

Letters	A a	B b	C c	D d	E e	F f	G g	H h	I i	J j
Wade System	a	pe	ts'e	te	ê	ef	ke	ha	i	chieh

Letters	K k	L l	M m	N n	O o	P p	Q q	R r	S s	T t
Wade System	k'e	el	em	ne	o	p'e	ch'iu	ar	es	t'e

Letters	U u	V v	W w	X x	Y y	Z z
Wade System	u	ve	wa	hsi	ya	tse

V is used only to produce foreign and national minority words, and local dialects. The written form of the letters follows the customary written form of Latin letters.

Note 1. Seven categories of syllables as represented by the characters 知, 摸, 詩, 日, 資, 雌 and 思 take i as their vowel. They are spelt as zhi, chi, shi, ri, zi, ci and si respectively.

Note 2. The sound êrh is spelt er. As a final, it is represented by r. Thus: ertong (兒童 children), huar (花兒 flower).

Note 3. When used alone, the vowel e is spelt as ê.

Note 4. Y is used as a semi-vowel in syllables beginning with i when not preceded by consonants. Thus: yi (衣), ya (呀), ye (耶), yao (腰), you (憂), yan (烟), yin (因), yang (央), ying (英), yong (雍).

W is used as a semi-vowel in syllables beginning with u when not preceded by consonants. Thus: wu (烏), wa (蛙), wo (窩), wai (歪), wei (威), wan (弯), wen (温), wang (汪), weng (翁).

Y is used as a semi-vowel in syllables beginning with ü when not preceded by consonants. In this case the two dots above u are omitted. Thus: yu (迂), yue (約), yuan (寃), yun (暈).

In syllables beginning with the consonants j, q and x, the two dots above u are also omitted. Thus: ju (居), qu (区) and xu (虛). But in syllables beginning with the consonants n or l the two dots must be retained. Thus: nü (女), lü (呂).

Note 5. When preceded by consonants, iou, uei and uen are spelt as iu, ui and un. Thus: niu (牛), gui (旧), lun (論).

Note 6. In annotating the Chinese characters, the letters ng can be simplified as ŋ.

Table 4.11 (*continued*)

2. CONSONANTS

Consonants	Illustrative Chinese Characters	Wade System	Approximate English Equivalents
b	玻	p	b as in "be"
p	坡	p'	p as in "par," strongly aspirated
m	摸	m	m as in "man"
f	佛	f	f as in "food"
d	得	t	d as in "do"
t	特	t'	t as in "ten," strongly aspirated
n	訥	n	n as in "nine"
l	勒	l	l as in "land"
g	哥	k	g as in "go"
k	科	k'	k as in "kind," strongly aspirated
h	喝	h	h as in "her," strongly gutturalized
j	基	ch (i)	j as in "jeep"
q	欺	ch' (i)	ch as in "cheek"
x	希	hs (i)	sh as in "she"
zh	知	ch	j as in "jump"
ch	蚩	ch'	ch as in "church," strongly aspirated
sh	詩	sh	sh as in "shore"
r	日	ĵ	r pronounced but not rolled, tending towards the z in "azure"
z	資	ts, tz	ds as in "deeds"
c	雌	ts'	ts as in "tsar," strongly aspirated
s	思	s, ss, sz	s as in "sister"

In annotating the Chinese characters, the letters zh, ch and sh may be simplified as ẑ, ĉ and ŝ.

Table 4.11 *(continued)*

3. VOWELS

Vowels	Illustrative Chinese Characters	Wade System	Approximate English Equivalents
a	啊	a	a as in "father"
o	喔	o	aw as in "law"
e	鵝	ê	er as in "her," the r being silent
i	衣	i	ea as in "eat"
u	烏	u	oo as in "too"
ü	汙	ü	as German "ü"

Each vowel may be followed by other vowels or consonants to form the following diphthongs or finals:

Diphthongs

Diphthongs	Illustrative Chinese Characters	Wade System	Approximate English Equivalents
ia	呀	ia	yah
ua	蛙	ua	wah
uo	窩	uo	wa as in "water"
ie	耶	ieh	ye as in "yes"
üe	約	yüeh	no English equivalent
ai	愛	ai	as pronoun "I"
uai	歪	uai	wi as in "wife"
ei	欸	ei	ay as in "way"
uei	威	ui, wei	as "way"
ao	熬	ao	ow as in "how"
iao	腰	iao	yow as in "yowl"
ou	歐	ou	ow as in "low"
iou	憂	iu	yee oo

Table 4.11 *(continued)*
Finals Ending in "N" or "Ng"

Finals	Illustrative Chinese Characters	Wade System	Approximate English Equivalents
an	安	ʾan	ahn
ian	烟	ien	ien as in "lenient"
uan	弯	uan	oo ahn
üan	冤	yüan	no English equivalent
en	恩	ên	as "earn"
in	因	in	een as in "keen"
uen	温	wên	won as in "wonder"
ün	量	yün	no English equivalent
ang	昂	ang	ahng
iang	央	iang	i ahng
uang	汪	uang	oo ahng
eng	the final as in "哼"	êng	no English equivalent
ing	英	ing	ing as in "sing"
ueng	翁	wêng	no English equivalent
ong	the final as in "瘋"	ung	oo ng
iong	雍	yung	y oong

4. TONE MARKS

To indicate tones, the following marks are used:

First tone	Second tone	Third tone	Fourth tone
—	∕	∨	∖
mā	má	mǎ	mà
媽 (mama)	麻 (hemp)	馬 (horse)	罵 (to scold)

The tone marks are put above the main vowels of syllables. When a syllable is neutral, no tone mark is called for. Thus: hǎu ma (好嗎 Is it good?)

5. THE DIVIDING SIGN

When a syllable preceded by a, o or e immediately follows another syllable and is liable to run into each other and cause confusion, the dividing sign " ' " is used. Example: pi'ao (皮袄 fur coat); without the sign it is piao (漂 to float).

Source. Reform of the Chinese Written Language (1958), pp. 55–59.

over thousands of years, many Chinese loanwords have long been part of its vocabulary. According to tradition the Chinese scholar Wan-Shin introduced Chinese script to Korea in the 3rd century A.D., and it has been used ever since to write Korean literature, although many logograms are now written differently in Korean usage.

Initially, Chinese logograms were used phonetically to express the phonemes of spoken Korean (similar to Japanese *On* readings), and the resulting script was known as Idu. However this was never widely adopted, especially since the increasingly large number of Chinese loanwords were written with their original Chinese logograms (i.e., as in Japanese *Kun* reading). Soon after the Yi dynasty came to power in the late 14th century, printing with movable copper types was invented in 1403 under King Ta-chong (1401–1419). The large number of individual types needed to print Chinese ideograms may have led to the subsequent invention of an ingenious and very simple alphabetic script by King Se-chong (1419–1451) in the year 1446. The Koreans are thus the only people whose language was originally written in Chinese characters to substitute their own alphabetic script for it. Moreover this script is one of the few of which we know definitely when and by whom it was invented. The king had sent delegations of learned men to China and elsewhere to gain more knowledge about simpler writing systems, but when these committees continued their deliberations for more than three years, the king and a few of his friends proceeded to design a new script themselves, accomplishing the task within a few weeks[71]—a nice historical parallel to the "invention" of the new Turkish alphabet by Kemal Atatürk.

The new script was called *Ŏn-mun* (literally "word-sentence") and consisted of 28 letters. Revised during the years 1777–1781, it now comprises 24 letters (10 vowels and 14 consonants). Its unique characteristic is the analytic representation of phonetic features by parts of a letter, and some scholars therefore consider it "the most perfect phonetic system" ever devised for the writing of a language.[72] For example, ㄱ stands for /k/ and ㅋ for /kh/, the horizontal stroke inside the letter indicating the aspiration; the same graphic device is used for other aspirated consonants. A superficial similarity can be seen in Roman *b* and *p,* the ascender being written for the voiced and the descender for the unvoiced dental plosive; but this happens to be a coincidence, whereas in Korean script it is a systemic feature.

For a long time after its invention, however, literate Koreans held that Ŏn-mun was unworthy of scholarly use, fit only for less well-educated people of the lower classes, and they continued to write Korean in Chinese script. At the end of the 19th century the Korean government attempted to popularize the

[71]Eckardt (1928), p. C 9.
[72]Diringer (1968), p. 355.

indigenous alphabet, changed its name to Han'gŭl ("the Han [Great] letter"), and printed the official gazette in both Chinese and Han'gŭl script. Han'gŭl was also used by Christian missionaries, who realized that it was better suited to the spread of the Gospel among Koreans than was the Roman script—a very rare occurrence in missionary activities. Since 1949 the Korean alphabet has entirely replaced the Chinese characters in the People's Democratic Republic of Korea, where it is now called Chosŏn Muntcha ("Korean script") and is written from left to right. In the Republic of Korea, Han'gŭl is still written from top to bottom in conjunction with Chinese logograms, mainly to indicate affixes, particles, and the pronunciation for an ambiguous logogram, that is, in a manner somewhat similar to the use of *kana* in Japanese.

The Han'gŭl script did not become the subject of systematic Romanization until the late 1920s and early 1930s. The German Jesuit missionary A. Eckardt, one of the earliest Western scholars to devise a transliteration scheme, was followed by the French Orientalist M. Haguenauer,[73] whose scheme was mainly intended for the use of philologists, as it contained several special characters and many diacritical marks which made it unsuitable for bibliographic and cartographic purposes. The Japanese author Shimpei Ogura proposed another scheme in 1934 and stated that 27 different such schemes had previously been devised by various people. A practical scheme based only on Roman characters and containing only two diacritical marks was devised in 1939 by two Americans, G. M. McCune and E. O. Reischauer[74]; it was first applied by American authorities to the Romanization of Korean geographic and personal names during World War II.

Although the McCune-Reischauer scheme is based on English orthographic conventions and pronunciation, it is now the most widely used scheme for the Romanization of Korean script; it is employed by scholars and Orientalists in many countries as well as by almost all libraries and bibliographic services. The LC code refers to it as the code used for Romanization of Korean entries[75] but does not display the table itself. The BGN manual contains the complete tables and also gives instructions on the transcription of Korean names written in Chinese characters. These first have to be converted into Han'gŭl script with the help of special Korean–Chinese characters–Han'gŭl dictionaries, and the resulting Han'gŭl transcription must then be transliterated by the McCune-Reischauer system. Probably not much of the original form of names can be preserved by this system of double transcription and transliteration.

More recently three other Romanization systems for Han'gŭl have been introduced, two of which have official status. The Academy of Sciences in the

[73] Haguenauer (1933).
[74] McCune (1939). The scheme of Ogura is mentioned there, and details of his and some others' schemes are given in a comparative table together with the authors' own scheme.
[75] American Library Association (1959), p. 56.

Table 4.12 Romanization Schemes for Han'gŭl (a) Vowels and Diphthongs

Letter[1]	Name	McCune-R. (=LC)	Haguenauer	North Korea	South Korea	Yale
o ㅏ	a	a	•	•	•	•
ㅐ	ae	ae	ai	ai	•	ay
o ㅑ	ya	ya	•	•	•	•
ㅒ	yae	yae	yè	yai	•	yay
o ㅓ	ŏ	ŏ	ɔ	•	eo	e
ㅔ	e	e	•	•	•	ey
o ㅕ	yŏ	yŏ	yɔ	•	yeo	ye
ㅖ	ye	ye	•	•	•	yey
o ㅗ	o	o	•	•	•	•
ㅘ	wa	wa	oa	•	•	•
ㅙ	wae	wae	uɛ	wai	•	way
ㅚ	oe	oe	ue̯	oi	•	oy
o ㅛ	yo	yo	•	•	•	•
o ㅜ	u	u	•	•	•	wu
ㅝ	wŏ	wŏ	u	wo	weo	we
ㅞ	we	we	ue̯	•	•	wey
ㅟ	wi	wi	ui̯	•	•	•
o ㅠ	yu	yu	•	•	•	•
o ㅡ	ŭ	ŭ	ø	•	eu	u
ㅢ	ŭi	ŭi	øi	•	eui	uy
o ㅣ	i	i	•	•	•	•

290

Table 4.12   *(continued)* **(b) Consonants**

Letter[2]	Name	McCune-R. (=LC)	Haguenauer	North Korea	South Korea	Yale
ㄱ	kiyŏk	k, g	k, g, ṅ	k	g	k
ㄴ	niŭn	n	n, l, *	.	.	.
ㄷ	tigŭt	t, d	t, d, č	t	d	t
ㄹ	riŭl	l, r	r, l, n, *	r	.	l
ㅁ	miŭm	m	.	.	.	.
ㅂ	piŭp	p, b	p, b, m	p	b	p
ㅅ	siot	s	s, š, t, n	.	.	.
ㅇ	iŭng	ng	ṅ	.	.	.
ㅈ	chiŭt	ch, j	č, dž	ts	j	c
ㅉ		tch	tč	tss	jj	cc
ㅊ	ch'iŭt	ch'	č'	tsh	ch	ch
ㅋ	k'iŭk	k'	.	kh	k	kh
ㅌ	t'iŭt	t'	.	th	t	th
ㅍ	p'iŭp	p'	.	ph	p	ph
ㅎ	hiŭt	h	.	.	.	.

[1] The 10 basic vowels are indicated by an asterisk in the left margin; all other vowels and diphthongs are combinations of these basic letters.

[2] Reduplicated consonants (except ㅉ) are transliterated by doubling the relevant Roman letter in all schemes.

Democratic People's Republic of Korea published its scheme in 1957, and the Ministry of Education in the Republic of Korea promulgated an entirely different one in 1959. Neither resembles the McCune-Reischauer scheme where specific Korean phonemes are involved. A third scheme has been employed in the *Korean–English Dictionary*[76] compiled by scholars at Yale University, and this is now used in Korean language courses there. Table 4.12 displays five Romanization schemes for Han'gŭl.

[76] Martin (1967).

Cyrillization of Korean script for Russians has been discussed by Serdjučenko,[77] and the treatment of Korean names in Bulgarian transcription was studied by Văglenov and Kančev.[78]

2.3.8. Greek. The transliteration of Classical Greek was already fairly uniform in the days of Imperial Rome, and has become standardized since the translation of the New Testament from Greek into Latin by Erasmus in 1516. Indeed, none of the developers of early cataloging codes deemed it necessary to display a table of transliteration, since the educated reader was supposed to be familiar with Classical Greek names in their Latin form. The AU code referred simply to "Erasmic transcription"; the PI stated "Die altgriechischen Namen werden stets in der latinisierten Form angesetzt" (§87), and Greek titles were written in Greek without transliteration (§4.1). The BM code did not even mention Greek names or titles.

Since the literature of classical Greece forms a closed universe, and practically all names and titles have been Latinized, the transcription of Greek would not constitute much of a problem were it not for the differences in orthography and pronunciation between Classical and Modern Greek. Although Modern Greek uses exactly the same alphabet as Classical Greek, several letters are pronounced differently, notably β, which has now the sound of $[v]$, while $[b]$ is now written by the digraph $\mu\pi$ and $[d]$ is often written $\nu\tau$. This makes transliteration by purely phonetic transcription of each letter according to its "classical" sound clumsy or even outright misleading when retranscription of non-Greek names from their Grecized form is involved. The name of Baudelaire, for example, is given in Greek encyclopedias and reference books as Μπωντελαιρ, which becomes Mpōntelair when transliterated according to the rules for Classical Greek. This problem is, of course, not peculiar to Greek; it also occurs in retransliteration from other scripts, but many people, including those who devised transliteration schemes for Modern Greek, seem unaware of it or ignore it for the sake of a misunderstood and misapplied "uniformity of transliteration."

Separate transliteration of Modern Greek for bibliographic purposes was first mentioned as a possible option in Cutter's cataloging code, which contained a partial Romanization table of those single letters and digraphs (for diphthongs) that were to be transliterated differently. The troublesome digraph $\mu\pi$ was, however, not listed. The Library of Congress followed the same example (but included the rendering of $\mu\pi$ by b) in its "Rule 11," printed in the form of a card in 1905 and subsequently reprinted as a complete table in ALA 1908; the table was revised in ALA 1949 and published with further revisions in 1972.[79] The BM code of 1936 also contains a transliteration table for Modern Greek which,

[77]Serdjučenko (1960).
[78]Văglenov (1969).
[79]"Greek Romanization," *Cataloging Service,* Bulletin 104, April 1972, pp. 17–18.

however, is nearly identical with classical transliteration because β is rendered as *b*. Almost all later cataloging codes contain transliteration tables for Greek, but only six of these distinguish between Classical and Modern Greek (see Table 4.13).

An attempt to sidestep the problems caused by the discrepancies between Classical and Modern Greek by designing a "strict" and therefore "neutral" transliteration scheme was made in the British Standard B.S. 2979, the preface of which admitted that it "deals with the Greek alphabet without special regard to phonetic, etymological or other linguistic peculiarities of Ancient, Medieval and Modern Greek—in short, a straightforward rule-of-thumb system."[80] It would seem that a standard, by definition, should not be a "rule-of-thumb," but such are the follies perpetrated by those who chase the will-o'-the-wisp of "strict" transliteration. The principle was violated at any rate by retaining the traditional phonetic transcriptions of *th* for θ and *ps* for Ψ, while the equally traditional *ch* for χ was inexplicably eliminated in favor of *h;* this, in turn, made it impossible to use *h* to indicate ^{c}, the *spiritus asper,* as had been the usage for 2000 years. Thus ‘Eλλάς is to be rendered as ‘Ellas (not Hellas), and ‘'Oμηρος becomes ‘Omēros (not Homēros). The result is that many names or words transliterated according to this scheme do not appear in the traditional classical form found in all reference works and in scholarly treatises on ancient Greek literature, history, and geography; nor can a modern Greek name be rendered in a recognizable (much less pronounceable) form if it happens to contain any of the digraphs γγ, γκ, γξ, γχ, μπ, or ντ. This makes the scheme entirely unsuitable for bibliographical purposes.

The ISO recommendation ISO/R843 for transliteration of Greek[81] is virtually identical with B.S. 2979. The French national standard also follows the same example, but entries for modern Greek books in the *Catalogue général* of the Bibliothèque Nationale are now printed in Greek rather than subjecting the names of authors to the kind of transliteration demanded by AFNOR, although all other transliterations in the catalog comply with those French standards.

The Cyrillization of Greek would not seem to be a major problem for Russians since no references to it could be found in recent Soviet literature dealing with the problem of transcription. The rendering of Classical and Modern Greek names into Bulgarian, however, has been the subject of papers by Filipova[82] and Batakliev.[83]

Grecization, or the rendering of non-Greek names into Greek, on the other hand, seems to be a difficult matter for which no firm rules have been evolved as yet by Greek linguists. Greek encyclopedias often list foreign names in

[80]British Standards Institution (1958), p. 5.
[81]International Organization for Standardization (1968).
[82]Filipova (1964).
[83]Batakliev (1967).

Table 4.13 Romanization Schemes for Greek Script

Letter	Name	Std ISO, BSI / AFNOR, PL	BM	LC	BE	BU	CS	GE	IT, VC	NO	SP	SW	YU	Alphabete	BGN	EB
A α	alpha	a	•	•	°	•	•	•	•	•	•	•	•	°	•	°
B β	beta	b	•	•	•	•	°	•	•	•	•	•	•	•	•	°
o B β	vita		b	v	v	v		v,w	v	v				v	v	v
Γ γ	gamma	g	•	•	•	•	•	g,j,y	•	•	•	•	•	•	g,y	g,y
1)			n	n	n	n		n	n		n	n		n	n	n
Δ δ	delta	d	•	•	•	•	•	d,dh	•	•	•	•	•	°	•	•
E ε	epsilon	e	•	•	•	•	•	•	•	•	•	•	•	•	•	•
Z ζ	zēta	z	•	•	°	•	•	•	•	•	•	•	•	•	°	•
H η	ēta	ē	•	•	•	•	•	•	•	•	•	°	•	•	°	•
o H η	ita		e		i			i	i						i	i
Θ θ	thēta	th	•	•	•	•	•	•	•	•	•	•	°	°	•	•
I ι	iota	i	•	•	•	•	•	•	°	•	•	°	°	•	•	•
	subscript	j							i	i	,2					
K κ	kappa	k	•	•	•	•	°	k,c	•	k,c	•	•	•	•	•	•
Λ λ	lambda	l	•	•	•	•	•	•	•	•	•	•	°	•	•	•
M μ	mu	m	•	•	°	•	•	•	•	•	•	•	•	•	•	•
o M π			b	b	b	b		b	b					b	b	b
N ν	nu	n	•	•	•	°	•	°	•	•	•	•	•	•	•	•
o N τ			d	d	d	d		d	d					d	d	d
Ξ ξ	xi	x	•	•	°	•	•	•	•	•	°	°	•	•	•	•
O o	omicron	o	°	•	•	•	•	•	°	•	•	•	•	•	°	•

Table 4.13 *(continued)*

Letter	Name	Std (ISO, AFNOR BSI, PL)	BM	LC	BE	BU	CS	GE	IT, VC	NO	SP	SW	YU	Alphabete	BGN	EB
Π π	pi	p	•	•	•	•	•	•	•	•	o	•	•	•	o	•
Ρ ρ	rō	r	•	•	•	o	•	o	•	•	•	•	•	•	•	•
ᶜΡ ῥ	rhō	r	•	rh	•	•	•	rh	•	rh	o	rh	o	rh	•	rh
Σ σ ς	sigma	s	•	•	•	•	•	•	•	•	•	•	•	•	•	•
Τ τ	tau	t	o	•	•	•	•	•	•	•	o	o	•	•	•	•
Τ υ	upsilon	u	•	y	•	•	y	y	y	y	y	y	y	y	•	i
3)				u	u	u	u	u	u	u	u	u		u		
o 4)				u	f	f		f						f	i,u	v
o 5)				u	v	v		v						v	v	v
Φ φ	phi	f	ph	ph	•	ph	•	ph	ph	ph	ph	ph	ph	ph	—	ph
o Φ ϕ	phi				f		f							f	f	f
Χ χ	khi	h	ch	ch	ch	ch	•	ch	ch	ch	ch	ch	ch	ch	kh	kh
Ψ ψ	psi	ps	•	o	•	•	o	•	•	•	•	•	•	o	o	o
Ω ω	ōmega	ō	o	o	•	•	o	o	•	•	•	o	•	o	o	•
o ᶜ rough breathing		ʽ, '	*	h	h	h	h	h	h	h	h	•	o	•	•	*

Note. Modern Greek transcriptions are indicated by a circle in the left margin.

[1] Before γ, κ, ξ, χ.
[2] Comma beneath the vowel.
[3] In diphthongs.
[4] In diphthongs before δ, κ, π, σ, τ, φ, and χ.
[5] Before β, γ, δ, ξ, λ, μ, ν, ρ, and vowels.

various spellings, referring to one of them as the preferred form. George Washington is rendered into Greek variously as Γεώργιος, Βάσιγκτων, or Γεώργιος Ο᾽νάσιγκτων, with preference for the latter form, but Greek publications do not seem to follow any fixed rules.

2.3.9.   Thai.   The Thai language belongs to the Sino-Tibetan family and is a tonal language like Chinese. Because of its political independence Thailand (formerly called Siam) was never forced to adopt the Chinese script but developed its own alphabet, which in its modern form consists of 44 consonants (including *a* and *u,* which are not considered as vowels) and 30 vowel and tone indicators, written by various diacritical marks. The writing system is very complex, since certain syllables are written but not pronounced, while a number of consonants are pronounced differently when written initially, medially, or finally, or may not be pronounced at all. Moreover there is a marked difference in the pronunciation of literary language and cultivated speech as opposed to everyday popular language. In short, the orthography of the Thai language displays complex features that are quite similar to those of English orthography. The compounding of one set of complexities by another one, further aggravated by a number of letters three times that of the Roman alphabet and by the need to indicate five or six different tones, makes the difficulties of Romanizing the script formidable indeed.

After some attempts at phonetic transcription had been made by missionaries in the 19th century, the Royal Survey Department of Siam developed its own Romanization scheme for the rendering of Thai place names in 1910. The scheme was, however, very complicated, and another approach was suggested by the French scholar P. Petithuguenin to the Siam Society, namely the use of two schemes, a "literal" and a "phonetic" one.[84] The King of Siam, Vajiravudh, a linguist and gifted writer as well as an able ruler and statesman, also elaborated a dual system for the use of the court and for official documents, with the clear intention not of Latinizing the Thai language but only of rendering Thai names and words intelligible to foreigners.[85] He rejected a phonetic system, since the Thai language would need at least three different conversion schemes for the pronunciations in various parts of the country. Several Thai governmental bodies studied the problem during the 1930s, culminating in the publication of an official Romanization system by the Royal Institute of Thailand in 1941,[86] which consisted of a "precise" and a "general" scheme. The precise scheme was intended for the use of philologists, while the general one "is to be applied in case it is desired to facilitate pronunciation by foreigners, without intention of indicating the unpronounced letters and tones."

[84]Petithuguenin (1913).
[85]Vajiravudh (1913).
[86]Royal Institute of Thailand (1941).

The general scheme was adopted by the Board on Geographic Names, which now uses a later, somewhat simplified version, officially published in 1968 by the Royal Institute.[87] The LC scheme,[88] first published in 1958 and reissued in amended form in 1966, is also based on the general scheme of the Royal Institute but is somewhat more elaborate than the BGN version, using many diacritical marks (see Table 4.14). This scheme is now used by all libraries that have Romanized catalogs for their Thai collections. The BM catalog of Thai printed books is still in manuscript form, and no details of its Romanization scheme have been published.

The Romanization of Thai script is unique in several respects. It is the only Southeast Asian language for which a transcription system was devised not by foreign philologists but by native scholars and statesmen. It is also one of the few scripts for which a nationally devised scheme was adopted more or less unchanged by Western scholars, thus not offending the speakers of that language by artificial contraptions intended to please foreigners.[89] Also, despite being an intricate script for a complex writing system, it did not give rise to a plethora of mutually incompatible conversion schemes. The latter phenomenon is probably attributable to the fact that only a few Western libraries have had to deal with Thai literature.

2.3.10. Hebrew.   The Romanization of Hebrew script in systematic form dates back to the early Middle Ages, as described in Chapter 3. The rather strict transliteration used by St. Jerome (see Table 3.5) gave way in the Renaissance to Romanizations that tried to approximate the sounds of Hebrew as spoken in the Sephardic pronunciation. The schemes devised by (mostly non-Jewish) Hebrew philologists since the early works by Reuchlin,[90] Postel,[91] and Buxtorf[92] before those used in our own times are all characterized by attempts to indicate a

---

[87]Royal Institute of Thailand (1968).

[88]"Romanization: Languages of Burma and Thailand," *Cataloging Service,* Bulletin no. 76, October 1966.

[89]Nevertheless some unfortunate blunders were made by overzealous Romanizers of Thai script. To give but one example: the letter อ is the 43rd consonant, used to express a glottal stop similar to the Arabic ع (*'ayn*) but also serving as a vowel symbol, especially when written in an initial position and followed by a vowel proper. It is thus written as the first letter of the Thai transcription of *America*. American philologists decided to transcribe this letter for linguistic purposes as *q* (in order to express its value as a glottal stop). This feature was adopted by Cornell University in its Romanization scheme for Thai script. As a consequence, Thai titles beginning with the word *America* are there transcribed *Qamerika* and filed under *Q,* although this is in direct conflict with the practice used in Thailand and in Thai dictionaries and reference books. The Library of Congress did not, however, follow this example and transcribes the letter by an apostrophe when it appears in an initial position, as is its practice for the Arabic *'ayn.*

[90]Reuchlin (1506).

[91]Postel (1538).

[92]Buxtorf (1609).

Table 4.14   Romanization of Thai

Vowels				Consonants	Initial and medial	Final
อะ, อั	a	อัวะ	ua	ก	k	k
อา	ā	อัว, ว	ūa	ข, ฃ, ค, ฅ, ฆ	kh	k
อำ	am	ใอ,ไอ,อัย,ไอย	ai	ง	ng	ng
อิ	i	อาย	āi	จ	čh	t
อี	ī	เอา	ao	ฉ, ช, ฌ	ch	t
อึ	ư	อาว	āo	ญ	y	n
อือ	ū̶	อุย	ui	ฎ, ฏ, ท[1]	d	t
อุ	u	โอย	ōi	ฏ, ฎ	t	t
อู	ū	ออย	ǭi	ฐ, ฑ, ฒ[1] ฑ, ธ, ถ	th	t
เอะ, เอ็	e	เอย	œ̄ i	น, ณ	n	n
เอ	ē	เออย	ư̄ ai	บ	b	p
แอะ	æ	อวย	ūai	ป	p	p
แอ	ǣ	อิว	iu	ผ, พ, ภ	ph	p
โอะ, อ	o	เอียว	eo	ผ, ฟ	f	p
โอ	ō	เอว	ēo	ม	m	m
เอาะ	ǫ	แอว	ǣ o	ย	y	–
ออ	ǭ	เอียว	īeo	ร[2]	r	n
เออะ	œ	ฤ	rư	ล, ฬ	l	n
เออ, เอิ	œ̄	ฤ	ri	ว	w	–
เอียะ	ia	ฤ	rœ̄	ซ, ทร, ศ, ษ, ส	s	t
เอีย	īa	ฤๅ	rū̶	อ[3]	'	–
เอือะ	ư̶ a	ฦ	lư	ห[4] ฮ	h	–
เอือ	ư̶ a	ฦๅ	lū̶			

1. ท is usually romanized *th*, occasionally *d*, depending on the pronunciation as determined from a standard dictionary.

2. When ร follows another consonant and ends a syllable, it is romanized *n*, and the inherent vowel of the preceding consonant is represented by ǫ (e. g., นคร *nakhǫn*).

When รร follows another consonant and no other pronounced consonant follows in the same syllable, it is romanized *an* (e. g., สวรรค์ *sawan*), but if a pronounced consonant follows, it is represented by *a* (e. g., กรรม *kam*).

3. In four common words อ occurs preceding another consonant to mark a certain tone and is then not romanized.

4. When ห occurs preceding another consonant to mark a certain tone, it is not romanized.

Source. Cataloging Service, Bull. 76, October 1966.

(sometimes conjectural) pronunciation, while increasingly striving to express also all written characters, including those not pronounced and those pronounced identically although written with different letters and diacritical marks. Since these phonemic and phonetic transcriptions were often linked to the orthographic conventions of the languages for whose readers they were intended, a large variety of schemes resulted from the efforts of philologists alone. In the latter part of the 19th century compilers of dictionaries and encyclopedias often devised their own schemes for the benefit of the "educated laymen," based on one or the other of the current philological schemes but shorn of excessive use of diacritical marks and other embellishments. Then the *Jewish Encyclopedia,*[93] published in the beginning of this century, produced a scheme which was a simplified version of one proposed at the 10th International Congress of Orientalists in 1895, and this has been widely accepted for the Romanization of Hebrew in English-speaking countries. The same encyclopedia also contained one of the best accounts of the history of Hebrew transcription, not matched by any later work of reference.

Comparative tables of the major philological and other scholarly transcription schemes from the Renaissance to the present time have been compiled by W. Weinberg,[94] whose paper also treats the problem in its historical and linguistic aspects in a thorough and exhaustive manner.

The vexing problems of Hebrew Romanization caused by the large variety of existing schemes have been compounded since the latter part of the 19th century by various more or less dilettantic renderings produced by Jewish individuals and communities trying to Romanize Hebrew names (especially those of synagogues and other religious, educational, and philanthropic institutions) according to what, in their opinion, approximated the pronunciation of Hebrew in the respective orthography of various countries. Because some of these phonemic renderings are based on the Sephardic pronunciation while others are linked to various shades of Ashkenazic pronunciation, the confusion that besets "popular" Romanization of Hebrew has been increased.

Romanization of Hebrew for bibliographic purposes can be traced to the first BM catalog of Hebrew printed books (which was also the first of the British Museum's many separate catalogs for non-Roman scripts). In the preface to this work, compiled by the Hebraist Joseph Zedner and published in 1867, a brief list of Roman equivalents for Hebrew letters is given, following in some respects German rather than English practice (e.g., *ch* for ח).

The transliteration tables for non-Roman scripts commissioned by the ALA in 1885 (already mentioned under Arabic) also contained proposals for Hebrew which, however, were not published. ALA 1908 contained the scheme used by

[93]*Jewish Encyclopedia* (1901–05).
[94]Weinberg (1969–70).

the *Jewish Encyclopedia,* and in ALA 1949 that scheme was reprinted, but a revised version (including variant Romanizations for Yiddish), which had been adopted by the Library of Congress in 1948, was introduced and is still in force.

The PI scheme is largely similar to that of the ICO, except for the rendering of ׳ by *j*, in accordance with German orthography. Nine other national cataloging codes have Romanization tables for Hebrew, following either LC or PI practice, with some local variations. The codes of the Scandinavian countries and the Communist countries (except Poland) lack Romanization tables for Hebrew (see Table 4.15).

With the establishment of the State of Israel in 1948 it became necessary to codify and standardize the Romanization of Hebrew for the uniform rendering of personal and place names for governmental and cartographic use. The Academy of the Hebrew Language, which had begun to deal with the problem long before 1948 (when it was still the Council on Language), devised a two-tiered Romanization system[95] which was published in 1957 as an official decree. It consists of a "simple" and a "more exact" scheme that are mutually compatible but intended for different purposes. The simple scheme (indicated in Table 4.15 as "Academy I") has several homographs for different Hebrew letters having the same (or very similar) pronunciation, and is used for the Romanization of names and words in official publications (such as passports and birth certificates) intended to be read outside Israel also, for general cartography, for the postal service, street signs, and so forth. It is also used by the Jewish National and University Library in Jerusalem where a name or title occasionally has to be Romanized, for example, in cross-references from the Romanized form to the Hebrew form. The more exact scheme ("Academy II") is used when it is important to distinguish the original Hebrew letters in Romanization. The introduction to the system emphasizes that neither the strict nor the more exact scheme is intended for highly specialized philological purposes, since even the more exact scheme Romanizes the various vowel signs by a phonemic rendering (i.e., without complete distinction between all three diacritical marks pronounced $[a]$ or all four marks pronounced $[e]$, etc.).

The ISO Recommendation ISO/R259[96] is almost exactly the same as the more exact scheme of the Academy, the only difference being the rendering of ח by *h* instead of *ḥ*. (The philologists on the ISO committee could not possibly leave a nationally devised and officially adopted scheme entirely unchanged, and had to assert their scholarship at least by changing a subscript diacritical mark!) The ISO scheme also indicates every single vowel sign (for vocalized text only) in a manner that looks peculiar to anyone familiar with Hebrew pronunciation because it gives the impression that certain vowels are pronounced as if they were German umlauts, which is certainly not the case. The AFNOR schemes which

[95] Academy of the Hebrew Language (1957).
[96] International Organization for Standardization (1962).

follows the ISO scheme exactly, has been applied to the relevant sections of the *Catalogue général* of the Bibliothèque Nationale for books published since 1960.

The BGN scheme is almost exactly like that of Academy I, the only difference in this case being the letter כ which, in conformity with long-standing English tradition, is rendered by *kh* (not *ḵ*).

An ill-chosen mixture of Hebrew Romanization schemes is found in the new *Encyclopedia Judaica (EJ),*[97] which is expressly aimed at English-speaking readers. The *EJ* generally uses a scheme almost identical to that of the Library of Congress, except for צ, which is rendered by *ẓ* (not *ts* as in the LC scheme). Although theoretically justifiable on the grounds that a Romanization by one character is preferable to a (sometimes ambiguous) digraph, one wonders whether much was gained by *EJ* readers who were accustomed to finding names and words beginning with the letter צ in library catalogs and other reference works under *T*. Now they must look for them under *Z,* and to confuse matters still more, the *EJ* uses the transliteration *ts* for צ in Yiddish! In entries concerning linguistic and Biblical subjects, the *EJ* uses the Academy II scheme, but not consistently.[98]

In his paper on the Romanization of Hebrew, Weinberg stressed the necessity for a multiple system, but went far beyond the two schemes devised by the Academy of the Hebrew Language. He believes that no less than five types of Romanization are needed: (1) narrow transliteration, (2) narrow phonetic transcription, (3) broad transliteration-transcription, (4) phonemic transcription, and (5) popular transcription-transliteration. Of these, (1) and (5) are roughly equivalent to Academy II and I respectively, (2) is for the use of phoneticians only and cannot be standardized since it depends on dialects, diction, and so forth, while (3) and (4) are intended for philological purposes, using a phonetic alphabet. As a consequence the ANSI Standard Z39.25–1975 for the transcription of Hebrew,[99] which is largely based on Weinberg's work, contains four schemes (which are only partially compatible with each other). Three are intended for conventional writing or printing, while the fourth is designed for use with computer printout facilities. The "general purpose" and "more exact" schemes, designed for English-speaking users, are based on the Israeli pronunciation. The "narrow transliteration" scheme is, as its name implies, a strict transliteration scheme with unambiguous one-to-one equivalents made possible by diacritical marks. The "general purpose" scheme is recommended for use in library catalogs, which is consistent with the use of the Academy I scheme by the Jewish National and University

---

[97]*Encyclopedia Judaica* (1972).

[98]Weinberg (1975) examined the Romanization of the *EJ* critically and found that there is "carelessness, confusion and total lack of planning and coordination displayed in the area of romanization" (p. 24).

[99]American National Standards Institute (1975).

Table 4.15 Romanization Schemes for Hebrew (a) Consonants

Letter	Name	Standards							Cataloging codes						Other schemes		
		ISO, AFNOR	Academy I	Academy II	ANSI General	ANSI More exact	ANSI Narrow	Keypunch-compatible	BM	LC	PI	BE, IT, VC	PL	SP	BGN	EB	EJ
א	alef	*,ʾ[1]	•	•	•	•	ʾ	@	*	•	•	•	•	*	•	•	*
ב	bet	b	•	•	•	•	•	B	•	•	•	•	•	•	•	•	•
ב	vet	v	•	•	•	•	ḇ	B	b	•	b	•	b	b	•	•	•
ג	gimal	g	•	•	•	•	•	G	•	•	•	•	•	•	•	•	•
ג	gimal	ḡ	g	•	g	g	g̱	G	g	g	g	g	g	g	g	g	g
ד	dalet	d	•	•	•	•	•	D	•	•	•	•	•	•	•	•	•
ד	dalet	ḏ	•	d	d	d	•	Ḏ	d	d	d	d	d	d	d	d	d
ה	he	h	•	•	•	•	•	H	•	•	•	•	•	•	•	•	•
ו	waw	w	•	•	v	w,v	•	W	v	•	•	•	•	•	•	•	v
ז	zayin	z	•	•	•	•	•	Z	•	•	•	•	•	•	•	•	•
ח	ḥet	ḥ	ẖ	ẖ	ch	•	•	Ḥ	ch	•	•	•	•	•	ẖ	•	•
ט	ṭet	ṭ	t	•	t	•	•	Ṭ	t	•	•	•	•	•	t	•	t
י	yod	y	•	•	•	•	•	Y	•	•	j	•	j	•	•	•	•
כ,ך	kaf	k	•	•	•	•	•	K	c	•	•	•	•	•	•	•	•
כ,ך	kaf	ḵ	kh	•	ch	kh	•	₭	c	kh	k	kh	kh	k	kh	kh	kh
ל	lamed	l	•	•	•	•	•	L	•	•	•	•	•	•	•	•	•
מ,ם	mem	m	•	•	•	•	°	M	•	•	•	•	•	•	•	•	•
נ,ן	nun	n	•	•	•	•	•	N	•	•	•	•	•	•	•	•	•
ס	samek	s	•	•	•	•	•	S	•	•	•	•	•	•	•	•	•
ע	ᶜayin	ᶜ	'	•	*,'	•	•	&	*	•	•	•	•	•	•	•	*
פ	pe	p	°	•	•	•	•	P	•	•	•	•	•	•	•	•	•
פ,ף	fe	f	•	•	•	•	p̱	₱	•	•	•	•	•	•	•	•	•
צ,ץ	zade	ẓ	•	•	ts	ts	ṣ	¢	ts	ts	ṣ	ṣ	c	•	•	tz	ẓ
ק	qof	q	•	•	k	q,k	•	Q	k	ḳ	•	•	ḳ	•	•	•	k
ר	reš	r	•	•	•	•	•	R	•	•	•	•	•	•	•	•	•
ש	šin	š	sh	•	sh	sh	•	$	sh	sh	•	•	•	sh	sh	sh	sh
ש	śin	ś	°	s	s	•	•	$	°	•	•	•	s	s	•	s
ת	taw	t	•	•	•	•	•	T	th	•	•	•	•	•	•	•	•
ת	taw	ṯ	t	•	t	t	•	T	th	t	t	t	th	t	t	t	t

Table 4.15 *(continued* **(b) Vowels**

Vowel sign[2]	Name	Standards ISO³ AFNOR v	Standards ISO³ AFNOR nv	Academy I	Academy II	ANSI General	ANSI More exact	ANSI Narrow	ANSI Keypunch-compatible	BM	LC	PI	BE, IT, VC	PL	SP	BGN	EB	EJ
֥	qama<u>z</u> gadol	ą	a	•	•	•	•	ā	Ⱥ	•	•	ā	ā	•	•	•	•	•
ֿ	pataḥ	a	a	•	•	•	•	•	A	•	•	•	•	•	•	•	•	•
ּ	ḥaṭaf pataḥ	ă	a	•	ă	•	•	ă	%A	•	•	ă	•	ă	•	•	•	•
ֽ	zêrê ḥaser	e	e	•	é	•	•	ē	Ɇ	•	•	ē	ē	•	•	•	•	'
ֿ	zêrê male	ê	ê	e	é	e,é/ei	e,é/ei	•	ɆY	e	•	ē	•	e	e	e	e	e,ei
ֿ	segôl	ę	e	•	•	•	•	•	E	•	•	•	•	•	•	•	•	•
ֿ	segôl male	ę̂	ê	e	e	e	e	e(y)	EY	e				e	e	e	e	e
ֿ	ḥaṭaf segôl	ę̆	e	•	ĕ	•	•	ĕ	%E	•		•		•	ĕ	•	•	e
ֿ	ševa naᶜ	ĕ	e	•	ĕ	•	•	e⁴	%	•	•	•		e	•	•	•	•
ֿ	ḥîrîq	i	i	•	•	•	•	•	I	•	•	•	•	•	•	•	•	•
ֿ	ḥîrîq male	î	î	i	i	i	i	•	IY	i	i	ī	ī	i	i	i	i	i
ֿ	hôlam ḥaser	o	o	•	•	•	•	ō	O	•		•	•	•	•	•	•	•
ֿ	hôlam male	ô	ô	o	o	o	o	•	OW	o	o	ō	ō	o	o	o	o	o
ֿ	qama<u>z</u> qatan	ǫ	o	•	•	•	•	•	Ⱥ	•		•	•	•	•	•	•	•
ֿ	ḥaṭaf qama<u>z</u>	ŏ	o	•	ŏ	•	•	ŏ	%O	•		•	ŏ	•	ŏ	•	•	•
ֿ	šûrûq	u	u	•	•	•	•	•	U	•		•	•	•	•	•	•	•
ֿ	qubû<u>z</u>	û	û	u	u	u	u	•	W*	u	u	ū	ū	u	u	u	u	u

[1]Not realized when initial, otherwise '.

[2]The horizontal line represents the vocalized consonant.

[3]v = transliteration for vocalized text. nv = transliteration for nonvocalized text; only this version of ISO is considered here for comparison with other schemes.

[4]Small raised ᵉ, for example, bᵉ ṭaḥ.

Library in Jerusalem. The "keypunch-compatible transliteration" scheme is considered in Section 2.3.12 (p. 308).

Until recently Hebraization of names and words from non-Hebrew scripts was not subject to any hard and fast rules, although the matter has long been the concern of Israeli librarians because of the large number of translations from foreign languages and the inconsistent Hebraizations of authors' names which lead to difficulties in cataloging. The librarian M. Ben-Yehuda proposed some basic rules, covering the languages most often translated into Hebrew, in a paper published in 1968.[100] An official Hebraization scheme for the transcription of

[100]Ben Yehuda (1968).

names and words from languages written in Roman or Cyrillic script was published in the *Transactions* of the Academy of the Hebrew Language in 1970, but has not been issued separately in tabular form.[101] A phonetic-phonemic transcription scheme, it is far superior to any of the home-made Hebraizations used by translators, journalists, and publishers in Israel until now, but it has not yet been generally accepted. Hebraization of Arabic script, primarily for the rendering of personal and place names, was officially codified in 1931 by the Government of Palestine[102]; the scheme is still in use in Israel (see Chapter 2, Table 2.9, p. 127) and is also employed by the *EJ*.

Whereas Hebrew (like Cyrillic and Arabic) suffers from a surfeit of different Romanization schemes, Yiddish has been treated by only a few cataloging codes and other schemes. Hebrew and Yiddish are written in the same script, but a single scheme cannot be used for the Romanization of both because of the differences in orthography, especially regarding the use of consonants to indicate vowels in Yiddish. The problem is made still more complex by the "phonetic" orthography of Yiddish as written in the Soviet Union.[103] The Romanization of personal names is particularly difficult because it is common for a writer with a name of German or Slavic origin to spell his name according to Yiddish orthography when writing in Yiddish, but according to Hebrew orthography when writing in Hebrew. Conversely a name of Hebrew origin (or one containing Hebrew elements) is not subjected to the rules of Yiddish orthography, but is written as other Hebrew words in Yiddish, namely in "defective" Hebrew spelling (i.e., without indication of vowels) while Yiddish spelling rules are applied to the non-Hebrew parts of a name. An example is the name *Katzenelson* (the popular Roman spelling most often used by bearers of this fairly common name). The first part of the name (which folk etymology erroneously derives from the German "Katze") is actually an acronym formed by the initials of the name (or honorific title) צדק כהן *(kohen zedeq)*, "Priest of Justice," and is therefore written with an initial כ *(kaf)* and not with the letter ק *(qof)* as would be the case in phonemic Yiddish transcription. The second part of the name, however, is spelled ענעלסאן —, following Yiddish orthography. The same name in Hebrew is written כצנלסון. Transliteration according to ISO/R259 would result in the rendering Kaznelson for the Hebrew form, but in Kaz'n'lsan for the Yiddish spelling. While this might indicate to the initiated what kind of spelling and language were used in the original, it would not bring together the works of this author in bibliographic control tools.

One of the first attempts at a systematic Romanization of Yiddish was made by Salomon A. Birnbaum,[104] but his scheme, which was based on German orthography, was not widely accepted. The YIVO Institute for Jewish Research, which

[101] Academy of the Hebrew Language (1970).
[102] Palestine (1931).
[103] Erlich (1973).
[104] S. Birnbaum (1915, 1933).

had been instrumental in standardizing Yiddish orthography in 1936[105] (when the Institute's headquarters were in Vilna, then one of the main centers of Yiddish culture), published a phonemic Romanization scheme in 1949. This scheme was aimed at English-speaking users,[106] since America had become the center of Yiddish language and literature after the holocaust. It was adopted by the LC and published in ALA 1949, together with the one for Hebrew (although some letter combinations frequently used in Yiddish to write voiced sibilants are missing). The ISO prepared a standard for Yiddish transliteration; although still in draft form, it has already been used by the Bibliothèque Nationale in its new series of the *Catalogue général*.[107] The ANSI is also preparing a draft standard for the Romanization of Yiddish, to be published in 1977. It provides for a "general purpose" and a "narrow" transliteration scheme, as well as for a "keypunch-compatible" one, similar to the ANSI transliteration standard for Hebrew. The Romanization schemes presently in use for Yiddish and the ANSI draft are shown in Table 4.16.

Ladino, also written in Hebrew script, has not been the subject of a transliteration scheme, so far as is known, although the rules for transliteration of Hebrew cannot be applied without modification to this language either. The reason is probably that few libraries outside Spain or Israel have sizable holdings of books and manuscripts in Ladino. The few specialists who study this now almost extinct language employ their own *ad hoc* transcriptions for philological purposes.

2.3.11. Other Scripts. Romanization schemes for all other scripts listed in Table 4.6 have been devised by either the British Museum or the Library of Congress, and in some instances by one of the manuals. Other cataloging codes list one or more of these scripts, apparently according to the needs of the respective country's libraries and their holdings of documents in non-Roman scripts, as perceived by the editors of the codes. A survey of Romanization practices in libraries throughout the world has shown that this is in many cases insufficient, and most libraries must employ Romanization schemes from various sources in addition to those offered by their national cataloging codes.[108]

2.3.12. Conversion Schemes for Machine-Readable Records. The recording of bibliographical data in machine-readable form, which began on a large scale with the MARC system[109] and its more or less compatible counterparts in other countries, makes it necessary to represent the various diacritical marks and letters not included in the basic Roman alphabet of 26 letters in a machine-readable

---

[105]YIVO (1936).
[106]Weinreich (1949).
[107]Bibliothèque Nationale. Paris. *Catalogue général des livres imprimés . . . 1960–1969. Serie 2. Caractères non latins.* Tome 1. Caractères hébraïques, p. [v].
[108]Wellisch (1976).
[109]Library of Congress. Information Systems Office. (1970). "Expanded 8-bit ASCII character set for MARC II format," pp. 5–15.

Table 4.16 Romanization Schemes for Yiddish

Letter	Name	ISO (Draft)	LC	EJ, YIVO	ANSI (Draft) General	Narrow
א	štumer alef	ɔ	*	*	*	•
אַ	(paseḥ) alef	a	•	•	•	
אָ	komez alef	o	°	•	•	
ב	bes	b	•	•	•	•
בֿ	ves	v	°	•	•	
ג	giml	g	•	°	•	
ד	dalet	d	•	•	•	•
דזש	dalet-zayen-šin	ǧ			dzh	
ה	he	h	•	°	•	•
ו	vov	u	•	•	•	v
וּ	melupm vov	u	•	•	•	
וו	zvey vovn	v	•	°	•	•
וי	vov-yud	oy	°	•	•	
ז	zayen	z	•	•	•	
זש	zayen-šin	ž		zh	zh	
ח	hes	h	•	kh	kh	x
ט	tes	t	°	•	•	•
טש	tes-šin	č		tsh	tsh	
י	yud	y,i[1]	•	•	•	y
יי	zvey yudn	è	ey	ey	ey	
ײַ	paseḥ zvey yudn	ay	°	•	•	
כ	kaf	k	•	°	•	•
ך	ḵaf	ḵ	kh	kh	kh	
ל	lamed	l	°	•	•	•
מ	mem	m	°	•	•	•
נ	nun	n	°	•	•	•
ס	samek	s	•	•	•	•
ע	ayen	e	•	•	•	ʿ
פ	pe	p	•	•	•	
פֿ	fe	f	°	•	•	•
צ	zadiq	ẓ	ts	ts	ts	c
ק	qof	q	k	k	k	•
ר	reš	r	•	•	•	•
ש	šin	š	sh	sh	sh	ẝ
שׂ	śin	ś	s	s	s	
ת	tov	t	°	°	•	
ת	sov	s̲	s	s	s	2

[1] y when used as a consonant, i when used as a vowel.

306

form in order to facilitate not only the recording of Romanized names and words by mechanized equipment but also the exchange of coded data among various data bases. This means that in addition to the coding for the 26 basic Roman letters in upper- and lowercase, and the most common punctuation marks (which is already standardized), there must also be internationally agreed-upon standard codes for computer-internal storage of other graphemes, so that these can be printed on paper or displayed on a CRT screen.

The problems encountered, especially those arising from different methods already developed and used in the United States and in Germany, have been discussed by Kohl.[110] The most extensive survey of diacritical marks as presently used in the orthographies of living languages written in the Roman alphabet, and in the transliteration schemes for other scripts with a view to their coding for machine-readable data bases was made by J. Pirenne,[111] who did not, however, propose an actual coding scheme.

Basically two methods exist by which a computer code can be used to produce a printed image of a character. One is direct printout via a print chain or other mechanical device. The printing of a diacritical mark over, under, or inside a basic letter is performed either by printing two lines simultaneously, the first for letters, the second (without moving the printing head forward) for printing the diacritical mark, or by ''overprinting'' the line first printed with basic letters by another one in which only the diacritical marks are superimposed on the letters. Direct printout in either form is slow and therefore costly, and in addition is subject to errors caused by mechanical malfunctioning of the printing devices, but it can be used in on-line mode (including displays on a CRT screen). Another method is the use of computer codes to control a phototypesetting machine which prints the complete character from an image stored on film. This method gives better results, is less prone to errors, and does not waste costly computer time during the printing stage since it is used in off-line mode. A recently introduced variant of this method stores the character set in the form of a dot pattern coded by bit configurations on an internal disk. The dot patterns are scanned by a laser beam which activates a photoconductive surface, and the image is then printed on paper. Both photo-typesetting equipment and the laser-operated IBM 3800 Printing Subsystem are quite expensive at present.

Several ISO standards, at the time of this writing still in draft form but already used to some extent by the International Serials Data Systems (ISDS),[112] have been elaborated for the coded representation of characters other than the 26 basic letters of the Roman alphabet. One standard covers the ''Extended Latin al-phabet character set for bibliographic use,'' which includes not only modified letters (e.g., the German ß, the Danish ø, and the Icelandic þ) but also logographic

---

[110]Kohl (1972).
[111]Pirenne (1973).
[112]International Center for the Registration of Serial Publications (1973). Appendix I.

signs ($, £, #, etc.), punctuation marks not included on regular printout devices, and diacritical marks. This system will make possible the printing of most material that is Romanized according to the ISO or LC schemes.

However there also exists a need for the coded representation of transliterations without diacritical marks and special characters not available on regular computer printout devices. Few mechanized systems for the handling of bibliographic data (except for the large centralized and national ones) will be equipped in the near future with special printout facilities, nor will every computer user be able to use phototypesetting machines because of the high costs involved. The ISO has therefore also sought to devise standards for the conversion of ISO transliterations to normal computer printout (where special letters or diacritical marks must necessarily be represented by two or even three letters or punctuation marks); these are as yet only in draft form.

In this context it must also be mentioned that there are two related ISO draft standards: one for the coded representation of Slavic Cyrillic letters, the other for that of Greek letters. Both are intended for the direct printout of material in these scripts, without any transliteration.

An entirely different approach to the use of computers for transliteration is the one envisaged by Goldman and others[113] for Semitic languages, with particular emphasis on Hebrew. Here the intention is not to code an already existing transliteration but to develop a transliteration scheme having a strict one-to-one relationship between a Hebrew character and its conversion into a character found on any standard computer printout device. The authors claim that conversion from Hebrew to "computer-compatible transliteration" is practically automatic, and that it can be done by a typist who knows the 22 letters of the Hebrew alphabet and the conversion code. However the results are not "readable" for anyone unfamiliar with the scheme, and are entirely different from any other Romanization of Hebrew names and words (see Chapter 5, Figure 5.1, p. 323). The scheme is now a part of the ANSI standard for the Romanization of Hebrew, as already mentioned, but the claim made there that "it is also entirely suitable for bibliographic records" is untenable. Rather, the use of this scheme will probably be restricted to linguistic research, especially computer-aided investigations into style and origin of certain texts based on comparison of passages and word counts, for which it was originally designed.

* * *

Our *tour d' horizon* of the major scripts and their conversion schemes has concentrated on those in actual use today, especially in the bibliographic control tools governed by the rules of various cataloging codes that are purportedly all based on

---

[113]Goldman (1971).

"scientific" principles. The picture that emerges is not encouraging. It shows an incredible amount of variety and idiosyncratic usages where compatibility and standardization should be the guiding principle. Very often discrepancies between two otherwise compatible schemes are created by putting a little dot over instead of under a letter, by using a macron instead of an underlining, and other typographical niceties, the meanings of which are a mystery to anybody except a philologist adhering to a particular school of thought or fashion in transliteration.

The quotation from T. E. Lawrence at the beginning of this chapter is the expression of an eccentric mind and is obviously hyperbolic. Yet it does contain a grain of truth, and its author was quite justified in putting the term "scientific system" in quotation marks, although his judgment was certainly based more on intuition than on analysis. In the following chapter we examine the validity of the claims to scientific accuracy made for some conversion schemes, in particular for those that are said to be "strict transliterations," and we try to discover the underlying causes for the great variety and incompatibility of conversion schemes.

Five

The Requirements of Script Conversion

The transfer of words from one script into another is superfluous and a mere hindrance to a master of both. No English student of Siamese need write that language in the English alphabet for his own help. But if he writes about Siam or the Siamese for the English-speaking public; if Siamese news is to be repeated in British newspapers; if Siam is to be shown on British maps or in British atlases; if Siamese literature is to be catalogued in British libraries, the need for satisfactory ways of writing Siamese proper names in the English alphabet is immediate. Their transcription is therefore indispensable to public life.

M. Aurousseau. *The Rendering of Geographic Names*, pp. 50–51.

1 SOME MISCONCEPTIONS ABOUT SCRIPT CONVERSION

In the following analysis of requirements we must always keep in mind that script conversion is a universal transaction that occurs whenever two different scripts and writing systems come into direct contact, and that it is by no means restricted to the rendering of non-Roman scripts in Roman script. Anyone who writes in a language using the Roman script may at one time or another be required to render Russian, Arabic, Chinese, or other foreign names and words not written in Roman script, but a similar problem exists also for a Russian, Arabic, or Chinese writer who wishes to cite names and words written in one of the other scripts. This is equally "indispensable to public life" in the respective language communities.

All this should be obvious and self-evident, but unfortunately this is not the case. As we have shown in the foregoing chapters, the predominance of Western scholarship in all fields of knowledge since the days of the Renaissance lies at the root of the phenomenon that the vast majority of work on the rendering of dissimilar scripts has been performed in one direction only, namely from non-Roman into Roman scripts. It was somehow tacitly assumed that peoples who did not use the Roman script did not encounter the problems of script conversion, or if they did, their methods of dealing with the problem were entirely irrelevant to Western scholarship. In a world of global communications and with a genuine concern about universal bibliographic control, this view is, of course, no longer tenable.[1]

But script conversion has not only been equated with Romanization, it has also become almost axiomatic that only transliteration will yield "scientific" results, because it is based on intrinsically immutable graphemes of a source script and their one-to-one transformation into the graphemes of the Roman target script, and thus is independent of the vagaries and uncertainties of pronunciation and its graphemic approximation. This point of view at first seems quite logical, but it disregards several facts that make it impossible to apply the purportedly scientific principle uniformly and for all possible cases. Firstly, only fully alphabetical scripts such as Greek or Cyrillic can be subjected to a process of one-to-one transformations, whereas defectively written languages (that is, those in which most or all vowels are omitted in writing) can be transliterated only partially, if at all. Secondly, Chinese, Japanese, and Korean, which are written in logographic scripts, can only be transcribed phonologically because there is no one-to-one relationship between graphemes in the source and target scripts. Thirdly, the graphemes of the Roman script stand for many different and widely divergent phonemes in various languages, which causes, in effect, numerous one-to-many transformations for particular graphemes in any non-Roman source script, since no agreement has ever been reached among different language communities as to

[1] The famous Indian librarian S. R. Ranganathan was the first to draw attention to this phenomenon: "Till now, the Roman script has been playing the part of the host-script. This has been due to historical circumstances. For, the Renaissance phase of the present cultural cycle appeared in areas of Roman script a few centuries earlier than in areas of any other script. Therefore, during the last few centuries, transliteration had virtually meant transliteration into Roman script. This has become such a rigid part of the mental set of the cataloguers of the West that the reverse movement of transliteration seems to have very little chance to be recognized, even at international level. This is again due to a historical factor. For international bodies have been all along effectively confined to the membership of the West. Therefore, the idea produced by reflex action, on hearing the term transliteration, is that of the Roman script as the host-script. Therefore, the so-called International Catalogue Codes provide only for one-way transliteration. . . . In my recent experience with the UNESCO Project on the Rendering of Asian Names, I had found this mental set in the librarians of the West too rigid to be broken. They cannot dissociate transliteration from rendering. Nor do they see the reciprocal feature of transliteration. For them Rendering of Asian names is mostly transliteration in Roman script." (Ranganathan, 1964, p. 68.)

The first Western author who dealt briefly with the problem was R. Frontard (1961), who pointed out that transliteration could not always remain a one-way street. But the problem was officially recognized only in 1969, when the International Meeting of Cataloguing Experts in Copenhagen resolved that "In catalogues using other, i.e. non-Roman scripts, a uniform phonetic transcription should be used for each name." *(Libri* **20** (1970):110.)

which Roman letter should stand for a certain Greek or Cyrillic letter, even if pronunciation is ostensibly eliminated from consideration. Despite these quite obvious limitations of "strict transliteration," which are discussed in more detail in this chapter, conversion schemes for scripts that could not be made to fit the mold of that ideal model were almost always considered exceptions to the rule rather than indicators of the implausibility of such a rule.

Also, very few have recognized that script conversions in languages with other writing systems cannot be based on the principle of transliteration at all; this is entirely precluded by the widely divergent sound values of certain Roman letters in various languages (the same factor that prevents uniform transliteration), as well as by the more or less unphonetic orthographies of most languages written in Roman script, and similar orthographic limitations of languages written in other scripts. Any rendering of names or words into languages written in a non-Roman script, whether from Roman script (e.g., English into Russian, French into Greek) or from another non-Roman script (e.g., Arabic into Russian, Japanese into Greek) can only be performed by phonological transcription.

All Romanization schemes (especially those used in bibliographic control) are actually a mixture of transliteration and transcription. Several attempts have been made to account for this fact of life which flies in the face of the assertion made by some theoreticians that only "strict" and unambiguously reversible transliteration can be truly "scientific." It has been said that transliteration is really only a subspecies of transcription, thus confusing the issue and ignoring the fundamental differences between the two methods of script conversion. More recently it has been claimed that what is needed, particularly for bibliographic control, are "broad" and "narrow" transliteration schemes. While it is true that more than one method of script conversion may be needed for different purposes, as we demonstrate in detail in the following, the terminology used here (which has been borrowed from the related field of phonetics) is unfortunately generating a spurious dichotomy. "Broad" transliteration is said to be one that is aimed at laymen, while "narrow" transliteration is to be used for scholarly use (but it is almost never made clear who the "scholars" in question are, and in which field they exercise their scholarship). Those who use the terms "broad" and "narrow" as synonyms for "popular" and "scientific" when referring to transliteration, do not seem to realize that they are making two errors that compound each other. Firstly, the terms broad and narrow transcription (but *not* transliteration!), as used in phonetics, refer to equally scientific applications, each having a different purpose and use in different contexts.[2] Moreover, they are exclusively concerned with the phonology of a language, its phonemes, their articulation,

---

[2] Concise definitions of "broad" and "narrow" transcription can be found in Pei (1966). A more detailed explanation of the scope and purpose of the two methods is given in *Encyclopedia of linguistics, information and control* (1969), s.v. *Phonology,* and in its "Glossary."

their dialectal variants, and their use in the pronunciation of its words and phrases. Secondly, any transliteration mixed with phonological elements (no matter how broadly or narrowly applied) ceases to be transliteration and becomes, by definition, a transcription. The distinctions between broad and narrow cannot, therefore, refer to the audience at which a particular scheme for script conversion is aimed, but rather apply to the degree to which the pronunciation of a language written in a dissimilar source script is graphically indicated in a dominant target script.

Very often broad and narrow are also confused with the visual image of the graphemes used in a conversion scheme, the erroneous notion being that the lavish use of diacritical marks and signs other than letters of the basic alphabet are a hallmark of narrow, and therefore scientific, transcription, while broad transcription, using only regular letters, must necessarily be popular, and therefore unscientific. This is not necessarily so, and in any case broad transcription should never be equated with popular use; nor should it be assumed that a narrow transcription is the only scholarly one, unless "scholarly" is equated with "incomprehensible except to a small band of specialists."

The classification of conversion systems for scripts by assigning to them terms such as popular and scientific, broad and narrow, so freely used in the literature on the subject, written primarily by librarians and bibliographers, is in itself highly unscientific. These terms, at least when used within the domain of bibliographic control, are vague and ill-defined. While broad and narrow description are well-defined terms in linguistics, these epithets have never been defined for bibliographic purposes, and it is unlikely that any scientifically valid yardstick will be developed by which it can be ascertained when and by virtue of which added elements a broad transcription becomes a narrow one.

2   OPERATIONAL CRITERIA FOR REQUIREMENTS

A scientifically valid analysis of script conversion systems cannot be based on an artifically derived paradigm that pertains to only one or at best a few specific cases, then to be laboriously "adapted" to others. It must necessarily apply to all possible pairs of languages and scripts as well as to the different purposes for which script conversion is performed, and this can be achieved only through the use of operational criteria that are independent of language, and that can be well defined and evaluated as to their effectiveness.

When we look at what a script conversion system is expected to achieve, we can distinguish between

(a)   fields of application in which script conversion is a necessary technical operation; and

(b)   the requirements needed to fulfill the task satisfactorily.

As to fields of application, we analyze the four most important ones:

(i)   general or "popular" applications of script conversion;
(ii)   philology and linguistics;
(iii)   geography and cartography; and
(iv)   bibliographic control.

Regarding requirements, we distinguish between

(i)   systemic requirements; and
(ii)   functional requirements.

The systemic requirements are those that are inherent in the structure and form of a conversion system, namely general applicability, uniqueness of graphemic representation, simplicity of graphemic representation, and economy of space. The functional requirements are those that affect the mode of operation of a system, namely pronounceability, reversibility, and traditionality.

Each of these terms is defined and explained in the context of its particular field of application.

The analysis of conversion systems by these operational criteria will show that there is no single "scientific" system whose principles can be applied uniformly to all scripts and for all purposes, nor are there broad and narrow systems. Rather, there is a plurality of more or less justified but mutually incompatible requirements (often within the same field of application), so that a choice must be made among those requirements that are *optimally* needed to make the system work for a particular purpose or task.

3   REQUIREMENTS FOR GENERAL USE

By "general use" are meant those applications of script conversion whose target is the public at large, without taking into consideration the needs of specialists in any of the other fields of application. General use is also often called "popular," and many applications of script conversion are undoubtedly used by people who range from those who are just barely literate to those who are somewhat presumptuously known as "educated laymen." It is well to remember that in this age of specialization all of us are, of course, laymen, more or less well educated, which means that even though we may have a thorough knowledge of a limited area, we can hope to be knowledgeable in other fields only to a certain limited extent, but cannot aspire to deep and well-grounded knowledge, much less to scholarship.

Transcription for general use is thus the largest and most variegated field of application. Whenever a name or an expression in a foreign language and a dissimilar script has to be cited, it becomes necessary to transcribe it more or less faithfully in the script and writing system familiar to the readers of a certain target language. In the daily press, in radio and television broadcasts, in textbooks from grade school to university, in literature and commercial writings, the names of persons and places, and occasionally also the names of objects, single words, or short phrases, have to be made readable and also pronounceable, no matter how they were originally written in various scripts and writing systems. It must, however, be emphasized that general transcription is also often used in scientific texts aimed at highly sophisticated readers. Historical works must name persons and places; sociologists must describe communities and their customs, institutions, and forms of government whose indigenous names can often only be explained but not translated, and must thus be given in transcription. Physicists, chemists, mathematicians, astronomers, biologists, and medical researchers (to name only a few branches of the natural sciences where this is a quite common occurrence) must frequently transcribe the names of persons after which phenomena, laws, formulas and the like have been named. In the life sciences new names are constantly added to the ever-growing repertory of taxonomic nomenclature (with the additional twist that the transcribed names have also to be Latinized, following long-standing custom[3]).

All these applications of general transcription have one trait in common, namely that no fixed rules for transcription are followed by everyone in the rendering of names even from one and the same source language, and that consequently different transcriptions may exist for the same name, depending on whether it is encountered in a newspaper, in a general textbook, on a map, or in a novel. It is this chaotic state of affairs that has led practitioners in other fields (who of necessity must pay more attention to consistency in the rendering of names from dissimilar scripts into a dominant script) to look askance at the popular transcriptions, and to condemn them as being entirely unscientific. However, as we shall presently see, their own attempts at producing more scientific results in script conversion by adhering to elaborate schemes and rules has led to an even more chaotic situation.

General transcription admittedly does not follow any prescribed rules, since anybody who feels the need to render a name or expression from a dissimilar script into his own script and writing system is free to do as he sees fit. Nevertheless such transcriptions must fulfill at least three requirements to judge from the results found in innumerable books, journals, newspapers, and other media of communication intended for the general public. These are, in ascending order of

[3] Only a few writers on botanical and zoological taxonomy have dealt with the difficulties posed by the proper rendering and Latinization of names not originally written in Roman script. The problems of Latinization of Slavic names written in Cyrillic have been discussed by Buchanan (1956), Fennah (1957), and Vasil'kov (1960).

importance, pronounceability, simplicity of graphemic representation, and traditionality.

3.1. Pronounceability

A transcribed name or phrase must, first of all, be pronounceable by a person
who has never before seen it in writing. To achieve this the transcribed letters
should be pronounced as they are usually pronounced in the target language,
according to its writing system, without any further instruction or special rules
(since these cannot normally be given in the context of a newspaper article or in a
novel, etc.). Because of the vagaries of English spelling, some crude instructions
are occasionally given in English-language newspapers, where a foreign name
(not necessarily transcribed but often originally in Roman script) may be accompanied by a parenthetical note such as, "rhymes with," or "pronounced as,"
followed by a familiar English word.

Pronounceability of a general transcription does not necessarily mean that a
foreign name is pronounced even approximately as it is in the country of its
origin, but it can at least be spoken by those who read the rendering in Roman
script, which is one of the principal aims of general transcription.

3.2. Simplicity of Graphemic Representation

The transcription must enable anybody to write, type, or print it with a minimum
of effort, and in a manner that blends well with indigenous names and words in
the target language. Therefore the graphemes of the source script are transcribed
following as closely as possible the conventions of the writing system of the
target language. Characters that are difficult to write or print, especially letters
with diacritical marks (when not already conventionally used in the target script)
are generally avoided, and of course no special letters or signs are employed. But
simplicity does not necessarily mean brevity. Digraphs, trigraphs, and combinations of several letters are frequently used in general transcription if this serves
the requirement of pronounceability, although occasionally some concessions
may also be made to transliteration of graphemes in the source script contrary to
the demands of pronunciation. The name of the Soviet premier Никита
Хрущев, which had to be rendered into practically all the world's languages and
scripts, exhibits both features, as shown in Table 5.1. Digraphs and letter combinations abound in the Germanic and Romance languages, but even in the
related Slavic languages two- and four-letter combinations are needed to render
the single Cyrillic grapheme Ш . The Cyrillic e in the final syllable is in most
languages rendered by the equivalent Roman letter *e,* although *o* (as preferred in

Table 5.1 **Use of Letter Combinations for General Transcription in Different Languages, Exemplified by a Russian Name**

Russian	X	P	У	Ш	E	B
Croatian	H	R	U	ŠČ	E	V
Czech	CH	R	U	ŠČ	O	V
Polish	CH	R	U	SZCZ	O	W
English	KH	R	U	SHCH	E	V
German	CH	R	U	SCHTSCH	O	W
Swedish	K	R	U	SJTSJ	E	V
French	KH	R	OU	CHTCH	E	FF
Portuguese	KH	R	U	CHTCH	E	V
Spanish	J	R	U	SCH	E	F
Vietnamese	KHU-	R	U̯	S	Ê	P

Czech, Polish, and German) would give a better approximation to the Russian pronunciation in all of the languages shown (except in Swedish, where *o* is pronounced [u]. In Vietnamese diacritical marks not present in the source script are used because they form part of the conventional writing system of that language.

The difference between a word as spelled in the source script and its general transcription in "simple" graphemes can in extreme cases amount to twice and even three times the length. The Russian word защищающая * (10 letters) becomes *zashchishchayushchaya* (21 letters) in English, while in German transcription it is *saschtschischtschajuschtschaja* (30 letters). In both instances, however, the primary purpose is achieved, since it is relatively easy for a reader who does not know Russian to approximate the pronunciation, following only the conventions of the relevant orthography.

Even the ISO scheme for transliteration of Cyrillic script has to use the digraphs *šč, ju,* and *ja* to render ш, ю, and я respectively in the basic version, and the still more cumbersome *shch* for щ in the alternative version of the second edition. The preceding example would thus have 15 letters in the basic ISO transliteration: *zaščiščajuščaja.* The divergences in the rendering of ш and other Cyrillic letters are as much in evidence among other scientific transliteration schemes as they are in the much-maligned general or popular transcriptions.

3.3. Traditionality

When a certain form of transcription has been used consistently for a long time, and people have become well acquainted with it, it is normally followed in all areas of general transcription, even if it violates the requirement of pronounce-

*"Defender" (female) [of a title in sport].

ability; that is, either it cannot be pronounced according to the customary sound value of the letters, resulting in an arbitrary pronunciation that does not even approximate the actual one, or it cannot be pronounced at all. A good example is the English transcription "czar" for царь; the digraph *cz,* which is entirely foreign to the English writing system is here employed to represent the original [ts] sound, but is pronounced [z]! There is no justification for either the spelling or the pronunciation in any of the Slavic languages written in Roman script, because the letter combination *cz* occurs among Slavic orthographies only in Polish, where it represents the phoneme [tʃ], not [ts]. Moreover it is not at all difficult for an English speaker to pronounce [ts] because it is one of the phonemes of the English language. (It is only fair to point out that in many English textbooks the transcription *tsar* is used, but despite its better suitability as a transcription for English readers, it has almost never been used in newspapers, television captions, and so forth, because the spelling *czar* has already been sanctioned as the traditional one.)

The value put on traditionality has led to a paradoxical phenomenon. While philologists and bibliographers always dismiss general transcription practices peremptorily as not being based on any scientific rules, and therefore quite erratic and unpredictable, inconsistent, and mutually incompatible, it is a fact that today there is often apt to be more consistency in general transcription practices of the press, television, and books published in the language of a certain country than there is in the libraries and bibliographical tools of that same country. Once an authoritative source such as a prestigious newspaper, a mass circulation magazine, or a television network has used a certain transcription, it is rapidly picked up by hundreds of other newspapers, journals, and books; the wire services continue to use it, and the transcribed form of a name or a word becomes standardized to an amazing degree, simply by the self-perpetuating forces exerted by the mass media. To be sure, there is a sometimes appalling lack of consistency in the transcription of the same phoneme or grapheme from a dissimilar source script, such as when the Cyrillic letter ц [ts] is variously transcribed in *cz*ar, Kapi*tz*a, and Solzheni*ts*yn, but a look at the annual indexes of the London *Times, The New York Times, Time,* or *Newsweek* will show that there is little if any discrepancy in the spelling of such names and words by these influential news media once a certain form has been "established." Since these sources are also known to be careful about their spelling and grammar, the general public, including writers of books, are quite justified in taking their clues for transcription of foreign names from them, so as not to deviate from the established practice. The phenomenon of mutual conformity among the mass media is not restricted to the United States or to English language publications; it can also be observed in other countries and language communities. The form of a name first printed in *Le Monde* and *Paris Match* tends to become the French general transcription, the *Frankfurter Allgemeine Zeitung* and *Der Spiegel* set the tone for Germany, and so on.

4 REQUIREMENTS FOR PHILOLOGY AND LINGUISTICS

The earliest use of transcription for scientific purposes occurred in the field of philology, as described in Chapter 3. The comparative and historical study of languages, especially by German philologists during the first half of the 19th century, was primarily concerned with comparison of individual words and their sounds in various languages. Since the findings and theories of comparative philology had to be recorded and discussed in writing, there was an immediate need for transcription systems that would allow the more or less faithful description of sounds quite independently of the script (if any) in which the languages under investigation were written. Firstly, many languages had never had a writing system of any kind, and some of them were not even known to have actually existed (such as Proto-Indo-European), but at least hypothetical sound values could be ascribed to certain "words" in these languages. Secondly, although the Devanagari script produced a remarkably faithful rendering of the sounds of Sanskrit (the language first studied comparatively, and the one on which Sir William Jones based his system of phonetic transcription), it was soon discovered that the writing systems of other ancient languages did not give such an accurate rendering of their phonology and might be of as little use in discovering or describing the sounds of a long-forgotten language as present-day English spelling would be for future philologists 2000 years hence. Thirdly, the technology and economics of printing militated against extensive use of "exotic" scripts mixed with Roman script, hence the various phonetic transcription systems devised by Lepsius, Ellis, and many others in the 19th century.

Although the aims and scope of philology have changed considerably since those days, the prime functional requirement for a philological transcription system is still pronounceability; that is, it must make possible not only the graphical recording of the sounds of a language, but also the pronunciation (at least if the rules and special instructions for the pronouncing of each letter and sign of the transcription system are followed by the reader). Any link between such a phonetic technography and the writing system and orthography of a written source language is fortuitous at best.

The requirements for exact graphemic sound recording and pronounceability became even more stringent with the advent of modern linguistics, particularly phonetics, where scientific methods of graphemic representation of sounds uttered by human beings are needed. Physical phenomena that are measurable by objective methods must be represented by distinct and separate elements in a linguistic transcription. Linguists and phoneticists are thus not at all concerned with the writing system of any language they study, and do not actually *use* it (except, of course, when writing texts in their own language). They have only to *mention* it,[4] such as when a word or phrase that is to be analyzed phonetically,

---

[4]The distinction between "using" and "mentioning" has been explicated by Robert Fairthorne (1965).

morphologically, or syntactically must necessarily be written down, but whether, for example, the word *through* is so spelled or may be written as *thru* is of no consequence at all to the linguist.

Philologists, however, are also engaged in studies of lexicography, etymology, and the literary output of a language community. For these purposes they need graphemic conversion systems if the script of the language studied is dissimilar from the one they use to describe their work. Their foremost requirement has always been *reversibility*; a philological conversion system should ideally make it possible to reconstruct unambiguously and automatically in the source script any name or word that has been converted to the target script. This requirement obviously conflicts with the one for pronounceability, at least for languages written defectively, as is the case in Arabic, Persian, Turkish, Hebrew, and so forth, because vowels have to be supplied to make a transcription pronounceable. Reversibility is completely impossible to accomplish for logographic scripts such as Chinese and Japanese, for reasons already explored in Chapter 2 and discussed in more detail below in Section 3.4. This does not mean that the requirement of reversibility is unreasonable in principle; it is indeed the only method for full and unambiguous identification of the original form of names and words that have been converted from a source script to a target script. However for reasons that are inherent in many source scripts and writing systems it can be achieved only to a limited extent. For strictly scientific purposes, in philology two different and separate conversion systems are therefore employed, namely phonetic transcription (usually using a specially devised phonetic alphabet) for phonological purposes, and transliteration-transcription (using the dominant script, if necessary augmented by suitable adaptation of letters and symbols) for lexicographic and literary purposes. For defectively or logographically written languages, as pointed out, hybrid systems have to be used, and these are only partially or not at all reversible. The requirement of pronounceability, which is always realizable, at least to some degree (however imperfectly), thus takes precedence over the requirement of reversibility, which is only partially attainable.

The requirement of *traditionality*, which plays such a large role in general transcription, is also important in philology, particularly in those branches that deal with the so-called "classical" languages (i.e., those that dominated Western antiquity). The transliteration of Greek or Hebrew names and words poses the problem of whether to transliterate according to a philologically correct system (i.e., one that allows for reversibility) or to render Greek names in their conventional Latinized form, and Hebrew names in the form made familiar to readers by the relevant translation of the Bible. One of the most widely used scholarly schemes for the rendering of Greek names is the one first introduced by the editors of the *Journal of Hellenistic Studies* in 1903. In this system unique graphemic representation (a requirement discussed in the next section) is purposely disregarded in favor of "the practice of educated Romans of the Augustean age." In response to criticism of the inconsistencies of the scheme, it was stated editorially that

In consideration of the literary traditions of English scholarship, the scheme is of the nature of a compromise, and in most cases considerable latitude of usage is to be allowed.[5]

In a work of the highest philological standards, the *Cambridge Ancient History,* this "latitude of usage" has been carried even further:

In the spelling of Greek names the practice adopted by the *Journal of Hellenistic Studies* has in general been followed, but here and there, consistency has been yet further abandoned in order to present to the reader familiar names in their familiar forms. On occasion, convenience has been the guide.[6]

Scientific accuracy in the rendering of classical names (i.e., reversibility) can be sacrificed relatively easily for "convenience" because philologists are dealing here with a practically closed universe. New and hitherto unknown Greek names are not likely to be discovered in great numbers, if at all, and even a "new" name could probably always be rendered according to an established pattern of transcription. The bulk of Greek names from classical antiquity are well known in their Latinized form, and numerous reference works, indexes, and concordances can be used to verify the original spelling and its transcription. Regarding Hebrew names from Biblical times until about the beginning of the Christian era in Anglicized or otherwise transcribed forms, there is, of course, an entirely unambiguous backup system in the Hebrew text of the Bible and in the Talmud, to which reference can always be made by chapter and verse in order to identify a certain transcription and to render it, if necessary, in exact transliteration. (The "traditional" rendering of Hebrew names from later periods, particularly in bibliographic practice, poses problems of a different kind that are considered in Section 6.4, p. 345–346.)

Thus, in philology no less than in general practice, the requirement of traditionality may frequently override that of reversibility, even when the latter would be technically feasible.

Conversion systems for philology and linguistics must also fulfill two systemic requirements, namely general applicability and uniqueness of graphemic representation.

[5]*Journal of Hellenistic Studies* **52** (1932): lxix.
[6]*The Cambridge ancient history* (1926–1939), v. 4, p. viii.

4.1   General Applicability

A conversion system in this field must be applicable to the phonological description of *all* languages, living and dead, at least within the limits set by the kind of transcription used (obviously a narrow transcription will make it necessary to use more modified letters and special signs, while a broad transcription will make only restricted use of such graphemes). Transliteration systems must be applicable to all kinds of written communication and must cover a script in the various forms it appeared in over centuries. Thus a transliteration scheme for the use of Russian philologists must allow for the rendering of letters that are now obsolete but were used before 1918 and even before 1710.

4.2   Uniqueness of Graphemic Representation

This requirement implies a one-to-one relationship between each grapheme in a target script and a corresponding phoneme in the source language or a grapheme in the source script. For phonetic transcription this requirement is best summarized in a statement formulated by the phoneticians Paul Passy and Daniel Jones, the founders of the International Phonetic Association, and published in the Association's journal *Le maître phonétique* in 1888:

> There shall be a separate sign for each distinctive sound: that is, for each sound which, being used instead of another in the same language, can change the meaning of a word.[7]

This is the basis of the International Phonetic Alphabet (IPA) (see Appendix A) and all "broad transcriptions" of speech forms. A certain phoneme is always expressed by one and the same sign in the IPA, while conversely the reader of that sign is able to pronounce that phoneme (at least approximately, according to his ability to transform a written explanation of a sound into the actual sound). The worldwide acceptance of the IPA demonstrates that the two systemic requirements have been successfully achieved in transcription systems for philology and linguistics.

The requirement of uniqueness of graphemic representation applies equally to transliteration. Ideally one grapheme in the source script must be represented by one (and only one) grapheme in the target script. For scripts that have more than one set of characters, such as upper- and lowercase letters in Roman, Cyrillic, and Greek, and for scripts that include various forms of the same letter, such as Arabic and Hebrew, unique graphemes for each set or specific form are also required, because only complete and unique graphemic representation can assure full and unambiguous reversibility. Needless to say, this ideal has never been

---

[7] Quoted in Heffner (1964), p. 68.

achieved in any practical transliteration scheme intended to be readable by human beings; at least a few combinations of letters and signs have to be resorted to (on condition that such combinations are inseparable in the target script and cannot be mistaken for the concatenation of the same letters read separately). In transliteration systems intended for manipulation by computers, however, uniqueness of graphemic representation is an absolute requirement if the purposes of automatic reversibility and exact interpretation of each source grapheme are to be achieved (mainly for the purposes of computational linguistics and in statistical studies of style). In this case readability, pronounceability, and the production of an easily legible visual image are not of any importance, although the difficulties of checking the accuracy of a computer-produced transliteration from the printout are considerable, and may lead to errors and mistakes. Figure 5.1, adapted from Goldman and others,[8] illustrates this point clearly.

Uniqueness of graphemic representation is thus an absolute precondition for reversibility, but it should not be confused with it. When both the source script and the target script are alphabetical and do not normally conceal or suppress the graphic representation of phonemes, full and unambiguous reversibility is indeed assured by uniqueness. A transliteration system for Cyrillic script that assigns a unique Roman letter (or letter combination) to each Cyrillic letter is fully reversible. When the source script is alphabetical but defective (because it does not normally indicate certain graphemes that have to be supplied in transliteration from other sources, or by intimate knowledge of the language, its grammar, syntax, and morphology), uniqueness of graphemic representation does not

בְּרֵאשִׁית בָּרָא אֱלֹהִים אֵת הַשָּׁמַיִם וְאֵת הָאָרֶץ:

a

Bereshit bara elohim et hashamayim veet haarets

b

Bĕrešît bārā ĕlohîm et haššamayim wĕet haarez

c

B*¬R∉@SIYT B*∦R∦@ @¬ELOHIYM @∉T HAS*∦MAYIM W¬@∉T H∦@REÇ:

d

Figure 5.1. Transcription and transliteration of Hebrew vocalized text by conventional and computerized schemes. *(a)* Hebrew vocalized text (Genesis 1:1); *(b)* transcription according to LC; *(c)* transliteration according to ISO/R 259; *(d)* transliteration according to the computer scheme devised by E. A. Goldman and others (simulated).

[8] Goldman (1971), p. 263.

necessarily result in full reversibility. For example, the vowels in an Arabic or Hebrew word written defectively can be supplied and indicated by unique graphemes in transliteration, but the resulting concatenation of letters and diacritical marks, when reversed, does not result in exactly the same concatenation of corresponding letters in the source script. Only *some* letters (in this case the consonants) reappear unchanged after reversion, while the automatic and exact reversion of the supplied vowels results in additional characters that were not present in the source script. The process just described is based on the assumption that no errors or mistakes have been made in vocalizing the transcription, but this condition is often difficult to meet, not only because of insufficient knowledge of the source language on the part of the transcriber-vocalizer, but also because the vocalization of personal or place names does not always follow fixed rules and can only be performed by someone who is actually familiar with the correct form of a name.[9]

5. REQUIREMENTS FOR GEOGRAPHY AND CARTOGRAPHY

The rendering of geographical names has been treated exhaustively and authoritatively by M. Aurousseau[10] (for English) and by J. Breu[11] (for German). Both authors stated the problems, traced the history of various attempts to unify and standardize not only geographical nomenclature but also its transcription, and finally put forward some proposals for the solution of these problems.

One of the prime requirements in geography and cartography is the exact and unambiguous identification of places, for which two elements are necessary: the *position* and the *name*. Of these, position can always be ascertained in a

---

[9]The Hebrew surname ברקת , for example, can be vocalized and transcribed as either *Barqat* or *Bareqet;* both forms are correct and are used in Israel by different people. On the transliteration of Arabic place names, the BGN manual has the following to say: " . . . the transliterator must be able to identify the words used in the names and must know their standard written Arabic spelling, their proper vowel pointing, and how to eliminate pecularities resulting from dialectical variation. The problem is complicated in most Arabic-language areas by the fact that a large proportion of the geographic names are not available in the Arabic alphabet. . . . Even when Arabic script is available it is not always possible to determine the proper voweling from dictionaries and other reference tools." (United States, Board on Geographic Names, 1972, p. 5.)

An example of erroneous vocalization and subsequent faulty transcription can be found in *New Serial Titles,* where the Hebrew word for *information,* מידע (transcribed *meyda'* according to ISO, or *meda'* according to the LC scheme), in the title of an Israeli journal is rendered as *meyadde'a.* No such word exists in the Hebrew language, but the transcriber apparently could not find the word מידע (coined in the 1950s from the root ידע *to know*) in his dictionary, decided to vocalize it in some manner, and then duly transcribed it. The entry appears in *NST,* 1973, v. 1, p. 141, as *Aguddat ha-sifriyot ha-meyuhadot u-merkeze ha-meyadde'a be-Yisrael. Alon.* (ISSN 0021-2318.)

[10]Aurousseau (1947, 1957).

[11]Breu (1969).

scientific and exact manner by giving the coordinates of longitude and latitude; it can be used to resolve ambiguities caused by the same name in different places and for conflicts caused by variant forms of names for the same place. The existence of an alternative and independent means of identification for a physical location or feature on the surface of the earth makes the issue of absolute consistency in the rendering of names less of a problem in geography and cartography than it is in bibliography.

Regarding names, there are many difficulties, among them the vexing problem of places having several names in different languages, any of which may at one time or another have been the official one, depending on the political jurisdiction, as in the case of the city near the present border of Austria, Czechoslovakia, and Hungary, the name of which is known as Pressburg, Bratislava, and Pozsony respectively. Even more cumbersome is the problem most relevant to our study, namely how to transcribe names of places originally written in scripts other than the one known to users of maps and geographical literature.

Aurousseau considered this problem from the point of view of how to render geographical names written in non-Roman scripts into the Roman alphabet, more specifically for the benefit of English-speaking readers, but his remarks are valid also for the problems of, say, Russian users of maps printed in Cyrillic. He points out that:

The question is not the simple one of how to write foreign names phonetically in our alphabet, but how, if it be possible, to transcribe them so that they shall preserve their identity well enough to be recognized beyond doubt, either when read aloud, or when compared with the written originals, say on foreign maps.[12]

The phrase "if it be possible" indicates that the author had his doubts about whether these requirements could be fulfilled, and indeed in most cases they conflict with each other. If a name is to be "recognized . . . when read aloud," this implies that the transcription must try to convey to the reader the pronunciation as faithfully as it is possible under the circumstances, and within the limitations of geographical and cartographical script conversion. But when they are also to be "recognized . . . when compared with the written originals," strict transliteration is necessary, and this makes the first requirement difficult or impossible to fulfill. Aurousseau proposed a "dual system for the writing of geographical names," to be employed for technical and for popular purposes respectively. Regarding transcription, he advocated for both systems the use of the scheme devised by the Permanent Committee on Geographical Names for Official British Use (PCGN). For the popular version he stipulated that:

Should a foreign form . . . in English transliteration or transcription be phonetically misleading to the English public, its pronunciation be given in brackets . . . according to

[12] Aurousseau (1957), p. 51.

the principles used by the B.B.C. in its 'Broadcast English' series. (The alphabet used by the P.C.G.N.., being conventional, is only crudely phonetic, and its possibilities for imitated pronunciation are therefore limited.)[13]

He also considered the troublesome problem of traditional forms of names versus consistent and strict use of a writing system, and came reluctantly to the conclusion that the power of long-standing practice and convention cannot be broken by "improvements" made through the use of such a system, not even if promoted and used by official authorities:

The P.C.G.N. ... in its general lists of African, Asiatic and European names ... attempted to introduce a number of supposedly English spellings ... but ... the established English and foreign official forms have not been displaced by the suggested innovations ...

The main inference to be drawn from the tacit public rejection of improved forms of accepted names is that ... the uniformity which many, from Astley's editor to certain contemporary official authorities, have tried to establish, is unattainable in practice.[14]

The most recent acknowledgment of traditionality as a valid and necessary requirement for the rendering of geographical names comes from one of the most important official sources, namely the United States Government Printing Office which, although it permits the use of a "local official form" as an alternative, states that "the GPO preference is for the conventional English form."[15]

The PCGN system, devised under the chairmanship of Lord Edward Gleichen and revised by Aurousseau, who later became the Committee's secretary, is an adaptation of the transcription scheme used by the Royal Geographical Society since 1885; it is also known as the R.G.S. II system (after the revision of the first version in 1921). The original R.G.S. system stated clearly that it was primarily intended to convey the pronunciation of a name; it took "the true sound of the word as locally pronounced" as the basis for spelling but did not attempt more than "an approximation ... to the sound," because "a system which would attempt to represent the more delicate inflexions of sound and accent would be so complicated as to defeat itself."[16] In the preface to the PCGN system the latter reservation was dropped and it was flatly stated:

(a) that vowels are pronounced as in Italian and consonants as in English;
(b) that every letter is pronounced, and no redundant letters are used.

---

[13]Ibid., p. 95.
[14]Aurousseau (1947), p. 1.
[15]United States, Government Printing Office (1973), p. 70.
[16]Rules for the R.G.S. System, 1885, cited in Aurousseau (1957), p. 75.

The system aims at giving a close approximation to the *local* pronounciation; but it is recognized that in some languages, notably Russian, Greek and Arabic, the necessity for letter-for-letter transliteration often renders this impossible.[17]

Statement (b) is not quite correct, since the system employs eight digraphs, the letters of which are *not* separately pronounced, and the last sentence stipulates two requirements that are mutually contradictory. However it is fairly obvious that the emphasis is on transcription that allows the proper pronunciation of names by English-speaking people.

The U.S. Board on Geographic Names (BGN) uses a compilation of conversion systems, most of which are identical with the PCGN systems, and states in its preface:

BGN romanization systems include elements of both transliteration and transcription, and are applicable to personal names and to general use, as well as to geographic names.

Conventional forms are kept to a minimum . . . in some instances, however, a familiar conventional form may be deemed preferable to the use of a BGN romanization from an original non-Roman script. . . . Examples: . . . *Jerusalem* [instead of] (Yerushalayim, Al Quds).[18]

The acceptance of PCGN principles by the BGN implies that the main emphasis is on the pronounceability of transcribed names and words, but two other requirements are also stated: general applicability, and regard for traditional (i.e., Anglicized) forms of names.

Two international conferences on the subject of geographic names were convened by the United Nations in 1967 and 1972. At the first meeting it was resolved to set up a Working Group of Experts to study the question of conversion of scripts; at the second one the problem was dealt with in depth, procedural recommendations were made, and some practical solutions were adopted. The Committee on Writing Systems proposed that existing official Romanization schemes be employed when so used in a country "irrespective of its scientific qualities," and that otherwise

it is recommended that a system of romanization that has proved workable in international use, especially in linguistics, libraries and documentation, be adopted. If more than one such romanization system exists for a language, preference should be given to a system which enables reconversion to be performed with a maximum of exactitude and simplicity.[19]

[17]Gleichen (1944), p. xii. Emphasis in the original.
[18]United States. Board on Geographic Names (1972), pp. ii–iii.
[19]United Nations Conference on the Standardization of Geographical Names (1972). "Writing systems." Vol. 2, p. 173.

Although the authors of this statement did not seem to recognize that the requirements for transcription in linguistics have little to do with those used for geographical or bibliographical purposes, we are here concerned only with what can be gleaned from it regarding requirements actually stipulated by geographers. Here the element of back-transliteration is clearly stressed as a desirable feature of a system for the conversion of non-Roman scripts into the Roman script.

For most non-Roman scripts the United Nations Conference recommended the use of the BGN/PCGN system, which thus became at least partially an international standard for the rendering of geographic names, even though it does not fulfill the requirement of unambiguous back-transliteration recommended by the Committee on Writing Systems. For Arabic script and place names written in the Arabic language (but not for those in other languages written in Arabic) a new scheme, devised by Arabic geographers at the Conférence régionale des pays arabes pour la normalisation des noms géographiques, held in Beirut in 1971, was proposed. The scheme closely resembled the PCGN scheme, and it was subsequently adopted with some minor revisions.[20]

5.1   Functional Requirements

Based on the requirements stated in official international and national documents, as well as on those emphasized by Gleichen, Aurousseau, and many other geographers and cartographers who dealt with the problem of script conversion, we can now summarize the functional requirements for the purposes of this field. They are, in approximate order of preference, pronounceability, traditionality, and reversibility.

5.1.1   Pronounceability.   This requirement has the highest priority, and is the guiding principle of the most widely used system, the BGN/PCGN. It clashes, however, with the requirement of reversibility; whenever strict transliteration would result in unpronounceable forms of names, pronounceability takes precedence, and letters not originally written (mostly vowels) are supplied in the transcription to make pronunciation possible.

5.1.2   Traditionality.   Recognized explicitly or tacitly as a necessary requirement, undesirable in theory but nevertheless unavoidable in practice, traditionality conflicts with general applicability, reversibility, and economy of space, yet takes precedence over any of these.

5.1.3   Reversibility.   What has been said about this requirement in philology applies also to the rendering of geographic names. Although justifiable in theory, reversibility is difficult (and often impossible) to accomplish in practice

---

[20]*Ibid.,* "Transliteration of the Arabic alphabet." Vol. 2, p. 170.

and clashes with the requirements of pronounceability and traditionality, which take precedence over it in all actual applications.

5.2. Systemic Requirements

The systemic requirements of geographical script conversion are general applicability and economy of space.

5.2.1 General Applicability. Similar to what has been said about philological requirements, a conversion system used for geographical purposes must be applicable not only to names of places as written in a certain script, but also to personal names lacking an apparent or immediately obvious meaning which have only to be transcribed to approximate their local pronunciation, and to personal names and words denoting objects or properties, because any of these may form part of a geographical name that is customarily not translated but must be rendered in transcription. The Lobačevskij crater on the moon, the Novaja Zemlja archipelago, the city of Tel Aviv, or the Dodecanese islands are examples (the first one includes a personal name, and the others are not translated to "New Land," "Hill of Spring," or "Twelve Isles"). Although this requirement is expressly stated only in a few sources, it is implied by all writers on the subject. At first glance it might seem self-evident and easy to fulfill, but it often clashes with the requirement of traditionality which, if effectuated, may assign different sound values to certain letters used in transcription.

5.2.2 Economy of Space. This requirement is specific to geography but also has some importance for other applications, notably bibliographic control. It implies that a transcribed form of a name or word should not take up more space (i.e., consist of more letters) than the original spelling. Although only seldom discussed in the literature, it is nevertheless highly important in cartography, where space is at a premium and written names have to be squeezed into very small and cramped spaces so as not to obliterate other features on a map. It is, however, often difficult or even impossible to fulfill this requirement. As already pointed out in Section 3.1, certain Cyrillic letters need anything from two to seven Roman letters (depending on the language) in transcription, so that economy of space must often give way to the more important requirements of pronounceability and traditionality.

6 REQUIREMENTS FOR BIBLIOGRAPHIC CONTROL

6.1 The Quest for a Scientific Conversion Method

It is difficult to determine the requirements for script conversion in the field of bibliographic control from the evidence provided in statements made by librarians and bibliographers because these are often unclear, contradictory, and mutually inconsistent. Librarians who have written about the subject, as well as those who have to use the products of their efforts as displayed in catalogs and bibliographies, seem to agree only on one thing: the conversion of scripts for bibliographic control purposes creates more problems than it solves.

One of the earliest authors who considered the conversion of scripts in the context of library practice, and in its theoretical as well as practical aspects, was Francis E. Sommer, cataloger for Oriental languages in the Cleveland Public Library. He introduced the first of several papers he wrote on the subject with the following words:

The spelling in Roman letters of names and words taken from languages using a different script is a permanent source of confusion.[21]

This sentiment was echoed by C. Sumner Spalding of the Library of Congress more than two decades later, when he began an essay on the problems of transliteration:

Why transliterate? Should the question not arise *ab initio,* it could hardly escape attention once one becomes aware of the morass of problems transliteration involves.[22]

Sommer stressed that "the 'popular' transliterated forms . . . lack entirely a uniform system" and that

for scientific purposes—and this includes also library work—greater accuracy is required. . . . A scientific transliteration should convey to the initiated the spelling of the original script because it is not always feasible to reproduce the foreign script.[23]

Regarding the details of a "scientific" method for script conversion, Sommer elaborated on them in a later article:

We can either substitute for each letter of the foreign script one of our letters, modified, if necessary, by diacritical marks, or the words can be written down according to their sound, *which necessarily is less accurate and scientific* [my emphasis].[24]

Why phonetic transcription, for so long used in philology and linguistics, suddenly became "unscientific" when used in libraries was not made clear by Sommer. Actually, as an accomplished linguist, he knew better; already in his earlier paper he had refuted his own thesis by showing that Chinese names and

[21]Sommer (1933), p. 534.
[22]Spalding (1957), p. 3.
[23]Sommer (1933), p. 534.
[24]Sommer (1934), p. 892.

words could only be rendered in Roman script according to their pronunciation, and that "accurate" back-transliteration from Russian or modern Greek would make Western names (particularly English ones) unintelligible. The Russian rendering of *Hoover* would become *Guver,* and the Greek form of *Washington* would be *Ouasigktōn* in back-transliteration. Nevertheless he largely disregarded the instances in which "accurate" transliteration was not feasible, treating them as mere exceptions to the rule. In a passage worth quoting for what it reveals not only about the author's muddled views on script conversion but also about his prejudices in another field, he warns:

A bid for popularity through sacrifice of scientific accuracy and standardization does not promise any more success than the attempts to popularize good music by jazz-setting. In making any changes we should strive towards the universal goal of uniform sound-values and internationally accepted rules about the use of letters and other symbols.[25]

It apparently did not occur to him that to require "uniform sound-values" (which can be represented graphically, if at all, only by a phonetic alphabet such as IPA) would be in conflict with his postulate of "accurate" (i.e., unique and reversible) rendering of the spelling in a "foreign" script, quite apart from the fact that there is no "internationally accepted use of letters," since certain letters are used differently in the alphabets of various languages and have no "uniform sound-value" (e.g., the letters *c, h,* and *j*). The same postulates and inherent contradictions were reiterated in Sommer's final and most elaborate paper on the subject, in which he gave a succinct definition of what, in his view, constituted "scientific" transliteration for library purposes:

A scientific transliteration should account for each letter used in the original script. . . . The principle of scientific transliteration should be: *write what you see, not what you hear* [emphasis in the original].[26]

Having stated this principle, he then devoted the following seven pages to the exceptions that necessarily must be made to this rule in converting various scripts; he gave examples from Semitic languages, Bengali, Burmese, Tamil, Armenian, and Siamese, and noted that even the transliteration of Russian and Greek was not quite what it ought to be. . . . Thereupon he came reluctantly to the conclusion:

From the foregoing examples it appears that the principles used in transliteration are far from uniform and that few systems follow consistently either the spelling or the pronunciation.[27]

[25]Sommer (1933), p. 536.
[26]Sommer (1937), p. 495.
[27]*Ibid.,* p. 501.

Yet although Sommer was well aware that the lack of uniformity was due to a clash of "principles" (i.e., what we call here requirements), as well as to the inherent features of certain languages and their scripts which simply do not lend themselves to the "write what you see" treatment, he proceeded nevertheless to reassert and stipulate rigid formal conditions for "scientific" transliteration:

For a scientifically accurate, uniform transliteration we have to strive towards a triple goal:

First, the faithful rendering of the original spelling rather than the pronunciation, which can be considered in the choice of symbols.

Second, the use of one special symbol for each foreign character. This cannot be done without diacritical marks or arbitrary inventions. . . . Those who are skeptical in this respect should look at a Siamese printed text and admire the typographical feats of superimposing sometimes as many as three auxiliary marks on one letter. . . .

Third, scientific impartiality in the choice of symbols and international co-operation to bring the various systems into harmony.[28]

We have dwelt on Sommer's writings in such detail for two reasons. He was the first to formulate several of the requirements for script conversion in the field of bibliographic control from the librarian's point of view and in concise form (even though some of them are contradictory). He also influenced almost all subsequent American writers on the subject, who quoted him as an authority and largely perpetuated the view that "scientific" conversion of scripts for library purposes can be achieved only by strict transliteration, because this method alone assures unambiguous reversibility and reconstruction of a source script.

This dogmatic belief in reversibility as the primary functional requirement for bibliographic script conversion is still held by many librarians and bibliographers in our own time, and is reminiscent of the astronomers of the Ptolemaic school, who postulated that the sun and the planets must revolve in circles because this is the most "perfect" mode of movement, and who for so long tried to "save the appearances" in the teeth of evidence to the contrary by inventing epicycles and eccentrics, rather than considering that the orbits of these celestial bodies might be ellipses (quite apart from the fact that they do not revolve around the earth).

One of the most recent representatives of this school of thought is H. C. Wright, who concludes his thesis on the problems of metagraphy (the term he uses for conversion of scripts) by saying:

Because graphemes frequently do not have unitary phonetic values in many languages,

---

[28]*Ibid*. The first condition seems to imply that the spelling should be indicated by transliteration, while at the same time additional (phonetic?) symbols should indicate the pronunciation. This method would in most instances result in two parallel script conversions, one superimposed on the other—certainly not a practical method for bibliographic purposes.

protographic fidelity must plainly be understood to mean that phonemes are transcriptively expendable whenever two or more of them are indicated by the same orthograph. . . . Grapheme-phoneme noncorresponsions are observable in many languages and must be managed in bibliographic transcription by the principle of graphic priority and fidelity to the protextual orthographs. . . . Full protographic representation also means that silent orthographs must not be overlooked in transcription. . . . Such, then, is the role of graphic priority in metagraphy. Solutions to the problem of bibliothecal transcription must be sought in an understanding of the graphic nature of bibliography and the behavior of graphic symbols. There is no such thing as bibliophony.[29]

Wright thinks that it is possible to advocate such stringent requirements for bibliographic script conversion, and dismisses as entirely "unscientific" any hint at phonological transcription, because he limits his investigation to alphabetical scripts only, and in particular to Cyrillic and Greek, which happen to be amenable to an unambiguous conversion into Roman script. Had he also considered Semitic languages and their scripts, as well as Chinese and Japanese, he would have been forced to admit that there is indeed such a thing as "bibliophony" (even though nobody uses that term). It exists at least as an intermittent stage in the conversion process from a logographic source script to an alphabetic target script, when the final graphemic representation is one of phonemes or morphemes and not of graphemes, and is only partially or not at all reversible.

A somewhat more pragmatic approach was taken by H. S. Bushell who, in his introduction to the transliteration scheme for Cyrillic proposed by the Royal Society, stated as one of the necessary criteria, "The transliteration should give some indication of the pronunciation of the words," although he tempered this statement in the following paragraph by saying that it "is much the least important for bibliographical purposes and should always yield to the first [i.e., unambiguous reversibility] if it is impossible to satisfy both."[30] But this is just the point: while it is indeed possible in a transliteration scheme for Cyrillic to "satisfy both" requirements by giving precedence to the first, this is not so for most other scripts, including the Roman one when it has to be converted into another script.

Unambiguous reversibility is also stressed by German bibliographers and librarians, who likewise consider mostly the problems of transliteration from Cyrillic. A broader view is taken by Max Mangold, an expert on non-Roman scripts with the firm of Duden, publishers of the most authoritative German dictionaries. In his essay on the problems of transliteration and transcription he first emphasizes strict transliteration:

Eine möglichst strenge Transliteration ist die *wissenschaftliche Transliteration*. Sie ist

---

[29]Wright (1969), pp. 314–320.
[30]Bushell (1953), p. 4.

absolut eindeutig bei der Uebertragung der Ausgangssprache in die Zielsprache und ebenso absolut eindeutig bei der Rückübertragung aus der Zielsprache in die Ausgangssprache. Das ist die erste Forderung. . . . Sie erlaubt es, auf Grund der Lateinform die Originalform eindeutig wiederherzustellen. [Emphasis in the original.][31]

But he also points out that the only possibility to render logographic scripts is by phonemic transcription, which must, in his opinion, be unambiguously reversible in both directions:

Die phonetisch-orthographische Transkription muss absolut eindeutig sein in der Übertragung aus der Aussprache der Ausgangssprache in die Orthographie der Zielsprache. Wenn auch die Rückübertragung aus der Orthographie der Zielsprache in die Aussprache der Ausgangssprache eindeutig möglich ist, dann kann man von einer *wissenschaftlichen phonetisch-orthographischen Transkription* sprechen. Ist eindeutige Übertragung nur in der ersten Richtung möglich, so können wir von *volkstümlicher phonetisch-orthographischer Transkription* sprechen. In der Praxis haben wir es vielfach mit gemischten Methoden zu tun [emphasis in the original].[32]

Mangold's postulate of mutually reversible phonemic transcription of languages written in logographic script is actually impossible to fulfill, even when the conversion scheme provides for the tone values of Chinese, for example (as is the case in the original version of the Wade-Giles scheme). The problems posed by the many dozens of homophonous logograms in Chinese, or by the different "readings" of the same logograms in Japanese are not amenable to *any* kind of unambiguously reversible transcription, as is demonstrated conclusively in Chapter 6. In other words, according to Mangold's definition, even the strictest application of the Wade-Giles transcription system, with all diacritical marks, tone indicators, and so forth, remains a "popular phonetic-orthographic transcription," and cannot claim to be scientific in the sense defined by him. The fact that most libraries and bibliographic works omit tone indicators from Chinese transcription makes their practices even less scientific.

The author's statement about mixed methods and the following somewhat regretful remark show, however, that he is well aware of the fact that the ideal of scientific, that is, unambiguously reversible rendering of scripts, can rarely if ever be achieved in practice:

Auf den ersten Blick könnte man solche Mischungen von Transliteration und phonetisch-orthographischer Transkription als hybrid und inkonsequent ablehnen. Man darf aber nicht vergessen, dass diese Mischungen durch alte Überlieferungen bestimmt werden. . . . Man muss sich wohl mit dem alten Grundsatz der traditionellen gemischten Transkription abfinden.[33]

[31]Mangold (1965), p. 9.
[32]*Ibid.*, pp. 15–16.
[33]Ibid., p. 16.

This statement actually reveals a far more scientific attitude than the doctrinaire insistence on a principle that seeks to prescribe how things ought to be without bothering much about how they really are and above all why.

It is, of course, undeniable that transliteration, or the exact graphic rendering of the "Schriftbild" (particularly when based on a one-to-one correspondence) is easier to perform, is less prone to errors, and is to a certain degree even possible to automate, whereas transcription, or the graphic rendering of the "Lautbild,"[34] which is subject to constant changes in the phonology of a language and dialectal variances as well as to subjective interpretation of sounds, is much less exact, and cannot be applied consistently. But the "mixture" of transliteration and transcription that is the hallmark of practically all conversion schemes, is not at all caused only by old traditions (although this factor plays a certain role that is considered later on), but is primarily the result of two ineluctable facts:

1. Many languages are written in scripts that cannot be converted to other scripts without representing at least some of their phonological elements, or their "Lautbild";
2. Reading and comprehension of any written message are almost entirely dependent on verbalization or subvocalization of the words formed by a string of letters.

The following analysis of the underlying causes for these two facts shows that the quest for a scientific bibliographic conversion system, primarily based on reversibility, is a futile endeavor not unlike the alchemist's pursuit of the philosophers' stone. It does not, at any rate, transform the field so often grandiosely called "library science" into a true branch of science. In this context it is perhaps interesting to note that geographers and cartographers, people who work in a scientific discipline, never claim any scientific basis or value for the conversion systems they use. The PCGN system freely admits its inconsistencies and deviations from certain principles, and no one seems to bother. The system is acknowledged as being widely *used* by scientists, which alone is enough to make it respectable, even if no scientific principle is followed either in its design or in its application. Not so in librarianship, where a sometimes frantic search for professional identity and respectability in the eyes of other professionals has been going on for many decades without much success. Whether the pathetic insistence on the use of scientific methods for bibliographic script conversion is another manifestation of this quest for respectability is a topic best left to psychologists and sociologists who might wish to investigate this phenomenon.

---

[34]The terms *Schriftbild* and *Lautbild* were introduced into the literature of script conversion for bibliographic purposes by the Orientalist A. Brux (1941) in his essay on Hebrew and Aramaic transcription, and have been used since by several authors.

6.2. Graphemic and Phonological Features Affecting Reversibility

We first consider the roles played by graphemic and phonological features in the conversion of various scripts by systems of Romanization, and then compare these roles in conversion from Roman script (and other scripts) into any non-Roman script, that is, Arabization, Cyrillization, and so forth. The degree to which graphemic features can be converted uniquely and unambiguously determines the degree of reversibility possible for any particular pair of source and target scripts, while the phonological features that are necessary for conversion determine to what degree pronounceability must be an element of any conversion scheme.

Figure 5.2 shows in schematic form the extent to which graphemic features (*G*) and phonological features (*P*) determine the nature of Romanization schemes for various scripts. Complete and unambiguous reversibility can be attained in transliteration for Cyrillic, Greek, Georgian, and Devanagari as used in the writing systems of Sanskrit and Hindi; no attention need to be paid to pronounceability, at least theoretically. At the other end of the spectrum Chinese, Japanese, and Korean (written in Chinese logographic script) can only be Romanized by phonological transcription, and no unambiguous reversibility is possible. Romanization schemes for all other scripts fall somewhere in between, since some but not all of their graphemes can be reconstructed by reversion, whereas certain phonological elements not expressed by graphemes must be supplied in transcription, and certain graphemes may have to be omitted for various reasons.

Figure 5.3 shows the two features as they affect script conversion into any script and writing system other than the Roman, that is, Cyrillization, Arabiza-

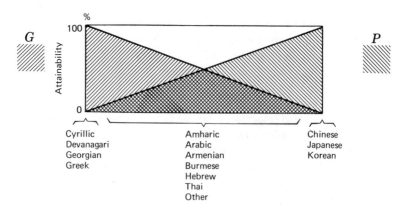

Figure 5.2.   Graphemic *(G)* and phonological *(P)* features characterizing Romanization schemes for various scripts.

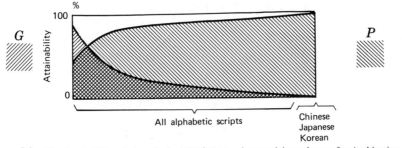

Figure 5.3.   Graphemic *(G)* and phonological *(P)* features characterizing schemes for Arabization, Cyrillization, Hebraization, Grecization, Sinization, Japanization, and so forth.

tion, Grecization, and so forth. The shape of the two curves for *G* and *P* indicates that most languages written in the Roman script (as well as those written in other scripts) can be converted only by phonological transcription and not by transliteration. Languages with a highly phonetic orthography such as Finnish or Turkish would occupy a place towards the left side of the diagram (since most but not all of their graphemes can be unambiguously and uniquely transliterated into Cyrillic, Arabic, etc.) whereas French and English would have a place somewhere near the right end of the spectrum, with other orthographies falling in between. The less phonetic the orthography, the more a conversion into another script must rely on phonological elements, and the fewer the graphemic features of the source script that can be rendered unchanged in the target script.

We can demonstrate this phenomenon by the example of Cyrillization of Roman script for Russian readers, which is statistically the second most frequent application of script conversion after Romanization. Unique and unambiguous Cyrillization (i.e., one that allows for complete reversibility) presupposes a one-to-one relationship between the Roman and Cyrillic letters. Naturally for each Roman letter a Cyrillic letter will be chosen that expresses as nearly as possible the same phoneme or one of its allophones, such as д for *d,* or ф for *f.* Many Roman letters, however, such as *c, g, h, j, s, v, x,* and *z* represent completely different phonemes in the orthographies of various languages, or even in the orthography of the same language (e.g., the various phonemes represented in English orthography by the letter *g*). For transliteration into Cyrillic only one letter can be chosen, say ц for *c;* this letter would then have to be used in Cyrillization whenever the letter *c* is written in any of the Roman source alphabets. Although this would be technically feasible, it would in most instances produce transliterated words and names that would be neither visually intelligible as the Cyrillized forms of the original words nor pronounceable. (Pronounceability means here only that a native Russian speaker could utter the transliterated word in some fashion; the importance of being able to do so is discussed later.) For example, the names *Chaucer, La Rochefoucauld,* or *Schocken* could be Cyrillized by strict transliteration (assuming here that *c* and *h* would be represented by ц and г) as Цгауцер, Ларсцгефоуцаулд, and Сцгоцкен respectively, but they would thereby become unintelligible (and also largely unpronounceable). Even Slavic names such as the Polish *Chodowiecki* or the Czech *Michalek* cannot be transliterated into Russian Cyrillic. The only instance in which true Cyrillic transliteration can actually be performed is in Serbo-Croatian, because this is virtually the same language written in two scripts. Consequently it was possible to designate one and only one letter in each script to represent the same phoneme, but digraphs have to be used for the Romanization of Russian Cyrillic letters not part of the Serbian alphabet, and the converse holds for the Cyrillization of Serbian letters not in the Russian alphabet.

In addition to the problems that would be caused by strict transliteration of the basic Roman letters into Cyrillic, there is also the question of how to transliterate letters that are modified by diacritical marks, since the Cyrillic script does not use any such marks except for the breve over the letter и (й) and sometimes a diaeresis over the letter e (ё). The umlauts *ä, ö* and *ü* could perhaps be rendered by writing ä, ö, and ÿ, but what could possibly be used as a Russian Cyrillic transliteration of *å, ç, ł, ţ, ş,* or *z*? Putting small circles, cedillas, slashes, tildes, and points over, under, or through Cyrillic letters would not mean anything to Russian readers, while digraphs (e.g., ao for *å,* and сз for *ç*) would often result in ambiguous reversibility, in addition to making the transliteration quite cumbersome and awkward to read. (In the Cyrillic alphabets designed for the languages of non-Slavic nationalities in the USSR, many diacritical marks and special letters are indeed being used, but these are language-specific and are quite incomprehensible for a Russian or Ukrainian reader.)

Strict transliteration according to the principle "write what you see" is therefore not feasible for the conversion of Roman script into the Cyrillic, and Cyrillization of non-Russian words and names is indeed performed exclusively by phonological transcription in which phonemes that are foreign to Russian (such as [h] or the nasalized vowels of French) are somehow approximated. *Chaucer* thus becomes Чосер /tʃosɛr/, *La Rochefoucauld* is transcribed as Ларошфуко /laroʃfuko/, *Schocken* becomes Шокен /ʃokɛn/, *Danton* is rendered as Дантон /danton/, and *Hegel* becomes Гегель /gegɛʎ/.[35] (This does

---

[35]The problem of transcription of foreign names into Russian has been treated by Starostin (1965) and by Giljarevskij (1969) from the point of view of Russian librarians. Their manual on the transcription of non-Russian personal, geographic, and object names first explains why transliteration into Russian Cyrillic is not practical, and then gives detailed instructions on the transcription of the most common given names and their orthographic characteristics from Czech, Danish, Dutch, English, Finnish, French, German, Hungarian, Italian, Norwegian, Polish, Portuguese, Romanian, Slovakian, Spanish, and Swedish, as well as from Bulgarian and Serbian, which, though written in Cyrillic script, need special transcription rules for conversion into Russian Cyrillic.

not imply, by any means, that a Russian reader, when pronouncing the Cyrillized name of an English, French, or German author, comes anywhere near the *actual* pronunciation of such names any more than does an English, French, or German reader when pronouncing a Romanized Russian name.) Phonological transcription may sometimes result in several variant renderings of a name. *Galsworthy,* for example, can theoretically be Cyrillized by no less than 72 different transcriptions (depending on how the letters *a, w, o,* and *th* are rendered); however, only a few versions have been used in Russian translations of his works, and only one, namely the form Голсуорти, has been recommended for biographical dictionaries and encyclopedias. Such Russian reference works generally also cite foreign names in the original script in parentheses, and contain indexes from the original to the Cyrillized form, which enables Russian readers to find such names in the source language in foreign catalogs, bibliographies, and reference works, or to compare the original with the Cyrillized form.

Phonological transcription precludes, of course, unique and unambiguous reversibility, but that is, after all, not different from the use of Romanization for the transcription of Chinese and Japanese names. It has been argued that it would be useful if the Russians would use "strict" transliteration when rendering foreign names in Cyrillic script, so as to facilitate back-transliteration into Roman script.[36] Any such attempt to "persuade" the Russians to adopt transliteration would not only be utterly futile but also presumptuous. The Russians transcribe foreign names and words to serve Russian-speaking readers, and to exercise bibliographic control in *their* libraries by methods suited to *their* language and script, and not to accommodate the need for back-transliteration of Cyrillized Western names in libraries that use the Roman script. Similar conditions prevail, *mutatis mutandis,* in Arabization, Grecization, Hebraization, and so on.

6.3. Psycholinguistic Factors and Pronounceability

We shall now consider the real causes for the "intrusion," as it were, of phonological features into otherwise "strict" transliteration schemes. Far from being regrettable aberrations or concessions reluctantly made to traditional practices, the allowances made for pronounceability in bibliographic script conversion are primarily the result of an intuitive response on the part of the makers and users of conversion schemes to fundamental psycholinguistic processes that

---

[36]In one of the more fanciful contributions to the problem of transliteration and retranscription of Cyrillic, David Franklin (1966) actually proposed such a course of action: "To solve our problems, we need to persuade the Russians to abandon the phonetic transcription approach for indicating English-type alphabet names in scientific contexts." Franklin does not indicate, however, by which means the Russians could be persuaded to make foreign names unreadable for their own people in order to "solve the problems" of English-speaking readers of translated texts. . . .

underlie the acts of reading and comprehending written messages. The use of the term ''pronounceability'' does not, of course, imply that transcribed names and words are always uttered *viva voce,* but refers rather to the fact that even for silent reading the verbalization and subvocalization of a string of letters is of the utmost importance for the reader's ability to read and, if possible, to comprehend what he has read. Research conducted during the last two decades into the physiological and psychological processes underlying the act of reading has made this abundantly clear.[37] ''There is little question that for many readers, if not most, the act of silent reading is accompanied by some manifestation of speech processes.''[38] Even if it could be argued that these findings do not always apply to highly skilled readers (among which librarians and bibliographers surely would count themselves), there is sound evidence that ''subvocalization increases for silent reading of text that is syntactically difficult, unfamiliar, or illegible.''[39] Since transcribed or transliterated names or words are, almost by definition, at first unfamiliar to the reader, and may also be difficult to read because of the abundance of diacritical marks used in certain transcriptions, it follows that verbalization or subvocalization is an indispensable element in the reading of names and words, not to mention entire phrases (such as titles) that are presented to a reader in converted form.

It might also be argued that transcribed or transliterated names and words are not meant to be ''read'' in the normal manner but rather looked at as concatenations of single letters that, if the key to the system is known, can be converted into the original letters and thus into names and words that can then be ''read'' in the normal way by someone familiar with the language. As we have seen, this assumption holds true only for certain scripts and languages, and it also fails to take into consideration that human beings do not read in this manner. Only machines ''read'' by recognizing letters (or rather their coded representations), combining them one by one into words, and comparing these with paradigms of words stored in their memory, to be accepted as valid words if they match or rejected if they do not. For human beings, however, the act of reading words does not consist in a mere mechanical adding up of component letters or of graphemic decoding of individual images of certain shapes, lines, curves, and so on; rather, it is a complex ''process of combining information from a variety of sources as needed to generate and confirm expectancies.''[40] One of the most important of these ''expected'' features is the tacit assumption that letters in an unfamiliar word would be pronounced as the letters in similar words and in

---

[37]See Geyer and Kolers (1974), especially section III.D, ''Verbal integration processes,'' pp. 216–222, and section IV, ''Flexible reading: control processes,'' pp. 225–228.
[38]*Ibid.,* p. 219.
[39]*Ibid.,* p. 220. See also Edfeldt (1959), whose studies of silent reading by electromyographic methods showed an increase in subvocalization as reading material became more difficult.
[40]*Ibid.,* p. 211.

similar concatenation with other letters according to the orthography and the graphotactics of the reader's language. Even when confronted with a nonsense word such as "plunkich," most English-speaking people will be able to pronounce it without any difficulty, although they do not know what it "means."[41] Any transliterated or transcribed word is thus instinctively read *as a word* and is consequently pronounced as any graphemically similar word would be, either alone or in context with other words of the language, and is written in the target script, whether or not it has "meaning," and it is also verbalized or (in silent reading) subvocalized.

Needless to say, such vocalization (aloud or silent) is a far cry from the actual pronunciation of a name or word in the source language, and a native speaker of that language would in most instances have difficulty understanding what was being uttered by the reader of a word transcribed into the target language and its script. But a bibliographic transcription that uses regular letters (i.e., not a phonetic alphabet) can never be more than an approximation to the actual pronunciation, and is not intended to convey it exactly. It fulfills its function adequately as long as the reader of a transcribed word can verbalize or subvocalize it at all in some manner, so as not to impede the smooth flow of his reading, or so as to enable him to utter it aloud if necessary.

The important point for our present analysis is, however, not that people try to pronounce any written word, and are also in most instances able to do so somehow; rather, it is that they pronounce it *differently, according to the spelling and pronunciation conventions governing their language and script.* The word "plunkich" (assuming it to be the transcription of some word in a dissimilar source script), as pointed out, will not pose any difficulties to English-speaking people, who will pronounce it /plʌnkitʃ/. A Frenchman will have some difficulties with the letter combination *nk,* which is foreign to his writing system and does not evoke any familiar pronunciation, so he might come up with something like /plœkiʃ/; a German speaker might pronounce the word /plunkiç/. In each case the expectation of the native speaker is oriented toward a certain letter or letter combination pronounced as in other familiar and phonetically spelled words of his language. Conversely any letter combinations that are unfamiliar because they do not occur in the writing system of a language, or any graphemes that are foreign to that writing system, constitute hindrances to smooth reading and to the necessary verbalization or subvocalization, and are therefore unconsciously rejected by native readers of a language. If, for example, the nonsense word cited above had been spelled "plunkish," it would again not

---

[41]No English-speaking child has ever had any difficulty reading and pronouncing the words of "Jabberwocky" when first encountering *Through the Looking-Glass,* although " 'twas brillig and the slithy toves, ..." do not at first "mean" anything. (Lewis Carroll himself produced some whimsical "explanations" for the nonsense words in Jabberwocky after the publication of the book.) Alice says, after having heard the poem: "It's *rather* hard to understand!"

be difficult at all for an Englishman, but would pose problems for a Frenchman or German, because their writing systems do not admit the letter combination *sh,* and consequently there is no received pronunciation for it. (We assume here that neither the Frenchman nor the German know anything about English spelling and pronunciation.) And if the nonsense word had been spelled "plunkiš," all three native speakers would be stumped (unless given special instructions). The English writing system does not contain any diacritical marks, while the French and German ones do have them, but not in conjunction with consonants nor in the form of a háček. But a Czech or Croatian reader would have no difficulty at all.

In practice, all bibliographical transliteration schemes contain elements of phonological transcription that owe their existence to deeply rooted habits of pronouncing letters in a certain way which are acquired when a child learns to read, and which are as difficult or impossible to change as are other phonetic traits of articulation such as intonation, stress, and pitch. It is therefore not surprising that even when absolute reversibility is at least theoretically possible, as in conversion from Cyrillic to Roman script, it is not performed in library practice. The LC scheme for Romanization of Cyrillic script (which is generally thought to be a "strict" transliteration scheme allowing for complete and unambiguous reversibility, and has therefore found such wide application in libraries) makes several concessions to pronounceability and exhibits features that are illogical from the point of view of strict transliteration. In some cases, namely the Cyrillic letters г, ё, и, and щ, the same letter is transliterated differently when it is *pronounced* differently in any of the six Slavic languages concerned, whereas the letter ц, identically pronounced in these languages, is rendered by different graphemes according to language. Actually the LC scheme uses six different transliteration tables for as many Slavic languages, four of which (Russian, Ukrainian, White-Russian, and Bulgarian) follow an "English" pattern with few or no diacritical marks, and are more or less pronounceable by English speakers, while two (Serbian and Macedonian) follow the "Croatian" pattern with many diacritical marks and sound values that are foreign to English pronunciation (see also Table 5.2, p. 349). The reason for this peculiar system is that the name of a Yugoslav author may appear on the title page of a book in either Roman or Cyrillic script, depending on whether the book has been published in Croatia or in Serbia. If the Serbian form of the name (in Cyrillic) were transliterated according to the scheme used for Russian Cyrillic, the Romanization would not coincide with the Croatian form of the name (in Roman script) used by the author himself as well as by the *Bibliografija Jugoslavija (BJ),* the Yugoslav national bibliography. But when a Russian author is translated into Serbian, his name is Romanized according to the LC scheme for Russian Cyrillic, since the original work has been Romanized in this form. When the book is also published in Croatian and is listed in *BJ,* there is then a clash between the Croatian

Romanization and the one used by the Library of Congress—exactly the thing that the use of various Romanization tables sought to avoid. At any rate the "correct" application of these so-called transliteration schemes demands an intimate knowledge of the six Slavic languages that are written in Cyrillic, and cannot merely be a mechanical substitution of Roman graphemes for Cyrillic ones, to be performed by library assistants with no reading ability of Cyrillic script, as is so often claimed as a partial justification for the practice of Romanization.

Indeed, none of the conversion schemes devised or revised during the past three decades by the Library of Congress for the Romanization of other scripts follows Sommer's "scientific" principle of "write what you see"; they are all mixtures of transliteration and transcription. The introductory note to the scheme for Hebrew and Yiddish even states quite unequivocally that "the transliteration [sic!] attempts to *represent the sound* of the Hebrew or Yiddish word"[42] [my emphasis]. In order to avoid cumbersome terminology as well as possible theoretical conflicts, the conversion schemes of the Library of Congress are now called "Romanization" systems. Yet the inherent conflict of principles cannot be resolved by simply calling the procedure by which a dissimilar source script is converted into the dominant Roman script "Romanization" instead of transliteration or transliteration-transcription. If, as has been postulated, only strict transliteration is a scientific method for bibliographic control, then, by definition, any intrusion or admixture of other subjective or "unscientific" methods will automatically render the scientific method invalid. If, on the other hand, it is recognized that all practical script conversion for bibliographic control can be based on transliteration only as far as this is technically feasible, and that it must also include elements of phonological transcription, then it is no longer possible to speak of transliteration as the only accurate and scientific method, nor to treat all phonological transcriptions as "exceptions" and troublesome but unavoidable distortions.

Incidentally, absolute and immutable adherence to the "Schriftbild" as the only scientific method acceptable for bibliographic control is not required either in theory or in practice of cataloging, the basic activity on which such control relies, and to which conversion of scripts is only ancillary. The spelling and form of a name, purportedly sacrosanct for the purposes of script conversion if we are to believe Sommer's maxim "Write what you see" and Wright's "principle of graphic priority and fidelity to the protextual orthographs," are sometimes changed and often completely disregarded in descriptive cataloging. The spelling *Shakspere,* when found on a title page, is converted to *Shakespeare,* and *Mark Twain* is entered as *Clemens, Samuel Langhorne,* in American library catalogs, yet these obvious deviations from "graphic priority and fidelity" are somehow

---

[42] American Library Association (1949), p. 249.

not considered to be "unscientific" in bibliographic control. Quite to the contrary, volumes have been written to justify them as the very acme of bibliographic accuracy and scholarly exactitude.

Finally, there is also a quite pragmatic reason for the inclusion of at least some rudimentary elements of phonological transcription in virtually all schemes of script conversion. A transcribed name or word is not always read silently. Indeed, in almost all situations in which a bibliographic citation is consulted, whether by librarians or by library users, the name of an author or the title of a work is also being talked about, however briefly and inaccurately. The library user who just looked up a reference in the catalog and now asks a librarian for further assistance does not point silently to what he copied from a card. A library assistant who is told to look up a certain book in a non-Roman script in the *National Union Catalog* to find out whether it has been cataloged is not only handed a slip of paper but is often *told* what name to look for. If there should be a discrepancy between the librarian's transcription and the one found in the reference tool (as is so often the case), there is almost bound to be some oral discussion of this fact with other librarians or language specialists. Even in an essentially nonverbal communication involving transcription, as in interlibrary loan procedures, some talking may take place at both ends about the author's name and the title of the work requested.

So far we have considered the two functional requirements of reversibility and pronounceability and have seen that, although the former is stressed as paramount by all librarians, in reality the latter takes precedence over it in almost all instances. We now turn to a third functional requirement of bibliographic script conversion.

6.4. Traditionality

The instructions given in various catalog codes regarding the rendering of Biblical names, names from classical antiquity, and other names that have become accepted in a form substantially different from a transcription or transliteration of the original name take precedence over the application of whatever conversion scheme is used for the source script. We thus find in library catalogs *Confucius* instead of *K'ung-tzŭ* or *K'ung Fu-tse, Lynceus* instead of *Lugkeios,* and *Catherine* instead of *Ekaterina*. One can even find *Tchaikovsky* and *Chaikovskiĭ* as variant renderings of exactly the same Russian name; the *British National Bibliography,* whose practice is followed by many British libraries, uses the "traditional" form for the name of the composer, while the "less well known" bearers of that name are transliterated according to the BSI scheme! From a British library comes the comment:

... a recurring problem is that of deciding between a correctly transliterated form of a name and a (fairly) well established form; we prefer "Cavafy" to "Kabaphes", for instance, but a decision is often influenced by existing headings in the catalogs as much as any other consideration.[43]

This is not the place to argue the validity or usefulness of various cataloging rules on the rendering of certain kinds of names. Here it is enough to state that these rules stress the need to adhere to traditional forms where these exist and to disregard, if necessary, the transcription practice otherwise followed to render names and words in a non-Roman script. One of the most characteristic examples of this procedure is the Anglo-American cataloging practice of rendering Hebrew names of Biblical origin in the form established by the Authorized Version of the Bible. The extension of this rule from Biblical characters to Jewish bearers of such names from the beginning of the Christian era until the end of the 19th century leads to sometimes grotesque results. Learned rabbis who lived in medieval France or later in Germany, Poland, or Russia, and who never set foot in England nor wrote a single line in the English language, sport Anglicized versions of their Biblical names, often linked to their mostly non-Hebrew surnames and other given names of post-Biblical or non-Biblical origin which are duly transcribed following Hebrew, Yiddish, or German pronunciation (not spelling!). The resultant entries are thus often a hodgepodge of transliteration, transcription, and traditional rendering that defies all reason, and they have, of course, no discernible connection whatsoever with the "Schriftbild" on the title pages of Hebrew commentaries on the Bible, rabbinical responsa, or other works in Hebrew. The following examples, culled at random from the *Catalogue of Hebrew Books* published by Harvard University Libraries, which are based on the practice of the Library of Congress, illustrate this (see Figure 5.4). In example *(a)* the form actually chosen consists of a Germanized spelling of the surname (note *ü* for the Hebrew or Yiddish phoneme [i]!), a phonetic transliteration of the first given name (Hebrew but not Biblical), and a "traditional" rendering of the second given name (a Biblical one). In example *(b)* the title page also happens to display a Romanized form of the name, supplied by a translator, namely *Salomon Rappoport;* here the spelling of the surname (with two *p*'s) has been disregarded, but the traditional form Solomon has been changed to Salomon, deferring to the German spelling. *Judah* is again rendered traditionally, and *Löb* is a Germanized spelling related neither to Hebrew nor to Yiddish or any "tradition" but based on the Biblical identification of the name Judah with

---

[43]Comment made in response to a questionnaire used in the survey by Wellisch (1976). The reference is to the name of the modern Greek poet Constantine Cavafi (1863–1933), who chose to Romanize his surname Καβαφης in this form.

	Hebrew name	Transcription that would result from correct application of Library of Congress scheme	Actual rendering in catalogs
(a)	חיים בן משה ליפשיץ	Lipshits, Hayyim ben Moshe	Lipschütz, Hayyim ben Moses
(b)	שלמה יהודה ליב רפאפורט	Rapaport (or Rapoport), Shlomo Yehudah Leib	Rapoport, Salomon Judah Löb
(c)	שלמה יצחקי	Shlomo Yitshaki	Solomon ben Isaac

Figure 5.4.   Rendering of Hebrew names in American library catalogs.

that of a lion (*Löwe* in German), which was popular among Ashkenazi Jews in the 17th and 18th century. In example *(c)* the name has been artificially constructed to fit the "traditional" mold. The name of the famous medieval rabbi and Bible commentator best known by his acronym *Raši* was (Rabbi) Šelomo Yizhaqi. The first part of the name (disregarding the title Rabbi) can readily be anglicized to *Solomon*, but the second part, derived from the Hebrew form of Isaac (meaning "the Isaacian") would not conform with the traditional form *Isaac* if transcribed. Therefore the word *ben* ("son of"), having roughly the same meaning and often found in Hebrew names but not used by Raši, is artificially inserted, which makes it possible to Anglicize the name almost completely to *Solomon ben Isaac*.

How all this can be reconciled with the lofty principles of "scientific accuracy" or "the representation of Hebrew sounds" must be left to the explanation of the learned transliterators of Hebrew in American libraries. Lest it be thought that the cult of traditionality is a phenomenon of the English-speaking library world, it should be pointed out that the catalog of the Bibliothèque Nationale in Paris follows the same practice. Biblical names are there generally rendered as they appear in the Douay version of the Bible:

Les auteurs anciens connus sous les noms bibliques sont catalogués sous la forme francisée de ces noms quand elle existe: Abraham, Isaac, Jacob, Moïse, Salomon, etc.[44]

Vive la petite différence. The catalog code of the Vatican naturally prescribes that Biblical names be entered in the form codified in the Vulgate, and other national catalog codes follow similar practices geared to the respective vernacular versions of the Bible.

Traditionality in librarianship and bibliography no less than in philology and geography thus takes precedence over reversibility and pronounceability, at least as far as general bibliographic practices are concerned.[45] Only in very

[44]Bibliothèque Nationale, Paris. *Catalogue général des livres imprimés* . . . , *1960–1969. Serie 2. Caractères non latins.* Tome 1. Caractères hebraïques. Paris, 1972, p. [iii].
[45]A notable exception from this practice is provided by S. R. Ranganathan, who postulates a "canon of ascertainability," and states in his *Theory of library catalogue:* "The cataloguer has no business to question the right of authors to transliterate or even mutilate their own names as they please. Any attempt to reconstruct the names of the authors so as to bring them into conformity with tradition or standard codes or philology or even semantics will be wronging the authors and will amount, in the long run, to courting chaos. Hence whatever the titlepage gives as the name of the author must be faithfully followed in accordance with the rule." (Ranganathan, 1938, p. 285).

specialized applications are traditional renderings of names rejected in favor of a more uniform application of a transcription system, but these instances are rare.

6.5. Systemic Requirements

6.5.1. General Applicability. This is a *conditio sine qua non* in bibliographic script conversion, since virtually any name or word written in a dissimilar script may have to be transcribed at one time or another, be it as a heading, a rendering of a title, a descriptive detail, or an annotation. But here too there is sometimes a clash with traditionality, the latter requirement gaining the upper hand.

6.5.2 Unique Graphemic Representation. This requirement has the next highest priority, particularly since reversibility is so strongly stressed as the most important functional requirement wherever feasible. As already pointed out, transliteration in the strictest sense with complete one-to-one equivalency of graphemes (as in the computer printout shown in Figure 5.1) can only be used for certain limited purposes that fall entirely outside the scope of present bibliographic control. It is, moreover, intended to be applied to consecutive text and not to bibliographic retrieval tags in the form of names or titles.

But even where at least unambiguous correspondence between source script and target script has been achieved by use of diacritical marks or digraphs (or both), as in the basic ISO system for transliteration of Cyrillic, mechanical or automatic conversion of bibliographic retrieval tags in the form of authors' names is possible only in theory and not always in practice. When the name of a Russian author is given at the head of a title page in its nominative form, it can indeed be mechanically transcribed with satisfactory results. However, if the author's name follows the title and is given in the genitive case (the Russian equivalent of the English practice to write "*by* John Doe"), it is written with a suffix, and a knowledge of Russian grammar is required to render the author's name in the nominative case, in the form in which it is to be entered in the catalog. The same is true for some other highly inflected languages.

6.5.3 Simplicity of Graphemic Representation. Diacritical marks and sometimes even specially devised letters and signs have always been a prominent feature of most transliteration and transcription schemes for bibliographic control purposes, especially those designed by teams of librarians and philologists. It is not difficult to discern the reasons for this. One is the simple arithmetic fact that practically all non-Roman scripts (with the exception of Greek and Hebrew) have a larger number of letters than the basic Roman alphabet, so that diacritical marks are necessary to distinguish between the same Roman letter when used for the transliteration of two or more letters in other scripts, if di- and trigraphs are to be avoided because of their ambiguity. The other reason is that philologists make ample use of diacritical marks and special letters and signs in phonetic transcription, and they are neither deterred by their complexity nor inclined to see the difficulties caused by these graphic marks in bibliographic control. Most practitioners in the library world, however, have always considered diacritical marks as a bothersome feature that should be avoided as far as possible—not only in English-speaking countries, where diacritical marks are naturally considered foreign to the conventions of the writing system, but even in Germany, France, and in the Scandinavian countries, where certain diacritical marks form part of the national writing system.

The earliest comprehensive conversion system for bibliothecal purposes, proposed in 1897 by the German librarian-philologist team of Kuhn and Schnorr von Carolsfeld,[46] mentioned briefly in Chapter 3 (p. 223), made ample use of diacritical marks and even included some Greek letters (for the transliteration of Arabic). But a review of this work by a librarian pointed out that diacritical marks had considerable drawbacks, and that one should use them only when "simple letters" could not be employed under any circumstances:

Wenn nun auch diese Unterscheidungszeichen schlechthin unentbehrlich sind, so bilden sie doch weder für den Leser, noch für den Schreiber, noch für den Drucker eine angenehme Zugabe; und auch dem Bibliothekar sind sie unbequem . . . Die verschiedensten Gründe sprechen also dafür, zu Unterscheidungszeichen nur dann zu greifen, wenn man mit einfachen Buchstaben auf keine Weise auskommen kann.[47]

In the introduction to the transliteration system for Cyrillic proposed by the Royal Society in 1953 one of the four "criteria by which a system for bibliographical use should be judged" is "[that] the system should not require diacritical marks that are not available to English printers."[48]

There are, however, other opinions, such as the one voiced by Sommer who considered the superimposition of as many as three different diacritical marks on a basic letter in the transcription of Siamese an "admirable typographical feat." (We must not forget that Sommer was a philologist first, and librarian only secondarily, so that the lavish use of diacritical marks was not a deterrent for him but rather the hallmark of scientific excellence.)

In the conversion schemes for Cyrillic script that are intended for the use of English-speaking people, diacritical marks are indeed largely avoided, since they are foreign to the writing system of English. For this reason, the basic ISO scheme for the transliteration of Cyrillic (which uses ž, č, š, and šč to render ж, ч, ш, and щ; i.e., a single diacritical mark on only three letters) was rejected by the British Standards Institution and by the American National Standards Insti-

---

[46]Kuhn (1897).
[47]O. Grulich, *Centralblatt für Bibliothekswesen* **14** (1897):305.
[48]Bushell (1953), pp. 3–4.

tute, which preferred the digraphs *zh, ch, sh,* and *shch* instead. Ironically, however, the Library of Congress, while using the same digraphs in its own set of transliteration schemes for Cyrillic, found it necessary to use ligatures over the six digraphs *ẑh, t͡s, i͡e, i͡o, i͡u,* and *i͡a,* thus not only using diacritical marks, but using unusual ones at that, which are available neither on commercially produced typefaces for printers nor on typewriters. To make matters still worse, the ligatures are not used uniformly to render the same Cyrillic grapheme, but are employed only for certain languages but not for others, as shown in Table 5.2. To add to the confusion, *i͡e* is used to transliterate the two different letters є and ѣ, while conversely ё is transliterated *ë* when it appears in Russian text, but *i͡o* when written in the White-Russian language. Needless to say, this is phonemic transcription and not transliteration, sacrificing unambiguous reversibility because the Cyrillic grapheme is the same in the alphabets of both languages, and only the pronunciation differs. (If this practice were applied to names written in Roman script, the name *Mexico,* would be so written in an English text but would be rendered as *Mekhiko* when it appeared in a Spanish text, since *x* is pronounced $[\chi]$ in Spanish, and this phoneme in turn is generally rendered by *kh* in transliterations aimed at English-speaking readers.)

Practically all modern conversion systems for scripts other than Cyrillic contain a multitude of diacritical marks and sometimes even special characters, particularly in the schemes for Arabic, Hebrew, and Devanagari and its variants and descendant scripts, thus flouting the requirement of simplicity of graphemic representation. Until recently this seemed to be a relatively minor problem. Until the 1950s the literary output of modern works in Arabic, Hebrew, and De-

Table 5.2   Inconsistent Transliterations of Cyrillic Letters in the Library of Congress Scheme

Cyrillic letter	Transliteration				
	Russian	Ukrainian	White-Russian	Bulgarian	Serbian
г	g	h	h	g	g
є	—	i͡e	—	—	—
ё	ë	—	i͡o	—	—
ж	zh	ẑh	zh	zh	ž
и	i	y	—	i	i
і	ī	i	i	—	—
х	kh	kh	kh	kh	h
ц	t͡s	ts	ts	ts	c
ч	ch	ch	ch	ch	č
ш	sh	sh	sh	sh	ś
щ	shch	shch	—	sht	—
ѣ	i͡e	—	—	i͡e	—

vanagari scripts to reach Western libraries was fairly small, so that only a handful of people—printers, specialist catalogers in libraries, and philologists as users of bibliographic tools—were affected. The printers who produced bibliographies and catalogs had to acquire special types if they wished to get this kind of business, and generally did so. Catalogers and bibliographers used specially devised typewriters with "library keyboards" that made it possible to type at least the more commonly used diacritical marks, or they resorted to inserting them by hand (a practice apparently still widely used by libraries even in technically advanced countries, to judge from specimens of transcribed catalog cards submitted by libraries in response to a survey.)[49] The technical developments in photo-offset and other "near-print" duplicating methods, and their increasing use for bibliographic purposes make diacritical marks inserted by hand an acceptable method for material published in book form.

But while advances in technology now allow for the lavish use of diacritical marks in the field of printing and reprography, other technological developments seem to necessitate their elimination altogether, mainly for economic reasons. The exchange of bibliographic data between libraries by means of telecommunications equipment, primarily teletypewriters, as well as the use of computers for direct printout of bibliographies and library catalogs, and finally the use of computer terminals with CRT screens for on-line communication became common in the late 1960s. This made it necessary to avoid almost entirely the use of diacritical marks in the transcription of foreign names and words, since these machines are normally not equipped to print or display accents, cedillas, ligature signs, and other diacritical marks. There is, of course, no technical reason why diacritical marks, either separately or precombined with certain basic letters, could not be built into the keyboards and printout devices of teletypewriters and computers. However only a limited market exists for these "frills" and their addition to the standard repertoire of graphic marks would result in considerably higher costs; consequently there is no incentive to produce such equipment commercially, and when it is needed, it must be custom-built. Thus, when on-line printout from teleprinters or computers is involved, the use of diacritical marks is virtually precluded.[50] This fact will no doubt influence the design of

---

[49]Wellisch (1976). See also Figure 6.8, p. 422.

[50]In 1975 the Library of Congress installed CRT terminals that can display a "full library character set" (i.e., the basic 26 letters in upper- and lowercase, the most common diacritical marks, and a number of logograms and punctuation marks). These terminals were custom-built to the specifications of the Library of Congress and may become commercially available in the near future.

When computers are used to control an off-line phototypesetting device, no limitations on the use of any graphic design exist other than suitable and standardized binary coding of each character. But such devices are at present economical only for large-scale production, and are beyond the means of most individual libraries even in the United States, not to speak of libraries in other countries. A Rolls-Royce can be equipped with the latest technical gadgets, but only a few can afford such a car; most people in the United States drive a Ford or a Chevrolet with standard equipment; in European

future transliteration and transcription schemes intended for international use and the exchange of bibliographic data between computerized systems and networks. Simplicity of graphemic representation, which formerly played a relatively insignificant role in bibliographic script conversion, may in the future become a major requirement.

6.5.4 Economy of Space. This requirement is of some importance for the production of catalog cards, where space is at a premium, and also for computer-produced book catalogs (printed or reproduced from direct printout), where the length of lines is sometimes restricted and each additional line adds to the costs of printing and reprinting. It has, however, not been emphasized at any time as a requirement for bibliographic script conversion. In practice it is always subordinated to other requirements.

6.6 Incompatibility of Requirements

The requirements of script conversion schemes used for bibliographic control are thus mutually incompatible. Table 5.3 shows where they clash with each other and which requirements emerge from such clashes as the dominant ones.[51] Starting with the systemic requirements, we see that uniqueness prevails over simplicity of graphemic representation, whereas the latter is dominant in a conflict with economy of space, most often in alliance with the requirements for traditionality and pronounceability. The predominance of the functional requirements of pronounceability and traditionality is practically total whenever a clash with another requirement occurs, while reversibility takes precedence only over simplicity of graphemic representation, a relatively minor requirement.

How can this result be reconciled with the claims of most writers on the subject, who assert that a strict one-to-one relationship between source and target script, and consequently unambiguous reversibility are the main requirements for conversion of scripts for bibliographic purposes? The principal reason for this

---

countries people drive smaller cars such as a Morris or Volkswagen; and for the inhabitants of developing countries, any car, even the smallest, is too expensive for almost anyone. So it is with a scheme intended to be of practical use in universal bibliographic control. It cannot be based on the premise that ultimately everybody will drive a Rolls-Royce.

[51]It is interesting to note that the conflict between requirements deemed necessary for bibliographic conversion schemes was recognized already by O. Grulich (see footnote 47): "Die beiden hauptsächlichsten Gesichtspunkte, von denen sich die Verfasser haben leiten lassen, sind: 1. möglichste Schonung bereits in weiten Kreisen eingebürgerter Umschreibungsweisen, und 2. möglichste Einheitlichkeit der Behandlung der verschiedenen Sprachen. . . . Aber freilich liegt die Hauptschwierigkeit überhaupt nicht in der Aufstellung solcher allgemein leitender Gesichtspunkte, sondern darin, dass die daraus abgeleiteten Grundsätze sich zum Teil durchkreuzen und gegenseitig einschränken. . . . " *(Centralblatt für Bibliothekswesen* **14** (1897):305.)

Table 5.3 Incompatibility of Requirements for Schemes of Script Conversion for Bibliographic Control Purposes

		Prevailing requirement					
	General applicability	Graphemic representation		Economy of space	Pronounce-ability	Reversib-ility	Tradition-ality
		Uniqueness	Simplicity				
General applicability							(X)
Uniqueness of graphemic representation			X		(X)		(X)
Simplicity of graphemic representation		(X)		X	(X)	(X)	
Economy of space			(X)		(X)		(X)
Pronounceability		X	X	X		X	
Reversibility			X		(X)		(X)
Traditionality	X	X		X		X	

X = Incompatibility.
(X) = Dominance of requirement listed in column head.

apparent paradox is that historically these requirements could be more or less fulfilled for the languages in non-Roman scripts with which Western librarianship was most often confronted, namely Greek and Cyrillic.

One of the first systems of script conversion on a major scale, the transliteration of Greek names and words into Latin, has remained virtually unchanged since the days of Imperial Rome. This conversion system evolved with an almost perfect one-to-one relationship between Greek and Latin letters. This was not difficult to achieve, because the Greek alphabet had almost the same number of letters as the Latin one, and each Latin letter had a fixed phonemic value which made unambiguous reversibility possible, if needed (although the Romans were probably not overmuch concerned with the correct spelling of their names in Greek—their main interest, as the politically dominant nation, was the simple and convenient rendering of Greek names and words in Latin). The principle of reversible transliteration thus established between two related languages in close cultural contact and with a partially shared script survived in an almost unbroken tradition through the Middle Ages, and was codified in the Renaissance for scholarship in general by Erasmus and for bibliographic purposes in particular by Conrad Gessner. Since transliteration was performed in one direction only, and the target language was always Latin, the system devised by the Romans continued to serve its purpose well enough. The adoption of the Roman script by many different languages—with their use of several letters to express widely divergent phonemes and their development of different ways to express the same phoneme or its allophones (as we have seen in Chapter 2)—changed this situation radically and made one-to-one transliteration essentially impossible. Any transliteration from a non-Roman script became a one-to-many transformation, especially when phonemes foreign to Greek or Latin, such as $\left[\int\right]$ and $\left[\text{ts}\right]$, were involved. In the case of transliteration from Greek this phenomenon did not immediately become obvious because of the strong force of tradition, which made most language communities adopt the form of names and words that had been devised by the Romans (although sometimes adaptations were made to approximate the pronunciation of Greek phonemes foreign to a modern language, e.g., when *Telemachus* was rendered as *Télémaque* in French).

When the problems of conversion of other scripts were encountered by philologists during the 18th century, it so happened that Sanskrit, the first to be treated methodically, had a very highly phonetic orthography that lent itself also to reversible transliteration. An Englishman, Sir William Jones, devised the system, and it was natural that he used the sound values of the Roman alphabet as used in the English language, thus setting a precedent later followed for most other Asian languages and scripts.

The next non-Roman script to have a major impact on the conversion practices of libraries was Cyrillic, whose literary output became significant during the 19th century, and whose importance has been steadily ascending until it is now second only to that of the Roman script. Cyrillic too is a fully alphabetic script that is amenable to reversible transliteration (although the fact that it has a larger number of letters than the Roman alphabet makes strict one-to-one transformations impossible unless diacritical marks or digraphs or both are used). In addition the variant orthographic conventions of the major European languages immediately made themselves felt, since the sibilants and gutturals that are so characteristic of the Slavic languages, and which are mostly expressed by single Cyrillic graphemes such as ж, х, ч, and щ were rendered in many different ways (see Table 2.1, p. 48).

Despite such obvious difficulties, the proponents of the "write what you see" theory believed that transliteration by strict one-to-one transformations, with the resulting unambiguous reversibility which seemingly worked so well for Greek, Sanskrit, and Cyrillic, was a fundamental principle or a kind of natural law that consequently should be the basis for all "scientific" script conversion schemes used in bibliographic control. The impossibility of achieving reversibility in the conversion of languages written in various other scripts, and especially not in those written in logographic scripts, was treated as an exception to the rule.

Our investigation of requirements has shown that reversibility cannot be a generally applicable principle in script conversion. In fact, in all conversion schemes presently in use throughout the world, pronounceability and traditionality take precedence over all other requirements if a clash occurs, even though both are based on the shaky foundation of ever-changing pronunciation, and its cumbersome and often impossible approximation by graphic representation, rather than on the much firmer principle of conversion of graphemes in the source script, which are immutable once they are written or printed in a document.

Long-standing traditions also play a decisive role in the retention of entire conversion schemes in libraries, even when a demonstrably better scheme is available or when a switch to another system would ensure more uniformity on the national as well as on the international level. The reverence for long-standing traditions and the subsequent reluctance to change familiar habits and working methods are here reinforced by the harsh demands of economics. Large libraries with millions of catalog entries find it impossible to change to another system of script conversion because of the staggering costs of retroactively changing the existing entries. This is precisely what happened in the Library of Congress when it was suggested that, in the interests of compatibility and international standardization, the adoption of the transliteration system for Cyrillic devised by the British Standards Association should be considered. To do so would have involved only a small number of changes in the tables, but

After lengthy study, and despite its recognition of the advantages of such a plan, the Library of Congress regretfully concluded in 1960 that the changes in its system essential for such agreement would force it to make very extensive changes in its catalogs at a cost quite beyond its means.[52]

The same line of reasoning is followed, no doubt, by many other large libraries, especially those that rely on the Library of Congress for the cataloging of non-Roman script documents. Only relatively few libraries have found it possible to change their systems for conversion of scripts entirely or even partially, and most of them have had to resort to the radical expedient of closing their old catalogs and starting new ones.

Serially published bibliographies and abstracting and indexing services should theoretically find it easier to switch to conversion systems that ensure greater compatibility between them, since they are not tied to any existing collection of documents and do not have to change any entries retroactively. Still, even these bibliographic tools must consider the lack of continuity in their annual indexes, which might be frustrating to the users on whose support they largely depend. It is a fact that most current bibliographies and abstracting and indexing services tend to stay with a conversion system to which they have committed themselves.

6.7   Conversion Practices of the World's Libraries

Tradition and economic necessity thus combine to perpetuate a chaotic situation in which not even the large libraries of one country or language community can agree on one transliteration or transcription scheme for any of the major scripts. Much less is there compatibility on the international level. The extent of this lack of uniformity and compatibility has been documented in a worldwide survey of libraries having substantial holdings of documents in a dissimilar script.[53]

The survey gathered data from 32 national libraries, 74 university libraries, 15 public libraries, and 25 special libraries, of which 9 are in Africa, 25 in America, 40 in Asia, 66 in Europe, 2 in Oceania, and 4 in the USSR. The reader can find full details in the source document, and we only summarize the most important findings. Table 5.4 shows the most widely used Romanization schemes for the eight most important non-Roman scripts. In this tabulation the Hepburn scheme for Japanese, the Wade-Giles scheme for Chinese, and the McCune-Reischauer scheme for Korean have been equated with the Library of Congress schemes, because the responses indicated that most libraries apply these Romanization schemes as practiced by the Library of Congress. The LC schemes, of course, predominate primarily because practically all North American libraries use

[52] Orne (1963), p. 4158.
[53] Wellisch (1976).

Table 5.4   The Most Widely Used Romanization Schemes

	Romanization schemes used					
Script	1st rank	Percent of all libraries	2nd rank	Percent of all libraries	3rd rank	Percent of all libraries
Cyrillic	LC	37	ISO	31	PI	14
Japanese	H (=LC)	91	Own	1		
Devanagari	LC	43	Own	23	Other	16
Arabic	LC	38	Own	17	ISO	16
Chinese	W-G (=LC)	83	Own	10	Pinyin	6
Korean	M-R (=LC)	82	Own	9	Other	9
Greek	LC	45	Own	19	ISO	18
Hebrew	LC	40	PI	19	Own	18
Other	LC	*	Own	*		

* = less than 1%.
H = Hepburn scheme.
ISO = International Organization for Standardization scheme.
LC = Library of Congress scheme.
M-R = McCune-Reischauer scheme.
PI = Preussische Instruktionen.
W-G = Wade-Giles scheme.
Own = a library's own (locally devised) scheme.

them. But even though LC schemes are also used to a certain extent in other countries (where they are often used in conjunction with locally devised "adaptations," thus obviating uniformity and compatibility), its overall rate of application to non-Roman scripts (except the logographic ones) hovers around 40% only. In other words, no one Romanization scheme for alphabetic non-Roman scripts is used by a clear majority of the world's libraries with large collections of documents in non-Roman scripts. If we consider also the Romanization practices of abstracting and indexing services, which form a huge segment of universal bibliographic control tools, there is even less uniformity, since it is known that these services do not use LC schemes to any extent, and most of them prefer to employ their own schemes.[54]

[54]Wellisch (1972), pp. 77–78.

Locally devised schemes are the second most widely used ones in libraries for all non-Roman scripts except Cyrillic (and for Hebrew they almost equal the use of PI, whose second place position for this script is due to the extensive Judaica holdings of European libraries). This is perhaps one of the most significant and disturbing results of the survey, because it means that, at least for alphabetic non-Roman scripts, about 20% of all libraries employ Romanization schemes that are, by definition, incompatible with those used in any other library or bibliographic tool. These homegrown schemes are often not made available even to readers of the respective libraries, who are literally left to guess at the original spelling of a Romanized name, or under which letter to look for a converted form of a name whose spelling in the source script they know. Here, indeed, Romanization generates "confusion worse confounded."

The survey also elicited data about the extent to which libraries have fully or partially Romanized catalogs. Table 5.5 shows that more than two thirds of all libraries Romanize all scripts, and more than 80% have at least partially Romanized catalogs. Less than 20% maintain separate catalogs for each script (most of the latter are Asian libraries which serve bi- or multilanguage, multi-script communities, which would obviously not benefit from any kind of Romanization). Table 5.6 provides a breakdown of libraries with separate catalogs by script and/or language, and Table 5.7 shows the extent to which bi- or multilingual communities are served by either Romanized or separate script catalogs.

The comments made by librarians who responded to the survey show that many of them are fully aware of the difficulties and pitfalls besetting Romanization. Most respondents complained about the proliferation of schemes and their inconsistent use. A typical response is the following:

Table 5.5   Romanized Catalogs versus Separate Catalogs by Script

Kind of catalog	National libraries	University libraries	Public libraries	Special libraries	Total number	Percent of all libraries ($N = 146$)
All scripts Romanized	20	53	8	17	98	67.1
Romanized Cyrillic and/or Greek but separate catalogs for other scripts	2	13	—	5	20	13.7
Separate catalogs for each script	10	8	7	3	28	19.2
Total	32	74	15	25	146	100.0

Table 5.6 Separate Catalogs by Script and/or Language

Script or language	National libraries Original script	National libraries Roman-ized	University libraries Original script	University libraries Roman-ized	Public libraries Original script	Public libraries Roman-ized	Special libraries Original script	Special libraries Roman-ized	Total number of separate catalogs Original script	Total number of separate catalogs Roman-ized	All libraries Number	All libraries Percent Original script	All libraries Percent Romanized
Cyrillic	2	1	3	3	1	1	—	—	6	5	90	7	6
Japanese	4	5	8	10	1	—	2	5	15	20	56	27	36
Chinese	4	6	4	9	1	—	2	7	11	22	69	16	32
Devanagari	4	3	4	5	—	—	1	3	9	11	44	21	25
Arabic	3	2	8	7	3	—	2	4	16	13	76	21	17
Persian	—	1	4	1	—	—	2	1	6	3			
Pushto	—	1	2	—	—	—	—	1	2	2			
Turkish	—	1	—	1	—	—	—	—	—	2			
Urdu	—	1	4	1	—	—	—	2	4	4			
Other	—	2	1	—	—	—	—	2	1	4			
Korean	3	5	2	5	1	—	1	2	7	12	45	16	27
Greek	—	—	1	—	—	1	1	1	2	1	66	3	2
Hebrew	4	3	6	5	1	1	—	2	11	11	67	16	16
Yiddish	2	—	2	—	1	—	—	—	5	—			

Note. Scripts are listed in order of book production (see Table 4.5); languages are listed alphabetically under each script.

Table 5.7 Catalogs in Libraries Serving Bi- or Multilingual Communities

Kind of catalog	National libraries	University libraries	Public libraries	Special libraries	Total number	Percent of all libraries (N = 47)
Romanized author/title headings	5	4	3	1	13	28
Separate catalogs by script or language	3	14	8	9	34	72
Total	8	18	11	10	47	100

Presence of ligatures for the same letter in one language, absence in another, e.g. Russian *zh* vs. Ukrainian *z̑h* . . . It seems that ligatures are not all that important, and should be abolished.

The LC practice of *not* using its own Romanization system for many geographic names, but using instead the form adopted by the Board on Geographic Names, or usage in the Columbia-Lippincott Gazetteer.

These remarks come from a large American university library. Another American university librarian complains, "East Asian languages: identical Romanization of same characters with different meanings." The respondent is apparently not aware that Chinese and Japanese can only be transcribed and not transliterated, so that a large number of homographs is unavoidable.

From Japan comes the comment, "There exist two systems of Romanization of the Japanese language . . . to the great puzzlement especially of foreigners."

One of the largest British libraries freely admits:

We are somewhat haphazard in transliterating the more exotic scripts and if we go to an outside expert . . . we do not necessarily enquire what standards he is adopting.

One wonders how the readers of this library are ever able to figure out which Romanization schemes have been used for one of the "exotic" scripts.

Finally, a Vietnamese special library that Romanizes Chinese and Japanese by Vietnamese orthography but does not Romanize other scripts succinctly address- es the problem of proliferating schemes:

Even if we would like to use an international transcription to accompany ours, we do not know which transcription to adopt, and we lack competent cataloger for the matter.

Several comments were made on the problems caused by the Romanization of Arabic, Hebrew, Japanese, Indonesian, and other names that are either rendered in widely different forms or are unintelligible when written in a Romanization or Cyrillization not accompanied by the original spelling. A British librarian says:

For Near Eastern and Indian names, the main problems are caused by the inconsistent forms used by authors, particularly when writing in different languages. It can easily happen that the same author will appear both in Arabic script and in a modified form of Cyrillic, and application of the standard transliteration schemes will result in two quite different forms of the name.

Regarding the Romanization of Hebrew names, the following comment points out some of the difficulties:

LC transliterates [Hebrew] family names according to transliteration tables only when author's preferred form is not known. As a result, two authors with the identical Hebrew family name may be transliterated differently (e.g., Carmi and Karmi), and this is a source of confusion to readers.

Several librarians who perform Romanization have come to the conclusion that the practice is either not very helpful to users or even counterproductive. The following comments speak for themselves:

For those who are versed in a language, e.g. Russian, cards written in Roman alphabet are rather inconvenient and difficult to use. (From a Japanese university library.)

[Romanization is] not appreciated by users who know the transliterated language. (From the library of an international agency serving a multilingual readership.)

Transliteration or transcription of non-Roman languages is rather complicated for the readers who can understand original materials. So it is desirable to be in original character in case of remarkable amount of volumes. (From a Japanese university library.)

Romanization is of questionable value in some languages such as Chinese. (From one of the oldest and most prestigious American university libraries with a large collection of Chinese material.)

We have the problem of acquainting users of the catalog with the transliteration scheme used. We are currently considering having an information leaflet specifically on transliteration schemes, and in addition putting explanatory cards in the card catalog. The problem with the latter is having the user find the cards: where should these be filed? Under "Russian language," for example, or "Russian language—Romanization," or where? (From another American university library.)

Russian and East Asian languages: searching problems due to existence of variant transliteration schemes. (From an American university library.)

The results of this survey confirm that there is indeed much diversity of

Romanization practices which inevitably leads to incompatibility of entries in catalogs and bibliographies. Only in the United States and Canada is there a large measure of uniformity because of the almost complete adoption of LC Romanization, and a similar but not quite as homogeneous situation prevails in Germany. In both instances uniformity is more easily achieved when a practically monolingual population is served. Characteristically, one of the few comments on problems encountered by a library on the American continent comes from a large Canadian library deploring the lack of transliteration schemes suitable for Francophones. The widely divergent practices of European libraries (other than the German ones) have their root as much in the phenomenon of having to serve readers speaking different languages as in the traditions on which their practice is based, and the sometimes staggering costs that would be involved in switching from one scheme to another for the sake of greater uniformity.

Not only do different libraries, even in the same country, use different Romanization schemes, but older university libraries in particular tend to use several Romanization schemes from various sources, often depending on which scheme had been published when Romanization was first practiced. Thus it is not unusual to find five or six different schemes being used for as many scripts, some of the schemes being the library's own invention, and others being adaptations of published schemes, with ensuing proliferation of local idiosyncrasies in the rendering of names and titles. One British university library reported even that various Romanization schemes were used for the same script in its different sectional libraries for the faculties of theology, law, medicine, and so forth!

A constantly recurring theme in comments is the difficulty experienced by many libraries in finding language experts to perform Romanization. Such difficulties are by no means encountered only by smaller libraries in less developed countries, as one might think. Even national libraries in highly developed industrial countries are struggling with the same problems, and their cataloging and Romanization backlogs will probably grow larger with the steadily increasing amount of literature in non-Roman scripts that is acquired by these libraries.

In the light of the evidence from this survey, which shows that script conversion in libraries, and in particular Romanization, leads to widely divergent results and incompatibility of bibliographic citations, the question necessarily arises whether the practice as performed by the majority of libraries throughout the world is indeed suitable as a control tool, or whether the goals of librarians and bibliographers on the one hand, and those of library users on the other hand would perhaps be better and more effectively served by other means. In the following chapter we analyze this question through the application of systems theory and the principles of cybernetics.

Table 5.8 Requirements for Schemes of Script Conversion for Various Fields of Application

Field of application	Systemic — General applicability	Systemic — Graphemic representation: Uniqueness	Systemic — Graphemic representation: Simplicity	Functional — Economy of space	Functional — Pronounceability	Functional — Reversibility	Functional — Traditionality
General	●	●	●		●	●	●
Philology	●	●	○		●	○	○
Geography	●		○	○	●		●
Bibliography				○	○	●	●

● Indispensable or strong requirement.
○ Optional or less important requirement.

7 SUMMARY

Our analysis of the operational requirements for schemes of script conversion in different fields of application has shown that these requirements are different for various fields and that the same requirement is given different weight in each field. Table 5.8 summarizes these findings in schematic (and necessarily oversimplified) form.

All schemes of script conversion are thus inevitably the result of compromises made by their designers between various and often mutually exclusive requirements, as has been demonstrated in detail for bibliographic applications. No scheme is entirely free from certain deficiencies which its designers and certain users (presumed by the designers to be in the majority) may consider minor while other users may consider them major flaws. This in turn often leads to the design of a new scheme which is promptly declared to be "better" or even "more scientific", even though the difference may sometimes lie only in the application of certain diacritical marks. As we have seen, there is no single "scientifically sound" or "correct" scheme even within one single field of application, much less are there such schemes that can be applied to more than one field without jeopardizing some or all of the requirements deemed important by the practitioners of certain disciplines. What is sound practice in philology and linguistics cannot always serve the purposes of bibliographic control, nor can schemes designed for cartography be used by philologists, and so on.

Six

Script Conversion in Bibliographic Control Systems

The moral is not to abandon useful tools; rather, it is, first, that one should maintain enough perspective to be able to detect the arrival of that inevitable day when the research that can be conducted with these tools is no longer important; and, second, that one should value ideas and insights that are to the point, though perhaps premature and vague and not productive of research at a particular stage of technique and understanding.

N. Chomsky. *Language and mind.* pp. 18–19.

1 ANALYSIS OF BIBLIOGRAPHIC CONTROL SYSTEMS

The difficulties and problems involved in the use of script conversion investigated in the preceding two chapters have often been deplored by librarians and bibliographers as well as by users of bibliographic control tools. But most writers on the subject came to the almost axiomatic conclusion that despite all inherent problems the method was still the only one by which effective control could be exercised over documents written in various scripts, in order to list them in bibliographies and catalogs and thus make them available to prospective users.

We now take a critical look at the axiom that script conversion acts as a regulating factor in bibliographic control, and try to determine whether it is actually capable of playing this role effectively. To do this in an objective and scientifically valid manner, we shall consider script conversion as one of the components in a system that is needed to keep the system in a viable state.

A system has been defined as "any entity, conceptual or physical, which consists of interdependent parts''[1] and more specifically as ''a set of components that work together for the overall objective of the whole.''[2] To analyze a system, it is necessary to examine its objectives, its environment (or constraints), its resources, its components and how they work toward the achievement of the objectives, and finally the management of the system.[3] In the following sections we consider the system known as a bibliographic control system (as defined in Definition 19), and focus our attention on the component of script conversion, especially in its form of Romanization. Thereafter we investigate the control functions of the system through the methods of cybernetics, the study of control in systems. Our examples are mainly taken from libraries and their catalogs because the problems involved are easiest to demonstrate in the case of this particular bibliographic control system, but it should be borne in mind that what is said of catalogs pertains also to other bibliographic control tools such as bibliographies, abstracting and indexing services, citation indexes, and certain reference books.

1.1 Objectives of a Bibliographic Control System

The objectives of a bibliographic control system were first explicitly stated in 1876 by the American librarian Charles Ammi Cutter who, in his *Rules for a Dictionary Catalog,* formulated them as follows:

1. To enable a person to find a book of which *(a)* the author, *(b)* the title, or *(c)* the subject is known;
2. To show what the library has *(d)* by a given author, *(e)* on a given subject, or *(f)* in a given literature.[4]

For our purposes, and enlarging Cutter's ''books'' to the more general ''documents,'' these objectives can be paraphrased and summarized as ''providing access to documents''; the system thus performs a *service* function for *users*.

In order to provide service and achieve the stated objectives, the system must be run and controlled by *operators*. These are persons who at various points in the system regulate it by using certain control tools. The term ''operators'' should be understood in its broadest sense as anybody who works inside the system as a cataloger, reference librarian, filer, stack attendant, and so forth. The goal of operators is to produce document surrogates and to display them in an

---

[1] Ackoff (1960), p. 2.
[2] Churchman (1968), p. 11.
[3] Ibid., pp. 29–30.
[4] Cutter (1904), p. 12. The rules were originally published in 1876. Cutter stated a third requirement regarding descriptive data as an aid to choice of edition and ''character'' of a book, but this is not relevant to our topic.

arrangement that follows a known and therefore predictable order, so as to exercise control over them, that is to say, to be able to identify a certain document on demand and to locate it if it is held in the system. The demand on the part of a user may be for any one of the six criteria enumerated by Cutter, or for any combination of them, but traditionally the approach to a document by the author's name has been considered the most important one. Consequently the operators are particularly concerned to fulfill Cutter's aim *(d)*, "to show what the library has by a given author," and to do so in such a manner that the smooth running of the system is not disturbed by documents that by their very nature do not fit into the predetermined framework. As we see later, every new document that is added to the collection constitutes a disturbance of the system, but not all documents create the same amount of disturbance, and most of them can be handled by certain well-established control methods. Documents that deviate most in their physical makeup from the majority of documents normally handled by the system create the most serious problems, but these too must ultimately be subjected to certain control methods, because otherwise they would become unmanageable and would have to be rejected by the system.

1.2   Bibliographic Control of Dissimilar Scripts

Documents handled by bibliographic control systems exhibit a bewildering variety of different features, most of which have to be subjected to regulating routines so that control can be achieved. Thus cataloging rules are explicitly aimed at creating order out of the chaos of authors' various and changing names, pseudonyms, anonymous writings, different titles for the same work, the same title for different works, and a whole host of other features of protean character that the rules try to reduce to order and known sequence. We are not concerned here with the details of these control measures other than noting that they form part of the regulatory processes in a bibliographic control system. We also ignore the control of the most variegated characteristic of documents, which at the same time is the most difficult one to cope with, namely their subject content, or Cutter's objectives *(c)* and *(e),* since it has no direct bearing on the control processes involved in the conversion of scripts.

The application of cataloging rules results in the production of a document surrogate which must, according to accepted bibliothecal practice, display a principal retrieval tag for that document, known in bibliographic terminology as the *main entry*.[5] Ideally this is the name of an author or, in the absence of a

---

[5] The validity of the main entry principle has been challenged by several authors, foremost among whom is M. N. Hamdi (1973), who proposed a restructuring of library catalogs according to title entry as the principal retrieval tag, which would eliminate most of the ambiguities and illogical features of main entry by author (including the problems generated by the conversion of names from one script to another, although Hamdi does not deal with this aspect).

known author, the title of a work, recorded exactly as it is given on the title page of a book or its equivalent in other documents. The name of the author and/or the title as given on the document surrogate must match those in the actual document in order to achieve bibliographic control, that is, to ascertain whether a document exists, and if so, to retrieve it on demand. (Other characteristics of the document such as edition, imprint, size, and so forth, are also needed for unambiguous identification and retrieval, but since these characteristics are not appreciably affected by script conversion, we can disregard them for the purposes of the following discussion.) Certain conditions often make it necessary to record the name of an author on a document surrogate in a form that is slightly or even substantially different from the one given on the title page of the actual document. Yet, somehow or other, a bibliographic control system must always refer to the form of a name or a title as given on the title page; if the main entry is recorded in a different form, cross references must be made from any other forms found in actual documents. If such references are lacking, the system cannot exercise full control because the original documents cannot be matched with their surrogates, and vice versa.

All this pertains to documents (and their surrogates) written in the dominant script of the documentary communication system. Additional problems inevitably arise when the input to that system also includes documents in dissimilar scripts.

In the specific context of bibliographic control, the dominant script is the one in which the majority of the documents handled by a bibliographic control system is written, in which all or most of the document surrogates are written, and which is primarily used in document storage and retrieval operations, such as assignment of subject headings, descriptors, and index entries; written formulation of requests; search of files; and written presentation of results.

While a document surrogate for a document in the dominant script is naturally also written in that script, a bibliographic surrogate for a document written in a dissimilar script can be produced by three different methods:

a. The document surrogate can be written throughout in the dissimilar script; this implies automatically that the document surrogates must be filed in as many separate author-title sequences as there are different scripts covered by a library catalog.

If this method is not feasible or desirable, either one of the following methods may be employed:

b. The document surrogate can contain the main retrieval tag (author's name or title of the work) in converted form, displaying all other bibliographic data in the dissimilar source script;

c. The document surrogate can be converted in its entirety to the dominant script; that is, not only the main retrieval tag but also all other bibliographic data are transcribed, and the dissimilar source script is not used at all.

Figure 6.1 illustrates the three methods as applied to a Russian book.

Method (*a*) results in an (ideally) isomorphic representation of the title page of an actual document, which allows the matching operation to be performed in the same manner as for documents in the dominant script. It therefore involves a minimal loss of information on the part of the user of the document who knows its language and script, but involves total loss of information on the document for anybody else, including the operators of the system (unless they too know the dissimilar script).

Method (*b*) results mostly in a distortion of isomorphic representation of the actual document, in which the main retrieval tag has no longer a one-to-one relationship to the relevant data on the title page, but is intelligible (and therefore controllable) to the operators of the system, though it may not be so to the users. All other data recorded on the document surrogate are again immediately accessible to the users but not to the operators. This method results in a partial loss of information for both sides; it favors, however, in most cases the goals of the operators over those of the users, who are no longer able to perform the matching operation directly but must use a conversion process. It also involves the operators in greater complexity when producing the document surrogate because of the need to print or write in two different scripts.

Method (*c*) also results in a distorted representation of the source document, with roughly the same intelligibility to the operators, but almost total loss of information to the users, since no part of the original data remains unchanged, and the matching process becomes extremely cumbersome and in many cases even impossible to perform. The completely transcribed document surrogate is, however, relatively easy to produce, which is an additional advantage from the point of view of the operators. (It should be noted that the services of a person knowledgeable in the language and script of the dissimilar source documents are needed for all three methods, and this constitutes therefore a fixed cost factor. The costs of producing the three different types of document surrogates varies only with the printing or display processes used.)

A survey of script conversion practices in the world's leading libraries with large collections of documents in dissimilar scripts, cited in Section 6.7 of the preceding chapter, showed clearly that methods (*b*) and (*c*) are the most widely used ones in those libraries that apply the control method of script conversion to documents in dissimilar scripts, and that this conversion is practically always made to the Roman script. In the following sections we therefore use the specific term ''Romanization'' instead of the more general one ''conversion of scripts,''

Городковъ, Н.
    Типографія Тобольскаго епархіальнаго братства.
ₗН. Городковъⱼ. Тобольскъ, Тип. Епархіальнаго братства, 1895.

(*a*)

Gorodkov, N
    Типографія Тобольскаго епархіальнаго братства.
ₗН. Городковъⱼ. Тобольскъ, Тип. Епархіальнаго братства, 1895.

(*b*)

```
Gorodkov, N
  Tipografīīa Tobol'skago eparkhīal'nago bratstva.
Tobol'sk, Tip. Eparkhīalnago bratstva, 1895.
```

(*c*)

Figure 6.1. Three possible forms of a document surrogate for a document in dissimilar script. (*a*) Document surrogate entirely in dissimilar script; (*b*) document surrogate with heading only in dominant script; (*c*) document surrogate entirely in dominant script.

because only the Roman script has been used as a means of bibliographic control over documents in non-Roman scripts on a large scale and exhaustively; that is, subjecting virtually *all* non-Roman scripts to Romanization. Although Cyrillization is employed to a certain extent in modern Russian bibliographic tools to list non-Cyrillic documents, it has never been used in the comprehensive manner in which Romanization dominates Western bibliographic practice.

    As to other scripts, most nations that use one of them have only recently begun to develop modern bibliographic control tools for their own literature or for the listing of translations of foreign works into their language.[6] Their librarians are generally not concerned with the transcription of bibliographic entries for works in Roman or Cyrillic script into, say, Arabic or Japanese script; in most instances they prefer to list such works separately according to the script in which they are written. Consequently Arabization or Japanization (or any other conversion *into* another non-Roman script) does not play a large role in the bibliographic control tools of the nations that do not use the Roman script. Rather, such script conversions are used in the field of "general" applications, namely for the transcription of foreign names and words in newspapers, periodicals, and books written in the vernacular, in cartography for the production of maps and atlases intended for the local population only, or for instruction in elementary schools to age groups that have not yet been taught the Roman script.

1.3   The Effectiveness of Romanization for Operators

As we have already seen in Chapters 3 and 5, the operators of most Western bibliographic control systems have tried to rationalize a largely misguided or misunderstood policy by claiming to use "scientific" methods, and by stressing the need for the exércise of control over documents in dissimilar scripts by people who do *not* know any foreign languages or scripts (clerical personnel in the ordering and acquisition departments, those who deal with interlibrary loan requests, and filers of catalog cards). We now examine whether Romanization actually constitutes an effective and efficient method for the performance of the first operation of a bibliographic control system, namely the production of document surrogates in a standardized and uniform format.

1.3.1   Romanization of Document Surrogates.   To achieve bibliographic control over documents in dissimilar scripts to the same degree and by the application of the same procedures used for documents in the dominant Roman script, three conditions must be fulfilled:

1. The Romanized form of an author's name or a title must be standardized;
2. The Romanized form must be unambiguously reversible, so as to allow a matching with the actual document, in order to assure that the document surrogate actually refers to that particular document; and
3. The place of Romanized document surrogates in an alphabetically arranged sequence must be uniquely predictable.

[6]These are listed in a series of international surveys, *Bibliographical services throughout the world,* published quinquennially since 1952 by UNESCO, and currently updated by bimonthly reports in the periodical *Bibliography, Documentation, and Terminology,* also issued by UNESCO.

However several factors make it difficult or even impossible to fulfill these conditions, particularly 1 and 3; as to condition 2, we have already shown in Chapter 5 that it is only partially attainable.

1.3.1.1 MULTIPLICITY OF SCHEMES. More than one Romanization system exists for each of the major non-Roman scripts, and most or all of them are used simultaneously by different libraries and bibliographic services. This means that, even when a certain Romanization scheme is applied consistently and uniformly (which is almost never the case), it allows only a very limited control, namely within the confines of the particular library catalog or bibliography that contains the Romanized entries, but not beyond. Other libraries and bibliographies may (and do) use other systems, not to speak of other sources and agents of bibliographic information such as publishers, booksellers, jobbers, and individual authors who design their own systems.

This problem has often been discussed by librarians, particularly with regard to Cyrillic script. Robert Gakovich, an American cataloger of Slavic languages, said:

> . . . a number of different transliteration systems are used throughout the world by various countries' libraries, institutions, book-dealers, etc. This especially becomes difficult in bibliographic searching. . . . Every time we give bibliographic searching to an entry . . . we have to keep in mind the various systems of transliteration. The same is true when we do our bibliographical searching in other national bibliographies, book catalogs, encyclopedias, etc. such as the British Museum Catalog, New York Public Library Catalog, and *Encyclopedia Britannica*. In this case, the searcher must be familiar with at least the major transliteration systems.[7]

The German librarian E. Richter, an authority on Cyrillic script and its transliteration, compiled a *Vergleichende Transkriptionstabelle*[8] as an aid to bibliographical searches in the large international bibliographical tools *Berliner Titeldrucke, Deutscher Gesamtkatalog,* and the catalogs of the Bibliothèque nationale in Paris, the British Museum, the Library of Congress, and the Kungliga biblioteket in Stockholm, in which, as we have seen in Chapter 4, the Russian name Юшкезич is found in four different alphabetical locations. Other examples are cited in E. P. Shaw's paper ''Transliteration—a game for the library sleuth,''[9] in which she traces the metamorphoses of the name of the Russian neurologist Владимир М. Вехтерев: His name is listed in *Index Medicus* (and in the bibliographical predecessors of this index journal) in no less than five forms (Bechtereff, Bechterev, Bechterew, Bekhtereff, Bekhterev) or in more than 20 if the variations in the rendering of his initials and the presence or

---

[7] Gakovich (1962), pp. 7–8.
[8] Richter (1955).
[9] Shaw, E. P. (1949), pp. 143–144.

absence of the preposition *von* are counted! In this case at least the "library sleuth" can always find the name under the same initial letter.

1.3.1.2   VARIANT FORMS OF PERSONAL NAMES.   The difficulties caused in the rendering of personal names by various Romanization schemes are compounded by the fact that many non-European names cannot be reduced to standardized forms in the Western style, which raises the question not only of which Romanization scheme to use but first of all which form of name to Romanize. The inherent futility of Western attempts to cast the names of Asian and African authors in the mold of European names by means of elaborate cataloging rules originally designed only for Western names was pointed out by the Indian librarian S. R. Ranganathan, who knew more about the problem than any Western librarian:

It is doubtful whether a cataloguer, who is not intimately familiar with the social practices connected with the formation of a Name-of-Person in a cultural group, can successfully and consistently pick out the Entry Element and the Secondary Element respectively. The individual variations—one may almost say idiosyncrasies—in making up one's own name may baffle even a cataloguer born in the same cultural group. . . . The greater the deviation of the cultural group of the cataloguer from that of a Name-of-Person, the greater will be the uncertainty. . . .

The impracticability of any one cultural group to render the Names-of-Persons of all other cultural groups will lead to inefficiency of service. Ultimately, such an inefficiency of service will be traceable to the insolubility of the problem of Name-of-Person by cataloging rules, however involved and however clever. Solution of the problem of rendering Names-of-Persons on a world-scale through a number of cataloguing rules is only an illusion.[10]

Most non-European names must be Romanized phonologically, which demands a knowledge of the "correct" pronunciation; added to this are widely varying onomastic customs which make it difficult and sometimes impossible to ascertain what constitutes a "name" for the purposes of cataloging. This is the case for many Arabic,[11] Bengali,[12] Urdu,[13] Persian,[14] and Hebrew[15] names, to name only a few for which Romanization is particularly cumbersome and often ambiguous. Romanization becomes an exercise in futility for Japanese names, since it depends on certain modes of "reading" the *kanji* characters, and intimate personal knowledge is often needed to render them in the form by which its

[10]Ranganathan (1964), pp. 226–227.
[11]Sheniti (1961).
[12]Huq (1970).
[13]Dogra (1973).
[14]Sharify (1959).
[15]Edelmann (1963).

bearer was known or as he wishes it to be pronounced.[16] The Romanization of Japanese titles poses further difficulties because even native Japanese readers cannot always agree on word division, which may result in quite different Romanizations and translations.

When one considers this chaotic situation to which the multiple Romanization systems add still more complexity, it is difficult to understand why so many authors who write on the problems of script conversion in libraries deplored the "popular" transcriptions of, say Пушкин, in various languages which result in the forms Pushkin, Pouchkine, Puschkin, Pusckin, Puszkin, Puskin, Puşkin, Poesjkin, Pusjkin, Puškin, and so on. They inevitably came to the conclusion that such terrible confusion could not be tolerated in libraries, which would have to employ "scientific" transliteration methods. As shown by the preceding examples (which are by no means isolated instances but represent the rule rather than the exceptions), the purportedly scientific bibliographic transcriptions do not appreciably differ from those arrived at by "popular" methods, either in their construction or in the variety of forms they exhibit. It seems to be rather a matter of taste whether one prefers the "scientifically" created confusion and ambiguity over the "popular" variety. Naturally the remedy prescribed is almost always adherence to a single system (preferably the one used in the author's own library, all others being considered either "unscientific" or otherwise unsuitable), although at least one librarian, J. T. Shaw,[17] recommended the simultaneous use of no less than four systems of transliteration for Cyrillic, for different kinds of documents and classes of users—this in the interest of greater uniformity and scientific accuracy! *Difficile est satiram non scribere.*

1.3.1.3 INCONSISTENT APPLICATION OF ROMANIZATION SCHEMES. Despite all well-meant efforts to persuade libraries and bibliographic services to employ a single Romanization system for a particular script, they are unlikely to change or abandon the various systems they use—for sociolinguistic reasons as well as for financial, administrative, and prestige-related reasons. In many instances, even within the same library or bibliographic service, more than one Romanization system is used for the same script, depending on such factors as source language, the period in which a document was created, or the kind of document. In large, old collections different Romanization methods for the same script have sometimes been employed during various periods, with the result that the same author or title is Romanized differently depending on the time when the document was processed. Decisions on which Romanization schemes to use for a particular language or script are not based on clear and unambiguous rules but on personal judgments made by catalogers or language experts—a procedure that defies any attempt at standardization and unification, and is entirely unpredictable for users

---

[16]O'Neill (1972).
[17]Shaw, J. T. (1967).

of the system. Even when a specific Romanization scheme has been adopted for the conversion of a certain script, it is often not applied consistently if the requirements of traditionality or pronounceability are deemed to be more important.

An additional element of inconsistency is often introduced by a fairly high degree of uniformity in the rendering of foreign names and words in the annual indexes of newspapers, magazines, and journals of a general nature, at least within one country or language community. Such indexes are in themselves important bibliographic tools which are frequently consulted by the "general" user, but libraries that keep these indexes in their reference rooms almost always offer in their catalogs a Romanization that is substantially at variance with the one found in general indexes.

1.3.1.4 LOCAL ADAPTATIONS.   Even when a library follows a published Romanization scheme for a certain script, local "adaptations" are often made for various reasons. Since these are normally not publicized and are applied only within a particular library (and even there not always consistently), a bibliographical search for a transcribed name or title is made still more difficult, and control (except by the local cataloger or reference librarian) becomes illusory.

1.3.1.5 INADEQUATE REVERSIBILITY.   Even when unique and unambiguous reversibility is theoretically possible to achieve, as in the Romanization of Greek or Cyrillic script, it is in practice sacrificed for pronounceability or traditionality. For all other scripts, particularly the logographic ones, it is not possible to achieve at all, as shown in Chapter 5.

1.3.1.6 PRONENESS TO ERRORS.   Even a well-trained Romanizer who is familiar with the source language and its script and writing system occasionally makes factual mistakes; that is, he may transcribe a character in the source script by an inappropriate Roman letter, or he may inadvertently skip a letter or add one where none is needed (this happens not infrequently in transcription of Arabic and Hebrew script where vowels have to be Romanized which are not expressed in the original). Such mistakes are further compounded by errors in typing, keypunching, and printing, which inevitably occur as they do in any kind of writing. However such mistakes and errors are bound to appear with much greater frequency in the spelling of Romanized words or names that have a "quaint" (i.e., unfamiliar) look, both to a reader who knows the source language (and who is not used to see its words in Romanized garb) and to a reader of the target language (to whom Romanized words do not mean anything since he does not know the source language). The reasons for the higher frequency of errors and mistakes are threefold. Firstly, a writer is apt to make more mistakes when writing an unfamiliar and "complicated" word than in writing familiar words. Secondly, transcribed words cannot be verified as to their correct spelling in any dictionary. Thirdly, a writer who makes a mistake in spelling is much less likely to detect it when he proofreads the text himself, but in the case of a transcriber of a dissimilar script, he himself may often be the only one able to check his own work for accuracy. This results in oversights of errors another proofreader might have detected.

When matching of document surrogates with the actual documents or with references to them is done visually and by human beings, an obvious error may be spotted and compensated for by a knowledge of the source language on the part of the reader. However, if the matching process is performed by someone who does not know the source language, or if it is done by a machine, even the slightest error results in a mismatch and in attendant complete loss of information.

1.3.2 Romanization in Alphabetization. We now consider the second purpose of a bibliographic control system, namely the arrangement of document surrogates in a unique and predictable sequence, in other words, the alphabetical filing of entries, as it is affected by Romanization.

1.3.2.1 ALPHABETIZATION OF ENTRIES ORIGINALLY IN ROMAN SCRIPT. The amalgamation of names and words in different languages written in the Roman script into one unbroken alphabetical sequence has been an accepted practice ever since bibliographical lists and indexes were compiled. In the late 15th and early 16th centuries this did not cause any difficulties, since relatively few vernaculars had attained the level of written communication, and fewer still were transliterated. Also, because of the dominant position of the Latin language, whose orthography did not use any diacritical marks, these were as yet little used in the writing systems of European vernaculars and were not employed in the transliteration of Greek and Hebrew (the two scripts most often converted into Roman). Therefore practically all names and words could be interfiled in one alphabet without difficulty, because only the basic forms of Roman letters were used. When, however, letters were modified by diacritical marks to express the phonemes of various languages for which the basic Roman letters alone were not sufficient, the question of alphabetizing the modified letters arose. This problem was solved in various ways in the writing systems of various languages. English did not have to cope with diacritical marks at all, so it seemed only natural to disregard them also when they appeared in foreign words, and to alphabetize them "as if" they were only basic letters. The French, although they use a number of diacritical marks on vowels and consonants, decided to follow the same principle. The Germans could never agree among themselves whether to file the umlauts *ä, ö,* and *ü* as basic vowel letters or "as if" written *ae, oe,* and *ue* (this, in turn, led in due course to two different filing methods for umlauts in Anglo-American bibliothecal practice also). The Swedes decided to file their modified letter *å* and the umlauts *ä* and *ö* at the end of the alphabet as separate letters, thus entirely separating the basic letter *a* from its modifications by 25 intervening letters, and so on. Alphabetical filing therefore actually involves an artificial amalgamation of as many alphabets as there are languages written in Roman script, where the differences between these individual alphabets are disregarded in the interests of creating one unified sequence in which the place of each entry is unique and therefore predictable. Once the spelling of a name or a word in its authorized form is known, it can (at least in theory) occupy one and only one place in the file, and this place is predetermined by the position of individual letters in the word and by the place of that letter in the basic Roman alphabet. The alphabetical interfiling of names and words in different languages and orthographies is made possible by two facts. First, no matter how many different Roman alphabets are amalgamated, they all belong to the actual writing systems of natural languages. Secondly, the authorized spelling of the names or words can be verified by using dictionaries and other bibliographical tools of these languages; that is to say, there exist certain control tools that are independent of the bibliographic control system (and its alphabetical filing subsystem), and these can be used to regulate the input to the system.

1.3.2.2 ALPHABETIZATION OF ROMANIZED ENTRIES.   The interfiling of Romanized names or words into such a unified alphabetical sequence introduces, however, entirely different elements which inherently are not subject to authorized regulation and are therefore uncontrollable. The "alphabets" created by Romanization schemes are in fact "pseudoalphabets." Although they formally constitute subsets of the Roman script, they are not part of the actual writing system of any natural language; rather, they have been artificially imposed on certain languages by foreigners "as if" these languages were written in Roman script. Consequently the Romanized spelling of names and words cannot be verified in dictionaries or other reference works because these do not exist. There are no Russian, Arabic, Persian, Hindi, Hebrew, and so forth, dictionaries in which the words of these languages are listed in Romanized form and in the alphabetical order of the Roman script. There are, to be sure, Japanese dictionaries of this kind, but they are of little value for bibliographic control because *(a)* the Romanization methods of these dictionaries are often not consistent with the Hepburn system as used (and modified) by Western libraries; and *(b)* the homography of a large number of Japanese words written in Roman script (or in *katakana*) makes it impossible to identify them without the relevant *kanji* characters, which turns the Romanization into an exercise in futility for anyone not familiar with *kanji* script. These dictionaries are therefore useful to the Japanese who actually use them for alphabetization purposes, but not to anyone unfamiliar with their language and script.[18]

[18] "Strange as it may seem to the uninitiated, it is common for a Japanese to look up a Japanese word in its Romanized form and in its alphabetical order, rather than to seek it according to the Chinese

1.3.2.3 THE INEFFICACY OF INTERFILING ROMANIZED ENTRIES. The ambiguities created by the application of various conversion schemes inevitably result in the filing of Romanized entries of certain names or words in completely different parts of the alphabet, depending on the catalog or bibliography and the scheme employed by it, as already demonstrated by several examples. This may also occur when a library employs more than one Romanization scheme for the same script. The English word *central,* for example, has an almost exact equivalent in all Slavic languages, derived from the same Latin root, at least as far as the first seven letters are concerned (only the suffixes differ somewhat). The Cyrillic form is Централ–, written identically in Russian and in Serbian; but when transliterated according to the LC Romanization schemes, the Russian word is rendered as *tsentral-,* whereas the Serbian equivalent becomes a Romanized *central-,* thus dispersing entries that are not only etymologically identical but that are also written in the same script and spelling.

The place of Romanized entries in an alphabetical sequence is therefore neither unique nor predictable, since a name or word beginning with the same letter in the source script may appear in entirely different alphabetical positions. The choice of position may be known only to the makers of a bibliographic list, not to its users, including operator-users who are themselves makers of such lists but who follow different Romanization practices.

In the preceding section we mentioned mistakes and errors that inevitably occur in any kind of transcription. Once they pass through the stage of proofreading undetected, they reach the filer who, whether he be a human being or a machine, is not able to spot them and interfiles the entries in their ''correct'' position in the alphabetical sequence, only to bury such entries forever if the mistake affects the first few letters of a name or a word.

Thus the interfiling of Romanized entries in one unbroken alphabetical sequence that also contains entries for languages originally written in Roman script is not a suitable method for achieving effective control over documents in dissimilar scripts held in a library or listed in a bibliography. The method is used because it is based on long-standing tradition, and because it is a facile way of treating a bothersome library problem with a minimum of inconvenience to the operators. Whether this serves also the best interests of library users (other than operator-users) was until a few years ago of little concern to the library world.[19]

---

character order or the *i-ro-ha* order. I have been informed that the easiest way for a Japanese to ascertain the identity of a Chinese character is to look up the word that it represents in a Japanese–English dictionary, in which the Japanese words are shown in Romanized form in alphabetical order.'' (Palmer, 1931, p. 119.)

[19]So far, only one librarian has dared to question the effectiveness of interfiling Romanized entries: ''We pay homage to the idea of the 'integrated catalogue,' as we do to that of the 'integrated collection.' But exactly what are we integrating here? Sounds? If so, then why don't we interfile *f* and *ph?* Letters? Then why do we file *ä* as *ae?* Perhaps we are integrating people—Arabs and Israelis, Russians and Americans—all in the name of world cooperation. Seriously, though, I contend that the

1.4   The Effectiveness of Romanization for Users

So far we have examined the effectiveness of script conversion almost entirely from the point of view of the system operators, whereas the effects of this operation on the users of the system have only been mentioned in passing. For an analysis and proper assessment of Romanization from the point of view of users of a bibliographic system, it is important to realize that the term "users" is somewhat ambiguous, entailing at least two dichotomies of interests and needs that result in different goals. One such dichotomy exists between the needs and goals of nonprofessional or "general" users versus those of professional users or operators of the system. The other exists between the needs and usages of a particular language community and those of the rest of the world's language communities.

1.4.1   "General" Users versus Operator-Users.   The "general" user, for whose benefit a bibliographic control system is ostensibly designed, is any member of the community served by a documentary communication system. When using the system his goal is essentially to find out what other people have said about a particular subject, or in which form they expressed nonverbal communications (such as music, pictures, or sculptures), and in which documents such statements, opinions, data, or artistic expressions have been recorded. Cutter's objectives *(a)* to *(c)* (see p. 365) anticipate the most-used avenues of approach to these documents, and they imply that the user ultimately has to read or otherwise assimilate the information conveyed by a book or other document in visible, audible, or tactile form.

In saying that either the author or the title of a work is "known" to the user, Cutter recognized that the user has a certain image (written or visualized) of names or phrases, and that the catalog should "enable" him to match it successfully against a similar image recorded in the bibliographic control system. To be able to do this, the user expects that a document surrogate will help him to locate the desired document, and that it is as free from distortion as possible or, in other words, that it is an isomorphic representation of the identifying characteristics of the document. The user who approaches the system from the outside brings to it only those basic skills of written communication commonly shared by literate members of his language community, that is, a knowledge of the order of the alphabet and an ability to read and write. He expects these skills to be sufficient to enable him to find, with the help of the bibliographic control system, any document the author or title of which is known to him and which he is able to write down.

---

various alphabets of the world are unlike things, and that there is a loss of information in the process of transcription." (Weinberg, 1974, p. 21.)

On the general attitude of librarians who blandly disregard the needs of users, see Draper (1964), who said that this is a disease, best characterized by the name *bibliothecal solipsism*.

There is, however, another kind of user: a system operator using the system himself. Examples of this are catalogers looking up entries in the catalog they themselves created and reference librarians using the catalog made by their colleagues. Filers of cards in a card catalog, while performing a function of system management in implementing a control process, are at the same time also constantly using the catalog and getting feedback from their own operations and the resulting product. These operator-users have considerably more knowledge about the system, and therefore stand a much better chance to succeed in using it for a search than the "general" user, who is normally not familiar with cataloging and filing rules which demand much more than a mere knowledge of the alphabet.[20]

Most of the problems regarding the effective use of bibliographic control systems by general users are caused by system operators who expect other users to have the same basic knowledge about the control methods used that they possess. Because they are so often cast into the roles of users, they tend to think that all users are similar to them in negotiating the system. General users who are unable to negotiate the system so as to find what they want are admonished to "learn" the system, often without being given a clue as to what constitutes the rules of the game, and exactly how the operators achieve control within the system.

This latent conflict (which sometimes erupts into open antagonism and mutual frustration) is caused by the different objectives and goals on the part of system operators and general users, and sometimes leads to completely different attitudes toward the results achieved by control methods. In other words, control methods that satisfy the legitimate goals of the system operators may be meaningless or detrimental to the legitimate goals of the general users of the system. This is particularly true when documents in a dissimilar script have to be handled. To be sure, the operators of the system do not generally deny the legitimacy of the users' goals, but they sometimes find it quite difficult to fulfill those goals, because they very often clash with their own. Now "the test of the objective of a system is the determination of whether the system will knowingly sacrifice other goals in order to attain the objective,"[21] and faced with such a test, the operators' goals will normally gain the upper hand, because if they do not

---

[20] Alphabetical filing, and in particular that of bibliographic data such as authors' names and titles of works, cannot always be performed by just sorting on one letter until the next different letter appears in the sequence. For a long time it was thought that alphabetization demanded nothing more than "a knowledge of the ABC's," and that it was therefore a clerical or purely mechanical task, although the need for whole books of elaborate rules for library filing belied this facile assumption. When library filing began to be performed by mechanized sorting, it was soon discovered that bibliographic filing is not at all a mindless mechanical task. Although most of the basic filing rules could be reduced to an algorithm, there remained a residue of filing problems that could not be programmed because their correct application demands decisions depending on factors unrelated to the ordinal arrangement of letters, and based on the interpretation of meaning in a certain context. For further discussion of these issues see Cartwright (1970), Davison (1970), and Rather (1972).

[21] Churchman (1968), p. 31.

achieve them, the existence of the system itself as designed by them is threatened, and consequently their own position may be in jeopardy. No disaster befalls the operator if the users' goals are not fulfilled; those users may go elsewhere to get what they want, and there are in any case enough other users of the system who accept it as it is.

We can illustrate this by an example. Assume that a librarian has to make a list of all books by Mark Twain that his library possesses. He can do this quickly and effectively because his control system, the catalog, lists all these books under the author's real name, Samuel Langhorne Clemens. The librarian knows this because he has been taught that the proper functioning of his control system depends, among other things, on the listing of pseudonymous authors under their real names. He will be able to ascertain how many and which of Mark Twain's books the library possesses, as well as where on the shelves they may be found. If Romanization is used for the cataloging of editions in dissimilar scripts, he will also be able to list any Russian, Arabic, or Japanese translations of, say *Huckleberry Finn*. If language specialists provide him with the proper Romanization, this control tool makes him master of any language and script ever devised without having to know even a single character or letter other than the 26 letters of the Roman alphabet. This fact reinforces the operator's belief in the control methods devised by him to attain his primary goal: complete and uniform control over the entire collection of documents in his library.

When, however, a general user enters the library and looks for a book by Mark Twain, he cannot find anything under that name, not knowing that all works by this author are found only under "Clemens," and perhaps not being able or willing to follow up an intricate system of cross-references which are hard to locate (if they are provided at all). If that reader leaves the library without having achieved his goal, he may be disappointed, but no damage will be done to the system: the library and its catalog will continue to exist. If, however, users who know Russian, Arabic, or Japanese come to the library, which, they have been told, has translations of Mark Twain's works in these languages, they will not find written records in the catalog that match their written or visualized image of the name Mark Twain in Cyrillic, Arabic, or Japanese script; much less would it occur to them to look for Clemens, Samuel Langhorne. These readers too would not achieve their goal, but that would have even less of an adverse impact on the system (which, according to the views of many operators, was not set up to serve foreigners anyway).

The latent or open conflict between the goals of general users and operator-users exists both where Romanization is used for bibliographic control purposes and in other fields of application, such as in geography and cartography. An exception may be the field of philology and linguistics, in which the operators are virtually identical with the users, or nearly so. Philologists write primarily for their colleagues in the profession, and they use transliteration or transcription to illustrate features of a language and a script that (mostly for technical reasons) cannot be easily printed in the original form. In the case of phonetics there is actually no way to write about the phenomena other than by using a phonetic transcription scheme which is supposed to be familiar to other phoneticists. Criticism of certain phonological transcription schemes or of the mode of their application is by no means infrequent, but it is always on the professional level, that is to say, between philologists themselves, and not between philologists as operators of a system and some "outside" or general users.

1.4.2 Script Conversion in the Usage of Different Language Communities.

The problems that arise for users of script conversion in different language communities are best illustrated by an example. The English-speaking language community needs a system to convert Russian names and words into Roman script as used in the writing system of English. This has to be done for the needs of professionals in various fields as well as for general users, and at least two systems may be needed to accomplish this. Both systems will be viewed by Russians as a (more or less distorted) mirror image of their own language and script, and several such mirror images exist, as each language community transcribes Russian Cyrillic in the way best suited to its script and writing conventions. At the same time the Russians need a conversion system, developed by themselves, for the purpose of making Russian names and words intelligible to the outside world, primarily to those who write in the Roman script. Such a system may differ considerably from those developed by English, French, German, and other scholars. Since the Russian conversion system cannot satisfy the writing system of all non-Russian languages, it must be geared to only one of them, say English. Alternatively several systems of conversion could be developed for various languages and perhaps for various alphabets. But the Russians also have to cope with Cyrillization of foreign scripts, and—as with Romanization for Western needs—they may have to develop at least two systems of conversion, one for professionals and one for more general purposes. These conversion systems (one for each script and each language) will in turn be seen by the respective language communities outside of the USSR as (distorted) mirror images of their own languages and scripts. Figure 6.2 shows these inter- and intralanguage relationships in schematic form.

Aurousseau, whose work we already cited in Chapter 5, was one of the first scholars to recognize these relationships when he suggested a "dual system for the writing of geographical names": one for "technical," that is, professional use by geographers for geographers; the other for "popular" use, that is, for the general public, and in other contexts where an exact rendering of names is unnecessary.[22] His proposal (which in fact has been more or less accepted by many mapmakers and writers on geographical subjects) was aimed at the En-

---

[22] Aurousseau (1957), pp. 92–95.

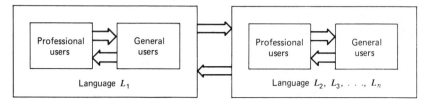

Figure 6.2. Relationships between the needs of intra and interlanguage groups of users of script conversion.

glish-speaking world only, taking into consideration the conventions of English spelling and pronunciation as well as traditional English place names. But as a geographer, a gifted linguist, and a keen observer of international relationships, Aurousseau was aware that the rendering of geographical names in one language and script has repercussions on other peoples and languages which cannot be dismissed as merely being the business of "those foreigners." He concluded his proposal with the words:

Whether we like it or not, geographical names have to be considered from two opposed positions, that of our own language and that of the rest of the world.

The clear recognition of the forms of geographical names which are most acceptable as good spoken English, and of the written forms which are best suited to our closer dealings with other countries, will help to maintain the clarity, precision and character of our language, and the dignity of our relations with peoples abroad who do not speak it.[23]

Thus, rather than striving for an elusive "international" system, he acknowledged the necessity of a plurality of national systems to be used for professional and for general purposes, with each system being adapted to the needs and usages of a particular language and its script, while trying to preserve, as far as possible, the pronunciation of place names in other languages, so dear to the speakers of those tongues. Admittedly such a plurality of systems is easier to maintain in geography than in other fields because geographers have a control system that is independent of language: it is always possible to identify a point or an area by latitude and longitude, even when its name is not clear, in dispute, or unknown.

The conclusions of the British geographer are equally valid for the bibliographic control of documents in dissimilar scripts, but here the interests of the operators have so far always been given top priority, while the "dignity of people who do not speak their language" has scarcely been respected. The needs of those who actually wish to use documents in dissimilar scripts for the sake of their information content are not served unless they are prepared to gain access to

[23]Aurousseau (1957), p. 95.

them through a tortuous route, and by deciphering a code to which the key in most instances is not provided. Since only professional cryptographers enjoy this kind of intellectual challenge, most potential users of documents in dissimilar scripts find it exceedingly difficult and often outright impossible to gain access to the material they need in libraries where such access is provided only in the Roman script.

1.4.3 Romanization as a Barrier to Access. For the general user of documents in dissimilar scripts who intends to read them in a library in which the Roman script is the dominant one, access is provided almost exclusively through Romanization. The degree to which the method is effective depends on the source script that is being Romanized, on the extent to which unambiguous reversibility is possible, and on the amount of energy and time a user is willing to spend on the decoding, reversion, and matching process that is necessary to identify the name of an author or the title of a work. Usually the method is indeed not effective, and acts as a barrier rather than as an avenue of access to the desired documents. The first and most formidable obstacle in the way of a general user is the lack of a publicly available key to the Romanization scheme used. But even a user fortunate enough to obtain such a key will encounter serious difficulties when trying to convert names of authors, names of corporate bodies, and above all, titles of works to their original form. He will also be hampered by the complete absence of any cross-references from the form of names in a non-Roman source script to their Romanization.

1.4.3.1 LACK OF ACCESSIBILITY TO KEYS. We have already shown in Chapter 4 that Romanization schemes are generally not widely publicized or easily accessible, and that few of the large printed catalogs, general bibliographies, or abstracting and indexing systems indicate clearly which scheme they apply and what kind of adaptations are made to it. While system operators generally have access to the Romanization schemes and know how they are applied, the general user has in most instances no key to the particular Romanization scheme of a catalog or bibliography, and is consequently not in a position to perform the operations necessary to establish an unambiguous matching between an actual document (or a reference to it) and the document surrogate in Romanized form.

1.4.3.2 NAMES OF PERSONAL AUTHORS. A reader who knows the spelling of a name in the source script can, if he is dedicated enough, indeed often find the Romanized form, although this may involve him in a time-consuming and tortuous search. He must first find the correct filing place of the first letter or letters of the name, which may sometimes demand that he check three or four likely places, as, for example, when a Russian name begins with any of the letters е, ж, х, ц, ш, щ, ю, or я; he must then match each letter of the original spelling with its Romanized equivalent (either mentally, or more often with pencil and paper). Even though modern names seldom consist of more than about 20 letters, some current Indian or classical Arabic names may be considerably longer, so that the matching process cannot be done in less than a minute or so and may take considerably longer.

This operation is not made easier by the fact that the order of letters is not the same in the source and target alphabets, which constitutes a psychological barrier. A reader familiar with, say, Russian intuitively seeks the letter *B* near the beginning of the alphabetical sequence, since it is the second letter of the Russian alphabet (as it is also in the Roman one). It involves some mental acrobatics not to look under the graphically identical Roman letter, but instead in the 22nd place of the English alphabet, under *V* (the transliteration of Cyrillic B). Conversely, Ф is the 21st Russian letter, but its Romanization *F* is the sixth in English, and so on. The delays and errors in the matching process caused by this phenomenon should not be underestimated.

Having patiently compared the Romanization with the original spelling, the searcher may often succeed in the case of Russian or Greek names, but his efforts may become more frustrating when Arabic, Hebrew, Persian, Urdu, or Indian names are involved, and they become almost or entirely hopeless when Chinese or Japanese names are being sought. *Huang I-hu* may also appear as *Wong Yat-lok* and *Hajime* may also be *Hitoshi, Osamu, Masashi,* or five other different Japanese names. Of course, the better known the name of an author is, the more likely it is that at least some Romanized form of his name is familiar to the searcher, who may have seen it in Western translations or citations, or in reference books (although the Romanization in an encyclopedia or biographical dictionary may not always be what he will find in a library catalog or bibliography). In any case the searcher must be something of a detective to successfully hunt down his quarry, as E. P. Shaw saw quite clearly when she entitled her paper on these problems "Transliteration: a game for the library sleuth."

1.4.3.3 NAMES OF CORPORATE BODIES. Romanization of the names of corporate bodies (i.e., the "authors," for cataloging purposes, of governmental and other institutional publications) poses greater obstacles to successful matching. First of all, the name of a government department, institution, or society as given in bibliographical entries may be quite different from the one that appears in a publication (for reasons that have nothing to do with Romanization *per se* but with the rules of cataloging). Secondly, the names of corporate bodies are frequently quite long and involved, especially if subordinate entities such as "department," "division," and "office," form part of the heading and if their equivalent expressions in foreign languages are Romanized. In these cases the matching process may become exceedingly difficult and time-consuming, the more so since there are only few reference works in which the Romanized form of foreign corporate names can be verified.[24] (At best, one can find the names of

[24]Aman (1973) compiled such a list for the government departments of Arab states.

ministries and major governmental departments or the names of universities, and scientific or professional societies, but not their subdivisions, branches, and minor offices, or committees and the like).

1.4.3.4 TITLES. The greatest difficulties result from the Romanization of titles, because these often consist of phrases, not of the relatively short words used as names. For anonymous works, and in particular serials, the Romanization of titles is the equivalent of the conversion of author names, but it is often much more complicated to perform as well as to decipher for identification. Nevertheless in many instances title Romanization is unavoidable as a part of bibliographic practice (though not necessarily for control purposes).

Romanization of titles for works that are bibliographically listed under their authors is, however, almost entirely an exercise in futility. To a reader who does not know the language it does not mean anything, and he cannot look up the Romanized words in a dictionary in the form in which they appear; instead, he would be much better served by a translation into his language, since a title often reveals the subject matter of a work. For the reader who is familiar with the language and the script of a work, the Romanization of the title is a serious and often insurmountable obstacle that results in partial or even total loss of information. For him only the original title gives direct access and allows immediate matching with the original work or citation, while a Romanized one involves him in a decoding and matching operation of such extent, complexity, and time expenditure that few people are ready to perform it, quite apart from the fact that the longer the title, the larger the number of errors in Romanization that may occur during the various stages of original Romanization in manuscript form, typing, proofreading, and printing.

A typical example of a Romanized Russian title is

Mel'chuk, I. A. I. Urovni predstavlenija vyskazyvanij i obshchee stroenie modeli "smysl-tekst". II. Slovoobrazovanie i konvercija.

It is not too difficult or time-consuming to match and verify the author's name. But comparing 92 letters with the relevant transliteration tables (in this case, the ISO R/9, 2nd edition, employing the option of Anglo-American practice) would take at least 8 minutes, assuming that no more than 5 seconds were spent in the looking-up, comparison, and writing of each letter, and that the user either has the conversion tables in his head or has them ready on his desk—all of which is not quite realistic to assume, to say the least. Does anyone really expect a busy scientist, engineer, or student to spend his time on such laborious deciphering, sometimes bordering on cryptanalysis? At that, the example just cited is a relatively "easy" one, since it involves two scripts that are fully alphabetic and unambiguously reversible. But titles Romanized from Arabic, Hebrew, and other Asian scripts are more difficult to decipher because of partial reversibility and the many potential sources of errors caused by such things as faulty vocalization. Thus transcribed Chinese or Japanese titles become "a riddle wrapped in mystery inside an enigma." *Kuan yü fa chan kuo min ching chi ti ti i ko wu nien (i chiu wu san nien tao i chiu wu ch'i nien) chi hua chih hsing chieh kuo ti kung pao* is a Chinese title of not unusual length, but an English reader cannot make sense of it; nor for that matter can a Chinese, unless the Chinese characters are also displayed.[25]

The main reason for the wholesale Romanization of titles in library catalogs and in some bibliographies is the need for a secondary filing medium after the main entry, so as to differentiate between several works by the same author. In other words, the only persons for whose immediate benefit the "title Romanized" note is made are the filers (or the keypunchers who prepare input data for a computer). Formerly this note was printed on the bottom of Library of Congress cards, while the title in the original script was displayed on top, beneath the author heading. In 1970 it was decided to print the Romanized title for Chinese and Japanese works on a line between the author heading and the title in the original script, and this practice was extended to all non-Roman titles in 1973 (see Figure 6.3) because

certain libraries . . . have expressed a need for a device that will enable paraprofessionals handling the cards to distinguish romanizations of titlepage titles from uniform titles. . . .[26]

One may well ask whether it makes sense—administratively, financially, and not least, intellectually—to employ highly trained language specialists to laboriously produce Romanizations which are of use neither to those who know the

---

[25]The example is taken from Lee-Hsia Hsu Ting (1966), who also provides the Chinese original and the English translation, "A report on the result of the implementation of the First Five-Year Plan (1953–1957) for national economy" (p. 10). The author states that "there does not seem to be any necessity to transliterate '1953' and '1957'" (which in the Chinese original are given in Arabic numerals!). He does not see any advantage in Romanization of Chinese titles, and pleads for translation: "Though it is extremely difficult to translate the titles of many Chinese classics, to translate the titles of works of non-fiction written in *pai-hua* (colloquial style) is not nearly so impossible a task. Many titles when Romanized mean nothing to most readers, but may make good sense if translated" (pp. 9–10).

In 1973 the Toronto Public Libraries decided to abandon the practice of author and title transliteration for Chinese books because, "The main complaint of the readers has been that without seeing the Chinese characters it is impossible to read off the meaning of these headings. A title which often gives a clue to the content of a book becomes utterly meaningless when transliterated and often cannot be uniquely identified" (Kishibe, 1974, p. 4).

On the transliteration of Russian titles, Podborny (1959) states: "Im allgemeinen hat aber ein transliterierter Titel ohne Uebersetzung für einen Leser, der das Russische nicht beherrscht, wenig Sinn' (p. 211). Weinberg (1974) agrees: " . . . title transliteration gives no information to the user who is not familiar with the language of the article and makes life difficult for the user who is" (p. 24).

[26]*Cataloging Service,* Bulletin 105, November 1972, p. 15.

Nemirovskiĭ, Evgeniĭ L'vovich.
Начало славянского книгопечатания. Москва, "Книга," 1971.

269 p. 22 cm. 2.00rub   USSR 71–VKP

At head of title: Е. Л. Немировский.
Includes bibliographical references.

1. Printing—History—Poland.   2. Books—History—Slavic countries.   I. Title.

➝ Title romanized : Nachalo slavi̇an-
skogo knigopechataniia.

Z163.X44   72–324165

Library of Congress   ◯   72 [2]

(a)

Fel'dman, Boris Aleksandrovich.
➝ [Gazetnoe proizvodstvo]
Газетное производство. Москва, "Книга," 1972.

319 p. with illus. 22 cm. 2.28rub   USSR 72–VKP

At head of title: Б. А. Фельдман.
Bibliography : p. 313–[315]

1. Printing, Practical.   2. Printing, Practical—Make up.
3. Newspapers.   I. Title.

Z244.F39   73–312152

Library of Congress   ◯   73 [2]

(b)

Figure 6.3. Romanization of titles on Library of Congress cards. *(a)* "Title romanized" note as given on cards until December 1972; *(b)* Romanized title interposed between heading and title in non-Roman script as given on cards since January 1973.

script nor to those who do not, except for the "paraprofessionals" whose mind-numbing task is to drop cards into catalog drawers and for subarrangement of entries by mechanical sorting devices. Once this has been done, the whole thing loses its justification. The practice of making added title entries that display the transliterated title (and which are filed by the artificial letter sequence of Romanized words) is no more than an empty ritual without any useful purpose. People who know the title in the original will almost never be able to duplicate its Romanization so as to find it in its alphabetical sequence, whereas the Romanized title entry, if by chance encountered by a reader who does not know the language, appears to him as only so much gibberish. At the very least the language specialists now employed to perform Romanization could also produce a translation of the title into the dominant language; in most instances this would take up only a fraction of the time now spent on Romanization, and would be of benefit to people other than filers and other paraprofessionals, but this is never done in present library practice.[27] From an economic point of view, the lack of such translations constitutes an "opportunity cost," a benefit that the resources used to produce a certain output could produce if they were used in an alternative way. A title translation, to be sure, can never serve as an unambiguous means of identification for a source document; this function can only be fulfilled by the title in the original script (and by other bibliographical data), supplemented by control codes, if necessary. But a title often tells more about the subject of a document than the subject headings assigned to it by a cataloger, and its translation can aid a user who does not know the language of a document in his decision whether to accept a document as relevant to a subject inquiry, and if so, whether to ask for a translation of the work in whole or in part.

It must be pointed out here that the practice of title Romanization without translation is most prevalent in library catalogs and in references appended to articles; abstracting and indexing services generally translate a foreign title into the language of their abstracts or predominant readership, sometimes accompanied by Romanization, but more often only by an indication of the original language. A survey that covered 42 abstracting and indexing services (including most of the world's large discipline- and mission-oriented ones) showed that practically all provided title translations in one form or another, especially for those titles written in a non-Roman script.[28]

1.4.3.5 LACK OF CROSS-REFERENCES. The simple expedient of making cross-references from a name in dissimilar script to its Romanized form as given

---

[27] This was not always so. The first version of the ALA cataloging rules, published in 1883, made a translation of "all titles not in the classic, Romance or Teutonic languages" mandatory. Cutter's rules made such translations optional, and so did the AA code of 1908; but even that option was dropped from the ALA code published in 1949 and also from its successor, the present *Anglo-American cataloging rules* of 1967.

[28] Wellisch (1972), p. 80.

in a particular catalog or bibliography (e.g., Юшкевич, *see* Juškevič), which would perhaps be even more helpful to users than an explanation of the Romanization scheme as such, has almost never been employed in any library. The reason for this lack of cross-references is that this would necessitate the establishment of one or more files of names and words in dissimilar scripts, requiring the services of language and script experts which are not available in many libraries. Sometimes cross-references are made from forms of Romanization not used by that library to the one employed (e.g., Iouchkevitch, *see* Juškevič), but these cannot always cover all possibilities, nor are they as helpful as would be cross-references from an author's name in the original form to its Romanization.

1.5 Changing Needs of Users

The picture emerging from our analysis of the needs and goals of system operators and users is one of an apparent conflict caused by essentially irreconcilable goals that the system is expected to achieve through the use of a certain method, namely Romanization. We explore this aspect in more detail in Section 3. But the presently perceived conflict between operators and users is also due to far-reaching changes in the nature and needs of library patrons which took place over the past two generations, and which has not yet been sufficiently recognized or acted on by libraries, which are by their very nature among the most conservative organizations in society. This phenomenon has been analyzed during the past few years by several writers; it is pertinent to our subject to quote three of them, all librarians and former deans of library schools, who are also innovators in the field of information provision and critical observers of their own profession. Robert S. Taylor has this to say:

Libraries have traditionally been concerned only with the information base—that is, with the gathering, collecting and organizing of the artifacts of information. . . . [They] have focused their attention only on the package, a result of the acquisitive syndrome of the middle class culture of the past four hundred years. Our concern with people has been relatively recent, and not terribly successful because the concern has been passive and reactive rather than dynamic and creative.[29]

Paul Wasserman states:

Libraries remain predominantly passive agencies . . . oriented powerfully to the book rather than to the client. . . . The consequence of past choices has noticeably linked libraries to the requirements of particular segments in the culture—in the public library to the literate middle class, in academia to the humanistic professor. . . . The institution and

[29]Taylor (1973), p. 67.

those who practice in it have identified libraries as the servant of scholarship and they have been astonishingly indifferent to perceiving alternative responses and responsibilities.[30]

And the doyen of American librarianship, Jesse H. Shera, who for more than 40 years tirelessly stressed the social responsibility of librarians and the role of the library as a social agency, sounded a warning:

The concept of *service* is the foundation upon which the library system is built, and it is here that the effectiveness of acquisition and organization are translated into reality and their effectiveness proved. A library that is nothing more than an accumulation of materials, however expertly chosen, that are only "marked and parked" will not long receive support if nothing is done to encourage its use.[31]

Taylor, Wasserman, Shera, and many others deal with the problem of change in libraries and the attitude of librarians toward their constituencies from a general point of view, and give many examples of the practices and methods that tend to alienate the actual or potential library clientele or even to make it impossible for prospective users to benefit from the information media the library should provide to those who need them. As Americans they naturally consider only the needs of a practically monolingual population, and the suitable provision (or rather the lack of it) of information media written or otherwise recorded in their own language and script. The collection, control, and use of documents in dissimilar scripts, however, demonstrates as perhaps no other activity in librarianship the woeful inadequacy of methods devised in a distant past for the purportedly perceived needs of a highly specialized clientele, which are still applied in our own time to the needs of an entirely different kind of user.

For hundreds of years Western libraries have collected works in Arabic, Persian, Chinese, and other "exotic" languages and scripts, not so much because of what they contained but rather because of their outlandish nature, their value as physical objects as embodied in artistic and precious bindings and in the beauty of their calligraphy and illumination, and quite generally because they tended to enhance the prestige of a library and its owner (often a prince, a rich merchant, or a retired public official). Exotic manuscripts and books were thus little more than museum exhibits, because few if any people were able to *read* them. It was not until the late 18th and early 19th centuries that scholars actually began to study documents in Oriental scripts for what they contained rather than merely gazing at their bindings and illustrations, and such scholars were inevitably Westerners who had become more or less well acquainted with the language and script of a people and its literature, often as a

[30]Wasserman (1972), p. 4.
[31]Shera (1974), p. 158.

result of earlier commercial, military, and administrative activity in one of the colonies of their homeland. The libraries of universities, learned societies, and academies in Western Europe (and to a lesser degree also in the United States) during the 19th century were thus frequented by learned gentlemen who had the means and the leisure to indulge in the study of exotic literature, as professional or amateur philologists. But it practically never happened that a native Arab, Persian, or Chinese reader came to these libraries to study his own literature, since the number of literate people in Asian and African countries was exceedingly small; travel was dangerous, complicated, and above all very costly; and the politics of the colonial powers effectively prevented even the literate ''natives'' from coming to Europe.

The librarians of scholarly libraries housing exotic literature were themselves often trained philologists, like Schleiermacher and Lepsius, or they relied on philological expertise to catalog these works, when, toward the end of the 19th century, libraries began to make systematic efforts to organize their holdings, and to make them accessible by means of catalogs. It was thus essentially a case of philologists serving fellow philologists, and the methods of bibliographic control involving transcription and transliteration were not only well known to the users who wished to study documents in dissimilar scripts but were also suited to their needs: the decipherment of manuscripts and the study of the language and literature of various peoples.

We must also remember that before 1900 practically no modern scientific or technical literature was written in any script other than the Roman (even Russian contributions were rather sparse, and few of them reached Western libraries). ''Civilization'' inevitably meant Western civilization, and the only languages considered to be the vehicles of its ideas and achievements were those that had also become the languages of colonization—and all were written in Roman script. Manuscripts and books written in other scripts were studied not so much for their intrinsic religious, historic, or literary content but rather as sources for theological, historical, or philological treatises *about* them, their authors (if known), and their cultural environment.

This situation began to change gradually after World War I and has gained tremendous momentum since the end of World War II, when the newly independent states of Asia and Africa began to encourage indigenous scientific and technological activities, the results of which were often published in the vernacular, both to serve the citizens of those countries and as a matter of national pride. (When ''scientific publications'' are mentioned, most people tend to think of physics and chemistry, where the bulk of publications are printed in Roman script because they are written in Western languages, primarily English, even by non-English scientists. Yet even in these disciplines the number of publications in Russian and Japanese is steadily growing, while in the life sciences, particularly botany and zoology, a large number of treatises about local plants and animals are published in the vernacular of a country, and thus in a great variety of scripts. The same is true to some degree in medicine and in many branches of technology.) Furthermore Western textbooks are increasingly translated into other languages, many of them in non-Roman scripts. All these are not only acquired by Western libraries but are actively sought by those users who are fluent in the languages and scripts of various peoples, among them students sent abroad and native scholars who wish to pursue further studies outside their homeland. Incidentally, it often happens that these users find a more complete collection of books and periodicals in the language and script of their homeland in large American or European research libraries than they could ever find in their own countries—both because of the scarcity and poor development of libraries there and, even more so, because concentrated efforts are now made by American libraries to acquire virtually everything published in a foreign country through various acquisition programs (the Farmington plan, book procurement under Public Law 480, the National Program for Acquisition and Cataloging, and comprehensive buying activities of individual libraries), whereas often no equivalent collection effort is made by any local library or information center in the country of origin itself.

Thus there is now a sometimes spectacular rise in the number of books, periodicals, and other documents in various non-Roman scripts which are collected by libraries, as well as a completely different and diversified readership that includes not only philologists, but also researchers whose scholarship is devoted to sciences other than the study of language and literature, and technologists, engineers, and "general" readers who merely want to read books in a language and script they know and understand, even though they happen to live outside their own country and language community, either temporarily or permanently. Their legitimate needs—to gain direct access to documents written in their own language and script, so as to use them as information sources—are badly served by a system that allows access only through an intricate and cumbersome system devised for philological purposes and used by librarians to exercise control over those documents as physical objects only without giving the slightest attention to their possible use as information sources by those for whom they were written. Philologists may not find an Arabic or Hindi treatise on civil engineering or cattle breeding of particular interest, and a Western engineer or agronomist will almost certainly find more suitable textbooks in English, French, or German. But to the foreign student at a Western university whose mother tongue is Arabic or Hindi, these books will offer a great deal of help, at least in the initial stages of his study, and he might find in them some applications to local conditions which will be valuable to him on his return to his homeland.

1.6   Changing Attitudes of Operators

The attitude of librarians began to change somewhat in the 1950s as they became more service-oriented, in part because of the impact of information services provided (primarily in the scientific-technological fields) by what was then called "documentalists," and perhaps also as a result of studies on library use and users that were initiated at that time, and which are still being pursued to find out how libraries serve their users, and how users react to the provision of such services.

In the late 1950s a few librarians also began to make a plea on behalf of the users of documents in dissimilar scripts, in consideration of the sorry plight of those subjected to the practices of completely Romanized libraries. C. S. Spalding of the Library of Congress asked:

Why, indeed, transliterate? Is the Thai scholar (or the Persian, or the Gujarati) better served by catalog entries using transliterated rather than vernacular forms of writing? It would take a more daring man than I to uphold the affirmative of this proposition. Even when the transliteration system is known to all or most nationals and scholars using the collections, the defense of its use for these readers would be difficult to support. And many times the system may be foreign to the ken or obnoxious to the taste of many of these readers; in such cases, transliterated entries are still more difficult to justify.[32]

One could hardly put the case against transliteration and for the interests of users more eloquently and convincingly, and it is the more astonishing that Mr. Spalding nevertheless found himself compelled to draw the opposite conclusion, as we have seen (p. 226). But only a few years later transliteration was considered "undesirable" by David T. Ray, an expert on the cataloging of Southeast Asian publications:

Cataloging in transliteration is theoretically possible. But in any extensive program it is, I think, undesirable. For one thing, vernacular materials must be readily located by native speakers of Southeast Asian languages, either faculty or students, who are already on our campuses. A Thai student preparing a thesis or dissertation on a subject connected with Thailand does not want to be obliged to puzzle out his native language in the strange garb of transliteration.[33]

Attention was finally also focused on the needs of users in countries in which two or more languages are spoken, and in which several different scripts are used simultaneously by various language communities. The International Federation of Library Associations (IFLA) devoted an entire session of its 1971 General Council at Liverpool to "the problems of the multi-language multi-script

[32]Spalding (1957), p. 3.
[33]Ray (1971), p. 94.

catalogue.'' The papers dealt with multiscript catalogs in India, Hong-Kong, Singapore, and Yugoslavia, and in particular with suggestions for a general manual on the organization and management of multiscript catalogs. When these papers were published in the IFLA's journal *International Cataloguing,* the editor stated in the preface:

There is no one problem of the multi-language multi-script catalogue, nor one solution. But there are some factors common to all situations: in every instance, the readers' requirements must be borne in mind: in each case, readers' habits may change, with consequent changes in a library's book stock arrangement and catalogue.[34]

During the first half of the 1970s, when the euphoric preoccupation with electronic gadgetry as a panacea for all library and information problems had evaporated together with the lavish amounts of money available to libraries in the United States, and when the interests of the consumer began to become paramount, more and more voices were also raised to condemn the complacency of library operators and their preoccupation with efficient methods to the detriment of adequate service to library users. We cite here only two typical contributions, one from a librarian, the other from a management consultant, both of whom are much concerned about the relationship between libraries and their users. The librarian D. L. Roth considered the following to be one of the contributing factors to the declining use of conventional libraries by scientists:

Library procedures are too often designed for the convenience of librarians. In short, libraries have not developed a user orientation. . . . Current emphasis on the mechanical aspects of acquisitions and cataloguing not only overlooks the prime importance of collection usage but also fails to realize that the giving function must be expanded to include self-service use. . . . Unless libraries are sucessful in the area of uniting book and reader, their very existence, as we currently know them, is threatened.[35]

And Peter Drucker, the renowned management expert, told an audience of librarians:

Find out who [your] publics are and probe for their information needs. Discover the image of the library as they see it and work toward making them happy and satisfied—rather than keeping librarians comfortable. Discover your publics' needs, and you will have defined your service objectives.[36]

The present practices of Romanization were most eloquently challenged from

---

[34]*International Cataloguing* **1** (1972):6. The four papers are by Siew (1971), Stipčević (1971), Elrod (1972), and Mehta (1973).
[35]Roth (1974), pp. 93–94.
[36]Drucker (1976), p. 6.

the point of view of the user by Bella Weinberg, a librarian specializing in the treatment of Hebrew and Yiddish literature:

Let us now turn to the poor user who is unlucky enough to be searching for a work in a non-Roman alphabet in a completely modern, Romanized library. First of all, the schemes are not posted: one could not fit them on the little cards in the catalogue that show "How to use this catalogue", and they are usually not available at the reference desk. The librarian on duty has never heard of Pushtu, let alone reads it, and the poor user is left to imagine all possible transliterations for the Arabic letters before him.

Let us look at another link in the chain of documentation—the scholar writing an article on Pushtu literature for a journal. He has neither the Library of Congress system nor Qasimi's dissertation before him. He uses an *ad hoc* transcription scheme for his citations, which other scholars will copy, and which students will take to the library only to search in vain for the items. . . .

The more we think of users, the less rationale we find for transliteration. If people take the trouble to learn another alphabet, why should they have to learn an additional artificial system to get access to material in that alphabet? . . .

Our libraries must rid themselves of "non-Roman alphabet phobia" and allow their multi-lingual readers some form of direct access to material in foreign scripts.[37]

Thus service to the user and provision for the most direct access to documents—rather than the building of ever-growing collections and the application of methods that are most convenient for operators—are now seen as the prime responsibility of libraries and any other documentary communication system.

1.7 Romanization in Asian and African Bibliographic Systems

The Romanization practices of Western libraries, frustrating as they are to foreign readers, can be at least partially justified by long-standing tradition and by the demands of those users who know only the Roman script but need some indication of what exists in other languages and scripts (however badly Romanization may serve these needs). But the practice has also been exported by zealous Western librarians who were asked to organize the libraries of Asian and African countries, and who rather naively thought that the methods used at home must inevitably be applied abroad, in a different cultural environment. One of the few to disagree with this practice is J. M. Elrod, a Canadian librarian with extensive experience in several Asian countries:

---

[37]Weinberg (1974), pp. 27–29. The reference to Qasimi concerns an unpublished doctoral dissertation on the cataloging of Urdu, Pushto, and Panjabi.

Present Anglo-American rules assume that the approach to the collection will be through the roman alphabet in author and title entry and through English in subject headings. This assumption cannot be made in a collection which serves patrons many of whom know neither the roman alphabet nor English. The librarian in a country with a perfectly good alphabet, character system, or syllabary of its own would find little reason to transliterate authors and titles in his own language into the roman alphabet nor to use English subject headings.[38]

When Romanization practices are imposed on the libraries and bibliographic tools of countries in which a user naturally expects to find documents organized in his own language and script, it becomes nothing but the tangible expression of haughty disdain for the indigenous culture on the part of foreign librarians who blandly graft their systems on the records of that culture for the sake of "efficiency" and in the name of "introducing modern methods."[39] Unfortunately some librarians in Asian and African countries (especially those who received their training in England or in the United States) adopt these practices without considering the consequences to their countrymen whom they are supposed to serve.[40] By using the Roman script as a control tool, they seem to say that the indigenous script, though producing the national literature, is not good enough to be used for the organization of those books and other documents. By degrading the traditional values of their own culture they may end by degrading themselves as well as the image of their libraries in the eyes of their fellow citizens. The misuse of Romanization in this manner may well be one of the last remaining vestiges of Western colonialism in Asia and Africa.[41]

[38] Elrod (1972), p. 7.

[39] Typical of this attitude is the article by J. F. Harvey (1973) entitled "Adapting American library science for Iranian use." Harvey had the impudence to state that "almost no one in Iran understands the more advanced and scholarly phases of any subject." His paper drew a sharp rebuke from B. Nestor (1974).

[40] One of the countries whose libraries suffer particularly from an Anglocentric education of its librarians is India: "In India at the moment, many of the graduates from the schools of library science are trained through the English medium, with British and American tools and codes, and catalogue practice is given with books in English: cataloguers with this training are not well equipped to solve the problems which face them every day in an Indian public library" (Mehta 1973, p. 5). "The present library science teaching in [India] is wholly oriented to the English language and hardly prepares the student in the systematic cataloguing of books in his own language" (Sharma, 1973, p. 36).

[41] The results of the worldwide survey of libraries discussed at the end of Chapter 5 indicate that the general trend in most Asian and African libraries is now toward separate bibliographic control tools (catalogs) in the vernacular for the respective indigenous literature, and in many cases for every dissimilar script, so that users can be served in their own languages and scripts rather than by a circuitous and cumbersome detour via a foreign script and by tortuous (and often faulty) transcription. Almost 80% of all university libraries, 73% of public libraries, and 90% of special libraries provide direct access to documents in the original script and language. Only national libraries in

1.8 The Usefulness and Limits of Romanization

It would be foolish to claim that Romanization (or any other kind of script conversion) in itself is either impractical or unnecessary. Quite the contrary, in our age, which has reduced the time needed to cover vast physical distances to a matter of a few hours, people of different cultures who speak and write different languages in different scripts meet more frequently than ever. Consequently the written records of various peoples and cultures also come into frequent contact with each other through translations of literature and in the news dispatches of the press, radio, and television. This is now also more than ever a multidirectional phenomenon. The Western world, which largely uses the Roman script, must constantly render Russian, Arabic, Hebrew, Indian, Chinese, Korean, and Japanese names (to mention only some of those most commonly encountered) in a form in which they can be read and pronounced by people who do not know those languages and scripts. To the same extent, Russian or Bulgarian authors of books and editors of newspapers and journals must render such names and words for the readers of Cyrillic script, and Chinese or Japanese authors and editors must make the names of foreign personalities and events intelligible to their readers. Script conversion is also a necessary operation for writers of books and articles in the fields of history and geography, in zoology and botany, and in many other areas, wherever persons or places have to be mentioned. It is also indispensible in cartography to make the names of places intelligible to map users, regardless of what script is used in those places. In short, in all spheres of human communication and wherever the records of various cultures written in different scripts have to be made intelligible and accessible to those who wish to know about them, script conversion is the only means of smoothly integrating names and words into texts written in a particular script.

But our analysis has shown that script conversion, and in particular Romanization, is stretched beyond the limits of its usefulness when it is applied as a bibliographic *control tool,* a task it is inherently incapable of fulfilling effectively. We have tried to demonstrate this by an empirical approach, mainly based on the observation and interpretation of operational requirements for script conversion as they are actually applied by system operators, and on the analysis of the impact these methods have on system users. It might well be argued that such an approach to the problem results in an evaluation that is as subjective as the different opinions on these matters voiced over the years by librarians, bibliographers, and others who became interested in the topic of script conversion. Yet our findings about the inadequacy of Romanization as a bibliographic control tool are reinforced and corroborated by the laws of cybernetics, which are independent of value judgments and are applicable to all control processes.

Asian countries show a preference for unified Romanized catalogs, possibly because of the example set by the Library of Congress, whose cards are widely used in these libraries.

2   THE CYBERNETICS OF SCRIPT CONVERSION

2.1   Regulation in Open Dynamic Systems

In order to understand how cybernetics, the science of regulation and control in systems, can be used to analyze the functioning of a bibliographic control system, it is first necessary to consider a model of an open dynamic system, that is, a system having a patterned activity of receiving an input from an external environment and transforming it into an output. Such a system need not be a physical or material one but can also be a conceptual system.

In its simplest form an open dynamic system exists in an environment T and is able to function properly if E, its set of essential variables, is kept within certain assigned limits, namely a subset of states η. The system may, however, be subject to outside influences or disturbances D that threaten the viable states of E through *variety*, which is the set of discriminable ways in which D could adversely affect E. To keep itself in viable states η the system must have a regulatory component R that can be coupled to T so as to form a subsystem B whose purpose is to block the flow of unwanted variety from D to E (see Figure 6.4).

The problem of regulation in an open dynamic system is therefore the following. If D, T, E, and η are given, the regulatory mechanism R, when coupled to T, must act to keep E within the limits of states η. It does this by blocking the transmission of variety from D to E. A classical example of such a system is the thermostatically controlled water bath, where D is the set of possible disturbances, such as cold air or the addition of cold water, E is the temperature of the water bath, which is to be kept within a desired range η of, say, 36° to 38° C, and R is the thermostat which, together with the environment T (the bathtub, pipes, fittings, etc.), forms the subsystem B that keeps the temperature constant by blocking the variety introduced at D.[42]

All regulation processes in a dynamic system are subject to the *Law of Requisite Variety,* first formulated by W. Ross Ashby: "Only variety in R can force down variety due to D; only variety can destroy variety."[43] The law can be expressed by the equation

$$V_E = \frac{V_D}{V_R} \tag{1}$$

---

[42] The description of a system with a controlled regulator mainly follows the one in Ross W. Ashby's *An introduction to cybernetics* (1956), especially Chapters 11 and 12, to which the reader is referred for more detail. Most, but not all, of the components of a system are labeled by the letters chosen by Ashby.

[43] Ashby (1956), p. 207.

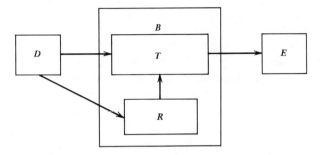

Figure 6.4.   Diagram of immediate effects in a regulated system.

or, if the values are measured logarithmically,

$$V_E = V_D - V_R \qquad (2)$$

where V_E is the variety in the outcomes of the essential variables E, or the
output of the system;

V_D is the variety in the disturbance D, or the input to the system;

V_R is the variety in the regulator R.

The minimum value of V_E, namely 1 (or 0, if measured logarithmically), can be achieved only when the variety in R equals the variety in D. Since V_D is generally given and fixed, V_E can be lessened only by an increase in V_R

The Law of Requisite Variety is also valid for regulation in nonphysical systems. Laurence B. Heilprin has shown that it is also applicable to conceptual systems, particularly those involving the processes of communication.[44] Since bibliographic control systems are parts of communication systems (more particularly, documentary communication systems), it follows that they too are systems to which the law applies.

2.2   Bibliographic Control as a Cybernetic System

A bibliographic control system B receives input of documents D, each of which constitutes a disturbance that introduces variety into the system. The environment T, together with a suitable regulator R, seeks to reduce this variety to an acceptable level, so that the system output E, namely document surrogates, will be in a viable state η, achieved when the following three conditions are satisfied:

1. Document surrogates must *identify* each document uniquely by certain characteristics listed according to a control routine C_1, the rules for descriptive cataloging and subject indexing.

[44]Heilprin (1974a,b).

2. They are *recorded* (written) by graphic signs known to the operators and users of the system, and conveying meaning to at least some of the latter; the graphic signs and the manner of their application are controlled by a control routine C_2, the orthographic rules of a language'. writing system.
3. They are formatted in such a manner that it is possible to *arrange* them in a sequence of prescribed and known order (alphabetical, alphanumerical, or numerical), following a control routine C_3, the filing rules of the system.

In an ideal bibliographic control system, in which all three conditions have been fulfilled, each document is represented by one or more document surrogates, depending on the kind and number of characteristics by which the document is to be made retrievable. Each document surrogate is assigned to a unique and therefore predictable place from which it can be retrieved on demand. In other words, each document surrogate can have one and only one place in the system, and that place is determined by the strict and logical application of three control routines, C_1, C_2, and C_3, by the operators. The users, on the other hand, provided that they also have full knowledge of the control routines and the rules of their application, and provided further that they apply them in exactly the same strict and logical manner in which the operators created the document surrogates, are able to predict the exact place of any document surrogate, and can therefore find it; they may ultimately also retrieve the document itself if it is held in the store of a documentary communication system.

Needless to say, in reality the operators of the system are not always able to make completely logical and consistent decisions about the applications of cataloging, spelling, and filing rules because these rules themselves are not always logical and consistent. Nor do users of the system always know these rules, or, even if they do know them, they may apply the rules in a manner different from the one chosen by the operators, unless the users are identical with the operators, that is, the catalogers or reference librarians looking up entries in a catalog they themselves compiled. In the following discussion, however, we assume that the system is an ideal one, and we digress only occasionally to look at conditions as they are in real-life applications.

2.3   Control of Documents Written in the Dominant Script

2.3.1   Control Operations.   Figure 6.5 shows the simplest form of modeling the control operations and regulation processes that take place when documents D_1, written in the dominant script of a system, are handled by its bibliographic control routines (i.e., the "normal" procedure). Let us now consider those bibliographic control routines that result in an output E satisfying the three conditions already mentioned, and in particular the kind of transformations that take place.

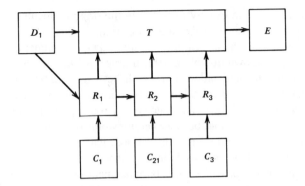

Figure 6.5.   Control and regulation in a bibliographic control system for documents written in the dominant script.

The first operation has as its aim the *identification* of a document. The characteristics by which a document is identified may be the author's name, the title, edition, place, or year of publication, the number of pages or volumes, and so forth, in other words, all or some of the data normally recorded in a bibliographic citation. The control routine C_1 consists of a catalog code and its appurtenant rules of application and interpretation. The transformation is *homomorphic*[45] as far as the characteristics of the document are concerned. Obviously the whole text is not transformed into a document surrogate, nor is the whole text of the title page (from which most of the document characteristics are normally taken). Generally also fewer details of those characteristics are actually recorded. The title or the publisher's name may be abridged; only one place of publication may be given even though two or three are printed on the title page; the various pictures, drawings, sketches, and maps in a document may be reduced to just the abbreviation "ill."; and so on. On the other hand, in some instances more details, provided from sources outside of the document itself, may be recorded: where the title page has "G. B. Shaw" the document surrogate may have "George Bernard Shaw," a short title may be augmented, notes about the document may be added, and so on.

The second operation has as its aim the *recording* of data. The document surrogates are written in the characters of the dominant script, following a control routine C_{21} that directs the operators to transcribe (here used in the sense "to write a copy of") the characters in which the identifying characteristics of a

---

[45] A homomorphism is a many-to-one transformation of a complex structure that preserves invariant a simpler substructure. This interpretation broadens the original mathematical concept (which is more narrowly defined) to a concept of far wider scope. Its applicability to cybernetics was recognized in the late 1950s by several authors, notably W. R. Ashby (1956) and Stafford Beer (1959). Homomorphic transformations were first applied to information science by L. B. Heilprin and F. L. Goodman (1965). Heilprin (1974a) developed the idea further in his paper "On access to knowledge in the social sciences and humanities, etc." (p. 31).

document are expressed exactly as found in the original document. It is therefore, by definition, an *isomorphic* transformation.

The third operation has as its aim the *arrangement* of document surrogates in a desired sequence, known in bibliographical usage as "filing," that is performed according to the standard order of the alphabet used, sometimes modified by special filing rules needed for bibliographic purposes and supplemented by numerical order. These together constitute control routine C_3. The result is again a *homomorphic* transformation, because certain words (e.g., articles written at the beginning of a filing medium) are disregarded, letters modified by a diacritical mark are filed as if they were basic letters, and so forth.

The control routine provides for subarrangement under one characteristic by another set of characteristics, and further subarrangement in descending hierarchical order, until the document surrogate can be assigned to a unique place in the alphabetical or numerical sequence. Thus a bibliographic list may be arranged by authors' names. When one name, say Smith, occurs more than once, it is subarranged by forenames in alphabetical order, and more than one work by John Smith is subarranged by title; if there is more than one John Smith, they are distinguished by further information, such as dates of birth and death.

2.3.2   Control by Operators.   Control routine C_1 can only be performed by skilled operators who are familiar with the script and language in which a document is written, since it is necessary to read and comprehend a document in order to distinguish between author, title, publisher, and other identifying data. These operators must also determine the subject of a document and decide on appropriate retrieval tags, resulting in main and added entries for author and title, subject headings, classification marks, and so on. Control routine C_{21} is also usually performed by the same specialists so as to minimize errors in transcribing of data.

Most documents handled by control routines C_1 and C_{21} are written in the language of the community predominantly served by a bibliographic control system. Thus, in a British or American library, they would be written in English. When documents in other languages written in Roman script have to be handled by a predominantly English-oriented system, operators who are skilled in those languages have to perform control routines C_1 and C_{21}, applying them in exactly the same way as for English documents. This results in document surrogates written in Roman script, and once these have been produced, all other operators of the system can exercise a certain measure of control over the foreign-language documents, because they need only know the dominant script in which the document surrogates have been written but do not necessarily have to know any of the languages written in that script.

To retrieve a document it is only necessary to match a request for it (written in the dominant script used by the system) with the relevant document surrogate.

This matching process may be performed by human beings when a certain latitude of errors and slight mismatching is permissible because of the human aptitude to recognize context and to substitute the correct configuration of graphic signs for one that is slightly or even considerably off the mark. If it is to be performed by machines, the input, i.e., the request, must be absolutely perfect as to spelling, word order, and punctuation so as to produce a match with the stored document surrogate.

Thus the operators of a documentary communication system need neither "understand" the documents they provide (i.e., know the meaning of strings of graphic signs which form words and sentences) nor interpret their titles, but they can retrieve requested documents by the application of certain control routines. This is an example of the axiom that "in cybernetics the concept of communication is less specific than in information science" and that "communication" does not imply that the two terminals between which it takes place necessarily "understand" the signals transmitted through a communication channel as *meaningful* messages.[46]

In summary, the regulators R of the system are effective in reducing the potentially threatening variety in the input D to an acceptable level by transforming it into an orderly pattern so that E stays within its assigned limits, the states η.

2.3.3 Control by Users. The control processes that serve the goals of operators can serve the goals of users of the system equally well, as long as all documents and their surrogates are written in the dominant script. In the case of foreign-language documents, the control operations are indeed even more useful, because readers of documents in a particular foreign language are by definition expected to know and understand that language, either because they are native speakers, or because they have acquired a more or less complete mastery of it. In the latter case their command of a foreign language may be aided by the use of bilingual dictionaries. Such dictionaries form standardized auxiliary control devices that are outside of the system itself but they can be resorted to in order to gain better control over the meaning of document surrogates.

An example will illustrate this point. A document written in Hungarian (a European language containing very few words based on Latin or Greek roots which are so common to most other European languages and which often make it possible to glean a modicum of meaning from them even without actual knowledge of those languages) results in a document surrogate that is written in Roman script. This document surrogate, however, is completely incomprehensible to an English-speaking librarian, to whom the words will appear to be no more than strings of nonsense syllables. Yet, if the words have been accurately transcribed

---

[46]Heilprin (1974b), p. 124.

by control routine C_{21}, they will convey sense and meaning to an Hungarian user. Moreover both librarian and user may have recourse to a Hungarian-English dictionary, which will serve as a point of reference and authority for the words. If a spelling error has occurred, it can be corrected, and within certain limits it is even possible for someone without a knowledge of Hungarian to extract some minimal meaning from the seemingly meaningless strings of syllables and letters. (This does not imply, by any means, that translation from a foreign language can be accomplished by people totally ignorant of this language, its grammar, syntax, and idioms, just by looking up word by word in a dictionary, especially if the language in question is highly inflected or is an agglutinating one, as is the case in Hungarian or Turkish.)

Minor difficulties may sometimes occur regarding the filing of entries according to control routine C_3, because the conventions of alphabetical order are not the same in all languages, but this does not constitute an unsurmountable obstacle to effective control by users. The exceptions to the conventional filing sequence of the Roman alphabet are so few that it is easy for users to learn and remember them. For example, a Swedish user of an English-language catalog will have to remember to look for words or names beginning with $\ddot{A}$ or $\mathring{A}$ under A, not after Z, as is the custom in his own country.

2.4   Control of Documents Written in Dissimilar Scripts

2.4.1   Control by Operators.   When documents D_2, written in dissimilar scripts, have to be handled by a bibliographic control system, the operators are faced with a completely different situation and a potential threat to the orderly functioning of their system. The kind of variety introduced by documents in one or more dissimilar scripts threatens to prevent any effective control if only those regulation methods are employed that are normally used to handle documents D_1, written in the dominant script.

A dissimilar document D_2, (e.g., a Russian book) is first subjected to control routine C_1; that is, it is cataloged by a language specialist who knows the Cyrillic script and the Russian language. Routine C_1 results, however, in a document surrogate that would drive E outside the acceptable limits of η, because it no longer satisfies condition (2): it is written in a script not understood by the operators of the system. And since control routine C_3 cannot be performed by filers familiar with the filing routine, because a completely different set of characters is involved, condition (3) cannot be met either. Thus, if document surrogates written in Cyrillic were allowed to reach E, they would play havoc with it, there being no known and predictable order in which to arrange them among the Roman-script document surrogates.

This situation calls for a different regulator that can cope with the increased amount of variety introduced into the system by documents D_2. According to the Law of Requisite Variety, in order for R to do this effectively, it must be equipped with an amount of variety at least equal to or exceeding that of D_2. The regulating mechanism most often used in Western bibliographic control systems is script conversion or Romanization, which (in theory) is able to match each dissimilar character with a corresponding Roman letter and can therefore perform one-to-one transformations that ultimately reduce the threatening variety in D_2 to an orderly pattern similar to the one produced by control and regulation processes applied to documents D_1.

The regulator R_{22} now employed to handle the variety in D_2 is governed by a control routine C_{22} (the rules of a Romanization scheme), and R_{22} takes the place of regulator R_{21}. The diagram of immediate effects for the bibliographic control of a document in dissimilar script now follows the sequence shown in Figure 6.6. A document D_2, written in a dissimilar script, enters the system, is subjected to control routine C_1 by regulator R_1, then to conversion of script S by control routine C_{22} governing regulator R_{22}, and is finally acted on by regulator R_3, which is now able to follow control routine C_3 "as if" D_2 had been written in the dominant script. It is thereby transformed to E, where conditions are again held within the acceptable limits of η. In other words, the variety in document D_2 that threatened to drive E outside the limits of η acceptable to the operators has been blocked by the application of regulator R_{22}. This apparently satisfies the goals of the operators and makes the system viable from their point of view: documents in dissimilar scripts are "reduced" to document surrogates in the dominant script which can be integrated with other such document surrogates. They are now "readable"; that is, they can be filed by the same rules of alphabetization that are applicable to other document surrogates. But whereas documents originally written in the dominant script are uniquely and predictably identifiable by their

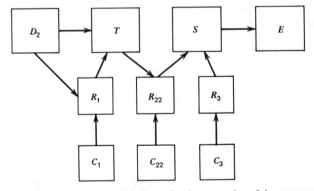

Figure 6.6.   Control of documents in dissimilar scripts by conversion of document surrogates from the dissimilar to the dominant script.

surrogates, this is only rarely the case for documents written in dissimilar scripts, because the conversion process is in most instances not an unambiguously reversible one-to-one transformation. In other words, the variety in regulator R_{22} is almost always *smaller* than the one introduced into the system by documents D_2. The document surrogates produced at E, though superficially resembling those for documents D_1, are actually no longer within the acceptable limits of states η.

2.4.2   The Conversion Process.   The conversion process that results in S should ideally consist of an isomorphic transformation in which a one-to-one relationship obtains between a character in the dissimilar script and its representation by a character of the dominant script. Only such an isomorphic transformation can make reversibility between the two scripts possible, so as to achieve exact reconstitution of a converted text in the source script. As shown in Chapter 5, one-to-one transformations in the conversion from a dissimilar source script to a dominant target script can be performed in principle only by transliteration in which each letter of the source alphabet has its unique and unambiguous equivalent in the target alphabet. However, because of certain features inherent in most alphabetic source scripts, the schemes employed for their conversion to other scripts must often resort to many-to-one or one-to-many transformations, so that the resulting transliterations are no longer isomorphic but become *distorted* transformations, with consequent distortions in the reconstitution of the source text. This fact invalidates the claim that transliteration makes it possible to identify unambiguously *any* original document if the transliteration scheme is applied in reverse. At best this is true only for *some* documents, and even then only between certain source and target scripts, such as Cyrillic to Roman and back to Cyrillic.

However, since there are as many different Roman alphabets as there are languages using this script, Romanization is always, in a sense, a one-to-many transformation. For example, several Cyrillic letters may be Romanized differently, depending on the alphabet of the target language. The opposite is true for Cyrillization, Arabization, and so forth, where many-to-one transformations must be made, namely from many Roman alphabets to the one alphabet used by the respective language. This is why such script conversions are performed not by transliteration but exclusively by transcription, that is, not on the purely graphemic level but only on the phonological level.

Transcription schemes for logographic (and for certain syllabic) scripts are without exception many-to-one transformations that cannot be disambiguated by reversion of the process; therefore they cannot be used for control purposes aimed at the unique identification of documents. In the case of Chinese the Wade-Giles transcription in its original form distinguishes between about 400 different syllables pronounced in four tones, which results in approximately 1600 different strings of Roman letters, diacritical marks, and raised numerals, representing some 10,000 Chinese logograms. The variety in Romanized output achieved through the full Wade-Giles regulator is therefore

$$V_E = \frac{10,000}{1,600} = 6.25 \tag{3}$$

a number that is already high enough to prevent any unambiguous identification of a Chinese logogram from its Romanized form. However, as we have seen in Chapter 4, in bibliographic practice the Wade-Giles transcription is used without the tone indicators and most diacritical marks, which reduces its variety to somewhat less than 300 unique strings of Roman letters.[47] Consequently the variety in Romanized Chinese bibliographic entries cannot be less than

$$V_E = \frac{10,000}{300} = 33.3 \tag{4}$$

This means that, on the average, any Romanized syllable may stand for any of more than 30 different logograms having completely different meanings. Actually some Romanizations, such as *hsi* or *shih,* may have more than a hundred different realizations in logographic form (see also Chapter 2, footnote 21).

In Japanese the possible variety in the output generated by the Hepburn Romanization (or any other transcription scheme) is even larger because Japanese words consist of from one to five (and sometimes more) syllables, and every Chinese logogram used to write a syllable may have from 2 to more than 200 different Japanese "readings" consisting of a combination of one or more of the 48 syllables that form the repertory of the Japanese language.

In short, far from producing unique document surrogates for documents in dissimilar scripts by isomorphic transformations, the transcription of logographic scripts inevitably results in distorted homomorphic transformations, that is, an output E that is no longer within the viable limits of states η as stipulated for a bibliographic control system.

Recognizing that there are many different conversion schemes for almost every script, we have already shown that, when more than one bibliographic system is involved, effective control of documents in dissimilar script is almost or entirely impossible. From a cybernetic point of view, adequate control can be achieved, at least in theory, for a limited number of scripts when only one control routine C_{22} is consistently applied to them within the confines of one bibliographic system (i.e., in the catalog of one library or in the compilation of one bibliography). But no bibliographic control system can stand alone; it must constantly interact with other bibliographic control systems of various kinds,

[47] J. D. Anderson (1974), p. 58.

such as publishers' trade lists, booksellers' stock lists, references to desired works submitted by users (which are products of personalized bibliographic control systems), bibliographies of all kinds, and last but not least, the bibliographic control tools of other libraries, either in the same country or throughout the world. Many of these bibliographic control systems use different control tools C_{221}, C_{222}, C_{223}, . . . , C_{22n} for the same language and script, with the well-known result that the document surrogates produced by them are mutually incompatible, sometimes to such a degree that there is not even an auxiliary subroutine for the conversion of the products of control routine C_{221} to those of control routine C_{222}, and so on. The solution to this problem is, of course, the long-cherished dream of most library operators, namely conversion systems for each script that are universally agreed upon and also universally and uniformly applied by everyone concerned with bibliographic control, from authors and translators to editors, publishers, booksellers, and, finally, librarians and bibliographers. Such a utopian state of affairs is unlikely to happen in the foreseeable future. Control of documents in dissimilar scripts by means of script conversion is not even feasible within the confines of a single bibliographic control system; much less is it possible to exercise such control in several separate but cooperating systems. At best a number of libraries may agree to use the same conversion schemes (but even then there may be discrepancies in application which make cooperative control difficult or even illusory), or a national or international agency may decide to use one set of conversion schemes that other libraries will have to accept if they wish to benefit from the bibliographical services provided by that agency.

Cybernetically, however, the proliferation of control routines constitutes only a special case of the one considered here in principle, and it does not affect the validity of the general argument. Rather the various document surrogates generated as output E by systems using different control routines C_{221}, C_{222}, C_{223}, . . . C_{22n}, form themselves disturbances D_{21}, D_{22}, D_{23}, . . . D_{2n}, with which each individual bibliographic control system has to cope by applying its own control routines.

In summary, the application of control routine C_{22} to documents in dissimilar scripts does not provide the operators with the same kind of absolute control that can be achieved by a control routine C_{21} applied to documents in the dominant script. No matter how well control routine C_{22} is applied, a certain amount of unwanted and potentially harmful variety in D_2 is transmitted through B to E; that is to say, the text of most document surrogates will not be unambiguously reversible to the source script so as to restore the exact identifying characteristics of a document in that script.

2.4.3 Control by Users.   "Users" in the case of documents written in the *dominant* script are all persons able to read that script (even though, as discussed in Section 2.3.3, not all are able to understand every language written in that script). The users of documents in *dissimilar* scripts, however, by definition constitute a minority among the community served by a documentary communication system. They are the ones able to read and understand one or more languages written in a script that is incomprehensible to the majority of the system's users as well as to all or most of its operators. In the following discussion of control by users it must constantly be kept in mind that we are dealing only with that minority of users who are actually capable of making use of documents in dissimilar scripts and who are most likely to derive any benefit from such a collection.[48]

The operators of most Western bibliographic control systems in which the Roman script is the dominant one tend to view documents in dissimilar scripts as a disturbance and a potential threat to the proper functioning of their system. The users of such documents, on the other hand, actually *need* the variety exhibited by these scripts, and they expect a bibliographic control system to preserve it rather than to destroy it through a regulation process. Regardless of whether a user is a native speaker of a foreign language or whether he has learned it (and its script) to the degree that he is able to read a text, his reference to an author's name or to a title will be in the script used by that language, either in written form or as visualized when the name or title is remembered. The users thus expect to find documents written in a dissimilar script by means of document surrogates written in that same script.

A bibliographic control system using conversion of scripts, however, presents its users with document surrogates written in the dominant script only, and in the process of conversion from dissimilar to dominant script the identifying characteristics of a document are distorted or even totally destroyed. From the users' point of view, therefore, the output E of a fully Romanized system has been driven beyond the acceptable limits of states η.

If a document surrogate has been produced by means of strict transliteration, there is at least a theoretical chance that the document surrogate can be reconverted to the original script, thus allowing the recovery of the meaning of the words. But if it has been made by transcription, especially from logographic

---

[48] It is sometimes argued that even persons who do not know a foreign language and its dissimilar script can make limited use of books and other documents written in that script. The illustrations in a Russian, Chinese, or Japanese book can be appreciated without any knowledge of languages, and the calligraphy of Persian manuscripts is pleasant to behold even if the text cannot be read and understood. Since users who do not know dissimilar scripts constitute the majority, their needs ought to be given preference over those of the minority—hence Romanization of entries for documents in dissimilar scripts. But this is a spurious argument, because written communication depends for its effect on the comprehension of texts, and if Western libraries collect large quantities of Russian, Chinese, or Japanese books, they cannot justify the existence and maintenance of such collections by their visual and other aesthetic values only. Books and periodicals are meant, after all, to be read. If only a minority of users are able to do that, they must be given access and retrieval facilities that are as good and effective as those provided for documents in the dominant script.

scripts, the meaning is in most instances irretrievably destroyed. Both methods confront the user with an initially unintelligible string of letters, and put the burden of decipherment on him.

The essential difference between this situation and the one concerning a Hungarian book in a Roman script catalog is the following. To an English-speaking operator a Hungarian or transliterated Russian document surrogate looks equally unintelligible (if he does not know those languages); both seem to be mere strings of letters that apparently form words but do not convey any meaning. As we have seen, the riddle of the Hungarian document surrogate can be solved, at least partially, by using a dictionary as a standard key for the decipherment of meaning (and the native Hungarian speaker would, of course, not need such a key since he would be able to grasp the meaning immediately). The transliterated Russian document surrogate, however, remains equally meaningless to both operator and user, because there are no standard dictionaries in which transliterated Russian words and their equivalent Russian spelling in Cyrillic can be verified. Instead the user who wishes to read a Russian book by a certain author must himself figure out the original spelling of the author's name or the title of a work. If the reader is to succeed in this task, at least two conditions must be fulfilled by the operators:

1. The conversion system (control routine C_{22}) must be made known to all users.
2. The conversion system must be applied consistently and without any errors.

Even assuming that these ideal conditions are fulfilled (which is rarely if ever the case in reality), so much of the variety in document D_2 is destroyed in the conversion process that, from the user's point of view, the document is almost or even completely unrecognizable. This is the case in particular when the whole document surrogate has been converted to the dominant script and no trace of the original script remains. The user is confronted with a distorted image at best, and he must rely on evidence twice removed (a surrogate of a surrogate) in order to gain even that distorted information from the system.

Thus the system whose purpose is rendering a service to its users, and which therefore ought to be what the Germans aptly call "benutzerfreundlich," turns out to be anything but that. The users derive little if any benefits from the control methods employed by the operators, and are pretty much left to their own devices.

Incidentally, such a system is also uneconomical, since the measure of performance of a system designed to provide a service is equal to the benefit to its users minus the cost of rendering the service. In the case of providing access to documents in dissimilar scripts by means of Romanized document surrogates, the benefit to users is small or even nonexistent, while the cost of producing the service is quite high and at any rate much higher than the average cost of producing surrogates for documents in the dominant script.

2.5   The Conflict between Operators and Users

As we have seen, neither operators nor users of a bibliographic control system can actually gain effective control over documents written in dissimilar scripts by means of script conversion. The operators of the system are, however, seldom aware of this fact, or rather, they are reasonably satisfied with the system because it seems to achieve their goals and because they have a vested interest in keeping the system going, no matter what the users may think of it, or whether their goals are achieved.

This conflict between operators and users about the methods of control over documents in dissimilar scripts can be seen as another result of the Law of Requisite Variety as applied to a very large system. According to Ashby, the capacity of a regulator R to reduce variety in D is limited when the variety in D is very large (as indeed it is in the case of documents in dissimilar scripts). In this instance

The law of requisite variety enforces a . . . strategy on the would-be regulator and controller: he should try to get near his maximum. . . .[49]

Consequently the operators of the system try to exercise maximum control with means that best achieve *their* goals.

Their maximum (or optimum) is, however, not compatible with that of the system's minority users, who have a different goal and would also like to achieve maximal or at least optimal control, albeit with different means. For them a document D_2 is not perceived as being written in a dissimilar script at all. When a user who knows Russian wishes to use a Russian book, this becomes for him, from the moment this decision has been made and until he can actually read it, a document in a dominant script—the script that "dominates" his intention to communicate through graphic signs with a person who had something to say about a subject in Russian. Consequently the bibliographic control method desired by a user for a Russian book is a document surrogate written in Cyrillic script and filed according to the Cyrillic alphabet together with document surrogates for other Russian books.

But since the application of such control methods would affect the conventional Western bibliographic control system in an adverse manner, and most or all of its operators would lose control over documents in dissimilar scripts, the operators are naturally motivated to use methods that preserve both the system as they know it and their own position in it, rather than accommodating the interests of a minority among their users.

This conflict, particularly the efforts made by the operators to employ control tools that preserve the status quo, is typical for many organizations managed as if

[49] Ashby (1956), p. 245.

they were a closed system. This has been observed by social scientists who based their conclusions also on the cybernetic theories of Ashby and on the related systems theory of Ludwig von Bertalanffy,[50] especially his principle of equifinality, according to which a system can reach the same final state by a variety of paths:

Moves towards tighter integration and coordination are made to insure stability, when flexibility may be the more important requirement. Moreover, coordination and control become ends in themselves rather than means to an end. They are not seen in full perspective as adjusting the system to its environment but as desirable goals within a closed system. . . .

One error which stems from this kind of misconception is the failure to recognize the equifinality of the open system, namely that there are more ways than one of producing a given outcome. In a closed physical system the same initial conditions must lead to the same final result. In open systems this is not true even at the biological level. It is much less true at the social level.[51]

In the model of a bibliographic control system considered here, the operators and the users of the system appear to be cast in the role of players at a game in which the dice are usually loaded in favor of the operators, while the users are most often the losers. Even though this is at present the case in many real-life situations, to draw such a conclusion would be based on a false analogy caused by viewing the system as if it were a closed one in which the output E could be produced by one kind of regulator only, namely Romanization. But a bibliographic control system is actually an open one whose desired output can be achieved by various control operations, and there need not be any antagonism between the goals of operators and users, because both are equally interested in the proper functioning of the system. Regulation of the system should thus work in such a way that neither operators nor users will lose and that both are able to achieve their legitimate goals, namely an output E that is effective from the point of view of the operators and useful from the point of view of the users. If a certain control method does not achieve this kind of regulation, it must be discarded in favor of other control methods, or some of the components of the system may have to be modified in order to make it work properly.

The reason for the failure of control routine C_{22}, the Romanization (or other script conversion) of document surrogates, to satisfy the legitimate goals of operators and users alike is not its faulty or imperfect construction, but rather the disturbance caused by documents in dissimilar scripts, which by their very nature are not amenable to control by this method. Conversion of scripts is a type of control routine that cannot achieve the necessary regulation by reducing the

[50]Bertalanffy (1973).
[51]Katz and Kahn (1966), pp. 26–27.

disturbing variety in D_2 in such a manner that the output E is still in a viable state η as required by the inherent and proclaimed purposes of the system, namely the provision of unique and predictable access to all documents in a documentary communication system for all of its users. In cybernetic terms noise is generated in a communications channel by irreducible variety at the input; to overcome this irreducible variety and to achieve a viable output in the form of unique identification requires additional parallel channels for permanent error correction.

The logical conclusion is that *the problem of control over documents in dissimilar scripts cannot be solved by purely graphemic transformations*.

What is needed for the control of documents in dissimilar scripts in bibliographic control systems is thus not a set of ''better'' transliteration or transcription schemes, but an entirely different approach that avoids the essentially unsolvable problem of converting one script into another in a perfect and universally applicable manner.

3 ALTERNATIVE METHODS OF BIBLIOGRAPHIC CONTROL

3.1 Bibliographic Control without Script Conversion

Even the most ardent champions of Romanization have always admitted that the practice is more a hindrance than a help to those who can read other scripts, but they insist that Romanization has to be performed in the interests of catalogers and reference librarians as well as for the benefit of Western scholars. At present, many people also think that Romanization is a precondition for universal bibliographic control performed with the aid of machines. But, as we have seen, the operators of library systems are not as well served by Romanization as they would like to think, because, far from producing universal control, the method tends to generate universal bibliographic chaos concealed by a varnish of artificially imposed ''alphabetical order.'' Regarding the service rendered by Romanization to ''scholars'' (a term that in this context is often restricted to the students of philology and other branches of the humanities), it is of questionable value. Orientalists, historians, ethnographers, and others frequently complain about the deficiencies and inanities of this or that transcription found in library catalogs and in bibliographies, whenever these do not coincide with the conversion scheme favored by that scholar in his own field of specialization. As for the Western reader in general, we have seen how difficult it is to find the name of an author when it is given only in transcription, and how meaningless the Romanization of titles is to anyone who does not know the language of the original.

But even assuming that a particular class of scholars is served to a certain extent by Romanization, the questions must be asked: What about service to the now much larger and ever-growing class of scholars and students in other scientific disciplines? What help is given to general readers who happen to have a good knowledge of languages written in non-Roman scripts and who therefore have a legitimate need of direct access to documents written in such scripts? Until now their interests have been treated with benign neglect, to put it mildly. But is it really possible in this day and age to neglect or even to deny the needs of a sizable segment of the user population of libraries and the needs of those who need bibliographic tools as a key to the world's literature in scripts other than the Roman? Does not this seriously impair the *raison d'être* of libraries as perceived today, namely to be service-oriented agencies of a community? And should libraries continue to collect documents in dissimilar scripts when they do not have the necessary expertise to make intelligent use of them, being content merely to "mark and park" them in a way that makes it exceedingly difficult or outright impossible for a user to gain direct access to them?

These questions can find rational and viable answers only if conversion of scripts, and Romanization in particular, is no longer considered either as sacrosanct or as a panacea for all the woes that beset librarians because of the proliferation of documents in dissimilar scripts.

One of the most significant achievements of the scientific method has been to show conclusively which problems cannot be solved at all and which ones cannot be solved with certain methods, so that the endeavors of theoreticians, system operators, and system users in the broadest sense could be devoted to those problems that are amenable to solution and to methods that achieve their intended aim. Once it had been shown that the squaring of the circle was impossible to perform by ruler and compass, it ceased to be a problem with which mathematicians were concerned and became a historical curiosity. The *perpetuum mobile* exercised the minds of serious mechanical inventors only until the formulation of the laws of thermodynamics which proved the impossibility of ever achieving such a thing; thereafter it became the domain of knaves and fools.

When analyzed by scientific methods, the idea of effective bibliographic control over all the world's documents through script conversion has now also been exposed as an elusive dream. It therefore seems imperative to search for alternative methods of control that will be of equal benefit to the operators and users of bibliographic control systems, and which will ultimately provide a sound basis for truly universal bibliographic control of all mankind's graphic records in whatever script they may be written.

This conclusion immediately raises a number of questions:

1. Are the methods of transliteration and transcription obsolete or useless in bibliographic work? If not, when and to which extent should they be applied?
2. What are the alternative methods for effective control of documents in dissimilar scripts?

3. Will such alternative methods be amenable to handling by computers and other automated equipment?
4. How can a changeover to alternative methods be effectuated without disruption of the functioning of existing bibliographic tools and with minimal costs to the producers of such tools?

The answer to the first question has essentially been given in Section 1.8 of this chapter. Here it remains only to reaffirm that script conversion by means of transliteration and transcription can and must be used for many bibliographic purposes, such as the rendering of names and words in translations, in subject headings, and in index entries to translated works or translated title citations, in references to the names of persons and places, and so on. They also fulfill an important function in bibliographic citations (e.g., in the indication of the title of a periodical as a source), provided that the converted form of a name or a title is not the *only* means of identification and that adequate provision is made to supply the user with a minimum of bibliographic data in the source script, which will enable him to identify the original document.

When conversion of scripts is no longer used as the sole means of identification for documents in a dissimilar script, it will become less important to use only one particular scheme or to make transcriptions in a manner that satisfies mainly the needs of specialists, i.e., with a plethora of diacritical marks and special characters. Conversion schemes can be simple or sophisticated, depending on their intended use; above all, they can be made compatible, at least on a national level, with the orthographic and phonological conventions of the language community served by a documentary communication system.

This means that an English, French, or German rendering of a Russian name will not necessarily have to be mutually compatible, provided that other and more reliable means of identification are employed for bibliographic control purposes. It will then matter little that the transcriptions are made according to what a native English, French, or German user is best able to read and pronounce. Actually, as we have seen, the conversion practices of libraries in various countries differ considerably from each other despite all efforts at standardization, and it would be futile to hope for a unification of the various systems in the foreseeable future, since it is virtually impossible, for technical as well as economical reasons, to change the vast accumulations of bibliographical data in the catalogs of large libraries and in bibliographic reference tools. Moreover even the more or less strict transliteration schemes have always made allowance for linguistic differences, thereby violating the very principle and *raison d'être* of script conversion as a control tool and resulting in awkward compromises with consequent loss of control and information. This has made transliteration "a custom more honor'd in the breach than the observance."

While reliance on alternative control tools will thus make it possible to tolerate a certain amount of divergence in the rendering of names and words on a *national* level, there will remain the need for conversion schemes that are *internationally* recognized and applied in situations where preference cannot be given to any national scheme or to one that is rooted in the psycholinguistic habits and graphemic conventions of a certain language community. The Romanization of serials titles by the International Centre for the Registration of Serial Publications in Paris is an example (although concordances of Romanized titles with the titles in their original script ought also to be published to ensure their unambiguous identification).

Consequently the ISO's activities in the field of standards for script conversion should be aimed at revision of the existing *Recommendations* for transliteration with a view to their applicability in bibliographic control, and toward the design of conversion schemes for scripts not yet covered. This ought to be done, however, with the clear understanding that truly international conversion schemes cannot satisfy the often divergent demands of philologists and other specialists, or the long-standing traditions of certain language communities, but will serve solely as perhaps somewhat mechanistic transformations of graphemes from script A to script B for purely technical purposes. They will serve as an international switching code, from and to which national or specialized script conversions may be made as needed. In certain cases, namely where a true one-to-one relationship between source and target script can be established (as is fortunately the case with Cyrillic, the script in which today the majority of all non-Roman documents is written), it will be possible to do this almost entirely with the help of automated methods.

A detailed answer to the question of alternative methods would go beyond the scope of this study. A problem of such magnitude and diversity as the design of suitable methods for bibliographic control of documents in all the world's scripts is obviously a task that can be tackled only by groups of experts, preferably under the auspices of international agencies such as UNESCO, the International Federation of Documentation (FID), the IFLA, and the ISO, to name only those that are most intimately concerned with Universal Bibliographic Control.

The following suggestions for practical solutions are therefore made only in barest outline, in the hope that they will be investigated in the framework of Universal Bibliographic Control. We wish to emphasize at the outset that these suggestions are mainly based on methods that are already in use for various other bibliographic control purposes. These suggestions also take into consideration existing conditions in the world's libraries and in other bibliographic enterprises, and recognize various technical and economic constraints, while at the same time aiming at better control of documents in dissimilar scripts, and at improved access to such documents for people who need them as information sources.

Nothing would be easier than to design an ideal blueprint for a "universal" method to achieve these aims, but it would remain a sterile paper-and-pencil exercise, because libraries would find it impossible to implement it for organizational, financial, and other reasons, and the compilers of bibliographies as well as the editors of abstracting and indexing services would not submit to it. Our suggestions are meant to be practical, and we realize that they will not result in perfect solutions. But the quest for perfect solutions is the hallmark of fanatics or impractical dreamers, and we wish to avoid the pitfalls of both extremes, because it seems to us that many of the troubles that beset bibliographic control today can be traced to a utopian belief in panaceas and in perfectionism, held by librarians of a bygone age. We agree with the British librarian Wilfred Ashworth:

There is another thing for which the classical librarian can be blamed: . . . his firmly-held idea that there is a perfect answer to every problem. If one believes this, it is logical enough to imagine that the safest way to ensure finding that answer is to have access to everything—hence the massive collections.[52]

3.2 Centralization of Collections in Dissimilar Scripts

The last sentence of the quotation just cited implies that massive collections are not always the ideal or the only possible solution to the problem of effective provision of books and other documents to those in need of information sources. A research report on acquisition policies in Canadian university and college libraries, with the significant subtitle "Are total world coverage and non-duplication of resources part of an impossible dream?"[53] came to similar conclusions. The investigator found that libraries, instead of making frantic efforts to cover everything from everywhere by means of standing orders and comprehensive acquisition programs, should be assigned collecting responsibilities based on subject allocations and organized on a regional basis, and that the criterion for acquisition of certain materials should be their potential use rather than sheer quantity.

What has been recommended for subject collections is even more relevant for collections in dissimilar scripts. The Farmington Plan has already resulted in the concentration of material in certain lesser-known languages and scripts in a few designated libraries in the United States, and similar agreements exist among university libraries in Germany and in Scandinavia.[54] But the acquisition of

---

[52] Ashworth (1974), p. 67.

[53] Ettlinger (1973).

[54] The Farmington Plan, initiated in the United States in 1947, provides for the acquisition of at least one copy of any scholarly publication from abroad by selected libraries to which certain subject areas and languages are assigned by mutual agreement. In Germany a project called *Sondersammelgebiete* was started in 1949, according to which certain university and special libraries acquire at least one copy of books and periodicals published outside Germany, with certain libraries covering the "difficult" languages. The Scandia Plan operates among the university libraries of Denmark, Norway, and Sweden in a similar manner.

books and manuscripts in exotic languages and scripts is still considered a status symbol in many libraries, although they do not have the resources to handle such documents adequately and would be better advised to leave that task to those libraries that have the means necessary to cope with the resulting problems. A library with no Russian cataloger, no Russian-speaking reference librarian, and no facilities for typing or printing Russian catalog entries has today no business collecting Russian books and periodicals. Both its local users and others throughout the country would be better served if any Russian material held by a library that is "illiterate" in Cyrillic were sent to a national library or to selected large research libraries that have the necessary resources to deal with such documents and to put them to good use. The local users, if in need of Russian material, could always be served by means of photocopies, microreproductions, and interlibrary loan of actual documents, provided that at least one key library in a country, state, or region specializes in the acquisition and bibliographic control of Russian books and other documents. A user's request, written in Russian, could not be handled directly, to be sure, by the local librarians, but if told that the request is for a Russian book, they would at least know to which library to channel such a request. Even in a country as large as the United States, only one or at most few libraries would have to be responsible for documents in scripts in which the literary output is small and which are used only by a limited number of people.

3.3   Catalogs by Script and Language

Libraries that deal with documents written in a certain script because they have the necessary personnel and expertise should reorganize their catalogs by script (and in some instances, notably for Arabic, Hebrew, and Chinese script, also by language). At first sight, this might be considered a revolutionary development for most Western libraries. But the choice lies between a continuation of the present practice of wholesale Romanization which creates bibliographic chaos under a thin veneer of apparent order, at steep costs for the operators and with small or nonexisting benefits for the users, and a system that is demonstrably less costly (because several stages of conversion are eliminated) and offers increased benefits to the users (which constitute an indirect cost reduction). When the issue of Romanized catalogs versus separate catalogs is considered from the point of view of its cost effectiveness, the arrangement of separate catalogs by script will appear in a different light, not least to library administrators who have to allocate limited resources where they can be used to best advantage.

Moreover the idea is far from new or untried. Separate catalogs for certain scripts, notably Chinese and Japanese, are or have been maintained in several American libraries with large East Asian collections. Separate card catalogs in

Hebrew script (at least for titles of works) are kept in the Library of Congress and in other libraries with substantial Judaica collections. The technical as well as economical feasibility of a separate catalog by script has recently been demonstrated by the New York Public Library Research Libraries which, beginning in 1976, have listed Hebrew titles (though not yet authors' names) in the original script in a separate part of their book catalog (see Figure 6.7).

The Bibliothèque Nationale in Paris has kept separate catalogs by script since 1960. Its librarian in charge of East Asian language material, Mme. Christiane Rageau, considers this practice to be useful also for other libraries and bibliographies. In a paper read at the 29th International Congress of Orientalists in Paris in 1973, she stated:

Les choix des pays asiatiques eux-mêmes devraient être les seuls choix valables. . . . Pour les bibliographies nationales, l'exemple de celle de Singapour qui parait depuis 1967, est intéressant a noter: elle donne en 4 langues et trois écritures la liste en trois séries des publications du pays. Dans la perspective de Contrôle bibliographique universel, comment se fera l'exploitation des notices par les autres bibliothèques? Gardera-t-on les notices d'ouvrages chinois et tamoul en écriture originale dans les catalogues des bibliothèques étrangères? La question devrait être envisagée avant tout en fonction de la rapidité et du côté pratique.[55]

The major national and research libraries in the Soviet Union have always maintained separate catalogs by script, both for author and title sequences, and in the classified subject sections.[56] The same practice is followed by many libraries in Yugoslavia, where the coexistence of two scripts for one language makes this practically a necessity. Most university and public libraries of Asian and African countries with multilingual and multiscript populations are naturally arranging their catalogs by script and language as the only practical solution to the problem.

Lest it be thought that only library users in Europe and in Asian countries prefer catalogs by script and language, it is worthwhile to cite the opinion of an American scientist whose subject, zoology, makes it necessary to use Russian references frequently:

. . . the practice of giving literature citations and making library cards in the Cyrillic alphabet should be encouraged. It takes little more time to learn the letters than to master

[55]Rageau (1973), pp. 11–12.
[56]An American delegation of librarians visiting Soviet libraries in 1960 "was very much interested in the way in which the cards for books printed in different kinds of characters (e.g., Arabic, Chinese, Bengali, and Hindi) were filed sequentially, without transliteration, behind the cards for Russian books under each subject heading in the main classified catalogs, instead of being organized into separate linguistic catalogs. But in the author catalogs separate files were used for books in different language groups" (Ruggles and Swank, 1962, p. 74).

אברהם רימון. יגור. 729 [1968 or 9]
118 p. illus., facsims., ports. 23 cm. NN
75-4767310 LC 78-281840
[*PWZ (Rimon) 75-5655]

אברי בן שדה-נחום. [שדה-נחום, קיבוץ
שדה-נחום, 1968?]
24 p. illus. 25 cm. Cover title. Microfiche (neg.) 1
sheet. 11 x 15 cm. (NYPL FSN 20,371) Title
romanized: Avri. NN 75-4817634 LC 72-950297
[*XMH-629]

אגודות ההתעמלות והספורט בארץ-ישראל
לפני מלחמת העולם הראשונה.
Simri, Uriel, 1925-
[ירושלים] 1968.
54 p. NN 76-4173135 LC 70-950231
[*PRR 75-5590]

האגרון.
Saadiah ben Joseph, gaon, 892?-942.
ירושלים, האקדמיה ללשון העברית [1969]
584, xix, p. NN 74-4789794 LC 70-952019
[*PCK 74-2713]

אגרות.
Moses ben Maimon, 1135-1204.
ירושלים, מוסד הרב קוק [1972]
172 p. NN 75-4770494 LC 72-950393
[*PPO 75-4460]

אדם וצלו.
Murad, Emil, 1931-
[תל-אביב] אל"ף [1970]
46 p. NN 74-4876345 LC 77-953468
[*PSF 75-4548]

האדם לבדו ...
Arigur, Isaac, 1902-
תל-אביב, חושן, 1970.
1 v. Vol. 1. NN 75-4767346 LC 74-952639
[*PBP 75-5651]

האדם על הירח.
Kasher, Menachem Mendel, 1895-
[ירושלים] 1970?
70 p. NN 76-4060162 LC 73-952076
[*PNK 75-5716]

אדמו"רי טשרנוביל.
Klapholz, Israel Jacob.
[בני-ברק] 731 [1971]
1 v. Vol. 1. NN 75-4714179 LC 77-953433
[*PQV 75-5591]

ספר אדרא קדישא.
Idra raba.
ירושלים
[S. E. Margolyot,
732
i. e. 1972] 147, [4] p. NN 76-4044500 LC
72-950678
[*PQG 75-5633]

א. טללי אורות.
Kook, Abraham Isaac, 1865-1935.
ירושלים, 733 [1972 or 3]
24 p. NN 75-4815894 LC 74-950534
[*XMH-685]

א. ספר מבין חידות.
Joseph ben David, of Eshva, d. 1771.
[ירושלים, 733
i. e. 1972 or 3] 1 v. (various pagings) NN
75-4422815 LC 75-950160
[*PDM 75-2376]

אבא בן-יעקב; לזכרו. [דגניה א'] הוצאת
דגניה א', 728 , [1967 or 8]
40 p. ports. 23 cm. Microfiche (neg.) 1 sheet. 11
x 15 cm. (NYPL FSN 21,862) Title romanized: Aba
Ben-Ya'akov. NN 76-4067166 LC HE68-3242
[*XMH-624]

אביתר. נחשול הוכה בסלע; סיפור חייו של
אביתר כהן. [נערך והובא לדפוס ע"י חבריו
לנשק. תל-אביב, צוות, 731]
i. e. 1970 or 1971] 96 p. NN 75-4711589
LC 70-954379
[*PWZ (Kohen, E.) 75-5605]

אבן שלמה.
Bible. O. T. Esther. Hebrew. 1971 or 2.
מגלת אסתר ... עם פירוש ... אליהו מווילנא,
ובסופו ... ביאורים ... מהרה"ג אברהם בן
הגרא ... ומהגאון דוד לוריא. ונלה עליו
פירוש על ברכות יוצר אור ועל תפלת השמע
... מהרה"ג מוהר"א ... וארשא [647]
i. e. 1886 or 7]
יצא לאור מחדש על ידי זונדל ברמן.
ניו-יארק, דפוס א. י. פריעדמאן,732
[1971 or 2]
52, 144, 54-68 p. NN 75-4709077 LC
74-950274
[*PDV (Esther) 75-5565]

אברהם אבינוס לעבן און שאפונג.
Rosmarin, Aaron, 1896-
ניו יארק, אום פאבלישינג קא., 724 [1964]
180 p. NN 75-4169780 LC 74-951393
[*PDY (Abraham) 75-779]

אברהם אוליצקי [במלאות שנה לפטירת
אברהם אוליצקי. עמיר, קיבוץ השומר
הצעיר עמיר, 1967]
[28] p. illus., ports. 24 cm. Cover title.
Microfiche (neg.) 1 sheet. 11 x 15 cm. (NYPL FSN
20,374) Title romanized: Avraham Olitski. NN
75-4817672 LC 79-950260
[*XMH-625]

אברהם אמר. בית השיטה, 728 [1967 or 8]
43 p. illus. 17 cm. Cover title:
אמר
Microfiche (neg.) 1 sheet. 11 x 15 cm. (NYPL FSN
21,845) Title romanized: Avraham Amar. NN

Figure 6.7. Hebrew titles in the computer-produced book catalog of the New York Public Library Research Libraries. (From the *Dictionary Catalog of The Research Libraries*. Reproduced by kind permission of the New York Public Library, Astor, Lenox and Tilden Foundations.)

some one of the transliteration systems, and many rather monstrous difficulties are thus avoided.[57]

3.3.1 Production of Entries in Dissimilar Alphabets.

Advances in library technology have made card catalogs somewhat of an anachronism in technologically advanced countries, where large and medium-sized libraries are now increasingly switching to more sophisticated forms, such as computer-produced catalogs in book form and on microfilm, and on-line catalogs. But it is safe to assume that the card catalog will remain in use for several decades, not only in many libraries in technically advanced countries but certainly in less affluent and developing countries unable to afford the hardware necessary for the utilization of other forms of cataloging. The question of how to produce catalog cards in non-Roman scripts must therefore be addressed.

Contrary to conventional opinion, the production of catalog cards in various scripts does not constitute a major technical problem. Where cards are now being typed entirely in Romanized form (see Figure 6.8, (*a*) and (*b*)), with diacritical marks often laboriously inserted by hand, overtyping, or typing between lines —all very time-consuming and errorprone methods—this is not so much because of a lack of technical resources as because of a deliberate policy. If typewriters in non-Roman scripts were provided, the language experts now employed to Romanize entries and to check the work of typists for accuracy would probably be able to type entries in the original script much faster and with fewer errors. Technical advances in typewriter design now make it possible to type several scripts on the same IBM Selectric machine, by exchanging only balls with different type fonts. IBM even designed a machine that can type scripts running from right to left, such as Arabic and Hebrew, in addition to typing left-to-right scripts (all one has to do is to put on the appropriate ball and to press a lever that governs the movement of the ball in the desired direction). Where cards are now being printed or typed in a dissimilar script except for a Romanized heading (as is the practice of the Library of Congress and many other libraries), the technical and typographical resources obviously exist to print the whole entry in that script (see Figure 6.8, *(c)*–*(g)*).

Catalog cards with headings in non-Roman scripts could, of course, no longer be filed by clerks who are illiterate in those scripts. The task of filing (for so long considered "simple" and requiring only the barest minimum of training and intellectual level, until the difficulties encountered in the design of computer filing showed it to be a highly complex operation) would indeed often have to be performed by the same language specialists who created the entries, or it would

---

[57]The quotation is from a letter to the editor, published as one of several such contributions to the discussion of an article by Razran (1959) on the transliteration of Russian in *Science* **130** (28 August 1959), p. 484.

(a) A h a w a i n ī al-Buḫārī, Abū-Bakr Rabīʿ Ibn-Aḥmad
al-: HIDĀJAT al-mutaʿallimīn fi 'ṭ-ṭibb. Bi-ihtimām-
i Ǧalāl Matīnī.
Mašhad: Čāpẖāna-i Dānišgāh-i Mašhad 1344 h.š.
(1965). 68,918 S. 8° [Pers.]

(b) ḴAZWĪNĪ (MUḤAMMAD MAHDĪ AL-KĀẒIMĪ AL-).

--- [Khaṣā'iṣ al-shīʿa.] [Arab.]
[Baghdād, 1922.]

(c) [KAZANSKAYA.] Казанская история. Подготовка текста,
вступительная статья и примечания Г.Н. Моисеевой.
Под ред. В.П. Адриановой-Перетц.

(d) KAZANTZAKIS (NIKOS).

--- Οἱ ἀδερφοφάδες. Μυθιστόρημα. Ἑβδόμη ἐκδ.

(e) Negrul᾽, Aleksandr Mikhaĭlovich
(Vinogradarstvo)
Виноградарство; с основами ампелографии
и селекции. Москва, Гос. изд-во с.-х.
лит-ры, 1952.

(f) Abgarian, Gevorg V
"Սեթբռոսի պատմութjունր" եվ Անանունի
տոեղձվածը [զրtg] Գ. Վ. Արզարjան: Եթե-
վան, Հաjկական ՍՍՌ Գիտությունների Ակադե-
միաjի Հրատ., 1965:

(g) CHIANG Chien-po 蔣 建 白
CHUNG-KUO chiao-yü wen-t'i
中 國 教 育 問 題
Education en Chine.
台 北 ， 正 中 書 局
1972.- 21 cm., 305 p.

Figure 6.8. Specimens of Romanized entries from various libraries.

at least have to be done by people who know a certain script and the rules for its orderly arrangement. The price of filing would be higher, but so would the value of the service rendered to users by a retrieval tool offering direct and unambiguous access to documents in the same manner in which a Roman catalog offers this service for documents written in Roman script.

For computer-produced catalogs (either in book form or in microform on roll film or microfiches) cold-type composition by computer-controlled phototypesetting devices or by cathode ray tube (CRT) photography is the obvious solution, because practically any character can be reproduced by these methods once its image has been stored mechanically or electronically,[58] and entries can also be alphabetized automatically by a suitable program, as shown in Figure 6.7. Computer-controlled cold-type printing is at present still quite costly if only relatively few copies of a document are to be produced, as would be the case for the catalog of an individual library. But not every library or bibliographic service would need such sophisticated devices to produce its own multiscript catalogs, because master entries would be provided mainly by large central libraries or by national bibliographies in countries where a particular non-Roman script is dominant, such as in the Singapore example. Other libraries in need of catalog entries could then make copies on cards or on slips to be stripped into photomechanically produced pages of book catalogs by inexpensive photolithographic processes or even by an office-copying process.

Where direct printout is necessary, this can now also be provided by teletypewriters and other devices in either on-line or off-line mode, as demonstrated by a pilot project at the National Bureau of Standards in the United States.[59]

3.3.2 Production of Entries in Logographic Scripts.

These methods for mechanized production of catalog entries are admittedly better suited to alphabetic scripts than to logographic ones, namely Chinese, Japanese, and Korean. In these scripts it is difficult to generate the many thousands of different images of the characters, and additional difficulties arise concerning their sequential ordering (the equivalent of alphabetic filing in other scripts). However, as far as bibliographic control of logographically written documents is concerned, it is not absolutely necessary to produce the images of the characters themselves by means of a computer or other automatic device. A method of representing Chinese logograms by different yet unambiguous graphemes has been used for many years, long before the first modern computers

---

[58] Law (1974). Photocomposition can easily reproduce any alphabetic script written with unconnected characters, such as Roman, Cyrillic, Greek, or Hebrew, but even the cursive script of Arabic has been made amenable to computer-controlled photocomposition through the efforts of Pierre MacKay (1976, 1977).

[59] Duncan and Garvin (1974).

were even thought about; it uses the simple expedient of assigning four-digit serial numbers to each character in a key table or dictionary. Chinese telegrams have been sent by means of the Standard Telegraphic Code for decades without much difficulty, and the National Science Foundation recommended the use of the Chinese numerical telegraph code for scientific work with Chinese texts.[60] The numbers assigned to Chinese characters in a Chinese–English dictionary have also been used to identify names and titles in scholarly works.[61]

Although writing Chinese by numbers is a cumbersome method when done manually, it seems to be well suited for treatment of Chinese script by computer. Input of text can be in numerical form only, while output may be either in the same numerical form or in the form of the corresponding logograms, depending on the kind of printing or display equipment used. Purely numerical output makes it necessary for a user to look up the characters in an index or in a key dictionary to which the numbers refer—a process that, although somewhat slow, often requires far less of a Chinese reader's time than trying to figure out which of the many different meanings of the Romanized syllable *shih,* for example, is the one contained in a Chinese title. Output of actual Chinese characters is, however, now also well within the capabilities of computers and their ancillary equipment. The National Diet Library in Tokyo produces catalog cards and printed bibliographies by computer-controlled printing devices which generate 336 *kana* signs (both *katakana* and *hiragana* in three different typefaces and sizes), 3965 *kanji* characters, 418 Roman letters in various typefaces, including boldface and italic, 95 numerals, and 214 symbols (see Figure 6.9).[62]

In the United States, IBM has developed the IBM Chinese Keyboard, a device based on the radicals of Chinese logograms; it has two keyboards, one a matrix of the 214 radicals, the other a 128 × 128 matrix of characters, a combination that allows the input and reproduction of practically all Chinese logograms. Another method, also using equipment designed by IBM, has been developed at Université Laval (Québec) by Marion R. Finley.[63] It is said to be capable of

---

[60]"Use of the Chinese telegraph code by groups working with Chinese texts has been recommended by the Foundation . . . in order to avoid the multiplicity of transliteration systems. . . . '' (National Science Foundation. 11th annual report. Washington, D.C., 1961. Pp. 127–128).

[61]George Sarton used the numbers assigned to Chinese logograms in the *Chinese–English dictionary* by H. A. Giles in order to make the transcription of Chinese names unambiguous, as explained in v. 1, pp. 47–48, of his *Introduction to the history of science* (Sarton, 1927), for example, K'ung³ Fu¹ Tzǔ³ (6605, 3612, 12317).

[62]"Printed catalogue cards of the National Diet Library: their preparation and distribution.'' *National Diet Library Newsletter,* no. 36 (1973):1–6. See also Japan. National Diet Library (1974?), Tanabe (1972), p. 169, and Oda (1974). Numerical coding of Chinese characters by the Chinese telegraph code for computer input, producing direct output of the characters by means of computer graphics has been successfully employed by K.-F. Lee at the University of Leeds for linguistic analysis of Chinese texts; see Lee (1975).

[63]Finley (1974). Other input and output devices for Chinese logograms are discussed in Stallings (1975), where an extensive bibliography on the subject can be found.

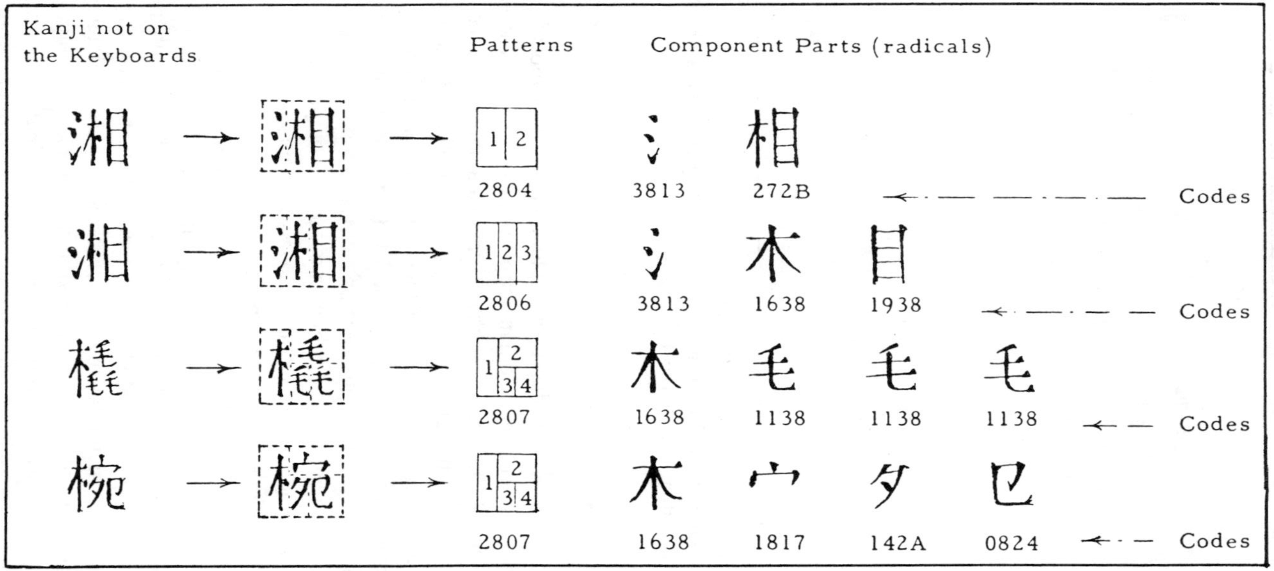

Figure 6.9 Computer-produced Japanese script. (*a*) Direct printout of radicals and generation of complex characters by suitable combination of radicals, controlled by numerical input.

KA234
2   井 口　海 仙 （1900–　　 ）
           茶室の案内
              京都　淡交社　昭和43（1968）
              216p（図版共）　19 cm　（茶の湯ライブラリー　4 ）

785953   1.茶室　I.書名　II.叢書名

KA234-2   Iguti, Kaisen
791.6   500円
                                             [民][図]69-3245

(*b*)

Figure 6.9. (*b*) Specimen of actual printout in Japanese and English, produced by the National Diet Library system. (Courtesy National Diet Library, Tokyo.)

constructing and displaying Chinese characters, using a keyboard not much larger than one for conventional Roman script, but its main purpose is to solve the difficult problem of filing Chinese characters in a unique sequence by means of a two-dimensional formal grammar that yields a quasi-algebraic formula for each character. While these and other devices are still in the prototype stage, another device made by the same firm, the IBM 3800 Printing Subsystem, is fully operative. It consists of a high-speed printer for data processing, using laser beams that scan dot matrixes and which are capable of producing output in several different typefaces; the machine can also produce all *katakana* signs (although it is not equipped to print Chinese characters).

Pending the outcome of Finley's research into automatic and unambiguous filing of Chinese characters which may constitute a breakthrough in solving a problem that has baffled and frustrated the Chinese and Japanese themselves, a partial solution is offered by a purely numerical system, because the numbers assigned to characters, when arranged by their ordinal value, will automatically result in an arrangement of characters linked to that of a key dictionary. Such a numerical filing system would admittedly not always yield perfect and unambiguous results, but it would constitute a more reliable control tool than the completely ambiguous and largely meaningless transcriptions now used for the bibliographic control of Chinese, Japanese, and Korean documents.

In summary, there are no major conceptual or technical obstacles to the organization of library catalogs or bibliographies by script and language. Their feasibility, as pointed out, has been demonstrated by many libraries throughout the world, and the possibilities offered by modern technology for their production, maintenance, and reproduction now make it much easier to provide such retrieval tools.

3.4 Identification of Authors

Unique identification of an author has always been one of the cornerstones of Western cataloging theory and practice, although the validity of this postulate has never been established theoretically, and seems to be based merely on long-standing tradition and the specialized needs of certain bibliographers. Be that as it may, the principle that works (albeit not without considerable difficulties) for European names, following the pattern Given name(s)–Surname, breaks down when it is applied to African and Asian names structured according to completely different cultural patterns. What constitutes the "main" part of a person's name (the equivalent, for cataloging purposes, of the European surname) is difficult or even impossible to decide even in that person's native country. When a sometimes quite arbitrary Romanization is added to an artificially contrived rendering of an author's name, the result is often a form impossible to retrieve by anyone except the cataloger or bibliographer who concocted that form.

In 1952 UNESCO appointed a committee under the chairmanship of S. R. Ranganathan to deal with the problem of cataloging Asian names, but it did apparently not achieve the desired results because the report was never formally published. The committee found, however, that Muslim names were the most difficult ones to catalog, a conclusion confirmed in a study on one particular type of such names, namely Bengali ones:

Bengali personal names . . . behave like fifth columnists in the catalog. Rather than being an instrument of support for identification of the works concerned, the pattern and structure of the names subverts all efforts to bring all related works together.[64]

What has been said here about Bengali names applies equally to Arabic, Persian, Urdu, and particularly to Indonesian names. Regarding the latter, several Indonesian and Malaysian librarians and library committees from both countries could not come to an agreement on cataloging principles for these names because of the bewildering variety in structure, elements, and the way they are used by authors, to which are added the problems caused by the Latinization of Muslim names in the two countries since 1949.[65]

[64]Huq (1970), p. 70.
[65]Tairas (1972), Pattipilohy (1974).

It therefore seems to be much more effective to list an author's name in the form in which he himself put it on the title page of his work, either in the original script or in whatever Romanization he may have chosen, even if it does not conform to any particular transcription scheme used by a library, because it would then be recorded in the form in which the author apparently wishes to become known in the Western world. If that form varies from title to title and the same author appears as, say, Mahmud, Makhmud, and Mahmood, then so be it. Cross-references from such various Romanized forms to an author's name in the original script would often be more effective in keeping the bibliographical records of a person's work together than an artificially contrived Romanization. It is important to realize that often users' references are to an author's name as given on the title page of a work and not necessarily in the form chosen as a "correct" Romanization of that name by a particular library.

Unique identification of an author by only one form of his name is, however, often very important. The difficulties involved in ascertaining a standardized form of a name are almost as great with Western names written in Roman script as they are for names appearing in various transcriptions, as has been demonstrated by Blanken, who suggested the tentative assigning of numerical codes to authors' names.[66] Such numbers would be independent of any script, and would therefore serve the purposes of Universal Bibliographic Control much better than the most elaborate and "accurate" Romanization. We already have International Standard Book Numbers (ISBN)[67] and International Standard Serial Numbers (ISSN)[68]; the design of an International Standard Author Number (ISAN), which in the past has been dismissed as impracticable, should now be given serious consideration. Its successful implementation would obviously depend on the cooperation of national bibliographies throughout the world. While these were either rudimentary or nonexistent in most Asian and African countries only a decade ago, an infrastructure of national libraries and national bibliographies now exists in many of these countries. Thus the allocation of author identification numbers on the national level seems to be feasible to a large extent; the nationally assigned numbers could then be integrated into an international framework of ISAN numbers.

3.5   Identification of Monographs

The unambiguous identification of monographic works is of equal if not larger importance than that of authors. Here too an internationally recognized numbering system that is independent of script or language will be much more conducive to effective Universal Bibliographic Control than even the best possible conver-

---

[66]Blanken (1971), p. 62.
[67]Neubauer and Selbmann (1974).
[68]Rosenbaum (1972), Koster (1973).

sion of the author's name and the title of a work in a dissimilar script. For works published after 1969 in many Western countries the ISBN number can be used; for a very large part of the world's older literature published before 1956, there now exist the numbers given to works listed in the *National Union Catalog: pre-1956 imprints* (London: Mansell, 1968–), which will be completed in 1979. Works not assigned ISBN or "Mansell numbers" (as the *NUC* numbers have become known) could be identified by means of a Universal Standard Book Number (USBN), as proposed by Ayres.[69] A USBN number would consist of an 18-digit numerical code, identifying a monograph by language, date, type of main entry, title, edition, volume, and publisher. Tests performed with such a code on a large sample from the *British National Bibliography* have shown that the degree of accuracy (or unique identification) is about 97%, an excellent result considering the enormously large variety of input data that had to be reduced to unique numerical codes.[70]

Another identification method that could serve as an alternative for works as yet without a number or as an additional safeguard against possible mistakes, would be an adaptation of the "fingerprint" method, first used in the compilation of a union catalog of early books in the libraries of Oxford, Cambridge, and the British Museum.[71] This technique, which made it possible for clerical staff without any bibliographical training to match duplicate copies of the same work by mechanically comparing 18 characters on certain lines of predetermined pages, proved to be quite successful. The method would probably work well for the identification of even the most difficult documents, including those written in logographic scripts. Romanization of certain Chinese characters on predetermined pages could here serve a real identification purpose, since the meaning of the characters would be irrelevant, and only their exact sequence and matching with an established fingerprint would be of significance for Universal Bibliographic Control.

USBN (if internationally adopted) or a combination of ISAN, ISBN, and other book number, with a fingerprint identification where necessary, would constitute a completely unambiguous means of control for any monographic publication. Language specialists and trained bibliographers would be needed only to identify and "tag" a document either at the source (in the country of publication) or, where this would not be feasible, at designated bibliographic centers in various parts of the world. The numerical coding of authors and works would do for monographic documents what the map grid does for the unique identification and location of places in cartography. No matter how many different names a place may have, and how they may be written in different languages

[69] Ayres (1974).
[70] Beale and Lynch (1975).
[71] *Computers and early books* (1974).

and scripts, its location on a map is unmistakably fixed by latitude and longitude. Since the codes would be entirely numerical, they could be used equally well in all countries, and they could be handled by clerical personnel and printed by normal teleprinter or computer printout. It would thus be possible to order photocopies of documents in any script from libraries anywhere, or to request interlibrary loans, all without the necessity for anyor 2 involved in these transactions either to know foreign scripts or to handle difficult and highly ambiguous script conversions.

3.6   Identification of Serials

The bibliographic control of serials by numerical codes is already a reality, since the allocation of International Standard Serial Numbers (ISSN) is rapidly covering most of the world's periodicals and other serially published documents. This means that the Romanization of the titles of serials written in a non-Roman script is now of less importance for direct control purposes than it was only a few years ago. Since the International Centre for the Registration of Serial Publications in Paris uses the ISO transliteration schemes for Romanization purposes, these will probably become more widely used in Romanization of titles in bibliographic citations. However even if the English-speaking countries continue to use their traditional Romanization schemes for bibliographic citations of serial titles, bibliographic control will not be appreciably affected since the ultimate authority for the identification of a particular serial will always remain its ISSN. In other words, what has been envisaged for monographic works is already well on its way to realization for serially published documents.

3.7   Subject Entries in Different Scripts

The arrangement of entries for works on a specific subject, whether in library catalogs or in subject bibliographies, is inherently independent of the script in which such entries are written. In subject catalogs with verbal subject headings (which are most common in the United States and in some other countries) it has almost always been the custom to interfile Roman script entries with those in other scripts under the same heading, the entries in non-Roman scripts being arranged by their Romanized author or title headings.[72] The only difference in a subject file with non-Roman entries in the original script lies in the filing principle, which must be based on an ordinal arrangement other than the Roman

[72]One of the best examples for this kind of subject arrangement in a catalog is the *Library of Congress Catalog: Books: Subjects*.

alphabet. There is only one other universally agreed-upon system, namely ordinal numbers, which means that entries are to be filed by *date*. Since the date of publication or issue is in almost all scripts given in Arabic numerals (or can be so indicated on the document surrogate), it is therefore a filing medium that lends itself easily to both manual and mechanized filing routines.

Filing of bibliographic entries by date is quite common in many subject catalogs today (regardless of the script of the entries) because it results in a more helpful sequence than the arbitrary juxtaposition of entries on the same subject by alphabetical order of author names. The method will in many instances also take care of the problem of which order to use for filing entries in various scripts, because it actually happens infrequently that works are written on exactly the same subject in various scripts and in the same year. When this does occur, a sequence of scripts and languages must be decided upon arbitrarily. As long as that sequence is made known to the users of a catalog or bibliography, it matters little whether it is by language family, by "importance" of a script, or by whatever other criterion.

Where subject catalogs are arranged in classified sequence (as is the case, for example, in Great Britain and in many European countries), the same procedure can be followed, namely subarrangement under one classification mark by date. This has the added advantage that classification marks are independent of language, and do not force a catalog user interested in, say, Russian books on a certain subject to look them up under an English subject heading (as is the case in a verbal subject heading catalog), since subject indexes to classification systems can be provided in more than one language.[73]

3.8 Entries in Bibliographies and Indexes

So far our proposals have dealt mainly with library catalogs. But entries in dissimilar scripts must also be handled in bibliographies, in abstracting and indexing services, and in back-of-the-book indexes.

This is mainly a technical problem of typography. When traditional hot-type composition is used, it should not be more difficult for modern printers to insert Cyrillic, Greek, Arabic, Hebrew, or other scripts among Roman entries than it was for the early printers in the 16th century who produced beautiful multiscript books with the most primitive technical facilities. Indeed modern printing and typesetting techniques make it much easier to print text in more than one script than was possible even a few decades ago. Coldtype composition can solve the problem of typefonts for different scripts without any difficulties. The production of text in more than one script, however, requires the services of expert typeset-

---

[73] Elrod (1972).

ters or editors of photocomposed copy, which means that most printed bibliographies with entries in dissimilar scripts will have to be produced in central locations where such expertise is available.

Regarding bibliographies produced from typewritten text or by other "near-print" methods, all of which rely on some reprographic process, it is not too difficult to insert entries in non-Roman scripts into a master copy, either manually or by reproduction from some other source. If it is difficult or impossible to list the entries themselves in the original script, so that names of authors have to be transcribed and titles have to be translated, then at least an index to names and titles in non-Roman scripts should be provided. This practice is quite common in bibliographies and nonfiction books printed in non-Roman scripts, especially in Russian and Japanese reference tools. In consecutive text, names of persons, places, or objects written in Roman script are generally printed in parentheses after the first transcription in order to provide an unambiguous identification of those names for the reader of a non-Roman text (see Figure 6.10). There is no reason why a reciprocal practice of listing names in non-Roman scripts could not be followed in Roman script publications, especially in bibliographies and indexes, where identification of authors' names is important.

3.9   The Role of Computers

The application of computers and other automated machinery to the bibliographic control of documents in dissimilar scripts has already been discussed in connection with the production of catalog entries for such documents. In concluding this brief survey of methods other than script conversion, we wish only to warn against the misuse of computers, now often advocated in the name of standardization and accommodation to the facilities provided by data processing equipment, namely the complete Romanization of document surrogates for documents in dissimilar scripts. If this became the general practice in Universal Bibliographic Control, it would be a disaster from the point of view of the users of such documents.

But this need not happen. It is simply not true that, in order to be integrated into the MARC system[74] or similar computerized bibliographic control systems, records for documents in non-Roman scripts need to be completely Romanized, nor is it axiomatic that MARC and similar systems must become immense monolithic data bases. For a long time it has been realized that a complete and universal record of everything that has ever been written in any branch of knowledge would not only be impossible to compile but would also be utterly impractical—hence the separate bibliographic services providing abstracts and

---

[74]Library of Congress. MARC Development Office. 1974.

О МЕСТУ FERDINANDA DE SAUSSURA, АЛЕКСАНДРА БЕЛИЋА И LEONARDA BLOOMFIELDA У ЛИНГВИСТИЦИ XX ВЕКА

1. Тематско повезивање ове три крупне научне индивидуалности јединственим системом изучавања није једноставно. Временски фактор је у овом случају најмањи проблем. Могло би се чак рећи да би управо време у коме се Фердинанд де Сосир (F. de Saussure), Александар Белић и Леонард Блумфилд (L. Bloomfield) јављају било један од аргумената који такво изучавање оправдава. Седамдесетак година научне делатности F. de Saussura и А. Белића тече паралелно.[1] L. Bloomfield је рођен 1897. године. Једанаест година је млађи од А. Белића, а своје научне погледе на језик први пут је експлицитније изложио 1914. године[2]; дакле, годину дана после смрти Saussurove.

У ово време догађају се крупне, квалитативне промене у развојним токовима лингвистичке мисли, па је од несумњивог интереса указати на ставове и опредељења изразитијих носилаца идеја и стваралаца у лингвистици тога времена.

2. Велик део научних активности А. Белића и L. Bloomfielda падају у исто време, али се ипак ретко подударају. И један и други очигледно одлично познају Saussurovo учење, али по правилу експлицитно не прихватају ни резултате тога учења, ни метод који је Saussure изградио. А. Белић, додуше, признаје значај Saussurovog лингвистичког

---

[1] Први рад Александра Белића, објављен 1897. године је: Замѣтка о славянскомъ житіи св. Пятки-Петки. Извѣстія отдѣленія русскаго языка и словесности императорской академіи, наукъ II, 1045—1047.

F. de Saussure умро је 1913. године када је Белић био већ формиран научни радник, добро познат у тадашњој Србији, а и у словенском свету. До 1913. године имао је већ педесетак објављених радова, од којих су неки били у теоријској вези са новим струјањима у лингвистици, нпр. Из новије лингвистике I—III, СКГл VI, 742—749, 996—1006, 1246—1255. и др.

[2] B. Introduction to the Study of Language, New York 1914. г.

Figure 6.10. Treatment of names in Roman script in a text written in Cyrillic script. This is the first page of a Serbian article by Dušan Jović ["The place of Ferdinand de Saussure, Aleksandar Belić and Leonard Bloomfield in 20th-century linguistics"]. Jужнословенски Филолог (*Južnoslovenski filolog*) 29(1–2) (1972):51–80. In the heading, the names of de Saussure and Bloomfield are not transcribed (although they have the Serbian suffix -*a* for grammatical reasons) and are set in a typeface that blends well with the Cyrillic one. In the text the names are transcribed into Serbian only once, when first mentioned, with the original spelling given in parentheses (lines 4 and 5); thereafter the names are printed in Roman script, both in the main text and in the footnotes.

indexes in the fields of chemistry, biology, medicine, physics, engineering, and many other branches of science and technology, as well as in the social sciences and humanities. By the same token there is no reason why there should not be a MARC section of records in Roman script, and several others for non-Roman scripts from which catalog entries and other bibliographic data could be generated in separate sequences. The technical facilities to do this, either in the form of conventional printed output or in visual displays of on-line systems exist already. As mentioned in Section 3.3. of this chapter, automated equipment can now reproduce practically any script at a speed and convenience unattainable only a few years ago.

The traditional methods of script conversion, and in particular Romanization, are no longer suitable for modern bibliographic control purposes. To perpetuate the practice which was devised for essentially different purposes and for use with manual methods, and to use a computer to do the same old thing just a little faster for the sake of so-called cooperation and "efficiency" would be an appalling misuse of this most versatile machine. The computer need not become an instrument of mindless uniformity for uniformity's sake. Indeed, far from imposing total Romanization on automated bibliographic control systems, it can actually provide services of a kind and scope that until a few years ago were beyond the technical and economic means of conventional systems.

While faster and more comprehensive technical services to users of libraries and bibliographic tools will increasingly depend on computers and their ancillary devices, the task of making the intellectual content of those services accessible will remain the responsibility of human beings, acting as mediators between two groups of human beings: the originators of written records and those who have a need for those records. To do this, librarians, bibliographers, and any other persons involved in bibliographic control must be knowledgeable and resourceful. Being knowledgeable should, however, not be confused with a pretension of omniscience or the ability "to know all languages by the mastery of one" (as John Ray claimed to be able to do 300 years ago).[75] If, in other words, librarians continue to use the crutches of Romanization to pretend that they can dance where they cannot even walk alone, they will eventually be found out as intellectual frauds. But if they use the resources of automation and communication technology wisely, they will be relieved from much mindless drudgery, and will be able to devote their energies and skills to the task that is at the heart of their profession: to provide rapid and accurate access to the records of all mankind, whenever and wherever they may have been created, and in whatever graphic form they may have been written.

---

[75] Ray (1675).

Appendix A

THE INTERNATIONAL PHONETIC ALPHABET

	Bi-labial	Labio-dental	Dental and Alveolar	Retroflex	Palato-alveolar	Alveolo-palatal	Palatal	Velar	Uvular	Pharyngal	Glottal
CONSONANTS											
Plosive	p b		t d	ʈ ɖ			c ɟ	k g	q ɢ		ʔ
Nasal	m	ɱ	n	ɳ			ɲ	ŋ	N		
Lateral Fricative			ɬ ɮ								
Lateral Non-fricative			l	ɭ			ʎ				
Rolled			r						ʀ		
Flapped			ɾ	ɽ					ʀ		
Fricative	ɸ β	f v	θ ð s z	ʂ ʐ	ʃ ʒ	ɕ ʑ	ç ʝ	x ɣ	χ ʁ	ħ ʕ	h ɦ
Frictionless Continuants and Semi-vowels	w ɥ	ʋ	ɹ				j (ɥ)	(w)	ʁ		
VOWELS							Front Central Back				
Close	(y ʉ u)						i y ï ʉ ɯ u				
Half-close	(ø o)						e ø ɤ o				
Half-open	(œ ɔ)						ɛ œ ɜ ɞ ʌ ɔ				
Open	(ɒ)						a ɶ ɑ ɒ				

(Secondary articulations are shown by symbols in brackets.)

OTHER SOUNDS.—Palatalized consonants: ṭ, ḍ, etc. Velarized or pharyngalized consonants: ł, đ, ẕ, etc. Ejective consonants (plosives with simultaneous glottal stop): p', t', etc. Implosive voiced consonants: ɓ, ɗ, etc. ɼ fricative trill. ơ, ʚ (labialized θ, ð, or s, z). ƪ, ʓ (labialized ʃ, ʒ). ʇ, ʗ, ʖ, ʔ, ʘ (clicks, Zulu c, q, x). ɺ (a sound between r and l). ʍ (voiceless w). ɪ, ʏ, ʊ (lowered varieties of i, y, u). ɘ (a variety of ə). ɵ (a vowel between ø and o).

Affricates are normally represented by groups of two consonants (ts, tʃ, dʒ, etc.), but, when necessary, ligatures are used (ʦ, ʧ, ʤ, etc.), or the marks ͡ or ͜ (t͡s or t͡ʃ, etc.). c, ɟ may occasionally be used in place of tʃ, dʒ. Aspirated plosives: ph, th, etc.

LENGTH, STRESS, PITCH.—ː (full length). ˑ (half length). ˈ (stress, placed at beginning of the stressed syllable). ˌ (secondary stress). ˉ (high level pitch); ˍ (low level); ˊ (high rising); ˏ (low rising); ˋ (high falling); ˎ (low falling); ˆ (rise-fall); ˇ (fall-rise). See Écriture phonétique internationale, p. 9.

MODIFIERS.—̃ nasality. ̥ breath (l̥ = breathed l). ̬ voice (ş = z). ˙ slight aspiration following p, t, etc. ̣ specially close vowel (ẹ = a very close e). ̨ specially open vowel (ę = a rather open e). ̫ labialization (n̫ = labialized n). ̪ dental articulation (t̪ = dental t). ̡ palatalization (ż = z̡). ˔ tongue slightly raised. ˕ tongue slightly lowered. ˒ lips more rounded. ˓ lips more spread. Central vowels ï (= ɨ), ü (= ʉ), ë (= ə˔), ö (= ɵ), ë̤ (= ɘ˕), ö̤ (= o̝). ̩ (e.g. n̩) syllabic consonant. ̯ consonantal vowel. ʃ variety of ʃ resembling s, etc.

Appendix B

The following draft for a new introduction to ISO standards on conversion of scripts, based partially on a proposal by the author was approved by the Subcommittee on Conversion of Written Languages (ISO/TC46/SC2) in November 1976. After its ratification by ISO members it will be included in all relevant ISO standards. A separate statement on "Principles for logographical writing systems" is in preparation.

GENERAL PRINCIPLES OF CONVERSION OF SYSTEMS OF WRITING

1 Definitions

The words in a language, which are written according to a given system (the converted system), sometimes have to be rendered according to a different system (the conversion system), normally used for a different language. This operation is often followed for historical or geographical texts, cartographical documents and in particular for bibliographical work in every case where it is necessary to write words supplied in various alphabets in a manner that allows intercalation with other words in a single alphabet so as to enable a uniform alphabet classification to be made in bibliographies, catalogues, indices, toponymic lists, etc.

The two basic methods of conversion of a system of writing are transliteration and transcription.

Transliteration is the operation which consists of representing the characters* of an entirely alphabetical system of writing by the characters of the conversion alphabet.

In principle, this conversion should be made character by character: each character of the alphabet converted is rendered by one character, and one only, of the alphabet of conversion, this being to ensure the complete and unambiguous reversibility of the alphabet of conversion in the alphabet converted.

---

* A *character* is an element of a system of writing, whether or not alphabetical, that represents a phoneme, a syllable, a word or even prosodical characteristics of the language by using graphical symbols (letters, diacritical marks, syllabic signs, punctuation marks, prosodical accents, etc) or a combination of these signs (a letter having an accent or a diacritical mark, e.g. *â, è, ö,* is therefore a character in the same way as a basic letter).

If transliteration character by character is not possible, it may be necessary to use digraphs or diacritical marks in order to obtain complete reversibility. Transliteration may provide a result that cannot be used phonetically.

Retransliteration is the operation which consists of converting the characters of an alphabet of conversion to those of the alphabet converted. This operation is the exact opposite of transliteration; it is carried out by applying the rules of a system of transliteration in reverse order so as to reconstitute the transliterated word to its original form.

Transcription is the operation which consists of representing the characters of a language, whatever the original system of writing, by any other phonetic system of letters or signs.

A transcription system is of necessity based on the orthographical conventions of a language of conversion and its alphabet. The users of a transcription system must therefore have a knowledge of the language of conversion to be able to pronounce the characters correctly. Transcription is therefore not strictly reversible.

Transcription may be used for the conversion of all writing systems. It is the only method that can be used for systems that are not entirely alphabetical and for all logographical systems of writing (Chinese, Japanese, etc).

To carry out *Romanization* (the conversion of non-Latin systems of writing to the Latin alphabet) it is possible to use either transliteration or transcription or a combination of these two methods, according to the nature of the system converted.

2 A system of conversion proposed for international use may call for compromise and the sacrifice of certain national customs. It is therefore necessary for each community of users to accept concessions, abandon certain customs where necessary and fully abstain in every case from imposing as a matter of course solutions that are actually justified only by national practice (e.g. as regards pronunciation, orthography, etc). However, these concessions would obviously relate only to the use that a country makes of its national system of writing: when this national system is not converted, the characters constituting it must be accepted in the form in which they are written in the national language.

Similarly, when a country itself uses a given system to write its own language in a system of writing different from the original system of writing of that language, this system is a preferential candidate to become the standardized international system inasfar as it is compatible with the other principles mentioned above.

3 Where necessary, the systems of conversion should specify an equivalent for each character, not only the letters but also the punctuation marks, numbers, etc. They should similarly take into account the arrangement of the sequence of characters that make up the text, e.g. the direction of the script, and specify the way of distinguishing words and of using separation signs and capital letters, following as closely as possible the customs of the language(s) which use the converted system of writing.

PRINCIPLES FOR ALPHABETICAL WRITING SYSTEMS

4   The conversion may be made at *various levels*. The first level is that of completely reversible *stringent conversion* which is necessary to attain in full the aims given in clause 1. This conversion applies all principles of conversion without exception. It does not permit variants. The conventional systems of stringent conversion should be applied as such without any change to meet national or regional customs as regards pronunciation or orthography.

The second level is that of *simplified conversion*. This simplification may be made necessary, for example, by the use of machines that do not accept all the alphabet characters required for stringent conversion. This method of conversion may allow variants; it is recognized that it does not permit complete reversibility.

Nevertheless, it should be deduced by simplification of the stringent method of conversion and not based on different principles. It may therefore be the subject of international agreements.

The third level is that of *popular conversion* which, for example, should enable the same foreign names to be written in a uniform manner in the newspapers of a given country. It is obliged to take into account (for example) phonetic practice, and therefore can only be national.

Subcommittee 2 grants priority to research into a system of transliteration applying the principles of stringent conversion, which, if necessary, will then be used as a basis for work on simplified conversion.

5   In cases where several languages use the same basic alphabet, possibly with various changes to certain characters in the systems of writing the various languages (e.g. the various Cyrillic alphabets), the system of transliteration of these alphabets should reproduce a character in the same way when it has undergone the same change and reproduce by other means any differing characters or those altered in other ways.

6   If the conversion alphabet gives a different form to the same character according to its place in the word (like the Arabic alphabet or the Greek alphabet which has two forms for Sigma) the conversion alphabet will use one single character of constant form. On the other hand, if the conversion alphabet contains two characters that are equivalent but distinctly different (such as *j* and *x* in Spanish), the conversion alphabet will render them in the form of two different characters.

References

This list contains all works referred to in the footnotes by name and date, arranged in one alphabetical sequence by author's name or by title. Works originally written in non-Roman scripts are listed in Romanized form; titles have not been Romanized but are given in brackets in English translation. Full bibliographical data are given in the original script in separate sections at the end of the Roman-script part of the list.

Works pertinent to the topic of script conversion are marked by an asterisk (*). These constitute, however, only a small fraction of the voluminous literature on this subject. A comprehensive listing is found in Hans H. Wellisch, *Transcription and transliteration: an annotated bibliography on conversion of scripts* (Silver Spring, Md.: Institute of Modern Languages, 1975).

The abbreviations [s.l.] *(sine loco)* and [s.n.] *(sine nomine)* are used when the place of publication or the name of the publisher (or printer) of a work is unknown or could not be ascertained.

Abdulaziz, M. H. "Tanzania's national language policy and the rise of Swahili political culture." In *Language use and social change*. London: Oxford University Press, 1971. Pp. 160–178.

*Academy of the Hebrew Language. ["Rules for the transliteration of Hebrew script into Roman script."] *See* (1957) האקדמיה ללשון העברית

*Academy of the Hebrew Language. ["Transcription from foreign languages into Hebrew."] See האקדמיה ללשון העברית (1970)

441

Ackoff, R. L. "Systems, organizations, and interdisciplinary research." *General Systems Yearbook* **5** (1960):1–8.

*Adelung, J. C. *Mithridates, oder allgemeine Sprachenkunde, mit dem Vaterunser als Sprachprobe in beynahe fünf hundert Sprachen und Mundarten.* Berlin: Vossische Buchhandlung, 1817.

Akzin, B. *State and nation.* London: Hutchinson, 1964.

*Allen, C. G. "Russian transcription of Chinese names." *Journal of Documentation* **16** (1960):80–91.

*Allworth, E. *Nationalities in the Soviet East; publications and writing systems: a bibliographical directory and transliteration tables for Iranian- and Turkic-language publications, 1818–1945 located in U.S. libraries.* New York: Columbia University Press, 1971.

Aman, M. M. *Arab states author headings.* New York: St. John's University Press, 1973.

*Ambrogio, T. *Introductio in chaldaicam linguam, syriacam atque armenicam, & decem alios linguas; characterum differentium alphabeta, circiter quadraginta* . . . . Papiae: I. M. Simoneta, 1539.

American Library Association. *Catalog rules; author and title entries,* American edition. Chicago: ALA, 1908.

American Library Association. *A.L.A. cataloging rules for author and title entries* . . ., 2nd ed., edited by Clara Beetle. Chicago: ALA, 1949.

American Library Association. "Manual of romanization, capitalization, punctuation, and word division for Chinese, Japanese, and Korean." In its *Cataloging rules of the American Library Association and the Library of Congress: additions and changes, 1949–1958.* Washington, D.C.: Library of Congress, 1959, pp. 47–56.

American Library Association. *Anglo-American Cataloging Rules.* Chicago: ALA, 1967.

*American National Standards Institute. *System for the Romanization of Arabic.* New York: ANSI, 1972. (Z39.12–1972.)

*American National Standards Institute. *System for the Romanization of Japanese.* New York: ANSI, 1972. (Z39.11–1972.)

*American National Standards Institute. *Romanization of Hebrew.* New York: ANSI, 1975. (Z39.25–1975.)

*American National Standards Institute. *System for the Romanization of Slavic Cyrillic characters.* New York: ANSI, 1976. (Z39.24–1976.)

*Anderson, J. D. "The arrangement of Chinese language author-title catalogs." *Library Quarterly* **44** (1974):42–59.

*Anderson, O. B. *A concordance to the five systems of transcription for standard Chinese.* Atlantic Highlands, N.J.: Humanities Press, 1975.

The Apocrypha and Pseudepigrapha of the Old Testament in English. . . . Edited by R. H. Charles. Oxford: Clarendon Press, 1913.

Aristeas to Philocrates (Letter of Aristeas). Edited and translated by M. Hadas. New York: Harper, 1951.

Aristoteles. *On interpretation.* Translated by H. P. Cook. Cambridge, Mass.: Harvard University Press, 1938. (Loeb classical library.)

Ashby, W. R. *An introduction to cybernetics.* London: Chapman & Hall, 1956.

Ashworth, W. "The information explosion." *Library Association Record* **76** (1974):63–68.

*Aurousseau, M. "Unresolved problems in geographical nomenclature." *Scottish Geographical Magazine* **63** (1947):1–10.

*Aurousseau, M. *The rendering of geographical names*. London: Hutchinson, 1957. (Reprinted, Westport, Ct.: Greenwood Press, 1975.)

Ayres, F. H. "The Universal Standard Book Number (USBN): a new method for the construction of control numbers for bibliographic records." *Program*, **8** (1974): 166–173.

*Baba, S. [Bibliographical Romanization of non-Roman characters.] *See* 馬場重徳

*Bachmaier, A. *Pasigraphisches Wörterbuch zum Gebrauche für die deutsche Sprache*. Augsburg: [s.n.], 1868.

Bacon, F. *The advancement of learning*. In his *Works*, v. 4, edited by J. Spedding (et al.). London: Longmans, 1858–1874.

Bacon, R. *Fr. Rogeri Bacon opera quaedam hactenus inedita*. Edited by J. S. Brewer. London: HMSO, 1859. (Rerum Britannicarum medii aevi scriptores; 15.)

Bacon, R. *The Opus maius. . . .* Edited by J. H. Bridges. Oxford: Clarendon Press, 1897–1900.

Bacon, R. *The Opus maius*. Translated by R. B. Burke. New York: Russell & Russell, 1962.

*Baskakov, N. A. ["The present state of scripts for Turkic languages in the USSR and their future improvement."] *See* Баскаков, Н. А. (1967).

Baskakov, N. A. ["Problems of the improvement of alphabets for Turkic languages in the USSR"] *See* Баскаков, Н. А. (1972).

*Batakliev, G. ["Pronunciation and transcription of ancient Greek names in Bulgarian."] *See* Батаклиев, Г.

Beale, D. D.; M. F. Lynch. "An evaluation of, and improvement on, Ayres' Universal Standard Book Number." *Program* **9** (1975):35–45.

*Beck, C. *The Universal Character by which all the nations in the world may understand one another's conceptions, reading out of one common writing their own mother tongues*. London: Weekley, 1657.

*Becher, J. J. *Spirensis character, pro notitia linguarum universalis*. Francofurti: W. Serlin, 1661.

Beer, S. *Cybernetics and management*. London: English University Press, 1959.

*Behn, W., and P. Greig. "Islamic filing." *The Indexer* **9** (1974):13–15.

*Ben Yehuda, M. ["Spelling in the Hebrew catalog."] *See* בן־יהודה, מ.

Bertalanffy, L. von. *General system theory; foundations, development, applications*. Harmondsworth: Penguin Books, 1973.

Biblia polyglotta. . . . London: Th. Roycroft, 1657.

Bibliographical services: their present state and the possibilities of improvement. Washington, D.C.: Unesco/Library of Congress, 1950.

Bigg, C. *The Christian Platonists of Alexandria*. Oxford: Clarendon Press, 1886.

Bin Haji Mohammad, A. R. *Ejaan baharu: a complete guide with easy references to the New Spelling System for Bahasa Malaysia*. Kuala Lumpur: Madatini, 1972.

*Birnbaum, E. "Transliteration of Ottoman Turkish for library and general purposes." *Journal of the American Oriental Society* **87** (1967):122–156.

*Birnbaum, S. A. *Praktische Grammatik der jiddischen Sprache für den Selbstunterricht . . .* Wien: A. Hartleben, 1915.

*Birnbaum, S. A. "Umschrift des ältesten datierten jiddischen Schriftstücks." *Teuthonista* **8** (1931/32):197–207.

*Birnbaum, S. A. "Die Umschrift des Jiddischen." *Teuthonista* **9** (1933):90–105.

*Blanken, R. R. "The preparation of international author indexes, with particular reference to the problems of transliteration, prefixes, and compound family names." *Journal of the American Society for Information Science* **22** (1971):51–63.

Blyden, E. W. *Christianity, Islam, and the Negro race.* Edinburgh: Edinburgh University Press, 1887. (Reprinted 1967.)

Bodmer, F. *The loom of language.* New York: Grosset & Dunlap, 1944.

Bouchard, J.-J. *Monumentum Romanum Nicolao Claudio Fabricio Perescio.* . . . Romae: Typis Vaticanis, 1638.

Bowers, J. "Language problems and literacy." In *Language problems of developing nations.* New York: Wiley, 1968, pp. 381–401.

Boxer, C. R. *The Christian century in Japan, 1549–1650.* Berkeley: University of California Press, 1951.

Boyle, R. *The works of the Honourable Robert Boyle.* Edited by T. Birch. London: Rivington, 1772.

*Braun, F. "Die Latinisierung der russischen Schrift." *Archiv für Schreib- und Buchwesen* **4** (1930):139–144.

*Braun, H. "Die alphabetische Katalogisierung von Werken in arabischer, persischer und türkischer Sprache. *Zeitschrift für Bibliothekswesen und Bibliographie* **11** (1964):9–32.

Bregzis, R. *Machine readable bibliographic records: criteria and creation.* Minneapolis: ERIC Clearinghouse for Library and Information Sciences, 1970.

Breu, J. "Die Transkription in der Kartographie." *Mitt. d. österreichischen geographischen Gesellschaft* **111** (1969):222–247.

*British Academy. "Transliteration of Slavonic. . . ." *Proceedings of the British Academy* **8** (1917/18):523–542.

British Museum. Department of Printed Books. *The catalogue of printed books in the British Museum.* London: The Museum, 1841.

*British Museum. Department of Printed Books. *Rules for compiling the catalogue of printed books, maps and music in the British Museum.* London: The Museum, 1936.

*British Standards Institution. *British standard for transliteration of Cyrillic and Greek characters.* London: BSI, 1958. (B.S. 2979:1958.)

*British Standards Institution. *British standard for the transliteration of Arabic characters.* London: BSI, 1968. (B.S. 4280:1968.)

*British Standards Institution. *Romanization of Japanese.* London: BSI, 1972. (B.S. 4812:1972.)

Brockelmann, C. *Geschichte der arabischen Literatur.* Leiden: Brill, 1937.

Brutis, Petrus de. *Victoria contra Judaeos.* Vicenza: Simon Bevilaqua, 1489.

*Brux, A. A. "Arabic-English transliteration for library purposes." *American Journal of Semitic Languages and Literature* **47** (1930): Supplement.

*Brux, A. A. "Simplified system of Hebrew–English and Aramaic–English transliteration." *American Journal of Semitic Languages and Literature* **58** (1941):57–69.

*Buchanan, R. E. "Transliteration of Greek and Latin in the formation of names of zoological taxa." *Systematic Zoology* **5** (1956):65–67.

Bullokar, W. *Book at large for the amendment of orthographie for English speech.* . . . London: Denham, 1580.

Bundy, M. L. "Conflict in libraries." *College and Research Libraries* **27** (1966):253–262.

*Bushell, H. S. *The transliteration of Russian, Serbian and Bulgarian for bibliographic purposes.* London: Royal Society, 1953.

Buxtorf, J. *Thesaurus grammaticus linguae sanctae Hebraeae.* . . . Basilea: Typis C. Waldkirch, 1609.

Calvet, M. "The elaboration of basic Wolof." In *Language use and social change.* London: Oxford University Press, 1971, pp. 274–287.

The Cambridge Ancient History. Cambridge: Cambridge University Press, 1926–1939.

The Cambridge History of the Bible. London: Cambridge University Press, 1963.

*Carr, D. "New official Romanization of Japanese." *Journal of the American Oriental Scoiety* **59** (1939):99–102.

Carroll, J. B. *The study of language.* Cambridge, Mass.: Harvard University Press, 1953.

Cartwright, K. L. "Mechanization and library filing rules." *Advances in Librarianship* **1** (1970):59–94.

*Castagné, J. A. "La latinisation de l'alphabet turk dans les républiques turkotatares de l'URSS." *Revue des Etudes Islamiques* **(1927):**321–353.

*Castagné, J. A. "Le mouvement de latinisation dans les républiques soviétiques musulmanes et les pays voisins (documents de presse russe)." *Revue des Etudes Islamiques* **(1928):**559–595.

Catford, J. C. *A linguistic theory of translation.* London: Oxford University Press, 1965.

Chadwick, H. *Early Christian thought and the classical tradition: Studies in Justin, Clement and Origen.* New York: Oxford University Press, 1966.

Chadwick, J. *The decipherment of Linear B.* Cambridge: Cambridge University Press, 1958.

Chakraborti, M. L. *Bibliography in theory and practice.* Calcutta: World Press, 1971.

*Chamberlayne, J. *Oratio Dominica in diversas omnium fere gentium linguas versa et propriis cuiusque linguae characteribus expressa. . . .* Amstelodami: Typis G. & D. Goerei, 1715.

Chao, Y. R. *Language and symbolic systems.* Cambridge: Cambridge University Press, 1968.

Chaplin, H. I. *A manual of Japanese writing.* New Haven: Yale University Press, 1967.

Charen, T. *MEDLARS indexing manual.* Bethesda, Md.: National Library of Medicine, 1972.

*Chatterji, S. K. *A Roman alphabet for India.* Calcutta: University of Calcutta, 1935.

Cheke, Sir J. *The Gospel according to St. Matthew. . . .* Translated into English from the Greek . . . by Sir John Cheke . . . London: W. Pickering, 1843.

Cherry, C. *On human communication,* 2nd ed. Cambridge, Mass.: MIT Press, 1966.

Chomsky, N. *Language and mind.* New York: Harcourt Brace, 1968.

Chu, Yu-kuang. *A comparative study of language reforms in China and Japan.* Saratoga Springs, N.Y.: Skidmore College, 1969.

Churchman, C. W. *The systems approach.* New York: Dell, 1968.

*Cohen, J. "On the project of a universal character." *Mind* **43** (1954):48–63.

*Cohen, M. La grande invention de l'écriture et son evolution. Paris: Imprimerie nationale, 1958.

Coleman, J. S. *Nigeria: background to nationalism.* Berkeley: University of California Press, 1958.

*Comenius, J. A. *Janua linguarum reserata. . . .* Lesnae: [s.n.], 1631.

Comenius, J. A. *Pansophiae prodromus. . . .* London: [s.n.], 1639.

Comenius, J. A. *A reformation of schooles. . . .* London: [s.n.], 1642.

Comenius, J. A. *Via lucis. . .* Amsterodami: Apud C. Cunradum, 1668.

Comenius, J. A. *The way of light of John Amos Comenius.* Translated into English . . . by E. T. Campagnac. Liverpool: Liverpool University Press, 1938.

*Commission Internationale de Coopération Intellectuelle. *L'adoption universelle des caractères latins.* Paris: [s.n.], 1934.

Computers and early books. London: Mansell, 1974.

Conference on Access to Southeast Asian Research Materials. Proceedings, edited by C. Hobbs. Washington, D. C.: [s.n.], 1971.

Cornelius, P. *Languages in seventeenth- and early eighteenth-century imaginary voyages*. Paris: Droz, 1965.

Corpus inscriptionum latinarum . . . Berolini: Apud G. Reimerum, 1862–

Cutter, C. A. *Rules for a dictionary catalog*. Washington, D. C.: Government Printing Office, 1876.

*Dalgarno, G. *Ars signorum, vulgo character universalis et lingua philosophica*. . . . Londini: J. Hayes, 1661.

*Danişman, N. "Transcription de l'alphabet arabe." *Revue des Etudes Islamiques* **9** (1935):97–103.

Dante Alighieri. *Dante's treatise "De vulgari eloquentia."* Translated by A. G. Ferrers Howell. London: K. Paul, 1890.

Davison, K. "Rules for alphabetic filing by computer." In *U. K. MARC project*. Newcastle-upon-Tyne: Oriel Press, 1970.

*Dekleva, B. *Uniform Slavic transliteration alphabet (USTA)*. Berkeley: University of California, 1973.

DeMott, B. "The sources of John Wilkins' philosophical language." *Journal of English and Germanic Philology* **57** (1958):1–13.

Descartes, R. *A discourse on method*. Translated by J. Veitch. London: Dent, 1912.

*Diringer, D. *The alphabet: a key to the history of mankind*, 3rd ed. New York: Funk & Wagnall, 1968.

*Dogra, R. C. "Cataloguing Urdu names." *International Library Review* **5** (1973):351–377.

*Dogra, R. C. "Notes on Hindi names." *International Library Review* **8** (1976):327–347.

*Dougherty, C., et al. *Chinese character indexes*. Berkeley: University of California Press, 1963.

Draper, H. "Librarian vs. scholar-user." *Library Journal* **98** (1964):1907–1910.

Drucker, P. "Managing the public service institution." *College & Research Libraries* **37** (1976):4–14.

*Duncan, B. C., and D. Garvin. *Complete clear text representation of scientific documents in machine-readable form*. Washington, D. C.: National Bureau of Standards, 1974. (NBS Technical Note; 820.)

Durant, W. *The age of faith*. New York: Simon & Schuster, 1950.

Dziatzko, K. *Instruction für die Ordnung der Titel im alphabetischen Zettelkatalog der Königlichen und Universitätsbibliothek zu Breslau*. Berlin: A. Asher, 1886.

Eckardt, A. "Der Ursprung der koreanischen Schrift." *Mitteilungen der deutschen Gesellschaft für Natur- und Völkerkunde Ostasiens* **22**(C) (1928):1–20.

*Edelmann, R. "The treatment of names in Hebrew characters and title entry for Hebrew books." In *International Conference on Cataloguing Principles. Paris, 1961*. London, International Federation of Library Associations, 1963, pp. 277–279.

Edfeldt, A. W. *Silent speech and silent reading*. Stockholm: Almquist & Wiksell, 1959.

Edgerton, W. F. "Egyptian phonetic writing, from its invention to the close of the nineteenth dynasty." *Journal of the American Oriental Society* **60** (1940):473–506.

*Edmonds, C. J. "Suggestions for the use of Latin characters in the writing of Kurdish." *Journal of the Royal Asiatic Society* **(1933):** 643–650.

Edmundson, H. *Lingua linguarum, the naturall language of languages, in a vocabulary . . . contrived and built upon analogy.* London: [s.n.], 1658.

Ellis, A. J. *A plea for phonotypy and phonography: or, Speechprinting, speechwriting.* Bath: [s.n.], 1845.

*Ellis, A. J. *The essentials of phonetics, containing the theory of a universal alphabet, together with its practical application to the reduction of all languages . . . to one uniform system of writing. . . .* London: Pitman, 1848.

Ellis, A. J. *On early English pronunciation. . . .* London: Trübner, 1869–1889.

*Elrod, J. M. "The two-language collection with the bilingual reader." *International Cataloguing* **1** (1972):6–9.

*Emerton, J. A. "The purpose of the second column of the Hexapla." *Journal of Theological Studies* **7** (1956):79–87.

*Emerton, J. A. "Were Greek transliterations of the Hebrew Old Testament used by Jews before the time of Origen?" *Journal of Theological Studies* **21** (1970):17–31.

Encyclopedia Judaica. Jerusalem: Keter Publ. House, 1972.

Encyclopedia of Islam. 2nd ed. Leiden: Brill, 1954– .

Encyclopedia of linguistics, information and control. London: Pergamon, 1969.

*Erlich, R. "Politics and linguistics in the standardization of Soviet Yiddish." *Soviet Jewish Affairs* **3** (1973):71–79.

Ettlinger, J. R. T. *Nation-wide rationalization of acquisition policies in Canadian college and university libraries: are total world coverage and non-duplication of resources part of an impossible dream?* Ottawa: Association of Universities and Colleges of Canada, 1973.

Fairthorne, R. A. "'Use' and 'Mention' in the information sciences." In *Education for information science. Proceedings of the symposium. . . ., Warrenton, Virginia, September 7–10, 1965.* Edited by L. B. Heilprin et al. Washington, D.C.: Spartan Books, 1965, pp. 9–12.

*Fennah, R. G. "Transliteration of Greek words." *Systematic Zoology* **6** (1957):194.

*Filipova-Bajrova, M. ["Pronunciation and transcription of Greek names in Bulgarian."] *See* Филиппова-Байрова, М.

Finley, M. R. "On the formal description of Chinese characters." In *International symposium on computers and Chinese input/output systems, 1st, Taipei, 1973.* Taipei: Academia Sinica, [1974?].

Finley, M. R. "Problème de la classification des charactères chinois." In *Open conference on information science in Canada. 2nd, Winnipeg, 1974. Proceedings.* Ottawa: Canadian Association for Information science, 1974, pp. 163–180.

Firth, J. R. *The tongues of men.* London: Watts, 1937. (Reprinted, London: Oxford University Press; 1964.)

Fonti Ricciane: documenti originali concernenti Matteo Ricci. . . . Editi da Pasquale M. D'Elia. Roma: Libreria dello Stato, 1942–49.

*Foord, E. "The transliteration of Russian." *Nature* **29** (August 2, 1917):454–455.

Francis, F. C. "The catalogues of the British Museum. 3. Oriental printed books and manuscripts." *Journal of Documentation* **7** (1951):170–183.

*Franklin, D. "Reversible punctuation Russian transliteration." *American Documentation* **17** (1966):142–145.

*Fritz, J. F. *Orientalisch- und occidentalischer Sprachmeister, welcher nicht allein hundert Alphabete nebst ihrer Aussprache . . . sondern auch das Gebet des Herrn in 200 Sprachen und Mund-Arten . . . mittheilet.* Leipzig: C. F. Gessner, 1748.

*Frontard, R. "Transliteration codes and their international standardization." *Unesco Bulletin for Libraries* **15** (1961):78–82.

Funke, O. *Zum Weltsprachenproblem in England im 17. Jahrhundert.* Heidelberg: C. Winter, 1929. (Anglistische Forschungen; 69.)

*Gakovich, R. "The problem of transliteration of Slavic languages." *University of Wisconsin Library News* **13** (1962):7–12.

*Garnier, C. *T.R.G. Méthode de transcription rationelle générale des noms géographiques s'applicant a toutes les écritures usitées dans le monde.* . . . Paris: Leroux, 1899.

*Gelb, I. J. *A study of writing: the foundation of grammatology,* 2nd ed. Chicago: University of Chicago Press, 1963.

Gerlach, A. C. "Geography and map cataloging and classification in libraries." *Special Libraries* **52** (1961):248–251.

Gerlach, W. *Physik und Sprache.* München: Bayerische Akademie der Wissenschaften, 1953.

*Germany. Bundesdruckerei. *Alphabete und Schriftzeichen des Morgen- und des Abendlandes,* 2. Aufl. Berlin: Bundesdruckerei, 1969.

*Gessner, C. *Mithridates. De differentiis linguarum, tum veterum tum quae hodie apud diversas nationes in toto orbem terrarum in usu sunt Conradi Gesneri observationes.* Tiguri: Excudebat Froschoverus, 1555.

Geyer, J. J., and P. A. Kolers. "Reading as information processing." In *Advances in Librarianship* **4** (1974):175–237.

*Giles, H. A. *A Chinese–English dictionary,* 2nd ed., rev. London: Quaritch, 1912.

*Giljarevskij, R. S., and N. V. Krylova. ["Transliteration of bibliographic entries in the languages of the USSR with letters of the Roman alphabet."] *See* Гиляревский, (1960).

*Giljarevskij, R. S., and B. A. Starostin. [*Foreign names and designations in Russian texts, a reference book.*] *See* Гиляревский, (1969).

Gill, A. *Logonomia anglica, qua gentis sermo facilius addiscitur.* Londini: J. Beale, 1619.

*Gleichen, E. *Alphabets of foreign languages transcribed into English, according to the RGS II system,* 2nd ed., rev. London: Royal Geographical Society, 1944. (Royal Geographical Society technical series, no. 2.)

*Goldman, E. A., et al. "A 'computer-compatible' Semitic alphabet." *Hebrew Union College Annual* **42** (1971):251–278.

Gombrich, E. H. "The visual image." *Scientific American* **227** (3) (1972):82–96.

*Goodhart, L. *The Universal Character: projects for a universal language developed during the seventeenth and early eighteenth centuries. A study of the background of Swift's satire on language in the Voyage to Laputa.* New York: Columbia University, 1952.

*Görner, F. "Entwurf einer Neuregelung der Transliteration kyrillischer Alphabete als Anlage zu den Regeln für die alphabetische Katalogisierung (RAK)." *Nachrichten für Dokumentation* **25** (1974):217–220.

Graberg, M. L. von. "Neueste deutsche Forschung zur Geschichte der Bibliotheken Alexandreia's (1955–1971)." *Libri* **24** (1974):277–301.

Great Britain. Commissioners Appointed to Inquire Into the Constitution and Government of the British Museum. *Report . . . with minutes of evidence.* . . . London: HMSO, 1850. (Reprinted in N. Brault. *The great debate on Panizzi's rules in 1847–1849: the issues discussed.* Los Angeles: University of California, School of Library Service, 1972.)

*[*Great Japanese–Russian dictionary.*] *See* Большой японско–русский словарь.

*Gregory, J. W. "Russian transliteration." *Nature* **78** (May 14, 1908):42–43.

*Guggenheim-Grünberg, F. "Zur Umschrift deutscher Mundarten des 14./15. Jahrhunderts mit hebräischer Schrift." *Zeitschrift für Mundartforschung* **24** (1956):229–246.

*Haguenauer, M. "Système de transcription de l'alphabet coréen." *Journal asiatique* **122** (1933):145–161.

Hamdi, M. N. *The concept of main entry as represented in the* Anglo-American Cataloging Rules: *a critical appraisal with some suggestions: author main entry vs. title main entry.* Littleton, Colo.: Libraries Unlimited, 1973.

Hamilton, C. E. *Code for descriptive cataloging.* Berkeley: University of California Central Library, 1953.

Harman, D. "Illiteracy: an overview." *Harvard Educational Review* **40** (1970):228–230.

Hart, J. *An orthographie, conteyning the due order and reason, howe to write or paint thimage of mannes voice, most like to the life or nature.* London: W. Serres, 1569. (Reprinted in Sir Isaac Pitman. *A manual of phonography.* London: Pitman, 1850.)

Harvey, J. F. "Adapting American library science for Iranian use." *Focus on International and Comparative Librarianship* **4** (1973):27–31.

Hase, T., and C. Iken. *Thesaurus novus theologico-philologicus.* . . . Amstelodami: [s.n.], 1732.

*Hatsukade, I. "Die Reform der japanischen Nationalschrift: Geschichte der Reformbestrebungen." *Gutenberg-Jahrbuch* **7** (1932):27–43.

Hayes, A. P. "The functionally illiterate adult: who is he, where is he, why is he?" In *Public library service to the illiterate adult: proceedings of a seminar, March 9–11, 1972.* Edited by G. M. Casey, Detroit: Wayne State University, [1973?], p. 1–57.

Heffner, R.-M. S. *General phonetics.* Madison: University of Wisconsin Press, 1964.

Heilprin, L. B., and F. L. Goodman. "Analogy between information retrieval and education." *American Documentation* **16** (1965):163–169.

Heilprin, L. B. "On access to knowledge in the social sciences and humanities, from the viewpoint of cybernetics and information science." In *Access to the literature of the social sciences and humanities: proceedings of the Conference.* . . . *New York City, April 5 and 6, 1972.* Flushing, N. Y.: Queens College Press, 1974a, pp. 23–43.

Heilprin, L. B. "Operational definitions." In *Information science: search for identity. Proceedings of the 1972 NATO Advanced Study Institute on Information Science.* . . . Edited by A. Debons. New York; Dekker, 1974b, pp. 115–138.

*Henze, P. B. "Politics and alphabets in Inner Asia." *Journal of the Royal Central Asian Society* **(1956)**:29–51.

*Henze, P. B. "Alphabet changes in Soviet Central Asia and Communist China." *Journal of the Royal Central Asian Society* **(1957)**:124–136.

*Hepburn, J. C. *A Japanese and English dictionary.* London: Trübner, 1867.

Hess, R. L. *Ethiopia: the modernization of autocracy.* Ithaca: Cornell University Press, 1970.

*Hexapla. *Origenis Hexaplorum quae supersunt.* . . . Edited by F. Field. Oxford, Oxford University Press, 1875.

*Hirsch, S. A. "Early English Hebraists: Roger Bacon and his predecessors." *Jewish Quarterly Review* **12** (1899–1900):34–88.

*Hirth, F. "Umschreibung chinesischer Schriftzeichen in dem für Schriftzwecke modifizierten Dialekt von Peking." In Internationaler Orientalisten-Kongress, 13. Hamburg, 1902. *Verhandlungen.* Leiden: Brill, 1904.

Hobbes, T. *Hobbes's* Leviathan, *reprinted from the edition of 1651* . . . Oxford: Clarendon Press, 1909.

*Hsia, Tao-tai. *China's language reforms*. New Haven: Yale University, Institute of Far Eastern Languages, 1956.

*Hsin, Hua. [*Handbook of English names, transcribed into Chinese.*] See 羊 华

Hugo, H. *De prima scribendi origine et universa rei literariae antiquitate*. . . . Antwerpiae: Apud B. et J. Moretos, 1617.

*Hunter, Sir W. W. *The Imperial gazetteer of India* . . . , 2nd ed. London: Trübner, 1885–87.

*Huq, A. M. A. "A study of Bengali Muslim personal names. . . . " Pittsburgh: University of Pittsburgh, Graduate School of Library and Information Sciences, 1970. (Ph.D. thesis.)

Ickelsamer, V. *Ein teütsche Grammatica, darauss einer von im selber mag lesen lernen*. [s.l.: s.n., 1527?] (Reprinted, Freiburg i.B.: Mohr, 1881.)

*Imart, G. "Le mouvement de 'Latinisation' en U.R.S.S." *Cahiers du monde russe et sovietique* **6** (1965):223–239.

*India. Ministry of Education. *A standard system of Roman transliteration*. New Delhi: The Ministry, 1958. (*Its* Publication no. 259.)

Instruktionen für die alphabetischen Kataloge der preussischen Bibliotheken vom 10. Mai 1899. 2. Ausg. in der Fassung vom 10. August 1908. Wiesbaden: Harrassowitz, 1966. (Reprint.)

*International African Institute. *Practical orthography of African languages*. Oxford: Oxford University Press, 1930. (Reprinted 1962.)

International Centre for the Registration of Serial Publications. *Guidelines for ISDS*. Paris: The Centre, 1973.

*International Organization for Standardization. *International system for the transliteration of Cyrillic characters*. Geneva: ISO, 1954. (ISO/R9.) Superseded by 2nd ed., 1968. 3rd ed. in preparation.

*International Organization for Standardization. *International system for the transliteration of Arabic characters*. Geneva: ISO, 1961. (ISO/R233.)

*International Organization for Standardization. *Transliteration of Hebrew*. Geneva: ISO, 1962. (ISO/R259.)

*International Organization for Standardization. *International system for the transliteration of Greek characters into Latin characters*. Geneva: ISO, 1968. (ISO/R843.)

International Organization for Standardization. *Documentation. Bibliographical references: essential and supplementary elements*. Geneva: ISO, 1975. (ISO 690.)

*International Organization for Standardization. Technical Committee ISO/TC 46 "Documentation." *Transliteration of alphabets of non-Slavic languages using Cyrillic characters*. Berlin: The Committee, 1972. (ISO/DIS 2805.)

*International Phonetic Association. *The principles of the International Phonetic Association*. London, IPA, 1949.

Jakobson, R., and M. Halle. *Fundamentals of language*. 's-Gravenhage: Mouton, 1956. (Janua linguarum; studia memoriae Nicolai van Wijk dedicata.)

Japan. National Diet Library. *The processing system of Japanese bibliographic data of the National Diet Library*. Tokyo: The Library, [1974?].

*Jensen, H. *Geschichte der Schrift*, 2. Aufl. Berlin: Deutscher Verlag der Wissenschaften, 1958.

The Jewish encyclopedia. New York: Funk & Wagnall, 1901–05.

Jones, D. *Differences between spoken and written languages*. London: International Phonetic Association, 1948.

Jones, R. F. "Science and language in England of the mid-seventeenth century." *Journal of English and Germanic Philology* **31** (1932):315–331.

*Jones, Sir William. "A dissertation on the orthography of Asiatick words in Roman letters." *Asiatick Researches* **1** (1788):1–56.

*Jopson, N. B. "Russian transliteration." *Slavonic Review* **12** (1934):704–713.

Kahle, P. E. *The Cairo Geniza*. London: Oxford University Press, 1947.

Kainz, F. *Psychologie der Sprache*, 4. Aufl. Stuttgart: Enke, 1967.

*Karlgren, B. *The Romanization of Chinese*. London: China Society, 1928.

Katz, D., and R. L. Kahn. *The social psychology of organizations*. New York: Wiley, 1966.

Kenkyusha's new Japanese–English dictionary, 4th ed. Tokyo: Kenkyusha, 1974.

*Kennedy, G. A. *A beginner's English–Chinese vocabulary*. New Haven: Yale University, 1944. (Mirror series A; 10.)

*Kircher, A. *Polygraphia nova et universalis ex combinatoria arte detecta*. Romae: Ex typographia Varesii, 1663.

*Kishibe, K. "Cataloguing books in Chinese." *International Cataloguing* **3**(1) (1974):4.

*Knowles, J., and L. Garthwaite. *Oriental Braille: one alphabet for the blind for all Oriental languages*. London: British and Foreign Bible Society, 1902.

*Knowles, J. *Our duty to India and Indian illiterates: roman letters for Indian languages*. London: Christian Literature Society for India, 1910.

*Knowles, J. *A common alphabet for Indian languages: or, 53 alphabetic letters for 20,000 syllabic symbols*. Eastbourne: W. H. Christian, 1913.

Kohl, E. "Zeichensatz und Zeichenverschlüsselung bibliographischer Daten." In *The exchange of bibliographic data and the MARC format*. München: Verlag Dokumentation, 1972, pp. 79–99.

Koster, C. J. "International Standard Serial Numbers and the International Serials Data System." *Libri* **23** (1973):70–72.

*Kowalski, T. *Karaimische Texte in Dialekt von Troki*. Kraków: Nakładem Polskiej Akademji Umiejętności, 1929.

*Kuhn, E. W. A., and H. Schnorr von Carolsfeld. *Die Transcription fremder Alphabete. . . .* Leipzig: Harrassowitz, 1897.

Language and linguistics in the People's Republic of China. Edited by W. P. Lehmann. Austin, Texas: University of Texas Press, 1975.

Language use and social change: problems of multilingualism, with special reference to Eastern Africa. Edited by W. H. Whiteley. London: Oxford University Press, 1971.

*Laures, J. *Kirishitan bunko: a manual of books and documents on the early Christian missions in Japan*. Tokyo: Sophia University, 1940.

Lavelle, L. *La parole et l'écriture*. Paris: L'Artisan du livre, 1947.

Law, G. T. "Cold type composition: its impact on library and information science." *Journal of the American Society for Information Science* **25** (1974):319–326.

Lee, K.-F. "Input/output problems of Chinese characters and the use of COCOA." *Association for Literary and Linguistic Computing Bulletin* **4** (1975):4–10.

*Legeza, I. L. *Guide to transliterated Chinese in the modern Peking dialect*. Leiden: Brill, 1968.

Legros, L. A. *Typographical printing surfaces*. London: Longmans, 1916.

Lenin, V. I. *Collected works*. Moskva: Progress, 1966.

*Lepsius, R. *Uebertragung fremder Schriftsysteme und bisher noch ungeschriebener Sprachen in europäische Buchstaben.* Berlin: W. Hertz, 1855.

*Lepsius, R. *Standard alphabet for reducing unwritten languages and foreign graphic systems to a uniform orthography in European letters.* London: Seeleys, 1855. A second, enlarged ed. published under the same title, London: Williams & Norgate, 1863.

Lewis, B. *The Arabs in history.* New York: Harper, 1966.

Lewis, B. *The emergence of modern Turkey,* 2nd ed. London: Oxford University Press, 1968.

Library of Congress. *A catalog of printed books represented by Library of Congress printed cards issued to July 31, 1942.* Ann Arbor: Edwards Bros., 1942–1946.

Supplements and cumulations published until 1955. Continued by *The National Union Catalog: a cumulative author list representing Library of Congress printed cards and titles reported by other American libraries.* Washington, D.C.: Government Printing Office, 1956– .

Library of Congress. Information Systems Office. *Books: a MARC format.* Washington, D.C.: The Library, 1970.

Library of Congress. MARC Development Office. *Information on the MARC system,* 4th ed. Washington, D.C.: The Library, 1974.

Literacy and world population. Washington, D.C.: Population Reference Bureau, [1975]. (*Population Bulletin,* **30** no. 2)

*Lodwick (or Lodowyck), F. *A common writing: whereby two, although not understanding one the others language, yet by the helpe thereof, may communicate their minds one to another.* London: [s.n.], 1647.

*Lodwick, F. *The groundwork and foundation laid (or so intended) for the framing of a new perfect language: and an universall or common writing.* London: [s.n.], 1652.

*Löhr, H. "Die Transliteration japanischer Wörter über die kyrillische in die lateinische Schrift." *Informatik* **18** (5) (1971):48–52.

The Lord's Prayer in five hundred languages. . . . London: Gilbert & Rivington, 1905.

Lundell, J. A. "Principes d'écriture." In *A grammatical miscellany offered to O. Jespersen on his seventieth birthday.* Copenhagen: Levin & Munksgaard, 1930, pp. 345–361.

Ma, J. T. *Elementary Chinese for American librarians: a simple manual.* Hanover, N. H.: Oriental Society, 1968.

*Macaev, S. A., and V. G. Orlov. [*Manual for transcription and orthography of Chinese words.*]
See Масаев, С.А.

MacKaye, P. "Computer processing for Arabic script documents; proposal for a standardized code." In *Les arabes par leurs archives, (xvie-xxe siécles). Paris, 1974.* Paris: Centre national de la recherche scientifique, 1976, pp. 257–271. (Colloques internationaux du CNRS, no. 555.)

MacKaye, P. "Setting Arabic with a computer." *Scholarly Publishing* **9** (1977):142–150.

*Magyar Tudományos Akadémia. *A kínai nevek és szavak magyar átírása.* Budapest: MTA, 1952.

Maitra, S. "The public library and adult education in India." *International Library Review* **6** (1974):55–60.

Makal, M. *Un village anatolien: récit d'un instituteur paysan.* Paris: Plon, 1963.

Mangold, M. *Transliteration und Transkription.* Mannheim: Bibliographisches Institut, 1965.

*Marsden, W. "On a conventional Roman alphabet, applicable to Oriental languages." In *Miscellaneous works.* London: Parbury, Allen & Co., 1834.

*Martin, S. E., et al. *A Korean–English dictionary.* New Haven: Yale University Press, 1967.

*Mathews, R. H. *Mathews' Chinese–English dictionary,* rev. American ed. Cambridge, Mass.: Harvard University Press, 1943.

*Matušík, A. *Alphabetum et orthographia universalis, ex naturae et artis observationibus deducta.* . . . Rozniaviae: J. Kek, 1837.

Mazrui, A. A. "Islam and the English language in East and West Africa." In *Language use and social change.* London: Oxford University Press, 1971, pp. 179–197.

*McCune, G. M., and E. O. Reischauer. "Romanization of the Korean language." *Transactions of the Royal Asiatic Society, Korean Branch* **29** (1939):1–55.

Meecham, H. G. *The Letter of Aristeas: a linguistic study.* . . . Manchester: Manchester University Press, 1935.

*Megiser, H. *Specimen quadraginta diversarum . . . linguarum et dialectorum.* . . . Francoforti: Ex typographeo Ioannis Spiessii, 1593.

*Megiser, H. *Thesaurus polyglottus: vel, dictionarium multilingue: ex quadringentis circiter . . . linguis.* . . . Francofurti ad Moenum: Sumptibus auctoris, 1603.

Megiser, H. *Institutionum linguae turcicae libri quattuor.* . . . Lipsiae: Sumptibus auctoris, 1612.

Mehta, J. C. "Cataloguing problems in Delhi Public Library." *International Cataloguing* **2**(1) (1973):5–6.

Meigret, L. *Le tretté de la grammere françoeze.* Paris: C. Wechel, 1550.

Middleton, J. H. *The remains of ancient Rome.* London: Black, 1892.

*Millás-Vallicrosa, J. M. "Sobre una moderna dejación de la escritura aljamiada hebraico-española." *Sefarad* **10** (1950):185–186.

*Minsheu, J. *Ductor in linguas. The guide into tongues. Cum illarum harmonia, et etymologiis, originationibus, rationibus et derivationibus.* . . . Londini: J. Browne, 1617.

*Mish, J. L. "The transliteration of Oriental languages in chemical literature." *Journal of Chemical Education* **32** (1955):137–138.

Moid, A. *Urdu language collections in American libraries.* Urbana, Illinois: University of Illinois, 1964. (Ph.D. thesis.)

*Monier-Williams, Sir Monier. *Applications of the Roman alphabet to the expression of Sanskrit and other Eastern languages.* . . . London: Allen, 1881.

*Monier-Williams, Sir Monier. "The duty of English-speaking Orientalists in regard to united action in adhering generally to Sir William Jones's *Principles of transliteration,* especially in the case of Indian languages; with a proposal for promoting a Uniform International Method of Transliteration so far at least as may be applicable to proper names." *Journal of the Royal Asiatic Society* (**1890**):607–629.

*Morison, W. A. "The adaptation of the Latin alphabet to Russian." *Slavonic Review* **12** (1934):430–435.

Mountford, J. "Writing-system: a datum in bibliographical description." In *Towards a theory of librarianship.* . . . Metuchen, N. J.: Scarecrow Press, 1973, pp. 415–449.

*Musaev, K. M. [*Alphabets of the languages of the peoples of the USSR*] *See* Мусаев, К. М. (1965).

*Musaev, K. M., ed. [The orthography of Turkic literary languages in the USSR] *See* Мусаев, К. М. (1973).

*Naim, C. M. "Arabic orthography and some non-Semitic languages." In *Islam and its cultural divergence: studies in honor of Gustave von Grunebaum.* Edited by G. L. Tikku. Urbana, Ill.: University of Illinois Press, 1971, pp. 113–144.

*Nedkov,B.["On the correct spelling of Arabic place names and personal names."]*See* Недков, Б.

Neill, S. *Colonialism and Christian missions.* London: Butterworth, 1966.

*Neiswender, R. "Russian transliteration—sound and sense." *Special Libraries* 53 (1962):37–41.

Nelson, A. N. *The modern reader's Japanese–English character dictionary,* 2nd ed. rev. Rutland, Vt: Tuttle, 1966.

Nestor, B. "To adapt, or not to adapt, Western librarianship." *Focus on International and Comparative Librarianship* 5 (1974):4.

Neubauer, K. W., and S. Selbmann. "Application of International Standard Book Numbers (ISBN) in libraries." *Unesco Bulletin for Libraries* 28 (1974):125–130.

Nida, E. A., and W. L. Wonderly. "Communication roles of languages in multilingual societies." In *Language use and social change.* London: Oxford University Press, 1971, pp. 57–74.

Nolan, E., and S. A. Hirsch. *The Greek grammar of Roger Bacon and a fragment of his Hebrew grammar.* Cambridge: Cambridge University Press, 1902.

North, E. M., ed. *The book of a thousand tongues, being some account of the translation and publication of all or part of the Holy Scriptures.* . . . New York: Harper, 1938.

*Nurmakov, N., ed. [*The October alphabet: results of the introduction of the new alphabet among the peoples of the RSFSR*] See* Нурмаков, Н.

*Oda, Y. "The processing system for Japanese bibliographic data in the National Diet Library." *International Cataloguing* 3(4) (1974):7–8.

O'Neill, P. G. *Japanese names: a comprehensive index by characters and readings.* New York: J. Weatherhill, 1972.

Orne, J. "Transliteration of modern Russian." *Library Journal* 88 (1963):4157–4160.

*Ošanin, I. M. [*Chinese–Russian dictionary*] 3rd ed. *See* Ошанин, И. М.

*Palestine. Government. *Transliteration for Arabic and Hebrew into English, from Arabic into Hebrew, and from Hebrew into Arabic, with transliterated lists of personal and geographic names for use in Palestine.* Jerusalem: Goldberg's Press, 1931.

*Pallas, P. S. *Linguarum totius orbis vocabularia comparativa.* . . . *See* Паллас, П. С.

*Palmer, F. M. "Value of Russian to reference librarians." *College and Research Libraries* 6 (1945):195–198.

*Palmer, H. E. *The principles of Romanization, with special reference to the Romanization of Japanese.* Tokyo: Maruzen, 1931.

Parsell, J. R. *World fonetic alfabet,* 3rd ed. New York: [s.n.], 1946.

Parsons, E. A. *The Alexandrian library.* . . . Amsterdam: Elsevier, 1952.

*Pattipilohy, F. C. "Problemen bij het catalogiseren van 'Oriëntal' collecties." *Open* 6 (1974):371–375.

Pei, M. *Glossary of linguistic terminology.* New York: Doubleday, 1966.

Pei, M. *Language for everybody.* New York: Devin-Adair, 1956.

*Petithuguenin, P. "Method for Romanizing Siamese." *Journal of the Siam Society* 9(3) (1913):1–9.

Phonetic transcription and transliteration. Proposals of the Copenhagen Conference, April 1925. Oxford: Clarendon Press, 1926.

Pinner, H. L. *The world of books in classical antiquity,* 2nd ed. London: Allen & Unwin, 1958.

*Pirenne, J. *Bilan des signes diacritiques et lettres spéciales pour la translittération universelle sur ordinateur.* Paris: Centre National de la Recherche Scientifique, 1973.

Plato. *Cratylus.* With an English translation by H. N. Fowler. Cambridge, Mass.: Harvard University Press, 1926. (The Loeb Classical Library.)

Plato. *Theaetetus.* With an English translation by H. N. Fowler. Cambridge, Mass.: Harvard University Press, 1921. (The Loeb Classical Library.)

*Podborny, J. G. "Zu einer international einheitlichen Umschreibung der kyrillischen Buchstaben." *Babel* **5** (1959):207–212.

*Postel, G. *Linguarum duodecim characteribus differentium alphabetum, introductio ac legendi modus longe facilimus.* Parisiis: Apud D. Lescuier, 1538.

*Preisigke, F. *Namenbuch, enthaltend alle griechischen, lateinischen, ägyptischen, hebräischen, aramäischen, arabischen und sonstigen semitischen und nicht-semitischen Menschennamen, soweit sie in griechischen Urkunden . . . Aegyptens sich vorfinden.* Heidelberg: Selbstverlag, 1922.

Rageau, C. "Les problèmes d'acquisition et de catalogage des ouvrages en langues d'Asie." Rapport présenté au 29e Congrès internationale des Orientalistes. Paris: 1973.

Ranganathan, S. R. *Theory of library catalogue.* Madras: Madras Library Association, 1938.

Ranganathan, S. R. *Classified catalogue code, with additional rules for dictionary catalogue code,* 5th ed. Bombay: Asia Publishing House, 1964.

Rather, J. C. "Filing arrangement in the Library of Congress catalogs." *Library Resources and Technical Services* **16** (1972):240–261.

Ray, D. T. "The need for cooperative cataloguing of Southeast Asian publications." In *Conference on Access to Southeast Asian Research Materials. Proceedings.* Edited by C. Hobbs. Washington, D.C.: [s.n.], 1971.

Ray, J. *A philosophical essay for the reunion of languages, or the art of knowing all by the mastery of one.* Oxford: [s.n.], 1675.

*Razran, G. "Transliteration of Russian." *Science* **129** (April 24, 1959):1111–1113.

Reform of the Chinese written language. Peking: Foreign Languages Press, 1958.

Rejaf Language Conference. *Report.* London: Government of Sudan, 1928.

Reuchlin, J. *De rudimentis hebraicis.* . . . Phorce: In aedib. Th. Anselmi, 1506.

Rhodes, A. de. *Catechismus pro iis qui volunt suscipere baptismum, in octo dies divisus. Phép giảng tám ngày.* . . . Romae: Typis S. Congregatio de Propaganda Fide, 1651a.

*Rhodes, A. de. *Dictionarium annamiticum, lusitanum et latinum.* . . . Romae: Typis S. Congregatio de Propaganda Fide, 1651b.

Ricci, M. *De christiana expeditione apud Sinas suscepta, ab Societate Iesu.* . . . Lugduni: Sumpt. H. Cardon, 1616.

*Ricci, M. [The miracle of Western characters.] [s.l.: s.n.], 1598.

*Richter, E. *Vergleichende Transkriptionstabelle als Hilfsmittel zum Auffinden russischer Schriften in den grossen internationalen Allgemeinbibliographien; mit Erläuterungen.* Göttingen: [s.n.], 1955.

Rosenbaum, M. "International Serials Data System." *International Cataloguing* **1**(4) (1972): 4–6.

*Rost, R. "Universal syllabics; a new method of learning to read, applicable to all languages." In *The Lord's Prayer in three hundred languages.* . . . London: Gilbert & Rivington, 1891, p. 85.

Roth, D. L. "The needs of library users." *Unesco Bulletin for Libraries* **28** (1974):92–94.

*Royal Institute of Thailand. "Notification of the Royal Institute concerning the transcription of Thai characters into Roman." *Journal of the Thailand Society* **33**(1) (1941):49–65.

*Royal Institute of Thailand. *Romanization guide for Thai script.* Bangkok: The Institute, 1968.

Ruggles, M. J. and R. C. Swank. *Soviet libraries and librarianship.* Chicago: American Library Association, 1962.

Sarton, G. *Introduction to the history of science.* Baltimore: Williams & Wilkins, 1927–1948.

Saussure, F. de. *Cours de linguistique générale,* 4e éd. Paris: Payot, 1949.

*Schleiermacher, A. A. E. *Alphabet harmonique pour transcrire les langues asiatiques en lettres européens: mémoire que l'Institut Royal de France a couronné en 1827.* Prospectus. Darmstadt: [s.n.], 1835a.

*Schleiermacher, A. A. E. *De l'influence de l'écriture sur le langage: mémoire . . . suivi de grammaires barmane et malaie et d'un aperçu de l'alphabet harmonique pour les langues asiatiques.* . . . Darmstadt: J. W. Heyer, 1835b.

Schleiermacher, A. A. E. *Bibliographisches System der gesamten Wissenschaftskunde.* Braunschweig: Vieweg, 1852.

*Schleiermacher, A. A. E. *Das harmonische oder allgemeine Alphabet zur Transcription fremder Schriftsysteme in lateinische Schrift, zunächst in seiner Anwendung auf die slawischen und semitischen Sprachen.* Darmstadt: Jonghaus, 1864.

*Schott, G. *Scholia steganographica.* . . . Norimbergae: Sumptibus J. A. Endteri, 1687.

*Schröpfer, J. *Hussens Traktat "Orthographia Bohemica"; die Herkunft des diakritschen Systems in der Schreibung slawischer Sprachen und die älteste zusammenhängende Beschreibung slawischer Laute.* Wiesbaden: Harrassowitz, 1968.

Schulte-Albert, H. G. "Cyprian Kinner and the idea of a faceted classification." *Libri* **24** (1974):324–337.

*Seitz, R. O. "Japlish, the Japanese brand of English." *Special Libraries* **53** (1962):30–34.

*Serdjučenko, G. P. ["On Russian transcriptions of Oriental languages."] *See* Сердюченко, Г. П.

Serdjučenko, G. P. *Elimination of illiteracy among peoples without alphabets.* Moskva: USSR Commission for UNESCO, 1965. [This document is probably in Russian, but the reference to it in Bowers (1968) is in English, and I was unable to verify it in other sources—H.H.W.]

Seton-Watson, H. *Nationalism old and new.* Sidney: Sidney University Press, 1965.

*Ševčik, A. "Translittération." *Revue de la Documentation* **14** (1947):21–22.

*Sharify, N. *Cataloging of Persian works: including rules for transliteration, entry and description.* Chicago: American Library Association, 1959.

Sharma, C. D. "Cataloguing practice in some Indian university libraries." *Unesco Bulletin for Libraries* **27** (1973):33–39.

*Shaw, E. P. "Transliteration: a game for the library sleuth." *Bulletin of the Medical Library Association* **37** (1949):142–145.

*Shaw, J. T. *Transliteration of modern Russian for English-language publications.* Madison: University of Wisconsin Press, 1967.

Sheniti, M. "Treatment of Arabic names." In *International Conference on Cataloguing Principles, Paris, 1961.* London: IFLA, 1963, pp. 267–276.

Shera, J. H. "Mechanization, librarianship and the bibliographic enterprise." *Journal of Documentation* **30** (1974):153–169.

Shera, J. H., and M. E. Egan. "Prolegomena to bibliographic control." *Journal of Cataloging and Classification* **5** (1949):17–19.

Siew, K. Y., and C. S. Choo. "Problems of the multi-language, multi-script library: multi-language catalogues in the National Library, Singapore." *International Calaloguing* **1** (1972):5–7.

Smith, F. *Understanding reading: a psycholinguistic analysis of reading and learning to read.* New York: Holt, Rinehart & Winston, 1971.

Smith, Sir Thomas. *De recta et emendata linguae Graecae pronuntiatione.* Lutetiae: R. Stephanus, 1568.

*Sommer, F. E. "Transliteration problems." *Library Journal* **58** (1933):534–536.

*Sommer, F. E. "Books in foreign script in the public library." *Library Journal* **59** (1934):892–893.

*Sommer, F. E. "Co-ordinated transliteration in libraries." *Library Quarterly* **7** (1937):492–501.

*Spalding, C. S. "Transliteration of vernacular alphabets; cooperative cataloging of vernacular materials; and cataloging treatment of pamphlet materials." In *Conference on American Library Resources in Southern Asia.* Washington, D.C.: [s.n.], 1957.

*Spalding, C. S. "Romanization Reexamined." *Library Resources & Technical Services* **21** (1977): 3–12.

Sprat, T. *History of the Royal-Society of London, for the improvement of natural knowledge.* London: J. Martyn, 1667.

Stalin, J. V. *Marxism and linguistics.* New York: International Publishers, 1951.

*Stallings, W. "The morphology of Chinese characters: a survey of models and applications." *Computers and the Humanities* **9** (1975):13–24.

*Starostin, B. A. [Transcription of proper names; a practical manual], 2nd ed. *See* Старостин, Б. А.

Stein, G. "Poetry and grammar." In *Lectures in America.* New York: Random House, 1935.

Stipčević, A. "The new Yugoslav cataloguing rules and their application in Yugoslav libraries." *International Cataloguing* **1** (1972):7–8.

Stokes, R. *Bibliographical control and services.* London: Deutsch, 1965.

Strype, J. *The life of ... Sir Thomas Smith.* London: Roper, 1698.

Strype, J. *The life of ... Sir John Cheke.* London: Wyat, 1705.

Swete, H. B. *An introduction to the Old Testament in Greek. . . .* Cambridge: Cambridge Universi. Press, 1902.

Tairas, J. N. B. "Some aspects of descriptive cataloguing standardization in Indonesia." In *International cooperation in Orientalist librarianship. . . .* Canberra: National Library of Australia, 1972, pp. 58–82.

Tanabe, H. "Library automation in Japan." In *International cooperation in Orientalist librarianship. . . .* Canberra: National Library of Australia, 1972, pp. 165–170.

Taylor, R. S. *Curriculum design for library and information science.* Syracuse: Syracuse University School of Library Science, 1973.

Tertullian. *Apology. . . .* With an English translation by T. R. Glover. Cambridge, Mass.: Harvard University Press, 1931. (The Loeb Classical Library.)

Thompson, L. C. *A Vietnamese grammar.* Seattle: University of Washington Press, 1965.

*Tien, H. C. *A guide to the new Latin spelling of Chinese.* Hongkong: Oriental Book Co., 1962.

*Ting, Lee-Hsia Hsu. "Problems of cataloging Chinese author and title entries in American libraries." *Library Quarterly* **36** (1966):1–13.

Tory, G. *Champ fleury.* Translated into English and annotated by G. B. Ives. New York: Grolier Club, 1927. (Reprinted, New York: Dover, 1967.)

*Trevelyan, Sir C. E. *Papers originally published at Calcutta in 1834 and 1836 on the application of Roman letters to the languages of Asia.* London: [s.n.], 1854.

Trigault, N. *Litterae Societatis Iesu e regno Sinarum.* . . . Augustae Vindelicorum: Apud C. Mangium, 1615a.

Trigault, N. *Rei christianae apud Iaponios commentarius.* . . . Augusta Vindelicorum: Apud C. Mangium, 1615b.

Trigault, N. *De christianis apud Iapanios triumphis.* . . . Monachii: [s.n.], 1623.

Trigault, N. *Regni Chinensis descriptio.* . . . Lugduni Batavorum: Ex officina Elzeviriana: 1639.

*Trigault, N. [The Western scholar's aid for ear and eye.] [S.l.:s.n.], 1626.

Turnbull, G. H. *Hartlib, Dury and Comenius.* Liverpool: University Press, 1947.

*Ubriatova, E. I. ["Problems of script and orthography in the languages of the peoples of the USSR who use alphabets based on the Russian."] *See* Убрятова, Е. И.

Union of Soviet Socialist Republics. [All-Union Standards Committee.] *See* СССР. Всесоюзний Комитет Стандартов.

UNISIST/ICSU-AB Working Group on Bibliographic Descriptions. *Reference manual for machine-readable bibliographic descriptions.* Compiled by M. D. Martin. Paris: Unesco, 1974.

United Nations Conference on the Standardization of Geographical Names, 2nd, London, 1972. *Second United Nations conference on the standardization of geographical names, London, 10–31 May 1972* . . . New York: United Nations, 1974. (E/CONF. 61/4)

*United States. Board on Geographic Names. *Romanization guide.* Washington. D.C.: [s.n.], 1972.

United States. Government Printing Office. *Style manual.* Rev. ed. Washington, D.C.: GPO, 1973.

Urquhart, Sir Thomas. *Logopandecteison, or an introduction to the Universal Language.* . . . London: G. Calvert, 1653. (Reprinted, Edinburgh: 1834.)

*Văglenov, M. ["Pronunciation and transcription of Japanese names in Bulgarian."] *See* Въгленов, М. (1968).

*Văglenov, M., and I. Kančev. ["Pronunciation and transcription of Korean names in Bulgarian."] *See* Въгленов, М. (1969).

*Vajiravudh, King of Siam. "The Romanization of Siamese words." *Journal of the Siam Society* **9**(4) (1913):1–10.

*Vajiravudh, King of Siam. "Notes on the proposed system of Siamese words into Roman characters." *Journal of the Siam Society* **10**(4) (1913):25–33.

Varossieau, W. W. *A survey of scientific abstracting and indexing services.* . . . The Hague: International Federation for Documentation, 1949. (Publication FID; 236.)

*Vasil'kov, B. P. "On the Latinization of authors' names written after the names of taxa." *Taxon* **7** (1960):199–200.

Venkatachari, P. N. "Production and marketing of books in India." *International Library Review* **6** (1974):61–64.

Verein Deutscher Bibliothekare. Kommission für Alphabetische Katalogisierung. *Regeln für die alphabetische Katalogisierung (RAK).* Frankfurt/Main: V. Klostermann, 1965–

*Vocabularium bibliothecarii. 2nd ed. Edited by A. Thompson. Paris: Unesco, 1962.

*Volney, C.-F. *Simplification des langues orientales, ou méthode nouvelle et facile d'apprendre les langues arabe, persane et turque avec des caractères européens.* Paris: Imprimerie de la république, III [i.e., 1794].

*Volney, C.-F. *L'Alfabet européen appliquée aux langues asiatiques; ouvrage élémentaire utile a tout voyageur en Asie.* Paris: Firmin-Didot, 1819.

*Von Ostermann, G. F. *Manual of foreign languages for the use of librarians, bibliographers,* *research workers, editors, translators and printers,* 4th ed., rev. New York: Central Book Co., 1952.

*Wade, T. *Yü-yên tzŭ-êrh chi . . . : a progressive course designed to assist the student of colloquial Chinese.* London: Trübner, 1867.

*Wagner, E. *Regeln für die alphabetische Katalogisierung von Druckschriften in den islamischen Sprachen (arabisch, persisch, türkisch). . . .* Wiesbaden: Harrassowitz, 1961.

Ward, S. *Vindiciae academiarum: containing some briefe animadversations upon Mr. Webster's book, stiled, The examination of academies.* Oxford: L. Lichfield, 1654.

Wasserman, P. *The new librarianship: a challenge for change.* New York: Bowker, 1972.

Webster, J. *Academiarum examen: or, The examination of academies. Wherein is discussed and examined the matter, method, and customes of academick and scholastick learning, and the insufficiency thereof discovered and laid open. . . .* London: G. Calvert, 1654.

*Weil, G. "Ein unbekannter türkischer Transkriptionstext aus dem Jahre 1489." *Oriens* **6** (1953):239–265.

*Weinberg, B. "Transliteration in documentation." *Journal of Documentation* **30**(1974):18–31.

*Weinberg, W. "Translateration and transcription of Hebrew." *Hebrew Union College Annual* **40–41** (1969–70):1–32.

*Weinberg, W. "The Romanization of Hebrew in the new *Encyclopedia Judaica." Language Sciences* **8** (1975):23–24.

*Weinreich, U. *College Yiddish. . . .* New York: YIVO, 1949.

*Weinreich, U. "The Russification of Soviet minority languages." *Problems of Communism* **2**(6) (1953):46–57.

Wellisch, H. H. *A survey of indexing and abstracting services for water resources engineering.* College Park, Md.: Water Resources Research Center, 1972.

Wellisch, H. H. *Transcription and transliteration: an annotated bibliography on conversion of scripts.* Silver Spring, Md.: Institute of Modern Languages, 1975.

*Wellisch, H. H. "Script conversion practices in the world's libraries." *International Library Review* **8** (1976):55–84.

*Wheeler, G. F. "Latinization: a study in Middle Eastern language reform." *Journal of the Royal Central Asian Society* **24** (1937):591–604.

White, A. D. *A history of the warfare of science with theology in Christendom.* New York: Appleton, 1896. (Abridged ed., New York: Free Press, 1965.)

*Wieger, L. *Chinese characters: their origin, etymology, history, classification and signification. . . . ,* 2nd ed. Hsien-hsien: Catholic Mission Press, 1927. (Reprinted, New York: Dover, 1965.)

Wiener, N. *Cybernetics.* Cambridge, Mass.: MIT Press, 1948.

Wilkins, J. *Mercury: or, The secret and swift messenger. . . .* London: I. Maynard & T. Wilkins, 1641.

Wilkins, J. *Mathematicall magick. . . .* London: Gellibrand, 1648.

Wilkins, J. *Essay towards a Real Character, and a philosophical language.* London: Gellibrand, 1668.

Wilson, P. *Two kinds of power: an essay on bibliographical control.* Berkeley: University of California Press. 1968.

*Wood, M. M. "Latinizing the Turkish alphabet." *American Journal of Sociology* **35** (1929–30):194–203.

*Wright, H. C. "Metagraphy and graphic priority; a discursus for catalogers." Cleveland: Case Western Reserve University, 1969. (Ph.D. thesis.)

Wrolstad, M. E. "A manifesto for visible language." *Visible Language* **10** (1976):5–40.

*YIVO Institute for Jewish Research. [*Rules for Yiddish orthography.*] See ייװאָ

Young, R. F. *Comenius in England.* London: Oxford University Press, 1932. (Reprinted, New York: Arno Press, 1971.)

*Zavadovskij, Yu. N. ["On a systematic transcription and transliteration for Hamito-Semitic languages."] *See* Завадовский, Ю. Н.

Zuntz, G. "Aristeas studies II: Aristeas on the translation of the Torah." *Journal of Semitic Studies* **4** (1959):109–126.

Авторский указатель

Баскаков, Н. А., ред. *Вопросы совершенствования алфавитов тюркских языков СССР.* Москва: «Наука», 1972.

Баскаков, Н. А. «О современном состоянии и дальнейсем совершенствовании алфавита для тюркских языков народов СССР». *Вопроси Языкознания* 16 (5) (1967):33–46.

Батаклиев, Г. «Изговор и транскрипция на старогръцките имена в българския език». *Български Език* 17 (1967):543–550.

Большои японско–русский словарь. Москва: Советская Энсиклопедия, 1970.

Въгленов, М. «Изговор и транскрипция на японски имена в българския език». *Български Език* 18 (1968):54–63.

Въгленов, М., и И. Кънчев. «Изговор и транскрипция на корейски имена в българския език». *Български Език* 19 (1969):280–287.

Гиляревский, Р. С., и Н. В. Крылова. «Транслитерася библиографических опнсаний на языках народов СССР латинскими буквами». *Советская Бильиография* 5 (63) (1960):37–44.

Гиляревский, Р. С., и Б. А. Старостин. *Иностранные имена и насвания в русском тексте.* Москва: Международные Отношения, 1969.

Завадовский, Ю. Н. «О системах транскрипции и транслитерации для хамито-семитских языков». *Семитске Языки* (1963):171–185.

Мацаев, С. А. *Посовие по транскрипци и правописанию китайских слов.* Москва: «Наука», 1966.

Мусаев, К. М. *Алфавиты языков народов СССР.* Москва: «Наука», 1965.

Мусаев, К. М., ред. *Орфография тюркских литературиых языков СССР.* Москва: «Наука», 1973.

Недков, Б. «За правилно писане на арабските собствени имена—лични и географски.» *Български Език* 13 (1963):138–141.

Нурмаков, Н., ред. *Алфавит Октября: итоги введения нового алфавита среди народов РСФСР. Сборник статей.* Москва: Власть Советов, 1934.

Ошанин, И. М. *Китайско–русский словарь,* изд. 3. Мосва: Гос. изд. Иностранных и национальных словарей, 1959.

Паллас, П. С. *Сравнительные словари всѣхъ языковъ и нарѣчій* ...
Linguarum totis orbis vocabularia comparativa. ...Petropolis: Typis
I. C. Schnoor, 1789.

СССР. Всесоюзний Комптет Стандартов. *Транслитерация русских слов
латинскими буквами.* Москва: ВКС, 1971. (ГОСТ 16876-71.)

Сердюченко, Г. П. «О русской транскрипции для языков зарубежного
востока.» *Проблемы Востоковедения* 2(3) (1960): 91–107.

Старостин, Б. А. *Транскрипция собственных имен: практическое посо-
бие,* изд. 2. Москва: Книга, 1965.

Убрятова, Е. И. «Вопросы графики и орфографии языков народов СССР,
пользующихся алфавитами на русской основе». В *Вопросы термино-
логии.* Москва: 1961, стр. 92–99.

Филипова-Байрова, М. «Изговор и транскрипция на гръчките имена в
българския език.» *Български Език* 14 (1964): 195–201.

מפתח המחברים

האקדמיה ללשון העברית. כללי התעתיק מכתב עברי לכתב לטיני.
ירושלים: האקדמיה, תשט"ז-תשי"ז [1957].

האקדמיה ללשון העברית. "התעתיק מלועזית לעברית." זכרונות האקדמיה
17 (תש"ל [1970]): 25-32; 66-77; 83-94; 97-120.

בן-יהודה, מ.   "הכתיב בקטלוג העברי." יד לקורא 9 (1968): 85-92.

ייווא. תקנות פון יידישן אויסלייג. ווילנע: ייווא, 1937.

著 者 索 引

辛华. 英语国家姓名译名手册. 北京: 商务印书馆, 1965.
  （翻译参考资料）

馬場重德. 非羅馬字の羅馬字(書誌的)飜字. 東京:
  学術文献普及会, 1968.

Index

Entries are filed in a single alphabetical sequence, word by word. Abbreviations and acronyms are filed as words. References are to pages. Footnotes are indicated by the letter *n*, illustrations by an asterisk after the page number. The word "language" is sometimes abbreviated by *l*.

All place names, including those transcribed from a non-Roman script, are listed in standard English spelling.

Chinese and Japanese personal names and titles in transcription are identified in brackets by the serial numbers of characters as listed in Mathew's *Chinese-English Dictionary* and Nelson's *The Modern Reader's Japanese-English Character Dictionary* respectively; in a few instances, it was not possible to ascertain the Chinese characters from the Romanized form of a Chinese or Japanese name as cited in a source. Modern Chinese and Japanese authors writing in Western languages, identified by [m], are listed in the form that appears in their publications.

Separate indexes in Cyrillic, Greek, Arabic, Hebrew, Chinese, Japanese, and Korean script are provided after the index in Roman script.

Указатель

Εὑρετηριον

索引

索 引